S0-AVK-521

CANADA'S OLYMPIC HOCKEY TEAMS

THE COMPLETE HISTORY 1920–1998

ANDREW PODNIEKS

Canadian Olympic Association

Doubleday Canada Limited

Canadian Cataloguing in Publication Data

Podnieks, Andrew
Canada's Olympic hockey teams : the complete history, 1920–1998

ISBN 0-385-25688-4

1. Hockey – Canada – History. 2. Winter Olympics – History. I. Title.

GV848.4.C3P62 1997 796.962'66 C97-930705-8

Cover and text design by Joseph Gisini, Andrew Smith Graphics, Inc.
Front and back cover photographs courtesy the Canadian Olympic Association
Printed and bound in Canada by Webcom Limited

Published in Canada by
Doubleday Canada Limited
105 Bond Street
Toronto, Ontario
M5B 1Y3

Contents

Acknowledgements

The author wishes to thank many people for aiding and abetting his efforts to produce what will hopefully be regarded as a worthy addition to the Canadian hockey library: the ever-supportive, consummately passionate Hockey Hall of Fame threesome of Jefferson Davis, Phil Pritchard, and Craig Campbell, and everyone else at the HHOF in T.O.; Dr. Jon Redfern and Geri Dasgupta, who began the whole literopolis; Dean Cooke, my agent provocateur; the incomparable group at Doubleday, especially Don Sedgwick, Christine Innes, Janine Laporte, and Anne Holloway, for tackling all that I throw their way; everyone at the Canadian Olympic Association: Richard Stamper, Lisa Diamond, and Justin Kingsley in Toronto; Sylvia Doucette and all the Donini-pizza eating staff at Maison Olympique in Montreal; Lucie Leclerc-Rose in Ottawa; Bob Nicholson at the CHA in Calgary; Rick Morrocco at the Centre of Excellence; the ever-wonderful Mr. Frank Selke; Birger Nordmark, who happily shared his research and information; Al Purvis and Denis Brodeur for help with photographs; all the players who happily gave of their time and Olympic experiences, particularly Billy Dawe, Ralph Hansch, Murray Dowey, Reg Schroeter, Denis Brodeur, Ken Reardon, Terry O'Malley, and Brian Conacher; and as usual, last but most, my mother, for taking the necessary time to raise me right proper.

350 West Georgia St.
Vancouver, B.C.
Canada V6B 6B1
VPL
Vancouver Public Library
Gift of
VANCOUVER CANUCKS
BOOSTER CLUB
member of
Vancouver Public Library's
legacy fund,
1997

EVERY BOY'S DREAM IN CANADA IS TO PLAY IN THE NATIONAL HOCKEY LEAGUE and to play in the Olympics wearing the Canadian sweater. For the first time ever, Canada's top NHL players will be donning the Canadian jersey and playing for their country in the 1998 Olympic Games in Nagano, Japan.

Andrew Podnieks has assembled a superb history of Canadian hockey at the Olympics leading to — and including — the 1998 Games. There has never been a book published on Canada's Olympic hockey teams in such depth as this publication. Readers will find all the facts and stories extremely interesting as they walk themselves through the many great moments in Olympic hockey history.

In 1998, the Canadian players, both from the NHL and the first ever Women's Olympic Team, will be trying to reach their ultimate goal in winning gold medals in Nagano. This book provides readers with an excellent opportunity to understand hockey at the Olympics, and profiles many of the players who have competed for our country and lived the Olympic dream.

BOB NICHOLSON
SENIOR VICE-PRESIDENT
CANADIAN HOCKEY

FOR THE HOCKEY TRADITIONALIST THIS IS A MUST-READ BOOK ON CANADA'S history at the Olympics.

It is fitting that this well-researched book is being published on the eve of the Nagano Olympics where two new chapters will be written in Olympic Hockey history. This will mark the first Olympics for Women's Hockey and also the first Olympics where professionals will represent Canada.

As Chef de Mission of Canada's Olympic team, which will be the largest ever to represent our country, I highly recommend this book for your hockey collection and reading enjoyment.

BRIAN WAKELIN
CHEF DE MISSION, CANADA
XVIII OLYMPIC WINTER GAMES
NAGANO, JAPAN

ONE OF THE GREATEST THRILLS AN ATHLETE CAN EXPERIENCE IS TO REPRESENT his or her country in international competition. For the members of Team Canada, the Olympic experience in Nagano, Japan will be a highlight for many of our NHL careers.

© Ed Mahan Photography

Although I never competed in the Olympic Games, some of my fondest memories are from playing international hockey. Two particular events that stand out are when Team Canada won the 1972 Summit Series in Moscow and the first Canada Cup in 1976. Both were experiences I will never forget. To stand on the blue line in Moscow, after having defeated the Russians by a goal, and hear the country's national anthem being played, was an unbelievable experience. Just as gratifying was winning the Canada Cup four years later on our home ice where we had total fan support throughout the tournament. Words cannot describe the emotion and excitement of winning in those surroundings. Those memories still remain as some of the great thrills that I had in hockey.

Although the Canadian team competing in Nagano will be very talented, in no way would I label our club the "Dream Team" of the Olympics. That phrase was derived in the 1992 Olympics in Barcelona where there was never any doubt that the United States Olympic basketball team would win easily. Our roster will be filled with great NHL players, but so will the other teams. To label our team a "Dream Team" would indicate our team is clearly better than all the other countries, and that is simply not the case.

I am excited about NHL hockey players being eligible for competition in the Nagano Olympics. Having professional athletes participate in the Olympics is not an entirely new concept. Even the so-called "amateur" athletes who competed in the Olympics are getting paid in some form. There is no reason to penalize a professional athlete because he or she is earning a living. Receiving a salary for one's profession should not prevent one from competing in the Olympics.

It is my hope that the relationship between the NHL and the Canadian Hockey Association becomes stronger. The NHL could do more for young hockey in Canada. The Canadians are still producing 65 percent of all NHL players. Yet, neither the NHLPA or the NHL is doing enough to keep NHL teams in Canada and to keep producing these players. When we start hurting our source of young players, the game will end up paying for it down the road. The CHA does a marvellous job of representing Canada the best it can with players who do not make the NHL. But the CHA will need more financial support in the future to ensure it remains successful.

The solution for this dilemma would be for the NHLPA and the NHL to work together. They should forget about power, control, and competition with each other; this drives teams out of Canada. The two should work together to ensure that hockey succeeds all across North America. The sport's popularity is finally starting to get the recognition it richly deserves, but it should not come at the expense of losing hockey's roots.

BOB CLARKE
GENERAL MANAGER, TEAM CANADA
1998 OLYMPICS, NAGANO

Introduction

Canada's hockey success at the Olympics has been unmatched by any competing nation since the sport was introduced in 1920 at the Summer Games in Antwerp. Yet, despite our many successes and occasional disappointments, there has never been any careful documentation or examination of the teams that have represented our country over the years. Canada has won more Olympic hockey medals than any other nation, won more games, scored more goals, recorded more shutouts and participated in more Winter Olympics than any other country. But for the longest time these achievements have been put in negative perspective by those who point out that Canada last won a gold medal in 1952. These same critics neglect to mention that when the Russians began playing in 1956 and started winning regularly, their elite "pros" were playing our university students.

As readers will discover, the history of Olympic hockey has been an ongoing battle over the definition and interpretation of that ever-malleable term "amateur." This is why Canada has not won gold in so long, and why we did not even enter teams for the 1972 and 1976 Winter Games. For these reasons, it is difficult for a young fan of today to understand why it was not until 1992 that Canada could hope to send even some of its best players to the Games (at which time, not coincidentally, we started winning medals again). The 1998 Nagano Olympics, however, will be the first time we are sending the finest Canadian hockey players — pro or amateur — to the Olympics.

The arrival of the Dream Team games, though, brings with it a poignant sense of loss, a sense that the existence of amateurs is no longer even acknowledged. There is little purity and integrity left in sport, little desire to allow athletes to compete solely for the love of the game. As a result, the singular honour of representing one's country and of excelling simply for the sake of competing against those who excel in other countries has been diminished if not lost altogether. For the young, hockey-playing boy of today, the nocturnal gold medal message is clear — the Olympic dream cannot be realized unless he makes it to the NHL.

This book consists of four elements: (1) stories, anecdotes and a written history of each Olympics, keeping in mind the development of hockey and the Olympics and of Canada's role along the way; (2) game summaries and end of Games statistics for every game Canada has played at the Olympics and for every player who has participated; (3) photographs, many before never previously published, for each

Olympics, providing important visual documentation of the way the game has been played; (4) a complete Fact, Guide, and Record Book, listing every Canadian player, every statistic, achievement and trivia from 1920–1994, the first of its kind ever published.

Read, discover, and enjoy, and in February 1998, during the wee, wee hours of the morning, remember — Go Canada Go!

ANDREW PODNIEKS
TORONTO 1997

CHAPTER 1

The Games of the VIIth Olympiad

ANTWERP, BELGIUM

April 23–September 12, 1920
(Winter Olympics held April 23–29, 1920)

Mike Goodman

Antwerp was chosen at the 18th IOC Session in Lausanne, Switzerland on April 5, 1919 to host the 1920 Olympics. Other bids came from Amsterdam, Budapest, Havana, Atlanta, Cleveland, and Philadelphia.

These Olympics were historic for three reasons: this was the first time the Olympic oath was taken by a competitor (Victor Boin), the first time the Olympic flag was flown, and the first time doves were released from the stadium as a symbol of peace.

FINAL PLACINGS

GOLD MEDAL
Canada

SILVER MEDAL
United States

BRONZE MEDAL
Czechoslovakia

FOURTH PLACE
Sweden

TEAM CANADA • 1920

WINNIPEG FALCONS

Wally Byron, *GOALIE*

Bobby Benson, *DEFENCE*
Connie Johannesson, *DEFENCE*

Frank Fredrickson, *CENTRE (CAPTAIN)*
Chris Fridfinnson, *FORWARD*
Mike Goodman, *LEFT WING*
Slim Halderson, *RIGHT WING*
Allan "Huck" Woodman, *ROVER*

Gordon Sigurjonson, *COACH*
H.A. Axford, *MANAGER*
William Hewitt, *SECRETARY*

THE WINNIPEG FALCONS

The Falcon Hockey Club began playing in 1908 when the Viking and Athletic Clubs joined forces, but disbanded after only one season. In 1912, H.A. Axford, Bill Fridfinnson, John Davidson, and Harvey Benson reorganized the Falcons with a new group of young players, winning the Independent Intermediate League their first winter of competition.

The following year the team moved up to the more skilled, three-team Independent Senior League, playing Portage La Prairie and Selkirk, and winning the championship in just their second season. For 1915–16, they played in Division II of the Patriotic League, along with Winnipeg and Vics. The entire team then joined the army in 1916 and played hockey for the 223rd Battalion. When they returned from overseas they captured the championship for Western Canada the same season.

Incredibly, five members from the 1912 team helped the Falcons this Olympic year — Frank Fredrickson, Bobby and Harvey Benson, Wally Byron, and Connie Johannesson (although Harvey Benson didn't make the trip to Antwerp). With this superb nucleus, this mostly Icelandic–Canadian contingent played together for a number of years, developing a bond as team-mates both on and off the ice and becoming one of the greatest early-era teams in Canadian amateur hockey history.

Rather than selecting an all-star team at the last minute, the Canadian Olympic Committee felt that the group of amateur players most deserving to represent Canada — and the team most likely to win — would be Canada's amateur titleists, the Allan Cup champions. To qualify for the Allan Cup finals, the Falcons whipped the Fort William Maple Leafs in Winnipeg by scores of 7–2 and 9–1 before carrying on to Toronto to play Varsity (the University of Toronto team) in a two-game total-goals series for amateur supremacy in Canada and the right to travel to Belgium as Canada's national hockey team. Jaded Torontonians, who thought they had the best hockey players in the country, were treated to great "western" hockey. The result was that the Varsity team was hammered 8–3 on March 28 and 3–2 the following night before a stunned Hogtown crowd. The Falcons were Allan Cup champions and on their way to Belgium.

THE TRIP

Getting to the host city was a significant part of Olympic participation in the early days of the Games. The total cost of the voyage from Canada to Antwerp was estimated at $10,000, a colossal sum that was collected from Allan Cup receipts as well as from handsome donations from both the Manitoba government ($2,000) and the City of Winnipeg ($500). After winning the Allan Cup, the Falcons carried on directly from Toronto to Ottawa and then to Montreal, where they were welcomed by William Northey, Allan Cup trustee, and members of the Montreal AAA (Amateur Athletic Association) team. The Falcons arrived in Saint John, New Brunswick on April 3, where they boarded the CPR steamship *SS Melita* two days later.

The voyage to Liverpool took a week and was reasonably uneventful, save for team captain Frank Fredrickson's falling out of his bunk and hurting his head. The ship's carpenter, meanwhile, carved two dozen hockey sticks from "rough" wood the team had obtained in Montreal; these were the only sticks the Falcons would

The Winnipeg Falcons *en route* to Antwerp aboard the *SS Melita*.

be using in the Olympics! The players also met four pilots on deck who volunteered to fly the team on the last leg of their journey from London to Antwerp. Foul weather, however, eventually scuppered these plans, so the team left for Antwerp by ship from Dover to Ostend.

HOCKEY AT THE OLYMPICS

There were two equally influential reasons why hockey was finally made an Olympic event, albeit as a demonstration sport, at these 1920 *Summer* Games. (The first Winter Olympic Games were held in 1924.) One reason was that for the first time, the International Olympic Committee was able to secure commitments to compete from at least five European nations — Belgium, France, Switzerland, Sweden, and the newly created Czechoslovakia (Germany and Austria, because of their involvement in World War I, were not allowed to participate in these Games). The second reason was that the managers of Antwerp's Le Palais de Glace stadium refused to allow their building to be used for figure skating unless hockey were included in the package! Because these two technicalities took time to arrange, it was not until mid-January that the competing nations (the five Europeans, as well as Canada and the United States) were informed of the event's inclusion in the Olympics.

RULES OF PLAY

The rules of the Games called for seven-man hockey (the six modern positions as well as a rover) and games would be divided into two twenty-minute halves separated by a ten-minute intermission. Tie games would go into overtime until a winner was decided. No substitutes were allowed, and if a man were injured, one from the other team had to come off the ice to even things up. This happened in the second half of Canada's game against Sweden when Connie Johannesson was injured. Both teams played six a side while he recovered from blocking a shot, and in the five minutes he was off Canada scored five goals.

Canadian rules of play were adopted for these Olympics, thanks entirely to the force of argument presented by William Hewitt (father of Foster), whose knowledge of hockey brought him instant respect in the international hockey community. In fact, the International Ice Hockey Federation (IIHF) was so impressed by Hewitt they gave him the honour of refereeing the first match in the history of Olympic hockey, Sweden vs. Belgium. Incredibly, there were *four* goal judges, two at each end, a *group* of timekeepers, and a penalty-timer who took his place in the corner of the rink, isolated from his colleagues. Such was the success of Hewitt's competitive, yet gentlemanly, interpretation of the rules as a referee that, at IOC meetings during the course of the Games, the Committee decided to adopt Canadian rules of play for all future international competitions.

While crossing the Atlantic, the players trained as often as their stomachs would permit.

Hewitt described the goal nets at the Antwerp Ice Palace as more like "folded gates" than the nets used in Canada, and although painted the traditional red, they were secured to the ice only by short nails. The dimensions of the natural-ice rink were miniscule by Canadian standards, just 165 feet long by 58½ feet wide. The rink was obviously built to accommodate figure skating and ice dancing, not hockey. The boarding was paneled and painted white, making bounces irregular and unfaithful. During games, netting was hoisted all around the rink to protect fans.

Interestingly, chairs and tables were placed at one end and side of the rink so those patrons who wished to dine and drink while watching the hockey action — and listen to an orchestra which played ceaselessly from morning till dark — could do so comfortably (early outdoor luxury boxes, as it were!).

Before each game, the national anthems of the competing teams were played, and after the final bell, "O, Canada" was played again to honour the winning team, the spectators standing in due respect.

THE SKINNY ON CANADA'S OPPONENTS

Sartorially speaking, team Canada players appeared in black and yellow uniforms with a large maple leaf sewn across the breast of the jersey. They were flummoxed by the appearance of two members of the French team, one who sported a long black beard, the other who was in his early forties and bald!

The Swedes came to the tournament familiar primarily with another form of hockey called bandy, a game which used short sticks like those in field hockey, and a large rubber ball. They were delighted and bemused by the "flat" Canadian ball (puck). Bandy was played on ice, but players wore speed skates and the playing area was as large as a soccer field. Thus, the Swedes were elegant skaters, but had little ability to stop and start like the Canadians and even less experience in the art of body-checking.

Also, the Swedes dressed like soccer players, wearing virtually no upper-body padding, no shin guards, and very crude hockey gloves. The goaler wore what Hewitt described as "a cross between a blacksmith's apron and an aviator's coat." As far as their play was concerned, the Swedes improved immensely in their first few days in Antwerp, most notably in their ability to check and control the puck, by watching the Canadians practise. However, when Canada's Mike Goodman refused to sell the Swedes his skates after the tournament (all the Americans gladly turned a profit), they became certain Goodman had a motor concealed in the tube of his boot or blade somewhere! A month before leaving for Europe, Goodman had, in fact, won the North American speed skating championship.

The Czechs, meanwhile, were dismissed by Hewitt out of hand: "They run on their skates with clumsy movements and use wrist shots and their play is all individual." The Americans, with so many Canadians on their team (see below), were clearly the only other competition in the tournament.

OLYMPIC ELIGIBILITY

As this was the first time hockey had been included in competition at the Olympics, there arose a dispute, particularly between the Canadians and Americans, as to which players were eligible to play for which country. More specifically, Canadians felt on principle that the United States was not playing fair when the Americans submitted a team list that included no fewer than *seven* Canadian-born players.

However, the Belgian Olympic Committee ruled the list was acceptable, and again spelled out the rules for eligibility to enlighten those who might have been unsure:

> ***Admission:***
> Only amateur athletes to be admitted to the Olympic Games.
>
> ***Necessary conditions for the representation of any given country:***
> It is necessary to be a native of any given country or a naturalized citizen of same or of the sovereign power to which said nation forms a part.
>
> Whoever has once taken part in the Olympic Games as a citizen of any given nation, cannot be admitted in any future Olympiad as a candidate for any other nation, even if he has been naturalized in that country save and excepting cases of conquest or the creation of fresh states duly ratified by treaty.
>
> In case of naturalization, the naturalized subject must supply adequate proofs that he was an amateur in his native country up to the time of his change of nationality.

THE FINISH AND RETURN

On the evening of April 27, after winning the gold medal the previous day, the Falcons were fêted royally as guests of the Canadian Pacific ocean service officers in Antwerp. Two nights later, the team received their medals, and after the ceremony Mike Goodman gave a performance of trick-skating during a hugely popular show by the figure skaters. The appreciative crowd demanded an encore from Goodman, and only Goodman.

After departing Antwerp, the players visited the battlefields of Belgium and France before carrying on to Paris, where Winnipeg Mayor Waugh was awaiting their arrival with a sumptuous banquet prepared in their honour. Frank Fredrickson and team coach Gordon Sigurjonsson left for Iceland, while the rest of the team set sail from Le Havre on May 5 aboard the *SS Grampian*. Their departure was something of a miracle as all seamen and dock workers were on strike. Le Havre was a madhouse, and the *Grampian* was the only vessel to leave as scheduled.

Ten days later the Falcons reached Quebec City, and went directly to Montreal and the next day to Toronto, where they were honoured non-stop for the balance of the day, beginning with a lunch given by the Sportsmen's Patriotic Association.

Later, they were guests of the City of Toronto at the Royal York Hotel, where Mayor Tommy Church welcomed the team with open arms, gifts, stories, and entertainment. Sheriff Paxton presented William Hewitt with a monocle to complete the

team secretary's formal attire. After Jack Slack sang a few songs, Mayor Church invited everyone to a night of boxing. He reminded one and all that the first fight on the card was scheduled for 8:30 P.M. sharp, and they all proceeded to the Arena Gardens (Mutual Street Arena).

The final celebration, of course, awaited the players in their home town. They reached Winnipeg on May 22, and were given a huge parade downtown leading to Wesley College field where they were presented the Allan Cup. After the ceremonies, the team was given its final banquet of the season, at the Fort Garry Hotel before some 400 honoured guests. The World's Champions then settled down to enjoy a peaceful summer.

The Competition

TOURNAMENT FORMAT

The "Bergvall" system of elimination was employed, that being a unique knockout format between the nations in the first round. Those who won went on to compete for the gold medal; those who lost games to the champion — Canada — played another knockout series for the silver; and those who lost games to the silver medalists — the United States — went on to play for the bronze (France, owing to the luck of the draw, received a bye in the first playdown and thus qualified right away for the gold medal round).

THE OPPOSITION

BELGIUM • Maurice Deprez, François Franck, Paul Goeminne, Jean-Maurice Goossens, Paul Loicq, Phillippe von Volcksom, Gaston van Volxem, François Vergulet

CZECHOSLOVAKIA • Adolf Dusek, Karel Hartmann, Karel Kotrba, Josef Loos, Vilem Loos, Jan Palous, Jan Peka, Karel Pesek-Kada, Josef Sroubek, Otakar Vindys, Karel Walzer

FRANCE • Jean Chaland, Pierre Charpentier, Henri Couttet, Georges Dary, Jacques Gaittet, Leonhard Quaglia, Alfred de Rauch

SWEDEN • Wilhelm Arwe, Erik Burman, Seth Howander, Albin Jansson, Georg Johansson, Einar Lindqvist, Einar Lundell, Hansjacob Mattsson, Nils Molander, Sven Safwenberg, Einar Svensson

SWITZERLAND • Rodolphe Cuendet, Louis Dufour, Max Holzbauer, Marius Jaccard, Bruno Leuzinger, Paul Lob, Rene Savoie, Max Sillig

UNITED STATES • Ray Bonney, Anthony Conroy, Herbert Drury, Edward Fitzgerald, George Geran, Frank Goheen, Joe McCormick, Larry McCormick, Frank Synott, Leon Tuck, Cyril Weidenborner

FINAL STANDINGS

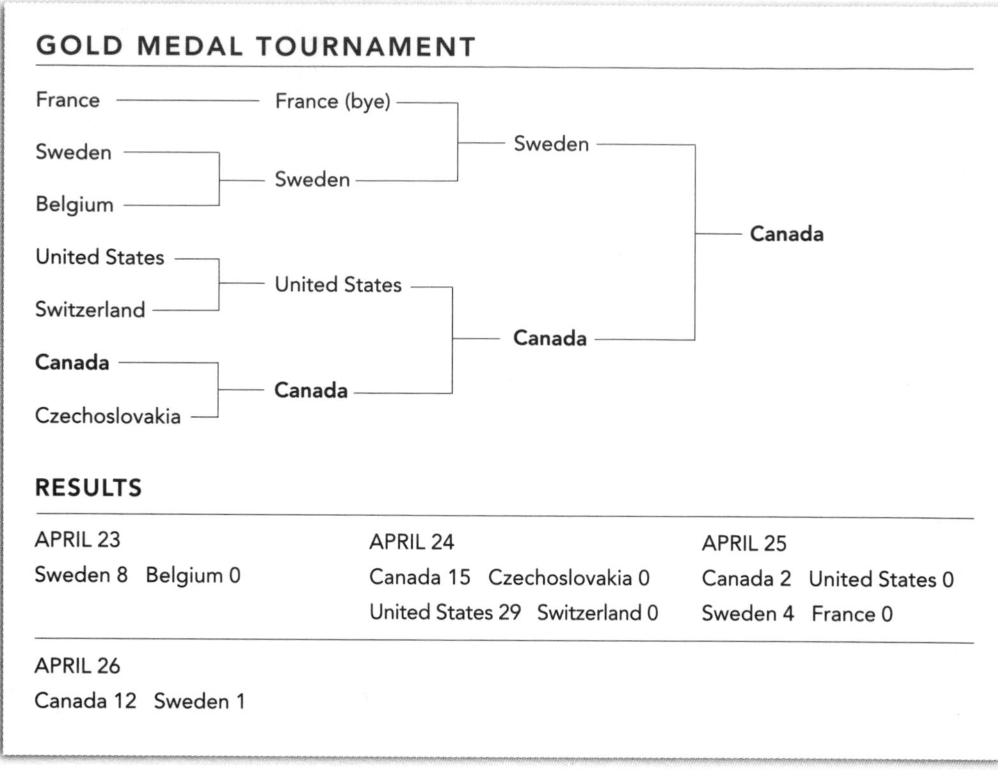

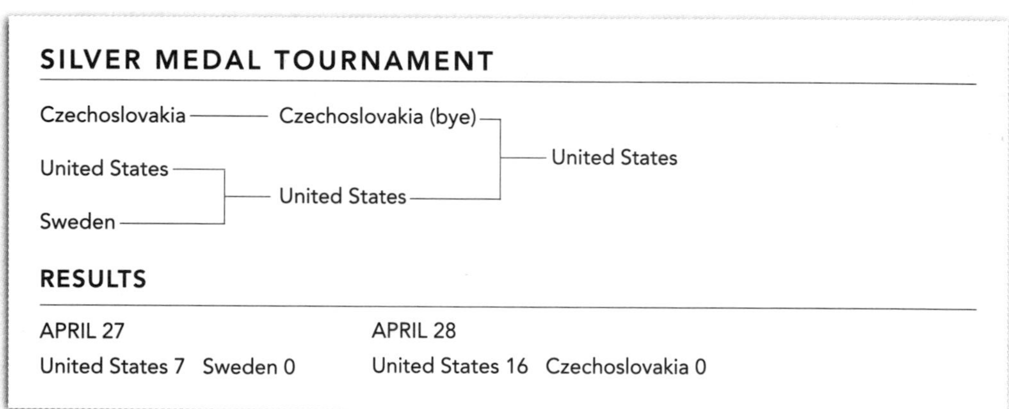

BRONZE MEDAL TOURNAMENT

Czechoslovakia — Czechoslovakia (bye) —
Sweden —
Switzerland — Sweden —
— Czechoslovakia

RESULTS

APRIL 28
Sweden 4 Switzerland 0

APRIL 29
Czechoslovakia 1 Sweden 0

TEAM CANADA GAME SUMMARIES

APRIL 24 • Canada 15 Czechoslovakia 0

FIRST HALF (20 minutes)
Canada 10 Czechoslovakia 0

SECOND HALF (20 minutes)
Canada 5 Czechoslovakia 0

penalties:
Canada — none
Czechoslovakia — three minors

GOAL SCORING
Canada Halderson • 7 goals
Fredrickson • 4 goals
Goodman • 2 goals
Johanneson • 1 goal
Woodman • 1 goal

IN GOAL
Canada — Byron
Czechoslovakia — Dusek

APRIL 25 • Canada 2 United States 0

FIRST HALF (20 minutes)
No Scoring
penalties: *Goheen (US)*

SECOND HALF (20 minutes)
1. Canada, Fredrickson • 11:00
2. Canada, Johanneson • 18:00
penalties: *Fredrickson (Can), Fredrickson (Can-major), Goheen (US-major)*

IN GOAL
Canada — Byron
United States — Bonney

APRIL 26 • Canada 12 Sweden 1

FIRST HALF (20 minutes)
1. Canada, Halderson • 1:15
2. Canada, Fridfinnson • 1:55
3. Canada, Fredrickson • 5:20
4. Sweden, Svensson • 15:58
5. Canada, Fredrickson • 16:00
6. Canada, Fredrickson • 17:35

SECOND HALF (20 minutes)
7. Canada, Goodman • 3:47
8. Canada, Benson • 8:09
9. Canada, Fredrickson • 9:15
10. Canada, Fredrickson • 9:30
11. Canada, Fredrickson • 14:55
12. Canada, Halderson • 16:20
13. Canada, Fredrickson • 19:02

IN GOAL
Canada — Byron
Sweden — Howander

TEAM CANADA FINAL STATISTICS • 1920

	GP	G	A	P	Pim	
Frank Fredrickson	3	12	—	12	2	
Slim Halderson	3	9	—	9	—	
Mike Goodman	3	3	—	3	—	
Connie Johannesson	3	2	—	2	—	
Bobby Benson	3	1	—	1	—	
Chris Fridfinnson	3	1	—	1	—	
Allan Woodman	3	1	—	1	—	
IN GOAL	**GP**	**W-L-T**	**Mins**	**GA**	**SO**	**Avg**
Wally Byron	3	3–0–0	120	1	2	0.50*

** average converted for consistency based on 60-minute games*

CHAPTER 2

The First Olympic Winter Games

CHAMONIX, FRANCE

January 25–February 5, 1924

In June 1922, the French Olympic Committee invited representatives from around the world to a special meeting outlining plans for an International Sports Week in Chamonix in early 1924 involving tournaments in hockey, skating, and skiing. Officially, the original title of the competition was "Semaine internationale des sports d'hiver," but on May 29, 1925 the IOC amended its mandate to include winter games. Thus, the 1924 event is now considered the First Winter Olympics (hockey, remember, had been a demonstration sport at the 1920 SUMMER Games at Antwerp).

TEAM CANADA • 1924

TORONTO GRANITES

Jack Cameron, *GOAL*
Ernie Collett, *GOAL*

Dunc Munro, *DEFENCE (CAPTAIN)*
Beattie Ramsay, *DEFENCE*

Hooley Smith, *CENTRE*

Cyril "Sig" Slater, *LEFT WING*
Harry Watson, *LEFT WING*

Bert McCaffery, *RIGHT WING*
Harold McMunn, *RIGHT WING*

Frank Rankin, *COACH*
William Hewitt, *GENERAL MANAGER*

FINAL PLACINGS

GOLD MEDAL
Canada

SILVER MEDAL
United States

BRONZE MEDAL
Great Britain

FOURTH PLACE
Sweden

FIFTH PLACE (tie)
Czechoslovakia
France

SEVENTH PLACE (tie)
Belgium
Switzerland

THE TORONTO GRANITES

The Granites was a team formed by ex-servicemen from the Great War. From the time they began competing in the Ontario Hockey Association (OHA) in 1919–20 until they disbanded (after the 1924 Olympics), the team was virtually unbeatable. They won the John Ross Robertson Cup in 1920, 1922, and 1923 (OHA Senior champions), and were runners-up to the University of Toronto in 1921.

The team qualified as Canada's Olympic representatives by winning the Allan Cup in successive seasons. In 1922, they beat the Regina Victorias 6–2 and 7–0 in games played in Toronto, and in 1923 they beat the University of Saskatchewan 11–2. However, some Granite players from these teams — Alex Romeril, Hugh Fox, Don Jeffrey, and Jack Aggett — were unable to make the trip overseas and were replaced by amateurs from the west (Harold McMunn from Winnipeg's Falcon Hockey Club) and east (Sig Slater from Montreal's Victoria Hockey Club).

Once the final roster had been established, the team played exhibition games against the best amateur teams in Toronto, Hamilton, Sault Ste. Marie, London, Niagara Falls, Ottawa, Kingston, and Montreal, finishing their tour with a sound 4–1 win over the Abeyweits of Charlottetown in a game played at Saint John, New Brunswick.

THE TRIP

The Granites left Toronto on Monday, January 6, 1924 and were joined in Montreal by Canadian champion figure skaters Melville Rogers and Cecil Eustace Smith. In Saint John, the contingent was completed by Charles Gorman, speed skating champion. The group left New Brunswick aboard the *SS Montcalm* on January 11, arrived in Liverpool on the 19th, and continued on to London and Paris, reaching Chamonix on the 22nd, where they booked into the Chamonix Palace Hotel, a short distance from the Olympic Stadium.

In an early attempt to get first-hand information for its readers, the *Toronto Telegram* hired left-winger Harry Watson to write two highly enjoyable journal-style reports for the paper, one while crossing the Atlantic, the other from Chamonix. The intent was to save the paper money by not sending a reporter overseas, to get one player's opinions and observations of the trip, and to provide social commentary on the international event. Watson's coverage was both playful and evocative.

> Jan. 11, 1924 — Today is a memorable day in the lives of the Canadian Olympic team for, having finished up our Canadian tour, we are finally on our way on the *RMS Montcalm* for Chamonix to defend the world's championship against all comers from Jan. 29 to Feb. 5, 1924.
>
> The trip started in a not too promising manner as the Bay of Fundy was on its bad behaviour and certainly showed its mean disposition with a wind, rain, and fog storm from the time we set sail till the morning of Jan. 12. The result was that most of us remained on deck till pretty late. Hooley Smith had bet me $10 that he wouldn't be seasick, but about 11 P.M. was counted out by Referee

P.J. Mulqueen. At this time Hooley's main cry was "And we've got to come back!"

Breakfast on the 12th was a very sad affair, as Jack Cameron, Ramsay, Rankin, and myself were the only members to appear. This was the day of Dunc Munro's famous quotation: "Why the —— don't they hold the games at Oakville?" He was afraid he was going to die; the next day he was afraid he wasn't going to die.

Sunday was a beautiful day, quite warm and sunny. All who were capable attended service in the dining room. Some stayed through the whole service; others walked, ran, or lurched towards the stairs at different intervals for reasons known only to themselves.

Monday the 14th, the majority of the team were able to sit up and take nourishment, but Dunc was still feeling the effects of the first night. A shuffle-board contest was arranged by Mr. Hewitt, which was won by Miss Edna Mulqueen and myself after some real battles. A deck tennis tournament was won by Jack Cameron and Maude (Jim) Smith. As usual, St. Andrew's College boys to the fore, as it should be.

Tuesday the 15th, the boys were all feeling pretty well, so a little exercise was indulged in, throwing the medicine ball, skipping, and a few jogs around the deck to finish off. Still perfect weather.

Wednesday the 16th was celebrated with a repetition of Tuesday's training and a concert by the crew in aid of Seamen's Charities. The concert was very good and ended in Mr. Mulqueen auctioning an autographed picture of the team for $25 to Mr. Scott of the Montreal *Gazette*. Hooley told Mr. Scott he was crazy, as he would have sold him a dozen for $5.

Thursday much of the same with Jack Cameron and myself still holding the record for not having missed a meal; also for Jack's winning of a progressive bridge party, the prize being a box of cigarettes, and the winner being a non-smoker, his room-mate H.E.W. has taken possession of the prize.

Friday the 18th — At 5:30 this morning we passed the Fastnet Lighthouse and so are practically in port. We dock at Liverpool early tomorrow and from there to London. It has been a wonderful and delightful trip, and our only hope now is that we can get to Chamonix at the earliest opportunity, so that we may start heavy training again and justify the confidence that has been placed in us and retain for Canada supremacy in the hockey world.

Chamonix, France. Jan. 24 — The Olympic team arrived at Liverpool on the 19th, and after much taking of pictures by the *Daily Mail,* etc., and hunting for baggage, we left for London at 11:00 A.M. arriving at 2:00 P.M. after a very enjoyable trip. Hooley Smith thought the English trains were toys but found out differently later, as we covered the 200 miles in less than four hours.

After registrating at the Cecil we (Dunc Munro, Cameron, Hooley, and self) set out on a tour of inspection. At this stage two and six was the only coin the others knew and everything was figured in how many 2.6's. We had a lot of fun: bought a lot of stuff and arrived back at the Cecil satisfied and tired. I took the boys from there to the famous home of roast beef — Simpson's — and we sure did justice to England's finest roast. From there we went to see the "Beauty Prize" at the Winter Garden, which was very good. Bed at 11:45 P.M. as our train left at 10 A.M. the next day.

The next thing I knew was a voice over the phone informing Cameron and I that it was 9:40 and they were leaving the hotel. Needless to say, we thought our chances of catching the train very slim, but we arrived at the station at 9:59, no collars, boots undone — but in time. Capt. Munro was very annoyed but it turned out he had omitted our room number when giving instructions as to being called, so he had to take it back.

We had a wonderfully calm trip from Dover to Calais and from there to Paris, passing the Canadian cemetery at Etaples, which is wonderfully well kept by the French: also other places of great interest.

Arrived at Paris at 6:30 P.M. and immediately inquired for seats at the "Follies Bergéres", which we obtained and the whole team trotted there *en masse*. Boxes, if you please, and a wonderful time was had by all, the best parts of which I will withhold until I hear from the censor.

Opening ceremonies, Chamonix, 1924.

The following day, the 21st, we were treated to a wonderful trip all around Paris by the president of the French Olympic committee. It is surely a wonderful place and the new Olympic stadium is a splendid structure, having a running track 1,000 metres around and a seating capacity of 60,000.

We left Paris at 8:30 P.M. on the 21st, travelling all night in what they term a "couchette" or sleeping car. They supply the beds but no blankets, which we found out after we had left Paris.

We arrived at Chamonix about 11:30 A.M. on the 22nd after a wonderful trip by electric train through the mountains. So far we have been unable to get on ice, as it is very mild, but everybody is in good physical condition and as soon as we get ice, as Bert McCaffery says, from then on we go.

THE GAMES

All games were played outside, on natural ice, on a European size rink, quite unfamiliar to the Canadians who were used to smaller confines that created a more physical game. Also, the boards were only about a foot high, thus preventing the Canadians from using them with the skill they did back home, particularly for hitting and passing. Additionally, netting was put up at both ends to prevent the "loss" of pucks. Ice conditions were often so poor that the boards had to be relocated almost daily to ensure the best possible patch of ice was being used!

From the time the Granites arrived, the weather varied in the extreme, from warm sun to heavy rains. These conditions were not ideal for hockey, and the Canadians were unable to have even one practice to acclimatize themselves to the already alien rink. On January 25, they made an attempt to skate but were quickly whisked off the ice after complaints from Norway, Sweden, and Finland, all of which claimed Canada had not scheduled the practice. In order to stay in shape the Canadians did road work, running and the like. None of these obstacles hampered the team, which was vastly superior to the competition and easily retained the gold medal the Winnipeg Falcons had won for Canada at the 1920 Olympics at Antwerp.

SUPERFLUOUS TENDING OF THE GOAL

Such was the strength of the Canadian team that goaler Jack Cameron had a tough time maintaining his interest in games that saw him literally idle from start to finish. Legend has it that Cameron frequently skated to the boards to chat up the young ladies who were in attendance. Later in life, he denied the allegations but did impart one interesting anecdote by way of replacement gossip: "The only girl I remember," he recalled, "was a little blonde 11-year old figure skater on the Norwegian team. When she wasn't competing, she sat on our bench. Her name was Sonja Henie and she was a great booster of the Granites." The pulchritudinous Henie finished last in competition that year, but in the next Games dazzled the world with her gold medal-winning performance and went on to become both a professional skater and popular film star.

THE FINALS

Even before play to decide the gold medal between the Canadians and Americans began, there was controversy. Both William Hewitt and W. S. Haddock, managers for the Canadians and Americans respectively, refused the official proposal to draw the referee's name from a hat. Both men agreed that choosing an official from among the continental countries competing (Britain, France, Sweden, Belgium, Switzerland, and Czechoslovakia) would likely leave this important game in the hands of an inexperienced man. In the end, negotiations resulted in Hewitt proposing Paul Loicq of Belgium and Haddock selecting La Croix of France. Hewitt objected that La Croix might be related to the American goalie of the same name. A coin toss settled the argument, and Loicq became the referee.

The weather for the game was perfect — clear and cold — producing hard, fast ice. The US won the right to choose which end they preferred after referee Loicq ruled that that choice belonged to the team whose captain was older! Irving Small bested Dunc Munro in that department and elected to defend the west end, meaning Canada had to play into the sun for the first and third periods. The start of play was further delayed while the captains argued with Loicq over his interpretation of body-checking.

There was clearly an air of animosity to the game, created in part by Harry Watson's remark earlier that Canada would win 10 or 12 to nothing. Less than two minutes after the puck had been faced off, Watson was bleeding from the nose and American Willard Rice had been knocked out by Smylie's stick. By the end of the game, the Americans were exhausted and gasping for breath, and the Canadians tired but victorious thanks to the heroic and skilful play of their star forward trio of Watson, Smith, and McCaffery.

THE HONOURS

At a sumptuous banquet the night of the victory, February 3, 1924, Count Clary, chairman of the French Olympic Committee, wrote a note to his Canadian counterpart that read: "Le Comte Justinien Clary presents his compliments to Mr. Hewitt with all his admiration for your splendid hockey team and your brilliant final victory."

The Canadians returned to Paris and agreed to play an exhibition match with Great Britain on a circular rink 120 feet in diameter. As Hooley Smith confessed, however, the tour was beginning to weigh heavily on the players, and this Paris match was particularly enervating: "Between the champagne parties, excursions to the Follies Bergéres and the like, we were pooped out, and the only way we could get a rest during the exhibition game was to shoot the puck up among the champagne drinkers at the tables surrounding the rink. It was messy but effective."

The T. Eaton Co. entertained the team with a dinner and dance at the Claridge Hotel before the Granites carried on to London. There, the Canadian Club of Great Britain honoured them with a reception and dance at the British Columbia Hall. The team set sail for the Dominion on February 25th aboard the *SS Metagama* and received wonderful receptions on their arrival in Saint John, Montreal, and Toronto, where they were given a huge civic welcome and a grand parade from Union Station up Bay Street to City Hall, a fitting end to an immensely successful, 58-day Olympic trip.

The Competition

TOURNAMENT FORMAT

Eight nations were divided into two groups of four teams each and played a round-robin series within each group. The top two teams advanced to the finals. Preliminary round games between teams that advanced to the finals were "carried over." Thus, although there were four teams in the final round-robin, each only played two additional games versus teams in the other qualifying group. The preliminary games consisted of three 15-minute periods, but the finals were NHL-regulation: three 20-minute periods, and all were played at the Stade Olympique du Mont Blanc. Goalies were still not permitted to drop to their knees.

Interestingly, for these early Olympics, *players* often served as referees for matches they didn't play in. For instance, Dunc Munro refereed the Belgium–United States game, while Beattie Ramsay handled both the France–Great Britain match and the France–United States game. The aforementioned Loicq, who officiated the Canada–US game, was himself a player on the French team.

THE OPPOSITION

BELGIUM • Paul van den Broeck, Charles van den Driessche, Henri Louette, Andre Poplimont, Louis de Ridder, Frederick Rudolph, Victor Verschueren, Gaston van Volckxsom

CZECHOSLOVAKIA • Jaroslav Fleischmann, Miroslav Fleischmann, Ludvik Hofta, Jaroslav Jirkovsky, Jan Krasl, Vilem Loos, Josef Malecek, Jan Palous, Jaroslav Pusbauer, Jaroslav Rezac, Josef Sroubek, Jaroslav Stransky, Otakar Vindys

FRANCE • Andre Charlet, Pierre Charpentier, Jacques Chaudron, Raoul Couvert, Albert Hassler, Charles Lavaivre, Joseph Monard, Calixte Payot, Philippe Payot, Alfred de Rauch, Maurice del Walle, G.F. de Wilde

GREAT BRITAIN • William Anderson, Lorne Carr-Harris, Colin Carruthers, Eric Carruthers, George "Guy" Clarkson, Cuthbert Ross Cuthbert, George Holmes, Hamilton Jukes, Edward Pitblado, Blane Sexton

SWEDEN • Ruben Allinger, Vilhelm Arwe, Erik Burman, Birger Holmqvist, Gustaf Johansson, Hugo Johansson, Karl Josefson, Ernst Karlberg, Nils Molander, Einar Ohlsson

SWITZERLAND • Fred Auckenthaler, Louis Dufour, Emil Filliol, Max Holzboer, Maurice Jaccard, Ernest Jaquet, Bruno Leuzinger, Ernest Mottier, Peter Muller, Rene Savoie, Wilhelm de Siebenthal, Donald Unger, Andre Verdeil

UNITED STATES • Clarence "Taffy" Abel, Harry Drury, Alphonse Lacroix, John Langley, John J. Lyons, Justin McCarthy, Willard Rice, Irving Small, Frank Synnott

FINAL STANDINGS*

* *Austria was supposed to participate but withdrew just before the Games began*

PRELIMINARY ROUND • GROUP A

	GP	W	L	T	GF	GA	P
Canada	3	3	0	0	85	0	6
Sweden	3	2	1	0	18	25	4
Czechoslovakia	3	1	2	0	14	41	2
Switzerland	3	0	3	0	2	53	0

RESULTS

JANUARY 28
Canada 30 Czechoslovakia 0
Sweden 9 Switzerland 0

JANUARY 29
Canada 22 Sweden 0
Czechoslovakia 11 Switzerland 2

JANUARY 30
Canada 33 Switzerland 0

JANUARY 31
Sweden 9 Czechoslovakia 3

PRELIMINARY ROUND • GROUP B

	GP	W	L	T	GF	GA	P
United States	3	3	0	0	52	0	6
Great Britain	3	2	1	0	34	16	4
France	3	1	2	0	9	42	2
Belgium	3	0	3	0	8	45	0

RESULTS

JANUARY 28
United States 19 Belgium 0

JANUARY 29
Great Britain 15 France 2

JANUARY 30
Great Britain 19 Belgium 3
United States 22 France 0

JANUARY 31
France 7 Belgium 5
United States 11 Great Britain 0

MEDAL ROUND

	GP	W	L	T	GF	GA	P
Canada	3	3	0	0	47	3	6
United States	3	2	1	0	32	6	4
Great Britain	3	1	2	0	6	33	2
Sweden	3	0	3	0	3	46	0

RESULTS

CARRY OVER GAMES
Canada 22 Sweden 0
United States 11 Great Britain 0

FEBRUARY 1
Canada 19 Great Britain 2
United States 20 Sweden 0

FEBRUARY 3
Canada 6 United States 1
Great Britain 4 Sweden 3

TEAM CANADA GAME SUMMARIES

(assists, penalties, and times not recorded)

JANUARY 28 • Canada 30 Czechoslovakia 0

IN GOAL

Canada — Cameron

Czechoslovakia — Stransky

FIRST PERIOD (15 minutes)

1. Canada, Watson
2. Canada, McCaffery
3. Canada, Smith
4. Canada, Watson
5. Canada, Smith
6. Canada, Smith
7. Canada, Watson
8. Canada, unknown*

** the goal was scored so quickly the statistician didn't see the shooter and was unable to give official credit to any particular player*

SECOND PERIOD (15 minutes)

9. Canada, Ramsay
10. Canada, Watson
11. Canada, Munro
12. Canada, Slater
13. Canada, Slater
14. Canada, Smith
15. Canada, McMunn
16. Canada, Watson
17. Canada, Watson
18. Canada, McCaffery
19. Canada, Ramsay
20. Canada, Watson
21. Canada, Watson
22. Canada, Watson

THIRD PERIOD (15 minutes)

23. Canada, Watson
24. Canada, Ramsay
25. Canada, Munro
26. Canada, Watson
27. Canada, Munro
28. Canada, McMunn
29. Canada, McMunn
30. Canada, McCaffery

JANUARY 29 • Canada 22 Sweden 0

IN GOAL

Canada — Collett

Sweden — Ohlsson
(replaced for about five minutes in the 2nd by Joseffson after being hit by a shot)

FIRST PERIOD (15 minutes)

1. Canada, Munro
2. Canada, Smith
3. Canada, McCaffery
4. Canada, McCaffery
5. Canada, Ramsay

SECOND PERIOD (15 minutes)

6. Canada, Watson
7. Canada, Slater
8. Canada, McCaffery
9. Canada, Watson
10. Canada, Watson
11. Canada, Ramsay
12. Canada, Ramsay

THIRD PERIOD (15 minutes)

13. Canada, Watson
14. Canada, Watson
15. Canada, Ramsay
16. Canada, Smith
17. Canada, Smith
18. Canada, Watson
19. Canada, Smith
20. Canada, Munro
21. Canada, Munro
22. Canada, Ramsay

JANUARY 30 • Canada 33 Switzerland 0

FIRST PERIOD (15 minutes)

1. Canada, McCaffery
2. Canada, Watson
3. Canada., Watson
4. Canada, Watson
5. Canada, Ramsay
6. Canada, Munro
7. Canada, McCaffery
8. Canada, Watson

SECOND PERIOD (15 minutes)

9. Canada, Munro
10. Canada, Smith
11. Canada, Watson
12. Canada, Watson
13. Canada, Watson
14. Canada, McCaffery
15. Canada, Watson
16. Canada, McCaffery
17. Canada, Watson
18. Canada, Munro
19. Canada, Smith

THIRD PERIOD (15 minutes)

20. Canada, Smith
21. Canada, Smith
22. Canada, Watson
23. Canada, Watson
24. Canada, Munro
25. Canada, Watson
26. Canada, McCaffery
27. Canada, Smith
28. Canada, Watson
29. Canada, Ramsay
30. Canada, Munro
31. Canada, McCaffery
32. Canada, McCaffery
33. Canada, McCaffery

IN GOAL

Canada — Cameron
Switzerland — Savoie

FEBRUARY 1 • Canada 19 Great Britain 2

FIRST PERIOD (15 minutes)

1. Canada, McCaffery
2. Canada, Watson
3. Canada, Smith
4. Great Britain, C. Carruthers
5. Canada, McCaffery
6. Great Britain, C. Carruthers
7. Canada, McMunn
8. Canada, McCaffery

SECOND PERIOD (15 minutes)

9. Canada, Smith
10. Canada, Munro
11. Canada, Munro
12. Canada, Smith
13. Canada, Munro
14. Canada, McCaffery

THIRD PERIOD (15 minutes)

15. Canada, Smith
16. Canada, Munro
17. Canada, Watson
18. Canada, McCaffery
19. Canada, Watson
20. Canada, McMunn
21. Canada, Slater

IN GOAL

Canada — Collett
Great Britain — Carr-Harris

FEBRUARY 3 • Canada 6 United States 1

IN GOAL

Canada — Cameron

United States — Lacroix

FIRST PERIOD (20 minutes)

1. Canada, Watson • 5:00

2. Canada, Watson • 8:00

3. United States, Drury • 8:50

penalties: *Smith (Can) & Abel (US)*

SECOND PERIOD (20 minutes)

4. Canada, Smith • 11:00

5. Canada, McCaffery • 12:00

6. Canada, Munro • 16:20

penalties: *Watson (Can) & Abel (US), Smith (Can) & Abel (US)*

THIRD PERIOD (20 minutes)

7. Canada, Watson • 12:00

penalties: *Munro (Can) & Synnott (US)*

TEAM CANADA FINAL STATISTICS • 1924

	GP	G	A	P	Pim
Harry Watson	5	36	—	36	2
Bert McCaffery	5	20	—	20	—
Hooley Smith	5	18	—	18	4
Dunc Munro	5	16	—	16	2
Beattie Ramsay	5	10	—	10	—
Harold McMunn	5	5	—	5	—
Sig Slater	5	4	—	4	—
unknown	—	1	—	—	—

IN GOAL	GP	W-L-T	Mins	GA	SO	Avg
Jack Cameron	3	3–0–0	150	1	2	0.40*
Ernie Collett	2	2–0–0	90	2	1	1.33*

* *average converted for consistency based on 60-minute games*

CHAPTER 3

The Second Olympic Winter Games

ST. MORITZ, SWITZERLAND

February 11–20, 1928

At the 24th session of the IOC at Prague in 1925, St. Moritz was awarded the 1928 Games over Davos and Engelberg, two other small Swiss towns.

Dr. Joe Sullivan

TEAM CANADA • 1928

UNIVERSITY OF TORONTO GRADUATES

Norbert "Stuffy" Mueller, *GOAL*
Dr. Joe Sullivan, *GOAL*

Frank Fisher, *DEFENCE*
Roger "Rod" Plaxton, *DEFENCE*
John "Red" Porter, *DEFENCE (CAPTAIN)*
Ross Taylor, *DEFENCE*

Hugh Plaxton, *CENTRE*

Dr. Lou Hudson, *RIGHT WING*

Dave Trottier, *LEFT WING*

Charlie Delahey, *FORWARD*
Grant Gordon, *FORWARD*
Bert Plaxton, *FORWARD*
Frank Sullivan, *FORWARD*

Conn Smythe, *COACH*
William Hewitt, *MANAGER*

FINAL PLACINGS

GOLD MEDAL
Canada

SILVER MEDAL
Sweden

BRONZE MEDAL
Switzerland

FOURTH PLACE
Great Britain

FIFTH PLACE
France

SIXTH PLACE
Czechoslovakia

SEVENTH PLACE (tie)
Belgium
Austria

NINTH PLACE
Poland

TENTH PLACE
Germany

ELEVENTH PLACE
Hungary

THE UNIVERSITY OF TORONTO GRADUATES

The formation of the team was as simple as its name implies — a group of players who graduated from the U of T and went on to establish themselves in the Ontario Hockey Association. After winning the OHA title, the Grads travelled to Vancouver to meet Fort William in the Allan Cup finals. They won this too, although the scores were close, the first a 2–2 tie, then a 3–2 overtime loss and 4–1 win to force an unusual, tie-breaking, fourth game, which the Grads won 2–1 (after 20 minutes of overtime) and with it the right to represent Canada at the Olympics.

To prepare themselves for international competition, the Grads spent most of January playing exhibition matches to hone their skills. They played the University Club of Boston in Boston before returning to Canada to play teams *en route* to Halifax, where they set sail for St. Moritz. They played in Dunnville, Ontario on January 11, London on the 14th, Toronto the 16th, Kingston the 18th, the Vics in Montreal the 19th, and Halifax the 21st. They lost only once all month, the second game against Boston, and this marked but the third time in two years the team had been beaten (by the Marlies in S.P.A. competition 4–3 the previous year, and the aforementioned 3–2 loss to Fort William in the Allan Cup series in Vancouver on March 28, 1927).

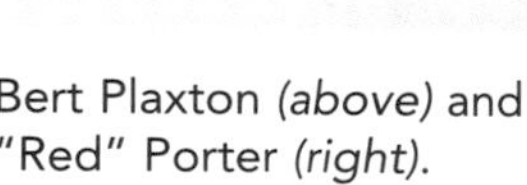

Bert Plaxton *(above)* and "Red" Porter *(right)*.

The last game in Canada was particularly satisfying for the team. They encountered heavy snowstorms and drifts from Montreal to Halifax via Moncton, but although tired and despite going straight from the station to the rink, the team was roused by an enormous crowd of 8,000 packed into the new Forum. The Grads played an all-star team from the Maritimes and won handily, and the fans were further treated to a speed-skating race featuring Dave Trottier and Ross Taylor of the Grads against two Maritimers. Trottier won the race in 16 seconds (in a building the size of Maple Leaf Gardens). His first prize was a silver cigarette case. In addition, all Olympians received a pen knife by way of "good luck" from their Halifax supporters. The next day, January 22, they set sail at 4 P.M. aboard the Red Star liner *SS Arabic*.

THE TEAM, ALTERED

Controversy crept into the Grads' preparations when coach Conn Smythe was not allowed to add two players — Wes Kirkpatrick and Dick Richards — to the Olympic roster for St. Moritz. Two of his players — Joe Sullivan and Hugh Plaxton — lobbied over Smythe's head to get their relatives on the squad instead, threatening to boycott the Games if their brothers were not selected to the Olympic team. Smythe was livid and refused to go overseas without the men to whom he had promised positions. However, Frank Sullivan, Bert Plaxton, and Roger Plaxton were put on the team and Kirkpatrick, Richards, and Smythe were left in Canada.

THE TRIP

The team arrived in Cherbourg, France in a record-setting six days, 18 hours, and carried on directly to Antwerp the next day, January 29. The crossing, just as it had in 1924, took its toll on the players' health: Dave Trottier and Red Porter were in sick bay for two days, Hugh Plaxton for a day, and Lou Hudson gave up a meal or two to the high waves.

The Canadians maintained fighting trim by jogging laps around the deck, Ross Taylor regimenting himself to 24 laps a day. W.A. Fry of Dunnville, the former president of the Ontario Hockey Association, was also on board, providing song sheets of popular music and keeping spirits up. The skiers and skaters on board carried on from Antwerp to St. Moritz, but the Grads remained at the Grand Hotel in Belgium the rest of the week to recover and get their bearings. They practised daily at the Palais de Glace in Antwerp, the same sheet where the Canadians had won the 1920 gold medal.

While in Antwerp, the Grads also had a chance to see the sights and explore a new culture for the first time. Team captain Red Porter wrote of his experiences for the *Toronto Star:*

> A strange mingling of Belgian customs with the modern innovations of America is the salient impression brought home forcibly to the average visitor to this progressive kingdom. Expensive American cars sweep over the same cobblestones that are traversed by the little two-wheel pushcarts of the peasants under which small dogs in harness strain their backs...
>
> Among the money-luring devices invented for the "benefit" of tourists is the "café de luxe." There are about 20 in Antwerp, but no Belgians attend them. Some are about the size of a corner drugstore and others quite palatial. A man generally stands at the door outside with an official cap and informs the gullible that it costs nothing to enter. That lends an air of mystery immediately and some of the Canadian Olympic team became "gullible" very quickly. The man with the official cap always forgets to inform his victims that it might cost considerable to "get out." It does.
>
> ...One larger one we entered, with a ballroom in the rear and similar methods of management, had an orchestra of 10 pieces and

many attendants and more girls. You are spotted for "an American" long before you are seated, and no sooner had we arrived through a long hallway into the ballroom than the orchestra blared forth louder than ever, and the saxophone player started to sing "Ain't She Sweet" in English...Shortly after, when we rose to go after listening to a few numbers by the cabaret performers and surviving the frantic smiles of the "champagne-sirens," there was a noticeable movement of people towards us.

As ham sandwiches did not seem to be very profitable to such a place, the idea was now to take out the profit in tips. First the performers passed their plates, then the waiters their trays, and just as everything looked to be over the door men, now augmented in numbers, bowed low and pleaded for just a "trifle pour bière."

LEAVING BELGIUM

As a fond farewell to the city, the team's regulars and substitutes put on a spectacular Blue and White exhibition game at the Palais for the Belgian Olympic Committee, an evening that was a huge success according to star left winger Dave Trottier:

> ...the spectators were kind enough to consider almost every play as something marvellous, as something to applaud. It was real kind of them and something our fellows appreciated though at a loss to understand why all the enthusiasm.
>
> An orchestra graced the occasion and our appearance on the ice was signalled by an outburst of Belgian cheering that rather startled the boys. Evidently the Canadian soldier is still fresh in the

> minds of the Belgian people and we certainly benefited by it.
>
> The game itself was just one of those exhibition affairs, and with the rink poorly lighted and filled with tobacco smoke it was hard to even see the puck...
>
> As the game ended the entire audience jumped to its feet and gave three hearty cheers for the Grads. We enjoyed the game and certainly appreciated the wholehearted reception the people of Antwerp gave us.

The Grads arrived leisurely in St. Moritz on February 5, staying at the palatial Grand Hotel, from which many events of the Games could be seen from the balconies. The men were eager to defend the World's Championship earned so impressively by the Toronto Granites in 1924.

THE WEATHER

The opening ceremonies for the Olympics were accompanied by bitter cold and a snowstorm. A mere 300 spectators took up the challenge and welcomed the competitors from 25 nations as the parade proceeded to the ice rink where the athletes took the Olympic oath. Just four days later, however, on February 15, conditions were so mild that all events were postponed and organizers feared the Games might have to be cancelled. The ice on the rink had been reduced to slush, which wreaked havoc with the half-completed 10,000-metre speed-skating event. Within 48 hours, though, the cold returned and the Games were completed without futher meteorological influence.

SOME FREE TIME

Because of their acknowledged superiority, Canada was excused from the preliminary round of matches, and the team had some time on its hands while the other 10 nations fought their way to the medal round. On February 12, the Grads were invited to play in the small town of Zuoz, an experience documented by goalie Joe Sullivan for the *Toronto Star:*

> We do not play our first championship game till Feb. 16. Meanwhile we are not allowed to take part in any other pastime till our games are over. That means skiing, bobsledding and other interesting diversions are barred to us right now...
>
> Today, just to keep in trim, we played an exhibition game with Zuoz, a boys' school near here. It is about two hours' ride by train. We were royally received. The team was greeted with a band at the station and walked through an archway of hockey sticks, the boys of the school holding them and acting as a guard of honour. This school, specializing in modern languages, is modelled somewhat after Upper Canada College, Ridley, or St. Andrew's. They have a regular outdoor rink with a wonderful ice surface.
>
> After the game we were honoured with a luncheon, during

which we were praised most highly...We returned later in the day to find St. Moritz crowded with tourists who have been attracted to the Olympic Games. Interest is being taken in all branches of sport and, of course, our hockey team is being regarded as the favourite. A large crowd always watches our practices and we invariably give them something worth looking at. The Europeans particularly seem amazed at our skill and speed. All I hope now is that we can do as well in the games as we show in practice. If we do, then there is no doubt that we shall win our games easily and take back the world hockey championship with us.

STYLE OF PLAY: CANADA VS. EUROPE

Dave Trottier spent much of his spare time sizing up the oppostion and drew this assessment:

> These European teams play a rough and ready game of close checking and that means that it will be hard to score against them if they can match our speed.
>
> Some of these players are exceptionally fine skaters, especially those from Switzerland and Norway, but their stickhandling and the finer points of hockey team play, fast snappy passing, pokechecking, dodging a man, drawing a defence or goaler out — all these, instinctive in a Canadian player, are as yet an undeveloped art with the Europeans...
>
> Our team should have no difficulty in beating anything I have seen but we are going to take no chances, and a game is never won until the final whistle blows.

Opening ceremonies with the hockey rink in the background.

THE POST-OLYMPIC EXHIBITION

After the gold medal triumph, the Grads took their remarkable show on the European road, as it were. They played in Vienna, Berlin, Paris, and London, the last leg of their whirlwind tour, before heading home. While in London, they were given a dinner and dance following their game and left for Liverpool on March 9. The next day, they boarded the *Celtic,* the world's largest liner, back to Canada. While on board, all passengers were asked to look out for a plane flown by W.R. Hinchcliffe and Elsie Mackay, a brave couple trying to follow in the transatlantic footsteps of Charles Lindbergh. Sadly, the plane was never spotted and the couple never found.

Exactly a week later, the Grads docked at Halifax and were promptly whisked off to an arena for another exhibition game. They travelled to Toronto via Quebec City and Montreal, and were met at Union Station by a huge procession of University of Toronto students who marched them up Bay Street through a ticker-tape parade to City Hall. On March 22, the last in an exhausting line of honours, the Grads were given a dinner by the University of Toronto Sports Club attended by Conn Smythe, U of T president Robert Falconer, P.J. Mulqueen (Canadian Olympic Committee chairman), and all the athletes from the U of T.

POSTSCRIPT

Dr. Lou Hudson, the team's right winger, later became friends with the Barilko family in Timmins. It was Lou's brother, Henry, who piloted the Fairchild 24 plane that went missing August 27, 1951 while he and Leaf hero Bill Barilko were flying to the far north on a fishing expedition. Lou had originally planned to join the two, but the weight of the three men might have been too much for the small craft and he stayed home. The wreck was not discovered until January 6, 1962.

The Competition

TOURNAMENT FORMAT

All 10 European teams were placed in three divisions to play round-robin preliminary matches. One team from each division moved on to the medal round. Because of the team's universally acknowledged superiority, Canada received a bye directly into the medal round, which again was set up as a round-robin schedule for the four finalists. All games still consisted of three 15-minute periods.

Game rules still prohibited the goalie from falling to his knees (an early NHL rule as well) and defencemen couldn't kick the puck in their own end. Unlike the one-foot boards of 1920, these were five feet high, an unusual though not problematic height. The rink was just slightly wider than NHL standards at 200 feet x 90 feet.

As in the previous Olympics, Canadian players also acted as referees; this time Red Porter and Frank Fisher had the whistle-blowing honours bestowed upon them by the IOC.

THE OPPOSITION

AUSTRIA • Herbert Bruck, Walter Bruck, Jacques Dietrichstein, Hans Ertl, Josef Gobel, Hans Kail, Herbert Klang, Ulrich Lederer, Walter Sell, Peregrin Spevak, Hans Tatzer, Herman Weiss

BELGIUM • Andre Bautier, Roger Bureau, Hector Chotteau, Albert Colon, Francis Frank, William Hoorickx, Willy Kreitz, Jean Meens, David Meyer, Mark Pelzer, Jacques van Reysschoot, Pierre van Reysschoot, Jean van den Wonwer

CZECHOSLOVAKIA • Wolfgang Dorasil, Karel Hromadka, Jan Krasl, J. Lichnovski, J. Ludvig, Josef Malecek, Jan Peka, Jaroslav Rezac, Miroslav Stiegenhofer, Josef Stroubek, Jiri Tozicka

FRANCE • Armand Charlet, Raoul Couvert, Albert Hassler, Jacques Lacarriere, Philippe Lefebvre, Francois Mautin, Calixte Payot, Philippe Payot, Leonhard Quaglia, Alfred de Rauch, Gerard Simond

GERMANY • Gustav Jaenicke, W. Kittel, Franz Kreisel, Matthias Leis, F. Rammelmayr, Erich Romer, Walter Sachs, H. Schmid, Martin Schrottle, Marquard Slevogt, Alfred Steinke

GREAT BRITAIN • William Brown, Colin Carruthers, Eric Carruthers, Cuthbert Ross Cuthbert, Bernard Fawcett, Harold Greenwood, Frederick Melland, G.E.F. Rogers, Blane Sexton, William Speechley, Victor Tait, Charles Wyld

HUNGARY • Miklos Barcza, Frigyes Barna, Matyas Farkas, Tibor Heinrich, Peter Krempels, Istvan Krepuska, Geza Lator, Sandor Minder, Bela Ordody, Jozsef de Revay, Bela Weiner

POLAND • Tadeusz Adamowski, Edmund Czaplicki, Alexander Kowalski, Wlodzimierz Krygier, Lucjan Kulej, Stanislaw Pastecki, Alexander Sluczanowski, Josef Stogowski, Karol Szenajela, Alexander Tupalski, Kazimierz Zebrowski

SWEDEN • Carl Abrahamsson, Emil Bergman, Birger Holmqvist, Gustaf Johansson, Henry Johansson, Nils Johansson, Ernst Karlberg, Erik Larsson, Bertil Linde, Sigurd Oberg, Vilhelm Petersen, Kurt Sucksdorf

SWITZERLAND • Gianni Andreossi, Murezzan Andreossi, Robert Breiter, Louis Dufour, Charles Fasel, Albert Geromini, Fritz Kraatz, Adolf Martignoni, Heinrich Meng, Anton Morosani, Luzius Ruedi, Richard Torriani

FINAL STANDINGS

PRELIMINARY ROUND • POOL A

	GP	W	L	T	GF	GA	P
Great Britain	3	2	1	0	10	6	4
France	3	2	1	0	6	5	4
Belgium	3	2	1	0	9	10	4
Hungary	3	0	3	0	2	6	0

RESULTS

FEBRUARY 11
Great Britain 7 Belgium 3
France 2 Hungary 0

FEBRUARY 12
Belgium 3 Hungary 2
France 3 Great Britain 2

FEBRUARY 16
Great Britain 1 Hungary 0
Belgium 3 France 1

PRELIMINARY ROUND • POOL B

	GP	W	L	T	GF	GA	P
Sweden	2	1	0	1	5	2	3
Czechoslovakia	2	1	1	0	3	5	2
Poland	2	0	1	1	4	5	1

RESULTS

FEBRUARY 11
Sweden 3 Czechoslovakia 0

FEBRUARY 12
Sweden 2 Poland 2

FEBRUARY 13
Czechoslovakia 3 Poland 2

PRELIMINARY ROUND • POOL C

	GP	W	L	T	GF	GA	P
Austria	2	1	0	1	4	4	3
Switzerland	2	1	1	0	5	4	2
Germany	2	0	1	1	0	1	1

RESULTS

FEBRUARY 11
Austria 4 Switzerland 4

FEBRUARY 12
Germany 0 Austria 0

FEBRUARY 16
Switzerland 1 Germany 0

MEDAL ROUND

	GP	W	L	T	GF	GA	P
Canada	3	3	0	0	38	0	6
Sweden	3	2	1	0	7	12	4
Switzerland	3	1	2	0	4	17	2
Great Britain	3	0	3	0	1	21	0

RESULTS

FEBRUARY 17
Canada 11 Sweden 0
Switzerland 4 Great Britain 0

FEBRUARY 18
Canada 14 Great Britain 0
Sweden 4 Switzerland 0

FEBRUARY 19
Canada 13 Switzerland 0
Sweden 3 Great Britain 1

TEAM CANADA GAME SUMMARIES

(assists and penalties not recorded)

FEBRUARY 16 • Canada 11 Sweden 0

FIRST PERIOD (15 minutes)
1. Canada, Trottier • 3:00
2. Canada, H. Plaxton • 3:30
3. Canada, Hudson • 13:30
4. Canada, Trottier • 14:00

SECOND PERIOD (15 minutes)
5. Canada, Trottier • 5:00
6. Canada, Sullivan • 8:00
7. Canada, H. Plaxton • 8:30
8. Canada, Trottier • 9:10

THIRD PERIOD (15 minutes)
9. Canada, Trottier • 5:00
10. Canada, Hudson • 6:30
11. Canada, Sullivan • 2:00

IN GOAL
Canada — Sullivan
Sweden — Johansson

FEBRUARY 18 • Canada 14 Great Britain 0

IN GOAL
Canada — Mueller
Great Britain — Speechley

FIRST PERIOD (15 minutes)
1. Canada, H. Plaxton • 4:00
2. Canada, Trottier • 6:00
3. Canada, B. Plaxton • 7:00
4. Canada, Hudson • 11:00
5. Canada, Hudson • 14:00
6. Canada, Porter • 14:30

SECOND PERIOD (15 minutes)
7. Canada, H. Plaxton • 2:00
8. Canada, H. Plaxton • 4:30
9. Canada, Fisher • 11:30
10. Canada, H. Plaxton • 3:00

THIRD PERIOD (15 minutes)
11. Canada, H. Plaxton • 3:00
12. Canada, Trottier • 4:45
13. Canada, B. Plaxton • 9:15
14. Canada, H. Plaxton • 12:15

FEBRUARY 19 • Canada 13 Switzerland 0

IN GOAL
Canada — Sullivan
Switzerland — Martignoni

FIRST PERIOD (15 minutes)
1. Canada, Taylor • 5:00
2. Canada, H. Plaxton • 11:00

SECOND PERIOD (15 minutes)
3. Canada, Porter • 5:00
4. Canada, Trottier • 8:15
5. Canada, H. Plaxton • 8:45
6. Canada, Porter • 9:15
7. Canada, Trottier • 10:00
8. Canada, Taylor • 14:30

THIRD PERIOD (15 minutes)
9. Canada, H. Plaxton • 2:10
10. Canada, Trottier • 3:10
11. Canada, Trottier • 3:40
12. Canada, Trottier • 5:25
13. Canada, H. Plaxton • 8:55

TEAM CANADA FINAL STATISTICS • 1928

	GP	G	A	P	Pim
Hugh Plaxton	3	12	—	12	—
Dave Trottier	3	12	—	12	—
Lou Hudson	3	4	—	4	—
Red Porter	3	3	—	3	—
Frank Sullivan	3	2	—	2	—
Bert Plaxton	1	2	—	2	—
Ross Taylor	1	2	—	2	—
Frank Fisher	1	1	—	1	—
Charles Delahey	1	0	—	0	—
Grant Gordon	1	0	—	0	—
Roger Plaxton	1	0	—	0	—

IN GOAL	GP	W-L-T	Mins	GA	SO	Avg
Joe Sullivan	2	2–0–0	90	0	2	0.00
Stuffy Mueller	1	1–0–0	45	0	1	0.00

CHAPTER 4

The Third Olympic Winter Games

LAKE PLACID, UNITED STATES

February 4–13, 1932

At the 28th IOC session in Lausanne, Switzerland on April 10, 1929 Lake Placid was awarded the 1932 Games over Montreal and several other American cities.

Romeo Rivers

TEAM CANADA • 1932

THE WINNIPEGS

William Cockburn, *GOAL (CAPTAIN)*
Stanley Wagner, *GOAL*

Roy Hinkel, *DEFENCE*
Hugh Sutherland, *DEFENCE*

George Garbutt, *CENTRE*
Walter Monson, *CENTRE*
Harold "Hack" Simpson, *CENTRE*

Bert "Spunk" Duncanson, *LEFT WING*
Romeo Rivers, *LEFT WING*
Aliston "Stoney" Wise, *LEFT WING*

Clifford Crowley, *RIGHT WING*
Victor Lindquist, *RIGHT WING*
Norm Malloy, *RIGHT WING*
Kenneth Moore, *RIGHT WING*

Jack Hughes, *COACH*
Lou Marsh, *MANAGER*

FINAL PLACINGS

GOLD MEDAL
Canada

SILVER MEDAL
United States

BRONZE MEDAL
Germany

FOURTH PLACE
Poland

THE WINNIPEG HOCKEY CLUB

In the first three Olympics, Canada had no trouble winning the gold medal each time. The teams representing the country were dominant and performed with the brilliance that was expected of them. However, the nomination of the Winnipeg Hockey Club to represent Canada in Lake Placid did not arouse the usual optimism. Far from it. Right from the get-go this was seen as a weak team, one that had won the Allan Cup convincingly over the Hamilton Tigers a year ago and that was current senior Canadian champion, to be sure, but somehow lacking the lustre and superiority of previous winners.

More specifically, the Canadian Olympic Association was worried about the lack of scoring ability on the team and was strongly in favour of adding players to the Winnipegs at the last minute to remedy this deficiency. To wit, they lost two games 1–0 and tied another 0–0 in the weeks leading up to the Games during competition in the Winnipeg City League in which they played (a total of six goals in seven league games), and the COA felt it had precedent on its side in wanting to alter the roster of a team going to the Olympics. When Hugh Fox, Alex Romeril, Jack Aggett, and Don Jeffrey could not accompany their Toronto Granites mates for the 1924 Games, Harold McMunn and Sig Slater were added to the club at the last minute. On the positive side, the Winnipegs had allowed only three goals in those seven league games and were considered the finest defensive team ever to play in Canada.

In this spirit, Walter Monson and Norm Malloy of the Senior A Selkirk Fisherman, and Bert Duncanson, a noted Junior A star, were added to this 1932 'Pegs team for offensive support. And, just before heading east to Toronto for their final two pre-Olympic exhibition games, the Winnipegs were given Norm Malloy of the Selkirks and Nelson Crutchfield of McGill Univeristy. However, on the advice of his parents, Crutchfield declined the Olympic offer a few days later, leaving the Winnipegs with too little time to add a replacement. The team reinstated Clifford Crowley, whose place was to have been taken by Crutchfield.

As final tune-ups for the Games, the 'Pegs played an exhibition match that consisted of two 30-minute exhibition periods in Toronto — one with the National Sea Fleas, the other with the Marlboros — on January 29, and a last game in Niagara Falls three days later before leaving for Lake Placid. To fans in Toronto, the 'Pegs played true to form, and the media were relentless in their criticism after the team was held without a goal over the 60 minutes and allowed one (to the Sea Fleas). One headline ran "Scoreless Wonders of the West Lived up to Reputation," and Lou Marsh's column underneath was equally derisive, beginning with, "Goals were as scarce as watercress in the Gobi desert up at the Gardens last night. When the statisticians got through adding up the counters they hadn't any more goals than One Eye Connelly has optics. The only one on the sheet was credited to the National Sea Fleas and there were three teams out there on the ice. The Canadian Olympic team drew a blank." This analysis paled next to the fantastic farewell reception the Winnipegs had received at the Amphitheatre at home when they beat the rival Selkirks 4-2 in their last league game four days earlier and were sent off with rousing home-town cheers and shouts of "Good luck, boys!"

CANADA-UNITED STATES FEUDING

Prior to and throughout these Games, the Americans did everything they could to bend the rules to their favour and distract the Canadians. Before arriving in Lake Placid, the US team played a game against the Boston Bruins for which fans paid for their tickets, and the Olympic team pocketed a large portion of the receipts. "I am of the opinion that under the amateur rules the United States team has professionalized itself by playing against the Boston Bruins," said P.J. Mulqueen, chairman of the Canadian Olympic Committee. The Americans argued by way of explanation that without this revenue they could not afford to go to the Games, but the fact remained that they had contravened the then strict rules for amateurs.

A distant view of the hockey rinks inside the speed-skating oval — not a spectator's delight.

Lou Marsh pointed out that team Canada could have done the same thing in Toronto, but knew this would be a serious violation of the rules and so declined. He observed that, "You can bet your last centime that if the shoe was on the other foot — and the Canadian team had played a pro club for any object where a gate was taken — there would be a protest!!" After pointing out their misgivings about the Americans, however, the Canadians, in true Conn Smythe spirit, refused to win a game off the ice and declined to launch a formal protest.

The Americans also frankly admitted to sending professional hockey players to the other two Olympics in which they competed, 1920 and 1924, again a basic violation of the prime tenet of the very existence of the Games. Stanley Woodward, in a column in the New York *Herald Tribune,* confessed: "As a matter of fact, our 1932 Olympic hockey team is a strictly amateur outfit...this is our first amateur Olympic hockey team." As one example, Irving Small, a member of the 1924 US team, sued a hockey team shortly after those Games were over for what he claimed was back pay owed him for his play in an "amateur" hockey league! He was only one of many old pros to represent the United States in 1924.

The next kerfuffle came when the Olympic schedule was sent to the Canadian team and the 'Pegs discovered they were being asked to play nine games in 11 days. Organizers had pre-sold tickets to hockey games based on eight nations participating. When only four registered, they didn't want to refund money to purchasers, so instead committed the competing teams to play two additional "exhibition" games (one against a group of Lake Placid all-stars, the other against a visiting McGill University team), proceeds going, of course, to the US Olympic Association. The Canadians were furious, although they acquiesced, and sent their subs to play those games (at the risk, of course, of injury).

Lastly, the village of Lake Placid featured two hockey venues, one outdoors and vastly inferior with a seating capacity of 8,000, the other in an arena with excellent ice but with a capacity less than half that. More specifically, the outdoor rink was contained *inside* the speed-skating oval! Spectators could see only half the rink and even then needed binoculars to distinguish players. The extreme cold did nothing to improve the spectator-appeal of the games. Despite the poor weather, horrible outdoor ice conditions, and extremely poor attendance (average of 1,500) most of the tournament was played outside, again to the detriment of quality of play. Superior conditions favour the superior team; inferior conditions help to minimalize the skill differences between the great and merely good.

THE UNITED STATES TEAM

Lou Marsh, the Samuel Pepys of hockey, provided this enlightening bit of information about the Americans' uniforms: "All the defencemen wear a broad white band around their chests to distinguish them from the forwards. Any time a forward sees a player with this broad white band pass him going down the ice, he knows the defence is temporarily weakened and that he must cover up for a return rush." Also, the Americans blackened the area under their eyes to prevent the sun's glare from inhibiting their play, something the Canadians wished they had done during their sunny outdoor match against the United States.

One other note of interest was that the American goalie, Frank Farrell, wore glasses and a mask, and prior to the Canada–United States game, the face-off was delayed while he had his goalie pads strapped tightly so that they were of legal width. The rules stated that when a goalie's knees were together the pads could not be more than 20 inches wide. While Canadian goalie Cockburn's were well within the limit (18½ inches), the Americans, Poles, and Germans were all 21½ inches and ruled illegal (no penalties could be imposed beyond delaying the game until the proper width was adhered to).

The indoor rink was far more conducive to excellent hockey than the one outdoors on which Team Canada played most of its games.

THE AFTERMATH

When all was said and done, and the Canadians had pocketed their fourth successive gold medal, the feeling was that the Americans were catching up to Canada in skill. Both games were close (2–1 Canada, 2–2 tie) and the consensus was that if the Winnipegs were the best amateur team in Canada, the collective best from the US was not far behind. Thus, in order to maintain supremacy in future Olympiads, Canada could not count on one team to represent our hockey interests but had to create an all-star team of its own, one that would train together for a month, play exhibition games, make final cuts, and go to the Games knowing they were the best 15 amateurs in the country, regardless of club affiliation. This realization represented an extremely important development in the Olympic program and in how Canada saw its future representation being decided.

The Competition

TOURNAMENT FORMAT

Teams received two points for a win and one for a tie. With just four teams entered — Canada, Germany, Poland, United States — each team played a double round-robin, two games against each opponent. The team that had the most points by tournament's end won the gold; second most, silver; third most, bronze. Each game consisted of three, 15-minute periods.

An even more remarkable version of the two-referee system was accepted for these Games: all hockey matches were reffed by the same two men, Lou Marsh of Canada and Don Sands of the United States. This ensured high-quality refereeing throughout the tournament and fairness during the most important game featuring their two nations.

THE OPPOSITION

GERMANY • Rudi Ball, Alfred Heinrich, Erich Herker, Gustav Jaenecke, Werner Korff, Walter Leinweber, Erich Romer, Martin Schrottle, Marquardt Slevogt, Georg Strobl

POLAND • Adam Kowalski, Aleksander Kowalski, Wlodzimierz Krygier, Witalis Ludwiczak, Czeslaw Marchewczyk, Kazimierz Materski, Albert Maurer, Roman Sabinski, Kasimierz Sokolowski, Josef Stogowski

UNITED STATES • Osborn Anderson, John Bent, John Chase, John Cookman, Douglas Everett, Franklin Farrell, Joseph Fitzgerald, Edward Frazier, John Garrison, Gerald Hallock, Robert Livingston, Francis Nelson, Winthrop Palmer, Gordon Smith

FINAL TOURNAMENT STANDINGS

	GP	W	L	T	GF	GA	P
Canada	6	5	0	1	32	4	11
United States	6	4	1	1	27	5	9
Germany	6	2	4	0	7	26	4
Poland	6	0	6	0	3	34	0

RESULTS

FEBRUARY 4
Canada 2 United States 1 (OT)
Germany 2 Poland 1

FEBRUARY 5
United States 4 Poland 1

FEBRUARY 6
Canada 4 Germany 1

FEBRUARY 7
Canada 9 Poland 0
United States 7 Germany 0

FEBRUARY 8
Canada 5 Germany 0
United States 5 Poland 0

FEBRUARY 9
Canada 10 Poland 0

FEBRUARY 10
United States 8 Germany 0

FEBRUARY 13
Canada 2 United States 2 (OT)
Germany 4 Poland 1

TEAM CANADA GAME SUMMARIES

FEBRUARY 4 • Canada 2 United States 1 (10:00 OT)

FIRST PERIOD (15 minutes)
No Scoring
penalties: *none*

SECOND PERIOD (15 minutes)
1. United States, Everett (unassisted) • 2:05
penalties: *none*

THIRD PERIOD (15 minutes)
2. Canada, Simpson (unassisted) • 13:36
penalties: *Garrison (US), Palmer (US)*

FIRST OVERTIME (five minutes)
No Scoring
penalties: *none*

SECOND OVERTIME (five minutes)
3. Canada, Lindquist (unassisted) • 2:14
penalties: *Sutherland (Can), Malloy (Can)*

IN GOAL
Canada — Cockburn
United States — Farrell

FEBRUARY 6 • Canada 4 Germany 1

FIRST PERIOD (15 minutes)
1. Canada, Monson (Lindquist) • 1:45
2. Canada, Monson (Lindquist) • 12:20
penalties: *Simpson (Can), Lindquist (Can), Heinrich (Ger), Strobl (Ger), Jaenecke (Ger)*

SECOND PERIOD (15 minutes)
3. Canada, Malloy (Sutherland) • 9:16
4. Canada, Wise (Malloy, Sutherland) • 12:37
penalties: *Hinkel (Can)*

THIRD PERIOD (15 minutes)
5. Germany, Herker (Korff) • 13:58
penalties: *none*

IN GOAL
Canada — Cockburn
Germany — Leinweber

FEBRUARY 7 • Canada 9 Poland 0

FIRST PERIOD (15 minutes)
1. Canada, Rivers (Sutherland) • 10:45
2. Canada, Rivers (Lindquist) • 12:49
penalties: *Sokolowski (Pol)*

SECOND PERIOD (15 minutes)
3. Canada, Lindquist (Malloy) • 3:15
4. Canada, Monson (unassisted) • 3:40
5. Canada, Monson (Rivers) • 12:15
6. Canada, Simpson (Lindquist) • 13:09
7. Canada, Simpson (Monson) • 14:57
penalties: *none*

THIRD PERIOD (15 minutes)
8. Canada, Malloy (Simpson) • 6:42
9. Canada, Hinkel (Rivers) • 11:59
penalties: *Sutherland (Can), Simpson (Can)*

IN GOAL
Canada — Cockburn
Poland — Stogowski

FEBRUARY 8 • Canada 5 Germany 0

FIRST PERIOD (15 minutes)
1. Canada, Lindquist (Monson) • 2:44
2. Canada, Monson (Lindquist) • 4:52
penalties: *none*

SECOND PERIOD (15 minutes)
3. Canada, Garbutt (unassisted) • 2:46
penalties: *none*

THIRD PERIOD (15 minutes)
4. Canada, Rivers (Lindquist) • 5:20
5. Canada, Duncanson (unassisted) • 8:17
penalties: *Hinkel (Can), Ball (Ger)*

IN GOAL
Canada — Cockburn
Germany — Leinweber

FEBRUARY 9 • Canada 10 Poland 0

IN GOAL
Canada — Wagner
Poland — Stogowski

FIRST PERIOD (15 minutes)
1. Canada, Monson (unassisted) • 1:52
2. Canada, Simpson (unassisted) • 6:03
3. Canada, Rivers (Monson) • 8:40
4. Canada, Monson (unassisted) • 9:28
5. Canada, Malloy (Hinkel) • 14:10
penalties: *none*

SECOND PERIOD (15 minutes)
6. Canada, Sutherland (Rivers) • 11:11
penalties: *none*

THIRD PERIOD (15 minutes)
7. Canada, Simpson (Sutherland) • 4:35
8. Canada, Hinkel (unassisted) • 7:51
9. Canada, Moore (Monson) • 9:35
10. Canada, Wise (Sutherland) • 13:01
penalties: *Sabinski (Pol)*

FEBRUARY 13 • Canada 2 United States 2 (30:00 OT)

IN GOAL
Canada — Cockburn
United States — Farrell

FIRST PERIOD (15 minutes)
1. United States, Everett (Palmer) • 2:17
2. Canada, Simpson (unassisted) • 9:47
penalties: *Garrison (US)*

SECOND PERIOD (15 minutes)
3. United States, Palmer (Bent) • 13:38(pp)
penalties: *Nelson (US), Simpson (Can) & Malloy (Can)*

THIRD PERIOD (15 minutes)
4. Canada, Rivers (unassisted) • 14:10
penalties: *Hinkel (Can), Garrison (US), Monson (Can)*

FIRST OVERTIME (10 minutes)
No Scoring
penalties: *none*

SECOND OVERTIME (10 minutes)
No Scoring
penalties: *Monson (Can), Chase (US)*

THIRD OVERTIME (10 minutes)
No Scoring
penalties: *none*

TEAM CANADA FINAL STATISTICS • 1932

	GP	G	A	P	Pim
Walter Monson	6	7	4	11	4
Victor Lindquist	5	3	6	9	2
Romeo Rivers	6	5	3	8	0
Hack Simpson	5	6	1	7	6
Hugh Sutherland	6	1	5	6	4
Norm Malloy	5	3	2	5	4
Roy Hinkel	6	2	1	3	6
Stoney Wise	5	2	0	2	0
Bert Duncanson	1	1	0	1	0
George Garbutt	1	1	0	1	0
Kenneth Moore	1	1	0	1	0
Clifford Crowley	1	0	0	0	0

IN GOAL	GP	W-L-T	Mins	GA	SO	Avg
William Cockburn	5	4–0–1	265	4	2	0.91*
Stanley Wagner	1	1–0–0	45	0	1	0.00

** average converted for consistency based on 60-minute games*

CHAPTER 5

The Fourth Olympic Winter Games

GARMISCH–PARTENKIRCHEN, GERMANY

February 6–16, 1936

Walter Kitchen

At the 32nd meeting of the IOC in Vienna on June 8, 1933 the twin villages of Garmisch and Partenkirchen were awarded the 1936 Games over Montreal and St. Moritz. This Olympics was hosted by Adolf Hitler and his National Socialist party, and on his way to Garmisch, IOC president Henri Baillet-Latour saw a road sign that read "Dogs and Jews not allowed." Baillet-Latour demanded Hitler remove such signs, to which the Führer replied that, as a guest, Baillet-Latour should accept the host nation's culture. The IOC president replied that as long as the Olympic flag was flying he, not Hitler, was the host. Hitler agreed to remove the offending signs.

TEAM CANADA • 1936

PORT ARTHUR BEAR CATS

Francis "Dinty" Moore, *GOAL*
Arthur "Jakie" Nash, *GOAL*

Walter "Pud" Kitchen, *DEFENCE*
Ray Milton, *DEFENCE*
Herman Murray, *DEFENCE (CAPTAIN)*

Hugh Farquharson, *CENTRE*
Alexander Sinclair, *CENTRE*

Maxwell "Bill" Deacon, *LEFT WING*
Ralph St. Germain, *LEFT WING*

Dave Neville, *RIGHT WING*
Bill Thomson, *RIGHT WING*

Ken Farmer, *FORWARD*
Jim Haggarty, *FORWARD*

Norm Friday *(DID NOT PLAY)*
Gus Saxberg *(DID NOT PLAY)*

Al Pudas, *COACH*
Malcolm Cochrane, *MANAGER*

FINAL PLACINGS

GOLD MEDAL
Great Britain

SILVER MEDAL
Canada

BRONZE MEDAL
United States

FOURTH PLACE
Czechoslovakia

FIFTH PLACE (tie)
Germany
Sweden

SEVENTH PLACE (tie)
Austria
Hungary

NINTH PLACE (tie)
Italy
France
Japan
Poland

THIRTEENTH PLACE (tie)
Belgium
Latvia
Switzerland

THE PORT ARTHUR BEAR CATS

As was customary, the 1935 Allan Cup champions, the Halifax Wolverines, were selected to represent Canada at the 1936 Olympics. By late 1935, however, many of the players had moved away, were playing for different teams, or were no longer accessible. It became apparent that a reassembling of the team was impossible. The finalists for the Allan Cup that year, the Port Arthur Bear Cats, were logically regarded as the next best choice, and the CAHA asked them to represent Canada with the stipulation that players could be added if it felt such steps were necessary.

The Bear Cats spent much of January organizing their team, playing exhibition matches, and figuring out which players would be needed to augment the team before sailing January 18 for Germany. They split a four-game series with the Fort William Wanderers in late 1935 and early in the new year, before going to Toronto for more exhibition games against the Toronto Marlies. From there they moved on to Hamilton to play the Tigers, Brockville to play the Magedomas, Kingston to play Queen's University. They followed with games in Montreal, Moncton, and Halifax before leaving for Garmisch–Partenkirchen.

Originally, the Bear Cats added 11 players to their training squad: Ralph St. Germain, Herman Murray, and Dave Neville from the Montreal Royals; Sylvester Bubar, Vic Ferguson, Chummy Lawlor, and Ernie Mosher from the Halifax Wolverines, Pud Kitchen of the Toronto Dukes, Hugh Farquharson of Montreal Victorias, Dinty Moore of the Port Colborne Sailors, and Jim Haggarty, formerly of the Bear Cats now playing for the Wembley Canadians in Britain.

Port Arthur Bear Cats, Canada's hockey representatives at the 1936 Games in Garmisch.

THE FIRST CONTROVERSY...AND STILL IN CANADA

From the outset, this Olympics was fraught with unpleasant developments, changes in rules, dissatisfaction, and general chaos. It all began while the Bear Cats were in Toronto, and Canadian Olympic Committee president A.E. Gilroy received a demand from the four Halifax Wolverine players who had been added to the Bear Cats to help the team win the gold medal (Bubar, Ferguson, Lawlor, and Mosher). Incredibly, these four demanded "broken time" pay for their wives and families ($150 a month for three months), citing loss of income while they were away from home playing at the Olympics! Not only would this have tarnished the whole team's amateur status, it would have compromised the integrity of the team and the very reason for competing and defending Canada's honour as 1932 Olympic champions. These four were summarily dropped from the roster amid a chorus of Haligonian boos, leaving a much depleted but prouder team. They were immediately replaced by Kitchen, Farquharson, Moore, and Haggarty.

Play during Canada's 5–2 win over Austria in the preliminary round. Notice the huge goal crease.

THE SEND-OFF AND ARRIVAL

The Bear Cats, unfortunately, had scheduled their last exhibition match in Halifax. What was initially going to be a rousing send-off (with four of their own in the line-up) turned into a fiasco (now that they had been dumped). Locals were urging a boycott of the match, and those at the game hurled bottles at the Port Arthur goal in protest. The Canadian representatives won the game 5–2 to complete a successful 5–2 eastern swing, and the next night, January 18, boarded the *Duchess of Atholl* bound for the United Kingdom. They arrived at Greenock, Scotland on the 26th, took a train to London the next day, and left for Paris the day after. There they played their only continental exhibition before the Games began, against a French all-star team dubbed the Flying Frenchmen, winning handily 5–2, and arrived in Germany the following day, January 31.

THE OPENING CEREMONIES: FEBRUARY 6, 1936

Ideally, the aspirations and achievements of athletes have little to do with politics, the running of a country, or the governing of its people. However, it is difficult to look at these 1936 Games at Garmisch-Partenkirchen without remembering the opening ceremonies, which were presided over by the Reichsführer Adolf Hitler. A crowd of 80,000 filled the stadium and gave him a rousing ovation, the athletes and sports supporters from other countries wholly unaware of the horror Hitler would soon inflict on the world.

GAME CONDITIONS

Canada's first game of these Olympics was played outside, on frozen Lake Riessersee, under the worst conditions imaginable. Fewer than 300 fans braved a blinding snowstorm to see a game frequently stopped while the ice was cleared enough to permit proper skating or the puck searched for in among the snowbanks. At one point, the game was delayed several minutes before the puck was discovered under the foot of an attendant! At the same time, the "Sammies" (a nickname used to describe the Americans) were playing inside, at the ice palace, before 8,000 comfortable patrons.

A dapper, 6-man crew cleans the ice during intermission.

THE OLYMPIC OATH

To understand the rules of the game, as it were, it is important to know the code each athlete is expected to adhere to before participating in the Olympic Games. An athlete: "(a) must not be, or knowingly have become, a professional in the sport for which he is entered or in any other sport; (b) must not have received reimbursement or compensation for loss of salary. A holiday given under the normal conditions of a business or profession, or a holiday accorded under the same conditions on the occasion of the Olympic games and provided that it does not lead to a reimbursement for lost salary, direct or indirect, does not come within the provision of Section b." Also, each athlete must sign the following declaration: "I, the undersigned, am an amateur according to the Olympic rules of amateurism."

The Olympic rules regarding amateurs are simple: "a competitor at the Olympic games must be an amateur in accordance with the rules of the international federation which governs his respective sport...and only those who are nationals or naturalized subjects of a country are eligible to represent that country in the Olympic games...the naturalized subject must give proof that he was an amateur in his native country at the time of changing his nationality." The association in each country for each sport must certify that each athlete is in good standing not only within that country but also within the international federation governing that sport. This last phrase was at the heart of the next controversy that ravaged almost beyond repair the ethics behind the very holding of the Games.

THE SECOND "AMATEUR" CONTROVERSY

Canada's pristine interpretation of the term "amateur," its desire to uphold before all else the stipulations and merits of the term, threw the British team into a paroxysm of anger after Canada complained about the status of two "English" players, Jimmy Foster and Alex Archer.

Both were ruled ineligible by the International Ice Hockey Federation the night before the Games opened, and the British response was to consider withdrawing from the competition altogether over this "injustice."

Canada's explanation for its protest stemmed not just from the fact that Foster and Archer had been playing with British clubs, but that they had formerly played in Canada, were, in fact, Canadians by birth, and transferred to English teams without first gaining the consent of the Canadian Amateur Hockey Association. Thus, they were automatically suspended in Canada and, by extension, in any other national federation that was run in accordance with the IIHF. The ruling affected not only these two but 16 other Canadians currently playing in British leagues, who may have hoped to play internationally for Britain now or in the future.

William Hewitt, long-time secretary of the CAHA, defended Canada's postition: "We wrote the international association early last fall detailing the situation regarding all players who had migrated to England without official permission. Surely it is the prerogative of a national governing body in sport to control its players. If the situation hits the English team, it is their own fault because they knew our attitude in plenty of time."

The Great Britain team had three other Canadians — Art Child, James Chappell, and Archibald Stinchcombe — who had secured the CAHA's permission to leave Canadian hockey and were playing under the Union Jack with Canada's blessing. Three days and two matches later, in a spirit of Olympic warmth, the Canadians withdrew their protest, though for the duration of the Games only. The International Association then adopted a new rule whereby "no native-born Briton may play in the Olympics for his native country unless he has lived in England the preceding five years."

TOURNAMENT FORMAT: THE FINAL CONTROVERSY THAT DECIDED GOLD

Both the Germans and Canadians were enraged by what they felt was tantamount to cheating by the Olympic authorities who announced only *after* the second round was over that second-round matches would count in third round standings, thus overturning the original rules under which all teams were thought to have been playing. This virtually eliminated Canada from a gold medal on account of their second-round loss to Great Britain. Canadian official P.J. Mulqueen called it "one of the worst manipulations in sporting history," and the *Times* editorial agreed, saying euphemistically, "it is regrettable that the Olympic hockey committee didn't publicly announce the regulations governing the tournament."

Upon returning to native soil, however, most of the Canadian players placed responsibility for the format confusion on their own officials. Left winger Ralph St. Germain said plainly: "The Olympic rules state that the hockey may be played either on an elimination or point system or both. Either through carelessness or dumbness, the officials neglected to find out what system was being used until after we were defeated by England." Team-mate Hugh Farquharson agreed: "No one realized, and the officials at least should have, that to lose that first game meant probable loss of the title. It would have made a big difference if that were known when we went into our game with England. That pool system has been in use over there for many years. There is no excuse for not completely understanding it before a Canadian team left Canada."

The Competition

TOURNAMENT FORMAT

The 15 entries were divided into four divisions (three of four teams, one of three teams) and played a round-robin series within each division. The top two countries then advanced to a semi-final round and the top two from that advanced to the finals. Any ties in the groupings would be decided by total number of goals scored in the Games. Games consisted of three 15-minute periods and each team could dress only 10 players. Three substitutes per game were allowed.

An extremely important, complex rule for the final round stated that any team that had beaten another in a previous round did not have to play against that same team in the finals. Instead, they were automatically given two points for the earlier win (the one win, therefore, counted two points in both the semi-final and final rounds for Britain at these Olympics). Thus, Canada's loss to Great Britain in the semi-finals virtually assured them of losing the gold medal, for they couldn't play the English in the final round to avenge the earlier defeat.

THE OPPOSITION

AUSTRIA • Franz Csongei, Friedrich Demmer, Josef Gobl, Lambert Neumaier, Oskar Nowak, Franz Schussler, Emil Seidler, Willibald Stanek, Hans Tatzer, Hans Trauttenberg, Rudolf Vojta, Hermann Weiss

CZECHOSLOVAKIA • Josef Bohac, Alois Cetkovsky, Karel Hromadka, Drahos Jirotka, Zdenek Jirotka, Jan Kosek, Oldrich Kucera, Josef Malecek, Jan Peka, Jaroslav Pusbauer, Jiri Tozicka, Ladislav Trojak, Walter Ullrich

GERMANY • Joachim Albrecht von Bethmann-Hollweg, Rudi Ball, Wilhelm Egginger, Werner George, Gustav Jaenecke, Karl Kogel, Alois Kuhn, Phillip Schenk, Herbert Schibukat, Georg Strobl, Paul Trautmann, Anton Wiedemann

GREAT BRITAIN • Alexander "Sandy" Archer, James Borland, Edgar Brenchley, James Chappell, John Coward, Gordon Dailey, John Davey, Carl Erhardt, James Foster, John Kilpatrick, Archibald Stinchcombe, James Wyman

HUNGARY • Miklos Barcza, Isvan Csak, Matyas Farkas, Andras Gergely, Laszlo Gergely, Bela Haray, Frigyes Helmeczi, Zoltan Jeney, Sandor Magyar, Sandor Miklos, Ferenc Monostori, Laszlo Rona, Ferenc Szamosi

LATVIA • Alexsis Ausinsch, Roberts Blukis, Janis Debris, Arvids Jurgens, Herberts Kuschiks, Roberts Lapainis, Karlis Paegle, Arvids Peterson, Adolfs Petrowski, Janis Rozitis, Leonidis Vedejs

SWEDEN • Stig Andersson, Sven Bergquist, Ruben Carlsson, Holger Engberg, Ake Ericson, Lennart Hellman, Torsten Johncke, Hermann Karlsson, Vilhelm Larsson, Yngve Liljeberg, Bertil Lundell, Bertil Norberg, Vilhelm Petersen

UNITED STATES • John Garrison, August Kammer, Philip LaBatte, John Lax, Thomas Moone, Eldrige Ross, Paul Rowe, Frank Shaughnessy, Gordon Smith, Francis Spain, Frank Stubbs

FINAL TOURNAMENT STANDINGS

ROUND ONE • GROUP A

	GP	W	L	T	GF	GA	P
Canada	3	3	0	0	24	3	6
Austria	3	2	1	0	11	7	4
Poland	3	1	2	0	11	12	2
Latvia	3	0	3	0	3	27	0

RESULTS

FEBRUARY 6
Canada 8 Poland 1
Austria 7 Latvia 1

FEBRUARY 7
Canada 11 Latvia 0
Austria 2 Poland 1

FEBRUARY 8
Canada 5 Austria 2
Poland 9 Latvia 2

ROUND ONE • GROUP B

	GP	W	L	T	GF	GA	P
Germany	3	2	1	0	5	1	4
United States	3	2	1	0	5	2	4
Italy	3	1	2	0	2	5	2
Switzerland	3	1	2	0	1	5	2

RESULTS

FEBRUARY 6
Switzerland 1 Italy 0
United States 1 Germany 0

FEBRUARY 7
Germany 3 Italy 0
United States 3 Switzerland 0

FEBRUARY 8
Germany 2 Switzerland 0
Italy 2 United States 1 (OT)

ROUND ONE • GROUP C

	GP	W	L	T	GF	GA	P
Czechoslovakia	3	3	0	0	10	0	6
Hungary	3	2	1	0	14	5	4
France	3	1	2	0	4	7	2
Belgium	3	0	3	0	4	20	0

RESULTS

FEBRUARY 6
Czechoslovakia 2 France 0
Hungary 11 Belgium 2

FEBRUARY 7
Czechoslovakia 5 Belgium 0
Hungary 3 France 0

FEBRUARY 8
France 4 Belgium 2
Czechoslovakia 3 Hungary 0

ROUND ONE • GROUP D

	GP	W	L	T	GF	GA	P
Great Britain	2	2	0	0	4	0	4
Sweden	2	1	1	0	2	1	2
Japan	2	0	2	0	0	5	0

RESULTS

FEBRUARY 6
Sweden 2 Japan 0

FEBRUARY 7
Great Britain 1 Sweden 0

FEBRUARY 8
Great Britain 3 Japan 0

ROUND TWO • GROUP A

	GP	W	L	T	GF	GA	P
Great Britain	3	2	0	1	8	3	5
Canada	3	2	1	0	22	4	4
Germany	3	1	1	1	5	8	3
Hungary	3	0	3	0	2	22	0

RESULTS

FEBRUARY 10
Great Britain 2 Canada 1
Germany 2 Hungary 1

FEBRUARY 12
Canada 15 Hungary 0
Great Britain 1 Germany 1
(30:00 OT)

FEBRUARY 13
Canada 6 Germany 2
Great Britain 5 Hungary 1

ROUND TWO • GROUP B

	GP	W	L	T	GF	GA	P
United States	3	3	0	0	5	1	6
Czechoslovakia	3	2	1	0	6	4	4
Sweden	3	1	2	0	3	6	2
Austria	3	0	3	0	1	4	0

RESULTS

FEBRUARY 10
Sweden 1 Austria 0
United States 2 Czechoslovakia 0

FEBRUARY 12
Czechoslovakia 4 Sweden 1
United States 1 Austria 0

FEBRUARY 13
Czechoslovakia 2 Austria 1
United States 2 Sweden 1

FINALS ROUND

	GP	W	L	T	GF	GA	P
Great Britain	3	2	0	1	7	1	5
Canada	3	2	1	0	9	2	4
United States	3	1	1	1	2	1	3
Czechoslovakia	3	0	3	0	0	14	0

RESULTS

CARRY OVER RESULTS
Great Britain 2 Canada 1
United States 2 Czechoslovakia 0

FEBRUARY 14
Canada 1 United States 0
Great Britain 5 Czechoslovakia 0

FEBRUARY 15
Canada 7 Czechoslovakia 0
Great Britain 0 United States 0

TEAM CANADA GAME SUMMARIES

FEBRUARY 6 • Canada 8 Poland 1

IN GOAL
Canada — Moore
Poland — Marchewczyk

FIRST PERIOD (15 minutes)
1. Canada, Thomson (unassisted) • 0:30
2. Canada, Thomson (unassisted) • 2:00
3. Canada, Farmer (unassisted) • 5:10
4. Canada, Kitchen (unassisted) • 12:30
5. Canada, Thomson (unassisted) • 14:51
penalties: *Ludwiczak (Pol)*

SECOND PERIOD (15 minutes)
6. Poland, Kowalski (Wolkowski) • 8:03
7. Canada, Farmer (Neville) • 12:03
8. Canada, Neville (Farquharson) • 14:00
penalties: *none*

THIRD PERIOD (15 minutes)
9. Canada, Thomson (unassisted) • 8:01
penalties: *none*

FEBRUARY 7 • Canada 11 Latvia 0

IN GOAL
Canada — Nash
Latvia — Lapainis

FIRST PERIOD (15 minutes)
1. Canada, St. Germain (Haggarty) • 8:00
2. Canada, St. Germain (Haggarty) • 12:00
penalties: *Ausinsch (Lat)*

SECOND PERIOD (15 minutes)
3. Canada, Farquharson (Neville) • 0:20
4. Canada, Farquharson (unassisted) • 4:20
5. Canada, Haggarty (St. Germain) • 5:00
penalties: *Jurgens (Lat)*

THIRD PERIOD (15 minutes)
6. Canada, Farquharson (unassisted) • 0:18
7. Canada, Neville (Farmer, Farquharson) • 5:42
8. Canada, Neville (Farquharson) • 8:04
9. Canada, St. Germain (Farquharson) • 11:15
10. Canada, Farquharson (St. Germain) • 13:58
11. Canada, Haggarty (unassisted) • 14:25
penalties: *none*

FEBRUARY 8 • Canada 5 Austria 2

IN GOAL
Canada — Moore
Austria — Weiss

FIRST PERIOD (15 minutes)
1. Canada, Thomson (Sinclair) • 4:03
2. Canada, Murray (Kitchen) • 5:30
3. Canada, Murray (unassisted) • 7:25
4. Canada, Farmer (unassisted) • 8:20
penalties: *none*

SECOND PERIOD (15 minutes)
5. Canada, Sinclair (unassisted) • 7:15
6. Austria, Nowak (unassisted) • 9:45(sh)
7. Austria, Nowak (Demmer) • 14:50
penalties: *Vojta (Aus)*

THIRD PERIOD (15 minutes)
No Scoring
penalties: *none*

FEBRUARY 10 • Great Britain 2 Canada 1

IN GOAL
Canada — Moore
Great Britain — Foster

FIRST PERIOD (15 minutes)
1. Great Britain, Davey (unassisted) • 0:20
2. Canada, St. Germain (Haggarty) • 12:30
penalties: *Farquharson (Can)*

SECOND PERIOD (15 minutes)
No Scoring
penalties: *none*

THIRD PERIOD (15 minutes)
3. Great Britain, Brenchley (Dailey) • 13:48
penalties: *none*

FEBRUARY 12 • Canada 15 Hungary 0

FIRST PERIOD (15 minutes)

1. Canada, Murray (unassisted) • 0:20
2. Canada, Farmer (unassisted) • 3:00
3. Canada, Neville (St. Germain, Farquharson) • 13:40
penalties: *none*

SECOND PERIOD (15 minutes)

4. Canada, Farmer (unassisted) • 6:25
5. Canada, Farmer (unassisted) • 7:00
6. Canada, Murray (unassisted) • 7:35
7. Canada, Farquharson (unassisted) • 8:05
8. Canada, Farquharson (unassisted) • 9:00
9. Canada, Farmer (Sinclair) • 9:50
10. Canada, Sinclair (unassisted) • 11:00
11. Canada, Thomson (unasssisted) • 11:50
12. Canada, Farquharson (Neville) • 14:40
penalties: *Magyar (Hun)*

THIRD PERIOD (15 minutes)

13. Canada, Farmer (unassisted) • 0:30
14. Canada, Thomson (unassisted) • 8:30
15. Canada, Farquharson (St. Germain) • 12:45
penalties: *Murray (Can), Barcza (Hun)*

IN GOAL

Canada — Moore
Hungary — Csak

FEBRUARY 13 • Canada 6 Germany 2

FIRST PERIOD (15 minutes)

1. Canada, St. Germain (Farquharson) • 6:15
penalties: *Schibukat (Ger), Neville (Can), Wiedemann (Ger)*

SECOND PERIOD (15 minutes)

2. Canada, Farquharson (St. Germain) • 3:50
3. Canada, Neville (Farquharson) • 7:20
4. Canada, Farmer (unassisted) • 12:05
penalties: *Kogel (Ger)*

THIRD PERIOD (15 minutes)

5. Germany, Wiedemann (unassisted) • 1:50
6. Canada, St. Germain (unassisted) • 5:10
7. Canada, Neville (Kitchen) • 8:15
8. Germany, Strobl (unassisted) • 14:35
penalties: *Thomson (Can), Schibukat (Ger), Neville (Can), Kogel (Ger)*

IN GOAL

Canada — Nash
Germany — Egginger

FEBRUARY 15 • Canada 7 Czechoslovakia 0

FIRST PERIOD (15 minutes)

1. Canada, Kitchen (Sinclair) • 9:23
2. Canada, Sinclair (Deacon) • 12:15
3. Canada, Farquharson (Farmer) • 12:45
4. Canada, Farmer (Farquharson) • 14:40
penalties: *none*

SECOND PERIOD (15 minutes)

5. Canada, Neville (Farmer) • 6:10
6. Canada, Murray (Farmer) • 10:25
penalties: *Pusbauer (Cz)*

THIRD PERIOD (15 minutes)

7. Canada, Farquharson (unassisted) • 4:50
penalties: *none*

IN GOAL

Canada — Nash
Czechoslovakia — Peka

FEBRUARY 16 • Canada 1 United States 0

FIRST PERIOD (15 minutes)

1. Canada, Neville (unassisted) • 2:35
penalties: *none*

SECOND PERIOD (15 minutes)

No Scoring
penalties: *LaBatte (US), LaBatte (US), LaBatte (US), Neville (Can), Lax (US)*

THIRD PERIOD (15 minutes)

No Scoring
penalties: *none*

IN GOAL

Canada — Moore
United States — Moone

TEAM CANADA FINAL STATISTICS • 1936

	GP	G	A	P	Pim
Hugh Farquharson	8	11	8	19	2
Ken Farmer	8	10	4	14	0
Dave Neville	7	8	3	11	6
Ralph St. Germain	4	6	5	11	0
Bill Thomson	8	7	0	7	2
Alex Sinclair	5	3	3	6	0
Herman Murray	8	5	0	5	2
Jim Haggarty	3	2	3	5	0
Pud Kitchen	6	2	2	4	0
Bill Deacon	4	0	1	1	0
Ray Milton	2	0	0	0	0

IN GOAL	GP	W-L-T	Mins	GA	SO	Avg
Dinty Moore	5	4–1–0	225	5	2	1.33*
Jakie Nash	3	3–0–0	135	2	2	0.89*

* *average converted for consistency based on 60-minute games*

CHAPTER 6

The Fifth Olympic Winter Games

ST. MORITZ, SWITZERLAND

January 30 – February 8, 1948

The Fifth Games were originally awarded to Sapporo, Japan at the 37th IOC session in Warsaw on June 9, 1937. Sapporo withdrew on July 16, 1938 and the Games were then awarded to St. Moritz on September 3, 1938. It, too, withdrew less than a year later, on June 9, 1939 and Garmisch–Partenkirchen was awarded but declined from hosting the Games which were eventually postponed because of World War II.

The Games were supposed to resume in 1944, with Cortina d'Ampezzo, Italy being given host honours at the 39th IOC session in London on June 9, 1939. Cortina received 16 votes in round two, just four more than Montreal and well ahead of Oslo (two votes). The persistence and horror of the war, however, were too great to contemplate a competition meant to celebrate universal participation. Resumption of the Games seemed far more practical and decent only after the end of the war and Cortina retracted its nomination.

The IOC Executive Board met next on September 4, 1946 and quickly awarded the Games to St. Moritz, the only other bid being an unimpressive one from Lake Placid. St. Moritz quickly got its Olympic house in order and was able to host the Games in true Olympian fashion.

FINAL PLACINGS

GOLD MEDAL
Canada

SILVER MEDAL
Czechoslovakia

BRONZE MEDAL
Switzerland

FOURTH PLACE
Sweden

FIFTH PLACE
Great Britain

SIXTH PLACE
Poland

SEVENTH PLACE
Austria

EIGHTH PLACE
Italy

TEAM CANADA • 1948

ROYAL CANADIAN AIR FORCE (RCAF) FLYERS

Aircraftsman 2 Murray Dowey, *GOAL*

Flying Officer Frank Dunster, *DEFENCE*
Aircraftsman 2 André Laperrière, *DEFENCE*
Flight Sergeant Louis Lecompte, *DEFENCE*

Aircraftsman 1 Orval Gravelle, *FORWARD*
Corporal Patrick "Patsy" Guzzo, *FORWARD*
Wally Halder (civilian), *FORWARD*
Aircraftsman 1 Ted "Red" Hibberd, *FORWARD*
George Mara (civilian), *FORWARD (CAPTAIN)*
Leading Aircraftsman Ab Renaud, *FORWARD*
Flying Officer Reg Schroeter, *FORWARD*
Corporal Irving Taylor, *FORWARD*

Hubert Brooks *(DID NOT PLAY)*
Roy Forbes *(DID NOT PLAY)*
Andy Gilpin *(DID NOT PLAY)*
Ross King *(DID NOT PLAY)*
Pete Leichnitz *(DID NOT PLAY)*

Sergeant Frank Boucher, *COACH*
Squadron Leader A. Gardner "Sandy" Watson, *MANAGER*

CANADA'S INTERNATIONAL HOCKEY BOYCOTT IN 1947

For years the CAHA had been displeased with the IIHF over a number of critical issues: the way amateur problems had been dealt with, and unfair rules that had been applied specifically against Canada (i.e., the controversy at the 1936 Olympics where previous scores were credited against Canada at the last minute in the final round). In 1940, George Hardy, an associate of the CAHA, organized the Independent Ice Hockey Association as a means of articulating this displeasure by announcing his new group was replacing the IIHF. The IIHF refused to acknowledge this new body, and in protest Canada boycotted the 1947 World Championships. In the spring of 1947, however, the IIHF attended the CAHA meetings in Canada and agreed to alternate the presidency of its own body between North America and Europe. In return, Canada abolished the IIHA and returned to international competition.

THE ROYAL CANADIAN AIR FORCE (RCAF) FLYERS

Despite Canada's supreme place in hockey, it was not until October 15, 1947, just 107 days before the first game of the 1948 Olympics was scheduled, that a decision was made to send a team to represent our country. This waffling was based on a clear disagreement in defining "amateur" when the IIHF met in Zurich to prepare for the Games. Al Pickard, president of the CAHA, felt the rules were too strict, thus encouraging "under-the-table dealings" on the part of other countries, notably the United States, when trying to assemble a team of superior talent. In the end, it was felt that the greater injustice would have been not to participate at all, but the RCAF, who sported some of the finest "pure" amateurs in the country, volunteered their services. The CAHA gladly approved, and in their position as Canada's organizer vouched to pay for the players' expenses both to St. Moritz and while in training at the Auditorium in Ottawa (though costs towards the latter would be minimal as the players stayed at the Princess Alice Barracks on Argyle Street, right next door to the arena).

Goalie Murray Dowey watches the play as the Flyers head up ice.

PUTTING THE TEAM TOGETHER

Initial rumours had Red Dutton being named coach of the team, not only because of his long hockey record as player and president of the NHL, but also because he had lost both his sons in the war while they were serving with the RCAF. However, it was decided that Corporal Frank Boucher, coach of the RCAF team in the Ottawa City League, would be the more appropriate choice to cull talent from all stations across the country. Boucher had plenty of NHL experience (14 years) and also was a member of the RCAF overseas team that was highly regarded in amateur circles.

Boucher's father, George "Buck" Boucher, was put in charge of selecting and inviting troops to training camp. He would act as coach and decide the final team in Ottawa while son Frank would take over full coaching duties in Switzerland. On October 19, the first players began arriving in Ottawa for try-outs, a process which eventually took much longer than expected. The first three were recruits from Winnipeg: F/L Jack Maitland, LAC Oscar Kleppe, and Sgt Lionel Bergeron. Three from the Toronto Station also arrived: F/L Bill McLeod, LAC Frank Hammond, and LAC Howard Kelly. Two players from Trenton were Sgt Nick Sargent and Sgt D. Sherman, and from Edmonton came F/O Bert Paxton. Arriving the next day were Del Sherman of Ottawa and Tom Moore of Montreal. Five new arrivals appeared October 29: AC1 Steve Chmara, AC1 Arthur Schultz, AC1 Arnold Metson, LAC Al Burgoin, and Roy Forbes.

Three days later, Boucher cut eight men and added three others: LAC Johnny Rhude, LAC Bill Grady, and Cpl Doug Lyon. Amid the confusion of who was able to do what how well, the next day, coach Boucher added another seven players to try-outs: Buck Buchanan, Ross Waugh, Gus Baudais, Al Lavery, George Wilson, Larry Paget, and Chuck Rafuse, followed shortly by Cpl Ross King, Sgt Andy Gilpin, and LAC Len Beatch.

By November 19, Boucher had the majority of the team selected, giving 13 players positions on the 17-man roster but only with the ever-present caveat, "if, before the team sails [January 8, 1948], other players prove of greater value, we will definitely make some changes." The 13 were: defencemen Jack Seymour, Louis Lecompte, Stan Molinari, Jack Maitland; forwards Orval Gravelle, Len Beatch, Irving Taylor, Hubert Brooks, Tommy Moore, Andy Gilpin, Roy Forbes, Dick Thomas, Patrick Guzzo. Five days later, Trev Williams and Ross King were selected as goalies for the Canadians and three days before their first exhibition match, Louis Bergeron and George Wilson were included to fill the roster.

DISHEARTENING PREPARATION

Hopes for the team in its present incarnation were destroyed December 14, 1947 in an exhibition game when the McGill Redmen thrashed the RCAF Olympic team 7–0 in their first match. Boucher immediately called replacements for a try-out, obtaining four players from the New Edinburgh entry of the Senior City Hockey League: Ted Hibberd, Reg Schroeter, Ab Renaud, and Pete Leichnitz. These additions clearly made a difference, leading the Flyers to an 8–4 win over Belleville of OHA Intermediate league shortly after. It was not, though, enough of a convincing victory to make everyone optimistic. In fact, Art Rice-Jones, manager of the Calgary Junior Buffaloes of the Southern Alberta Junior League, wanted to play a best-of-three challenge match with the RCAF, the winner to go on to the Olympics. Rice-Jones made the pitch because of "the doubtful ability of the RCAF hockey team." While his insult may have been justified, his brazenness was all for naught: the games never took place.

Action during Canada's gold medal-clinching 3–0 win over the Swiss.

Just 10 days before sailing, three newcomers made such an impression they made the team almost on the spot: defenceman André Laperrière, from the University of Montreal, and forwards George Mara and Wally Halder. Also added was goalie Dick Ball, who took over as the number one man in the nets, thus allowing Boucher to cut both Joe Tunney and Trev Williams, capable goalies both, but not up to Olympic snuff (also cut were Jack Seymour and Jack Maitland). Thus, in the two weeks leading up to the Games, the team had changed character and personnel almost completely.

Three days before sailing, a major disruption occurred when goaler Ball was diagnosed by team doctors with a lung condition that rendered him unable to travel and forced him to leave the team. A new goalie was needed instantly, and Ball himself suggested Murray Dowey of the Barkers (see below) in the Toronto Mercantile Hockey League, a worthy suggestion that was to be the most important the RCAF could have made. Dowey arrived just in time to take the train to New York, where the RCAF team sailed for England on January 8.

THE TORONTO CONNECTION

In a promotion after the Games, Barker's Biscuits put a quarter-page ad in the *Toronto Star* congratulating Canada on bringing home another Olympic gold, and also pointing out that three members of the team were not only born in Toronto but played for the Barker's Hockey Club. Furthermore, it was noted that Murray Dowey was able to attend the Games after being granted a leave of absence by the Toronto Transportation Commission (TTC), Wally Halder as sales director of Willards Chocolates, and George Mara as an agent with George E. Mara Manufacturers.

THE TRIP AND ITINERARY

While boarding the *Queen Elizabeth* in New York, LAC Roy Forbes, former bombardier, summed up a nation's joy and sorrow in sailing the Atlantic when he commented, "this is a bit different than the last time I crossed on the Lizzie — I was lugging a kitbag then."

The squad arrived in Southampton, England on January 15, where they began a very long hockey journey that included more than 40 non-Olympic games and would keep them in Europe until the end of April. It began with a series of preparatory games leading up to competition in St. Moritz and then a full slate of continental games in Switzerland, Czechoslovakia, France, Belgium, Holland, and Sweden. Their first game, just a day after arriving in port, was a 5–5 tie with Streatham, followed the next night by a 7–6 win over the Brighton Tigers. They lost to Le Racing Club de Paris 5–3 on January 21, beat Zurich 6–3 on the 24th, lost to Basel 8–5 on the 25th, and beat Davos decisively 10–3 the next night before leaving for the real McCoy in St. Moritz.

WHAT TO BRING?

Each member of the team received a "suggested personal kit" list for their Olympic voyage:

1. Kitbag
2. Suitcase
3. RCAF greatcoat
4. Civilian overcoat
5. Civilian hat
6. RCAF cap
7. RCAF uniform
8. Lounge suit
9. Light trousers
10. One pair of boots
11. One pair of shoes
12. One pair of overshoes
13. One pair of slippers
14. Four RCAF shirts
15. Four civilian shirts
16. Ties (civilian and RCAF)
17. Underwear (suggested two suits long, four undershirts and shorts)
18. Sweater (heavyweight)
19. Gloves (RCAF and civilian)
20. Socks (suggested six pairs civilian and four pairs RCAF)
21. Pyjamas (suggested two pairs flannelette)
22. Dressing gown
23. Scarf (one woollen and one silk)
24. Handkerchiefs (suggested dozen white and a half-dozen RCAF)
25. Belt
26. Braces
27. Parka
28. Flying boots (issued)
29. Blazer
30. Shoe polish (to be shared by several members)
31. Button polish (to be shared by several members)

Final words of advice were appended to the list: "As soap is on ration in many European countries, members must bring at least six large bars apiece. Towels are frequently not provided in European hotels at present. Each member should bring at least two towels. Many such hotels are not equipped for electric razors, hence it is advised to bring a safety razor and blades."

THE AMERICAN CONTROVERSY...AGAIN

Long before Enrico Celio, president of the Swiss Olympic Federation, pronounced the Games begun, the United States began a fight that almost cost the world the cancellation of the whole Games, disrupted the competition for most of the Olympics, and relegated hockey to a non-official event until only a couple of days remained, and again threw into disrepute a country which continued to use "impure" amateurs in Olympic competition.

The conflict heated up December 30, 1947 and involved two American hockey bodies — the American Hockey Association (AHA), the Amateur Athletic Union (AAU) — and the IIHF. The IIHF had always stated that athletes could not participate in the Olympics unless they were endorsed by their own country's governing body. In this case, the AAU had run amateur hockey in the States since 1930, but had been expelled by the IIHF the previous year because the AAU had refused to support those players who made up the Americans' national team, all of whom played under the auspices of the "professional" AHA. But the IIHF recognized the AHA before the AAU, and thus welcomed the AHA, *not* the AAU, to the Games even though it was a league that *paid* its players.

The AAU refused to acknowledge these players because, according to their pamphlet, "the AHA players were openly paid salaries. Beyond the continued use of the name 'amateur' in connection with its hockey, there were few pretensions."

Daniel Ferris, secretary-treasurer of the United States Amateur Athletic Union, concurred:

> If there is surrender [to the IIHF] on this point in hockey, a similar situation is bound to arise in basketball, boxing, figure skating, and other arena sports with popular appeal. The AAU has been charged by the US Olympic Association with the responsibility of conducting amateur hockey in this country and it will not abdicate to any body that does not subscribe to the principles of amateurism for which it stands. The AAU will stand firm on this issue. If the uncertified AHA team competes in the Olympics, the death knell of amateur sports may be sounded.

Avery Brundage, chairman of the US Olympic Committee, the American governing body that controlled all amateur sports in the States, threatened the AHA with total withdrawal of the US from the Games if it sent its team over. The IIHF countered by threatening to withdraw all other hockey teams from the Games if the AHA were banned. The battle now was one of will and stubbornness, the USOC supporting the AAU, the IIHF supporting the AHA. "It isn't a question of which hockey team should play," Brundage said. "It is, one, whether the Olympic Games are for amateurs or for business institutions like the AHA, and two, whether the National Olympic Committee has the sole authority to certify entries as international rules specify or whether anybody can get into the picture." At the very moment Brundage spoke, the AHA team was arriving in St. Moritz and the AAU team was on its way.

The gold medal Flyers prepare for the presentation ceremonies.

Meanwhile, the Swiss Olympic Organizing Committee had also already formally accepted the AHA application, much to the dismay of Brundage, and the executive committee of the International Olympic Committee then put forth its opinion — that both US entries be denied. This, too, was rejected by the Swiss committee, and the possibility of hockey being removed altogether from Olympic competition grew more real. On January 20, the US Olympic Committee upped the ante by voting 68 to 6 in favour of withdrawing all American athletes from the Games if the AHA were allowed to participate in the Games, to which St. Moritz mayor Carl Nater replied: "That's nice."

Just before the US was to play its first game of the tournament, the IOC relegated hockey to an "unofficial" event, a mere demonstration sport, as it were, sending the sport's reputation careering back to the 1920 Summer Olympics as a mere experiment and rendering the Games a competitive farce. Then, on February 7th, a compromise was reached whereby only the US entry would be considered unofficial by the IOC. The team — the *AHA* team — would play all opponents and be placed in the standings, and other teams' results versus the US would count, but the Americans could not qualify for a medal. This meant that the hockey games continued, but only under a dark cloud and the promise of a stormy future for the game. More importantly, it threw the sport into disrepute, and the IOC even gave public consideration afterward to barring hockey from all future Olympic Games.

CANADA'S GAMES

Because of the late assembly of the final team, the relatively poor exhibition results, and the huge AAU/AHA controversy, Canada entered these Olympics quietly and not as the runaway favourite expected once again to romp to victory.

The team played all of its games outdoors, and this caused havoc on a couple of occasions when snowstorms almost forced the cancellation of matches already under way. The refereeing was particularly European-partisan, and the penalties against Canada became a running joke for both team Canada and its opposition.

The final game of the tournament, a 3–0 Canadian victory over the home-town Swiss side, was genuinely farcical especially considering that it was the game that decided the gold medal. During the last two periods, when it became clear the Swiss were outclassed and on their way to losing, the crowd hurled snowballs at the Canadian skaters. The officiating was so biased it led the Flyers' trainer, Cpl George McFaul, to comment, "We played eight men — the Swiss players and the referees — and still beat 'em!"

When the final bell was rung, the Canadians leaped onto the ice *en masse* and posed for a team picture at centre ice. They then ascended the podium where they were given their gold medals by Marcel Heninger, chairman of the Swiss Olympic Committee. Going to the dressing room, the Flyers blew kisses to the crowd. One player found a Union Jack and hooked it onto his stick while he walked, and once in the room the players demanded a speech from coach Boucher, who gallantly complied: "Fellows," he said, "I am proud of you. I want to thank you all, and that goes for the boys who didn't play. You're a great gang, and I knew you'd do it." Wally Halder was hailed as the best forward in Canada, and special accolades went to goalie Murray Dowey, the last-second replacement, who recorded a remarkable five shutouts in eight games. Early in the tournament, he went 226:07 minutes without allowing a goal, and he finished off with 196:10 shutout minutes.

Dowey was also part of an interesting bit of Olympic trivia. Near the end of the team's first game, he caught the puck and threw it forward accidentally, a no-no in international hockey (the puck had to be put behind the goal after a save). Dowey was therefore given a two-minute penalty and had to serve it himself! Defenceman André Laperrière took Dowey's stick and glove and played goal the last eight seconds of the game while Dowey sat in the penalty box, the only time such an oddity has occurred to team Canada in Olympic history.

FOR WHOM THE BELLS TOLL

Flying Officer Hubert Brooks of the Canadian team married his sweetheart of four years, Birthe Grontved of Denmark, at a ceremony in a small church in St. Moritz

Medal ceremonies: Canada wins gold, Czechoslovakia *(left)* silver, and Switzerland *(right)* bronze.

attended by the whole squad February 10. The bridesmaid was none other than Canadian Olympic figure-skating champion and gold medalist Barbara Ann Scott. Brooks, who toured with the Flyers but did not play in the Olympics, met his wife-to-be while he was a member of the missing persons research team in Europe during the war. He was one of five men on the Flyers to have received the Military Cross, awarded after his escape from a German prisoner-of-war camp, but the greatest honour of all was to have his team-mates at his wedding. The best man was team manager Sandy Watson, but the beautiful Barbara Ann stole the show when she acquiesced to photographers' demands to kiss the groom for their cameras.

THE TOURING

Once the Olympics ended, the Canadians again set out on a lengthy series of exhibitions, beginning with games in Switzerland and Czechoslovakia. They played a three-game series for the Jean Potin Cup in Paris where they were also fêted by the Canadian Embassy, then played games in The Hague and Stockholm. In Sweden, they were wined and dined nightly, before playing twice in London and returning to Kircaldy, Scotland for a final round of six games. The Flyers had a chance to play the Old Course at St. Andrew's (no report on scores!) and were entertained at the Garden Clover Club in London before heading home on March 31 aboard the *Queen Mary*. They arrived in New York exactly one week later, where a dinner in their honour was given by the Canadian Club in the posh Waldorf Astoria Hotel. They then struck out for Ottawa, where further receptions, galas, luncheons, and parades greeted them. To mark their return, they staged an exhibition against a team made up of NHL and QSHL players (won by the pros 6–3) before the squad bid each other adieu and disbanded.

The Competition

TOURNAMENT FORMAT

With nine teams entered, all were placed together with a simple round-robin format used as the schedule. Teams received two points for a win, one for a tie. In the final game, an overtime period would be played, but no overtime would be played throughout the balance of the round-robin. Teams could take 15 players to the Olympics, but only 12 (including a spare goalie) could dress for any one game. For the first time, all games now consisted of three 20-minute periods.

In the case of a tie in the standings after the round-robin, goal *average* would decide the final positions. This meant dividing the goals scored by goals against. For instance, Canada scored 69 and gave up 5 for a figure of 13.8. The Czechs, by comparison, scored 80 but surrendered 18 for an average of just 4.3. That is how Canada won the gold in St. Moritz.

THE OPPOSITION

AUSTRIA • Albert Bohm, Franz Csongei, Friedrich Demmer, Egon Engel, Walter Feistritzer, Gustav Gross, Adolf Hafner, Alfred Huber, Julius Juhn, Oskar Nowack, Jorg Reichel, Johann Schneider, Willibald Stanek, Herbert Ulrich, Fritz Walter, Helfried Winger, Rudolf Wurmbrandt

CZECHOSLOVAKIA • Vladimir Bouzek, Augustin Bubnik, Jaroslav Drobny, Premsyl Hajny, Zdenek Jarkovsky, Vladimir Kobranov, Stanislav Konopasek, Bohumil Modry, Miloslav Pokorny, Vaclav Rozinak, Moroslav Slama, Karel Stibor, Villibald Stovik, Ladislav Trojak, Josef Trousilek, Oldrich Zabrodsky, Vladimir Zabrodsky

GREAT BRITAIN • George Baillie, Leonard Baker, James Chappell, J. Gerry Davey, Frederick Dunkelman, Arthur Green, Frank Green, Frank Jardine, John Murray, John Oxley, Stanley Simon, William Smith, Archibald Stinchcombe, Thomas Syme

ITALY • Claudio Apollonio, Giancarlo Bassi, Mario Bedogni, Luigi Bestagini, Giancarlo Buchetti, Carlo Bulgheroni, Ignacio Dionisi, Arnaldo Fabris, Vincenzo Fardella, Aldo Federici, Umberto Gerli, Dino Innocenti, Constanzo Mangini, Dino Menardi, Otto Rauth, Franco Rossi, Gianantonio Zopegni

POLAND • Henryk Bromer, Mieczyslaw Burda, Stefan Csorich, Tadeusz Dolewski, Alfred Gansiniec, Thomas Jasinski, Miecszlaw Kasprzycki, Boleslaw Kolasa, Adam Kowalski, Eugeniusz Lewacki, Jan Maciejko, Czeslaw Marchewczyk, Mieczyslaw Palus, Henryk Przezdziecki, Hilary Skarzynski, Maksymillian Wiecek, Ernest Ziaja

SWEDEN • Ake Andersson, Stig Andersson, Stig Carlsson, Ake Ericson, Rolf Ericson, Svante Granlund, Arne Johansson, Rune Johansson, Gunnar Landelius, Klas Lindstrom, Lars Ljungman, Holger Nurmela, Bror Petterson, Rolf Pettersson, Kurt Svanberg, Sven Thunman

SWITZERLAND • Hans Banninger, Alfred Bieler, Heinrich Boller, Ferdinand Cattini, Hans Cattini, Hans Durst, Walter Durst, Emil Handschin, Heini Lohrer, Werner Lohrer, Reto Perl, Gebhard Poltera, Ulrich Poltera, Beat Ruedi, Otto Schubiger, Richard Torriani, Hans Trepp

UNITED STATES • Robert Baker, Ruben Bjorkman, Robert Boeser, Bruce Cunliffe, John Garrity, Donald Geary, Goodwin Harding, Herbert van Ingen, John Kirrane, Bruce Mather, Allan Opsahl, Fred Pearson, Stanton Priddy, Jack Riley, Ralph Warburton

FINAL STANDINGS

	GP	W	L	T	GF	GA	P
Canada	8	7	0	1	69	5	15
Czechoslovakia	8	7	0	1	80	18	15
Switzerland	8	6	2	0	67	21	12
United States	8	5	3	0	86	33	10
Sweden	8	4	4	0	55	28	8
Great Britain	8	3	5	0	39	47	6
Poland	8	2	6	0	29	97	4
Austria	8	1	7	0	33	77	2
Italy	8	0	8	0	24	156	0

RESULTS

JANUARY 30
Canada 3 Sweden 1
Czechoslovakia 22 Italy 3
Poland 7 Austria 5
Switzerland 5 United States 4

JANUARY 31
Czechoslovakia 6 Sweden 3
Great Britain 5 Austria 4
Switzerland 16 Italy 0
United States 23 Poland 4

FEBRUARY 1
Canada 3 Great Britain 0
Czechoslovakia 13 Poland 1
Switzerland 11 Austria 2
United States 31 Italy 1

FEBRUARY 2
Canada 15 Poland 0
Czechoslovkia 11 Great Britain 4
Sweden 7 Austria 2

FEBRUARY 3
Canada 21 Italy 1
United States 5 Sweden 2

FEBRUARY 4
Switzerland 12 Great Britain 3
Czechoslovakia 17 Austria 3
Poland 13 Italy 7

FEBRUARY 5
Canada 12 United States 3
Switzerland 8 Sweden 2
Austria 16 Italy 5
Great Britain 8 Poland 2

FEBRUARY 6
Canada 0 Czechoslovakia 0
Switzerland 14 Poland 0
Sweden 4 Great Britain 2
United States 13 Austria 2

FEBRUARY 7
Canada 12 Austria 0
Czechoslovakia 7 Switzerland 1
Sweden 23 Italy 0
United States 4 Great Britain 3

FEBRUARY 8
Canada 3 Switzerland 0
Great Britain 14 Italy 7
Sweden 13 Poland 2
Czechoslovakia 4 United States 3

TEAM CANADA GAME SUMMARIES

JANUARY 30 • Canada 3 Sweden 1

IN GOAL
Canada — Dowey
Sweden — A. Johansson

FIRST PERIOD
1. Sweden, Lindstrom (Nurmela) • 2:35
2. Canada, Mara (Guzzo) • 4:35
penalties: *Renaud (Can)*

SECOND PERIOD
3. Canada, Halder (Renaud) • 2:07
penalties: *R. Ericson (Swe)*

THIRD PERIOD
4. Canada, Schroeter (Lecompte) • 0:35
penalties: *Nurmela (Swe — minor, misconduct), Laperrière (Can), R. Ericson (Swe), Dunster (Can), Dowey (Can)*

FEBRUARY 1 • Canada 3 Great Britain 0

IN GOAL
Canada — Dowey
Great Britain — Simon

FIRST PERIOD
1. Canada, Schroeter (Renaud) • 1:08
penalties: *Davey (GB), Schroeter (Can), Baillie (GB), Halder (Can), Guzzo (Can)*

SECOND PERIOD
2. Canada, Mara (unassisted) • 3:47
penalties: *Murray (GB), Syme (GB), Syme (GB), Halder (Can), Halder (Can), Oxley (GB), Oxley (GB), Guzzo (Can), Lecompte (Can)*

THIRD PERIOD
3. Canada, Halder (Lecompte) • 16:00
penalties: *A. Green (GB), Guzzo (Can), Guzzo (Can), Hibberd (Can), Dunster (Can), Dunster (Can), Baker (GB)*

FEBRUARY 2 • Canada 15 Poland 0

IN GOAL
Canada — Dowey
Poland — Maciejko

FIRST PERIOD
1. Canada, Renaud (Halder) • 1:55
2. Canada, Lecompte (unassisted) • 10:50
3. Canada, Schroeter (Halder) • 12:21
4. Canada, Schroeter (Halder) • 15:16
5. Canada, Gravelle (Guzzo) • 19:21
penalties: *Renaud (Can)*

SECOND PERIOD
6. Canada, Renaud (unassisted) • 2:40
7. Canada, Guzzo (Mara) • 4:03
8. Canada, Halder (Schroeter) • 6:30
9. Canada, Halder (unassisted) • 7:50
10. Canada, Mara (Guzzo) • 7:54
11. Canada, Schroeter (Renaud) • 16:32
penalties: *none*

THIRD PERIOD
12. Canada, Halder (Renaud) • 4:03
13. Canada, Gravelle (Mara) • 11:11
14. Canada, Laperrière (Mara) • 14:26
15. Canada, Mara (Guzzo) • 15:50
penalties: *Kolasa (Pol), Laperrière (Can)*

FEBRUARY 3 • Canada 21 Italy 1

FIRST PERIOD

1. Canada, Halder (Lecompte) • 0:45
2. Canada, Dunster (unassisted) • 3:12
3. Canada, Hibberd (unassisted) • 4:02
4. Canada, Mara (unassisted) • 5:48
5. Canada, Mara (Hibberd) • 6:01
6. Canada, Schroeter (Halder, Renaud) • 6:50
7. Canada, Halder (Renaud) • 7:00
8. Canada, Mara (unassisted) • 9:00
9. Canada, Halder (Renaud) • 14:52
10. Canada, Guzzo (Mara) • 16:40
11. Canada, Hibberd (Mara) • 17:12
penalties: *Laperrière (Can)*

SECOND PERIOD

12. Canada, Hibberd (Mara) • 2:13
13. Canada, Renaud (Schroeter) • 6:14
14. Canada, Mara (unassisted) • 7:00
15. Canada, Halder (Laperrière) • 12:00
16. Canada, Schroeter (Renaud) • 16:00
17. Canada, Gravelle (Mara) • 19:00
penalties: *none*

THIRD PERIOD

18. Canada, Halder (unassisted) • 0:10
19. Canada, Guzzo (unassisted) • 2:00
20. Italy, Menardi (unassisted) • 8:00
21. Canada, Guzzo (Mara) • 9:00
22. Canada, Mara (unassisted) • 12:00
penalties: *Laperrière (Can)*

IN GOAL

Canada — Dowey
Italy — Zopegni

FEBRUARY 5 • Canada 12 United States 3

FIRST PERIOD

1. Canada, Halder (unassisted) • 0:30
2. Canada, Mara (Hibberd) • 6:30
3. United States, Cunliffe (Mather) • 14:45
4. Canada, Halder (Schroeter, Renaud) • 19:50
penalties: *Lecompte (Can), Halder (Can), Mara (Can)*

SECOND PERIOD

5. Canada, Halder (Renaud, Schroeter) • 0:30
6. Canada, Lecompte (Hibberd) • 2:00
7. Canada, Mara (unassisted) • 4:00
8. Canada, Halder (unassisted) • 5:40
penalties: *Lecompte (Can), Lecompte (Can), Renaud (Can), Riley (US)*

THIRD PERIOD

9. United States, Priddy (unassisted) • 0:20
10. Canada, Halder (unassisted) • 2:00
11. Canada, Halder (unassisted) • 3:10
12. United States, Cunliffe (unassisted) • 4:30
13. Canada, Schroeter (Halder) • 12:30
14. Canada, Mara (Hibberd) • 13:40
15. Canada, Mara (Guzzo) • 17:45
penalties: *Lecompte (Can), Riley (US)*

IN GOAL

Canada — Dowey
United States — Harding

FEBRUARY 6 • Canada 0 Czechoslovakia 0

FIRST PERIOD

No Scoring
penalties: *Mara (Can)*

SECOND PERIOD

No Scoring
penalties: *Laperrière (Can), Rozinak (Cz)*

THIRD PERIOD

No Scoring
penalties: *Mara (Can), Slama (Cz), Dunster (Can)*

IN GOAL

Canada — Dowey
Czechoslovakia — Modry

FEBRUARY 7 • Canada 12 Austria 0

IN GOAL
Canada — Dowey
Austria — Huber

FIRST PERIOD
1. Canada, Halder (unassisted) • 1:00
2. Canada, Schroeter (Halder) • 4:10
3. Canada, Halder (unassisted) • 9:38
4. Canada, Mara (Guzzo) • 14:48
5. Canada, Schroeter (unassisted) • 16:30
penalties: *none*

SECOND PERIOD
6. Canada, Halder (unassisted) • 0:50
7. Canada, Schroeter (Halder) • 1:40
8. Canada, Mara (unassisted) • 3:10
9. Canada, Renaud (Halder) • 6:13
10. Canada, Mara (unassisted) • 15:10
penalties: *none*

THIRD PERIOD
11. Canada, Mara (Guzzo) • 0:40
12. Canada, Halder (unassisted) • 4:08
penalties: *none*

FEBRUARY 8 • Canada 3 Switzerland 0

IN GOAL
Canada — Dowey
Switzerland — Banninger

FIRST PERIOD
1. Canada, Halder (Schroeter) • 4:23
penalties: *Lecompte (Can), Halder (Can — major)*

SECOND PERIOD
2. Canada, Guzzo (Mara) • 3:13
penalties: *Boller (Swi), Boller (Swi), Laperrière (Can), Trepp (Swi), U. Poltera (Swi), W. Durst (Swi), Halder (Can — major), Gravelle (Can)*

THIRD PERIOD
3. Canada, Schroeter (unassisted) • 7:34
penalties: *Boller (Swi) & Hibberd (Can), Ruedi (Swi), Laperrière (Can), Gravelle (Can), Halder (Can)*

TEAM CANADA FINAL STATISTICS • 1948

#		GP	G	A	P	Pim
6	Wally Halder	8	21	8	29	20
8	George Mara	8	17	9	26	6
10	Reg Schroeter	8	12	5	17	2
12	Ab Renaud	8	4	10	14	6
17	Patsy Guzzo	8	5	7	12	8
11	Ted Hibberd	8	3	4	7	4
4	Louis Lecompte	8	2	3	5	12
16	Orval Gravelle	7	3	0	3	4
5	André Laperrière	8	1	1	2	14
3	Frank Dunster	8	1	0	1	8
1	Murray Dowey	8	0	0	0	2
7	Irving Taylor	1	0	0	0	0

#	IN GOAL	GP	W-L-T	Mins	GA	SO	Avg
1	Murray Dowey	8	7–0–1	480	5	5	0.62*
5	André Laperrière	1	0–0–0	1	0	0	0.00*

** Laperrière played in goal the last eight seconds of the game January 30 vs. Sweden when goalie Dowey was penalized*

Canada has yet to lose to Poland in seven Olympics dating back to 1932. In those games, Canada has outscored the Poles 59–2, including this modest 5–1 win at the 1980 Olympics.

Polish players Henryk Janiszewski (#5) and Wieslaw Jobczyk (#8) wear unique mouthguards in play during the team's 5–1 loss to Canada, February 14, 1980.

Dutch goalie Ted Lenssen protects his crease in the first game of the Lake Placid Olympics. Notice the odd placement of the jersey number on the front of his sweater. Canada won easily, 10–1.

Goalie Paul Pageau played in four games at the 1980 Games and later played once for the L.A. Kings.

Canadian goalie Paul Pageau makes the save as Joe Grant (#7) and Ron Davidson (#6) move in to help. Russia beat Canada 6–4, February 20, 1980.

Team Canada 1984 began each game with an inspirational goal crease meeting, though the team finished a disappointing fourth in Sarajevo.

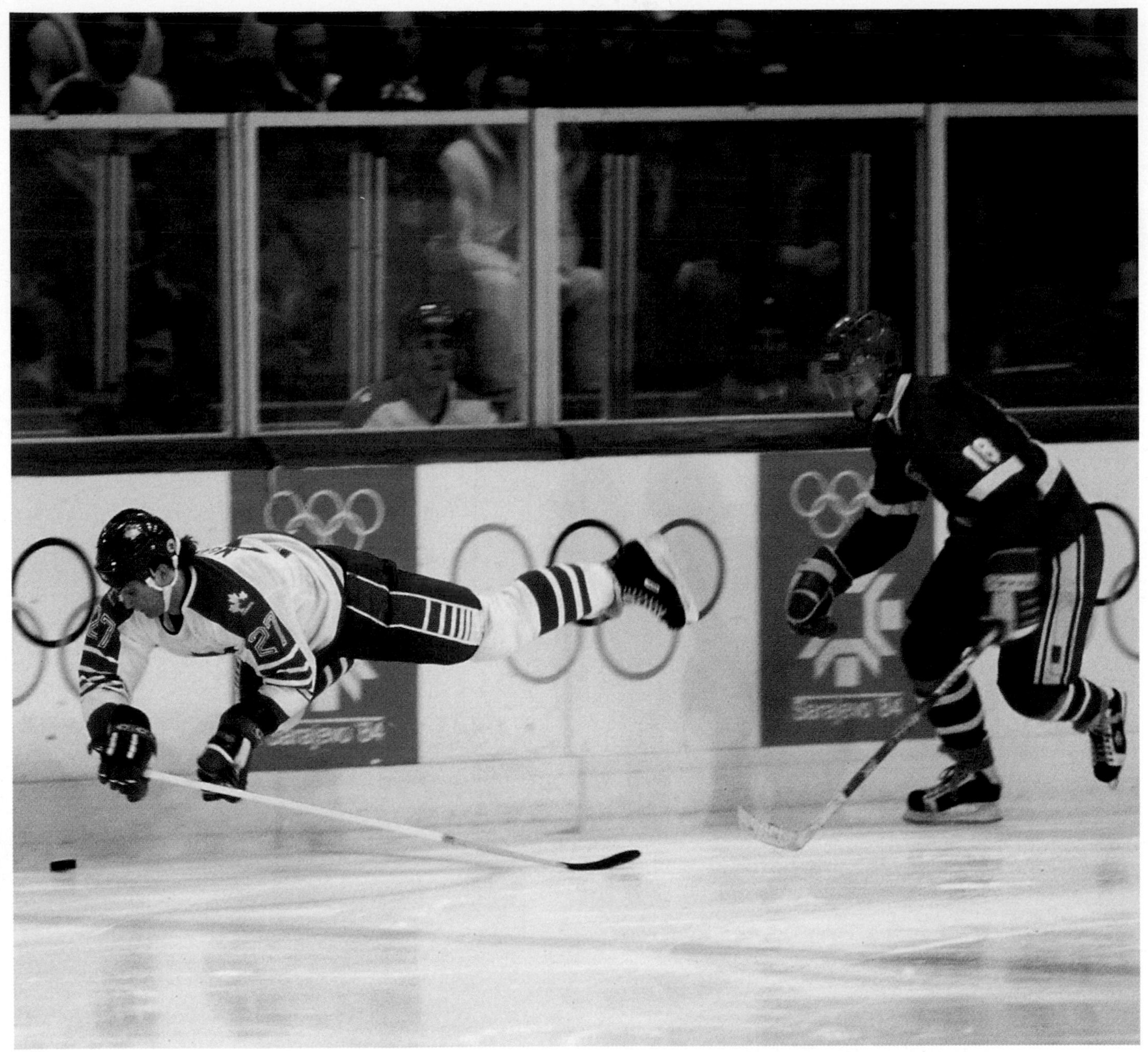

Canada's Kirk Muller flies through the air while Czech forward Darius Rusnak chases the loose puck. There was no penalty on the play and the Czechs went on to win 4–0, the first of three consecutive shutout defeats suffered by the Canadians at the 1984 Games.

Mario Gosselin played almost every minute for Canada at the Sarajevo Games in 1984. Here he wears the new team jersey that lasted through the 1994 Olympics.

Goalie Mario Gosselin watches the puck hit the crossbar while defenceman James Patrick checks an oncoming Russian, Mikhail Vasiliev. The Russians won the game 4–0.

Kevin Dineen did not have a point in seven games at Sarajevo but joined Hartford after the Olympics. After three years with the Flyers, he is back with Carolina (née Hartford) and is now in his 14th NHL season.

Russian Aleksandr Gerasimov gives and receives a little interference. Canada's 4–0 loss in Sarajevo, February 17, 1984, eliminated the team from the medal chase.

Soviet captain ("K") and current 39-year-old Detroit Red Wing Vyacheslav Fetisov fights with Carey Wilson for puck possession.

Goalie Mario Gosselin and team captain Dave Tippett celebrate another victory over the US, this a 4–2 win to open the 1984 Games. Since 1920, Canada has lost just twice in 13 Olympic games played vs. the Americans.

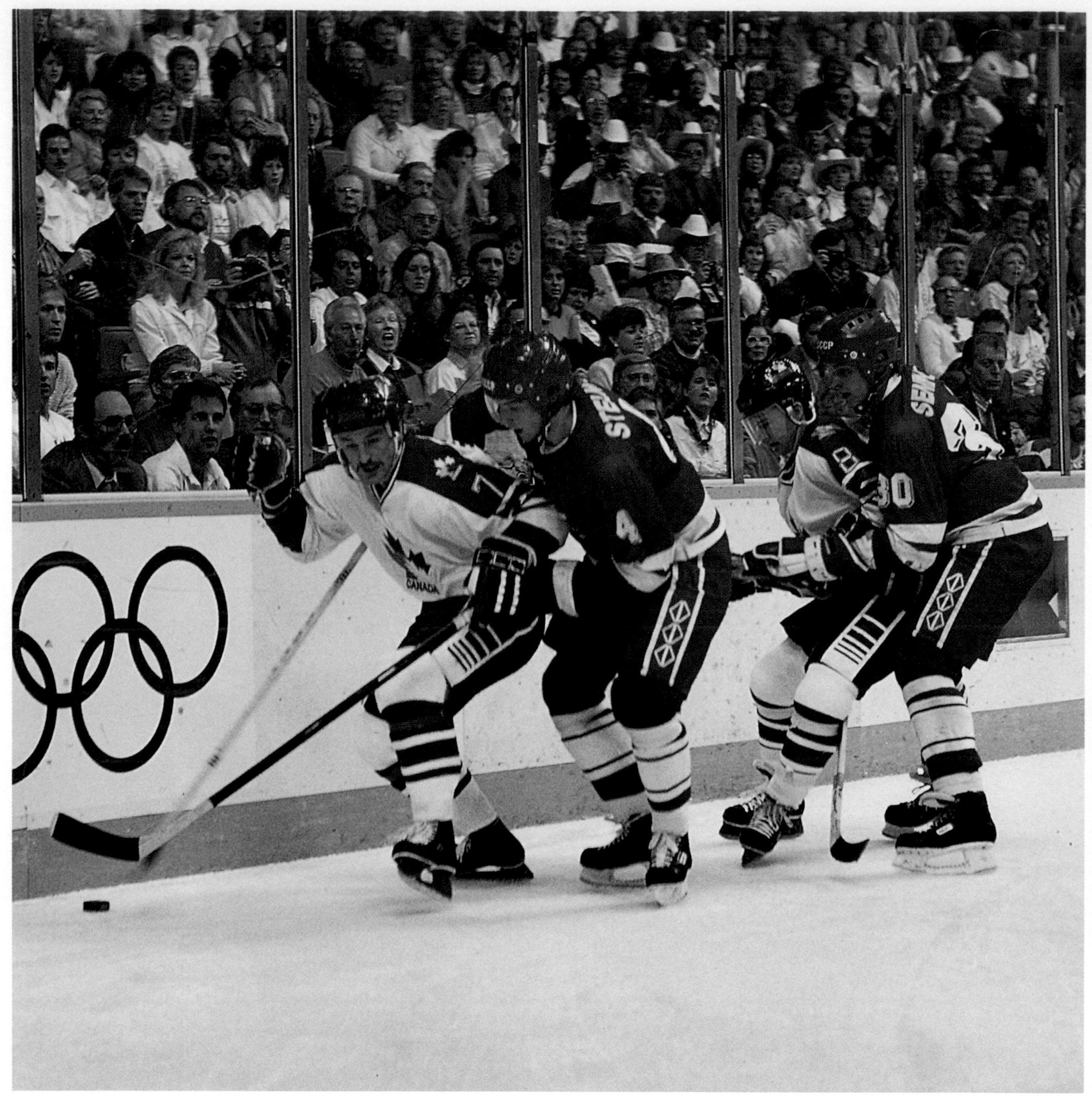

Two Soviets do a good job tying up their men (Wally Schreiber (#7) and Brian Bradley (#8)) along the boards at the 1988 Games in Calgary.

Defenceman Zarley Zalapski was one of the brightest prospects to emerge from the '88 Games. He signed with Pittsburgh after the Olympics and is currently with the Flames in Calgary.

Canadians Serge Boisvert (#12) and Wally Schreiber (#7) battle for a loose puck during a 5–0 loss to the Russians in Calgary, the only team to have beaten Canada more than three times since 1920.

CHAPTER 7

The Sixth Olympic Winter Games

OSLO, NORWAY

February 15–25, 1952

At the 41st IOC session in Stockholm on June 21, 1947, Oslo (with 18 votes) was awarded the 1952 Games over Cortina d'Ampezzo (nine votes) and Lake Placid (one vote).

Billy Dawe

TEAM CANADA • 1952

EDMONTON MERCURYS

Ralph Hansch, GOAL
Eric Patterson, GOAL

John Davies, DEFENCE
Don Gauf, DEFENCE
Bob Meyers, DEFENCE
Tom Pollock, DEFENCE
Al Purvis, DEFENCE

George Abel, FORWARD
Billy Dawe, FORWARD (CAPTAIN)
Bruce Dickson, FORWARD
Billy Gibson, FORWARD
David Miller, FORWARD
Gordie Robertson, FORWARD
Louis Secco, FORWARD
Frank "Sully" Sullivan, FORWARD
Robert Watt, FORWARD

Lou Holmes, COACH
Jim Christianson, MANAGER

FINAL PLACINGS

GOLD MEDAL
Canada

SILVER MEDAL
United States

BRONZE MEDAL
Sweden

FOURTH PLACE
Czechoslovakia

FIFTH PLACE
Switzerland

SIXTH PLACE
Poland

SEVENTH PLACE
Finland

EIGHTH PLACE
West Germany

NINTH PLACE
Norway

THE EDMONTON MERCURYS

The Mercurys' selection by the CAHA to represent Canada at these Games differed slightly in rationale from the usual process of simply penning in the name of the Allan Cup champions. While teams from the west were still considered the best in Canada in 1951, the Western Senior A league had gone from being an amateur congregation in 1950 to semi-pro in 1951, thus disqualifying most of the teams and players from Olympic eligibility. The Mercurys, an Intermediate club, were still highly regarded and through both their performance on ice and their clean record as amateurs they were invited to represent Canada in Oslo.

The Mercurys got to Europe early — by mid-December 1951 — and stayed well after the Games were over, playing an extensive series of exhibition games throughout the Continent, at first to prepare themselves for the competition and then to promote their excellent skills and high standards of play and delight fans unused to seeing such a calibre of hockey.

This was the first time a Canadian team travelled to the Games by plane, leaving from Montreal and arriving at Prestwick, Scotland on January 5, 1952. There, bedecked in white Stetsons, the Mercs were greeted by W. Duncan, president of the Scottish Ice Hockey Association, and Ross Low, manager of Ayr Arena. Less than an hour later, the Canadian boys were on the ice playing their first exhibition game, a 6–3 win over the Ayr Raiders. They played two more games in Scotland, then a series in London, and carried on to the Continent for more Olympic tune-ups.

THE GUIDING LIGHT

The team was backed financially by Jim Christianson of Edmonton, a car dealer who provided the $100,000 needed to tour Europe and participate in the Olympics, and who, as owner, named the team after a brand of Fords he frequently sold. Christianson was in many ways a remarkable man and great hockey fan. He revived the Junior Oil Kings franchise which went on to win a Memorial Cup, and as owner of one of the most successful Lincoln Mercury dealerships in the country, his business acumen was indisputable.

While in Norway with the team, he contracted a virus and was ill for most of the Games. Upon his return to Canada, he again became ill and died a short time later. The Ford Motor Company then appointed a dealer principal who oversaw operations for the next decade or so, and when he died, Mercs defenceman Al Purvis was named the next dealer principal. Purvis then got a number of his Olympics team-mates on board as shareholders (Miller, Gauf, and Dawe) or employees, each managing a division of the operations. Over the years, he bought back their shares, and to this day Al Purvis runs the Waterloo Mercury dealership in Edmonton, now celebrating 50 years of operation.

AN ACCIDENT

The European tour was immensely successful for the Mercurys. Everywhere they went, they amazed fans who had never seen such speed and strength coupled with unparalleled skill. And everywhere the Mercs went, they won. The only unpleasant incident in their travels was a bus accident just outside Oslo. Coach Lou Holmes

explained: "The wheels locked as we rounded a curve on the highway and the bus went over a ditch and toppled against a tree." David Miller received a gash on his face, Tom Pollock cut his arm, and George Abel hurt his back. While the experience was emotionally unnerving, none of the injuries was serious, and within an hour another bus picked them up and took them to the great outdoor Jordal Amfi stadium in Oslo, where 10,000 fans watched the Canucks beat the Norwegian aggregation 7–2 in an exhibition on the site where most of the Olympic games would be played (along with nearby Daalenenga Stadium, another outdoor rink).

Miller was also the centre of a small dispute initiated by the Czechs, who claimed he had played semi-pro hockey several years earlier for Streatham in England. The Olympic Committee listened to the argument but dismissed the protest. Miller didn't miss a minute of action.

IN MEMORIAM

Flags were flown at half mast throughout the Games to mourn the death of King George VI of England, whose untimely passing grieved all Canadians and Britons alike. Back home, the New York Rangers-Toronto game at Maple Leaf Gardens was postponed by Major Conn Smythe, the first time in team history this had been done, to allow all Canadians time to pay proper respect to the King.

A CABLE OF SUPPORT

Halfway through the Games, the gold medal team of 1948 sent a cable to the team trying to continue the Olympic reign: "Former members RCAF Flyers, 1948 Winter Olympic champs and all of RCAF, pulling for Mercs. Confident you will bring home Olympic title. Good luck and best wishes."

MR. ZERO — RALPH HANSCH

Ralph Hansch is the answer to one of the more unique trivia questions about the history of Canadian hockey at the Olympics: who is the only goalie to wear "0" ? Having worn the number all through peewee and minors, Hansch saw no reason to alter his good luck number now that he had arrived at the biggest tournament of his life. The IOC frowned on the idea, however, and asked him to switch to a "real" number. He refused, but the IOC put a rule in its books making the future wearing of this digit illegal.

THE INFLAMMATORY EUROPEAN MEDIA

The Canada–Czech game and the US–Swiss game were thrown into a very bad light when reporters focused on two non-fights instigated by a Canadian and an American, respectively. Both Gordie Robertson of Canada and, more seriously, Joe Czarnota of the States received major penalties for waving at an opponent, but Zurich's leading paper, *Neue Zuricher Zeitung*, was outraged, commenting: "We have neither the words nor the space to describe in detail what some of these rowdies drilled in circus business considered permissible. It is now time to ask whether this pollution of European ice hockey through overseas teams should not be halted. One can be certain that neither the Canadians nor the Americans would let themselves be criticized. However, what seems good enough for their players and their public need not be held up as a model for European circumstances." The editorial concluded by questioning "whether an ice hockey tournament under such unfavourable auspices might not better be stricken from the Olympic program."

During the Czarnota incident, Norwegian fans threw orange peels onto the ice and screamed "Chicago Gangsters" at the players. When asked to comment, Norway's Prime Minister Oscar Torp defended the brand of hockey on display: "Just ignorance of the mainly-Norwegian crowd," he concluded. "People should understand that the penalties make ice hockey a human game. When the boys get so het up that they do something wrong or get too rowdy — OK, give them two minutes to cool down and think it over. Ice hockey is a terrific display, not only of teamwork but also of technique and bodily strength. So, of course, the lads will hurt each other now and then."

The next day, after an hour's meeting by the IIHF, under the directorship of Dr. Fritz Kraatz, the fire was doused. No suspensions were levied and the games went on as planned.

BODY-CHECKING

International rules had always been at odds with the Canadian style of play with respect to body contact in hockey. That is, while the IOC had adopted Canadian rules way back in 1920, there had always been disagreements regarding the interpretation of those rules, particularly about checking. Europeans considered it a goon tactic, something used to intimidate the opposition, and not relevant to the skills pursuant to the game. Obviously, Canadians saw things differently.

Incredibly, it wasn't until 1968 that the Olympic body-checking rule was changed to the NHL rule. Until then, hitting in the offensive zone was prohibited.

In other words, the defenceman could check his man coming in on him, but the forechecker could not hit the defenceman with any purpose.

In this excerpt from a radio interview conducted by Foster Hewitt, Bunny Ahearne, European president of the IIHF, admitted differences persisted between the Canadian and European styles of play:

> **FH:** Are the Europeans as strong as their records would indicate from recent encounters with Canadian teams?
>
> **BA:** Well, that's a difficult question, Foster, because, as you know, we don't have any body-checking in Europe and it's very difficult to form a comparison between our European teams here and your own teams in Canada. There's no question that the Czechoslovakian team is a first-class team, and if you eliminate the body-checking, they would stand up to any team in Canada.
>
> **FH:** Now I understand that body-checking is still in the rules, it's just the means of interpretation...
>
> **BA:** That's right, Foster. The International Ice Hockey Federation adopted the CAHA rules, but unfortunately they overlooked the rules of interpretation, and that's what caused all the problem.
>
> **FH:** And there seems to be quite a mess!
>
> **BA**: Oh, very definitely.
>
> **FH:** Well, do these tours by Canadian teams help stimulate interest in hockey?
>
> **BA:** There's no question at all about that, Foster. Every year, every hockey country in Europe looks forward to seeing the Canadian teams play because Canada, after all, is the mother of hockey and they want to see how the Canadian teams play the national game.

THE WRAP-UP

After winning gold, the Mercurys travelled through Belgium, Holland, Sweden, Norway, Switzerland, Italy, and England again. All in all, they won 45 of the 50 games they played, the last a 7–2 win over the Earl's Court Rangers, before flying home April 1, 1952. They were greeted at the airport by Edmonton Mayor William Hawrelak, provincial government officials, wives, friends, fans, and well-wishers. They disembarked with the same white Stetsons they had paraded into the Olympic Stadium six weeks earlier and went in a 20-car motorcade to Edmonton's downtown where bands and a large crowd formed a parade. That evening, the Chamber of Commerce, as well as city and provincial politicians, hosted a lavish banquet in their honour.

THE AFTERMATH

Canada had been so far the superior hockey-playing nation in the world since 1920, and part of our teams' mandate had always been to tour Europe in good faith to promote hockey, Canada, and Canadian skills. In return, the players were culturally

Nearly all of Edmonton came out to greet the Mercs upon their return home.

enriched by the time spent in these countries and certainly enjoyed the games. However, they received no remuneration beyond living expenses (they were, after all, amateurs) and, worse, were frequently berated, most often during tense games at the Olympics, for incorporating too much the physical side of the game into play. This criticism exasperated the CAHA, which felt increasingly that travelling teams had little to gain and much to lose.

Thus, the following year, the feeling was that Canada should not send a touring team to the World Championships in Switzerland, a decision made officially by CAHA president W.B. George but one fully supported by everybody. As George rationalized: "Every year we spend $10,000 to send a Canadian hockey team over to Europe to play 40 exhibition games. All of these games are played to packed houses that only enrich European coffers. In return, we are subjected to constant, unnecessary abuse over our Canadian style of play." Outgoing CAHA president Doug Grimston was more diplomatic in assessing the situation as it pertained to the Oslo Games, though his conclusions were similar in substance: "Hockey, as played in Europe, is a different game than what we play in Canada and I felt that our boys did exceptionally well under different rules and 'strange' refereeing. We play a more robust game, which is frowned on in Europe."

THE CAVEAT

> "European teams have improved considerably the last few years and, with some proper coaching, could be mighty troublesome to Canada."

So said Doug Grimston after watching the swift development of teams during the course of the Oslo Games. He went on to observe that, "European teams lack stamina, especially on power-plays, and they are timid when it comes to bodily contact." But, he warned, if these problems could be eradicated, many countries could become superior hockey-playing nations. By the time the next Olympics arrived, his words had proved timely and prescient.

The Competition

TOURNAMENT FORMAT

All nine countries were placed in a single division, and the schedule was again a simple round-robin format, each nation playing all others once. There would be no overtime in the event of a tie after 60 minutes of regulation play. If two teams were tied in the standings and a medal were at stake, they would play an extra playoff game. In case of a tie between three teams, the team with the better goal differential (goals allowed subtracted from goals scored) would be given the better placing in the final standings.

THE OPPOSITION

CZECHOSLOVAKIA • Slavomir Barton, Miloslav Blazek, Vaclav Bubnik, Vlastimil Bubnik, Miloslav Charouzd, Bronislav Danda, Karel Gut, Vlastimil Hajsman, Jan Lidral, Miroslav Novy, Miloslav Osmera, Zdenek Pycha, Miloslav Rejman, Jan Richter, Oldrich Sedlak, Jiri Sekyra, Josef Zahorsky

FINLAND • Yrjo Hakala, Aarne Honkavaara, Erkki Hytonen, Pentti Isotalo, Matti Karumaa, Ossi Kauppi, Keijo Kuusela, Kauko Makinen, Pekka Myllyla, Christian Rapp, Esko Rehoma, Matti Rintakoski, Eero Saari, Eero Salisma, Lauri Silvan, Unto Vitala, Jukka Vuolio

GERMANY • Karl Bierschel, Markus Egen, Karl Enzler, Georg Guggemos, Alfred Hoffmann, Engelbert Holdereid, Walter Kremershof, Ludwig Kuhn, Dieter Niess, Hans Georg Pescher, Fritz Poitsch, Herbert Schibukat, Xaver Unsinn, Heinz Wackers, Karl Wild

NORWAY • Jan Erik Adolfsen, Arne Bergh, Egil Bjerklund, Per Dahl, Bjorn Gulbrandsen (I), Bjorn Gulbrandsen (II), Finn Gundersen, Arthur Kristiansen, Gunnar Kroge, Jonny Larntvet, Annar Pedersen, Roar Pedersen, Ragnar Rygel, Leif Solheim, Oivind Solheim, Roy Strandem, Per R. Voigt

POLAND • Michal Antuszewicz, Henryk Bromowicz, Kazimierz Chodakowski, Stefan Csorich, Rudolf Czech, Alfred Gansiniec, Jan Hampel, Marian Jezak, Eugeniusz Lewacki, Roman Peszek, Hilary Skarzynski, Konstanty Swicarz, Stanislaw Szlendak, Zdzislaw Trojanowski, Adolf Wrobel

SWEDEN • Gote Almqvist, Ake Andersson, Hans Andersson, Stig "Tvilling" Andersson, Lars Bjorn, Gote Blomquist, Thord Flodquist, Erik Johansson, Gosta Johansson, Rune Johansson, Sven Johansson, Ake Lassas, Holger Nurmela, Hans Oberg, Lars Pettersson, Lars Svensson, Sven Thunman

SWITZERLAND • Hans Banninger, Gian Bazzi, François Blank, Bixio Celio, Reto Delnon, Walter Durst, Emil Golaz, Emil Handschin, Paul Hofer, Willy Pfister, Gebhard Poltera, Ulrich Poltera, Otto Schlapfer, Otto Schubiger, Alfred Streun, Hans Trepp, Paul Wyss

UNITED STATES • Ruben Bjorkman, Leonard Ceglarski, Joseph Czarnota, Richard Desmond, André Gambucci, Clifford Harrison, Gerald Kilmartin, John Mulhern, John Noah, Arnold Oss, Robert Rompre, James Sedin, Allen Van, Donald Whiston, Kenneth Yackel

FINAL STANDINGS

	GP	W	L	T	GF	GA	P
Canada	8	7	0	1	71	14	15
United States	8	6	1	1	43	21	13
Sweden	8	6	2	0	48	19	12*
Czechoslovakia	8	6	2	0	47	18	12*
Switzerland	8	4	4	0	40	40	8
Poland	8	2	5	1	21	56	5
Finland	8	2	6	0	21	60	4
Germany	8	1	6	1	21	53	3
Norway	8	0	8	0	15	46	0

* *Because of identical point totals and goal differential, Sweden and Czechoslovakia played an extra game to determine third place (the winner was also considered European champion). The Swedes won that game 5–3.*

RESULTS

FEBRUARY 15
Canada 15 Germany 1
Sweden 9 Finland 2
Czechoslovakia 8 Poland 2
United States 3 Norway 2

FEBRUARY 16
Switzerland 12 Finland 0
Czechoslovakia 6 Norway 0
Sweden 17 Poland 1
United States 8 Germany 2

FEBRUARY 17
Canada 13 Finland 3
Sweden 4 Norway 2
Czechoslovakia 6 Germany 1
Switzerland 6 Poland 3

FEBRUARY 18
Canada 11 Poland 0
Sweden 7 Germany 3
Switzerland 7 Norway 2
United States 8 Finland 2

FEBRUARY 19
Canada 4 Czechoslovakia 1
United States 8 Switzerland 2

FEBRUARY 20
Finland 5 Norway 2
Poland 4 Germany 4

FEBRUARY 21
Canada 11 Switzerland 2
Czechoslovakia 11 Finland 2
Germany 6 Norway 2
Sweden 4 United States 2

FEBRUARY 22
Canada 3 Sweden 2
Czechoslovakia 8 Switzerland 3
Finland 5 Germany 1
United States 5 Poland 3

FEBRUARY 23
Canada 11 Norway 2
Sweden 5 Switzerland 2
Poland 4 Finland 2
United States 6 Czechoslovakia 3

FEBRUARY 24
Canada 3 United States 3
Czechoslovakia 4 Sweden 0
Switzerland 6 Germany 3

FEBRUARY 25
Poland 4 Norway 3
Sweden 5 Czechoslovakia 3
(replay, to break bronze medal tie)

TEAM CANADA GAME SUMMARIES

FEBRUARY 15 • Canada 15 Germany 1

IN GOAL
Canada — Hansch
Germany — Wackers

SHOTS ON GOAL

Canada			
14	10	20	**44**
Germany			
7	6	4	**17**

FIRST PERIOD
1. Canada, Davies (Gibson) • 4:12
2. Canada, Gibson (Dawe) • 9:18
3. Germany, Kremershof (unassisted) • 11:20
4. Canada, Robertson (Gibson) • 16:05
5. Canada, Gibson (unassisted) • 16:13
6. Canada, Miller (unassisted) • 16:25
7. Canada, Watt (unassisted) • 16:53

penalties: *Pescher (Ger) 19:50*

SECOND PERIOD
8. Canada, Gibson (Robertson) • 0:50(pp)
9. Canada, Sullivan (Miller) • 2:56
10. Canada, Miller (Sullivan) • 9:14
11. Canada, Miller (Sullivan) • 13:14
12. Canada, Miller (unassisted) • 15:54
13. Canada, Purvis (unassisted) • 18:00
14. Canada, Gibson (Robertson) • 19:23

penalties: *Dawe (Can) 5:50*

THIRD PERIOD
15. Canada, Miller (Sullivan) • 17:20
16. Canada, Gauf (unassisted) • 19:37(pp)

penalties: *Guggemos (Ger) 18:10*

FEBRUARY 17 • Canada 13 Finland 3

IN GOAL
Canada — Hansch
Finland — Myllyla

SHOTS ON GOAL

Canada	**44**
Finland	**7**

FIRST PERIOD
1. Canada, Secco (unassisted) • 0:51
2. Canada, Dawe (Gibson) • 5:40
3. Finland, Honkavaara (unassisted) • 7:12
4. Canada, Dickson (Abel) • 10:10
5. Canada, Miller (Sullivan) • 11:20
6. Canada, Meyers (unassisted) • 11:32
7. Finland, Kuusela (unassisted) • 14:14
8. Canada, Abel (Secco) • 19:59

penalties: *none*

SECOND PERIOD
9. Canada, Robertson (Dawe) • 3:25
10. Canada, Miller (unassisted) • 9:29
11. Canada, Gibson (Robertson) • 11:30
12. Canada, Gibson (unassisted) • 13:28
13. Canada, Pollock (unassisted) • 18:45

penalties: *Robertson (Can)*

THIRD PERIOD
14. Canada, Gibson (Dawe) • 1:12
15. Canada, Meyers (unassisted) • 7:05
16. Finland, Silvan (unassisted) • 8:32

penalties: *Isotalo (Fin), Salisma (Fin)*

FEBRUARY 18 • Canada 11 Poland 0

IN GOAL
Canada — Patterson
Poland — Szlendak

SHOTS ON GOAL

Canada			
16	13	9	**38**
Poland			
2	4	1	**7**

FIRST PERIOD
1. Canada, Watt (Davies) • 12:40
2. Canada, Dawe (unassisted) • 13:55
3. Canada, Abel (Secco) • 17:25

penalties: *none*

SECOND PERIOD
4. Canada, Robertson (Gibson) • 13:58
5. Canada, Abel (Davies) • 15:15
6. Canada, Abel (Dickson) • 15:50

penalties: *Davies (Can) 3:59, Pollock (Can) 6:01, Miller (Can) & Swicarz (Pol) 11:10*

THIRD PERIOD
7. Canada, Gauf (Robertson) • 9:05(pp)
8. Canada, Davies (Dickson) • 9:10
9. Canada, Dickson (Abel) • 9:53
10. Canada, Gibson (Dawe) • 14:20
11. Canada, Sullivan (Watt) • 18:20

penalties: *Bromowicz (Pol) 2:05, Bromowicz (Pol) & Gibson (Can) & Gansiniec (Pol) 7:25, Davies (Can) 19:58*

FEBRUARY 19 • Canada 4 Czechoslovakia 1

FIRST PERIOD

1. Czechoslovakia, Charouzd (Gut) • 5:21(pp)

2. Canada, Gibson (Pollock) • 13:21

penalties: *Va. Bubnik (Cz) 2:28, Sullivan (Can) 4:32, Robertson (Can) 8:25, Osmera (Cz) 18:20*

SECOND PERIOD

3. Canada, Dickson (unassisted) • 10:20

penalties: *Vl. Bubnik (Cz) 2:05, Gauf (Can) 6:00, Barton (Cz) 7:36, Purvis (Can) 11:07, Watt (Can) 15:40, Rejman (Cz) 15:47*

THIRD PERIOD

4. Canada, Robertson (unassisted) • 1:37

5. Canada, Gibson (unassisted) • 5:10

penalties: *Pollock (Can) 1:59, Davies (Can) 7:19, Osmera (Cz) 8:22, Vl. Bubnik (Cz) 8:45, Robertson (Can — major) 10:16, Gibson (Can) & Rejman (Cz) 18:13*

IN GOAL

Canada — Hansch

Czechoslovakia — Richter

SHOTS ON GOAL

Canada	13	11	8	**32**
Czechoslovakia	8	7	7	**22**

FEBRUARY 21 • Canada 11 Switzerland 2

FIRST PERIOD

1. Canada, Davies (unassisted) • 8:15

2. Canada, Dawe (Robertson) • 10:35

3. Canada, Sullivan (unassisted) • 17:44

4. Canada, Sullivan (unassisted) • 18:25

penalties: *none*

SECOND PERIOD

5. Canada, Miller (Watt) • 2:10

6. Canada, Miller (Sullivan) • 2:56

7. Canada, Sullivan (Watt) • 10:45

8. Canada, Gibson (Dawe) • 14:20

9. Canada, Dickson (unassisted) • 17:58

penalties: *Gibson (Can) 3:28*

THIRD PERIOD

10. Switzerland, Trepp (unassisted) • 2:02

11. Canada, Purvis (Abel) • 5:59

12. Switzerland, Hofer (unassisted) • 8:54

13. Canada, Gibson (unassisted) • 13:55

penalties: *none*

IN GOAL

Canada — Patterson

Switzerland — Wyss

SHOTS ON GOAL

Canada	17	14	10	**41**
Switzerland	4	8	9	**21**

FEBRUARY 22 • Canada 3 Sweden 2

FIRST PERIOD

1. Sweden, Pettersson (unassisted) • 1:30

2. Sweden, Oberg (unassisted) • 9:22

3. Canada, Secco (Abel) • 13:00

penalties: *E. Johansson (Swe) 10:20, Gauf (Can) 15:40*

SECOND PERIOD

4. Canada, Abel (unassisted) • 18:04

penalties: *none*

THIRD PERIOD

5. Canada, Dawe (Gibson) • 19:40

penalties: *none*

IN GOAL

Canada — Hansch

Sweden — Flodquist

SHOTS ON GOAL

Canada	12	14	10	**36**
Sweden	4	2	3	**9**

FEBRUARY 23 • Canada 11 Norway 2

First Period

1. Canada, Dickson (Abel) • 0:25

2. Canada, Pollock (Secco) • 1:59

3. Norway, Rygel (unassisted) • 4:15

4. Canada, Gibson (Davies) • 9:03

5. Norway, Bergh (unassisted) • 13:10

6. Canada, Davies (Gibson, Abel) • 17:59

7. Canada, Abel (unassisted) • 19:40

penalties: *none*

SECOND PERIOD

8. Canada, Watt (Miller) • 3:40

9. Canada, Miller (unassisted) • 5:25

10. Canada, Gibson (Dawe) • 6:45

penalties: *Secco (Can), Rygel (Nor), Pollock (Can)*

THIRD PERIOD

11. Canada, Gibson (unassisted) • 9:12

12. Canada, Dickson (unassisted) • 13:45

13. Canada, Dawe (Robertson) • 16:34

penalties: *none*

IN GOAL

Canada — Hansch

Norway — Dahl

SHOTS ON GOAL

unavailable

FEBRUARY 24 • Canada 3 United States 3

IN GOAL
Canada — Hansch
United States — Desmond

SHOTS ON GOAL

Canada	**58**
United States	**13**

FIRST PERIOD
1. Canada, Dawe (Gibson) • 18:48
2. Canada, Dickson (unassisted) • 19:06
penalties: *none*

SECOND PERIOD
3. United States, Mulhern (Kilmartin) • 13:03
4. United States, Bjorkman (unassisted) • 14:01
5. Canada, Gauf (unassisted) • 18:03
penalties: *Abel (Can) & Noah (US) 7:56, Yackel (US) 14:45*

THIRD PERIOD
6. United States, Sedin (unassisted) • 17:51
penalties: *none*

TEAM CANADA FINAL STATISTICS • 1952

#		GP	G	A	P	Pim
13	Billy Gibson	8	15	7	22	6
10	David Miller	8	10	2	12	2
8	George Abel	8	6	6	12	2
5	Billy Dawe	8	6	6	12	2
11	Sully Sullivan	8	5	5	10	2
14	Gordon Robertson	8	4	6	10	9
9	Bruce Dickson	8	7	2	9	0
2	John Davies	8	4	3	7	6
7	Robert Watt	8	3	3	6	2
12	Louis Secco	8	2	3	5	2
6	Donald Gauf	7	3	0	3	4
15	Tom Pollock	8	2	1	3	6
4	Al Purvis	8	2	0	2	2
3	Bob Meyers	2	2	0	2	0

#	IN GOAL	GP	W-L-T	Mins	GA	SO	Avg
1	Eric Patterson	2	2–0–0	120	2	1	1.00
0	Ralph Hansch	6	5–0–1	360	12	0	2.00

## CHAPTER 8

The Seventh Olympic Winter Games

CORTINA d'AMPEZZO, ITALY

January 26 – February 4, 1956

Denis Brodeur

At the 44th IOC session in Rome on April 28, 1949, Cortina (with 31 votes) was the popular choice to host the 1956 Games, beating out Montreal (again, this time with but seven votes), Colorado Springs, Colorado (two votes), and Lake Placid, New York (one vote). This was to be the first time the USSR entered the Winter Olympics (they first joined the Summer Olympics in 1952 in Helsinki).

TEAM CANADA • 1956

KITCHENER-WATERLOO DUTCHMEN

Denis Brodeur, *GOAL*
Keith Woodall, *GOAL*

Art Hurst, *DEFENCE*
Byrle Klinck, *DEFENCE*
Howie Lee, *DEFENCE*
Jack MacKenzie, *DEFENCE (CAPTAIN)*
Floyd Martin, *DEFENCE*

Billy Colvin, *CENTRE*
Ken Laufman, *CENTRE*
Bob White, *CENTRE*

Charlie Brooker, *LEFT WING*
Jim Logan, *LEFT WING*
Don Rope, *LEFT WING*
Gerry Théberge, *LEFT WING*

Buddy Horne, *RIGHT WING*
Paul Knox, *RIGHT WING*
George Scholes, *RIGHT WING*

Bobby Bauer, *COACH*
Ernie Gorman, *GENERAL MANAGER*

FINAL PLACINGS

GOLD MEDAL
USSR

SILVER MEDAL
United States

BRONZE MEDAL
Canada

FOURTH PLACE
Sweden

FIFTH PLACE
Czechoslovakia

SIXTH PLACE
Germany

SEVENTH PLACE
Italy

EIGHTH PLACE
Poland

NINTH PLACE
Switzerland

TENTH PLACE
Austria

THE KITCHENER-WATERLOO DUTCHMEN

The CAHA had an easy time selecting the Dutchmen as Canada's team for the 1956 Olympics, given that the K-Ws had won the Allan Cup the past two seasons. However, some replacements to the team that was competing in the five-team OHA Senior A would have to be made because of the amateur status required by Olympic rules. More specifically, Clare Martin, Bud Kemp, Joe Schertzel, Jack Hamilton, and Jack White were all professionals who had been reinstated for amateur play, which was fine for Senior OHA hockey, but not so fine for the Olympics.

To this end, the team signed forwards Bob White and Jim McBurney to replace the pros in November, and in early January added Elmer Skov, George McLagan, and Art Hurst as possible final reinforcements for the Olympic tournament. Unfortunately, these were players from Senior B and Junior B teams, worth barely a whisper in Canada but at the time thought to be good enough for international competition. In retrospect, the addition of five higher-calibre players would probably have made a significant difference in the team's performance.

A further complication arose when it was decided that the Dutchmen would have to play the full OHA schedule if they were to qualify for the playoffs and defend their rule as Allan Cup champions. In the past, amateur teams and players had little problem getting time off to ready themselves for the Olympics. For the Dutchies, representing Canada meant cramming many extra games before and after the Olympics into an even tighter time frame to meet league schedule requirements. At the start of December, for instance, they played five games in seven nights, a pace that would do nothing to improve the team's chances in Cortina.

GETTING THERE

The Dutchies played their last OHA game on January 14, flew from Malton to Prestwick, Scotland the next day, and played their first exhibition game that night. All the while, they were hearing talk from all quarters of an expected gold medal, the whole nation fully anticipating the customary triumphant return three weeks hence. "We didn't come over here to lose" was the succinct answer from manager Ernie Gorman when asked of his team's chances.

The Italian and German players were all conceding top spot to the Canadians, and even Louis Lecompte, a Canadian referee at the Games, compared his nation to the Russians and found the latter wanting: "I don't think the Russians are as strong as last year [at the World Championships] and a number of other teams are much stronger," he opined. "The Canadians look like a happy gang of kids on the ice, and can they ever go! The Russians often carry the puck within ten feet of the net and then pass instead of shoot. You can't get goals that way."

The K-Ws beat the Paisley Pirates 6–5 in a game against mostly Canadian expatriates, one intended more to familiarize the Dutchmen with European rules (such as, no body-checking in the offensive zone) than to provide suitable training for the Games.

The next morning at 4 A.M., the team flew to Prague for further Olympic-conditions preparation, playing the Czechs on outdoor rinks as they would be doing for all their games in Cortina. There they incurred but one minor penalty in the first game (compared to a dozen in the Paisley game) and beat the Czech "B" squad 9–1. The next night they didn't earn a single penalty and waltzed to a 10–1 win. Coach Bobby Bauer was delighted with his team's adjustment: "I think we have shown we can play top-flight hockey in the European style," he beamed after the victory.

To make matters even better, for the first time ever the Canadian team was being warmly greeted by media and fans alike for their fair play, sportsmanship, and extreme skill, while other teams, notably Russia and the US, were being accused of rough and dirty play. The Dutchmen arrived in Cortina a week early and used the time to train and accustom themselves to the high altitude of this beautiful town in the Italian Alps.

LET THE GAMES BEGIN — A COMIC OPENING

The battle for hockey supremacy is as emotional as it is physical, as much about being mentally tough and accepting any challenge as it is about superior technical skill with the puck. And so it was, at least in part, that Canada began these 1956 Games on a high note, teaming with the US to beat Germany — in a snowball fight!

As the athletes were lined up just outside the Olympic Stadium, preparing for the ceremonial walk in front of Italian president Giovanni Gronchi, one of the Germans threw a snowball Canada-ward. A Canadian shot back his own verbal volley: "For every snowball you throw, we will put five pucks in your hockey net tonight." At this prompting, the Germans *en masse* assailed the Dutchies with a barrage of snowballs. The Americans came to their neighbours' help, and while the three warring nations were whipping snow around, President Gronchi's car pulled up and he stepped out, right in the middle of snowball battle and three laughing hockey teams.

THE REFEREES

The 15 referees for the Olympics threatened to quit the Games just prior to their opening, citing poor accommodations and an IOC failure to reimburse them for out-of-pocket expenses. Once this problem was straightened out, the skill and competence of European officials was questioned. It was brought to the attention of Bunny Ahearne, European president of the IIHF, who then proposed ways of overcoming the poor skating ability of the Continental zebras.

Ahearne wanted to put the refs in some sort of cage that would be elevated above the ice, so they could make the calls from an easier vantage point and not have to skate all the while. He explained: "A spotlight would follow the referee up and down the rope ladder [leading to the cage], thus giving the fans a chance to blow off steam. The ice would be marked off into numbered areas for face-offs and the referee would announce over the loudspeaker the reason for penalties. One or two linesmen would be on the ice simply to handle face-offs and get between fighters." As history has shown, the idea went nowhere!

THE REFEREEING

Up until the medal round, the most surprising result for Canada was undoubtedly their narrow 3–1 win over their lowly hosts, the Italians. The previous day, the

Canucks had beaten Austria 23–0, a team Italy had only managed to tie 2–2 two days earlier. Canada would surely trounce Italy with equal embarrassment.

The refereeing of Germany's Hans Unger, however, went a long way to prove just how equalizing discriminatory judging could be in determining the outcome of a game. Over the first two periods alone, Canada was called for 10 penalties to Italy's two. The games still used a two-referee system, and of Canada's 10 infractions, nine were whistled by Unger. Twice Canada was down five men to three, and at one time Italy had seven men on the ice. Rather than call a too-many-men penalty, referee Unger blew the play dead and ordered Italy to send a man to the bench!

Canadian goalie Denis Brodeur (father of New Jersey's Martin) covers the puck while a Czech player is tied up in front by the toque-wearing Jack MacKenzie.

The normally taciturn Bobby Bauer called Unger "disgraceful," and Jimmy Dunn, president of the CAHA, immediately protested Unger's involvement in any further games involving Canada. Walter Brown of the IIHF tacitly conceded the biased refereeing by ensuring Unger and Canada never skated on the same sheet of ice again.

LOSING TO THE UNITED STATES

Canada's 4–1 defeat by the United States the night of January 31, 1956 virtually ensured Canada's loss of the gold medal to which the country seemed to have an almost inherited right since 1920. Thom Benson, in his broadcast for CBC radio, began his next day report with appropriate solemnity:

> Today, in this small mountain village, there was a funeral. The bells of the ancient church told the passing of a procession. The mourners chanted prayers as they trudged up the steep hills behind the coffin bearers. Those who were left were saying their farewells to a robust and lively friend.
>
> The cortege wound its way through narrow and twisted streets up past the Concordia Hotel. Inside that building, there was a similar ceremony where the inhabitants mourned the passing of an era. In the hotel was housed the Kitchener–Waterloo hockey team and all those other Canadians who aspired to Olympic heights in the field of amateur competition.
>
> There was no joy there, no happy words, no jubilation, for last night Canadian amateur hockey suffered a blow to its prestige from which it may never recover. The Kitchener–Waterloo team was beaten fairly and squarely by a team which would never make the junior finals in Canada. If you think saying that is easy, then you are greatly mistaken.

AFTER THE GAMES

On February 6, the Dutchmen were in Baden-Baden, in southern Germany, to play a two-game series against the RCAF Flyers (they won both, 15–4 and 15–5), flew to Soest, in the north, for one last game, and then left for London via Dusseldorf before heading home on the 10th. Back in Kitchener, the whirlwind season continued. The Dutchies were greeted by more than 4,000 fans in Kitchener–Waterloo and were serenaded around town atop a firetruck which took them to a civic reception led by Mayor Harry Ainlay. Balloons and streamers added to the festivities, and schools were closed an hour early to allow all the town's children to attend. Celebrations were short-lived, however, as the Dutchmen had to play seven games before February 20 to fulfill their OHA obligations, a brutally demanding conclusion to a long, exhausting season. One player, Howie Lee, decided to forego the rigours of completing the amateur season when he signed a pro contract with the Cleveland Barons of the AHL, playing his first game February 11 and helping his team beat Springfield 6–2.

THE AFTERMATH OF LOSING: ASSESSING THE DAMAGE

For Canada, the team didn't win a bronze medal as much as it lost a gold. The result was considered a dismal failure. It was the worst placing a Canadian team had achieved in 36 years of Olympic hockey. The result, however, was not without some benefit, signalling a new era in Olympic competition and a significant skewing of the amateur-professional dichotomy.

Soviet official Roman Kiselev was asked how much professional hockey players were paid in the USSR. His answer: "There are no professionals in Russia." So, while the Soviets operated a league of their own and trained their Olympians eight months or more of the year, apparently none of them actually made a ruble directly or indirectly. When asked who would win if the Soviets played Canada's best players — Howe, Richard et al. — Kiselev was equally terse, saying only that "Richard and Howe are not here [at the Olympics]."

By the same token, the Canadians in charge of the country's Olympic representatives were again questioning the team concept, suggesting again that an all-star team format would be better, if not essential, if Canada were to remain competitive in the years ahead, especially if the Russians were going to continue to send "non-professional" professionals to the Games and World Championships each time. Nor was it just the assemblage of the team that was of concern. The Russians prepared intensely for these two events year-round; the Canadians forced a club team to play a demanding schedule in league play right before the Games and expected the team to walk away with the gold.

Those days were at an end.

The Competition

TOURNAMENT FORMAT

Ten teams were divided into three groups, each playing a round-robin schedule within that group. The top two teams from each section then advanced to a six-team finals round. The team with the most points among the six (two points for a win, one for a tie) won the gold, with goal differential being the deciding factor in the event of a tie. If still tied, goals against average would be the last method to decide the winner. Tie games after 60 minutes of play would not be decided by overtime.

All referees were from Europe and all games were played at the new Olympic stadium, measuring 202 feet x 99 feet and seating 10,000. This was to be the last year hockey's medal-round games would be played outdoors and the last year Canada's jerseys would be made of wool.

THE OPPOSITION

AUSTRIA • Adolf Hafner, Wolfgang Joechl, Hermann Knoll, Kurt Kurz, Hans Moessmer, Robert Nusser, Franz Potucek, Alfred Puels, Hans Scarsini, Wilhelm Schmidt, Max Singewald, Fritz Spielmann, Gerhard Springer, Konrad Staudinger, Hans Wagner, Walter Znenahlik, Hans Zollner

CZECHOSLOVAKIA • Stanislav Bacilek, Stavomir Barton, Vaclav Bubnik, Vlastimil Bubnik, Jaromir Bunter, Otto Cimrman, Bronislav Danda, Karel Gut, Jan Jendek, Jan Kasper, Miroslav Kluc, Zdenek Navrat, Vaclav Pantucek, Bohumil Prosek, Frantisek Vanek, Jan Vodicka, Vladimir Zabrodsky

GERMANY • Paul Ambros, Martin Beck, Toni Biersack, Karl Bierschel, Markus Egen, Arthur Endress, Bruno Guttowski, Alfred Hoffmann, Hans Huber, Ulrich Jansen, Gunther Jochems, Rainer Kossmann, Rudolf Pittrich, Hans Rampf, Kurt Sepp, Ernst Trautwein, Martin Zach

ITALY • Giancarlo Agazzi, Rino Alberton, Mario Bedogni, Giampiero Branduardi, Ernesto Crotti, Gianfranco Darin, Giulians Ferari, Aldo Federici, Giovani Furlani, Francesco Machietto, Aldo Maniacco, Carlo Montemurro, Giulio Oberhammer, Bernardo Tomei, Carmine Tucci

POLAND • Henryk Bromowicz, Kazimierz Bryniarski, Mieczyslaw Chmura, Kazimierz Chodakowski, Rudolf Czech, Bronislaw Gosztyla, Marian Herda, Szymon Janiczko, Edward Koczab, Josef Kurek, Zdzislaw Nowak, Stanislaw Olczyk, Wladyslaw Pabisz, Hilary Skarzynski, Adolf Wrobel, Alfred Wrobel, Janusz Zawadzki

SWEDEN • Stig "Tvilling" Andersson, Lars Bjorn, Sigurd Broms, Stig Carlsson, Yngve Casslind, Sven Johansson, Vilgot Larsson, Ake Lassas, Lars-Erik Lundvall, Ove Malmberg, Nils Nilsson, Holger Nurmela, Hans Oberg, Ronald Pettersson, Lars Svensson, Hans Tvilling, Bertz Zetterberg

SWITZERLAND • Martin Riesen, Christian Conrad, Sepp Weingartner, Kurt Peter, Georg Rifsch, Milo Golaz, Rudolf Keller, Urs Frei, Paul Hofer, Hans Otto, Bernhard Bagnoud, Emil Handschin, Fritz Naef, Walter Keller, Hans Pappa, Otto Schlapper, Franz Berry

UNITED STATES • Wendell Anderson, Wellington Burnett, Eugene Campbell, Gordon Christian, William Cleary, Richard Dougherty, Willard Ikola, John Matchefts, John Mayasich, Daniel McKinnon, Richard Meredith, Weldon Olson, John Petroske, Kenneth Purpur, Donald Rigazio, Richard Rodenheiser, Edward Sampson

USSR • Yevgeny Babich, Usevolod Bobrov, Nikolai Chylstov, Aleksei Guryshev, Yuri Krylov, Alfred Kuchevsky, Valentin Kuzin, Grigory Mkrtchan, Viktor Nikiforov, Yuri Pantyuchov, Nikolai Puchkov, Viktor Shuvalov, Genrich Sidorenkov, Nikolai Sologubov, Ivan Tregubov, Dmitri Ukolov, Aleksandr Uvarov

FINAL STANDINGS

PRELIMINARY ROUND • POOL A

	GP	W	L	T	GF	GA	P
Canada	3	3	0	0	30	1	6
Germany	3	1	1	1	9	6	3
Italy	3	0	1	2	5	7	2
Austria	3	0	2	1	2	32	1

RESULTS

JANUARY 26
Canada 4 Germany 0
Italy 2 Austria 2

JANUARY 27
Canada 23 Austria 0
Italy 2 Germany 2

JANUARY 28
Canada 3 Italy 1

JANUARY 29
Germany 7 Austria 0

PRELIMINARY ROUND • POOL B

	GP	W	L	T	GF	GA	P
Czechoslovakia	2	2	0	0	12	6	4
United States	2	1	1	0	7	4	2
Poland	2	0	2	0	3	12	0

RESULTS

JANUARY 27
Czechoslovakia 4 United States 3

JANUARY 28
United States 4 Poland 0

JANUARY 29
Czechoslovakia 8 Poland 3

PRELIMINARY ROUND • POOL C

	GP	W	L	T	GF	GA	P
USSR	2	2	0	0	15	4	4
Sweden	2	1	1	0	7	10	2
Switzerland	2	0	2	0	8	16	0

RESULTS

JANUARY 27
USSR 5 Sweden 1

JANUARY 28
Sweden 6 Switzerland 5

JANUARY 29
Russia 10 Switzerland 3

MEDAL ROUND FINAL STANDINGS

	GP	W	L	T	GF	GA	P
USSR	5	5	0	0	25	5	10
United States	5	4	1	0	26	12	8
Canada	5	3	2	0	23	11	6
Sweden	5	1	3	1	10	17	3
Czechoslovakia	5	1	4	0	20	30	2
Germany	5	0	4	1	6	35	1

RESULTS

JANUARY 30
Canada 6 Czechoslovakia 3
USSR 4 Sweden 1
United States 7 Germany 2

JANUARY 31
United States 4 Canada 1
Sweden 5 Czechoslovakia 0
USSR 8 Germany 0

FEBRUARY 1
Canada 10 Germany 0
USSR 7 Czechoslovakia 4
United States 6 Sweden 1

FEBRUARY 2
Canada 6 Sweden 2
Czechoslovakia 9 Germany 3
USSR 4 United States 0

FEBRUARY 4
USSR 2 Canada 0
Sweden 1 Germany 1
United States 9 Czechoslovakia 4

TEAM CANADA GAME SUMMARIES

JANUARY 26 • Canada 4 Germany 0

IN GOAL
Canada — Brodeur
Germany — Jansen

SHOTS ON GOAL

Canada	**30**
Germany	**17**

FIRST PERIOD
1. Canada, Théberge (Laufman, Scholes) • 1:04
2. Canada, Théberge (unassisted) • 10:36
penalties: *Théberge (Can) 16:50*

SECOND PERIOD
3. Canada, Théberge (Scholes, Laufman) • 4:44
4. Canada, Logan (unassisted) • 5:45(sh)
penalties: *Martin (Can) 5:10, Hurst (Can) 11:42*

THIRD PERIOD
No Scoring
penalties: *Rope (Can) 8:32*

JANUARY 27 • Canada 23 Austria 0

IN GOAL
Canada — Woodall
Austria — Puels

SHOTS ON GOAL

Canada	**76**
Austria	**14**

FIRST PERIOD
1. Canada, Lee (Laufman) • 2:20
2. Canada, MacKenzie (Knox, Logan) • 10:08
3. Canada, Knox (MacKenzie) • 12:17
4. Canada, White (Brooker) • 16:29
5. Canada, Knox (unassisted) • 18:29
6. Canada, Knox (Logan) • 19:59
penalties: *none*

SECOND PERIOD
7. Canada, Logan (unassisted) • 0:20
8. Canada, Logan (MacKenzie, Klinck) • 0:42
9. Canada, Hurst (Brooker, White) • 3:21(pp)
10. Canada, Brooker (Rope, White) • 3:40
11. Canada, Scholes (Laufman) • 8:32
12. Canada, Brooker (Rope) • 9:43
13. Canada, MacKenzie (Knox, Logan) • 12:52
14. Canada, Laufman (Théberge) • 13:13
15. Canada, Théberge (Laufman) • 14:00
16. Canada, Scholes (Laufman) • 14:10
17. Canada, White (Klinck, Brooker) • 15:22
penalties: *Scarsini (Aus) 1:25, Klinck (Can) 3:59*

THIRD PERIOD
18. Canada, MacKenzie (Logan) • 5:37
19. Canada, Knox (unassisted) • 6:22
20. Canada, Théberge (Martin, Laufman) • 7:47
21. Canada, Knox (Martin) • 12:16
22. Canada, Théberge (Laufman, Hurst) • 12:31
23. Canada, Hurst (unassisted) • 19:10
penalties: *none*

JANUARY 28 • Canada 3 Italy 1

FIRST PERIOD

1. Italy, Crotti (Agazzi, Maniacco) • 10:21(pp)

2. Canada, Théberge (MacKenzie) • 18:35

penalties: *Hurst (Can) 1:10, Théberge (Can) 4:11, Scholes (Can) 8:57, Klinck (Can) 13:18, Bedogni (It) 19:39*

SECOND PERIOD

No Scoring

penalties: *Lee (Can) 4:44, Théberge (Can) 9:00, Lee (Can) 13:00, Agazzi (It) 13:51, Brooker (Can) 14:18, Hurst (Can) 14:22, Lee (Can) 18:29*

THIRD PERIOD

3. Canada, Brooker (Hurst) • 13:20

4. Canada, Scholes (unassisted) • 18:42(sh)

penalties: *Montemurro (It) 2:15, MacKenzie (Can) 16:58, Montemurro (It) 19:42*

IN GOAL

Canada — Brodeur

Italy — Ferrari

SHOTS ON GOAL

Canada	**47**
Italy	**20**

JANUARY 30 • Canada 6 Czechoslovakia 3

FIRST PERIOD

1. Czechoslovakia, Navrat (unassisted) • 14:18

2. Canada, Logan (Scholes, Martin) • 18:20

penalties: *Théberge (Can) 5:04, Bunter (Cz) 5:29, Martin (Can) 6:57, Vl. Bubnik (Cz) 11:37, Potucek (Cz) 15:02, White (Can) & Bunter (Cz) 18:07*

SECOND PERIOD

3. Czechoslovakia, Navrat (Gut) • 2:35(sh)

4. Canada, Théberge (Scholes, Laufman) • 7:26

5. Canada, Knox (unassisted) • 9:06

6. Canada, Knox (Logan) • 12:58

7. Czechoslovakia, Pantucek (Kasper) • 15:28(pp)

penalties: *Va. Bubnik (Cz) 0:55, Gut (Cz) 8:11, Hurst (Can) 8:30, Hurst (Can) 13:48*

THIRD PERIOD

8. Canada, Logan (MacKenzie, Knox) • 9:59

9. Canada, Rope (Brooker, Lee) • 12:15

penalties: *Martin (Can) 3:01*

IN GOAL

Canada — Brodeur

Czechoslovakia — Vodicka

SHOTS ON GOAL

unavailable

JANUARY 31 • United States 4 Canada 1

FIRST PERIOD

1. United States, Mayasich (unassisted) • 1:58

2. United States, Mayasich (Dougherty) • 9:23

penalties: *Hurst (Can) 4:15, Meredith (US) 6:35*

SECOND PERIOD

3. Canada, MacKenzie (Logan, Knox) • 13:00

penalties: *Hurst (Can) 0:09*

THIRD PERIOD

4. United States, Mayasich (unassisted) • 3:56

5. United States, Olson (Matchefts) • 7:40

penalties: *MacKenzie (Can — major) & Purpur (US — major) 14:58*

IN GOAL

Canada — Brodeur

United States — Ikola

SHOTS ON GOAL

Canada	10	16	13	**39**
United States	9	6	14	**29**

FEBRUARY 1 • Canada 10 Germany 0

FIRST PERIOD

1. Canada, Horne (unassisted) • 7:07

penalties: *Laufman (Can) 15:54*

SECOND PERIOD

2. Canada, Lee (Colvin) • 8:08

3. Canada, Rope (Colvin) • 8:56

4. Canada, Hurst (Logan) • 11:28(pp)

5. Canada, Scholes (Martin) • 14:37

penalties: *Hurst (Can) 5:41, Ambros (Ger) 10:13*

THIRD PERIOD

6. Canada, Rope (Colvin, White) • 3:37

7. Canada, Martin (MacKenzie) • 7:42

8. Canada, Logan (Knox, Hurst) • 12:12(pp)

9. Canada, MacKenzie (Knox) • 18:00

10. Canada, Théberge (Martin, Scholes) • 19:32

penalties: *Ambros (Ger) 11:21, Lee (Can) & Beck (Ger) 18:52*

IN GOAL

Canada — Woodall

Germany — Jansen

SHOTS ON GOAL

unavailable

FEBRUARY 2 • Canada 6 Sweden 2

IN GOAL
Canada — Woodall
Sweden — Casslind

SHOTS ON GOAL
unavailable

FIRST PERIOD
1. Canada, Logan (Lee, Knox) • 2:50
2. Sweden, Tvilling (unassisted) • 4:09
3. Canada, Rope (Colvin) • 7:59
4. Sweden, Johansson (unassisted) • 10:18
5. Canada, MacKenzie (unassisted) • 16:12
penalties: *none*

SECOND PERIOD
6. Canada, Scholes (Laufman, Théberge) • 19:15
penalties: *Martin (Can) 4:43, Malmberg (Swe) 6:42*

THIRD PERIOD
7. Canada, MacKenzie (Logan, Lee) • 16:48
8. Canada, Martin (unassisted) • 18:32
penalties: *Hurst (Can) 3:04, MacKenzie (Can) 8:38, Lee (Can) & Malmberg (Swe) 11:25, Laufman (Can) 19:41*

FEBRUARY 4 • USSR 2 Canada 0

IN GOAL
Canada — Woodall
USSR — Puchkov

SHOTS ON GOAL

Canada			
9	9	5	**23**
USSR			
3	3	3	**9**

FIRST PERIOD
No Scoring
penalties: *Rope (Can) 1:35, Knox (Can) 2:40, Lee (Can) 14:13*

SECOND PERIOD
1. USSR, Krylov (Kuzin) • 6:20
penalties: *Hurst (Can) 1:22, Sologubov (USSR) 3:37, Sidorenkov (USSR) 12:33*

THIRD PERIOD
2. USSR, Kuzin (Uvarov) • 0:37
penalties: *Martin (Can) 7:11, Hurst (Can) 12:31, Sidorenkov (USSR) 13:14, Martin (Can) 18:00*

TEAM CANADA FINAL STATISTICS • 1956

#		GP	G	A	P	Pim
11	Jim Logan	8	7	8	15	0
9	Paul Knox	8	7	7	14	2
12	Jack MacKenzie	8	7	5	12	9
8	Gerry Théberge	8	9	2	11	8
17	Ken Laufman	8	1	10	11	4
15	George Scholes	8	5	5	10	2
18	Charlie Brooker	5	3	4	7	2
3	Floyd Martin	8	2	5	7	12
14	Don Rope	8	4	2	6	4
5	Art Hurst	8	3	3	6	22
4	Howie Lee	8	2	3	5	12
19	Bob White	8	2	3	5	2
10	Billy Colvin	4	0	4	4	0
2	Byrle Klinck	4	0	2	2	4
16	Buddy Horne	3	1	0	1	0

#	IN GOAL	GP	W-L-T	Mins	GA	SO	Avg
1	Keith Woodall	4	3–1–0	240	4	2	1.00
1	Denis Brodeur	4	3–1–0	240	8	1	2.00

CHAPTER 9

The Eighth Olympic Winter Games

SQUAW VALLEY, UNITED STATES

February 18–28, 1960

Squaw Valley was awarded the 1960 Games at the 51st IOC session in Paris on June 14, 1955, defeating Innsbruck in the second round of voting by a slim 32–30 margin. In the first round, Garmisch–Partenkirchen and St. Moritz had been eliminated.

George Samolenko

TEAM CANADA • 1960

KITCHENER–WATERLOO DUTCHMEN

Don Head, *GOAL*
Harold "Boat" Hurley, *GOAL*

Moe Benoit, *DEFENCE*
Jack Douglas, *DEFENCE*
Harry Sinden, *DEFENCE (CAPTAIN)*
Darryl Sly, *DEFENCE*

Bob Attersley, *FORWARD*
Jim Connelly, *FORWARD*
Fred Etcher, *FORWARD*
Bob Forhan, *FORWARD*
Ken Laufman, *FORWARD*
Floyd "Butch" Martin, *FORWARD*
Bob McKnight, *FORWARD*
Cliff Pennington, *FORWARD*
Don Rope, *FORWARD*
Bobby Rousseau, *FORWARD*
George Samolenko, *FORWARD*

Bobby Bauer, *COACH*
Ernie Gorman, *GENERAL MANAGER*

FINAL PLACINGS

GOLD MEDAL
United States

SILVER MEDAL
Canada

BRONZE MEDAL
USSR

FOURTH PLACE
Czechoslovakia

FIFTH PLACE
Sweden

SIXTH PLACE
Germany

SEVENTH PLACE
Finland

EIGHTH PLACE
Japan

NINTH PLACE
Australia

THE RETURN OF THE KITCHENER–WATERLOO DUTCHMEN

The 1959 Allan Cup champion Whitby Dunlops declined the invitation to represent Canada at Squaw Valley, thus paving the way for the Dutchies to appear in their second successive Olympics. As in 1956, they were at a disadvantage right away, losing three of their top players — Bill Kennedy, George Gosselin, and Dick Mattiussi — to the pros.

Furthermore, the team was once again in the Senior OHA loop, meaning they had to finish off a gruelling 48-game schedule before leaving on a one-month exhibition tour on their way to Squaw Valley. This time, the other Senior A teams promised to help in any way they could as far as replacement players were concerned, provided they received replacements themselves and $500 per man loaned. To this end, the Dutchies got Bob Attersley, Fred Etcher, George Samolenko, and Harry Sinden from the Dunlops, Moe Benoit from the Belleville MacFarlands, Don Head from the Windsor Bulldogs, and Jack and Jim Connelly from the Chatham Maroons. The Montreal Canadiens also made Bobby Rousseau available for the team.

Rousseau's addition was an interesting story in itself, one that began with a future Leaf great, Dave Keon. On January 12, K–W manager Ernie Gorman announced that 19-year old St. Michael's College star centre Keon would be given a one-game trial the next night when the Dutchies played a home game against the Windsor Bulldogs. Keon was spectacular in the match, scoring once and setting up numerous chances while displaying his trademark stickhandling wizardry. He had, for all intents and purposes, made the Olympic team.

Canadians beat goalie Nikolai Puchkov during convincing 8–5 win.

The problem was that St. Mike's was willing to loan him to the Olympians for only a very restricted time, three games out west as part of the team's exhibition tune-up, and two weeks for the Games themselves. Wren Blair, a key member of the Olympic team's player committee, felt that in fairness to the other players, and to maximize the effectiveness of team cohesion, Keon would be needed for fully the next six weeks. At this point, St. Mike's coach, Father David Bauer, sympathetic but unbending, suggested Bobby Rousseau of the Brockville Canadiens, the Habs' farm team, to replace Keon. Montreal GM Frank Selke consented to the loan, Keon returned to St. Mike's, and Rousseau joined the Olympians.

To help the Dutchies financially, the twin cities of Kitchener–Waterloo established a committee to raise $17,000 for the team's expenses, including travel, doctors, trainers, extra baggage, and insurance. The money was raised mostly through a $2,000 donation from Conn Smythe, $1,000 from the Canadiens, and $12,000 through ticket sales for a car that was to be auctioned off.

Floyd Martin fights for the puck during last game of the Olympics to decide the silver medal. In pursuit are Russians Alfred Kuchevsky *(left)* and Konstantin Loktev.

K-W COACHING

Although the record books show Bobby Bauer coached this 1960 entry, he was by no means the man intended to be there. The Dutchies already had a coach the year before and at the start of this season, former Canadiens great Bill Durnan, but he quit the team after a six-game losing streak, forcing the Dutchies to find a replacement. Initially it was to have been Joe Primeau, then Ted Kennedy, then Happy Day, but none of these well-known ex-Leafs could get the time off necessary to prepare for the demanding task that lay ahead. They had all been out of hockey awhile and had successful business interests they wanted to nurture, and could not afford to abandon for the sake of such a short-term commitment. It was then that Bauer agreed to the challenge, despite the caustic, pessimistic words of NHL president Clarence Campbell, who declared that, "Canada's Olympic entry does not have the best management and coaching, which is needed if the team is to win."

The team left Kitchener-Waterloo on January 31, 1960 by chartered bus, using the drive west to squeeze in a two-week Western Canadian exhibition tour. They won all seven games they played before arriving in Squaw Valley just a few days prior to their first Olympic game.

CONTROVERSY ERUPTS AGAIN

The accommodations were lousy, the transportation ridiculous, the organization inept. The Soviet Union? Czechoslovakia? Some other Iron Curtain country? Nope...Squaw Valley, California. And this was just the beginning! The IIHF arrived in the Wild West and promptly blasted the US Olympic Committee on almost every hockey front and threatened to withdraw all European teams unless conditions were improved.

The schedule, for starters, was cruel. Teams were being asked to play eight games in 10 days, hardly a way to produce the best hockey. The indoor hockey rink was booked virtually day and night for figure skaters to practise and compete on, leaving all hockey teams to practise out of doors. But outdoors, there was little ice due to a pleasant thaw the previous few days. One morning, all six hockey teams showed up at the rink to practise. All were rebuffed by the figure skaters.

For the final weekend, American TV network CBS, which had paid $1 million to broadcast the Games, wanted the US and Canada to play the same afternoon the Russians wanted to meet the Canadians in what was conceded would be a game to decide gold. The schedule also called for three games to be played on opening day, even though opening ceremonies would require the use of the rink, rendering this scheme temporally impossible and the rink conditions "atrocious," according to officials from Canada, Czechoslovakia, and the USSR. Referring to the outdoor rink, IIHF president Bunny Ahearne commented, "I don't know how you can expect teams who come here from thousands of miles away to play on that slush. Surely there are other places in this country where conditions would be at least suitable."

George Samolenko is beaten to the puck by American goalie Jack McCartan.

After a three-hour meeting between the IIHF and Olympic officials, most of the problems were resolved. No games, save the consolation round matches, would be played outdoors. The three games scheduled for opening day would begin in the evening, though laughably the USSR-Germany match would begin at midnight. And, Canada and the US would play Thursday night — a good TV night — paving the way for a gold medal showdown Sunday afternoon between the Canadians and the Russians.

REDEFINING "AMATEUR"

In quintessentially Canadian fashion, our media spearheaded an assault on our own Olympic hockey players vis-à-vis their status as true amateurs, while saying nary a word about the Russians and Americans. Canadians had long felt that others may do as they please, but we would adhere to the virtues of the truest definition of the word amateur with our dying breath.

This time, it was pointed out that OHA Juniors received $60 a week, while Senior players (i.e., the Dutchmen) could receive as much as $130. And so our own media began an attack on the CAHA's ethics: If this wasn't pay, what was? If this did not compromise, nay, negate, the players' rank as amateurs, what would? The team was pilloried, the IOC excoriated, for their lax interpretation of the term amateur, and their willingness to overlook such heinous transgressions by the Canadians in the name of improving international competition. The argument was that even if a player were to receive a cardigan or sandwich from his parent organization, he was no longer an amateur, according to the definition set down on paper by the IOC.

However, two significant facts should have been taken into consideration before Canadian journalists castigated their Olympic compatriots. Firstly, most Senior A players in general, and K–W Dutchmen in particular, worked for a living. Darryl Sly, for instance, was a teacher in Elmira while he played, Ken Laufman sold real estate in Guelph, Don Labelle (who never made the Olympic squad) worked on the Montreal Stock Exchange. Rules and ethics had always permitted remuneration to players for the loss of real income. This had been the case since the 1920 Olympics, and was a practical way of ensuring that hockey would remain an Olympic sport, and Canada a vital participant.

Secondly, the much more serious level of deception by the Soviets, who adamantly refused to concede that players received *anything* from their team or government for playing should not have been overlooked. The CAHA, OHA, and every other hockey body in Canada openly acknowledged the salary system at the junior level, and could rightly justify it. In Russia, players had been training together for years under ideal circumstances. They were given government "jobs" but were never asked to actually work, did nothing but prepare year-round, and played hockey solely for the purpose of representing their country at the World Championships and Olympics. In exchange, they received free housing, food, clothing, and other necessities and perks. They were professionals, plain and simple.

Action around Team Canada's net as goalie Donald Head watches play closely.

LOOKING AHEAD TO MAJOR CHANGE

For the second Olympics in a row, the Canadians lost a game to the Americans and also failed to win the gold medal. This was indicative of two factors, both of which would have to be addressed if Canada were ever to remain atop the international hockey heap. First, the idea of taking a single club to represent the country no longer seemed possible. After all, this K–W team, an excellent amateur team, had, in the end, only eight original members on the final Olympic roster. Thus, the whole concept of choosing a team because the players knew each other and had played together for a long time, was thrown out the window. Rather than do things by halves, it was time to select the team player by player rather than attempt to fill huge gaps in one team's line-up. There were many highly skilled juniors and amateurs who weren't playing in the Games, partly because of the team concept, but mostly because the finest amateurs were quickly signed to pro contracts by the Big Six NHL teams.

Furthermore, the players competing for communist countries, most notably the USSR, were the 17 best players in that country. It is without any question that if the finest 17 Canadians in 1960 — Gordie Howe, Terry Sawchuk, Henri Richard, George Armstrong, Jean Béliveau *et al* — were permitted to represent Canada, we would have won the gold almost uncontested. However, the Olympic association was not bending on its amateur rule, so Canada clearly had to adapt to change by ensuring that for the 1964 Games the finest 20 hockey players in the country *not* signed to pro contracts represented Canada. Bobby Bauer was a respected, capable coach, the Kitchener–Waterloo Dutchmen had been Allan Cup champions twice, yet the team neither represented Canada's best amateurs nor won the gold medal.

THE OFFICIAL CAHA REPORT

After each Olympics, the president of the CAHA submitted a report in which the achievements and events of the Games were noted and examined. Gordon Juckes saw readily the problems that were facing the Canadian Olympic hockey team which had now failed to win Gold in eight years:

> In my opinion, there are a number of lessons for Canada in the 1960 Winter Olympic Games. Compared to other teams, ours was not banded together soon enough as a team unit. The CAHA's draft regulations, which we and Kitchener both hoped would provide our team with reinforcements well in advance, broke down for a number of reasons. It was the beginning of February — with the Olympics barely two weeks away — before Canada's complete Olympic team came together finally and conclusively. While we may have had the players, such a situation was simply putting too much on the shoulders of the management, the coach and the team as a whole. In the future I believe that team efficiency — even at a sacrifice of individual talent — is of prime importance, and coupled with that, of course, must go team spirit and determination. These characteristics can only be achieved if our Canadian team operates most of the season, prior to the Games, as a unit. That was the objective of the CAHA and of Kitchener in 1960, but unfortunately circumstances prevented it being attained.

The Competition

TOURNAMENT FORMAT

The format remained unchanged from the one used in Cortina d'Ampezzo in 1956. The nine competing countries were divided into three pools of three teams, each pool playing round-robin games with the others in their division. The top two teams from each pool then advanced to a six-team finals round-robin, the gold medal going to the team with the most points (two for a win, one for a tie). In the event of a tie in the standings, goal differential would decide the winner.

THE OPPOSITION

AUSTRALIA • Benjamin Acton, Ronald Amess, David Cunningham, Noel Derrick, Victor Ekberg, Bassel Hansen, Clive Hitch, Russell Jones, Noel McLoughlin, Allan Nicholas, Peter Parrott, Kenneth Pawsey, Robert Reid, John Thomas, Zdenek Tikal, Ivo Vesley, Kenneth Wellman

CZECHOSLOVAKIA • Vlastimil Bubnik, Josef Cerny, Bronislav Danda, Vladimir Dvoracek, Josef Golonka, Karel Gut, Jaroslav Jirik, Jan Kasper, Frantisek Maslan, Vladimir Nadrchal, Vaclav Pantucek, Rudolf Potsch, Jan Starsi, Frantisek Tikal, Frantisek Vanek, Miroslav Vlach, Jaroslav Volf

FINLAND • Yrjo Hakala, Raimo Kilpio, Erkki Koiso, Matti Lampainen, Esko Luostarinen, Pertti Nieminen, Veijo Numminen, Heino Pulli, Kalevi Rassa, Teppo Rastio, Jouni Seistamo, Seppo Vainio, Juhani Wahlsten, Juhani Lahtinen, Esko Niemi, Jorma Salmi, Vaito Soini

GERMANY • Paul Ambros, Georg Eberl, Markus Egen, Ernst Eggerbauer, Michael Hobelsberger, Hans Huber, Uli Jansen, Horst Metzer, Hans Rampf, Josef Reif, Otto Schneitberger, Siegfried Schubert, Horst Schuldes, Kurt Sepp, Ernst Trautwein, Xaver Unsinn, Leonhard Waitl

JAPAN • Chikashi Akazawa, Shinichi Honma, Toshiei Honma, Hidenori Inatsu, Atsuo Irie, Joji Iwaoka, Takashi Kakihara, Yoshihiro Miyazaki, Masao Murano, Isao Ono, Akiyoshi Segawa, Shigeru Shimada, Kunito Takagi, Mamoru Takashima, Mashyoshi Tanabu, Syoichi Tomita, Toshihiko Yamada

SWEDEN • Anders Andersson, Lars Bjorn, Gert Blome, Sigurd Broms, Einar Granath, Sven Johansson, Bengt Lindquist, Lars-Erik Lundvall, Nils Nilsson, Bert-Ola Nordlander, Carl-Geran Oberg, Ronald Pettersson, Ulf Sterner, Roland Stoltz, Hans Svedberg, Kjell Svensson, Sune Wretling

UNITED STATES • Roger Christian, William Christian, Robert Cleary, William Cleary, Eugene Grazia, Paul Johnson, John Kirrane, John Mayasich, Jack McCartan, Robert McVey, Richard Meredith, Weldon Olson, Edwyn Owen, Rodney Pavola, Lawrence Palmer, Richard Rodenheiser, Thomas Williams

USSR • Veniamin Alexandrov, Aleksandr Almetov, Yuri Baulin, Mikhail Bykov, Vladimir Grebenikov, Yevgeny Groshev, Nikolai Karpov, Alfred Kuchevsky, Konstantin Loktev, Stanislav Petuchov, Viktor Pryazhnikov, Nikolai Puchkov, Genrich Sidorenkov, Nikolai Sologubov, Yuri Tsitsinov, Viktor Yakushev, Yevgeny Yerkin

FINAL STANDINGS

POOL A

	GP	W	L	T	GF	GA	P
Canada	2	2	0	0	24	3	4
Sweden	2	1	1	0	21	5	2
Japan	2	0	2	0	1	38	0

RESULTS

FEBRUARY 18	FEBRUARY 20	FEBRUARY 21
Canada 5 Sweden 2	Canada 19 Japan 1	Sweden 19 Japan 0

POOL B

	GP	W	L	T	GF	GA	P
USSR	2	2	0	0	16	4	4
Germany	2	1	1	0	4	9	2
Finland	2	0	2	0	5	12	0

RESULTS

FEBRUARY 18	FEBRUARY 20	FEBRUARY 21
USSR 8 Germany 0	USSR 8 Finland 4	Germany 4 Finland 1

POOL C

	GP	W	L	T	GF	GA	P
United States	2	2	0	0	19	6	4
Czechoslovakia	2	1	1	0	23	8	2
Australia	2	0	2	0	2	30	0

RESULTS

FEBRUARY 18
United States 7 Czechoslovakia 5

FEBRUARY 20
Czechoslovakia 18 Australia 1

FEBRUARY 21
United States 12 Australia 1

CONSOLATION ROUND FINAL STANDINGS

	GP	W	L	T	GF	GA	P
Finland	4	3	0	1	58	11	7
Japan	4	2	1	1	33	30	5
Australia	4	0	4	0	8	58	0

RESULTS

FEBRUARY 22
Finland 14 Australia 1

FEBRUARY 23
Finland 6 Japan 6

FEBRUARY 24
Japan 13 Australia 2

FEBRUARY 25
Finland 19 Australia 2

FEBRUARY 26
Finland 19 Japan 2

FEBRUARY 27
Japan 12 Australia 3

MEDAL ROUND FINAL STANDINGS

	GP	W	L	T	GF	GA	P
United States	5	5	0	0	29	11	10
Canada	5	4	1	0	31	12	8
USSR	5	2	2	1	24	19	5
Czechoslovakia	5	2	3	0	21	23	4
Sweden	5	1	3	1	19	19	3
Germany	5	0	5	0	5	45	0

RESULTS

FEBRUARY 22
Canada 12 Germany 0
USSR 8 Czechoslovakia 5
United States 6 Sweden 3

FEBRUARY 24
Canada 4 Czechoslovakia 0
Sweden 2 USSR 2
United States 9 Germany 1

FEBRUARY 25
United States 2 Canada 1
Czechoslovakia 3 Sweden 1
USSR 7 Germany 1

FEBRUARY 27
Canada 6 Sweden 5
Czechoslovakia 9 Germany 1
United States 3 USSR 2

FEBRUARY 28
Canada 8 USSR 5
Sweden 8 Germany 2
United States 9 Czechoslovakia 4

TEAM CANADA GAME SUMMARIES

FEBRUARY 18 • Canada 5 Sweden 2

IN GOAL

Canada — Head

Sweden — Lindquist/Svensson *(Svensson replaced Lindquist near 19:00 of 1st)*

SHOTS ON GOAL

Canada			
11	12	19	**42**
Sweden			
9	7	7	**23**

FIRST PERIOD

1. Canada, Martin (Pennington) • 8:26
2. Sweden, Oberg (Granath) • 11:43(pp)
3. Canada, Attersley (Etcher, Douglas) • 17:03(pp)
penalties: *Pennington (Can) 2:57, Benoit (Can) 5:29, Attersley (Can) 11:07, Connelly (Can) 11:38, Svedberg (Swe) 16:59, Bjorn (Swe) 18:34*

SECOND PERIOD

4. Canada, Samolenko (Benoit, Attersley) • 11:00
5. Sweden, Lundvall (Nilsson) • 11:47
penalties: *Martin (Can — minor, misconduct) 14:28, Sly (Can) 18:14*

THIRD PERIOD

6. Canada, Etcher (Attersley) • 11:37(pp)
7. Canada, Etcher (Samolenko, Attersley) • 16:06(pp)
penalties: *Sly (Can — fighting major) & Johansson (Swe — fighting major) 5:57, Stoltz (Swe — major) 8:43, Nordlander (Swe) 14:04, Oberg (Swe) 14:57, Pennington (Can) 18:13*

FEBRUARY 20 • Canada 19 Japan 1

IN GOAL

Canada — Head

Japan — T. Honma/Tomita *(Tomita replaced Honma for part of 2nd only)*

SHOTS ON GOAL

Canada			
29	24	23	**76**
Japan			
4	1	9	**14**

FIRST PERIOD

1. Canada, Attersley (Etcher) • 4:52
2. Canada, Rousseau (unassisted) • 7:28
3. Canada, Etcher (Attersley) • 10:31(pp)
4. Canada, Sinden (Etcher) • 11:24
5. Canada, Samolenko (Attersley) • 11:51
penalties: *Takagi (Jap) 9:16, S. Honma (Jap) 18:22*

SECOND PERIOD

6. Canada, Attersley (Etcher) • 2:00
7. Canada, Sinden (Forhan, Rope) • 4:15
8. Canada, Rousseau (Sinden) • 5:54
9. Japan, Irie (Segawa) • 8:28
10. Canada, Samolenko (Etcher, Sinden) • 11:15
11. Canada, Martin (Connelly, McKnight) • 14:13
12. Canada, Connelly (Martin, McKnight) • 16:20
13. Canada, Rousseau (Forhan) • 19:26(pp)
penalties: *Miyazaki (Jap) 19:13*

THIRD PERIOD

14. Canada, Etcher (Attersley) • 3:37
15. Canada, Etcher (unassisted) • 4:59
16. Canada, Rope (unassisted) • 6:00
17. Canada, Martin (Benoit) • 8:35
18. Canada, McKnight (Martin) • 8:51
19. Canada, Samolenko (Douglas) • 11:45
20. Canada, Rousseau (Forhan, Rope) • 12:24
penalties: *Benoit (Can) 14:17*

FEBRUARY 22 • Canada 12 Germany 0

IN GOAL

Canada — Head

Germany — Hobelsberger

SHOTS ON GOAL

Canada			
20	12	12	**44**
Germany			
7	6	5	**18**

FIRST PERIOD

1. Canada, Etcher (Attersley, Samolenko) • 6:58
2. Canada, Etcher (Samolenko) • 7:10
3. Canada, Douglas (Martin) • 8:04
4. Canada, McKnight (Martin) • 8:41
5. Canada, Rope (Forhan) • 11:03
6. Canada, Attersley (Etcher) • 18:56(pp)
penalties: *Waitl (Ger) 18:00*

SECOND PERIOD

7. Canada, Douglas (Forhan) • 6:15
penalties: *Waitl (Ger) 6:45, Benoit (Can) 16:35*

THIRD PERIOD

8. Canada, Rope (Rousseau) • 3:40
9. Canada, Attersley (Etcher, Samolenko) • 6:01
10. Canada, Samolenko (Etcher) • 11:33
11. Canada, Douglas (Sinden, Attersley) • 12:17
12. Canada, Forhan (Rousseau) • 15:59
penalties: *none*

FEBRUARY 24 • Canada 4 Czechoslovakia 0

FIRST PERIOD
1. Canada, Sly (Connelly) • 6:41
2. Canada, Martin (Pennington, Sinden) • 16:45
3. Canada, Samolenko (Etcher, Benoit) • 18:22
penalties: *Pennington (Can) 2:03, Sinden (Can) 6:45, Jirik (Cz) 13:22*

SECOND PERIOD
4. Canada, Martin (Sly) • 11:36
penalties: *none*

THIRD PERIOD
No Scoring
penalties: *Benoit (Can) 3:28, Vanek (Cz) 9:33, Benoit (Can) 12:15, Sly (Can) 18:38*

IN GOAL
Canada — Head
Czechoslovakia — Nadrchal

SHOTS ON GOAL

Canada	14	16	6	**36**
Czechoslovakia	8	14	16	**38**

FEBRUARY 25 • United States 2 Canada 1

FIRST PERIOD
1. United States, R. Cleary (Mayasich) • 12:47(pp)
penalties: *Benoit (Can) 6:21, Williams (US) 8:41, Connelly (Can) 11:08*

SECOND PERIOD
2. United States, Johnson (unassisted) • 14:00
penalties: *Benoit (Can) 14:21*

THIRD PERIOD
3. Canada, Connelly (Martin, Laufman) • 13:38
penalties: *Pavola (US) 9:31*

IN GOAL
Canada — Head
United States — McCartan

SHOTS ON GOAL

Canada	8	20	11	**39**
United States	15	6	4	**25**

FEBRUARY 27 • Canada 6 Sweden 5

FIRST PERIOD
1. Sweden, Lundvall (Pettersson) • 1:35
2. Sweden, Broms (Sterner) • 4:36
3. Sweden, Johansson (Nordlander) • 14:55
4. Canada, Samolenko (Etcher) • 15:23
5. Sweden, Lundvall (Pettersson, Nordlander) • 18:22
penalties: *Douglas (Can) 7:33*

SECOND PERIOD
6. Canada, Connelly (Martin) • 16:41
penalties: *Oberg (Swe) 11:39*

THIRD PERIOD
7. Canada, Rousseau (Rope) • 3:11
8. Canada, Sinden (Laufman) • 11:17
9. Sweden, Lundvall (Svedberg) • 12:55
10. Canada, Benoit (Rousseau) • 15:32
11. Canada, Connelly (Laufman) • 17:31
penalties: *Martin (Can) & Broms (Swe) 4:05, Benoit (Can) 8:56, Svedberg (Swe) & Attersley (Can) & Connelly (Can — misconduct) 18:00*

IN GOAL
Canada — Head
Sweden — Svensson/Lindquist
(Lindquist replaced Svensson late in 3rd)

SHOTS ON GOAL

Canada	10	17	12	**39**
Sweden	8	14	11	**33**

FEBRUARY 28 • Canada 8 USSR 5

FIRST PERIOD
1. Canada, Etcher (Attersley) • 7:32
2. Canada, Sinden (Attersley, Etcher) • 18:12
3. Canada, Samolenko (Attersley, Sinden) • 18:27
penalties: *Baulin (USSR) 4:30*

SECOND PERIOD
4. Canada, Rope (Rousseau) • 2:37
5. USSR, Almetov (Alexandrov) • 5:28(pp)
6. USSR, Alexandrov (Sologubov, Loktev) • 5:51
7. USSR, Grebenikov (Bykov, Sologubov) • 9:56
penalties: *Benoit (Can) 5:18, Sinden (Can) 6:41, Rousseau (Can) 11:37, Baulin (USSR) 16:51*

THIRD PERIOD
8. Canada, Etcher (Attersley) • 5:33
9. Canada, Connelly (unassisted) • 6:48
10. Canada, Martin (Connelly, Laufman) • 7:53
11. USSR, Groshev (Sidorenkov) • 10:16
12. USSR, Pryazhnikov (Groshev, Baulin) • 15:02
13. Canada, Attersley (Etcher) • 19:52
penalties: *Douglas (Can) 8:16, Loktev (USSR) & Sinden (Can) 19:15, Douglas (Can) 19:55*

IN GOAL
Canada — Hurley/Head
(Head (two goals) replaced Hurley (three goals) near 15:00 of 2nd)
USSR — Puchkov

SHOTS ON GOAL

Canada	8	12	19	**39**
USSR	10	8	10	**28**

TEAM CANADA FINAL STATISTICS • 1960

#		GP	G	A	P	Pim
14	Fred Etcher	7	9	12	21	0
7	Bob Attersley	7	6	12	18	4
10	George Samolenko	7	8	4	12	0
15	Floyd Martin	7	6	6	12	14
20	Bobby Rousseau	7	5	4	9	2
2	Harry Sinden	7	4	5	9	6
18	Jim Connelly	7	5	3	8	14
16	Don Rope	7	4	3	7	0
9	Bob Forhan	6	1	5	6	0
5	Jack Douglas	7	3	2	5	6
12	Bob McKnight	3	2	2	4	0
6	Moe Benoit	7	1	3	4	18
17	Ken Laufman	4	0	4	4	0
4	Darryl Sly	7	1	1	2	9
8	Cliff Pennington	4	0	2	2	6

#	IN GOAL	GP	W-L-T	Mins	GA	SO	Avg
1	Don Head	7	5–1–0	385	12	2	1.87
1	Harold Hurley	1	1–0–0	35	3	0	5.14

GOALIE NOTES

1. *Head (two goals) replaced Hurley (three goals) near 15:00 of 2nd, February 28 vs. USSR*

Chapter 10

The Ninth Olympic Winter Games

INNSBRUCK, AUSTRIA

January 29 – February 9, 1964

At the 56th IOC session in Munich on May 26, 1959 Innsbruck was the runaway selection to host the 1964 Games (49 votes), Calgary receiving only nine votes and Lahti, Finland none.

TEAM CANADA • 1964

Ken Broderick, *GOAL*
Seth Martin, *GOAL*

Hank Akervall, *DEFENCE (CAPTAIN)*
Barry MacKenzie, *DEFENCE*
Terry O'Malley, *DEFENCE*
Rod Seiling, *DEFENCE*

Gary Begg, *CENTRE*
Gary Dineen, *CENTRE*
George Swarbrick, *CENTRE*

Roger Bourbonnais, *LEFT WING*
Terry Clancy, *LEFT WING*
Brian Conacher, *LEFT WING*

Ray Cadieux, *RIGHT WING*
Paul Conlin, *RIGHT WING*
Bob Forhan, *RIGHT WING*
Marshall Johnston, *RIGHT WING*

Father David Bauer, *COACH*
Dr. Bob Hindmarch, *MANAGER*

FINAL PLACINGS

GOLD MEDAL
USSR

SILVER MEDAL
Sweden

BRONZE MEDAL
Czechoslovakia

FOURTH PLACE
Canada

FIFTH PLACE
United States

SIXTH PLACE
Finland

SEVENTH PLACE
Germany

EIGHTH PLACE
Switzerland

NINTH PLACE
Poland

TENTH PLACE
Norway

ELEVENTH PLACE
Japan

TWELFTH PLACE
Romania

THIRTEENTH PLACE
Austria

FOURTEENTH PLACE
Yugoslavia

FIFTEENTH PLACE
Italy

SIXTEENTH PLACE
Hungary

THE DAWN OF A NEW ERA

Taking Gordon Juckes' 1960 report to heart, Father David Bauer had become increasingly concerned by Canada's poor showing in international competitions, and equally aware that our top amateur teams were no longer the cream of the crop, the absolute favourites, the shoe-in gold medalists. He was also very confident that academics and athletics could make successful bedfellows and that university students were just as capable of winning gold as any Russian congregation of talent. In June 1962, when the CAHA held its summer meetings in Toronto, Father Bauer proposed a system whereby the top amateurs in university and Senior A could play together for close to a year in preparation for major tournaments, specifically the Olympics and World Championships.

Canada's Ray Cadieux (#18) tries to get a shot off during the team's easy 14–1 qualifying win over Yugoslavia.

The CAHA embraced the concept wholeheartedly: the inaugural team would enrol at the Univeristy of British Columbia (with which Father Bauer had become affiliated after leaving St. Mike's) and play at its Kerrisdale Arena. This combination was, if nothing else, supposed to prevent potential pros from joining the NHL right away. In exchange, the players would get an education and living expenses (in other words, a scholarship), the experience of travelling, and the opportunity to represent Canada on an international level.

With little fanfare and plenty of confidence, Father Bauer officially began his term as Canada's national coach on August 21, 1963 when players gathered at UBC to begin training for the 1964 Olympics. This was Father Bauer's vision, his solution to the problems of assembling a truly amateur team, one that was both national and of the highest calibre. He invited the best amateurs he could think of to a training camp that would be maintained for the better part of half a year. No last-minute additions, no exhausted league team representation, no weak links. The team would practise together and tour together before heading to Innsbruck for the Olympics. The plan may not have been perfect, but the status quo was clearly the least desirable option. Change of any sort seemed progressive.

FATHER BAUER'S TEAM TOURS CANADA

The Olympians played a 33-game exhibition schedule in cities across the country, finishing with a 5–4 loss to the Toronto Marlies in a game played in London, only the eighth loss of their season. However, all of these games were against other amateur teams, not the much tougher NHL and AHL teams that would have, in the opinion of some of the players, given them much stiffer competition and, therefore, greater preparation and experience before facing the Russians and Czechs.

Goaler Seth Martin makes a dramatic save vs. Czechoslovakia.

THE EUROPEAN TOUR

Team Canada flew to Europe on January 6, 1964 to begin a 10-game pre-Olympic tour throughout January, a series that ended with a disappointing 5–4–1 record. They beat EV Fuessen (West Germany) 9–5 and 4–1; ERC Mannheim (a makeshift team of Canadians playing in Europe) 13–0, then tied them 4–4; lost twice to the Russians in Moscow 8–1 and 2–1; lost to the Czech Olympic team 6–0 in Prague, then beat the Czech "B" team two of three, winning 3–2 and 4–3, and losing 6–4. With this middling tour behind them, the Canadians went on to the Games, enriched by the experience but not intimidating opponents as had other Canadian teams in the past.

FATHER BAUER'S GESTURE

During play in the Canada–Sweden game, Carl Oberg, a Swedish forward, threw his broken stick in the Canadian bench as he skated to his own bench to get a new one. The stick hit an unsuspecting coach Bauer in the forehead, causing a cut to open. The Canadian players were furious, and were ready to defend their honour by pummelling Oberg and his team to full extent, but Bauer restrained his corps and pleaded for calmness.

After the game, IIHF president Bunny Ahearne suspended Oberg for one game for deliberately trying to injure Canada's coach. As well, the Swiss referee who failed to give Oberg a penalty on the play was also suspended for a game. In an expression of sportsmanship and forgiveness, Father Bauer invited Oberg to be his guest the next night to watch the Czechoslovakia–USSR game, a gesture that earned international acclaim for its kindness and sporting understanding.

That night, the two sat side by side at the Ice Stadium where the Canadians were given a huge cheer from the 11,000 fans. At the end of the Games, Father

Brian Conacher (#24) scores Canada's seventh goal in the team's first game vs. Switzerland.

Bauer was awarded a special gold medal for "the control he exercised over his players" during the stick throwing incident which easily could have turned into a full-scale brawl.

LOSS TO THE CZECHS

Canada's final two games of the tournament were against their toughest opposition, Czechoslovakia and the Soviet Union. In the Czech game, and in fact throughout the Olympics, Canada's Seth Martin was brilliant in goal, and with fewer than 10 minutes remaining, his team still had a slim 1–0 lead on Rod Seiling's second-period goal. However, on one enemy rush, a Czech player collided with Martin, who fell clutching his left leg. Injured though determined he tried to continue, but two minutes later had to come out of the net. Ken Broderick took his place, but with no warm-up and almost no Olympic experience he was at a serious disadvantage. The Canadians could not protect him, and Broderick was not as hot as Martin had been. The Czechs put three goals into the Canadian net in just eight minutes to win the game and deflate Canada's hopes for gold. They fought valiantly but lost the next game too, 3–2 to the Russians, leaving them in what they calculated to be the bronze medal spot.

MEDALS CONTROVERSY

What would the Olympics be without some controversy to cloud the athletic endeavours of the competitors? All through the tournament, it had been understood by Canada that in the case of a tie in the standings the victor would be decided based on goal differential versus games involving the top four teams only. Thus, on the final day of competition, a problem was foreseen when Sweden was beating Czechoslovakia, creating an inevitable second-place tie among three teams — Canada, the Swedes, and the Czechs. According to the system in place, USSR, with a perfect record of 7–0, would gain the gold, Sweden the silver (11 goals for, 10 against, +1 overall in games versus Canada, Russia, and Czechoslovakia), and Canada the bronze (-1 goal differential; the Czechs -5 finish fourth). Such was not to be. During the third period of the Sweden–Czech game, the IIHF directors, led by Bunny Ahearne, met and decided the tie break would be decided by goal differential against *all* teams, thereby pushing the Czechs into third and dropping Canada to fourth.

The Canadians score again vs. Yugoslavia in 14–1 win.

Even then, however, no official announcement was made. That night, the Canadian team, bedecked in its national colours, paraded smartly into the Ice Palace for the awards ceremonies, learning only then that they had been robbed of a medal. "Come on, fellas," said Father Bauer, "let's get out of here. We're not getting anything."

THE FINAL ANALYSIS

After beating the Czechs on the pre-Olympic tour in Brno, the Canadians were told by one Czech hockeyist that the players get 300 kronen for each win, 150 kronen for a tie, and nothing for a loss. Another Czech said that although the players were listed officially as factory workers, they rarely worked even a few hours a year but earned 4,000 kronen a month for playing hockey. A similar scheme existed in the Soviet Union.

Despite losing games to the "pros" of USSR and Czechoslovakia, Father Bauer was encouraged by the results of the program he had set up. "I hope we as a nation will cooperate from now on in this venture of playing true amateurs in this competition," he concluded. Little could he have known then how huge, successful, and comprehensive Canada's Olympic program would become during the next 30 years, all the result of a single suggestion in Toronto on a hot day in June 1962.

THE PLAYERS AND THE PONTIFF

As a man of the cloth, Father Bauer had as much influence off the ice as he did on it as coach. Following the disappointment of the Games, the Nationals played two exhibitions against Canadian Armed Forces teams stationed in West Germany and then travelled to Rome. Although it was winter in Canada and Austria, it was balmy in Italy, and the Canadians looked their part walking down the Via Condotti in their heavy Hudson Bay parkas! Father Bauer took the players to Vatican City where the Swiss Guards outside St. Peter's wanted to know which one was "Seeth," Canada's famous goalie, Seth Martin! Martin had become a legend in Europe after his play in the World Championships in 1961 and again in 1963, and was by far the most identifiable member of the team.

Father Bauer was able to arrange a private audience with His Holiness Pope Paul VI in the Room of Tapestry. There, the pontiff met the men and gave a brief speech about sportsmanship, the importance of the ideals of the Olympics, and the qualities of character acquired through sport. The team returned to Canada on February 22, medal-less from the Games but certainly more enlightened by the papal visit.

The Competition

TOURNAMENT FORMAT

Because of the number of teams entered — 16 — the Olympics began with a tricky little elimination round before the medal round, in which all teams played one game to decide whether they would be placed in Group A — the medal round, or Group B — the consolation round. Once the eight winners had been determined, a simple round-robin format was used, the winner being decided by points (two for a win, one for a tie, as always). In the event of a tie in the standings, the team with the better goal differential (goals allowed subtracted from goals scored) would finish ahead (see "Medals Controversy" for further details). If this calculation did not yield a winner, head-to-head wins would be decisive followed by goal average (goals scored divided by goals allowed).

THE OPPOSITION

AUSTRIA • Adolf Bachura, Horst Kakl, Dieter Kalt, Hermann Knoll, Eduard Moessmer, Tassilo Neuwirth, Alfred Puels, Josef Puschnig, Erich Romauch, Fritz Spielmann, Adelbert St. John, Gustav Tischer, Friedrich Turek, Fritz Wechselberger, Erich Winkler

CZECHOSLOVAKIA • Vlastimil Bubnik, Josef Cerny, Jiri Dolana, Vladimir Dzurilla, Josef Golonka, Frantisek Gregor, Jiri Holik, Jaroslav Jirik, Jan Klapac, Vladimir Nadrchal, Rudolf Potsch, Stanislav Pryl, Ladislav Smid, Stanislav Sventek, Frantisek Tikal, Miroslav Vlach, Jaroslav Walter

FINLAND • Raimo Kilpio, Juhani Latinen, Rauno Lehtio, Esko Luostarinen, Ilka Masikammen, Seppo Nikkila, Kalevi Numminen, Lasse Oksanen, Jorma Peltonen, Heino Pulli, Matti Reunamaki, Jauni Seistamo, Jorma Suokko, Juhani Wahlsten, Jarmo Wasama

GERMANY • Paul Ambros, Bernd Herzig, Michael Hobelsberger, Jansen, Ernst Kopf, Albert Loibl, Josef Reif, Otto Schneitberger, Georg Scholz, Siegfried Schubert, Dieter Schwimmbeck, Sepp, Ernst Trautwein, Wackerle, Leonhard Waitl, Helmut Zanghellini

HUNGARY • Joszef Baban, Arnad Bankuti, Janos Beszteri, Peter Bikar, Gabor Boroczi, Laszlo Jakabhazi, Joszef Kertesz, Lajos Koutny, Ferenc Loerincz, Gyoergy Losonci, Karoly Orosz, Gyoergy Raffa, Gyoergy Rozgonyi, Bela Schwalm, Matyas Vedres, Viktor Zsitva

ITALY • Giancarlo Agazzi, Isidoro Alvera, Heini Bacher, Enrico Benedetti, Vittorio Bolla, Giampiero Branduardi, Bruno Frison, Roberto Gamper, Bruno Ghedina, Ivo Ghezze, Francesco Machhietto, Giulio Oberhammer, Edmondo Rabanser, Alberto da Rin, Giafrance da Rin, Giulio Verocai

JAPAN • Shinichi Honma, Toshiei Honma, Atsuo Irie, Koji Iwamoto, Iasao Kawabuchi, Kimio Kazahari, Kimihisa Kudo, Hirovuki Matsuura, Nakano Minoru, Katsuji Morishima, Jiro Ogawa, Isao Ono, Masahiro Sato, Shigeru Shimada, Manoru Takashima, Masami Tanabu

NORWAY • Egil Bjerklund, Olav Dalsoeren, Bjoern Elvenes, Erik Fjeldstad, Thor Gundersen, Jan-Erik Hansen, Svein Hansen, Einar Larsen, Thor Martinsen, Oeystein Mellerud, Kare Oetsensen, Franz Olafsen, Per Olsen, Christian Petersen, Georg Smefjell

POLAND • Andrzej Fonfara, Bronislaw Gosztyla, Hendrik Handy, Tabeusz Kilanowicz, Josef Kurek, Gerd Langner, Jozef Manowski, Jerzy Ogoczyk, Stanislaw Olszyk, Wladislaw Pabisz, Hubert Sitko, Augustin Skorski, Josef Stefaniak, Sylvester Wilczek, Josef Wisniewski, Andrzej Zurawski

ROMANIA • Nicolae Andrei, Anton Biro, Anton Crisan, Zoltan Czaka, Ioan Ferencz, Iulian Florescu, Andrei Ianovitz, Ioan Ionescu, Alexandru Kalamar, Dan Mihailescu, Eduard Pana, Josif Safian, Geza Szabo, Juliu Szabo, Ion Tiriac, Dezideriu Varga

SWEDEN • Anders Andersson, Gert Blome, Lennart Haggroth, Lennart Johansson, Nils Johansson, Sven "Tumba" Johansson, Lars Lundvall, Eilert Maatta, Hans Mild, Nils Nilsson, Bert Nordlander, Carl Oberg, Uno Ohrlund, Ronald Pettersson, Ulf Sterner, Roland Stotlz, Kjell Svensson

SWITZERLAND • Franz Berry, Roger Chappot, Rolf Diethelm, Elvin Friedrich, Gaston Furrer, Oskar Jenny, Rene Keiner, Pio Parolini, Kurt Pfammatter, Gerald Rigolet, Max Ruegg, Walter Salzmann, Herold Truffer, Peter Wespi, Otto Wittwer

UNITED STATES • David Brooks, Herb Brooks, Bill Christian, Roger Christian, Paul Coppo, Daniel Dilworth, Dates Fryberger, Paul Johnson, Thomas Martin, James McCoy, Wayne Meredith, William Reichart, Donald Ross, Patrick Rupp, Gary Schmaltzbauer, James Westby, Thomas Yurkovich

USSR • Veniamin Alexandrov, Aleksandr Almetov, Vitaly Davydov, Anatoly Firsov, Eduard Ivanov, Viktor Konovalenko, Viktor Kuzkin, Konstantin Loktev, Boris Mayorov, Yevgeny Mayorov, Stanislav Petuchov, Aleksandr Ragulin, Vyacheslav Starshinov, Leonid Volkov, Victor Yakushev, Boris Zaitsev

YUGOSLAVIA • Aleksander Andjelic, Jan Bogo, Miroljub Djordjevic, Albin Felc, Anton Gale, Mirko Holbus, Jan Ivo, Marjan Kristan, Igor Radin, Ivan Rataj, Viktor Ravnik, Boris Renaud, Rasid Semsedinovic, Franc Smolej, Viktor Tisler, Virko Valentar

QUALIFYING ROUND RESULTS

JANUARY 27

Canada 14 Yugoslavia 1

Czechoslovakia 17 Japan 2

Switzerland 5 Norway 1

Sweden 12 Italy 2

Germany 2 Poland 1

Finland 8 Austria 2

USSR 19 Hungary 1

United States 7 Romania 2

Because these games were not part of the official Winter Olympics competition, the statistics from them do not count towards personal and team records.

FINAL STANDINGS

GROUP A • MEDAL ROUND

	GP	W	L	T	GF	GA	P
USSR	7	7	0	0	54	10	14
Sweden	7	5	2	0	47	16	10
Czechoslovakia	7	5	2	0	38	19	10
Canada	7	5	2	0	32	17	10
United States	7	2	5	0	29	33	4
Finland	7	2	5	0	10	31	4
Germany	7	2	5	0	13	49	4
Switzerland	7	0	7	0	9	57	0

RESULTS

JANUARY 29

Canada 8 Switzerland 0

Czechoslovakia 11 Germany 1

USSR 5 United States 1

JANUARY 30

Canada 3 Sweden 1

Finland 4 Switzerland 0

JANUARY 31

USSR 7 Czechoslovakia 5

United States 8 Germany 0

FEBRUARY 1

Czechoslovakia 4 Finland 0

USSR 15 Switzerland 0

Sweden 7 United States 4

FEBRUARY 2

Canada 4 Germany 2

Sweden 7 Finland 0

FEBRUARY 3

Canada 8 United States 6

FEBRUARY 4

USSR 10 Finland 0

Czechoslovakia 5 Switzerland 1

Sweden 10 Germany 2

FEBRUARY 5

Canada 6 Finland 2

Sweden 12 Switzerland 0

USSR 10 Germany 0

Czechoslovakia 7 United States 1

FEBRUARY 7

Czechoslovakia 3 Canada 1

Germany 6 Switzerland 5

USSR 4 Sweden 2

Finland 3 United States 2

FEBRUARY 8

USSR 3 Canada 2

Germany 2 Finland 1

Sweden 8 Czechoslovakia 3

United States 7 Switzerland 3

GROUP B • CONSOLATION ROUND

	GP	W	L	T	GF	GA	P
Poland	7	6	1	0	40	13	12
Norway	7	5	2	0	40	19	10
Japan	7	4	2	1	35	31	9
Romania	7	3	3	1	31	28	7
Austria	7	3	3	1	24	28	7
Yugoslavia	7	3	3	1	29	37	7
Italy	7	2	5	0	24	42	4
Hungary	7	0	7	0	14	39	0

RESULTS

JANUARY 30
Poland 4 Norway 2
Japan 6 Romania 4
Italy 6 Hungary 4

JANUARY 31
Poland 6 Romania 1
Japan 4 Norway 3
Austria 6 Yugoslavia 2

FEBRUARY 1
Austria 3 Hungary 0
Yugoslavia 5 Italy 3

FEBRUARY 2
Norway 9 Italy 2
Romania 5 Yugoslavia 5

FEBRUARY 3
Poland 6 Hungary 2
Japan 5 Austria 5

FEBRUARY 4
Yugoslavia 6 Japan 4

FEBRUARY 5
Poland 7 Italy 0
Romania 5 Austria 2
Norway 6 Hungary 1

FEBRUARY 6
Japan 4 Poland 3
Norway 4 Romania 2
Austria 5 Italy 3
Yugoslavia 4 Hungary 2

FEBRUARY 7
Norway 8 Austria 2
Poland 9 Yugoslavia 3
Romania 6 Italy 2
Japan 6 Hungary 2

FEBRUARY 8
Poland 5 Austria 1
Norway 8 Yugoslavia 4
Italy 8 Japan 6
Romania 8 Hungary 3

TEAM CANADA GAME SUMMARIES

JANUARY 29 • Canada 8 Switzerland 0

FIRST PERIOD

1. Canada, Seiling (MacKenzie) • 19:57

penalties: *Dineen (Can) 7:00*

SECOND PERIOD

2. Canada, Forhan (Johnston) • 0:27

3. Canada, Begg (Bourbonnais) • 6:46

4. Canada, Akervall (Bourbonnais) • 11:25

5. Canada, Dineen (Seiling) • 14:53

6. Canada, Swarbrick (Dineen) • 15:12

penalties: *Johnston (Can) 0:48, Jenny (Swi) 2:20, Berry (Swi) & Akervall (Can) 14:18*

THIRD PERIOD

7. Canada, Conacher (unassisted) • 3:18

8. Canada, Conacher (Bourbonnais) • 3:36

penalties: *Clancy (Can) 17:03, Can (too many men — served by Seiling) 19:14*

IN GOAL

Canada — Martin/Broderick *(Broderick (no goals) replaced Martin (no goals) to start 3rd)*

Switzerland — Rigolet

SHOTS ON GOAL

Canada	24	24	13	**61**
Switzerland	13	8	7	**28**

JANUARY 30 • Canada 3 Sweden 1

IN GOAL

Canada — Martin/Broderick *(Broderick (no goals) replaced Martin (one goal) to start 3rd)*

Sweden — Svensson

SHOTS ON GOAL

Canada	13	8	8	**29**
Sweden	19	14	13	**46**

FIRST PERIOD

1. Canada, Forhan (unassisted) • 5:05

penalties: *none*

SECOND PERIOD

2. Canada, Seiling (Swarbrick) • 7:17

3. Sweden, T. Johansson (L. Johansson) • 17:20(pp)

penalties: *Conacher (Can) 13:03, Conlin (Can) 14:24, Mild (Swe) 14:46, Begg (Can) 17:12*

THIRD PERIOD

4. Canada, Seiling (Dineen) • 4:15

penalties: *Oberg (Swe) & Dineen (Can) 8:13, L. Johansson (Swe) 12:30*

FEBRUARY 2 • Canada 4 Germany 2

IN GOAL

Canada — Martin

Germany — Jansen

SHOTS ON GOAL

Canada	13	7	13	**33**
Germany	8	11	9	**28**

FIRST PERIOD

1. Canada, Conacher (unassisted) • 4:10

2. Germany, Schubert (Reif) • 9:50(pp)

3. Canada, Dineen (Swarbrick) • 18:59

penalties: *Scholz (Ger) 6:25, Conlin (Can) 9:20, MacKenzie (Can) 19:32*

SECOND PERIOD

No Scoring

penalties: *Wackerle (Ger) 8:11, Conacher (Can) 13:00, Schubert (Ger) 14:09, Dineen (Can) 14:59, Ackervall (Can) 19:42*

THIRD PERIOD

4. Canada, Conacher (unassisted) • 2:52(pp)

5. Canada, Cadieux (Johnston) • 3:48

6. Germany, Trautwein (Sepp) • 17:45

penalties: *Ambros (Ger) 1:01, Wackerle (Ger) & O'Malley (Can) 8:02*

FEBRUARY 3 • Canada 8 United States 6

IN GOAL

Canada — Broderick

United States — Yurkovich/Rupp *(Rupp replaced Yurkovich late in 2nd)*

SHOTS ON GOAL

Canada	10	14	13	**37**
United States	17	16	18	**51**

FIRST PERIOD

1. United States, Westby (unassisted) • 0:12

2. Canada, Dineen (unassisted) • 3:23(pp)

3. United States, Johnson (Ross) • 11:15

4. United States, Johnson (Dilworth) • 18:30

penalties: *Brooks (US) 2:57*

SECOND PERIOD

5. Canada, Conacher (unassisted) • 0:43

6. Canada, Cadieux (Bourbonnais) • 6:20

7. Canada, Swarbrick (Dineen) • 7:18

8. Canada, Forhan (Clancy) • 10:25

9. Canada, Conacher (unassisted) • 11:25

10. Canada, Cadieux (Bourbonnais) • 16:28

penalties: *Cadieux (Can) 3:40, Martin (Can) & Dineen (Can) 12:35, Johnston (Can) 13:00*

THIRD PERIOD

11. Canada, Conacher (Swarbrick) • 2:29

12. United States, B. Christian (unassisted) • 7:40

13. United States, Reichart (unassisted) • 19:11

14. United States, Johnson (Coppo) • 19:37

penalties: *Seiling (Can) 2:35, MacKenzie (Can) & Westby (US) 3:22, Cadieux (Can) & Brooks (US) 6:24, Swarbrick (Can) 9:22, Cadieux (Can) 12:53, Johnston (Can) 13:09, R. Christian (US) 14:20*

FEBRUARY 5 • Canada 6 Finland 2

FIRST PERIOD

1. Finland, Wahlsten (unassisted) • 4:17

2. Canada, Cadieux (Conacher) • 10:19

3. Canada, Clancy (Dineen) • 19:01

penalties: *none*

SECOND PERIOD

4. Canada, Forhan (unassisted) • 2:47

5. Canada, Forhan (Dineen) • 7:22

6. Canada, Akervall (unassisted) • 19:15

penalties: *Cadieux (Can) 19:21*

THIRD PERIOD

7. Canada, Forhan (Dineen) • 6:12

8. Finland, Reunamaki (Pulli) • 6:50

penalties: *Seiling (Can) 19:36*

IN GOAL

Canada — Martin/Broderick
(Broderick (one goal) replaced Martin (one goal) to start 3rd)

Finland — Latinen

SHOTS ON GOAL

Canada			
17	12	13	**42**
Finland			
7	7	13	**27**

FEBRUARY 7 • Czechoslovakia 3 Canada 1

FIRST PERIOD

No Scoring

penalties: *Akervall (Can — major) 15:14*

SECOND PERIOD

1. Canada, Seiling (MacKenzie) • 14:05

penalties: *none*

THIRD PERIOD

2. Czechoslovakia, Klapac (unassisted) • 11:10

3. Czechoslovakia, Holik (unassisted) • 13:35

4. Czechoslovakia, Cerny (Tikal) • 19:01

penalties: *none*

IN GOAL

Canada — Martin/Broderick
(Broderick (three goals) replaced Martin (no goals) at 7:00 of 3rd)

Czechoslovakia — Nadrchal

SHOTS ON GOAL

Canada			
15	9	10	**34**
Czechoslovakia			
13	14	14	**41**

FEBRUARY 8 • USSR 3 Canada 2

FIRST PERIOD

1. Canada, Swarbrick (Johnston) • 5:57

penalties: *Dineen (Can) 12:50*

SECOND PERIOD

2. USSR, Y. Mayorov (B. Mayorov) • 10:49

3. Canada, Forhan (Seiling) • 13:40

4. USSR, Starshinov (Y. Mayorov) • 18:28

penalties: *Zaitsev (USSR) 14:30, Conacher (Can) 16:18*

THIRD PERIOD

5. USSR, Alexandrov (Almetov) • 1:36

penalties: *O'Malley (Can) 3:40, Davydov (USSR) 16:39*

IN GOAL

Canada — Broderick/Martin
(Martin (one goal) replaced Broderick (two goals) to start 3rd)

USSR — Konovalenko

SHOTS ON GOAL

Canada			
4	6	7	**17**
USSR			
12	8	19	**39**

TEAM CANADA FINAL STATISTICS • 1964

#		GP	G	A	P	Pim
9	Gary Dineen	7	3	6	9	10
13	Brian Conacher	7	7	1	8	6
14	Bob Forhan	7	7	0	7	0
3	Rod Seiling	7	4	2	6	6
12	George Swarbrick	7	3	3	6	2
8	Roger Bourbonnais	7	0	5	5	0
18	Ray Cadieux	7	4	0	4	8
10	Marshall Johnston	7	0	3	3	6
6	Hank Akervall	7	2	0	2	9
16	Terry Clancy	7	1	1	2	2
4	Barry MacKenzie	7	0	2	2	4
15	Gary Begg	7	1	0	1	2
11	Paul Conlin	7	0	0	0	4
2	Terry O'Malley	7	0	0	0	4
1	Seth Martin	6	0	0	0	2

#	IN GOAL	GP	W-L-T	Mins	GA	SO	Avg
1	Seth Martin	6	4–1–0	247	5	0*	1.21
1	Ken Broderick	6	1–1–0	173	12	0*	4.16

* *Broderick and Martin shared a shutout January 29 vs. Switzerland*

GOALIE NOTES

1. *Broderick (no goals) replaced Martin (no goals) to start 3rd, January 29 vs. Switzerland*

2. *Broderick (no goals) replaced Martin (one goal) to start 3rd, January 30 vs. Sweden*

3. *Broderick (one goal) replaced Martin (one goal) to start 3rd, February 5 vs. Finland*

4. *Broderick (three goals) replaced Martin (no goals) at 7:00 of 3rd, February 7 vs. Czechoslovakia*

5. *Martin (one goal) replaced Broderick (two goals) to start 3rd, February 8 vs. USSR*

CHAPTER 11

The Tenth Olympic Winter Games

GRENOBLE, FRANCE

February 6–17, 1968

Coach Jackie McLeod

Calgary was making a habit of finishing runner-up in the voting to host the Games, and 1968 was no exception. At the 62nd IOC session in Innsbruck on May 28, 1964, Lake Placid, Oslo, and Sapporo were all eliminated in the first round of balloting, Lahti in the second, and in the third round Calgary (Banff) finished bridesmaid to Grenoble.

TEAM CANADA • 1968

Ken Broderick, *GOAL*
Wayne Stephenson, *GOAL*

Paul Conlin, *DEFENCE*
Brian Glennie, *DEFENCE*
Ted Hargreaves, *DEFENCE*
Marshall Johnston, *DEFENCE (CAPTAIN)*
Barry MacKenzie, *DEFENCE*
Terry O'Malley, *DEFENCE*

Roger Bourbonnais, *FORWARD*
Ray Cadieux, *FORWARD*
Gary Dineen, *FORWARD*
Fran Huck, *FORWARD*
Billy MacMillan, *FORWARD*
Steve Monteith, *FORWARD*
Morris Mott, *FORWARD*
Danny O'Shea, *FORWARD*
Gerry Pinder, *FORWARD*
Herb Pinder, *FORWARD*

Jackie McLeod, *COACH*
Father David Bauer, *MANAGER*

FINAL PLACINGS

GOLD MEDAL
USSR

SILVER MEDAL
Czechoslovakia

BRONZE MEDAL
Canada

FOURTH PLACE
Sweden

FIFTH PLACE
Finland

SIXTH PLACE
United States

SEVENTH PLACE
West Germany

EIGHTH PLACE
East Germany

NINTH PLACE
Yugoslavia

TENTH PLACE
Japan

ELEVENTH PLACE
Norway

TWELFTH PLACE
Romania

THIRTEENTH PLACE
Austria

FOURTEENTH PLACE
France

CANADA'S PREPARATION: FATHER BAUER'S PROGRAM CONTINUES APACE

The dream that started in 1963 when Father Bauer established a national junior squad had now become part of Canada's yearly hockey operations, and the preparation for the 1968 Olympics began for Canada earlier than ever before when the players hit the ice at Dutton Arena at St.John's–Ravenscourt School in Fort Garry, Manitoba on August 9, 1967, fully six months before their first Olympic game. In the previous three years — that is, in the years following their disappointing fourth place finish at Innsbruck at the 1964 Games — Canada had placed only slightly better in international competition, finishing 4th, 3rd, and 3rd again at the World Championships won each year by the seasoned professionals from the USSR. While Father Bauer's ideals were clearly admirable, the simple fact of the matter was that the "national team" was comprised mostly of Canadian university students — amateurs to be sure, but unlikely to wrest the gold from the Soviets' grip.

Canada's Ted Hargreaves chases a loose puck.

The first few days of camp featured mostly newcomers and hopefuls, rookies who were eager to make an impression with coach McLeod early, a chance they would be given just a week later when the Nats faced a team of NHL All-Stars, including rookie-of-the-year Bobby Orr, and league veterans Carl Brewer, Ab McDonald, and Pete Stemkowski, in a charity match. In a new twist, the national team would also play as two teams for a number of months at varying tournaments, one playing out of Winnipeg in the Western Canadian Senior League, and the other, based in Ottawa, playing in the Quebec Provincial Senior League under alumnus Jack Bownass. This, coach McLeod felt, would give the greatest number of players the greatest opportunity to show their skills and prove themselves worthy of the final Olympic roster. At the same time, though, it divided the team and prevented the final squad from using this time to get to know one another on ice, thus creating a situation similar to previous years when the final team — the actual players who would go to the Olympics — weren't put together soon enough or for long enough.

Orr's appearance in Manitoba for the benefit game created a remarkable stir, but, ominously, he played just eight minutes before suffering a knee injury that kept him off ice until the start of the Bruins' training camp some three weeks later. To augment their games in the Western Senior League, which wouldn't provide a particularly stiff challenge for the Olympians, the team also played a number of tougher exhibition games in the coming months against the US Nationals, the Eastern Nationals, and a selection of NHL teams, and also partook in another pre-Olympic tournament in Prague.

Team Canada's first big test, however, was a tournament in Grenoble at the newly-built Olympic Stadium, featuring four countries — USSR, Czechoslovakia, and the States — that would surely be the Nats' chief opposition at the Games in February '68. Canada was impressive, winning the tournament and coming home proud and optimistic, but the road ahead was none too smooth for the team.

THE CANADIAN TOURNAMENT

For the second straight year, Canada hosted a world competition of its own, featuring itself, USSR, and Sweden as a further, necessary step to developing a cohesive team for the Olympics. The tournament consisted of two sets of round-robin play, four games in all for each team, and provided the Canadians with ample opportunity to suss out each country's talent while determining its own. As could have been expected, the Soviets won and Canada placed second, further highlighting the obvious discrepancies in talent that would surely be present at Grenoble.

CANADA'S PROPOSAL

In an effort to ameliorate the problems of amateur and professional, of sending NHLers to the Olympics or inexperienced, under-talented non-pros, Canada made a proposal to the IIHF whereby a six-team World League would be established, one team each from the Soviet Union, Czechoslovakia, Sweden, and the US, and two from Canada. This World League would not conflict with the World Championships or the Olympics, but would instead see a 20- or 30-game schedule adopted as a more formal structure to the loosely organized exhibition games that had long been used as preparation leading to the Olympics. Thus, the league would give the players needed top-notch experience without harming their amateur status.

When the concept was broached to the IIHF and its relevant member countries, however, there were too many objections and obstacles to overcome to make it practicable. Sweden's national team was an all-star team that couldn't remain intact for a full year without upsetting its league schedule; the Soviets objected to having two Canadian entries; others said their schedule for the coming year had already been planned. Also, the European countries were leery about doing something that might upset the current standard which saw the Canadians perform less than superbly. Why would they agree to help Canada's team improve? The suggestion was quickly forgotten.

Thus, Father Bauer's main concerns for the future of the national program remained unsolved, as he expressed after the IIHF rejected the World League: "We set up the national team concept four years ago on a four-year program...Now we must plan ahead as to whether we will continue to develop. The team can't go on

Team Canada vs. the Soviet Union, February 17, 1968.

living from hand-to-mouth year after year. Also, we must do something to counter the attractive offers some of our players are receiving from professional clubs." In short, since Father Bauer's national program had come into effect, hockey had become so much more complex that the team was still losing ground internationally. Father Bauer was still able to combine hockey and education for his players, but the quality of the teams he was assembling, even when collective soul and motivation were factored in, had little chance of winning in the international arena.

B-2 FORMS: A NEW OLYMPIC DECLARATION OF "AMATEUR"

While the ideal of a strictly amateur Games was becoming harder and harder, if not impossible, to maintain, the IOC introduced for 1968 a new pledge that virtually assured each and every hockey player at the Games was lying. It required each participant to read the rules and "on his honour" declare his status as an amateur. This included complying with a clause restricting participation to those: who have never received any sort of pay for playing his sport; whose training expenses did not exceed 30 days' worth in any calendar year; and — believe this! — who have no intention of turning pro at any time *after* the Games ended!

Frank Shaughnessy, Canada's chef de mission for these Olympics, could only help his team "rationalize" the signing of the contract by saying, "For example, probably every hockey player as a boy dreams of becoming a professional. But unless he has signed a professional contract, how can we signify his intentions?"

CANADA'S WINTER OLYMPIC BID

Attending the 1968 Games was a delegation of four men from Garibaldi, British Columbia who were there to study the practical and financial details of running an

Olympics. Garibaldi was readying a proposal it would make to the Canadian Olympic Association that August to persuade it to back the town as Canada's formal bid to host the 1976 Winter Games. One member of the contingent was Bob Tidmarsh, who felt very confident about Garibaldi's — and Canada's — chances: "I think the people [IOC delegates] are very sympathetic towards Canada. We've never had an Olympic bid...We [Garibaldi] have one great asset, and that is that all the facilities, or at least the facilities for all the events, will take place right on the same site. Places like Sapporo, and here at Grenoble, and places like Innsbruck, people have had to go great distances from the bobsled to the cross-country to the downhill. We at Garibaldi will have all this in one nice compact area so that all the competitors...would meet one another in a friendly, competitive atmosphere."

PASSPORTS

Moments before Canada's opening game of the tournament against West Germany, the players were ordered off the ice during the warm-up by an IIHF official who wanted to check the citizenship and validity of each and every player. Coach McLeod was obviously livid, as this was a detail that should have been looked after long before the drop of the first puck. Team Canada, unfazed, skated to an easy 6–1 win.

A STRANGE BUT SERENDIPITOUS OCCURRENCE

Although Canada had to settle for a bronze medal at these Games, it might well have been due to a very odd play at a critical time in the Canada–Czechoslovakia game that even that third-place finish was accomplished.

Canada had surged to an early 3–0 lead after two periods, and at intermission any gambler would have given excellent odds on Canada's winning the game. However, the Czechs came out as flying as the Nats were flat, and three minutes into the third had narrowed the gap to 3–2. They continued to press Ken Broderick's net for the tying goal, and then Danny O'Shea, on his way to the bench and furious with himself after having missed a breakaway, smashed his stick against the Plexiglas by Canada's bench. The glass shattered and the game was held up 10 minutes while it was replaced.

Goalie Ken Broderick loses his stick after making a save in Canada's 3–2 win over the US. Team-mate Danny O'Shea and Lenny Lilyholm react to the play.

Coach Jackie McLeod used the time-out to settle down his players and reinstitute a cohesive defensive plan for the rest of the game. Canada held on to win 3–2 and remained tied with the Czechs for second place at that point in the tournament.

McLeod admitted the break was truly lucky, "The guys somehow got their signals mixed and on both Czech goals we were caught with three men deep. After that delay, though, they settled down and played it right."

USSR 5 CANADA 0

More than 15,000 people packed the Stade de Glace in Grenoble to see this gold medal game, the vast majority chanting, "Canada! Canada!" The outcome of this match could be put in the simplest terms: a win meant a gold medal, a tie meant a silver, a loss meant a bronze.

While both teams maintained a blistering pace and hit fiercely and cleanly, the Russians got the upper hand under the most demoralising of circumstances — on a Canadian power-play. Anatoly Firsov's first period short-handed goal gave the Russians a 1–0 lead that held up until midway through the second period.

All along, it was the Canadians' ability to score, to finish their plays, that had been questioned, and no greater example of this weakness can be cited than the second period. The flip side to the argument, of course, is that the Russians got great goaltending. Either way, Russian goaler Konovalenko stopped Fran Huck close in and then Mott and Pinder in quick succession. Michakov went in alone on Ken Broderick on the counter-attack, and the USSR was up 2–0. The Redshirts followed with a goal early in the third to leave no doubt of the outcome, and two later goals merely affirmed Canada's loss.

Canada's Marshall Johnston celebrates his game-tying goal in the 3rd period of his team's win over the US as team-mate Terry O'Malley skates by.

THE POST-MORTEM

While a medal, albeit bronze, might have gone over well with just about any other hockey playing nation, it was a portentous achievement, to say the least, for Canada. After the Olympics, critics were fighting each other to be at the front of the coach-bashing line, not necessarily knocking Jackie McLeod in particular, but rather heaping praise on Russian leader Anatoly Tarasov as a man far more sage and erudite than his Canadian counterparts. They talked about how the Russians were on the ice every day, 10 months of the year, for five hours, practising every possible skill needed to win.

But the critics, by harping on the coaching, were missing the point. The Russians weren't outplaying and beating Canada's best; Canada's best weren't competing internationally. The Russian elite league was to the USSR what the NHL was to Canada — the place where all of that country's best played during the year. Imagine an NHL All-Star team playing in the Original Six as a seventh team, the absolute best being given many years' worth of preparation. *That* was the Russian team that beat Canada's university students 5–0.

Enough was enough. Canada was at a crossroads: to keep sending under-qualified players to the Games in the name of competition, amateur fair play, dedication, and upholding the Olympic ideal, or to do something drastic to voice our collective frustration and displeasure with the IOC and IIHF? Canada chose the latter. Either pros would represent the country in upcoming Games and World Championships, or Canada would not send a hockey team to international events.

The Competition

TOURNAMENT FORMAT

The top eight teams were grouped into a medal round section, each playing a round-robin schedule. The top team in the standings (two points for a win, one for a tie) would win the gold medal. In the event of a two-way tie, the winner of the head-to-head game would get the gold. If there were a tie between more than two teams, goal differential (goals against subtracted from goals scored) would be the deciding factor.

One odd international rule that continued through these 1968 Games was that the third period was divided into two halves. At the 10:00 mark, the buzzer would sound, play would stop, and teams would change ends as they did after each intermission. This ensured that each played 30 minutes (exactly half the game) at either goal. All games were played at Le Stade de Glace de Grenoble (capacity 15,000). For the first time, full body-checking in all areas of the rink was permitted.

THE OPPOSITION

AUSTRIA • Guenther Burkhart, Delgon, Gerhard Felfernig, Gerhard Hausner, Dieter Kalt, Klaus Kirchbaumer, Heinz Knoflach, Walter Konig, Josef Mossner, Karl Pregl, Josef Puschnik, Adelbert St. John, Paul Samonig, Gerd Schager, Heinz Schupp, Josef Schwitzer, Franz Scilcher, Klaus Weingartner

CZECHOSLOVAKIA • Josef Cerny, Vladimir Dzurilla, Josef Golonka, Jan Havel, Petr Hejma, Jiri Holik, Josef Horesovsky, Jan Hrbaty, Jaroslav Jirik, Jan Klapac, Jiri Kochta, Oldrich Machac, Karel Masopust, Vladimir Nadrchal, Vaclav Nedomansky, Frantisek Pospisil, Frantisek Sevcik, Jan Suchy

EAST GERMANY • Manfred Buder, Lothar Fuchs, Bernd Hiller, Klaus Hirche, Bernd Karrenbauer, Dieter Kratzsch, Hartmut Nickel, Rudiger Noack, Ullrich Noack, Helmut Novy, Dietmar Peters, Wolfgang Plotka, Bernd Poindl, Peter Prusa, Dieter Purschel, Wilfried Sock, Dieter Vogt, Joachim Ziesche

FINLAND • Matti Harju, Karl Johanson, Matti Kainonen, Veli-Pekka Ketola, Ilpa Koskela, Pentti Koskela, Pekka Kuusisto, Pekka Leimu, Seppo Lindstrom, Lasse Oksanen, Lalli Partinen, Esa Peltonen, Jorma Peltonen, Juha Rantasila, Matti Reunamaki, Paavo Tirkonen, Juhani Wahlsten, Urpo Ylonen

FRANCE • Claude Blanchard, Rene Blanchard, Bernard Cabanis, Michel Caux, Bernard Deschamps, Gerard Faucomprez, Patrick Francheterre, Joel Gauvin, Joel Godeau, Daniel Grando, Gilbert Itzicsohn, Philippe Lacarriere, Gilbert Lepre, Charles Liberman, Alain Mazza, Patrice Pourtanel, Olivier Prechac, Jean-Claude Sozzi

JAPAN • Takeshi Akiba, Nobuhiro Araki, Isao Asai, Yutaka Ebina, Takao Hikigi, Toru Itabashi, Minoru Ito, Kodji Iwamoto, Takaaki Kaneiri, Kimihisa Kudo, Kazuo Matsuda, Katsuyi Morishima, Toshimito Ohtsubo, Toru Okajima, Michihiro Sato, Mamoru Takashima, Kenji Toriyabe

NORWAY • Trygve Bergeid, Steinar Bjolbakk, Harald Brathen, Olav Dalsoeren, Tor Gundersen, Svein Haagensen, Svein Hansen, Bjorn Johansen, Thor Martinsen, Arne Mikkelsen, Kaare Oestensen, Per Olsen, Christain Petersen, Georg Smefjell, Terje Steen, Odd Syversen, Terje Thoen

ROMANIA • Ion Basa, Zoltan Czaka, Constantine Dumitras, Iulian Florescu, Zoltan Fogarasi, Ion Ghiorghiu, Ioan Ste. Ionescu, Alexandru Kalamar, Aurel Mois, Eduard Pana, Razvan Schiau, Valentin Stefanov, Mihai Stoiculescu, Gheza Szabo, Stefan Texe, Dezideriu Varga

SWEDEN • Folke Bengtsson, Arne Carlsson, Hans Dahllof, Svante Granholm, Henric Hedlund, Leif Henriksson, Leif Holmquist, Nils Johansson, Tord Lundstrom, Lars-Goran Nilsson, Bert-Ola Nordlander, Carl-Goran Oberg, Roger Olsson, Bjorn Palmquist, Lars-Erik Sjoberg, Roland Stoltz, Lennart Svedberg, Hakan Wickberg

UNITED STATES • Herb Brooks, John Cunniff, John Dale, Craig Falkman, Robert Paul Hurley, Thomas Hurley, Leonard Lilyholm, James Logue, Patrick Loyne, John Morrison, Lou Nanne, Robert Paradise, Larry Pleau, Bruce Riutta, Donald Ross, Pat Rupp, Larry Stordahl, Doug Volmar

USSR • Veniamin Aleksandrov, Viktor Blinov, Vitaly Davidov, Anatoly Firsov, Anatoly Ionov, Viktor Konovalenko, Viktor Kuzkin, Boris Mayorov, Yevgeny Michakov, Yuri Moiseyev, Viktor Polupanov, Aleksandr Ragulin, Igor Romichevsky, Vyacheslav Starshinov, Vladimir Vikulov, Oleg Zaitsev, Yevgeny Zimin, Viktor Zinger

WEST GERMANY • Heinz Bader, Lorenz Funk, Manfred Gmeiner, Gustav Hanig, Gunther Knauss, Ernst Kopf, Bernd Kuhn, Peter Lax, Horst Meindl, Josef Reif, Hans Schichtl, Alois Schloder, Josef Schramm, Rudolf Thanner, Leonhard Waitl, Heinz Weisenbach, Josef Volk

YUGOSLAVIA • Slavko Beravs, Albin Felc, Anton Gale, Miroslav Gojanovic, Rudi Hiti, Ivo Jan, Joze-Bogo Jan, Lado Jug, Ciril Klinar, Rudolf Knez, Janez Mlakar, Ivo Rataj, Viktor Ravnik, Franco Razinger, Franc Smolej, Roman Smolej, Viktor Tisler

FINAL STANDINGS

GROUP A CHAMPIONSHIP

	GP	W	L	T	GF	GA	P
USSR	7	6	1	0	48	10	12
Czechoslovakia	7	5	1	1	33	17	11
Canada	7	5	2	0	28	15	10
Sweden	7	4	2	1	23	18	9
Finland	7	3	3	1	17	23	7
United States	7	2	4	1	23	28	5
West Germany	7	1	6	0	13	39	2
East Germany	7	0	7	0	13	48	0

RESULTS

FEBRUARY 6
Canada 6 West Germany 1
USSR 8 Finland 0
Czechoslovakia 5 United States 1

FEBRUARY 7
USSR 9 East Germany 0
Sweden 4 United States 3

FEBRUARY 8
Finland 5 Canada 2
Czechoslovakia 5 West Germany 1

FEBRUARY 9
Canada 11 East Germany 0
Sweden 5 West Germany 4
USSR 10 United States 2

FEBRUARY 10
Czechoslovakia 4 Finland 3
Sweden 5 East Germany 2

FEBRUARY 11
Canada 3 United States 2
USSR 9 West Germany 1

FEBRUARY 12
Czechoslovakia 10 East Germany 3
Sweden 5 Finland 1
United States 8 West Germany 1

FEBRUARY 13
Canada 3 Czechoslovakia 2
USSR 3 Sweden 2

FEBRUARY 14
Finland 3 East Germany 2

FEBRUARY 15
Canada 3 Sweden 0
Czechoslovakia 5 USSR 4
United States 6 East Germany 4

FEBRUARY 16
Finland 4 West Germany 1

FEBRUARY 17
USSR 5 Canada 0
Czechoslovakia 2 Sweden 2
West Germany 4 East Germany 2
Finland 1 United States 1

GROUP B CONSOLATION

	GP	W	L	T	GF	GA	P
Yugoslavia	5	5	0	0	33	9	10
Japan	5	4	1	0	27	12	8
Norway	5	3	2	0	15	15	6
Romania	5	2	3	0	22	23	4
Austria	5	1	4	0	12	27	2
France	5	0	5	0	9	32	0

RESULTS

FEBRUARY 7
Yugoslavia 5 Japan 1
Romania 3 Austria 2

FEBRUARY 8
Norway 4 France 1

FEBRUARY 9
Romania 7 France 3
Yugoslavia 6 Austria 0

FEBRUARY 10
Japan 4 Norway 0

FEBRUARY 11
Austria 5 France 2

FEBRUARY 12
Japan 5 Romania 4
Norway 5 Austria 4

FEBRUARY 13
Yugoslavia 10 France 1

FEBRUARY 14
Norway 4 Romania 3

FEBRUARY 15
Japan 11 Austria 1

FEBRUARY 16
Yugoslavia 9 Romania 5

FEBRUARY 17
Japan 6 France 2
Yugoslavia 3 Norway 2

TEAM CANADA GAME SUMMARIES

FEBRUARY 6 • Canada 6 West Germany 1

IN GOAL
Canada — Stephenson
West Germany — Knauss/Schramm

SHOTS ON GOAL

Canada			
12	16	9	**37**
West Germany			
5	13	7	**25**

FIRST PERIOD
No Scoring
penalties: *Schichtl (WGer) 14:35*

SECOND PERIOD
1. Canada, Cadieux (Johnston, Huck) • 0:09
2. Canada, Dineen (MacMillan) • 4:29(pp)
3. Canada, Mott (Huck) • 6:08
4. Canada, Huck (Mott) • 11:35
5. West Germany, Kopf (Hanig) • 15:25(pp)
penalties: *Reif (WGer) 4:10, H. Pinder (Can) 13:15, MacKenzie (Can) 15:10*

THIRD PERIOD
6. Canada, Bourbonnais (MacKenzie, O'Shea) • 11:30
7. Canada, Bourbonnais (Hargreaves) • 19:55
penalties: *Thanner (WGer) 5:43, Huck (Can) 6:30, Thanner (WGer) 15:40, MacKenzie (Can) 16:07*

FEBRUARY 8 • Finland 5 Canada 2

FIRST PERIOD

1. Finland, Kainonen (unassisted) • 7:16

2. Finland, Oksanen (Ketola) • 12:59

3. Canada, O'Shea (Glennie, MacMillan) • 14:47

penalties: *Huck (Can) 3:51*

SECOND PERIOD

4. Finland, J. Peltonen (Leimu) • 13:06(pp)

penalties: *Johnston (Can) 12:51, Johanson (Fin) 13:26, O'Shea (Can) 13:56*

THIRD PERIOD

5. Finland, Koskela (unassisted) • 8:26

6. Canada, MacMillan (O'Shea) • 11:49

7. Finland, Wahlsten (unassisted) • 19:12(en)

penalties: *Glennie (Can) 3:29, Johanson (Fin) 9:35*

IN GOAL

Canada — Broderick

Finland — Ylonen

SHOTS ON GOAL

Canada	13	11	13	**37**
Finland	8	8	10	**26**

FEBRUARY 9 • Canada 11 East Germany 0

FIRST PERIOD

1. Canada, Hargreaves (O'Malley) • 3:40

2. Canada, O'Shea (Bourbonnais) • 6:38

3. Canada, Mott (Huck) • 9:08

4. Canada, Huck (Johnston, Dineen) • 18:21(pp)

penalties: *O'Shea (Can) 1:31, U. Noack (EGer) 12:05, Plotka (EGer) 18:08*

SECOND PERIOD

5. Canada, Bourbonnais (Johnston) • 1:21

6. Canada, Mott (Cadieux) • 1:55

7. Canada, Monteith (unassisted) • 12:51

8. Canada, Mott (MacKenzie) • 15:46

penalties: *none*

THIRD PERIOD

9. Canada, Mott (Huck) • 6:32

10. Canada, H. Pinder (unassisted) • 13:32

11. Canada, Huck (Johnston) • 18:19(pp)

penalties: *Dineen (Can) 9:41, Nickel (EGer) 17:11*

IN GOAL

Canada — Stephenson

East Germany — Purschel/Hirche *(Hirche replaced Purschel midway through 1st)*

SHOTS ON GOAL

Canada	18	18	15	**51**
East Germany	5	9	10	**24**

FEBRUARY 11 • Canada 3 United States 2

FIRST PERIOD

1. Canada, Cadieux (Johnston) • 12:35

2. United States, Pleau (unassisted) • 13:00

3. United States, Riutta (Cunniff) • 18:53

penalties: *Dineen (Can) 2:56, Glennie (Can) 8:55, O'Shea (Can) 16:04, Lilyholm (US — major) 20:00*

SECOND PERIOD

No Scoring

penalties: *Lilyholm (US) 11:29*

THIRD PERIOD

4. Canada, Johnston (O'Malley) • 2:28(pp)

5. Canada, Cadieux (Johnston) • 7:30

penalties: *Volmar (US) 0:50, Riutta (US) 13:42, Glennie (Can) 16:07, O'Malley (Can) 17:49*

IN GOAL

Canada — Stephenson/Broderick *(Broderick (no goals) replaced Stephenson (two goals) to start 2nd)*

United States — Rupp

SHOTS ON GOAL

Canada	7	11	17	**35**
United States	5	3	8	**16**

FEBRUARY 13 • Canada 3 Czechoslovakia 2

FIRST PERIOD

No Scoring

penalties: *Cz (too many men) 3:29, Glennie (Can) 8:18*

SECOND PERIOD

1. Canada, Huck (Cadieux) • 2:09

2. Canada, Bourbonnais (O'Shea) • 7:52

3. Canada, Cadieux (Huck) • 12:42

penalties: *none*

THIRD PERIOD

4. Czechoslovakia, Havel (Cerny) • 0:51

5. Czechoslovakia, Nedomansky (Holik) • 1:52

penalties: *none*

IN GOAL

Canada — Broderick

Czechoslovakia — Dzurilla

SHOTS ON GOAL

Canada	8	12	5	**25**
Czechoslovakia	12	11	11	**34**

FEBRUARY 15 • Canada 3 Sweden 0

IN GOAL
Canada — Broderick
Sweden — Holmquist

SHOTS ON GOAL

Canada			
12	10	5	**27**
Sweden			
5	12	8	**25**

FIRST PERIOD
1. Canada, Johnston (O'Shea) • 9:16
2. Canada, G. Pinder (Dineen) • 12:30
penalties: *Dineen (Can) 3:28, Huck (Can) 15:00*

SECOND PERIOD
No Scoring
penalties: *MacKenzie (Can) 3:07, Glennie (Can) 13:12, Lundstrom (Swe) 15:27, Granholm (Swe) & O'Shea (Can) 20:00*

THIRD PERIOD
3. Canada, O'Shea (Bourbonnais) • 14:52
penalties: *Huck (Can) 9:10*

FEBRUARY 17 • USSR 5 Canada 0

IN GOAL
Canada — Broderick
USSR — Konovalenko

SHOTS ON GOAL

Canada			
7	12	6	**25**
USSR			
11	5	16	**32**

FIRST PERIOD
1. USSR, Firsov (Vikulov) • 14:51(sh)
penalties: *Mott (Can) 9:28, O'Shea (Can) 11:57, Zimin (USSR) 13:56, G. Pinder (Can) 15:03*

SECOND PERIOD
2. USSR, Michakov (Moiseyev) • 12:44
penalties: *MacKenzie (Can) 0:38, Polupanov (USSR) 0:50, Johnston (Can) 16:34*

THIRD PERIOD
3. USSR, Starshinov (unassisted) • 1:21
4. USSR, Zimin (Starshinov, Davidov) • 8:44(pp)
5. USSR, Firsov (Vikulov) • 13:59
penalties: *Huck (Can) 8:18*

TEAM CANADA FINAL STATISTICS • 1968

#		GP	G	A	P	Pim
9	Fran Huck	7	4	5	9	10
10	Marshall Johnston	7	2	6	8	4
20	Morris Mott	7	5	1	6	2
8	Roger Bourbonnais	7	4	2	6	0
16	Ray Cadieux	7	4	2	6	0
18	Danny O'Shea	7	3	2	5	10
7	Gary Dineen	7	1	2	3	6
12	Billy MacMillan	6	1	2	3	0
11	Ted Hargreaves	7	1	1	2	0
4	Barry MacKenzie	7	0	2	2	8
2	Terry O'Malley	6	0	2	2	2
15	Gerry Pinder	7	1	0	1	2
14	Herb Pinder	2	1	0	1	2
17	Steve Monteith	7	1	0	1	0
5	Brian Glennie	7	0	1	1	10
3	Paul Conlin	7	0	0	0	0

#	IN GOAL	GP	W-L-T	Mins	GA	SO	Avg
1	Ken Broderick	5	3–2–0	280	12	1	2.57
21	Wayne Stephenson	3	2–0–0	140	3	1	1.29

GOALIE NOTES
1. *Broderick (no goals) replaced Stephenson (2 goals) to start 2nd, February 11 vs. United States*

CHAPTER 12

The 11th and 12th Olympic Winter Games

CANADA WITHDRAWS FROM INTERNATIONAL COMPETITION

1972 and 1976

At the 65th IOC session in Rome on April 26, 1966, Sapporo easily won the right to host the 1972 Games with 32 votes over Banff (second again, with 16 votes), Lahti (seven votes), and Salt Lake City (seven votes).

When the IOC met for the 70th time, in Amsterdam, on May 13, 1970, it awarded the 1976 Games to Denver. Vancouver had been eliminated from consideration in the first round of voting, Tampere, Finland in the second round, and Sion, Switzerland lost to Denver (39–30 votes) in the third. However, fearing that the Games would have a negative impact on its environment, Denver withdrew as host on November 12, 1972, and Innsbruck volunteered to replace the Americans as host city.

ESTABLISHING "HOCKEY CANADA"

As a result of winning the 1968 federal election, Prime Minister Pierre Trudeau fulfilled a campaign promise by commissioning a Task Force on Sports aimed at understanding amateur hockey in Canada and why its programs had become increasingly unsuccessful in the past decade. The committee concluded that one organizing body should be created to oversee all levels of amateur hockey and control all necessary plans for national and international competitions. To this end, Hockey Canada Inc. was formed on February 24, 1969. A charitable organization that comprised the CAHA, CIAU, Fitness and Amateur Sport, and the NHL's two Canadian teams, the Leafs and Canadiens, its mandate was as complex as its wording was simple: "To support, operate, manage, and develop a national team or teams for the purpose of representing Canadian international tournaments and competitions. To foster and support the playing of hockey in Canada and in particular the development of the skill and competence of Canadian hockey players and, in this connection, to cooperate with other bodies, groups and associations having similar or related purposes and objectives."

Initially, though, Hockey Canada felt that since Canada was being awarded host country honours for the World Championships in 1970 for the first time (to be co-hosted by Winnipeg and Montreal), its goal should be to make it an open competition, one in which Canada's professionals could compete. When the IIHF met at Crans-sur-Sierre, Switzerland in July 1969, the question of professional participation headed the agenda, both because of Canada's discontent with the current set-up and our status as host nation for the 1970 Worlds. The IIHF agreed to allow nine non-NHL pros into each tournament for one year, after which a full review would decide the long-term future of the practice (the theory being that if *some* pros were allowed to play, Canada would be mollified, but that NHLers were of too high a calibre for the Europeans' liking). It wasn't all Hockey Canada had hoped for, but organizers were optimistic nonetheless.

The first significant test for the rule was the Isvestia tournament in Moscow at Christmas 1969. Canada used only five pros and finished a close second, and as a result the IIHF held an emergency meeting on January 3, 1970 immediately after the tournament's conclusion. At this time, president Avery Brundage did an about-face and announced that any players competing with Canada's pros in the future would be forfeiting their amateur status and would not be eligible to compete at the Olympics. Hockey Canada members were red with rage.

THE WITHDRAWAL

> Canada has withdrawn from the phoney world of international hockey and the vast majority of Canadians will applaud this decision. There was no point in messing around further with such hypocrites as the Swedes and the Russians. Canada couldn't gain anything from associating in such shabby sporting company. If you lie down to wallow with the pigs, you're certain to get fleas.
>
> Jim Coleman, *Toronto Telegram,*
> Monday, January 5, 1970

Since its participation in competition in 1956, the Soviets had dominated world tournaments because, not to mince words, they cheated. In Canada, the term routinely coined was "shamateurs," for the Olympics was becoming an ethical farce, on the one hand staunchly upholding ideals of sportsmanship, fair play, and clean competition, on the other allowing professionals from communist countries to participate.

In response to the IIHF's decision to force Canada's hand and rescind the earlier "nine pros" agreement, Earl Dawson, president of the CAHA, declared point blank that if the non-NHL pros were not given full international sanctions, Canada would not host the Worlds, would withdraw from international competition altogether, and would not send teams on goodwill exhibition tours through Europe in the future.

At a meeting in Geneva shortly after this announcement, Dawson seemed also to have come up with a favourable counter-proposal: the World Championships would be scrapped and replaced with an invitational series featuring five teams. No medals would be awarded, and Canada could field any team it wanted without jeopardizing the Olympic status of anyone from any of the five countries — Canada, USSR, Czechoslovakia, Finland, and Sweden. While the other countries ruminated over the idea, Brundage made clear his belief that this *would* compromise the players' Olympic eligibility. The other teams quickly backed away from the idea, and Canada made the proud and correct choice — it followed through on its threat and withdrew from all international competitions, except the Olympics. Dawson explained: "Canada will enter a team of amateurs in the 1972 Olympic Games and we intend to question the eligibility of every other team and make ineligible any and all teams which have played professionally."

Reaction in Canada to the decision was swift, unanimous, and fully supportive. John Munro, federal minister of national health and welfare, was first in line to praise those who made the tough decision: "Our country has not been able to ice the best teams because of farcical regulations which made it impossible to use players with the same experience as those other countries used. Canada has *some* pride."

Meanwhile, players with the other countries weren't really as concerned over their Olympic status as they were about implementing any rule change that helped Canada. Russia feared the nine Canadian pros would be enough to end their seven-year hold on the World Championships; Sweden became host now that Canada withdrew, thus giving their team a better chance of winning; East Germany and Czechoslovakia would do nothing to offend Mother Russia.

Canada, internationally, was on its own. As Bob Pennington pointed out in a column in the *Toronto Telegram* on January 5, 1970, the day after the withdrawal: "Olympic rules give a tremendous advantage to any communist country. It would be naive to think that Russia would voluntarily change such a sweet set-up particularly if honesty meant handing over a world crown to the fathers of hockey [Canada]."

David Molson, president of the Montreal Canadiens, was equally effusive in praise. "I'm in full agreement with the decision," he said. "We should have done it 10 years ago. I'm glad we stood up to them and did not compromise. It is a matter of principle." Abroad, praise was equally high for the Canadians' stance. In Sweden, the newspaper *Dagens Nyheter* said that, "[IOC president Bunny] Ahearne has conducted this confused affair so badly that he should now leave his post. Otherwise there is a great risk that the cold war will be protracted." In Finland's *Ilta Sanomat*, the editors concurred. "It is no longer reasonable to distinguish between professionals and amateurs. The Russian world champions are no less professionals than the Canadians. It is unnecessary to speak of 'pure amateurs' in any country."

CONTINUED RESISTANCE

Following Canada's withdrawal from hosting the World Championships, Stockholm filled in as host city at the last minute. At the 1969 Worlds, Canada's games drew 40 percent of the total attendance. In Stockholm, total attendance for the championships was down — 40 percent.

At the fourth plenary session of the CAHA's annual meeting on May 27, 1970, President Earl Dawson gave the members a detailed account of what had transpired over the past year in the wake of Canada's withdrawal:

> I attended the congress of the IIHF in Stockholm this past March, and Fred Page, your past president, the North American vice-president of the IIHF, and Gordon Juckes, who is one of the members of the council, attended as well. Mr. Hay of Hockey Canada attended as an observer.

At this meeting, our position was to reintroduce a resolution that had been approved at the July meeting held in 1969 in Crans, Switzerland, and this is the resolution which gave us permission to use nine professionals on our national team. After some considerable discussion, we were finally permitted to reintroduce that resolution and had it defeated. That put us in the position that the congress, at least for the next year, adopted the position that there would not be an open tournament and Canada would not be permitted to use any professionals on their hockey team.

We had a number of meetings with practically every country that was over there. Every country approached us on the basis of having a team visit their country and return a visit to our country. Our attitude, until we left, was non-committal. We decided that we would stand pat. If we couldn't have any professionals on our team or were not permitted to have an open competition, we were not going to entertain any thought of exchanging visits or having any European team come here or us going there.

I think that the Soviets, the Czechs, Finland have not suffered the financial loss that the other teams such as Sweden suffered. Because the Swedes suffered a financial loss by Canada not appearing there for the Ahearne Trophy, plus the world tournament, they took a different stand than they had in January which was a complete about-face. Anything Canada was introducing at the congress meetings, the Swedes were prepared to support. As a matter of fact, they introduced a couple of resolutions which would have eased our position had they been passed.

As it worked out, the Russians and Czechs, as I told you, and Switzerland, Finland, most of the countries, had private meetings with us and they all wanted us to go over there and we could bring anybody we wanted on the team, including Bobby Orr or Bobby Hull, it didn't matter to them. But when we asked the question, "What happens in the world tournament?" they said that is different. You must revert to a completely amateur team. In view of that, and in view of the stand we had taken in September, we gave up the tournament on the principle of not being allowed to use the best Canadian players. It was my recommendation to the board of directors yesterday that we adopt the same stand for the next season. It was endorsed by the board with a unanimous endorsation, with two people abstaining from the vote.

What I am saying is that the board of directors of the CAHA adopted the position that there will be no exchange visits between European countries next year. Our position will remain the same. They will not come here, nor will we go there.

Despite the huge support for the decision, one very serious question remained. Regardless of the medal results at all these Russian-won Games, the experience of playing international hockey was absolutely invaluable for young Canadian players. Without such experience, how could Canada hope to keep producing top-notch players? And what about Hockey Canada, an organization swamped with young men who learned and grew through international participation? Was it not still honourable to compete and play by the rules, even if no one else did? In a special report for the *Telegram,* former Leaf coach Punch Imlach wrote: "The national team has come a long way and it would be folly to discontinue operations just because the [world] tournament has been changed ... I have always thought that the stronger the amateur leagues, the stronger the professionals. A good foundation is always good business."

The conflict, then, was twofold. On the one hand, any time a country competes in a tournament, it wants to win. Canada would certainly have won *all* the Olympics had NHLers played. On the other hand though, since Canada couldn't use pros, should it still compete for the sake of the experience, even knowing the team probably wasn't going to win? The problem was that despite competing, Canada's international reputation was taking a battering and the country's hockey morale was slipping. Canada now seemed second-best to Russia because it kept placing second in tournaments. Canada's amateurs were still phenomenal athletes at a world level, *among* the best, but clearly not *the* best. The time had come to compete one-on-one, our best versus their best, winner take all — accolades, bragging rights, and rankings.

THE SUMMIT SERIES

After beating Canada 5–0 in the 1968 Olympics, Soviet coach Anatoly Tarasov defiantly boasted that his team could beat any in the NHL. Soon he would get his chance to prove it. Hockey Canada, through sublime negotiations, led by NHL Players' Association president and player agent Alan Eagleson, arranged an eight-game tournament with the Russians, the very best players in Canada against any team that the Soviets could put together. The first four games would be played in Canada, the last four in Moscow. The dates were September 1–28, 1972.

The player selections for the two teams told a story in itself. The Russians had 13 players who had played at the Sapporo Winter Olympics earlier in the year and, incredibly, seven men who had played against Canada at the 1968 Winter Olympics at Grenoble. Team Canada had not one player for the Summit Series who had any international experience, fully indicating Canada had never had the chance to play its best at the world level while confirming that Russia used only its best at all times.

The series proved a defining moment in Canada's cultural and sporting history, easily the most remarkable example of the bond between national identity and sport uniting Canada from coast to coast. Down 3–1 in games with one tie, the Canadians had to win the last three matches, all in Russia, if they were to win the series and prove themselves the best, to erase the years of accusations of cheating and fraud they had hurled at the Russians each Olympics and World Championships.

Today, Canadians over 35 recall vividly where they were on September 28, 1972 when Foster Hewitt screamed across the nation's television sets that "Henderson has scored for Canada!" This remarkable Summit Series proved a number of things: Canada had better players, and many more of them, than Russia; Russia's "pro" team was the same as their "amateur" team; and the gap between them and us wasn't as great as we had thought. Canadian pride, integrity, fortitude, desire, and heart won the series and established a reputation that has won this country many, many games and medals over the years.

Despite the unparalleled success of this head-to-head matchup, the IOC and IIHF were no closer to allowing professionals to join the Olympic ranks than they were before 1972. Canada continued not to enter the Worlds or Olympics, and the Russians continued to win. When the 1976 Winter Games came along, both sides hadn't altered their feelings one iota. Canada wanted to use professionals; the IOC was adamantly opposed. Canada again did not send a hockey team, but this time it was not alone. Sweden, Norway, and East Germany also passed on the Games, a protest that was recognized by the IIHF but not the IOC as significant. In response, the IIHF announced that beginning in 1977, the World Championships would be open to professionals. Canada immediately announced its intention to compete the following year. No such declaration came from the IOC, however, and this time Alan Eagleson organized a true world championship, the inaugural Canada Cup. And, just to make sure the taint of "amateur," or, more rightly, "shamateur," would never darken the Canada Cup's doors, Eagleson announced that $150,000 in prize money was to be won, in addition to the beautiful trophy and international prestige!

The Canada Cup differed from the Summit Series in that six nations — Canada,

USSR, Czechoslovakia, Sweden, Finland, and the United States — would compete in a round-robin tournament, culminating with a best-of-three finals. This time, the Russians didn't even make the finals and, as to be expected, Canada won handily and dramatically over the Czechs when Darryl Sittler faked goalie Dzurilla outside and slid the puck into the open net. Canada had once again asserted its world hockey superiority.

THE 1977 WORLD CHAMPIONSHIPS: CANADA RETURNS

At the opening of the tournament in Vienna, IIHF secretary Walter Wasservogel openly defied the IOC, saying, "It's a big lie. They [the hockey players] are all professionals ... the people want to see the best athletes in the world, and the best athletes of the world are professional. My personal opinion is that if the Olympic Games aren't open in the next, let's say eight years, they are finished."

Perhaps the most significant event in the process of reconciliation between Canada and the IIHF came in the summer of 1975 when the IIHF replaced Bunny Ahearne with Gunther Sabetzki as president. Sabetzki immediately announced that getting Canada back on side was his top priority, and to this end Alan Eagleson represented Hockey Canada in meetings intended to solve the amateur-pro rift.

Negotiations focused on two events, the inaugural 1976 Canada Cup and Canada's participation in the 1977 World Championships in Vienna.

The IIHF agreed to sanction the Canada Cup and was, in turn, given a flat fee of $25,000, 5 percent of TV revenues generated by the five non-Canadian entries in the tournament, and a $100,000 bond guaranteeing Canada's commitment to the '77 Worlds. This agreement was definitely a trade-off. Canada got its Canada Cup, which it won in dramatic fashion, but even though it could now send pros to Vienna, the tournament was still held in early spring, from April 21–May 8, 1977, a time when the NHL playoffs were in full swing. Thus, the only real pros who could participate were those on NHL teams that did not make the playoffs or were eliminated quickly. They would be playing at the end of a 90-game season (exhibition and regular season), have virtually no time to gel as a team and become a unit, and have to adapt almost instantly to jet lag and a significant culture change. Further, while the team left Toronto on April 5, 1977 for an eight-game exhibition tour beginning in Göteborg, Sweden, nine more players arrived a week later in Düsseldorf after their teams had been eliminated from the first round of the playoffs. Thus, most of what was positive about the tour was offset by the infusion of new, unfamiliar players who had little time to fit in.

All in all, the gesture of allowing pros to participate at the World Championships was as hollow as it was generous. It was a sign of progress, but of microscopic proportions. The IIHF refused in future years to push the date of the Worlds back so as to allow better players to represent Canada, and the dates for submitting final rosters was, in reality, a precarious gamble for whoever coached the Canadian entry. Further, for 1977, the IIHF refused to allow Canadians to play without helmets, which, at the time, virtually all of them had done their entire careers (a problem that was as much psychological as athletic). In 1977, Team Canada beat the teams it should have beaten — United States, Czechoslovakia, Finland, West Germany, and Romania — but lost to Sweden and were hammered 11–1 by the Russians in the preliminary round. In the medal round, they clobbered the Swedes 7–0 and the Czechs 8–2 but were again thrashed by the Russians 8–1.

The IIHF got its way — Canada was back in the international picture — but Canada was still participating under a series of huge disadvantages. The Summit Series and the Canada Cup proved that Canada's best were consistently the best in the world — albeit narrowly — but hastily assembled teams couldn't possibly be expected to beat a Russian team that trained year-round with the express purpose of peaking for the World Championships. That was their Stanley Cup, and we would never win it with makeshift squads that were, for the most part, entirely unused to international competition, no matter how seasoned they were in the NHL.

Team Canada 1977 World Championships Roster:
Guy Charron, Ron Ellis, Phil Esposito, Tony Esposito, Rod Gilbert, Rick Hampton, Dennis Kearns, Ralph Klassen, Pierre Larouche, Al MacAdam, Wayne Merrick, Walt McKechnie, Wilf Paiement, Jean Pronovost, Phil Russell, Jim Rutherford, Dallas Smith, Greg Smith, Carol Vadnais, Eric Vail

1972 Sapporo Olympics

FINAL STANDINGS

GROUP A

	GP	W	L	T	GF	GA	P
USSR	5	4	0	1	33	13	9
United States	5	3	2	0	18	15	6
Czechoslovakia	5	3	2	0	26	13	6
Sweden	5	2	2	1	17	13	5
Finland	5	2	3	0	14	24	4
Poland	5	0	5	0	9	39	0

RESULTS

FEBRUARY 5
Sweden 5 United States 1
Czechoslovakia 14 Poland 1
USSR 9 Finland 3

FEBRUARY 7
Sweden 3 USSR 3
United States 5 Czechoslovakia 1
Finland 5 Poland 1

FEBRUARY 8
Czechoslovakia 7 Finland 1

FEBRUARY 9
Sweden 5 Poland 3
USSR 7 United States 2

FEBRUARY 10
USSR 9 Poland 3
Czechoslovakia 2 Sweden 1
United States 4 Finland 1

FEBRUARY 12
United States 6 Poland 1

FEBRUARY 13
Finland 4 Sweden 3
USSR 5 Czechoslovakia 2

GROUP B

	GP	W	L	T	GF	GA	P
Germany	4	3	1	0	22	10	6
Norway	4	3	1	0	16	14	6
Japan	4	2	1	1	17	16	5
Switzerland	4	0	2	2	9	16	2
Yugoslavia	4	0	3	1	9	17	1

RESULTS

FEBRUARY 6
Norway 5 Yugoslavia 2
Germany 5 Switzerland 0

FEBRUARY 7
Switzerland 3 Japan 3
Germany 6 Yugoslavia 2

FEBRUARY 9
Japan 3 Yugoslavia 2
Germany 5 Norway 1

FEBRUARY 10
Norway 5 Japan 4
Switzerland 3 Yugoslavia 3

FEBRUARY 12
Japan 7 Germany 6
Norway 5 Switzerland 3

FINAL PLACINGS

GOLD MEDAL
USSR

SILVER MEDAL
United States

BRONZE MEDAL
Czechoslovakia

FOURTH PLACE
Sweden

FIFTH PLACE
Finland

SIXTH PLACE
Poland

SEVENTH PLACE
West Germany

EIGHTH PLACE
Norway

NINTH PLACE
Japan

TENTH PLACE
Switzerland

ELEVENTH PLACE
Yugoslavia

1972 Summit Series

RESULTS

GAME 1 •	USSR 7	Canada 3 (Montreal)	GAME 5 •	USSR 5	Canada 4 (Moscow)
GAME 2 •	Canada 4	USSR 1 (Toronto)	GAME 6 •	Canada 3	USSR 2 (Moscow)
GAME 3 •	Canada 4	USSR 4 (Winnipeg)	GAME 7 •	Canada 4	USSR 3 (Moscow)
GAME 4 •	USSR 5	Canada 3 (Vancouver)	GAME 8 •	Canada 6	USSR 5 (Moscow)

1972 Innsbruck Olympics

FINAL PLACINGS

GOLD MEDAL
USSR

SILVER MEDAL
Czechoslovakia

BRONZE MEDAL
West Germany

FOURTH PLACE
Finland

FIFTH PLACE
United States

SIXTH PLACE
Poland

SEVENTH PLACE
Romania

EIGHTH PLACE
Austria

NINTH PLACE
Japan

TENTH PLACE
Yugoslavia

ELEVENTH PLACE (tie)
Switzerland
Norway

THIRTEENTH PLACE
Bulgaria

FINAL STANDINGS

GROUP A

	GP	W	L	T	GF	GA	P
USSR	5	5	0	0	40	11	10
Czechoslovakia	5	3	2	0	24	10	6
West Germany	5	2	3	0	21	24	4
Finland	5	2	3	0	19	18	4
United States	5	2	3	0	15	21	4
Poland	5	1	4	0	9	44	2

RESULTS

FEBRUARY 6
West Germany 7 Poland 4
USSR 6 United States 2
Czechoslovakia 2 Finland 1

FEBRUARY 8
USSR 16 Poland 1
Finland 5 West Germany 3
Czechoslovakia 5 United States 0

FEBRUARY 10
United States 5 Finland 4
Czechoslovakia 7 Poland 1
USSR 7 West Germany 3

FEBRUARY 12
United States 7 Poland 2
Czechoslovakia 7 West Germany 4
USSR 7 Finland 2

FEBRUARY 14
West Germany 4 United States 1
Finland 7 Poland 1
USSR 4 Czechoslovakia 3

GROUP B

	GP	W	L	T	GF	GA	P
Romania	5	4	1	0	23	15	8
Austria	5	3	2	0	18	14	6
Japan	5	3	2	0	20	18	6
Yugoslavia	5	3	2	0	22	19	6
Switzerland	5	2	3	0	24	22	4
Bulgaria	5	0	5	0	19	38	0

RESULTS

FEBRUARY 5
Yugoslavia 6 Switzerland 4
Romania 3 Japan 1
Austria 6 Bulgaria 2

FEBRUARY 7
Yugoslavia 4 Romania 3
Switzerland 8 Bulgaria 3
Austria 3 Japan 2

FEBRUARY 9
Yugoslavia 8 Bulgaria 5
Japan 6 Switzerland 4
Romania 4 Austria 3

FEBRUARY 11
Romania 9 Bulgaria 4
Japan 4 Yugoslavia 3
Switzerland 5 Austria 3

FEBRUARY 13
Japan 7 Bulgaria 5
Romania 4 Switzerland 3
Austria 3 Yugoslavia 1

1976 Canada Cup

FINAL STANDINGS ROUND ROBIN

	GP	W	L	T	GF	GA	P
Canada	5	4	1	0	22	6	8
Czechoslovakia	5	3	1	1	19	9	7
USSR	5	2	2	1	23	14	5
Sweden	5	2	2	1	16	18	5
United States	5	1	3	1	14	21	3
Finland	5	1	4	0	16	42	2

RESULTS

SEPTEMBER 2
Canada 11 Finland 2

SEPTEMBER 3
Sweden 5 United States 2
Czechoslovakia 5 USSR 3

SEPTEMBER 5
Canada 4 United States 2
Czechoslovakia 8 Finland 0
Sweden 3 USSR 3

SEPTEMBER 7
Canada 4 Sweden 0
Czechoslovakia 4 United States 4
USSR 11 Finland 3

SEPTEMBER 9
Czechoslovakia 1 Canada 0
USSR 5 United States 0
Finland 8 Sweden 6

SEPTEMBER 11
Canada 3 USSR 1
Sweden 2 Czechoslovakia 1
United States 6 Finland 3

CANADA CUP FINALS (best of three)

SEPTEMBER 13
Game 1 • Canada 6 Czechoslovakia 0

SEPTEMBER 15
Game 2 • Canada 5 Czechoslovakia 4 (OT)

CHAPTER 13

The 13th Olympic Winter Games

LAKE PLACID, UNITED STATES

February 12–24, 1980

Dan D'Alvise

When the IOC convened its 75th session, in Vienna, on October 23, 1974, it chose Lake Placid for the 1980 Games in an uncontested selection. No other country had come forward to offer either opposition or objection to the American bid.

TEAM CANADA • 1980

Bob Dupuis, *GOAL*
Paul Pageau, *GOAL*

Warren Anderson, *DEFENCE*
Joe Grant, *DEFENCE*
Randy Gregg, *DEFENCE (CAPTAIN)*
Terry O'Malley, *DEFENCE*
Brad Pirie, *DEFENCE*
Don Spring, *DEFENCE*
Tim Watters, *DEFENCE*

Glenn Anderson, *FORWARD*
Ken Berry, *FORWARD*
Dan D'Alvise, *FORWARD*
Ron Davidson, *FORWARD*
John Devaney, *FORWARD*
Dave Hindmarch, *FORWARD*

Paul MacLean, *FORWARD*
Kevin Maxwell, *FORWARD*
Jim Nill, *FORWARD*
Kevin Primeau, *FORWARD*
Stelio Zupancich, *FORWARD*

Doug Buchanan *(DID NOT PLAY)*
Cary Farelli *(DID NOT PLAY)*
Roger Lamoureux *(DID NOT PLAY)*
Ron Paterson *(DID NOT PLAY)*
Shane Pearsall *(DID NOT PLAY)*

Lorne Davis, *CO-COACH*
Clare Drake, *CO-COACH*
Tom Watt, *CO-COACH*
Rick Noonan, *MANAGER*
Father David Bauer, *MANAGING DIRECTOR*

FINAL PLACINGS

GOLD MEDAL
United States

SILVER MEDAL
USSR

BRONZE MEDAL
Sweden

FOURTH PLACE
Finland

FIFTH PLACE
Czechoslovakia

SIXTH PLACE
Canada

SEVENTH PLACE
Poland

EIGHTH PLACE
Romania

NINTH PLACE (tie)
Holland
Norway

ELEVENTH PLACE
West Germany

TWELFTH PLACE
Japan

The important thing in the Olympic Games is not to win, but to take part. The important thing in life is not the triumph but the struggle. The essential thing is not to have conquered but to have fought well.

Pierre, baron de Coubertin (1863–1937), founder of the modern Olympics

THE HOCKEY PROGRAM REBORN

Although Father David Bauer's dream of a national junior team came to fruition between 1963 and 1969, Canada's withdrawal from international hockey pretty much ended the need for the concept. However, with Canada's return to the World Championships in 1977 and the Olympics in 1980, Father Bauer was able to convince Hockey Canada to reinstitute his idea of one team that trained together for a full season. The argument was still sound and since there was none better, training camp opened in Calgary in August 1979 to full national support.

As before, players came mostly from Canadian universities, which was why Father Bauer selected coaches Tom Watt (University of Toronto) and Clare Drake (University of Alberta) to select the camp roster. Between them, Watt and Drake had won 11 of the previous 12 national titles, an achievement which certainly attested to their abilities to work with young players and their thorough knowledge of the CIAU (Canadian Intrauniversity Athletic Union). In certain cases, Watt and Drake also added Canadian players attending American colleges on scholarships, and those playing in other countries.

The players lived in the "Rig," portable dormitories donated by an oil company that had used them previously at a drilling site in Alaska, and they practised at the Calgary Corral. The team participated in the challenging Rudi Pravo tournament in Prague in September, played six games against NHL clubs (losing only

to Washington and the Rangers), won four of six exhibitions against the American national team, and then hosted a series of matches against the Moscow Dynamo, the Czech "B" team, and colleges across North America. In December, the team was divided into two groups, one heading for the Isvestia tournament in Moscow, the other to an important pre-Olympic tournament in Lake Placid.

LAST-MINUTE PLAYER CUTS

While Canada's national hockey team had been together for the better part of six months, paring the team down to the final Olympic roster to be submitted before the Games proved to be the unkindest cut of all for five of the players who had given their hearts to the program but were deemed unnecessary by the coaching staff. They were: Shane Pearsall, Ron Paterson, Doug Buchanan, Cary Farelli, and Roger Lamoureaux. Their efforts helped sustain the program, nurture the talent, and prepare Canada for the Olympics, and to be told to go home was, of course, part of the gamble of participating in the program, but still a devastating disappointment.

Kevin Maxwell fights for position with Yuri Lebedev during the always-important Canada–Soviet Union match.

THE CANADA–USSR SHOWDOWN

As usual, this game would almost certainly decide the gold medal. Despite being heavy underdogs, a team of university students going up against one that had been playing half a dozen years or more together (seven players in this lineup had been on the 1972 Summit Series team), the proud Canadians almost stole a victory. It wasn't until midway through the third that the Russians gained a lead they didn't relinquish, though earlier in the period a controversy broke out over Vladimir Golikov's hooked stick.

Team Canada alleged that Golikov had scored his third-period goal using an illegal blade (he scored late in the third, as well, to make the score 6–4). To get the proof, Canada's Stelio Zupancich went to the Russian bench to get Golikov's stick by force to show referee Jim Neagles, but Zupancich was stopped at the gate by coach Viktor Tikhonov. Shoving ensued, Neagles simply ignored the accusation, and the Russians carried on. "What we should have done," opined Ron Davidson afterwards, "was tackle Golikov and grab his stick before he got off the ice."

While both teams stood at their respective blue lines for the playing of the Russian national anthem after the Soviet victory, it was Canada that received a standing ovation from the supportive fans for their incredible fight, collegians playing stride for stride with the best Russia could offer. What was the difference in talent? These were the best players in the whole Soviet Union, while of the 20 members of the Canadian team, only nine had played more than two games in the NHL!

LAKE PLACID — POOR HOSTS

After the unpleasant Squaw Valley experience in 1960, the IOC was in no hurry to return to the United States for the Winter Games, but when no other country put in a bid for 1980, Lake Placid was given this Olympics by default. Unfortunately, the

Americans proved to be no better hosts this time round, as complaints rained down on the Lake Placid organizers, from fans right up to the IOC president himself.

On the first Saturday of the Games, more than 12,000 spectators were stranded while waiting for buses that never came. New York Governor Hugh Carey was forced to declare a limited state of emergency to get more buses to Lake Placid before travel within the pretty little town became all but impossible. Then, there was major trouble with tickets being wrongly or improperly issued. As these two problems began to overtake the running of the Games, another quarrel sprang up between ABC, the US network that had paid $15.5 million for the exclusive broadcasting rights, and certain newspapers, notably the *Washington Post*. The *Post* vilified ABC for ignoring the obvious issues of the plague-ridden Games, printing headlines such as "ABC Fouls Up On Games Foul-ups."

A column by Tony Kornheiser in the *Post* was even more scathing: "It seems clear that [ABC broadcaster Jim] McKay sees himself as the FDR [referring to former president Franklin Delano Roosevelt] of sportscasting; that he longs for the thrill of victory, sitting by the Olympic torch, all snuggy-pooh in his cashmere sweater, babbling along, setting a new world and Olympic record for most tripe spewed in any given hour."

While ABC staunchly defended its mandate and coverage, it made an enormous scheduling blunder. Somehow they managed to deny Americans the chance to see their hockey team beat the Russians 4–3 live, arguably the greatest game an American hockey team had ever played to date. Instead, ABC aired the game later, taped, after the fact, with all the drama and impact lost.

Also, the Lake Placid organizing committee had apparently given the problem of accommodation little serious thought. The athletes lived in a village which the IOC president referred to as a "jail." That description was more apt than he had realized, for after the Games the building would, indeed, become a minimum security prison. As for fans and ticket-holders, two choices were available: rent a nearby house for a month (minimum) for about $15,000, or stay well away from Lake Placid. Many tour companies were offering packages that included beds in Albany, Plattsburgh, and even Montreal, providing shuttles, even helicopters, to and from events!

THE NATIONAL HOCKEY DREAM REVIVED

While the Canadians may have lost on the scoreboard to the Russians that final afternoon in Lake Placid, they won the emotional battle and were so impressive that the result could almost be said to have kept Father Bauer's national program alive. "I think our objectives have been partially realized," he concluded, "but we have to hope that playing for their country doesn't obscure the other values to be derived from this experience. The whole rationale was to provide another option wherein some form of education could be involved, wherein some experiences other than hockey might be a part of human growth. These fellows have received pretty good coaching; they've improved their skills; hopefully this experience broadened their horizons. I think the game against the Russians brought all of these together."

Lou Lefaive, president of Hockey Canada, was equally buoyed by the results: "There's no question that the [national team] concept is one that we're going to keep alive and we'll try to keep as many of these players as we can. We're taking them to a tournament in Sweden in April almost as a unit ... we'll try to bring this team together, as many of them that we can, for the Pravda tournament, for the Isvestia tournament, and we'll be gearing towards next year's World Championship in Sweden." The concept of a national dream was still, however, very much a compromise between only competing and doing everything possible to win. Canada was allowed to have pros at the World Championships (governed by the IIHF) as compensation for guaranteeing a committment to the Olympics without pros (governed by the IOC).

Action from the only Canada–Holland game ever played at the Olympics, February 12, 1980.

However, while IIHF president Gunther Sabetszki was trying to convince the IOC to allow pros to participate in the Games, it was a gesture that carried with it few practical results because of the structure of the NHL season. A national amateur team was an excellent way of developing talent, but at the day's end that talent still wasn't likely to win a gold medal or be skilled enough to make the NHL.

Canada was clearly in a no-win situation. We looked bad sending university students with little chance of winning to the Olympics, but the best players in the country were not available to assure victory. Everyone knew Canada had the best players, and winning was as important to national morale as competing was to international sportsmanship.

The Competition

TOURNAMENT FORMAT

Twelve teams were divided into two groups and played a round-robin schedule in each division. The top two teams from each then advanced to a four-team, medal-round round-robin. In case of a tie in the standings, the winner of the head-to-head meeting would be awarded the superior position. Games tied after 60 minutes' regulation time would *not* be decided by an overtime period.

THE OPPOSITION

CZECHOSLOVAKIA • Jiri Bubla, Milan Chalupa, Vitezslav Duris, Miroslav Dvorak, Bohuslav Ebermann, Miroslav Frycer, Karel Holy, Frantisek Kaberle, Arnold Kadlec, Jiri Kralik, Karel Lang, Vincent Lukac, Jan Neliba, Jiri Novak, Milan Novy, Jaroslav Pouzar, Anton Stastny, Marian Stastny, Peter Stastny

FINLAND • Kari Eloranta, Hannu Haapalainen, Markku Hakulinen, Markku Kiimalainen, Antero Kivela, Jukka Koskilahti, Hannu Koskinen, Jari Kurri, Mikko Leinonen, Reijo Leppanen, Tapio Levo, Lasse Litma, Jarmo Makitalo, Esa Peltonen, Jukka Porvari, Olli Saarinen, Seppo Suoraniemi, Timo Susi, Jorma Valtonen, Ismo Villa

HOLLAND • Ron Berteling, Klaas van de Broek, Brian de Bruyn, John de Bruyn, Dick de Cloe, Rick van Gog, Corky de Graauw, Jack de Heer, Harry van Heumen, Henk Hille, Chuck Huizinga, Jan Janssen, William Klooster, Patrick Kolijn, Leo Koopmans, Ted Lenssen, Georg Peternousek, Al Pluymers, Frank van Soldt, Larrie van Wieren

JAPAN • Takeshi Azuma, Tadamitsu Fujii, Tsutomu Hanzawa, Yoshiaki Honda, Sadaki Honma, Hiroshi Hori, Yoshio Hoshino, Mikio Hosoi, Takeshi Iawmoto, Norio Ito, Katsuyoshi Kawamura, Mikio Matsuda, Minoru Misawa, Satoru Misawa, Hitoshi Nakamura, Iwao Nakayama, Hideo Sakurai, Hideo Urabe, Koji Wkasa

NORWAY • Trond Abrahamsen, Knut Andresen, Knut Fjeldsgaard, Stephen Foyn, Peystein Jarlsbo, Morten Johansen, Vidar Johansen, Oeivind Loesaamoen, Haakon Lundenes, Jim Martinsen, Thor Martinsen, Rune Molberg, Geir Myhre, Nils Nilsen, Tore Falk Nilsen, Erik Pedersen, Tom Roeymark, Morten Sethereng, Petter Thoresen, Tore Waalberg

POLAND • Stefan Chowaniec, Bogdan Dziubinski, Henryk Gruth, Leszek Jachna, Andrzej Janczy, Henryk Janiszewski, Wieslaw Jobczyk, Stanislaw Klocek, Leszek Kokoszka, Pawel Lukaszka, Andrzej Malysiak, Marek Marcinczak, Tadeusz Obloj, Jerzy Potz, Henryk Pytel, Dariusz Sikora, Ludwik Synowiec, Andrzej Ujwary, Henryk Wajtynek, Andrzej Zabawa

ROMANIA • Elod Antal, Istvan Antal, Dumitru Axinte, Ion Berdila, Traian Cazacu, Marian Costea, Sandor Gall, Alexandru Haauca, Gheorghe Hutan, George Justinian, Doru Morosan, Bela Nagy, Zoltan Nagy, Valerian Netedu, Constantin Nistor, Adrian Olenici, Marian Pisaru, Mihail Popescu, Laszlo Solyom, Doru Tureanu

SWEDEN • Mats Ahlberg, Sture Andersson, Bo Berglund, Hakan Eriksson, Jan Eriksson, Thomas Eriksson, Leif Holmgren, Tomas Jonsson, Per-Eric "Pelle" Lindbergh, William Lofquist, Harald Luckner, Bengt Lundholm, Per Lundquist, Lars Mohlin, Mats Naslund, Lennart Norberg, Tommy Samuelsson, Dan Soderstrom, Mats Waltin, Ulf Weinstock

UNITED STATES • William Baker, Neal Broten, Dave Christian, Steve Christoff, Jim Craig, Mike Eruzione, John Harrington, Mark Johnson, Rob McClanahan, Ken Morrow, John O'Callahan, Mark Pavelich, Mike Ramsey, William "Buzz" Schneider, Dave Silk, Eric Strobel, Bob Suter, Phil Verchota, Mark Wells

USSR • Helmut Balderis, Zinetula Bilyaletdinov, Vyacheslav Fetisov, Aleksandr Golikov, Vladimir Golikov, Aleksei Kasatonov, Valery Kharlamov, Vladimir Krutov, Yuri Lebedev, Sergei Makarov, Aleksandr Maltsev, Boris Mikhailov, Vladimir Myshkin, Vasily Pervukhin, Vladimir Petrov, Aleksandr Skvortsov, Sergei Starikov, Vladislav Tretiak, Valery Vasileyev, Viktor Zluktov

WEST GERMANY • Klaus Auhuber, Ulrich Egen, Bernhard Englbrecht, Hermann Hinterstocker, Martin Hinterstocker, Ernst Hofner, Udo Kiessling, Horst-Peter Kretschmer, Harald Krull, Marcus Kuhl, Holger Meitinger, Rainer Phillipp, Joachim Reil, Franz Reindl, Peter Scharf, Sigmund Suttner, Gerhard Truntschka, Vladimir Vacatko, Martin Wild, Hans Zach

FINAL STANDINGS

PRELIMINARY ROUND • Red Division

	GP	W	L	T	GF	GA	P
USSR	5	5	0	0	51	11	10
Finland	5	3	2	0	26	18	6
Canada	5	3	2	0	28	12	6
Poland	5	2	3	0	15	23	4
Holland	5	1	3	1	16	43	3
Japan	5	0	4	1	7	36	1

RESULTS

FEBRUARY 12
Canada 10 Holland 1
Poland 5 Finland 4
USSR 16 Japan 0

FEBRUARY 14
Canada 5 Poland 1
USSR 17 Holland 4
Finland 6 Japan 3

FEBRUARY 16
Finland 4 Canada 3
USSR 8 Poland 1
Holland 3 Japan 3

FEBRUARY 18
Canada 6 Japan 0
Holland 5 Poland 3
USSR 4 Finland 2

FEBRUARY 20
USSR 6 Canada 4
Finland 10 Holland 3
Poland 5 Japan 1

PRELIMINARY ROUND • Blue Division

	GP	W	L	T	GF	GA	P
Sweden	5	4	0	1	26	7	9
United States	5	4	0	1	25	10	9
Czechoslovakia	5	3	2	0	34	16	6
Romania	5	1	3	1	13	29	3
West Germany	5	1	4	0	21	30	2
Norway	5	0	4	1	9	36	1

RESULTS

FEBRUARY 12
Czechoslovakia 11 Norway 0
Romania 6 West Germany 4
Sweden 2 United States 2

FEBRUARY 14
Sweden 8 Romania 0
West Germany 10 Norway 4
United States 7 Czechoslovakia 3

FEBRUARY 16
Czechoslovakia 7 Romania 2
Sweden 5 West Germany 2
United States 5 Norway 1

FEBRUARY 18
Sweden 7 Norway 1
Czechoslovakia 11 West Germany 3
United States 7 Romania 2

FEBRUARY 20
Sweden 4 Czechoslovakia 2
Norway 3 Romania 3
United States 4 West Germany 2

MEDAL ROUND FINAL STANDINGS

	GP	W	L	T	GF	GA	P
United States	3	2	0	1	10	7	5
USSR	3	2	1	0	16	8	4
Sweden	3	0	1	2	7	14	2
Finland	3	0	2	1	7	11	1

CARRY OVER RESULTS

Russia 4 Finland 2
Sweden 2 United States 2

RESULTS

FEBRUARY 22
Czechoslovakia 6 Canada 1
(5th place game)

FEBRUARY 22
Finland 3 Sweden 3
United States 4 USSR 3

FEBRUARY 24
USSR 9 Sweden 2
United States 4 Finland 2

TEAM CANADA GAME SUMMARIES

FEBRUARY 12 • Canada 10 Holland 1

IN GOAL
Canada — Dupuis
Holland — Lenssen

SHOTS ON GOAL

Canada			
10	13	17	**40**
Holland			
10	5	5	**20**

FIRST PERIOD
1. Holland, de Graauw (de Cloe) • 1:56(sh)
2. Canada, Primeau (Devaney) • 4:04
3. Canada, Berry (Maxwell, O'Malley) • 11:40
penalties: *Hille (Hol) 1:34, D'Alvise (Can) 13:55, W. Anderson (Can) 14:50, Janssen (Hol) 15:32, Nill (Can) 18:20*

SECOND PERIOD
4. Canada, D'Alvise (O'Malley) • 6:52
5. Canada, Hindmarch (Devaney) • 15:02(pp)
penalties: *Primeau (Can) 1:17, Janssen (Hol) & Berry (Can) 3:36, W. Anderson (Can) 8:28, de Cloe (Hol) 14:49, de Heer (Hol) 19:49*

THIRD PERIOD
6. Canada, G. Anderson (Davidson, Nill) • 3:31
7. Canada, D'Alvise (Zupancich, Pirie) • 4:14
8. Canada, Devaney (Primeau, Hindmarch) • 10:35(pp)
9. Canada, Berry (Watters, Maxwell) • 11:11(pp)
10. Canada, Berry (Maxwell, MacLean) • 12:22
11. Canada, Hindmarch (MacLean, Davidson) • 18:11
penalties: *Berry (Can) 6:56, de Cloe (Hol — double minor) 9:07, Pluymers (Hol) & Devaney (Can) 15:55, MacLean (Can) 18:11*

FEBRUARY 14 • Canada 5 Poland 1

IN GOAL
Canada — Pageau
Poland — Wajtynek

SHOTS ON GOAL

Canada			
9	16	11	**36**
Poland			
8	6	11	**25**

FIRST PERIOD
1. Canada, Zupancich (Pirie, D'Alvise) • 3:17
penalties: *none*

SECOND PERIOD
2. Poland, Jobczyk (Zabawa) • 3:17
3. Canada, Watters (G. Anderson, Spring) • 10:56
4. Canada, Berry (Maxwell, MacLean) • 12:06
penalties: *none*

THIRD PERIOD
5. Canada, Devaney (Hindmarch, Gregg) • 7:42
6. Canada, Primeau (unassisted) • 13:29
penalties: *none*

FEBRUARY 16 • Finland 4 Canada 3

FIRST PERIOD

1. Finland, Peltonen (Suoraniemi) • 4:03

2. Canada, MacLean (Berry, O'Malley) • 14:22

3. Finland, Leppanen (Hakulinen, Levo) • 19:51

penalties: *Berry (Can) & Litma (Fin) 2:06, Nill (Can) 6:04, Saarinen (Fin) 8:21, D'Alvise (Can) 10:41, G. Anderson (Can) 11:02, Grant (Can) 17:51*

SECOND PERIOD

4. Finland, Koskilahti (unassisted) • 17:07

penalties: *Kurri (Fin) 11:52*

THIRD PERIOD

5. Canada, G. Anderson (Nill, Davidson) • 6:47

6. Finland, Suoraniemi (Leppanen) • 16:55(sh)

7. Canada, Primeau (Hindmarch, Devaney) • 17:09(pp)

penalties: *Primeau (Can) 11:59, Kurri (Fin) 15:20, Hindmarch (Can) & Litma (Fin) 17:25, Haapalainen (Fin) 18:12*

IN GOAL

Canada — Dupuis

Finland — Valtonen

SHOTS ON GOAL

Canada	9	8	16	**33**
Finland	9	11	6	**26**

FEBRUARY 18 • Canada 6 Japan 0

FIRST PERIOD

1. Canada, Devaney (Zupancich, D'Alvise) • 9:36(pp)

2. Canada, Primeau (unassisted) • 14:35

penalties: *Maxwell (Can) 4:02, Wkasa (Jap) 5:02, Nakayama (Jap) 7:44, Honda (Jap) 18:30*

SECOND PERIOD

3. Canada, MacLean (Maxwell) • 3:17

4. Canada, Davidson (unassisted) • 6:19

penalties: *Urabe (Jap) & D'Alvise (Can) 9:27, Maxwell (Can) 11:02, Berry (Can) & Nakamura (Jap) 14:46, Zupancich (Can) 15:26, Urabe (Jap) 16:27, Fujii (Jap) 17:44, Devaney (Can) & Nakamura (Jap) 18:40*

THIRD PERIOD

5. Canada, W. Anderson (unassisted) • 1:27

6. Canada, Hindmarch (unassisted) • 10:22

penalties: *Nakamura (Jap) 7:37, Urabe (Jap) 12:13, Azuma (Jap) & Devaney (Can) 18:07*

IN GOAL

Canada — Pageau

Japan — M. Misawa

SHOTS ON GOAL

Canada	13	12	23	**48**
Japan	5	6	2	**13**

FEBRUARY 20 • USSR 6 Canada 4

FIRST PERIOD

1. Canada, Nill (Davidson, G. Anderson) • 1:35

2. USSR, Balderis (Skvortsov, Zluktov) • 13:42

penalties: *Hindmarch (Can) 6:08, Gregg (Can) 10:47*

SECOND PERIOD

3. Canada, Gregg (unassisted) • 0:19

4. Canada, Pirie (Zupancich, D'Alvise) • 2.38

5. USSR, Kasatonov (Krutov) • 19:47

penalties: *Fetisov (USSR) 5:10, MacLean (Can) 6:44, Kasatonov (USSR) 7:58, G. Anderson (Can) & Kasatonov (USSR) 10:49, Pirie (Can) 15:45*

THIRD PERIOD

6. USSR, Mikhailov (Golikov) • 1:53

7. USSR, Golikov (Makarov) • 2:05

8. Canada, D'Alvise (unassisted) • 3:05

9. USSR, Mikhailov (Starikov) • 8:41

10. USSR, Golikov (unassisted) • 16:51

penalties: *Can (too many men) 14:16*

IN GOAL

Canada — Pageau

USSR — Tretiak

SHOTS ON GOAL

Canada	6	11	9	**26**
USSR	12	5	18	**35**

FEBRUARY 22 • Czechoslovakia 6 Canada 1

IN GOAL

Canada — Dupuis/Pageau *(Pageau (4 goals) replaced Dupuis (2 goals) at 2:14 of 1st)*

Czechoslovakia — Kralik

SHOTS ON GOAL

Canada			
9	7	5	**21**
Czechoslovakia			
14	4	9	**27**

FIRST PERIOD

1. Czechoslovakia, Frycer (Novy, Pouzar) • 1:38

2. Czechoslovakia, A. Stastny (unassisted) • 2:14

3. Czechoslovakia, M. Stastny (Bubla, A. Stastny) • 7:16

4. Czechoslovakia, A. Stastny (M. Stastny, P. Stastny) • 12:47

5. Czechoslovakia, M. Stastny (A. Stastny, P. Stastny) • 13:19

penalties: *D'Alvise (Can) 5:00, Novak (Cz) 7:54, Pouzar (Cz) & Primeau (Can) 18:58*

SECOND PERIOD

6. Canada, Devaney (Grant, Hindmarch) • 8:01

penalties: *Kadlec (Cz) 15:04*

THIRD PERIOD

7. Czechoslovakia, M. Stastny (P. Stastny) • 17:18

penalties: *M. Stastny (Cz) 9:01, MacLean (Can) 11:28*

TEAM CANADA FINAL STATISTICS • 1980

#		GP	G	A	P	Pim
15	John Devaney	6	4	3	7	6
20	Dave Hindmarch	6	3	4	7	4
18	Dan D'Alvise	6	3	3	6	8
19	Ken Berry	6	4	1	5	8
21	Kevin Primeau	6	4	1	5	6
17	Paul MacLean	6	2	3	5	6
6	Ron Davidson	6	1	4	5	0
11	Kevin Maxwell	6	0	5	5	4
9	Glenn Anderson	6	2	2	4	4
22	Stelio Zupancich	6	1	3	4	2
12	Jim Nill	6	1	2	3	4
3	Brad Pirie	6	1	2	3	2
24	Terry O'Malley	6	0	3	3	0
4	Randy Gregg	6	1	1	2	2
5	Tim Watters	6	1	1	2	0
2	Warren Anderson	6	1	0	1	4
7	Joe Grant	6	0	1	1	2
8	Don Spring	6	0	1	1	0

#	IN GOAL	GP	W-L-T	Mins	GA	SO	Avg
29	Paul Pageau	4	2–1–0	238	11	1	2.77
1	Bob Dupuis	3	1–2–0	123	7	0	3.41

GOALIE NOTES

1. *Pageau (4 goals) replaced Dupuis (2 goals) at 2:14 of 1st, February 22 vs. Czechoslovakia*

CHAPTER 14

The 14th Olympic Winter Games

SARAJEVO, YUGOSLAVIA

February 7–19, 1984

At the 80th IOC session in Athens on May 18, 1978, Sarajevo beat out Sapporo, Japan in the second round of voting 39–36 votes (Göteburg, Sweden had been eliminated in the first round) to host the 1984 Games.

Coach Dave King

TEAM CANADA • 1984

Darren Eliot, *GOAL*
Mario Gosselin, *GOAL*

Warren Anderson, *DEFENCE*
Robin Bartel, *DEFENCE*
J.J. Daigneault, *DEFENCE*
Bruce Driver, *DEFENCE*
Doug Lidster, *DEFENCE*
James Patrick, *DEFENCE*
Craig Redmond, *DEFENCE*

Russ Courtnall, *FORWARD*
Kevin Dineen, *FORWARD*
Dave Donnelly, *FORWARD*
Pat Flatley, *FORWARD*
Dave Gagner, *FORWARD*
Vaughn Karpan, *FORWARD*
Darren Lowe, *FORWARD*
Kirk Muller, *FORWARD*
Dave Tippett, *FORWARD (CAPTAIN)*
Carey Wilson, *FORWARD*
Dan Wood, *FORWARD*

Dave King, *COACH & GENERAL MANAGER*
George Kingston, *ASSISTANT COACH*
Jean Perron, *ASSISTANT COACH*

FINAL PLACINGS

GOLD MEDAL
USSR

SILVER MEDAL
Czechoslovakia

BRONZE MEDAL
Sweden

FOURTH PLACE
Canada

FIFTH PLACE
West Germany

SIXTH PLACE
Finland

SEVENTH PLACE
United States

EIGHTH PLACE
Poland

NINTH PLACE
Italy

TENTH PLACE
Norway

ELEVENTH PLACE (tie)
Austria
Yugoslavia

PUTTING TEAM CANADA 1984 TOGETHER

The ideal situation for coach Dave King and his staff heading towards the 1984 Games would have mirrored that of virtually every other coach since Canada and hockey began at the Olympics in 1920: select a team, keep it training together for six months, and enter the Games as the most skilled group of amateurs in the country. However, the roster that appeared at the training camp in August 1983 to prepare for the Games and the one that King listed on the official score sheet for the first Olympic game were vastly different, thanks to the addition of new players (Kirk Muller and Russ Courtnall, for instance), injuries (Joe Grant, Gord Sherven and George Servinis), and the inevitable international squabble over who was amateur and who professional.

Dave Donnelly helps defend against a Finnish attack during Canada's 4–2 win on February 11.

One player who was caught between the national team and the NHL was Michel Petit of the Vancouver Canucks. Originally, the Canucks had agreed to loan Petit to the Nats until the Olympics were over, then have him rejoin the NHL team in February '84. However, NHL rules stated that a junior could not be promoted to the NHL after January 1 of any season unless there were an injury on the parent club. In other words, if Petit were to join Team Canada in September '83, he couldn't count on playing for the Canucks until September '84. The Canucks thought too highly of their prospect to lose him for that long, and so, after starting the year with the Olympians (joining the team October 6), Petit was recalled before the year was out and never made the Sarajevo sojourn at all.

A similar controversy on a smaller scale unfolded in the form of J.J. Daigneault, the only junior on the team, who was playing for Longueuil in the QMJHL. Longueuil contended he was under contract to the club and couldn't simply join the national team without permission, which he did anyway. It took a bit of negotiating and legal wrangling, but he was finally able to remain with Dave King after receiving Longueuil's permission. Daigneault was becoming part of an evermore active group of young players who craved the international experience, both for the culture of the sport and as a means of being exposed to a higher calibre of competition.

A year later, Team Canada '84 team-mate Pat Flatley would look back and call his decision to play "the best thing I ever did," citing the huge improvements he had made in his game under the tutelage of King. "I developed quickness, which I didn't have before. The Olympic coaches taught me techniques for getting into open ice — again, something you really need in the NHL ... I didn't have the remotest idea about playing in the neutral zone. For that matter, I didn't know much about defensive hockey at all. But by the time the Olympics were over, I'd received a very thorough education."

THE EXHIBITION SEASON

Team Canada held two regional camps, one in Montreal (June 3–8) and one in Winnipeg (June 9–13), before the 49 invited players appeared on the scene at home base in Calgary to begin preparations for the Olympics. On August 30, new sweaters packed, numbered, and laundered, the team, pared to 26 men, headed to Sweden for a six game tour (and a record of 3–2–1) before heading home to allow coach King to re-evaluate the early roster successes and worries. From September 20 to October 1, team Canada played seven games against NHL clubs, beginning with a close 4–3 loss to the Calgary Flames and a 4–4 tie the next night. The Nats beat Minnesota 6–3 before suffering a resounding defeat to the remarkable Edmonton Oilers 11–5. They lost again to Calgary 9–5, tied Vancouver 3–3, and beat Winnipeg 6–3 to finish with a respectable 2–3–2 record.

After that, the team had a week off before beginning a pressure-packed 11-game series with the Americans. They won resoundly, 5–2–4. A series of exhibition games against minor pro teams took them to Christmas and the final round of cuts for King, barring last-minute additions (which, inevitably, came in January). The flux of the roster took its toll on the players' nerves in the new year, as the team went virtually winless in January. Every day players were wondering whether they would be replaced by someone "better," even though they had been with the team for months. For most, the Olympics could not start quickly enough.

THE CHANGEABILITY OF DETERMINING ELIGIBILITY

One rule change of significance that Gunther Sabetzki had managed to get the IOC to agree to was to allow pros who had played 10 games or less in the NHL to participate in the Olympics, including those who had played for NHL affiliates or who had signed a pro contract, but had yet to play a pro game. Four members of the Canadian team who played through the exhibition season with Team Canada, and were expecting to go to the Olympics, fell into this category — Dan Wood (St. Louis Blues), Mario Gosselin (Quebec Nordiques), Mark Morrison (New York Rangers), and Don Dietrich (Springfield Indians of the American Hockey League).

Dave King hoped to bring Islanders' rookie goalie Kelly Hrudey to Sarajevo as well; however, in late January 1984 he played his 11th game on the Island, thus making himself ineligible, even by Canada's standards. The big peeve, though, came from the Americans, who felt that the IOC and IIHF had agreed to the 10-NHL game plan after they had selected their Olympic team, a claim Alan Eagleson vehemently denied, explaining that the United States was represented in Munich in April 1983 during the World Championships when the rule was introduced and accepted. William Simon, president of the US Olympic Committee was not prepared to accept the decision to allow any pro Canadians of any calibre to participate: "Our stance is well known ... A professional is not allowed to participate in the Olympic games. If they [Canada] play professionals, we will protest."

This stance set off one of the most bitter feuds ever between the Canadians and Americans, although more than anything else it was a boardroom battle. The Americans tried to intimidate the Canadians further by threatening to revoke the NCAA scholarships of any Canadians on the Olympic team or in American college or university if Team Canada played with any of the four "professionals" at the Olympics! The Canadian government parried that thrust by assuring that those university players who were caught in the middle would be fully reimbursed for any losses suffered over the fallout of this controversy.

THE RULING

The Americans were relentless on this issue and increased the intensity of this brouhaha as their first game of the Olympics — versus Canada — approached. The IOC was forced to meet and decide whether any or all of Dietrich, Morrison, Wood, Gosselin, and Courtnall were eligible to play under what were now new rules. The Olympic delegation finally decided that those who "have played one game in the National Hockey League" would *not* be allowed to play in the Games, but everyone else could! Thus, Mark Morrison and Don Dietrich were ruled ineligible while Gosselin, Wood, and Courtnall were allowed to play.

The ruling was flagrantly biased against Canada, although it was a small concession on the IOC's part in that non-NHL pros were, all of a sudden, able to play in the Olympics and not just the World Championships. Consider the unfairness, though: Morrison played nine games with the New York Rangers, and Dietrich six games with the Chicago Black Hawks and they couldn't play. The ruling also disqualified Jim Corsi and Rick Bragnalo of Italy and Greg Holst of Austria. However, the IOC did allow anyone who played professionally in the WHA, AHL, IHL, or on any club team in Europe to play. In other words, the IOC was saying that the NHL was the *only* league in the world that it — the IOC — acknowledged paid its players! Among those players who *could* play at the Olympics were Rick Cunningham, 300-game veteran of the WHA, and Eric Kuhnhackl, veteran of the West German pro league. As Team Canada forward Carey Wilson pointed out, "The difference between a professional and amateur is not whether you're paid a salary, but whether you're paid a big or small salary."

The result for the Americans was just the opposite of what they had intended. The Canadians were motivated beyond words for that now pride-important opening game. "After all the stuff we had been through here," now-eligible goaler Gosselin said, "we decided that the US trying to give us all that bull was the end. Losing the two players from a team that's very close got us mad and we decided to set things right again on the ice." Gosselin was great in goal, stopping 37 of 39 shots, and Carey Wilson scored three times and added an assist, as Canada solidly shut down the Americans 4–2. Team USA was *en route* to another disappointing seventh place finish at these Games.

Doug Lidster collides with Finland's Raimo Summanen.

THE MEDAL ROUND

While Canada did its job in the preliminary round to advance for a chance at a medal, its performance during the finals was heartbreaking. In fact, counting the loss to Czechoslovakia in the preliminaries, which was carried over to count in the medal round, Canada did not score a goal in three games, its worst drought in 64 years of Olympic competition. Scoring, though, had been this squad's problem all year, and it was for this reason Canada had added Russ Courtnall and Kirk Muller to the team after the two had competed in the World Junior Championships in Sweden. But neither of these two 18-year-olds, nor anyone else for that matter, could find the range against the Russians (4–0) or the Swedes (2–0), and Canada finished a distant fourth in the medal round.

"TRETIAK, TRETIAK!"

The calls of "Tretiak, Tretiak!" were heard loud and clear while the Sarajevo Games went on, but they came from a building much closer to home than might have been expected — the Montreal Forum. Vladislav Tretiak had long admired Canada in general, and Montreal in particular, going back to the Summit Series, and then the great New Year's Eve 3–3 tie in 1975 at the Forum vs. the Canadiens. The Habs had hoped Tretiak would be the first Russian-trained player to join the NHL, and were so optimistic, in fact, they used their 9th-choice (138th overall) in the 1983 Entry Draft to stake a claim to him. They offered the Soviet Union Ice Hockey Federation $500,000 for his release, but Moscow said *nyet,* until after the Olympics.

Meanwhile, the Habs weren't doing so well. The night Guy Lafleur scored four points to become the all-time Montreal point-getter, the team blew a comfortable

6–3 lead and lost to Vancouver 7–6 in the Forum. That's when the fans, as derisive as New York Yankee fans in baseball, began their "Tretiak, Tretiak!" chants. Alas, it was wasted breath, for the Russians never really came close to releasing their hero goalie to the NHL.

DOPING

In the IIHF "Statutes and By-Laws" of 1978, there was included a detailed account of how drug testing should be implemented. Of the nine-point process, the eighth is the most interesting: "Refreshing drinks for the tested players, about 10 bottles per game."

During the Olympics, the IOC met regularly to discuss how plans and events were unfolding. After the session of February 16, 1984, they reached one conclusion regarding dope tests for hockey players:

> Due to the accident that occured [sic] yesterday after the game FIN–USA, when the two Finnish players selected for doping tests arrived fully dressed 58 minutes after they have [sic] received the doping documents into the doping room. The IOC has suggested that from now on only two bottles of beer shall be given to each player in question.

Canada's Carey Wilson jostles with Austrian goalie Michael Rudman and defender Richard Cunningham.

AFTER THE OLYMPICS — THE NHL

After the Winter Games ended and Canada's fourth place finish was in the books, the team travelled to Paris for exhibition games against the Soviet and Czech "B" teams, as well as a West German team, before heading home and disbanding. The next stop for Team Canada was the 1984 Canada Cup. Not surprisingly, our best beat everyone else's best — again. Only one player, James Patrick, played for both the Olympic team and Canada Cup team for Canada in 1984. Incredibly, fully 18 members of the 1984 Russian Olympic team also played in the Canada Cup. Of the Canadian Olympians, each and every member to play at the 1984 Games went on to play in the NHL!

While the Canada Cup victory boosted the country's morale (the team was made up entirely of NHLers), the national hockey program as a whole was still, as ever, in flux. If a national amateur program were to stay in place for the next four years, it would need strong international competition, but this was impossible when the pros now dominated the World Championships roster and the Juniors at the World Junior Championships had Major Junior A affiliation in Canada (thus restricting their international eligibility). The current national program was the best at nurturing that talent, but it risked becoming an isolated junior team with no place to play. Yet the pros showed no signs of closing down the NHL for the 1988 Games at Calgary, thus placing the future of an Olympic medal squarely on the amateur program.

The Competition

TOURNAMENT FORMAT

The 12 teams were divided into two groups of six, all teams playing a round-robin schedule within each group. The top two teams from each group then advanced to a four country round-robin medal round with the results from the qualifying round between qualifying teams counting in the finals round as well. Thus, because of this carry over, the four teams in the medal round-robin each played two games, not three. In the event of a tie in the preliminary round standings, head-to-head results would be the first determining factor. If that game were a tie, then overall goal differential would decide the issue.

THE OPPOSITION

AUSTRIA • Thomas Cijan, Leopold Civec, Richard Cunningham, Konrad Dorn, Johann Fritz, Fritz Ganster, Kevin Greenbank, Kurt Harand, Bernie Hutz, Rudolph Koenig, Helmut Koren, Eddy Lebler, Giuseppe Mion, Helmut Petrik, Martin Platzer, Herbert Poek, Peter Raffl, Michael Rudman, Krunoslav Seculic, Brian Stankiewicz

CZECHOSLOVAKIA • Jaroslav Benak, Vladimir Caldr, Frantisek Cernik, Milan Chalupa, Miloslav Horava, Jiri Hrdina, Arnold Kadlec, Jaroslav Korbela, Jiri Kralik, Vladimir Kynos, Jiri Lala, Igor Liba, Vincent Lukac, Dusan Pasek, Pavel Richter, Darius Rusnak, Vladimir Ruzicka, Jaromir Sindel, Radoslav Svoboda, Eduard Uvira

FINLAND • Raimo Helminen, Risto Jalo, Arto Javanainen, Timo Jutila, Erkki Laine, Marcus Lehto, Mika Lehto, Pertti Lehtonen, Jarmo Makitalo, Anssi Melametsa, Hannu Oksanen, Arto Ruotanen, Simo Saarinen, Ville Siren, Arto Sirvio, Petri Skriko, Raimo Summanen, Kari Takko, Juka Tammi, Harri Tuohimaa, Jorma Valtonen

ITALY • John Bellio, Marco Capone, Gerard Ciarcia, Robert Depiero, Cary Farelli, Norbert Gasser, Grant Goegan, Adolf Insam, Fabrizio Kasslatter, Erwin Kostner, Michael Mair, Michael Mastrullo, Lodovico Migliore, Thomas Milani, Gino Pasqualloto, Martin Pavlu, Constantine Priondolo, Norbert Pruenster, Adriano Tancon, David Tomassoni

NORWAY • Trond Abrahamsen, Cato Andersen, Arne Bergsen, Per Arne Christainsen, Aage Ellingsen, Stephen Foyn, Joern Goldstein, Oeistein Jarslbo, Roy Johansen, Jon Magne Karlstad, Erik Kristiansen, Sven Lien, Oeyvind Loesamoen, Oerjan Loevdal, Jim Marthinses, Geirtore Myhre, Erik Nerell, Bjorn Skaare, Petter Thoresen, Frank Vestreng

POLAND • Janusz Adamiec, Marek Cholewa, Andrzey Chowaniec, Jerzy Christ, Josef Chrzastek, Czeslaw Drozd, Bogdan Gebczyk, Henrik Gruth, Andrzej Hachula, Andrezej Hanisz, Leszek Jachna, Wieslav Jobszyk, Stanislaw Klocek, Andrzey Nowak, Wlodzimierz Olszewski, Bogdan Pawlik, Jan Piecko, Henryk Pytel, Gabriel Samolej, Dariusz Sikora, Krystian Sikorski, Jan Stopczyk, Ludwik Synowiec, Robert Szopinski, Andrzej Ujwary, Andrzey Zabawa

SWEDEN • Thomas Ahlen, Per-Erik Eklund, Thomas Eklund, Bo Ericsson, Lars Erikson, Peter Gradin, Mats Hessel, Peter Michael Hjalm, Goran Lindblom, Tommy Morth, Leif Nordin, Jens Ohling, Rolf-Lennart Riddervall, Thomas Rundquist, Tomas Sandstrom, Karl Sodergren, Mats Thelin, Arne Thelven, Gote Walitalo, Mats Waltin

UNITED STATES • Mark Behrend, Scott Bjugstad, Robert Brooke, Chris Chelios, Rich Costello, Mark Fusco, Scott Fusco, Steven Griffith, Paul Guay, Gary Haight, John Harrington, Tomas Hirsch, Al Iafrate, David A. Jensen, David H. Jensen, Kurt Kleinendorst, Mark Kumpel, Pat Lafontaine, Robert Mason, Corey Millen, Ed Olczyk, Gary Sampson, Tim Thomas, Phil Verchota

USSR • Zinatula Bilyaletdinov, Sergei Chepelev, Nikolai Drozdetsky, Vyacheslav Fetisov, Aleksandr Gerasimov, Aleksei Kasatonov, Andrei Komutov, Vladimir Kovin, Aleksandr Kozhernikov, Vladimir Krutov, Igor Larionov, Sergei Makarov, Vladimir Myshkin, Vasily Pervukhin, Aleksandr Skvortsov, Sergei Starikov, Igor Stelnov, Vladislav Tretiak, Victor Tumenev, Michail Vasiliev

WEST GERMANY • Manfred Ahne, Ignaz Berndaner, Michael Betz, Bernhard Englbrecht, Karl Friesen, Dieter Hegen, Ulrich Heimer, Ernst Hofner, Udo Kiessling, Harold Kreis, Marcus Kuhl, Eric Kuhnhacki, Andreas Niederberger, Joachim Reil, Franz Reindl, Roy Roedger, Peter Scharf, Helmut Steiger, Gerhard Truntschka, Manfred Wolf

YUGOSLAVIA • Igor Beribak, Mustafa Besic, Dejan Burnik, Cveto Pretnar, Marjan Gorenc, Edvard Hafner, Gorazd Hiti, Drago Horvat, Igor Peter Klemenc, Joze Kovac, Vojko Lajovec, Blaz Lomovsek, Dominik Lomovsek, Drago Mlinarec, Murajca Pajic, Bojan Raspet, Ivan Scap, Matjaz Sekelj, Zvone Suvak, Andrej Vidmar

FINAL STANDINGS

PRELIMINARY ROUND • GROUP A

	GP	W	L	T	GF	GA	P
USSR	5	5	0	0	42	5	10
Sweden	5	3	1	1	24	15	7
West Germany	5	3	1	1	27	17	7
Poland	5	1	4	0	16	37	2
Italy	5	1	4	0	15	21	2
Yugoslavia	5	1	4	0	8	37	2

RESULTS

FEBRUARY 7
Italy 3 Sweden 1
West Germany 8 Yugoslavia 1
USSR 12 Poland 1

FEBRUARY 9
West Germany 8 Poland 5
USSR 5 Italy 1
Sweden 11 Yugoslavia 0

FEBRUARY 11
USSR 9 Yugoslavia 1
Sweden 1 West Germany 1
Italy 6 Poland 1

FEBRUARY 13
Sweden 10 Poland 1
Yugoslavia 5 Italy 1
USSR 6 West Germany 1

FEBRUARY 15
Poland 8 Yugoslavia 1
USSR 10 Sweden 1
West Germany 9 Italy 4

PRELIMINARY ROUND • GROUP B

	GP	W	L	T	GF	GA	P
Czechoslovakia	5	5	0	0	38	7	10
Canada	5	4	1	0	24	10	8
Finland	5	2	2	1	27	19	5
United States	5	1	2	2	16	17	4
Austria	5	1	4	0	13	37	2
Norway	5	0	4	1	15	43	1

RESULTS

FEBRUARY 7
Canada 4 United States 2
Finland 4 Austria 3
Czechoslovakia 10 Norway 4

FEBRUARY 9
Canada 8 Austria 1
Finland 16 Norway 2
Czechoslovakia 4 United States 1

FEBRUARY 11
Canada 4 Finland 2
Czechoslovakia 13 Austria 0
Norway 3 United States 3

FEBRUARY 13
Canada 8 Norway 1
Czechoslovakia 7 Finland 2
United States 7 Austria 3

FEBRUARY 15
Czechoslovakia 4 Canada 0
Austria 6 Norway 5
Finland 3 United States 3

MEDAL ROUND

	GP	W	L	T	GF	GA	P
USSR	3	3	0	0	16	1	6
Czechoslovakia	3	2	1	0	6	2	4
Sweden	3	1	2	0	3	12	2
Canada	3	0	3	0	0	10	0

CARRY OVER RESULTS

FEBRUARY 15
USSR 10 Sweden 1
Czechoslovakia 4 Canada 0

RESULTS

FEBRUARY 17
USSR 4 Canada 0
Czechoslovakia 2 Sweden 0
West Germany 7 Finland 4
(5th place game)
United States 7 Poland 4
(7th place game)

FEBRUARY 19
Sweden 2 Canada 0
USSR 2 Czechoslovakia 0

TEAM CANADA GAME SUMMARIES

FEBRUARY 7 • Canada 4 United States 2

IN GOAL

Canada — Gosselin

United States — Behrend

SHOTS ON GOAL

Canada			
15	12	11	**38**
United States			
7	19	13	**39**

FIRST PERIOD

1. Canada, Flatley (unassisted) • 0:27

2. United States, D.A. Jensen (unassisted) • 10:10

3. Canada, Wilson (Daigneault) • 12:02(pp)

penalties: *Donnelly (Can) 5:18, Iafrate (US) 10:36*

SECOND PERIOD

4. Canada, Flatley (Wilson) • 2:12

5. United States, D.A. Jensen (Chelios, Olczyk) • 13:54(pp)

penalties: *Chelios (US) 8:18, Flatley (Can) 8:53, Gagner (Can) 11:57, Hirsch (US) 16:41*

THIRD PERIOD

6. Canada, Wilson (Wood) • 9:19

penalties: *Bartel (Can) & Guay (US) 16:10*

FEBRUARY 9 • Canada 8 Austria 1

IN GOAL

Canada — Gosselin/Eliot

(Eliot (one goal) replaced Gosselin (no goals) to start 3rd)

Austria — Rudman

SHOTS ON GOAL

Canada			
17	17	9	**43**
Austria			
5	6	9	**20**

FIRST PERIOD

1. Canada, Donnelly (Patrick) • 3:00

2. Canada, Muller (Wilson, Driver) • 11:54(pp)

penalties: *Driver (Can) 6:49, Cunningham (Aus) 10:30, Redmond (Can) 13:45, Raffl (Aus) 17:20*

SECOND PERIOD

3. Canada, Muller (Patrick, Donnelly) • 0:13

4. Canada, Driver (Lidster) • 3:58

5. Canada, Tippett (unassisted) • 13:40

6. Canada, Wilson (Flatley) • 14:47

penalties: *Wilson (Can) & Civec (Aus) 7:56, Koenig (Aus) 16:53, Patrick (Can) 19:03*

THIRD PERIOD

7. Austria, Lebler (unassisted) • 0:20

8. Canada, Gagner (unassisted) • 9:34

9. Canada, Redmond (Lowe, Bartel) • 15:47

penalties: *Gagner (Can) 5:43, Donnelly (Can) 11:48, Hutz (Aus) & Dineen (Can) 16:17, Dineen (Can) 18:52*

FEBRUARY 11 • Canada 4 Finland 2

IN GOAL

Canada — Gosselin

Finland — Takko

SHOTS ON GOAL

Canada			
17	16	12	**45**
Finland			
11	8	8	**27**

FIRST PERIOD

1. Canada, Driver (Tippett) • 3:26

penalties: *Melametsa (Fin) & Tippett (Can) 0:52, Donnelly (Can) 14:24, Jalo (Fin) 15:32, Gosselin (Can — served by Flatley) 16:05*

SECOND PERIOD

2. Finland, Tuohimaa (unassisted) • 1:44

3. Finland, Skriko (unassisted) • 10:22

penalties: *Lehtonen (Fin) 7:24, Lidster (Can) 12:07*

THIRD PERIOD

4. Canada, Lowe (Muller) • 3:56

5. Canada, Redmond (Wilson, Flatley) • 9:03

6. Canada, Gagner (Courtnall) • 14:01

penalties: *Summanen (Fin) 5:23, Flatley (Can) 6:10, Lehto (Fin) 9:46, Summanen (Fin) 14:35, Courtnall (Can) 17:50*

FEBRUARY 13 • Canada 8 Norway 1

FIRST PERIOD
1. Canada, Courtnall (unassisted) • 9:44
2. Canada, Lowe (Flatley) • 10:53
penalties: *Foyn (Nor) & Bartel (Can) 0:45, Flatley (Can) 5:58, Jarslbo (Nor) 12:21*

SECOND PERIOD
3. Canada, Flatley (Lidster) • 5:14
4. Canada, Gagner (Courtnall) • 14:14
5. Canada, Driver (Patrick, Gagner) • 17:57(pp)
penalties: *Driver (Can) 6:51, Skaare (Nor) 10:48, Foyn (Nor) 17:20*

THIRD PERIOD
6. Canada, Daigneault (Gagner, Courtnall) • 6:37
7. Canada, Gagner (Daigneault) • 9:41(pp)
8. Norway, Foyn (Andersen) • 16:44
9. Canada, Gagner (unassisted) • 18:18
penalties: *Donnelly (Can) 3:35, Karlstad (Nor) 9:00, Flatley (Can — double minor) & Abrahamsen (Nor — double minor) 12:39*

IN GOAL
Canada — Gosselin/Eliot
(Eliot (one goal) replaced Gosselin (no goals) to start 3rd)
Norway — Goldstein/Marthinses

SHOTS ON GOAL

Canada	12	15	11	**38**
Norway	10	4	4	**18**

FEBRUARY 15 • Czechoslovakia 4 Canada 0

FIRST PERIOD
1. Czechoslovakia, Caldr (Pasek) • 17:16
penalties: *none*

SECOND PERIOD
2. Czechoslovakia, Liba (Lukac) • 2:02
penalties: *Kadlec (Cz) 18:19, Redmond (Can) 19:55*

THIRD PERIOD
3. Czechoslovakia, Svoboda (Liba) • 6:31
4. Czechoslovakia, Ruzicka (Hrdina, Horava) • 14:08
penalties: *Hrdina (Cz) 0:55, Cernik (Cz) & Dineen (Can) 12:53*

IN GOAL
Canada — Gosselin
Czechoslovakia — Sindel

SHOTS ON GOAL

Canada	15	12	9	**36**
Czechoslovakia	10	10	12	**32**

FEBRUARY 17 • USSR 4 Canada 0

FIRST PERIOD
No Scoring
penalties: *Driver (Can) 4:23*

SECOND PERIOD
1. USSR, Kovin (unassisted) • 11:31
2. USSR, Kozhernikov (Drozdetsky) • 14:19
penalties: *Patrick (Can) 0:15, Driver (Can) 8:07*

THIRD PERIOD
3. USSR, Skvortsov (Stelnov) • 14:41(sh)
4. USSR, Drozdetsky (unassisted) • 16:59
penalties: *Wilson (Can) 4:30, Gerasimov (USSR) 14:26, Wood (Can) & Stelnov (USSR) 17:49, Fetisov (USSR — double minor) & Dineen (Can) 19:31*

IN GOAL
Canada — Gosselin
USSR — Tretiak

SHOTS ON GOAL

Canada	5	5	5	**15**
USSR	14	14	10	**38**

FEBRUARY 19 • Sweden 2 Canada 0

FIRST PERIOD
No Scoring
penalties: *Donnelly (Can) 7:11*

SECOND PERIOD
1. Sweden, Gradin (P. Eklund) • 11:21
penalties: *Driver (Can) 4:36, Flatley (Can — match misconduct) 15:19, H. Erikson (Swe) 17:24*

THIRD PERIOD
2. Sweden, Sodergren (B. Erikson, P. Eklund) • 6:59(pp)
penalties: *Wilson (Can) 5:40, B. Erikson (Swe) & Gagner (Can) 8:02, Donnelly (Can) 8:57, H. Erikson (Swe) 9:24*

IN GOAL
Canada — Gosselin
Sweden — Riddervall

SHOTS ON GOAL

Canada	8	7	13	**28**
Sweden	4	13	5	**22**

TEAM CANADA FINAL STATISTICS • 1984

#		GP	G	A	P	Pim
19	Dave Gagner	7	5	2	7	6
26	Pat Flatley	7	3	3	6	70*
20	Carey Wilson	7	3	3	6	6
25	Bruce Driver	7	3	1	4	10
18	Russ Courtnall	7	1	3	4	2
14	Darren Lowe	7	2	1	3	0
27	Kirk Muller	6	2	1	3	0
9	James Patrick	7	0	3	3	4
3	Craig Redmond	7	2	0	2	4
23	Dave Donnelly	7	1	1	2	12
8	Dave Tippett	7	1	1	2	2
15	J.J. Daigneault	7	1	1	2	0
4	Doug Lidster	7	0	2	2	2
2	Robin Bartel	6	0	1	1	4
22	Dan Wood	7	0	1	1	2
16	Kevin Dineen	7	0	0	0	8
33	Mario Gosselin	7	0	0	0	2
5	Warren Anderson	7	0	0	0	0
31	Vaughn Karpan	7	0	0	0	0

* *including 60-minute match misconduct penalty*

#	IN GOAL	GP	W-L-T	Mins	GA	SO	Avg
33	Mario Gosselin	7	4–3–0	380	14	0	2.21
1	Darren Eliot	2	0–0–0	40	2	0	3.00

GOALIE NOTES:

1. *Eliot (one goal) replaced Gosselin (no goals) to start 3rd, February 9 vs. Austria*

2. *Eliot (one goal) replaced Gosselin (no goals) to start 3rd, February 13 vs. Norway*

CHAPTER 15

The 15th Olympic Winter Games

CALGARY, CANADA

February 13–28, 1988

Claude Vilgrain

Three cities were considered for the 1988 Games when the IOC held its 84th session in Baden-Baden, Germany, on September 30, 1981. Cortina d'Ampezzo, Italy was eliminated in the first round of voting, and in the second round Calgary (48 votes) easily defeated Falun, Sweden (31 votes) for the honour.

TEAM CANADA • 1988

Sean Burke, GOAL
Andy Moog, GOAL

Chris Felix, DEFENCE
Randy Gregg, DEFENCE
Serge Roy, DEFENCE
Tony Stiles, DEFENCE
Tim Watters, DEFENCE
Trent Yawney, DEFENCE
Zarley Zalapski, DEFENCE

Ken Berry, CENTRE
Mark Habscheid, CENTRE

Vaughn Karpan, LEFT WING
Wally Schreiber, LEFT WING

Gord Sherven, RIGHT WING
Claude Vilgrain, RIGHT WING

Serge Boisvert, FORWARD
Brian Bradley, FORWARD
Bob Joyce, FORWARD
Merlin Malinowski, FORWARD
Jim Peplinski, FORWARD
Steve Tambellini, FORWARD
Ken Yaremchuk, FORWARD

Rick Kosti (DID NOT PLAY)

Dave King, COACH & GENERAL MANAGER
Guy Charron, ASSISTANT COACH
Tom Watt, ASSISTANT COACH

FINAL PLACINGS

GOLD MEDAL
USSR

SILVER MEDAL
Finland

BRONZE MEDAL
Sweden

FOURTH PLACE
Canada

FIFTH PLACE
West Germany

SIXTH PLACE
Czechoslovakia

SEVENTH PLACE
United States

EIGHTH PLACE
Switzerland

NINTH PLACE
Austria

TENTH PLACE
Poland

ELEVENTH PLACE
France

TWELFTH PLACE
Norway

THE OLYMPIC WINTER GAMES COME TO CANADA

While Canada, thanks largely to its hockey team and figure skaters, had always been one of the most popular winter participants at the Olympics, bids for hosting the Games had always been turned down with predictable consistency. During the 1928 Games in St. Moritz, P.J. Mulqueen, chairman of the Canadian Olympic Committee, made an official request to allow Canada to host the 1932 Games. If accepted, he said, Montreal would be the host city, but that proposal didn't impress IOC delegates enough. In January 1956, while preparing for the Games at Cortina, Sydney Dawes, then president of the COC, said Canada had "an excellent chance" of getting the 1964 Games: "Delegates are continually coming up to me and asking why Canada doesn't bid for the Games," he said, noting that either Toronto or Vancouver would be ideal locations. Again, international enthusiasm waned and Canada was passed over.

Randy Gregg (left) and Steve Tambellini celebrate a goal.

After the brilliant performance in Squaw Valley in 1960 by Anne Heggtveit, who won Canada's first Olympic gold medal in the slalom, many felt Canada's heightened reputation would allow it to follow Innsbruck in 1964 as host of the '68 Games. Just after the 1960 Olympics ended, none other than hockey great Cyclone Taylor began promoting Garibaldi Provincial Park in British Columbia as the ideal place for the Olympics.

Four years later, Banff was touted as a sure thing for the 1968 Winter Olympics but lost to Grenoble by the slimmest of margins, 27 votes to 24. Banff had been part of the bidding since 1955, when the Calgary Olympic Development Association was formed. The CODA made a quick bid in 1959 for the '64 Games, a bid it knew it would lose but made anyway in the name of experience. By 1961, Banff had been accepted by the COA over five other British Columbia locations (Fernie, Rossland, Garibaldi Park, Manning Park, and Revelstoke) as the official Canadian site. However, after the 1968 loss, everyone felt that if Canada were to win a bid, it would have to move away from the Banff preference. Nearby Calgary was deemed the most favourable second option, and the COA once again began politicking and bargaining for Olympic position. When the IOC met in 1981, Calgary was an easy winner over Falun, Sweden and was awarded the honour of hosting the 1988 Olympic Winter Games.

THE BICKERING BEGINS EARLY

In the fall of 1984, the IOC decided to extend the hockey portion of the 1988 Games from 12 to 16 days in order to accommodate American television and generate extra revenue. The IIHF was furious. It had not been asked to approve the plan, and it immediately threatened to pull hockey from the Olympics altogether; federation rules did not allow tournaments it sanctioned to last longer than 12 days. Furthering its argument, the IIHF stated that too many of its member nations, primarily the Russians and Czechs, would have to start their league seasons too early to leave room for the extra four days at the Games, which they said was impossible. The good news was that the argument took place four years before the first scheduled game, and by 1988 in Calgary the dispute had been resolved and American TV had won the day.

THE SADDLEDOME

Host to all hockey games, the Saddledome was a state-of-the-art hockey palace. Geometrically, it was a "reverse hyperbolic paraboloid" of some three acres and had the world's largest suspended concrete roof. More colloquially, it was described as resembling a big saddle. The arena's interior was without pillars and visible supports; not a seat in the house was obstructed. The IIHF called it the finest international rink in the world, and with a seating capacity of 20,016 it was also the largest ever used at the Games. Unique in Canada, the ice surface could be expanded from NHL size to regulation Olympic size.

THE PROFESSIONALS ARE COMING TO TOWN

As early as October 20, 1986, IIHF president Gunther Sabetzki announced that any and all pros — no restrictions on age, numbers, or leagues — would be able to participate in the 1988 Olympics, making Calgary the first truly "open" Games for hockey. "There are no restrictions," Sabetzki declared. "Canada can use Wayne Gretzky if it wants to." NHL president John Zeigler, however, made it clear that what Canada wanted and what it got were two different things: "We put on a thousand events a year. Most of our sales are season tickets. I don't think it's fair to the customer if we say, 'You've paid $16 for your ticket — oh, by the way, for the next three weeks you're not going to see the Gretzkys, the Paul Coffeys, and the Bourques and so forth.' What would that do to the integrity of the competition?" Alas, the great opportunity put on the international table by Sabetzki had no takers.

While NHL players had been allowed to compete in the World Championships since 1977 (sanctioned by the IIHF), this was the first time they were allowed to play at the Olympics (sanctioned by the IOC). So, although the results were not remarkable — no NHL team actually allowed a top-notch star to leave — it did set the stage for 1998 in Nagano, where virtually every player on every contending team will have some pro experience. The days of raw rookies and part-time, hockey-playing amateurs were now truly over, though participating Canadians were hardly well paid. For the 1987-88 season, Team Canada members earned $12,000 and had to pay their own living expenses. Clearly, this was a labour of love and no one was going to get rich playing for the Olympics.

A SEGUE — THE WORLD JUNIOR CHAMPIONSHIPS

The participation of the USSR in the 1956 Olympic Winter Games had a profound influence on international hockey. While it was a scandalous system that allowed their "pros" to compete against our amateurs, everyone could see that this was a superior hockey-playing nation, one that could challenge Canada for world bragging rights on a regular basis. The Summit Series proved that although Canada had the better team and as a nation was certainly much deeper in talent, Russia's best could win on any particular day. Too, while the Canada Cups in 1976, 1981, 1984, 1987, and 1991 provided the best hockey on the planet, it was clear other nations, particularly Sweden, Finland, and Czechoslovakia, were not about to lose 20–0 or 30–0 against Canada as they had in the pre-war Olympics.

International competition in the 70s gained recognition as the only time hockey games could outdo the NHL for speed, calibre, and excitement. As part of this global expansion, the IIHF nations established the World Junior Championships in 1977, the same year Sabetzki allowed NHLers to play the World Championships. It made perfect sense in Canada, because clearly the Worlds were going to be dominated by the pros now that they were allowed in. This created a need to give junior players international experience of the highest level, and the World Juniors provided just that. A look at how Canada has fared between 1977 and 1997 shows that far from being second to Russia or losing ground in the international arena, Canada has once again proved to be the best hockey-playing nation in the world.

While the first few tournaments were not kind to Canada (only one gold medal in the first six years), Canada has dominated the competition since. In the last 13 years, there has been one fourth place finish, a sixth place in 1992, one disqualification after the brawl in Piestany, Czechoslovakia and an incredible nine gold medals. Canada's juniors have won the last five consecutive World Junior Championships, and have proved beyond a shadow of a doubt we continue to produce the finest players anywhere in the world.

BACK TO THE OLYMPICS AND THE PROS

Heading the list of Canada's pros was goaltender Andy Moog. A member of the Edmonton Oilers from 1980 to 1987, Moog was a three-time Stanley Cup winner in 1984, 1985, and 1987, but he was now sitting out in a contract dispute with Edmonton. Here was a proven, *bona fide* NHLer who was now allowed to play in the Olympics. Joining him, under more pleasant circumstances, was Oilers team-mate Randy Gregg. Gregg originally played for Canada at the 1980 Games as an amateur. He was taking the 1987–88 season off to pursue his dream of an Olympic medal, one which had eluded him when his team finished a disappointing sixth at Lake Placid. Gregg planned to rejoin the Oilers after the Olympics.

Many of the Gregg and Moog's team-mates were either to embark on a pro career as soon as the Olympics were over or already had pro experience and wanted the chance to represent Canada internationally. Tim Watters, another 1980 Olympian, was loaned at the last minute to the team by the Winnipeg Jets for whom he was playing; Ken Berry, another '80 alumnus, used the opportunity as a springboard to sign with Vancouver; Jim Peplinski and Brian Bradley were loaned

Quel surprise! Goalie Sean Burke is on his knees, defenceman Jason Woolley goes down, two Germans are toppled and the only one left standing is the Big E! Canada won the game 4–3 after a dramatic shootout in Albertville '92.

Canadian Kevin Dahl jostles for position with Germany's Axel Kammerer during Canada's dramatic 4–3 shootout victory to advance to the semi-finals in Albertville. The German "uniform" is probably the most featureless jersey ever used in Olympic play.

The Canadians mob goalie Sean Burke after he stopped Germany's Peter Draisaitl on the team's last shot of the sudden-death shootout. With the win, Canada advanced to the semi-finals vs. the Czechs.

Canada was, is, and always will be the hockey capital of the world. And, when a Canadian team represents the country abroad, a strong and vocal contingent is sure to follow. Albertville was no exception, as these red and white fans attest during the German match.

Sean Burke is Canada's international war horse. His play at the 1997 World Championships in Finland was the most recent in a long series of appearances as goalie for the team.

Canada's first game in Albertville in 1992 was against the home side. Canada scored a narrow 3–2 win *en route* to a silver medal. France finished eighth.

Eric Lindros fails to one-time this pass past French goalie Petri Ylonen, but Canada did get goals from Joe Juneau, Dave Archibald, and Kent Manderville to win the opening game of the '92 Games 3–2.

French captain Antoine Richer is given the old mid-ice tug to prevent him from breaking away. The French put up a good fight before going down 3–1 in Canada's second game of the 1994 Olympics.

Slovakia's Robert Petrovicky and Canada's Brad Werenka follow a loose puck in a preliminary round game. Lillehammer was the first Olympics in which Slovakia competed as an independent nation, having played previously with the Czechs and the Czech Republic.

Fabian Joseph goes down low to win the draw during Canada's 3–1 loss to the Unified Team for the gold medal in 1994.

Defenceman Jean-Yves Roy scored only one goal in Albertville, but it was the game winner in a 5–3 victory over Finland, February 25, 1994 and advanced Canada to a gold medal showdown with Sweden.

Action between the Canadians and Swedes in the last game of the 1994 Lillehammer Olympics. Sweden got a power-play goal with just 1:49 left in the game to tie the score 2–2 and force sudden death.

Paul Kariya is *the* superstar of his generation. Phenomenal acceleration, great hands, and superb passing skills will make his contribution to Canada's gold medal chances in Nagano essential.

Tense moments at the Canadian bench during the shootout as the team sits idly and watches when it should be playing sudden death overtime.

Mats Naslund is stopped cold by Corey Hirsch during the gold medal shootout eventually won by the Swedes 3–2.

The traditional handshake follows a shootout that was quick but not a very competitive way to decide the gold medal.

Swiss goalie Richard Bucher is beaten as team-mate Urs Burkhart (#12) ties up Merlin Malinowski.

to the team by the home town Calgary Flames (Paul Reinhart was also slated to join the team, but a back problem prevented his participation); Steve Tambellini was loaned by the Canucks and Ken Yaremchuk by the Leafs; Bob Joyce would join Boston and Trent Yawney Chicago right after the Games. And, at the other end of the spectrum, amateur Chris Felix had spent the last three years with the Olympic team, time that helped him mature as a player and persuaded Washington to take enough of an interest in him to sign him after the Games had ended.

There was also another kind of NHLer starting to appear at the Olympics: the skilled, speedy, small, and versatile forward. In NHL terms, the word versatile is a pejorative — a way of saying something nice about a player who possesses minimal NHL skills — but not to Dave King. Two such examples were Bradley and Serge Boisvert. Both were excellent players who looked much better on the larger, Olympic surface than on the cramped NHL sheet with its hooking, clutching, and grabbing that wore down smaller players. Bradley and Boisvert teamed with Wally Schreiber to form one of Canada's best lines — fast, defensively superb, and skilled enough to chip in offensively.

Many of the players on the team, however, were not seasoned NHLers. They were not dominant players in the league, but they had enough experience at top levels to be more prepared for the rigours of the Olympics than the amateurs of days gone by. The task of assembling the team was still great. For one, there was the persistent problem/bonus of late NHL player additions. On the one hand, any improvement in talent was welcome; on the other, it disrupted team chemistry and camaraderie, and left those who were scratched from the team feeling embittered. In addition, the more numerous the late additions, the more difficult would be the adjustments for the team and individuals alike. In some respects, it was better to have a less talented team together for six months than a slightly more talented team training together for just a couple of weeks.

Bob Joyce and Serge Roy were two men who made long-term committments to the Olympic program, but were not rewarded: Joyce was scratched from four of Canada's eight games and Roy from three. It was a well-known secret after the Games that the last-minute additions — of obviously very talented players — had a significant negative impact on what Randy Gregg termed the team's "oneness" between their excellent showing at the Isvestia tournament in December and the disappointing fourth-place showing at the Olympics just six weeks later.

THE PRE-OLYMPICS SCHEDULE

The Olympic team's exhibition schedule leading up to the Games was well-planned and highly successful. From September to November 1987 they had a record of 17–9–7 before entering the heart of their season. First, they played the Moscow Selects in an eight game series (which they won) and then headed to Moscow for the aforementioned Isvestia tournament (which they won, beating the USSR 3–2 in the finals). Canada was peaking at just the right time.

Having lost the Canada Cup and Isvestia to Canada, the Calgary Cup to the Czechs, and the World Championships to Sweden, the Russians were going into the Games without having won anything of significance in 22 months. On the one hand, the pressure was certainly on them to perform, on the other they were plenty motivated and knew the slump had to end some time. Further motivation came in

Bucher stops Canada's Serge Boisvert and Jim Peplinski in close.

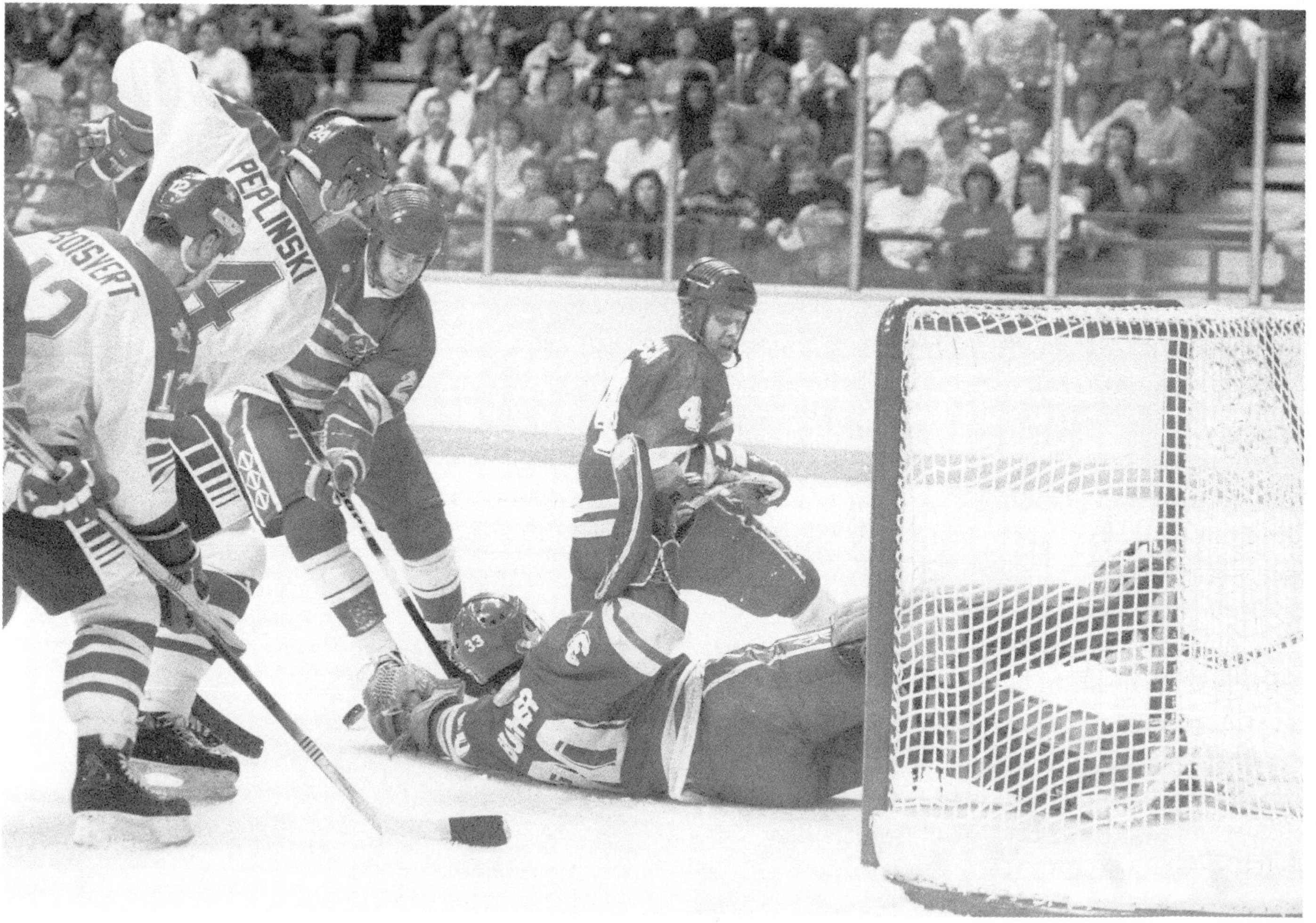

a guarantee from the Russian government that a gold medal would be worth $25,000 to each player!

CANADA'S "OTHER" CANADIANS

Because pros were now allowed to compete, and dual-citizenship laws were increasingly open in this evermore global village, there were many Canadian-born players on other hockey teams as well. In fact, three countries — Norway, Austria, and West Germany — could boast of having a starting goalie who was born and raised in Canada: Vernon Mott (Norway), Brian Stankiewicz (Austria), and Karl Friesen (West Germany). In all, 21 Canadians were playing for other countries in the Olympic hockey tournament, most of them having played pro in smaller European centres for a number of years, not good enough for the NHL, but not willing to abandon their Olympic dream.

OPENING GAME HISTRIONICS

Canada's first game, a 1–0 win over Poland, was watched by an incredible 3.7 million Canadians on national TV, but just before the opening face-off the Swedish contingent tried to play mind games with Canada. Sweden claimed that the goalie masks of Sean Burke and Andy Moog were illegal, and measurement proved them correct. Out went the fibreglass masks, in came unfamiliar shield-masks. The Canadians were also fined $100,000 by the IIHF for wearing uniforms that were not sanctioned; before the Games, all jersey rights had been bought by the Finnish company Tackla, but Canada insisted on wearing their standard uniforms instead.

Interestingly, this Swedish mask complaint was used by Canada itself towards the end of their 3–1 loss to Finland. Desperate, with 2:21 to go in the 3rd, they protested Jarmo Myllys's mask. They, too, were right, but were unable to cash in on the subsequent power-play and the final score remained 3–1 for Finland.

CANADA'S MEDAL HOPES

Because of the "unique" formula to determine the gold medal winner, Canada had one real shot for a medal, their first game against the Soviets. Although Canada qualified for the medal round by being tied with Finland and Sweden for first place in their preliminary group (with seven points each), they entered the medal round with a record of 0–1–1 because of their results against other qualifying teams (a loss to Finland and a tie with Sweden). Thus, Canada trailed Russia by three points *before* the medal round even began and had to beat the Russians to have any chance at all for the gold.

Canada played a solid first period, killing off two penalties and coming out of it scoreless, but just 45 seconds into the second Russia scored what proved to be the winner. Canada failed to score on its two power-play chances, and in the third the Russians threw their game into overdrive, scoring three goals and limiting Canada to just three shots. Russia 5, Canada 0.

A BRIEF SUMMATION

Despite the result, the inclusion of pros paved the way for future Olympics, when even more, higher-calibre players might be expected to play. The participation of goalie Moog, for instance, also added a new kind of player to the mix. Previously, there had been the amateur, then the minor pro who would never make it in the NHL, then the amateur who used the Olympic program to hone his skills above and beyond Junior A hockey as a path to the NHL. Now there was the holdout, the unhappy NHLer who could use the Olympics as a way of playing top level hockey while indicating to his team he wanted a new contract or a trade. This was to become a vital part of future Canadian Olympic teams, especially in 1994, and although it helped give Canada an improved squad, the ethical price was high. Was the Olympian who played for the pride, glory, and honour of his country being replaced by the spoiled pro who used the Canadian team as leverage and a threat in million-dollar NHL contract squabbles? The team might have been improving, but at what cost?

The Competition

TOURNAMENT FORMAT

The 12 teams entered in the Olympics were divided into two groups of six and then played a round-robin schedule within each division (five games per team). The top three teams in each pool then advanced to a medal round in which all previous results against opponents in the medal round counted. The other teams were placed in another pool to determine 7th–12th place rankings. Games were the regulation three 20-minute periods, with no overtime. In the case of a tie in the final standings, goal differential would be the deciding factor.

THE OPPOSITION

AUSTRIA • Thomas Cijan, Konrad Dorn, Kelvin Greenbank, Kurt Harand, Bernie Hutz, Werner Kerth, Rudolf Koenig, Gert Kompajn, Gunter Koren, Edward Lebler, Robert Mack, Manfred Muehr, Martin Platzer, Herbert Pok, Gerhanrd Pusnik, Peter Raffl, Robin Sadler, Andreas Salat, Michael Shea, Brian Stankiewicz, Johann Sulzer, Silvester Szybisti, Peter Znenahlik

CZECHOSLOVAKIA • Jaroslav Benak, Mojmir Bozik, Petr Briza, Jiri Dolezal, Ota Hascak, Dominik Hasek, Miloslav Horava, Jiri Hrdina, Jiri Lala, Igor Liba, Dusan Pasek, Radim Radevic, Petr Rosol, Vladimir Ruzicka, Bedrich Scerban, Jiri Seiba, Jaromir Sindel, Antonin Stavjana, Rudolf Suchanek, Eduard Uvira, David Volek, Peter Volek, Rostislav Vlach

FINLAND • Timo Blomqvist, Kari Eloranta, Raimo Helminen, Iiro Jarvi, Esa Keskinen, Erkki Laine, Erkki Lehtonen, Jyrki Lumme, Reijo Mikkolainen, Jarmo Myllys, Teppo Numminen, Janne Ojanen, Arto Ruotanen, Reijo Ruotsalainen, Simo Saarinen, Kai Suikkanen, Timo Susi, Jukka Tammi, Jari Torkki, Pekka Tuomisto, Jukka Virtanen

FRANCE • Peter Almasy, Paulin Bordeleau, Stephane Botteri, Phillippe Bozon, Jean-Marc Djian, Guy Dupuis, Patrick Foliot, Derek Haas, Michel Leblanc, Jean-Phillippe Lemoine, Jean Lerondeau, Stephane Lessard, Daniel Maric, François Ouimet, Franck Pajonkowski, Andre Peloffy, Denis Perez, Christian Pouget, Antoine Richer, Pierre Scmitt, Christophe Ville, Steven Woodburn

NORWAY • Cato Andersen, Morgan Andersen, Lars Bergseng, Arne Billkvam, Tor Eikeland, Age Ellingsen, Jarl Eriksen, Stephen Foyn, Jarle Friis, Rune Gulliksen, Geir Hoff, Roy Johansen, Erik Kristiansen, Truls Kristiansen, Orjan Lovdal, Vernon Mott, Jorgen Salsten, Petter Salsten, Tommy Skaarberg, Kim Sogaard, Sigurd Thinn, Petter Thoresen, Frank Vestreng, Marius Voigt

POLAND • Janusz Adamiec, Zbiginiew Bryjak, Krzysztof Bujar, Marek Cholewa, Jerzy Christ, Miroslaw Copija, Henryk Gruth, Andrzej Hanisz, Leszek Jachna, Andrzej Kadziolka, Jedrzej Kasperczyk, Franciszek Kukla, Piotr Kwasigroch, Jaroslaw Morawiecki, Ireneusz Pacula, Krzysztof Podsialdo, Jerzy Potz, Gabriel Samolei, Krystian Sikorski, Roman Steblecki, Marek Stebnick, Jan Stopczyk, Andrzej Swiatek, Jacek Szopinski, Robert Szopinski, Jacek Zamojski

SWEDEN • Peter Andersson, Mikael Andersson, Peter Aslin, Bo Berglund, Anders Bergman, Jonas Bergqvist, Thom Eklund, Anders Eldebrink, Peter Eriksson, Thomas Eriksson, Michael Hjalm, Lars Ivarsson, Mikael Johansson, Lars Karlsson, Mats Kihlstrom, Peter Lindmark, Lars Molin, Jens Ohling, Lars-Gunnar Pettersson, Thomas Rundqvist, Tommy Samuelsson, Ulf Sandstrom, Hakan Sodergren

SWITZERLAND • Olivier Anken, Gaetan Boucher, Patrice Brasey, Richard Bucher, Urs Burkhart, Manuele Celio, Pietro Cunti, Jorg Eberle, Felix Hollenstein, Peter Jaks, Jakob Kolliker, Andre Kunzi, Markus Leuenberger, Fredy Luthi, Fausto Mazzoleni, Gil Montandon, Thomas Mueller, Philipp Neuenschwander, Andreas Ritsch, Bruno Rogger, Peter Schlagenhauf, Renato Tosio, Thomas Vrabec, Roman Wager, Andreas Zehnder

UNITED STATES • Allen Bourbeau, John Blue, Greg Brown, John Donatelli, Scott Fusco, Guy Gosselin, Tony Granato, Craig Janney, James Johannson, Peter Laviolette, Steve Leach, Brian Leetch, Brad MacDonald, Cory Millen, Kevin Miller, Jeff Norton, Todd Okerlund, Mike Richter, Dave Snuggerud, Kevin Stevens, Chris Terreri, Eric Weinrich, Scott Young

USSR • Ilya Byakin, Vyacheslav Bykov, Aleksandr Chernykh, Vyacheslav Fetisov, Aleksei Gusarov, Valery Kamensky, Aleksei Kasatonov, Andrei Khomutov, Aleksandr Kozhevnikov, Igor Kravchuk, Vladimir Krutov, Igor Larionov, Andrei Lomakin, Sergei Makarov, Aleksandr Mogilny, Sergei Mylnikov, Vitaly Samoylov, Anatoly Semenov, Sergei Starikov, Igor Stelnov, Sergei Svetlov, Sergei Yashin

WEST GERMANY • Christian Brittig, Peter Draisaitl, Ron Fischer, Georg Franz, Karl-Heinz Friesen, Dieter Hegen, Georg Holzmann, Udo Kiessling, Horst-Peter Kretschmer, Harold Kries, Dieter Medicus, Andreas Niederberger, Peter Obresa, Helmut de Raaf, Joachim Reil, Roy Roedger, Peter Schiller, Josef Schlickenrieder, Manfred Schuster, Helmut Steiger, Bernd Truntschka, Gerd Truntschka, Manfred Wolf

FINAL STANDINGS

PRELIMINARY ROUND • GROUP A

	GP	W	L	T	GF	GA	P
Finland	5	3	1	1	22	8	7
Sweden	5	2	0	3	23	10	7
Canada	5	3	1	1	17	12	7
Switzerland	5	3	2	0	19	10	6
Poland	5	0	4	1	9	13	1*
France	5	1	4	0	10	47	0*

RESULTS

FEBRUARY 14
Canada 1 Poland 0
Sweden 13 France 2
Switzerland 2 Finland 1

FEBRUARY 16
Canada 4 Switzerland 2
Sweden 1 Poland 1
Finland 10 France 1

FEBRUARY 18
Finland 3 Canada 1
Poland 6 France 2*
Sweden 4 Switzerland 2

FEBRUARY 20
Canada 9 France 5
Finland 3 Sweden 3
Switzerland 4 Poland 1

FEBRUARY 22
Canada 2 Sweden 2
Finland 5 Poland 1
Switzerland 9 France 0

** Poland won the game 6–2 but was stripped of the win after forward Jaroslav Morawiecki tested positive for testosterone. He was banned from international competition for 18 months and France was officially awarded a 2–0 win, but not the points.*

PRELIMINARY ROUND • GROUP B

	GP	W	L	T	GF	GA	P
USSR	5	5	0	0	32	10	10
West Germany	5	4	1	0	19	12	8
Czechoslovakia	5	3	2	0	23	14	6
United States	5	2	3	0	27	27	4
Austria	5	0	4	1	12	29	1
Norway	5	0	4	1	11	32	1

RESULTS

FEBRUARY 13
West Germany 2 Czechoslovakia 1
USSR 5 Norway 0
United States 10 Austria 6

FEBRUARY 15
West Germany 7 Norway 3
USSR 8 Austria 1
Czechoslovakia 7 United States 5

FEBRUARY 17
West Germany 3 Austria 1
Czechoslovakia 10 Norway 1
USSR 7 United States 5

FEBRUARY 19
Czechoslovakia 4 Austria 0
USSR 6 West Germany 3
United States 6 Norway 3

FEBRUARY 21
USSR 6 Czechoslovakia 1
Austria 4 Norway 4
West Germany 4 United States 1

FEBRUARY 23
France 6 Norway 6 (11th place game — France wins shootout 2–0)
Austria 3 Poland 2 (9th place game)

FEBRUARY 25
United States 8 Switzerland 4 (7th place game)

MEDAL ROUND

	GP	W	L	T	GF	GA	P
USSR	5	4	1	0	25	7	8
Finland	5	3	1	1	18	10	7
Sweden	5	2	1	2	15	16	6
Canada	5	2	2	1	17	14	5
West Germany	5	1	4	0	8	26	2
Czechoslovakia	5	1	4	0	12	22	2

MEDAL ROUND RESULTS

Carry Over Results From Preliminary Round

FEBRUARY 13
West Germany 2 Czechoslovakia 1

FEBRUARY 18
Finland 3 Canada 1

FEBRUARY 19
USSR 6 West Germany 3

FEBRUARY 20
Finland 3 Sweden 3

FEBRUARY 21
USSR 6 Czechoslovakia 1

FEBRUARY 22
Canada 2 Sweden 2

MEDAL ROUND GAMES

FEBRUARY 24
USSR 5 Canada 0
Sweden 6 Czechoslovakia 2
Finland 8 West Germany 0

FEBRUARY 26
Canada 8 West Germany 1
Czechoslovakia 5 Finland 2
USSR 7 Sweden 1

FEBRUARY 27
Canada 6 Czechoslovakia 3

FEBRUARY 28
Sweden 3 West Germany 2
Finland 2 USSR 1

TEAM CANADA GAME SUMMARIES

FEBRUARY 14 • Canada 1 Poland 0

FIRST PERIOD
1. Canada, Habscheid (Sherven, Yawney) • 4:22
penalties: *Schreiber (Can) 6:05, Gruth (Pol) 12:16, Steblecki (Pol) 16:47*

SECOND PERIOD
No Scoring
penalties: *Felix (Can) 5:51, Gregg (Can) 18:48*

THIRD PERIOD
No Scoring
penalties: *none*

IN GOAL
Canada — Moog
Poland — Samolei

SHOTS ON GOAL

Canada	12	10	7	**29**
Poland	9	3	5	**17**

FEBRUARY 16 • Canada 4 Switzerland 2

IN GOAL
Canada — Burke
Switzerland — Bucher

SHOTS ON GOAL

Canada	18	14	13	**45**
Switzerland	6	9	8	**23**

FIRST PERIOD
No Scoring
penalties: *Brasey (Swi) 17:00*

SECOND PERIOD
1. Canada, Boisvert (Roy) • 4:05
2. Switzerland, Schlagenhauf (Kolliker, Boucher) • 11:15(pp)
penalties: *Jaks (Swi) 7:54, Burke (Can — served by Vilgrain) 11:09, Tambellini (Can) & Vrabec (Swi) 12:11, Boucher (Swi) 17:17, Habscheid (Can) 20:00*

THIRD PERIOD
3. Canada, Sherven (Zalapski, Berry) • 4:56
4. Canada, Yaremchuk (Malinowski) • 15:04
5. Canada, Habscheid (Berry, Sherven) • 16:01
6. Switzerland, Eberle (Neuenschwander) • 16:22
penalties: *Rogger (Swi) 10:29, Peplinski (Can) 19:57*

FEBRUARY 18 • Finland 3 Canada 1

IN GOAL
Canada — Burke
Finland — Myllys

SHOTS ON GOAL

Canada	12	13	14	**39**
Finland	11	11	4	**26**

FIRST PERIOD
1. Finland, Laine (Helminen, Jarvi) • 13:11
2. Finland, Laine (Helminen, Numminen) • 15:02
3. Finland, Lehtonen (Mikkolainen, Eloranta) • 19:20
penalties: *Lumme (Fin) 19:50*

SECOND PERIOD
4. Canada, Gregg (Tambellini) • 13:05
penalties: *Karpan (Can) 4:02, Suikkanen (Fin) 6:10*

THIRD PERIOD
No Scoring
penalties: *Blomqvist (Fin) 11:19, Myllys (Fin — served by Suikkanen) 17:39*

FEBRUARY 20 • Canada 9 France 5

IN GOAL
Canada — Moog
France — Djian/Foliot
(Foliot replaced Djian to start 2nd)

SHOTS ON GOAL

Canada	21	13	14	**48**
France	12	6	2	**20**

FIRST PERIOD
1. Canada, Boisvert (Zalapski, Tambellini) • 6:57
2. France, Bozon (Woodburn) • 8:16
3. Canada, Boisvert (Peplinski, Tambellini) • 9:36(pp)
4. Canada, Yawney (Habscheid, Roy) • 10:47(pp)
5. France, Richer (Perez, Bozon) • 16:16
6. Canada, Yaremchuk (unassisted) • 16:57
7. Canada, Malinowski (Schreiber, Felix) • 17:24
8. France, Bozon (Lemoine, Ville) • 17:57
9. Canada, Habscheid (Sherven, Berry) • 18:58
10. Canada, Tambellini (Boisvert) • 19:20
penalties: *Can (too many men — served by Sherven) 3:39, Lerondeau (Fr) 9:22, Almasy (Fr) & Fr (too many men) 10:31*

SECOND PERIOD
11. France, Bozon (Almasy) • 6:14
penalties: *Sherven (Can) 10:33*

THIRD PERIOD
12. Canada, Malinowski (Yaremchuk, Zalapski) • 6:34(pp)
13. France, Woodburn (unassisted) • 17:36
14. Canada, Felix (Roy, Habscheid) • 18:41
penalties: *Pajonkowski (Fr) 5:46, Berry (Can) 11:12, Roy (Can) 12:36, Perez (Fr) 13:30, Perez (Fr) & Peplinski (Can) 17:18*

FEBRUARY 22 • Canada 2 Sweden 2

FIRST PERIOD

1. Sweden, Eldebrink (Molin) • 2:23

2. Canada, Malinowski (Felix) • 6:34

penalties: *none*

SECOND PERIOD

3. Canada, Boisvert (unassisted) • 19:30

penalties: *Berglund (Swe) 13:54*

THIRD PERIOD

4. Sweden, Ohling (Johansson, Eriksson) • 8:26

penalties: *none*

IN GOAL

Canada — Burke

Sweden — Lindmark

SHOTS ON GOAL

Canada	10	10	5	**25**
Sweden	12	6	12	**30**

FEBRUARY 24 • USSR 5 Canada 0

FIRST PERIOD

No Scoring

penalties: *Gregg (Can) 1:20, Peplinski (Can) 5:31*

SECOND PERIOD

1. USSR, Yashin (Semenov) • 0:45

2. USSR, Bykov (Khomutov, Biakin) • 7:22(pp)

penalties: *Yaremchuk (Can) 6:07, Biakin (USSR) 12:09, Makarov (USSR) 19:37*

THIRD PERIOD

3. USSR, Mogilny (Lomakin) • 8:00

4. USSR, Krutov (Larionov, Fetisov) • 16:37

5. USSR, Makarov (Lomakin) • 18:16

penalties: *Makarov (USSR) & Gregg (Can) 16:04*

IN GOAL

Canada — Burke

USSR — Mylnikov

SHOTS ON GOAL

Canada	6	8	3	**17**
USSR	10	11	12	**33**

FEBRUARY 26 • Canada 8 West Germany 1

FIRST PERIOD

1. Canada, Boisvert (Roy, Bradley) • 19:34

penalties: *Can (too many men — served by Berry) 6:26*

SECOND PERIOD

2. West Germany, Hegen (G. Truntschka) • 5:45

3. Canada, Zalapski (unassisted) • 6:22

4. Canada, Yaremchuk (Gregg, Malinowski) • 9:46

5. Canada, Habscheid (unassisted) • 11:04

6. Canada, Berry (Sherven) • 11:20

penalties: *Yawney (Can) 6:54, Watters (Can) 7:29, Kiessling (WGer) 11:42*

THIRD PERIOD

7. Canada, Schreiber (Bradley, Boisvert) • 3:59(pp)

8. Canada, Boisvert (Schreiber) • 16:05

9. Canada, Habscheid (Roy, Yaremchuk) • 19:29(pp)

penalties: *Franz (WGer) 3:49, Yawney (Can) 5:21, Boisvert (Can) 12:01, Schuster (WGer) 17:24, Roedger (WGer) 17:43*

IN GOAL

Canada — Moog

West Germany — Schlickenreider/ Friesen *(Friesen replaced Schlickenreider at 11:20 of 2nd)*

SHOTS ON GOAL

Canada	7	17	14	**38**
West Germany	17	9	5	**31**

FEBRUARY 27 • Canada 6 Czechoslovakia 3

FIRST PERIOD

1. Canada, Boisvert (Roy) • 2:14

2. Czechoslovakia, Stavjana (Liba, Seiba) • 2:48

3. Canada, Joyce (Yaremchuk, Watters) • 9:00

4. Canada, Berry (Bradley, Roy) • 19:18(pp)

penalties: *Yawney (Can) 4:27, Benak (Cz) 9:52, Gregg (Can) 12:26, Zalapski (Can) 16:19, Liba (Cz) 17:40*

SECOND PERIOD

5. Czechoslovakia, Seiba (Liba) • 3:46

6. Canada, Sherven (Habscheid, Berry) • 4:52

7. Czechoslovakia, Ruzicka (Hrdina) • 13:50

penalties: *Horava (Cz) 7:33, Habscheid (Can) 11:13, Horava (Cz) 17:50*

THIRD PERIOD

8. Canada, Sherven (Bradley, Gregg) • 12:59

9. Canada, Sherven (unassisted) • 19:51(sh-en)

penalties: *Uvira (Cz) 1:04, Bozik (Cz) 3:22, Roy (Can) 9:55, Habscheid (Can) 18:40*

IN GOAL

Canada — Moog

Czechoslovakia — Hasek

SHOTS ON GOAL

Canada	9	11	10	**30**
Czechoslovakia	9	5	8	**22**

TEAM CANADA FINAL STATISTICS • 1988

#		GP	G	A	P	Pim
12	Serge Boisvert	8	7	2	9	2
14	Marc Habscheid	8	5	3	8	6
10	Gord Sherven	8	4	4	8	4
3	Serge Roy	5	0	7	7	4
13	Ken Yaremchuk	8	3	3	6	2
9	Ken Berry	8	2	4	6	4
16	Merlin Malinowski	8	3	2	5	0
11	Steve Tambellini	8	1	3	4	2
25	Zarley Zalapski	8	1	3	4	2
8	Brian Bradley	7	0	4	4	0
21	Randy Gregg	8	1	2	3	8
7	Wally Schreiber	8	1	2	3	2
23	Chris Felix	6	1	2	3	2
5	Trent Yawney	8	1	1	2	6
15	Bob Joyce	4	1	0	1	0
24	Jim Peplinski	7	0	1	1	6
2	Tim Watters	8	0	1	1	2
19	Vaughn Karpan	8	0	0	0	2
1	Sean Burke	4	0	0	0	2
18	Claude Vilgrain	6	0	0	0	0
4	Tony Stiles	5	0	0	0	0

#	IN GOAL	GP	W-L-T	Mins	GA	SO	Avg
35	Andy Moog	4	4–0–0	240	9	1	2.25
1	Sean Burke	4	1–2–1	239	12	0	3.02

CHAPTER 16

The 16th Olympic Winter Games

ALBERTVILLE, FRANCE

February 8–23, 1992

Dave Hannan

The 91st IOC session was held in Lausanne, Switzerland on October 17, 1986 and Albertville was awarded the Games of 1992 after five rounds of voting. Berchtesgaden, Germany was eliminated in the first round, Anchorage, USA in the second, Cortina, Italy in the third, Lillehammer, Norway in the fourth, and Sofia, Bulgaria and Falun, Sweden in the final round.

TEAM CANADA • 1992

Sean Burke, *GOAL*
Trevor Kidd, *GOAL*

Kevin Dahl, *DEFENCE*
Curt Giles, *DEFENCE*
Gord Hynes, *DEFENCE*
Adrien Plavsic, *DEFENCE*
Dan Ratushny, *DEFENCE*
Brad Schlegel, *DEFENCE (CAPTAIN)*
Brian Tutt, *DEFENCE*
Jason Woolley, *DEFENCE*

Dave Archibald, *FORWARD*
Todd Brost, *FORWARD*
Dave Hannan, *FORWARD*
Fabian Joseph, *FORWARD*
Joe Juneau, *FORWARD*
Patrick Lebeau, *FORWARD*
Chris Lindberg, *FORWARD*
Eric Lindros, *FORWARD*
Kent Manderville, *FORWARD*
Wally Schreiber, *FORWARD*
Randy Smith, *FORWARD*
Dave Tippett, *FORWARD*

Sam St. Laurent *(DID NOT PLAY)*

Dave King, *COACH & GENERAL MANAGER*
Terry Crisp, *ASSISTANT COACH*
Wayne Fleming, *ASSISTANT COACH*

FINAL PLACINGS

GOLD MEDAL
Unified Team

SILVER MEDAL
Canada

BRONZE MEDAL
Czechoslovakia

FOURTH PLACE
United States

FIFTH PLACE
Sweden

SIXTH PLACE
Germany

SEVENTH PLACE
Finland

EIGHTH PLACE
France

NINTH PLACE
Norway

TENTH PLACE
Switzerland

ELEVENTH PLACE
Poland

TWELFTH PLACE
Italy

TEAM CANADA'S HOCKEY SEASON

As had become customary, team Canada had been in training for the Olympics since August of the previous year, though the small crew of 18 players who showed up for the first day of camp, which included seven members from the 1988 Calgary Games, certainly did not even faintly resemble the final roster on opening night in Albertville six months later. In fact, of the returnees, only Sean Burke and Jason Woolley actually played in both Olympics. Of prime concern was the team's training centre in Alberta. Because the altitude at Albertville would be 500 metres higher, conditioning became a priority. Also, this would be Dave King's third trip to the Games with Canada; still medal-less, he, too, had something to prove this trip.

CANADA'S SMALL TOWNS

In the four years between Olympics, Canada's national team played many exhibition games against varying levels of competition, mostly in small Canadian cities that didn't often get the chance to see such quality of hockey. The team's itinerary included stops in Kapuskasing, New Liskeard, Iroquois Falls, and Elliot Lake in Northern Ontario, the remote Powell River in British Columbia, Maniwaki, Quebec, and Sherwood Park, and Red Deer in Alberta.

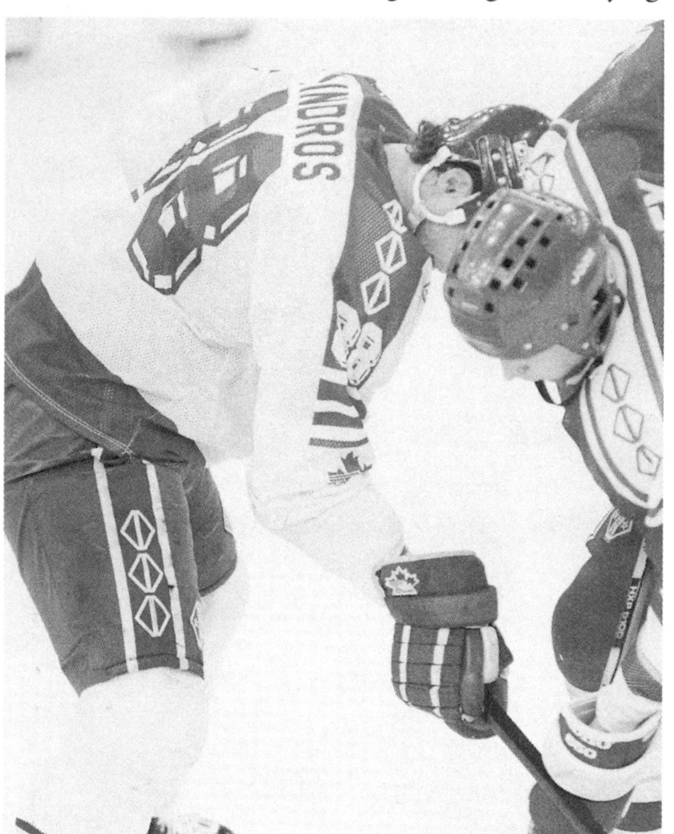

Perhaps most cherished of all was Canada's game against a Russian team in White Court, Alberta, where a local women's hockey team, the Hot Paddies, put up a $28,000 guarantee to bring the game there on January 1, 1992. Another gem of a game took place in Barrs Head, Alberta in a rink that could seat only 850 people. When the Olympians visited, 1,400 people paid between $25-$50 for once-in-a-lifetime seats. Fans in these remote cities were as encouraging in their telegrams and faxes as were those in the big cities, and all players appreciated and recalled the support with great affection. Over the decades, small-town Canada had provided the NHL and Olympic teams with as many great players as the country's metropolises; these games were not token symbols or publicity stunts but well-chosen ways of saying thanks to all the families in all the small places for making Canada the great hockey playing nation it was.

THE PROS ARE HERE

The 1988 Games had been a watershed event in officially allowing professionals to participate in the Olympics. Four years later, all teams were recruiting their country's pros with single-minded determination. The Swedes were perhaps the most successful in their efforts and thus became the early favourites to win gold. On their blue line would be Borje Salming, the 16-year Toronto Maple Leafs veteran. He was joined by Hakan Loob, Tommy Soderstrom, Mats Naslund, and Bengt

Gustafsson, all seasoned NHLers. The Finns also fielded a pro-preference team that included Kari Eloranta, Simo Saarinen, Hannu Virta, Ville Siren, Hannu Jarvenpaa, Raimo Sumanen, Petri Skriko, and Teemu Selanne. Money was playing an ever-increasing role in the Games. The Czechs were all guaranteed a new car (a Skoda, but a new car, nonetheless) if they brought home a medal, while the Russians were even more blunt about awarding their hockey players' success: a gold was worth $3,000 a player, silver $2,000, and bronze $1,000.

CANADA'S PROS

By the time the new year rolled around, "L'affaire Lindros" was in full swing in Quebec and across the country. In June 1991, the Quebec Nordiques drafted the hugely talented Lindros first overall in the Entry Draft, knowing full well that Lindros had no intention of signing with les Nords. Despite Lindros's repeated statements that his dislike of team president Marcel Aubut was the reason he wouldn't sign, the media, particularly the francophone writers, tore into Lindros for being anti-Quebec, anti-separatiste, and anti-French. Lindros calmly went back to Junior A with the Oshawa Generals, then took off for the World Junior Championships in Fussen, Germany, after which he joined the Olympians. He insisted the Nordiques trade him or lose him back into the draft two years down the road. Until then, he was going to play wherever he could at whatever level, but not in Quebec City and not with the Nordiques.

While "the Big E" was clearly the player of the year, the media circus that his life became was distracting equally to him and those around him. He had long outgrown his Oshawa days, and played most of the year in Junior more or less to stay in shape. When he played in the World Juniors, he was ill and ineffective, which helped neither his reputation on ice (the team didn't win gold) nor off it (being seen as manipulative and selfish). By the time he caught up with the Olympians, he was under such scrutiny and pressure to do something *big* it was almost certain not to happen. Lindros, not an Olympic medal, became the focus of attention, and no amount of talent or patriotism he may have possessed could have diverted the attention elsewhere. Like Andy Moog during the previous Olympics, but on a much grander scale, he was using the team as leverage in his dispute with the Nordiques. Nothing could have made people forget this fact, and nothing short of a gold medal could have redeemed him in the eyes of those most critical of his motives. Plain and simple, had any other team than Quebec drafted him, he would have been playing in the NHL in February 1992 and not in the Olympics. In the end, though, he was a key component in Canada's winning the silver medal, but perhaps as much a disruptive force to team concentration, cohesion, and confidence as a positive one.

Goalie Sean Burke was another example of an NHL pro joining the team, though his commitment was certainly of longer duration. After the 1988 Games, he led the New Jersey Devils to their first-ever playoff appearance, and when the team missed the post-season the following year, no one could rightly accuse him of being the culpable party. In 1989–90, he struggled and became less popular with the fans as back-up Chris Terreri began playing himself into the number one position. The following season (1990–91), when he found himself playing back-up to Terreri, Burke played out his option and asked to be traded. For some reason, GM Lou Lamoriello did not oblige, and so in September 1991 Burke committed to the Olympic team for the year. "It made our day when we found out Sean Burke would be with us," assistant coach Terry Crisp said. "You can't win a tournament like this without great goaltending and Sean gives us that. We couldn't believe how lucky we were to get him."

Dave Hannan playing stickless defence.

Dave Hannan was a lesser pro, another small, agile player with the Leafs whose career seemed at a dead end when the club tried to trade him but found no takers. As a last resort, GM Cliff Fletcher suggested Hannan try the Olympic team, an idea Dave King made palatable for the fleet-footed checking forward. "One of my selling points," King would later comment, "was that I could virtually guarantee Hannan would look great on the large Olympic ice surface. And he has. He's been one of our best players here."

Joe Juneau was in a slightly different boat, though in similar waters. Selected 81st overall by the Bruins in the 1988 Entry Draft, he rubbed Boston GM Harry Sinden the wrong way by demanding a one-way contract, that guaranteed that if he were demoted to the farm team, he'd still be paid his NHL salary. The Bruins balked, and Juneau played with the Olympians well enough to earn no fewer than four offers to play in Europe, though the NHL was obviously the budding star's first choice. Thus, he used his time with the team not only to learn and develop, but also to gain some bargaining leverage with the Bruins. It worked. He was instrumental in Canada's silver medal performance, and the Bruins wound up offering him a three-year deal with a healthy $300,000 signing bonus.

CANADA'S ROSTER — A SUMMARY

Putting together the team for the 1992 Olympics began the day after the '88 Games concluded, and Canada's entry in Albertville reflected the singular methods of hockey in Canada. Captain Brad Schlegel started with King in the fall of 1988 when Olympic on-ice preparations began in earnest. Todd Brost joined the team the next fall, and in 1990 Gord Hynes, Dave Archibald, Chris Lindberg, and Randy Smith began their tour of duty. This, then, was the core of the 1992 team, but at the same time King was adding and scratching from the line-up right up until

Sean Burke stops Peter Draisaitl on Germany's last penalty shot during Canada's 4–3 shootout victory.

days before the Games were set to begin, based on the availability of the pros.

The quality of the team had increased a little bit each year since Canada re-entered the Olympics in 1980, but the set-up still was nowhere near ideal. Having all amateurs would have been perfect from the point of view of preparation, but not if optimum results were being asked for. All top-notch pros would have been the route to go to maximize results, but that still was not feasible without a comprehensive agreement with the NHL, and that was not going to happen until the Americans decided the effort would be worth it.

The Competition

TOURNAMENT FORMAT

The 12 competing nations were divided into two pools of six teams each and played a round-robin schedule within each group. The top four teams from each then advanced to an elimination round showdown. The top team in group A played the fourth team in group B; the top team in group B played the fourth team in group A; the second team in group A played the third team in group B; the second team in group B played the third team in group A. The elimination playoffs (a quarter-finals, semi-finals and finals) represented a new way to bring excitement to the Olympics, through one-game eliminations.

In case of a tie in the standings in the preliminary round, goal differential in games played between those teams that were tied would be the deciding factor (for example, Canada tied with Unified Team and Czechs but wound up on top). In the preliminary round, a 10-minute sudden-death overtime period would follow a tie, after which the game would go in the books as a tie. In the elimination playoff round, there would be a 10-minute sudden-death overtime period, then a penalty shot-style shootout after 70 minutes if the game were still tied.

THE OPPOSITION

CZECHOSLOVAKIA • Patrick Augusta, Petr Briza, Leo Gudas, Miloslav Horova, Petr Hrbek, Otakar Janecky, Tomas Jelinek, Drahomir Kadlec, Kamil Kastak, Robert Lang, Igor Liba, Ladislav Lubina, Frantisek Prochazka, Petr Rosol, Bedrich Scerban, Jiri Slegr, Richard Smehlik, Robert Svehla, Oldrich Svoboda, Radek Toupal, Peter Veselovsky, Richard Zemlicka

FINLAND • Timo Blomqvist, Kari Eloranta, Raimo Helminen, Hannu Jarvenpaa, Timo Jutila, Markus Ketterer, Janne Laukkanen, Harri Laurila, Jari Lindroos, Mikko Makela, Mika Nieminen, Timo Peltomaa, Arto Ruotanen, Timo Saarikoski, Simo Saarinen, Keijo Sailynoja, Teemu Selanne, Ville-Jussi Siren, Petri Skriko, Raimo Summanen, Jukka Tammi, Pekka Tuomisto

FRANCE • Peter Almasy, Michael Babin, Stephane Barin, Stephane Botteri, Phillippe Bozon, Arnaud Briand, Yves Crettenand, Jean-Marc Djian, Patrick Dunn, Gerald Guennelon, Benoit Laporte, Michel Leblanc, Jean-Phillippe Lemoine, Pascal Margerit, Denis Perez, Serge Poudrier, Christian Pouget, Pierre Pousse, Antoine Richer, Bruno Saunier, Christophe Ville, Petri Ylonen

GERMANY • Richard Amann, Thomas Brandl, Andreas Brockmann, Peter Draisaitl, Ronald Fischer, Karl Friesen, Dieter Hegen, Michael Heidt, Ulrich Heimer, Joseph Heiss, Raimond Hilger, Georg Holzmann, Axel Kammerer, Udo Kiessling, Ernst Kopf, Jorg Mayr, Andreas Niederberger, Helmut de Raaf, Jurgen Rumrich, Michael Rumrich, Michael Schmidt, Bernd Truntschka, Gerd Truntschka

ITALY • Michael de Angelis, Jimmy Camazzola, Anthony Circelli, Georg Comploi, David Delfino, Giuseppe Foglietta, Robert Ginetti, Emilio Iovio, Bob Manno, Giovanni Marchetti, Rick Morocco, Frank Nigro, Robert Oberrauch, Diego Riva, Martino Soracreppa, William Stewart, Lucio Topatigh, John Vecchiarelli, Ivano Zanatta, Bruno Zarrillo

NORWAY • Arne Billkvam, Ole Dahlstrom, Jan Fagerli, Jarle Friis, Rune Gulliksen, Carl Gunnar Gundersen, Geir Hoff, Tommy Jacobsen, Tom Johansen, Jon Karlstad, Erik Kristiansen, Jim Marthinsen, Oystein Olsen, Eirik Paulsen, Marius Rath, Petter Salsten, Robert Schistad, Kim Sogaard, Petter Thoresen

POLAND • Janusz Adamiec, Marek Batkiewicz, Krzysztof Bujar, Marek Cholewa, Mariusz Czerkawski, Dariusz Garbocz, Henryk Gruth, Kazimierz Jurek, Andrzej Kadziolka, Waldemar Klisiak, Krzysztof Kuzniecow, Mariusz Puzio, Gabriel Samolej, Jerzy Sobera, Rafel Sroka, Andrzej Swistak, Robert Szopinski, Miroslaw Tomasik, Wojciech Tzacz, Slawomir Wieloch

SWEDEN • Peter Andersson, Charles Berglund, Patrik Carnback, Lars Edstrom, Patrik Erickson, Bengt-Ake Gustavsson, Mikael Johansson, Kenneth Kennholt, Patric Kjellberg, Petri Liimatainen, Hakan Loob, Mats Naslund, Roger Nordstrom, Peter Ottosson, Thomas Rundqvist, Daniel Rydmark, Borje Salming, Tommy Sjodin, Fredrik Stillman, Tommy Soderstrom, Jan Viktorsson

SWITZERLAND • Samuel Balmer, Sandro Bertaggia, Mario Brodmann, Andreas Buetler, Manuele Celio, Jorg Eberle, Keith Fair, Patrick Howald, Peter Jaks, Dino Kessler, Andre Kuenzi, Sven Leuenberger, Alfred Luthi, Gil Montandon, Reto Pavoni, Andre Rotheli, Mario Rottaris, Andreas Ton, Renato Tosio, Thomas Vrabec

UNIFIED TEAM • Sergei Bautin, Igor Boldin, Nikolai Borschevsky, Vyacheslav Butsayev, Vyacheslav Bykov, Yevgeny Davydov, Darius Kasparaitis, Yuri Khymlev, Andrei Khomutov, Andrei Kovalenko, Aleksei Kovalev, Igor Kravchuk, Vladimir Malakhov, Dmitri Mironov, Sergei Petrenko, Vitaly Prokhorov, Mikhail Shtalenkov, Andrei Trefilov, Dmitri Yushkevich, Aleksei Zhamnov, Aleksei Zhitnik, Sergei Zubov

UNITED STATES • Greg Brown, Clark Donatelli, Theodore Donato, Theodore Drury, David Emma, Scott Gordon, Guy Gosselin, Brett Hedican, Steve Heinze, Sean Hill, James Johannson, Scott Lachance, Ray LeBlanc, Moe Mantha, Shawn McEachern, Marty McInnis, Joe Sacco, Tim Sweeney, Keith Tkachuk, David Tretowicz, Carl Young, Scott Young

FINAL STANDINGS

PRELIMINARY ROUND • POOL A

	GP	W	L	T	GF	GA	P
United States	5	4	0	1	18	7	9
Sweden	5	3	0	2	22	11	8
Finland	5	3	1	1	22	11	7
Germany	5	2	3	0	11	12	4
Italy	5	1	4	0	18	24	2
Poland	5	0	5	0	4	30	0

RESULTS

FEBRUARY 9
Sweden 7 Poland 2
Finland 5 Germany 1
United States 6 Italy 3

FEBRUARY 11
Finland 9 Poland 1
Sweden 7 Italy 3
United States 2 Germany 0

FEBRUARY 13
Italy 7 Poland 1
Sweden 3 Germany 1
United States 4 Finland 1

FEBRUARY 15
Germany 5 Italy 2
Sweden 2 Finland 2
United States 3 Poland 0

FEBRUARY 17
Germany 4 Poland 0
Finland 5 Italy 3
Sweden 3 United States 3

PRELIMINARY ROUND • POOL B

	GP	W	L	T	GF	GA	P
Canada	5	4	1	0	28	9	8
Unified Team	5	4	1	0	32	10	8
Czechoslovakia	5	4	1	0	25	15	8
France	5	2	3	0	14	22	4
Switzerland	5	1	4	0	13	25	2
Norway	5	0	5	0	7	38	0

RESULTS

FEBRUARY 8
Canada 3 France 2
Czechoslovakia 10 Norway 1
Unified Team 8 Switzerland 1

FEBRUARY 10
Canada 6 Switzerland 1
Czechoslovakia 6 France 4
Unified Team 8 Norway 1

FEBRUARY 12
Canada 10 Norway 0
France 4 Switzerland 3
Czechoslovakia 4 Unified Team 3

FEBRUARY 14
Canada 5 Czechoslovakia 1
Switzerland 6 Norway 3
Unified Team 8 France 0

FEBRUARY 16
Unified Team 5 Canada 4
Czechoslovakia 4 Switzerland 2
France 4 Norway 2

CONSOLATION ROUND

FEBRUARY 18
Norway 5 Italy 3

FEBRUARY 19
Switzerland 7 Poland 2

FEBRUARY 20
Poland 4 Italy 1
(11th place game)
Germany 5 France 4
Sweden 3 Finland 2

FEBRUARY 21
Norway 5 Switzerland 2
(9th place game)

FEBRUARY 22
Finland 4 France 1
(7th place game)
Sweden 4 Germany 3
(5th place game)

QUARTER-FINALS

FEBRUARY 18
Canada 4 Germany 3
(OT & shootout)
United States 4 France 1

FEBRUARY 19
Czechoslovakia 3 Sweden 1
Unified Team 6 Finland 1

SEMI-FINALS

FEBRUARY 21
Canada 4 Czechoslovakia 2
Unified Team 5 United States 2

BRONZE MEDAL GAME

FEBRUARY 22
Czechoslovakia 6 United States 1

GOLD MEDAL GAME

FEBRUARY 23
Unified Team 3 Canada 1

TEAM CANADA GAME SUMMARIES

FEBRUARY 8 • Canada 3 France 2

IN GOAL

Canada — Burke

France — Ylonen

SHOTS ON GOAL

Canada			
12	10	7	**29**
France			
7	6	6	**19**

FIRST PERIOD

1. Canada, Juneau (Brost) • 7:05

2. France, Barin (Dunn, Laporte) • 17:11

penalties: *Dahl (Can) 1:18, Tippett (Can) 1:27, Lemoine (Fra) 11:06, Guennelon (Fra) 17:47*

SECOND PERIOD

3. Canada, Archibald (unassisted) • 0:50(pp)

4. Canada, Manderville (Plavsic, Lebeau) • 2:41

penalties: *Botteri (Fra) 0:24, Briand (Fra) & Lindberg (Can) 5:40, Poudrier (Fra) & Hynes (Can) 5:47, Ratushny (Can) 9:36, Pouget (Fra) 11:39, Ville (Fra) & Brost (Can) 15:16, Lebeau (Can) 17:39*

THIRD PERIOD

5. France, Barin (Almasy) • 0:59

penalties: *Archibald (Can) 10:59, Hannan (Can) 16:49*

FEBRUARY 10 • Canada 6 Switzerland 1

IN GOAL

Canada — Burke

Switzerland — Tosio

SHOTS ON GOAL

Canada			
11	15	11	**37**
Switzerland			
8	5	7	**20**

FIRST PERIOD

1. Canada, Lindros (Juneau) • 3:18(pp)

penalties: *Kessler (Swi) 2:22, Tosio (Swi) 6:02, Giles (Can) 10:20, Lindberg (Can) 12:57, Burke (Can) 15:01, Smith (Can) 19:52*

SECOND PERIOD

2. Canada, Juneau (Smith, Woolley) • 4:06(pp)

3. Canada, Lindros (Hynes, Hannan) • 5:47

4. Canada, Schreiber (Lindros, Lebeau) • 7:44

5. Canada, Juneau (Lindberg, Smith) • 15:43

penalties: *Rottaris (Swi) 2:34, Archibald (Can) & Beutler (Swi) 5:05, Archibald (Can — double minor) & Brodmann (Swi) 16:24*

THIRD PERIOD

6. Switzerland, Eberle (Vrabec, Luthi) • 0:47

7. Canada, Hynes (Smith, Lindros) • 18:19(pp)

penalties: *Beutler (Swi) 4:01, Brost (Can) 9:39, Archibald (Can) 13:40, Brasey (Swi — high-sticking major, game misconduct), Beutler (Swi — double minor) & Hannan (Can) 17:13*

FEBRUARY 12 • Canada 10 Norway 0

IN GOAL

Canada — Kidd

Norway — Schistad

SHOTS ON GOAL

Canada			
13	16	8	**37**
Norway			
4	15	0	**19**

FIRST PERIOD

1. Canada, Archibald (Hannan, Plavsic) • 1:57

2. Canada, Archibald (Lindros, Hannan) • 6:35

3. Canada, Schreiber (Manderville, Lindros) • 19:41

penalties: *Fagerli (Nor) 3:08, Giles (Can) 14:46*

SECOND PERIOD

4. Canada, Smith (Lindberg, Schlegel) • 0:24

5. Canada, Lebeau (Smith, Juneau) • 10:02(pp)

6. Canada, Dahl (Juneau) • 13:39

penalties: *Lindros (Can) 3:44, Hannan (Can) 7:44, Thoresen (Nor) 9:04, Hoff (Nor) & Hynes (Can) 12:32, Dahl (Can) 17:15*

THIRD PERIOD

7. Canada, Joseph (Schreiber, Juneau) • 6:25

8. Canada, Lindros (Lebeau, Lindberg) • 8:37

9. Canada, Hynes (Brost) • 10:26

10. Canada, Hynes (Juneau, Smith) • 19:50

penalties: *Archibald (Can) 1:48, Dahlstrom (Nor) 4:16, Can (too many men — served by Lebeau) 11:15*

FEBRUARY 14 • Canada 5 Czechoslovakia 1

FIRST PERIOD

1. Canada, Juneau (Lindros, Smith) • 3:33(pp)

penalties: *Zemlicka (Cz) 3:27, Ratushny (Can) 8:40, Tutt (Can) 13:28*

SECOND PERIOD

2. Canada, Archibald (Juneau, Lindros) • 10:12(pp)

3. Canada, Juneau (Hynes) • 16:46

4. Czechoslovakia, Kastak (Lang) • 19:37(pp)

penalties: *Gudas (Cz) 3:35, Smith (Can) 7:37, Lang (Cz) 9:26, Archibald (Can) 11:09, Schlegel (Can) 11:42, Dahl (Can) 12:25, Archibald (Can) 17:47, Burke (Can — misconduct) 19:37*

THIRD PERIOD

5. Canada, Hannan (Tippett, Manderville) • 1:35

6. Canada, Archibald (Woolley) • 15:23(pp)

penalties: *Zemlicka (Cz) 15:15, Tutt (Can) 18:11*

IN GOAL

Canada — Burke

Czechoslovakia — Briza

SHOTS ON GOAL

Canada

11	6	14	**31**

Czechoslovakia

14	10	10	**34**

FEBRUARY 16 • Unified Team 5 Canada 4

FIRST PERIOD

1. Unified Team, Mironov (Bykov, Kravchuk) • 8:05(pp)

2. Canada, Archibald (Hynes) • 11:03

3. Canada, Lindros (unassisted) • 13:22

4. Unified Team, Borchevsky (Prokhorov) • 14:35

5. Unified Team, Petrenko (Zhamnov, Mironov) • 15:20

penalties: *Tippett (Can) 6:18, Malakhov (Un) 9:07, Juneau (Can) 10:13, Hannan (Can) & Yushkevich (Un) 13:18, Tippett (Can) 19:38*

SECOND PERIOD

6. Unified Team, Kravchuk (Butsayev, Khmylev) • 14:33

penalties: *Bautin (Un) 6:54, Lindros (Can) 17:40*

THIRD PERIOD

7. Canada, Tippett (Hannan) • 3:39

8. Canada, Hannan (Brost, Tippett) • 8:50

9. Unified Team, Kravchuk (Khymlev) • 12:44

penalties: *Tippett (Can) & Davydov (Un) 11:10*

IN GOAL

Canada — Burke

Unified Team — Shtalenkov

SHOTS ON GOAL

Canada

4	8	7	**19**

Unified Team

19	14	19	**52**

FEBRUARY 18 • Canada 4 Germany 3 (10:00 OT & shootout)

FIRST PERIOD

1. Canada, Juneau (Lindberg, Woolley) • 9:38(pp)

2. Germany, J. Rumrich (Holzmann) • 12:40

3. Germany, Hegen (Brockmann, G. Truntschka) • 16:34

penalties: *Amann (Ger) 7:54*

SECOND PERIOD

4. Canada, Schlegel (Schreiber, Archibald) • 0:28

penalties: *M. Rumrich (Ger) 3:29*

THIRD PERIOD

5. Canada, Dahl (Smith) • 13:54

6. Germany, Kopf (Fischer) • 17:38

penalties: *Niederberger (Ger) 9:09*

OVERTIME (10 minutes)

No Scoring

penalties: *none*

SHOOTOUT

First Round (five shots each)

Canada • Lindros ~ missed

Germany • Draisaitl ~ missed

Canada • Archibald ~ missed

Germany • Hegen ~ missed

Canada • Woolley ~ SCORED (1-0)

Germany • G. Truntschka ~ missed

Canada • Schreiber ~ SCORED (2-0)

Germany • M. Rumrich ~ SCORED (2-1)

Canada • Juneau ~ missed

Germany • Brockmann ~ SCORED (2-2)

Second Round (sudden death)

Canada • Lindros ~ SCORED (3-2)

Germany • Draisaitl ~ missed

Canada won shootout 3-2; only Lindros was credited with a goal

IN GOAL

Canada — Burke

Germany — de Raaf

SHOTS ON GOAL

Canada

11	14	11	10	**46**

Germany

7	6	8	9	**30**

FEBRUARY 21 • Canada 4 Czechoslovakia 2

IN GOAL
Canada — Burke
Czechoslovakia — Briza

SHOTS ON GOAL

Canada			
12	11	8	**31**
Czechoslovakia			
16	8	9	**33**

FIRST PERIOD
1. Canada, Hannan (unassisted) • 1:58
2. Canada, Archibald (Woolley, Schlegel) • 10:43
3. Czechoslovakia, Svehla (Zemlicka) • 19:52
penalties: *Schlegel (Can) 3:20*

SECOND PERIOD
4. Czechoslovakia, Augusta (Zemlicka, Hrbek) • 3:22
penalties: *Woolley (Can) 7:05, Svehla (Cz) 10:00, Hynes (Can) 11:37, Zemlicka (Cz) 16:05*

THIRD PERIOD
5. Canada, Giles (Joseph, Juneau) • 3:59
6. Canada, Joseph (Brost, Hannan) • 17:48
penalties: *Kadlec (Cz) & Schreiber (Can) 0:48, Tippett (Can) 9:36*

FEBRUARY 23 • Unified Team 3 Canada 1

IN GOAL
Canada — Burke
Unified Team — Shtalenkov

SHOTS ON GOAL

Canada			
10	6	6	**22**
Unified Team			
10	15	12	**37**

FIRST PERIOD
No Scoring
penalties: *Mironov (Un) 7:41, Juneau (Can) 10:45, Joseph (Can) 12:33, Giles (Can) 16:01*

SECOND PERIOD
No Scoring
penalties: *Kovalev (Un) & Burke (Can) 0:32, Lindros (Can) 16:56*

THIRD PERIOD
1. Unified Team, Butsayev (Davydov) • 1:01
2. Unified Team, Boldin (Borschevsky, Prokhorov) • 15:54
3. Canada, Lindberg (Juneau, Woolley) • 17:20
4. Unified Team, Bykov (Khomutov) • 18:51
penalties: *Woolley (Can) 2:14, Zhamnov (Un) 8:33, Bautin (Un) 10:08, Archibald (Can) 10:45, Prokhorov (Un) 12:05, Shtalenkov (Un) 13:06*

TEAM CANADA FINAL STATISTICS • 1992

#		GP	G	A	P	Pim
9	Joe Juneau	8	6	9	15	4
88	Eric Lindros	8	5	6	11	6
12	Dave Archibald	8	7	1	8	18
10	Dave Hannan	8	3	5	8	8
22	Randy Smith	8	1	7	8	4
4	Gord Hynes	8	3	3	6	6
11	Chris Lindberg	8	1	4	5	4
5	Jason Woolley	8	0	5	5	4
16	Wally Schreiber	8	2	2	4	2
20	Patrick Lebeau	8	1	3	4	4
19	Todd Brost	8	0	4	4	4
8	Fabian Joseph	8	2	1	3	2
15	Dave Tippett	7	1	2	3	10
28	Brad Schlegel	8	1	2	3	4
18	Kent Manderville	8	1	2	3	0
6	Kevin Dahl	8	2	0	2	6
7	Adrien Plavsic	8	0	2	2	0
44	Curt Giles	8	1	0	1	6
1	Sean Burke	7	0	0	0	14
2	Dan Ratushny	8	0	0	0	4
3	Brian Tutt	8	0	0	0	4

#	IN GOAL	GP	W-L-T	Mins	GA	SO	Avg
1	Sean Burke	7	5–2–0	430	17	0	2.37
37	Trevor Kidd	1	1–0–0	60	0	1	0.00

CHAPTER 17

The 17th Winter Olympic Games

LILLEHAMMER, NORWAY

February 12–27, 1994

Paul Kariya

Lillehammer, unsuccessful in its 1992 bid, was awarded the 1994 Games when the IOC met for the 94th time on September 15, 1988 in Seoul, Korea. Sofia was eliminated in the first round of voting and Anchorage in the second. In the third round, Lillehammer received 45 votes and Ostersund, Sweden 39 votes.

The Lillehammer Games were held just two years after the 1992 Games in Albertville, France, a decision by the IOC to separate the Winter and Summer events, which previously had been held during the same calendar year. Henceforth, alternating Summer and Winter Olympics would be held every two years.

TEAM CANADA • 1994

Corey Hirsch, *GOAL*

Mark Astley, *DEFENCE*
Adrian Aucoin, *DEFENCE*
David Harlock, *DEFENCE*
Ken Lovsin, *DEFENCE*
Derek Mayer, *DEFENCE*
Brad Schlegel, *DEFENCE*
Chris Therien, *DEFENCE*
Brad Werenka, *DEFENCE*

Greg Johnson, *CENTRE*
Petr Nedved, *CENTRE*
Greg Parks, *CENTRE*
Todd Warriner, *CENTRE*

Fabian Joseph, *LEFT WING*
Paul Kariya, *LEFT WING*
Jean-Yves Roy, *LEFT WING*
Wally Schreiber, *LEFT WING*

Todd Hlushko, *RIGHT WING*
Chris Kontos, *RIGHT WING*
Dwayne Norris, *RIGHT WING*
Brian Savage, *RIGHT WING*

Manny Legace *(DID NOT PLAY)*
Alain Roy *(DID NOT PLAY)*

Tom Renney, *COACH*
Danny Dube, *ASSOCIATE COACH*
George Kingston, *DIRECTOR OF HOCKEY OPERATIONS*

FINAL PLACINGS

GOLD MEDAL
Sweden

SILVER MEDAL
Canada

BRONZE MEDAL
Finland

FOURTH PLACE
Russia

FIFTH PLACE
Czech Republic

SIXTH PLACE
Slovakia

SEVENTH PLACE
Germany

EIGHTH PLACE
United States

NINTH PLACE
Italy

TENTH PLACE
France

ELEVENTH PLACE
Norway

TWELFTH PLACE
Austria

BUILD-UP TO THE GAMES

The Canadian team began training in September 1993 and played perhaps their most ambitious series of tournaments and exhibition games in preparation for Lillehammer. Canada won a silver medal at the Telehockey Cup in Norway and again at the Nova Scotia International Cup. The team also played in the Globen Cup in Sweden, Deutschland Cup in Germany, and the Isvestia tournament in Moscow. They played a nine-game series against Russia, a four gamer with the American Olympians, and a series of matches against other Olympics-bound hockey nations such as the Czech Republic, Sweden, and Finland.

THE CANADIAN ROSTER

Team Canada's Lillehammer line-up was again an interesting blend of NHLers and NHL-aspirants, but perhaps the most notable absentee from the squad was Toronto Maple Leaf forward Glenn Anderson. Anderson signed with the Leafs for the 1993–94 season with a guarantee from GM Cliff Fletcher that he would make Anderson available to the national team at the appropriate time. Fletcher was only too happy to oblige, but, as it turned out, NHL rules stated that if Anderson were to leave the Leafs to play in the Olympics, he would have to clear waivers.

Corey Hirsch (right) talks to back-up Manny Legace.

Obviously, he would have been claimed by some team had Toronto put him on the open market, so the Leafs petitioned NHL commissioner Gary Bettman asking to receive special exemption for Anderson, seeing that his being put on waivers was not to get rid of him from the Leafs but to allow him to participate in the Games. Bettman, however, refused to help Anderson in his Olympic cause.

At least two US-based owners acknowledged they were against Anderson's loan because it would have improved Canada's chances of winning. Bettman justified his ruling by claiming that "we didn't want to be seen impacting the competition at the Olympics. I am sympathetic to Toronto and Mr. Anderson and what they're trying to do, but I'm not sympathetic to making a rule change for this particular exception."

In the end, it wasn't so much the rule change *per se* that was the problem. That it was being refused for a quality player implied that had someone talentless requested the exception, it would have been granted. Thus, the denial of a rule change was less about principle than about not wanting to increase Canada's chance of winning. The dispute became an international one, and more political than athletic, when Liberal MP John Nunziata met with Bettman in New York, and wound up angrily denouncing the commissioner in a media scrum right after his unsuccessful appeal.

New Canadian Petr Nedved ties up his man off the draw vs. Sweden.

Another controversy, one that ended more positively, involved Czech-born Canadian Petr Nedved. Nedved became a Canadian citizen in July 1993 after spending three years in the Vancouver Canucks organization, but that same summer became involved in a contract dispute that saw him walk out on the team and refuse to show up for training camp that fall. Nedved's desire was to play for Canada, but because of his citizenship change he had to sit on the sidelines until December 26, 1993 before the IIHF finally gave him clearance to play for his new country.

Even with the IIHF's backing, however, many observers weren't gung-ho about Nedved's inclusion, feeling that although having pros at the Games was desirable, doing so for contractual reasons rather than those of pure loyalty, compromised the composition of the team and the moral backbone of participation. Although on paper his addition was welcome, he was following in the slightly tarnished footsteps of Sean Burke (1992), Andy Moog (1988), and Eric Lindros (1992), who all obviously would have been playing in the NHL instead of the Olympics. Nedved adamantly refuted this cynical interpretation: "The thing is, I feel Canadian. Canada is my home, for now and forever. I wanted to be free, and Canada has made it possible. I am thankful to the country."

George Kingston, Canada's director of hockey operations, was quick to try to control the controversy: "This is not a marriage of convenience. From the beginning it was clear Petr wanted to be an Olympian because he wanted to do something for Canada. Playing for Canada is a win-win situation for everybody. Vancouver will get more value in a trade if Petr plays well ... Without a doubt, Petr brings a real offensive component to the team and he also brings a level of grit and experience."

One genuine success story in the Canadian line-up was goalie Corey Hirsch, who wound up playing every minute of the '94 Games for Canada (only the third time since 1920 that one goalie carried the whole load). Hirsch was the star of the AHL his first year as a pro (1992-93) and was confident he could earn a spot at training camp in 1993 with the New York Rangers. Such was not the case, and before the season started he was sent by the Broadway Blueshirts to Tom Renney's Olympic team, a move Hirsch saw as a demotion, a sign of failure. But by the time the Games were in full swing, he was on cloud nine. "I wouldn't have missed this for the world," he beamed. "This is just an awesome experience, the best thing that ever happened to me. And to think I started out lukewarm about the whole idea. I just didn't get it."

The best of the best — Paul Kariya.

His epiphany came the second day of the Games, after watching downhiller Edi Podivinsky fly down the mountain to win a bronze for Canada. "It hit me then, what I'd failed to appreciate, when I realized what a chunk of his life this guy had sacrificed to do that for Canada. I'll tell you ... it's a privilege to be associated even remotely with a person like that." Hirsch, too, was an inspiration to many young Olympic hopefuls after backstopping Canada to a silver medal at Lillehammer.

THE REST OF THE ROSTER

Team Canada came back from the Isvestia tournament a sorry lot, having scored just four goals in four games. This outcome led to a series of changes similar to those of other years, when one set of players stayed with the team for a long time to bolster the line-up and try to earn a spot but was then replaced by superior players at the last minute. Although Brett Lindros was injured and couldn't join the team, and Glenn Anderson had been refused the opportunity to play, others were able to come in and improve, among other things, the team's offence. Petr Nedved was one such player, as were Brad Werenka from the Edmonton Oilers organization and defenceman Mark Astley from his club in Switzerland. In all, close to a dozen new faces who hadn't played at the Isvestia in December were starters in Lillehammer six weeks later.

As for the rest of the roster, virtually every Canadian on the Olympic team went on to play in the NHL: Astley joined the Buffalo Sabres, Adrian Aucoin the Canucks, David Harlock the Leafs, and Todd Hlushko signed with the Flyers right after the Games. Greg Johnson became a Red Wing, Fabian Joseph an Edmonton Oiler, and Paul Kariya emerged as a *bona fide* superstar in Anaheim. Chris Kontos had 10 years of part-time NHL experience. Manny Legace became a Whaler in Hartford, Jason Marshall a St. Louis Blue, Derek Mayer signed with the Senators, Dwayne Norris joined Quebec, Jean-Yves Roy the Rangers, Brian Savage the Habs in Montreal, Chris Therien the Flyers, and Todd Warriner became a fine young player with the Leafs. Tom Renney, of course, moved on to become bench boss for the Canucks. All of these players gave further credence to the sound belief that Hockey Canada was doing its job, providing competition superior to any other these players could have gained in Junior or elsewhere in the world (outside the NHL), giving them an incredible national and emotional experience second to none, and providing the best training imaginable for a career in the NHL.

SHOOTOUT TO DECIDE GOLD

While this was the first time since Russia joined the Games in 1956, and Canada also participated, that the two countries did not play each other even once, the Olympics did not lack drama. What *kind* of drama was another question. After the preliminary round, the final eight teams played an elimination series of games, but because the IOC didn't want to risk sudden-death overtime going on too long, they took a page from soccer's controversial method of "play," and used shootouts to decide each game's winner. The resultant showdown concept was entertaining, nail-biting, and quick, but it was no way to determine which was the better team on a particular day or over a period of four years. A coin toss would have been as relevant.

Action from the gold medal game vs. Sweden, February 27, 1994.

When Peter Forsberg scored on the 13th shootout penalty shot and Paul Kariya missed his on the 14th, Sweden won the gold. But the excitement was missing. To have even just the finals decided by sudden-death overtime would at least be comforting, but the IOC and IIHF did not see it that way. Nagano will employ the same format. "It's not fair," stated Mats Naslund, even though his team won, echoing the sentiments expressed by the Canadians two years earlier when they beat Germany in a tense, but unexciting, shootout.

The Competition

TOURNAMENT FORMAT

The format was the same as that for the 1992 Olympics: the 12 competing nations were divided into two pools of six teams each and played a round-robin tournament within each group. The top four teams from each group then advanced to a playoff elimination round. The top team in group A played the fourth team in group B; the top team in group B played the fourth team in group A; the second team in group A played the third team in group B; and the second team in group B played the third team in group A. The elimination playoffs (quarter-finals, semi-finals, and finals) featured one-game playoffs, the winner still in contention for gold, the loser out of the running.

In the case of a tie in the standings in the preliminary round, goal differential in games played between those teams that were tied would be the deciding factor. In group B, for instance, Canada was given second place over Sweden because it had beaten the Swedes 3–2. In group A, with six points each, Germany, Czech Republic, and Russia were tied, but their ranking reflected the goal differentials (4–3 for Germany, 4–4 Czech Republic, and 6–7 for Russia). In the preliminary round, a 10-minute sudden-death period would follow a tie game, after which the game would go into the books as a tie. In the elimination round, the overtime period would be followed by a shootout until a winner was decided.

THE OPPOSITION

AUSTRIA • James Burton, Marty Dallman, Rob Doyle, Michael Guentner, Karl Heinzle, Herbert Hohenberger, Dieter Kalt, Werner Kerth, Martin Krainz, Wolfgang Kromp, Gunther Lanzinger, Englebert Linder, Manfred Muehr, Richard Nasheim, Michael Puschacher, Andreas Puschnik, Gerhard Puschnik, Gerald Ressman, Michael Shea, Brian Stankiewicz, Ken Strong, Martin Ulrich

CZECH REPUBLIC • Jan Alinc, Petr Briza, Jiri Dolezal, Pavel Geffert, Roman Horak, Miroslav Horava, Petr Hrbek, Martin Hustak, Otakar Janecky, Drahomir Kadlec, Tomas Kapusta, Kamil Kastak, Jiri Kucera, Bedrich Scerban, Tomas Srsen, Antonin Stavjana, Radek Toupal, Roman Turek, Jrir Veber, Jan Vopat, Jiri Vykoukal, Richard Zemlicka

FINLAND • Mika Alatalo, Vesa Haemaelaeinen, Raimo Helminen, Timo Jutila, Sami Kapanen, Esa Keskinen, Marko Kiprusov, Saku Koivu, Janne Laukkanen, Tero Lehterae, Jere Lehtinen, Mikko Makela, Jarmo Myllys, Mika Nieminen, Janne Ojanen, Marko Palo, Ville Peltonen, Pasi Sormunen, Mika Stroemberg, Jukka Tammi, Petri Varis, Hannu Virta

FRANCE • Benjamin Agnel, Stephane Arcangeloni, Stephane Barin, Stephane Botteri, Arnaud Briand, Sylvain Girard, Gerard Guennelon, Benoit Laporte, Eric Lemarque, Pierrick Maia, Christophe Moyon, Franck Pajonkowski, Denis Perez, Serge Poudrier, Pierre Pousse, Antoine Richer, Bruno Saunier, Franck Saunier, Michel Valliere, Stephane Ville, Steven Woodburn, Petri Ylonen

GERMANY • Richard Amann, Jan Benda, Thomas Brandl, Benoit Doucet, Georg Franz, Joerg Handrick, Dieter Hegen, Ulrich Heimer, Raimund Hilger, Torsten Kienass, Wolfgang Kummer, Mirko Ludemann, Joerg Mayr, Klaus Merk, Jayson Meyer, Andreas Niederberger, Helmut de Raaf, Michael Rumrich, Alexander Serikow, Leo Stefan, Bernhard Truntschka, Stefan Ustorf

ITALY • Michael de Angelis, Patrick Brugnoli, Jimmy Camazzola, Bruno Campese, Anthony Circelli, Luigi da Corte, David Delfino, Stefan Figliuzzi, Philip de Gaetano, Alexander Gschliesser, Leo Insam, Emilio Iovio, Maurizio Mansi, Robert Oberrauch, Gaetano Orlando, Martin Pavlu, Roland Ramoser, Michael Rosati, Vezio Sacratini, William Stewart, Lino de Toni, Lucio Topatigh, Bruno Zarrillo

NORWAY • Cato Andersen, Lars Andersen, Morgan Andersen, Vegar Barlie, Arne Billkvam, Svenn Bjornstad, Ole Dahlstrom, Jan Roar Fagerli, Morten Finstad, Geir Hoff, Tommy Jacobsen, Roy Johansen, Tom Johansen, Espen Knutsen, Erik Kristiansen, Trond Magnussen, Jim Marthinsen, Svein Norstebo, Marius Rath, Petter Salsten, Robert Schistad, Petter Thoresen

RUSSIA • Sergei Abramov, Sergei Berezin, Viacheslav Bezoukladnikov, Oleg Chargorodski, Sergei Chendelev, Oleg Davydov, Dmitri Denissov, Gueorgui Evtioukhine, Ravil Gousmanov, Igor Ivanov, Valeri Karpov, Alexei Kudachov, Andrei Nikolishin, Alexandre Smirnov, Sergei Sorokine, Andrei Tarassenko, Vladimir Tarassov, Sergei Tertychny, Pavel Torgaev, Igor Varitski, Alexandre Vinogradov, Andreo Zouiev

SLOVAKIA • Jergus Baca, Vladimir Buril, Jozef Dano, Jaromir Dragan, Eduard Hartmann, Oto Hascak, Branislav Janos, Lubomir Kolnik, Roman Kontsek, Miroslav Marcinko, Stanislav Medrik, Zigmund Palffy, Robert Petrovicky, Vlastimil Plavucha, Dusan Pohorelec, Rene Pucher, Miroslav Satan, Lubomil Sekeras, Marian Smerciak, Peter Stastny, Robert Svehla, Jan Varholik

SWEDEN • Hakan Algotsson, Jonas Bergkvist, Charles Berglund, Andreas Dackell, Christian Due-Boje, Niklas Eriksson, Peter Forsberg, Roger Hansson, Roger Johansson, Jorgen Jonsson, Kenny Jonsson, Tomas Jonsson, Patrik Juhlin, Patric Kjellberg, Hakan Loob, Mats Naslund, Stefan Ornskog, Leif Rohlin, Daniel Rydmark, Tommy Salo, Fredrik Stillman, Mikael Sundloev, Magnus Svensson

UNITED STATES • Mark Beaufait, James Campbell, Peter Ciavaglia, Edward Crowley, Theodore Drury, Mike Dunham, Peter Ferraro, Brett Hauer, Darby Hendrickson, Christopher Imes, Craig Johnson, Peter Laviolette, Jeff Lazaro, John Lilley, Todd Marchant, Matthew Martin, Travis Richards, Barron Richter, David Roberts, Brian Rolston, David Sacco, Garth Snow

FINAL STANDINGS

CONSOLATION ROUND

FEBRUARY 22
France 5 Austria 4
(OT & shootout)
Italy 6 Norway 3

FEBRUARY 24
Italy 3 France 2
(9th place game)
Norway 3 Austria 1
(11th place game)
Slovakia 6 Germany 5 (OT)
Czech Republic 5 United States 3

FEBRUARY 26
Czech Republic 7 Slovakia 1
(5th place game)
Germany 4 United States 3
(7th place game)

QUARTER-FINALS

FEBRUARY 23
Canada 3 Czech Republic 2 (OT)
Sweden 3 Germany 0
Russia 3 Slovakia 2 (OT)
Finland 6 United States 1

SEMI-FINALS

FEBRUARY 25
Canada 5 Finland 3
Sweden 4 Russia 3

BRONZE MEDAL GAME

FEBRUARY 26
Finland 4 Russia 0

GOLD MEDAL GAME

FEBRUARY 27
Sweden 3 Canada 2
(OT & shootout)

PRELIMINARY ROUND • POOL A

	GP	W	L	T	GF	GA	P
Finland	5	5	0	0	25	4	10
Germany	5	3	2	0	11	14	6
Czech Republic	5	3	2	0	16	11	6
Russia	5	3	2	0	20	14	6
Austria	5	1	4	0	13	28	2
Norway	5	0	5	0	5	19	0

RESULTS

FEBRUARY 12
Finland 3 Czech Republic 1
Russia 5 Norway 1
Germany 4 Austria 3

FEBRUARY 14
Czech Republic 7 Austria 3
Germany 2 Norway 1
Finland 5 Russia 0

FEBRUARY 16
Russia 9 Austria 1
Finland 4 Norway 0
Czech Republic 1 Germany 0

FEBRUARY 18
Finland 6 Austria 2
Czech Republic 4 Norway 1
Germany 4 Russia 2

FEBRUARY 20
Finland 7 Germany 1
Austria 4 Norway 2
Russia 4 Czech Republic 3

PRELIMINARY ROUND • POOL B

	GP	W	L	T	GF	GA	P
Slovakia	5	3	0	2	26	14	8
Canada	5	3	1	1	17	11	7
Sweden	5	3	1	1	23	13	7
United States	5	1	1	3	21	17	5
Italy	5	1	4	0	15	31	2
France	5	0	4	1	11	27	1

RESULTS

FEBRUARY 13
Canada 7 Italy 2
Sweden 4 Slovakia 4
France 4 United States 4

FEBRUARY 15
Canada 3 France 1
Sweden 4 Italy 1
Slovakia 3 United States 3

FEBRUARY 17
Canada 3 United States 3
Slovakia 10 Italy 4
Sweden 7 France 1

FEBRUARY 19
Slovakia 3 Canada 1
Italy 7 France 3
Sweden 6 United States 4

FEBRUARY 21
Canada 3 Sweden 2
Slovakia 6 France 2
United States 7 Italy 1

TEAM CANADA GAME SUMMARIES

FEBRUARY 13 • Canada 7 Italy 2

FIRST PERIOD

1. Canada, Nedved (Werenka, Kariya) • 7:32(pp)
2. Italy, de Toni (unassisted) • 8:16
3. Canada, Werenka (Kariya) • 19:40(pp)
penalties: *Werenka (Can) 2:31, Hirsch (Can) 3:59, Oberrauch (It) 6:54, Zarrillo (It) 12:08, Therien (Can) 14:49, Mansi (It) 18:31*

SECOND PERIOD

4. Canada, Schreiber (Mayer) • 1:24
5. Canada, Hlushko (Astley) • 7:43
6. Canada, Kontos (Savage) • 16:23
7. Canada, Kontos (Nedved) • 19:39
penalties: *Savage (Can) 2:04, Mayer (Can) 5:12, Brugnoli (It) 8:06, Nedved (Can) 12:52, Orlando (It) 13:37, Ramoser (It) 17:04*

THIRD PERIOD

8. Italy, Orlando (unassisted) • 7:13
9. Canada, Nedved (Kariya) • 14:58
penalties: *Therien (Can) 0:54, Harlock (Can) 2:31, Oberrauch (It) 9:24*

IN GOAL

Canada — Hirsch
Italy — Delfino/Rosati *(Rosati replaced Delfino to start 3rd)*

SHOTS ON GOAL

Canada			
12	14	12	**38**
Italy			
12	6	11	**29**

FEBRUARY 15 • Canada 3 France 1

FIRST PERIOD

1. Canada, Hlushko (Parks) • 2:26
penalties: *Agnel (Fr) 14:16, Parks (Can) 15:45, Lemarque (Fr) 17:49*

SECOND PERIOD

2. Canada, Hlushko (Parks) • 15:13
3. Canada, Warriner (Norris) • 19:43
penalties: *Lovsin (Can) 10:50*

THIRD PERIOD

4. France, Laporte (unassisted) • 2:39(pp)
penalties: *Schlegel (Can) 0:58, Woodburn (Fr) 3:38, Parks (Can) & Poudrier (Fr) 5:57, Mayer (Can) 7:51, Richer (Fr) 17:51*

IN GOAL

Canada — Hirsch
France — Ylonen

SHOTS ON GOAL

Canada			
11	13	11	**35**
France			
2	1	7	**10**

FEBRUARY 17 • Canada 3 United States 3

FIRST PERIOD

1. Canada, Norris (Savage, Warriner) • 4:46
penalties: *Lazaro (US) 1:20, Richter (US) 6:43, Martin (US) 8:32, Lilley (US) 14:04, Harlock (Can) 17:22, Werenka (Can) 19:03*

SECOND PERIOD

2. United States, Rolston (Sacco, Roberts) • 1:06
3. United States, Rolston (Beaufait, Roberts) • 9:43(pp)
4. Canada, Nedved (penalty shot) • 12:09
penalties: *Lovsin (Can) 2:11, Harlock (Can) 8:12, Parks (Can) 8:25, Hauer (US) 14:18*

THIRD PERIOD

5. Canada, Norris (unassisted) • 1:16
6. United States, Marchant (Roberts) • 19:32(pp)
penalties: *Rolston (US) 8:11, Nedved (Can) 10:31, Joseph (Can) 19:18*

IN GOAL

Canada — Hirsch
United States — Snow

SHOTS ON GOAL

Canada			
11	9	12	**32**
United States			
8	12	9	**29**

FEBRUARY 19 • Slovakia 3 Canada 1

IN GOAL
Canada — Hirsch
Slovakia — Hartmann

SHOTS ON GOAL

Canada				
	4	12	9	**25**
Slovakia				
	10	8	9	**27**

FIRST PERIOD
1. Canada, Kariya (unassisted) • 1:06
2. Slovakia, Dano (Palffy) • 17:13
penalties: *Mayer (Can) 3:56, Sekeras (Slo) 7:50, Schlegel (Can) 20:00*

SECOND PERIOD
3. Slovakia, Svehla (Janos) • 3:27(pp)
penalties: *Astley (Can) 2:44, Kontsek (Slo) 5:33, Schlegel (Can) 8:32, Varholik (Slo) 12:21, Svehla (Slo) 14:19, Parks (Can) & Petrovicky (Slo) 16:42*

THIRD PERIOD
4. Slovakia, Dano (P. Stastny, Baca) • 19:49(sh-en)
penalties: *Sekeras (Slo) 2:11, Kariya (Can) 9:50, Sekeras (Slo) 18:15*

FEBRUARY 21 • Canada 3 Sweden 2

IN GOAL
Canada — Hirsch
Sweden — Salo

SHOTS ON GOAL

Canada				
	9	11	10	**30**
Sweden				
	17	13	6	**36**

FIRST PERIOD
1. Canada, Kontos (Johnson) • 2:39
2. Sweden, Hansson (unassisted) • 8:57(pp)
penalties: *Harlock (Can) 3:20, Mayer (Can) 7:51, Salo (Swe) 13:32, Savage (Can) 18:55, Juhlin (Swe) 19:19*

SECOND PERIOD
3. Canada, Hlushko (unassisted) • 1:26
4. Sweden, Loob (Naslund) • 5:19
5. Canada, Nedved (Joseph) • 10:56
penalties: *Nedved (Can) 1:45, Mayer (Can) 5:28, Mayer (Can) 14:12, Johansson (Swe) 15:02, Kontos (Can) 17:22, Norris (Can) 18:07, Parks (Can) 18:46*

THIRD PERIOD
No Scoring
penalties: *Johansson (Swe) 2:27, Due-Boje (Swe) 5:36, Jonsson (Swe) 6:50, Can (too many men) 8:43, Rydmark (Swe) & Mayer (Can) 13:51, Due-Boje (Swe) 16:12*

FEBRUARY 23 • Canada 3 Czech Republic 2

IN GOAL
Canada — Hirsch
Czech Republic — Briza

SHOTS ON GOAL

Canada					
	6	6	8	4	**24**
Czech Republic					
	12	13	9	3	**37**

FIRST PERIOD
1. Czech Republic, Janecky (unassisted) • 19:34(sh)
penalties: *Hlushko (Can) 8:32, Mayer (Can) 10:57, Hlushko (Can) 16:35, Vykoukal (CR) 17:54*

SECOND PERIOD
2. Canada, Savage (unassisted) • 6:40
3. Czech Republic, Kucera (Janecky) • 15:42
penalties: *Norris (Can) 10:25*

THIRD PERIOD
4. Canada, Savage (Norris) • 14:35
penalties: *Alinc (CR) 1:21, Lovsin (Can) 9:07, Horava (CR) 10:21*

OVERTIME
5. Canada, Kariya (unassisted) • 5:54(pp)
penalties: *Horak (CR) 5:49*

FEBRUARY 25 • Canada 5 Finland 3

FIRST PERIOD
No Scoring
penalties: *Helminen (Fin) 0:11, Laukkanen (Fin) 7:03, Werenka (Can) 10:42*

SECOND PERIOD
1. Finland, Koivu (Peltonen) • 2:08(pp)
2. Finland, Keskinen (Virta) • 3:48
3. Canada, Hlushko (Joseph) • 15:59
4. Canada, Nedved (unassisted) • 19:24(pp)
penalties: *Lovsin (Can) 0:29, Aucoin (Can) & Stroemberg (Fin) 16:31, Kiprusov (Fin) 17:27*

THIRD PERIOD
5. Canada, Werenka (Johnson, Kariya) • 4:27
6. Canada, Roy (Werenka, Mayer) • 7:30(pp)
7. Canada, Parks (unassisted) • 14:19
8. Finland, Lehtinen (Nieminen, Keskinen) • 19:25
penalties: *Mayer (Can) 5:18, Ojanen (Fin) 6:52, Keskinen (Fin) 12:01*

IN GOAL
Canada — Hirsch
Finland — Tammi

SHOTS ON GOAL

Canada	5	12	16	**33**
Finland	6	16	11	**33**

FEBRUARY 27 • Sweden 3 Canada 2 (OT & shootout)

FIRST PERIOD
1. Sweden, Jonsson (Loob, Forsberg) • 6:10(pp)
penalties: *Astley (Can) 5:44, Rohlin (Swe) 16:58, Salo (Swe) 19:39*

SECOND PERIOD
No Scoring
penalties: *Hlushko (Can) & Jonsson (Swe) 4:17, Schreiber (Can) 9:11, Johansson (Swe) 11:46, Savage (Can) 13:37, Svensson (Swe) 17:38*

THIRD PERIOD
2. Canada, Kariya (Kontos, Johnson) • 9:08
3. Canada, Mayer (unassisted) • 11:43
4. Sweden, Svensson (Forsberg, Jonsson) • 18:11(pp)
penalties: *Werenka (Can) 17:50*

OVERTIME (10 minutes)
No Scoring
penalties: *none*

SHOOTOUT
First Round (five shots each)
Canada • Nedved ~ SCORED (1-0)
Sweden • Loob ~ missed
Canada • Kariya ~ SCORED (2-0)
Sweden • Svensson ~ SCORED (2-1)
Canada • Norris ~ missed
Sweden • Naslund ~ missed
Canada • Parks ~ missed
Sweden • Forsberg ~ SCORED (2-2)
Canada • Johnson ~ missed
Sweden • Hansson ~ missed

Second Round (sudden death)
Sweden • Svensson ~ missed
Canada • Nedved ~ missed
Sweden • Forsberg ~ SCORED (2-3)
Canada • Kariya ~ missed

** Sweden won shootout 3-2; only Forsberg was credited with a goal*

IN GOAL
Canada — Hirsch
Sweden — Salo

SHOTS ON GOAL

Canada	7	6	6	2	**21**
Sweden	6	16	16	4	**42**

TEAM CANADA FINAL STATISTICS • 1994

#		GP	G	A	P	Pim
9	Paul Kariya	8	3	4	7	2
93	Petr Nedved	8	5	1	6	6
7	Todd Hlushko	8	5	0	5	6
27	Chris Kontos	8	3	1	4	2
5	Brad Werenka	8	2	2	4	8
14	Brian Savage	8	2	2	4	6
10	Dwayne Norris	8	2	2	4	4
4	Derek Mayer	8	1	2	3	18
22	Greg Parks	8	1	2	3	10
12	Greg Johnson	8	0	3	3	0
18	Todd Warriner	4	1	1	2	0
8	Fabian Joseph	8	0	2	2	2
16	Wally Schreiber	8	1	0	1	2
25	Jean-Yves Roy	8	1	0	1	0
24	Mark Astley	8	0	1	1	4
28	David Harlock	8	0	0	0	8
6	Kevin Lovsin	8	0	0	0	8
44	Brad Schlegel	8	0	0	0	6
33	Chris Therien	4	0	0	0	4
1	Corey Hirsch	8	0	0	0	2
3	Adrian Aucoin	4	0	0	0	2

#	IN GOAL	GP	W-L-T	Mins	GA	SO	Avg
1	Corey Hirsch	8	5–2–1	495	18	0	2.18

CHAPTER 18

The 18th Olympic Winter Games

NAGANO, JAPAN

February 7–22, 1998

Nagano was awarded the 1998 Games at the IOC's 97th session held June 15, 1991 in Birmingham, England in the fourth round of voting, receiving 46 votes, four more than Salt Lake City, Utah. Ostersund, Sweden, Aosta, Italy and Jaca, Spain were eliminated in earlier rounds of voting.

When the IOC met in Budapest on June 16, 1995 in its 104th session, it awarded the 2002 Games to Salt Lake City which received 55 first-round votes, well ahead of Ostersund and Sion (both with 14 votes), and Quebec City (seven votes).

TEAM CANADA'S SCHEDULE

February 13 • vs. Group A Qualifier, 4:45 A.M.

February 14 • vs. Sweden, 4:45 A.M.

February 15 • vs. United States, 11:45 P.M.

February 18 • Quarter-finals, 11:45 P.M.

February 20 • Semi-finals, 11:45 P.M.

February 22 • Gold Medal Game, 11:45 P.M.

TOURNAMENT FORMAT

Teams in the round robin tournament at Nagano will be divided into two groups. Group C will include the Czech Republic, Finland, Russia, and one qualifier, and Group D will include Canada, Sweden, the United States, and another qualifier.

The two qualifiers will have survived a qualifying tournament featuring two like groups playing a round robin between February 7 and February 12. Group A consists of Austria, Italy, Kazakhstan, and Slovakia; Group B Belarus, France, Germany, and Japan. One winner from each group will advance to the medals round.

THE CANADIAN HOCKEY ASSOCIATION

The CHA came into being in July 1994, the result of a merger between Hockey Canada and the Canadian Amateur Hockey Association. It thus became the sole body for amateur hockey in the country and now governs all levels of national and international play. Its biggest task and greatest accomplishment has been to organize these levels so that communication, development, and cohesion are more easily achieved. To this end, the CHA has established Centres of Excellence in Toronto, Saint John, Calgary, and Vancouver to develop systems and programs that will enhance coaching and playing at all levels of hockey in Canada.

ORGANIZING THE ORGANIZERS

Perhaps the biggest task of all facing Canada in the upcoming Olympics is the proper coordination of the many groups, teams, and interests who will have a hand in organizing Team Canada for Nagano. Bob Nicholson, senior vice-president of the Canadian Hockey Association, selected the three men to run the on-ice show for Nagano on January 30, 1997—Bob Clarke, general manager of the Philadelphia Flyers; Bob Gainey, GM of the Dallas Stars; and Pierre Gauthier, GM of the Ottawa Senators. Opined Nicholson: "when we did our search and interviewed various general managers, we thought it would be best to have people who are involved in the day-to-day operations of NHL teams. In Clarke, Gainey, and Gauthier, I believe we have three of the sharpest minds in hockey...all three have impeccaable credentials for the formidable, high-pressure, and exciting challenge that lies ahead."

Interestingly, the CHA was the one body in the IOC that didn't want pros to join the Olympics, as Nicholson confessed: "All of the European countries, along with the US, wanted NHL players involved because they really thought it would give better exposure to hockey globally. We were the odd federation out, so we went on side with it." However, in order for the idea to reach fruition, much had to be worked out. The NHL had to plan and agree to stop play in the league for some 17 days; the NHL Players' Association, headed by Bob Goodenow, had to negotiate with the league regarding the closing, supplying the players to the various competing teams, and making practical arrangements for the players' participation. In the end, the labour turmoil that affected the NHL's start to the 1994-95 season went a long way to ensuring the players' participation at Nagano. The labour agreement subsequently worked out was an important ballast in creating trust and happiness among the NHL, its owners, its commissioner, and Goodenow. Without the long-term Collective Bargaining Agreement that was signed, the players would probably not have been heading to the Far East to play Olympic hockey.

Only once an agreement in principle had been arranged could the three-man executive of Clarke, Gainey, and Gauthier be named. As part of the national mandate, CHA coaches Andy Murray and Mike Johnston have been guaranteed places as assistant coaches, and here begins the complexities. The CHA (successor to the CAHA) runs Canada's international competitions. It is an amateur body and, of course, such events have traditionally been for amateurs only. It is odd, therefore, that Nicholson, an executive of an amateur organization, must decide who are the

Team Canada coach Marc Crawford *(opposite)*.

best *professional* executives to run the 1998 Nagano show. Furthermore, all negotiations with the IOC, the IIHF and the COA must be governed by the CHA, the amateur body in Canada. Now that the NHL has become involved, the CHA has to work with the NHL and vice versa, but each has a different approach.

Because of these Dream Team Olympics, virtually no juniors and young professional aspirants will have a chance of gaining international experience, which virtually every player from 1920 to 1994 has claimed was integral in his development. In other words, one concern is how this professional inclusion for Nagano will affect the next crop of young stars. While the argument that having all pros at Nagano will be spectacular, an equally valid one can be made that now, more than ever, is the time to revert to a strictly amateur team for Olympic hockey. Taken in an historic context, and given the original intentions of all the Olympic rules on eligibility, this view is easily rationalized.

For years, Canada gladly sent its finest pure amateurs to the Winter Olympics. But when the USSR entered in 1956 and other European countries started using players who were, for all intents and purposes, professional, Canada grew impatient and then angry at the imbalance. But the NHL of the nineties features a truly international blend of the best players in the world. *All* the finest Czechs, Russians, Finns, and Swedes play in the NHL. All are professional and extremely well paid. Thus, if original Olympic rules were to be imposed, all countries would have to field amateurs, non-NHLers. This would ensure a more level playing field and guarantee fairness never before achieved.

GM Bob Clarke *(below)* and Assistant GM Bob Gainey *(right)*.

1997 World Championships coaching staff with trophy: *(left to right)* Mike Johnston, Andy Murray, Wayne Cashman, and Rob Cookson.

CANADA'S COACH

Right on schedule, the three GMs announced Team Canada's head coach at a press conference in Toronto on July 15, 1997. Marc Crawford, Stanley Cup-winning coach of the Colorado Avalanche, was chosen because, as Clarke said, "he's the kind of coach who gets a team to play its best in a short, two-week run." Thus, the final management map can be drawn. At the top is Clarke with assistants Gainey, and Gauthier. Under them are coach Crawford, and under him are his front line colleagues, associate coach and CHA representative and head coach of the 1997 World Championship team Andy Murray, and assistants Wayne Cashman (NHL and 1997 World Championship assistant) and Mike Johnston (CHA assistant). Rob Cookson will coordinate video for the staff.

NAMING THE ROSTER

One day after being named Team Canada GM, Bob Clarke pronounced that, "there's no possible way you can have your team on August 1," thus contradicting an important piece of the negotiations that had been worked out with the IOC for NHL participation. It wouldn't be until some six weeks later that the IOC relented and allowed Canada until December 1 to name the roster, thus giving the GM troika time to assess the performance of the players during the first third of the 1997-98 season, and giving players on the selection bubble a chance to showcase themselves and prove themselves worthy of selection.

Previous to that, some players got a chance to prove themselves at the World Championships in Helsinki in April 1997. For the sake of continuity and experience, the three Olympic GMs had full control over the team sent to represent Canada there, with the one obvious limitation being that players on the team were on NHL clubs that didn't make the Stanley Cup playoffs. Thus, the World Championship team did not reflect at all what the GMs saw as the final Nagano roster.

Unlike selection for the 1996 World Cup, the Dream Team will be chosen

The Nagano coaching staff: *(left to right)* Mike Johnston, Wayne Cashman, Marc Crawford, Andy Murray, and Rob Cookson.

based on three considerations: (1) who is playing well as close to the tournament as can be judged? (2) what is the player's role on the team? (3) who can play on a European ice surface with international rules and European officiating? All three of these qualities testify to the advantage of having such a tournament during the season, and the difficulty involved in naming a team over the summer that will play before NHL training camps begin (as was the case with the World Cup).

In deciding who plays which role (question two), having the best four offensive centres in the NHL is not necessarily Team Canada's goal. Paul Kariya, Eric Lindros, and Joe Sakic are the three obvious choices (or Wayne Gretzky as a centre and Sakic moving to the wing), but the fourth line centre will almost surely be a checker, someone who can neutralize the other teams' best players. Also, big, slow men who played at the World Cup (notably Trevor Linden and Keith Primeau) will almost certainly be neglected for Nagano, their weaknesses far outstripping their merits on the large international ice sheet.

THE HECTIC SCHEDULE

Having Canada's best at the Olympics is something that has never happened before in the history of hockey at the Winter Olympics. Yet the logistics of participation, particularly for Nagano, is something less than ideal. Yes, the NHL will close down, but not for one hour longer than necessary. The players will have only four days to practise in Calgary before leaving for Japan, where they will play their first game just a few days later. They will have a 14-hour flight to Tokyo, a train ride into the city, and another four-hour train ride to Nagano. With millions of Olympic tourists clogging the transportation system, who's to say these times won't be, in actuality, much worse? These might be our best players, playing at mid-season when they are in peak physical condition, but we will not see them performing at the height of their powers.

CANADA'S 1996 WORLD CUP ROSTER

Rob Blake, Rob Brind'Amour, Martin Brodeur, Paul Coffey, Eric Desjardins, Theoren Fleury, Adam Foote, Ron Francis, Wayne Gretzky, Curtis Joseph, Claude Lemieux, Trevor Linden, Eric Lindros, Al MacInnis, Mark Messier, Scott Niedermayer, Lyle Odelein, Keith Primeau, Bill Ranford, Joe Sakic, Brendan Shanahan, Scott Stevens, Pat Verbeek, Steve Yzerman, Jason Arnott (alternate), Eric Daze (alternate), Ed Jovanovski (alternate)

Glen Sather, *COACH & GENERAL MANAGER*
Bob Gainey, *ASSISTANT GENERAL MANAGER*
Pat Quinn, *ASSISTANT GENERAL MANAGER*
Neil Smith, *ASSISTANT GENERAL MANAGER*
Marc Crawford, *ASSISTANT COACH*
Ed Johnston, *ASSISTANT COACH*
Andy Murray, *ASSISTANT COACH*

CANADA'S 1997 WORLD CHAMPIONSHIPS ROSTER

Rob Blake, Joel Bouchard, Sean Burke, Anson Carter, Steve Chiasson, Corey Cross, Shean Donovan, Bob Errey, Dean Evason, Jeff Friesen, Chris Gratton, Travis Green, Jarome Iginla, Bryan McCabe, Owen Nolan, Keith Primeau, Chris Pronger, Mark Recchi, Geoff Sanderson, Don Sweeney, Rick Tabaracci, Rob Zamuner

Bob Clarke, *GENERAL MANAGER*
Bob Gainey, *ASSISTANT GENERAL MANAGER*
Pierre Gauthier, *ASSISTANT GENERAL MANAGER*
Andy Murray, *HEAD COACH*
Mike Johnston, *ASSOCIATE COACH*
Wayne Cashman, *ASSOCIATE COACH*
Rob Cookson, *ASSOCIATE COACH (VIDEO)*

STATISTICS

Fact and Record Guide for Canada at the Olympics

Canada's All-Time Player Register

* played in the NHL
Pos = team finish
G = Gold
S = Silver
B = Bronze

YEAR	GP	G	A	P	Pim	Pos			
YEAR	GP	W-L-T	Mins	GA	SO	Avg	A	Pim	Pos

GEORGE ABEL • *b. February 23, 1916*

1952	8	6	6	12	2	G

HANK AKERVALL • *b. Port Arthur, Ontario, August 24, 1937*

1964	7	2	0	2	9	4th

***GLENN ANDERSON** • *b. Vancouver, British Columbia, October 2, 1960*

1980	6	2	2	4	4	6th

WARREN ANDERSON • *b. Creighton Mines, Ontario, April 13, 1952*

1980	6	1	0	1	4	6th
1984	7	0	0	0	0	4th
Totals	13	1	0	1	4	—

***DAVE ARCHIBALD** • *b. Chilliwack, British Columbia, April 14, 1969*

1992	8	7	1	8	18	S

***MARK ASTLEY** • *b. Calgary, Alberta, March 30, 1969*

1994	8	0	1	1	4	S

BOB ATTERSLEY • *b. Oshawa, Ontario, August 13, 1933*

1960	7	6	12	18	4	S

***ADRIAN AUCOIN** • *b. Ottawa, Ontario, March 7, 1973*

1994	4	0	0	0	2	S

***ROBIN BARTEL** • *b. Lanigan, Saskatchewan, May 16, 1961*

1984	6	0	1	1	4	4th

GARY BEGG • *b. Moosomin, Saskatchewan, December 29, 1940*

1964	7	1	0	1	2	4th

MOE BENOIT • *b. Valleyfield, Quebec, July 26, 1933*

1960	7	1	3	4	18	S

***BOBBY BENSON** • *b. Manitoba, May 18, 1894*

1920	3	1	—	1	—	G

***KEN BERRY** • *b. Burnaby, British Columbia, June 21, 1960*

1980	6	4	1	5	8	6th
1988	8	2	4	6	4	4th
Totals	14	6	5	11	12	—

***SERGE BOISVERT ("Beaver")** • *b. Drummondville, Quebec, June 1, 1959*

1988	8	7	2	9	2	4th

ROGER BOURBONNAIS ("Rog") • *b. Edmonton, Alberta, October 26, 1942*

1964	7	0	5	5	0	4th
1968	7	4	2	6	0	B
Totals	14	4	7	11	0	B

***BRIAN BRADLEY** • *b. Kitchener, Ontario, January 21, 1965*

1988	7	0	4	4	0	4th

***KEN BRODERICK** • *b. Toronto, Ontario, February 16, 1942*

YEAR	GP	W-L-T	Mins	GA	SO	Avg	A	Pim	Pos
1964	6	1–1–0	173	12	0+	4.16	0	0	4th
1968	5	3–2–0	280	12	1	2.57	0	0	B
Totals	11	4–3–0	453	24	1	3.18	0	0	B

+ shared shutout with Seth Martin on January 29, 1964 vs. Switzerland

YEAR	GP	G	A	P	Pim	Pos			
YEAR	GP	W-L-T	Mins	GA	SO	Avg	A	Pim	Pos
DENIS BRODEUR • *b. Montreal, Quebec, October 12, 1930*									
1956	4	3–1–0	240	8	1	2.00	0	0	B
CHARLIE BROOKER • *b. Toronto, Ontario, March 25, 1932*									
1956	5	3	4	7	2	B			
TODD BROST • *b. Calgary, Alberta, September 23, 1967*									
1992	8	0	4	4	4	S			
***SEAN BURKE** • *b. Windsor, Ontario, January 29, 1967*									
1988	4	1–2–1	239	12	0	3.02	0	2	4th
1992	7	5–2–0	430	17	0	2.37	0	14	S
Totals	11	6–4–1	669	29	0	2.60	0	16	S
WALLY BYRON • *b. September 2, 1894*									
1920	3	3–0–0	120	1	2	0.50	0	0	G
RAY CADIEUX • *b. Ottawa, Ontario, December 27, 1941*									
1964	7	4	0	4	8	4th			
1968	7	4	2	6	0	B			
Totals	14	8	2	10	0	B			
JACK CAMERON • *b. Ottawa, Ontario, December 3, 1902*									
1924	3	3-0-0	150	1	2	0.40	0	0	G
***TERRY CLANCY ("Prince"/"Whip")** • *b. Ottawa, Ontario, April 2, 1943*									
1964	7	1	1	2	2	4th			
WILLIAM COCKBURN • *b. Unknown*									
1932	5	4–0–1	265	4	2	0.91	0	0	G
ERNIE COLLETT • *b. 1895*									
1924	2	2–0–0	90	2	1	1.33	0	0	G
BILLY COLVIN • *b. Toronto, Ontario, December 3, 1934*									
1956	4	0	4	4	0	B			
***BRIAN CONACHER** • *b. Toronto, Ontario, August 31, 1941*									
1964	7	7	1	8	6	4th			
PAUL CONLIN ("Conk") • *b. Granton, Ontario, January 26, 1943*									
1964	7	0	0	0	4	4th			
1968	7	0	0	0	0	B			
Totals	14	0	0	0	4	B			
JIM CONNELLY • *b. South Porcupine, Ontario, October 7, 1932*									
1960	7	5	3	8	14	S			
***RUSS COURTNALL ("Rusty")** • *b. Duncan, British Columbia, June 2, 1965*									
1984	7	1	3	4	2	4th			
CLIFFORD CROWLEY • *b. Unknown*									
1932	1	0	0	0	0	G			
***KEVIN DAHL** • *b. Regina, Saskatchewan, December 30, 1968*									
1992	8	2	0	2	6	S			
***JEAN-JACQUES (J.J.) DAIGNEAULT** • *b. Montreal, Quebec, October 12, 1965*									
1984	7	1	1	2	0	4th			
DAN D'ALVISE • *b. New Toronto, Ontario, December 13, 1955*									
1980	6	3	3	6	8	6th			
RON DAVIDSON • *b. Prince Albert, Saskatchewan, July 16, 1957*									
1980	6	1	4	5	0	6th			

YEAR	GP	G	A	P	Pim	Pos			
YEAR	GP	W-L-T	Mins	GA	SO	Avg	A	Pim	Pos
JOHN "Jack" DAVIES • *b. Edmonton, Alberta, July 14, 1928*									
1952	8	4	3	7	6	G			
BILLY DAWE • *b. Cochrane, Alberta, June 8, 1924*									
1952	8	6	6	12	2	G			
MAXWELL "Bill" DEACON • *b. March 22, 1910*									
1936	4	0	1	1	0	S			
CHARLIE DELAHEY • *b. Pembroke, Ontario, 1905*									
1928	1	0	—	0	—	G			
JOHN DEVANEY • *b. Edmonton, Alberta, April 10, 1958*									
1980	6	4	3	7	6	6th			
BRUCE DICKSON • *b. April 22, 1931*									
1952	8	7	2	9	0	G			
***GARY DINEEN** • *b. Montreal, Quebec, December 24, 1943*									
1964	7	3	6	9	10	4th			
1968	7	1	2	3	6	B			
Totals	14	4	8	12	16	B			
***WILLIAM "Kevin" DINEEN** • *b. Quebec City, Quebec, October 28, 1963*									
1984	7	0	0	0	8	4th			
***DAVE DONNELLY ("Gonzo")** • *b. Edmonton, Alberta, February 2, 1963*									
1984	7	1	1	2	12	4th			
JACK DOUGLAS • *b. Trenton, Ontario, April 24, 1930*									
1960	7	3	2	5	6	S			
MURRAY DOWEY • *b. Toronto, Ontario, January 3, 1926*									
1948	8	7–0–1	480	5	5	0.62	0	2	G
***BRUCE DRIVER** • *b. Toronto, Ontario, April 29, 1962*									
1984	7	3	1	4	10	4th			
BERT "Spunk" DUNCANSON • *b. Winnipeg, Manitoba, October 2, 1911*									
1932	1	1	0	1	0	G			
FRANK DUNSTER • *b. Ottawa, Ontario, March 24, 1921*									
1948	8	1	0	1	8	G			
***BOB DUPUIS** • *b. Blind River, Ontario, August 26, 1952*									
1980	3	1–2–0	123	7	0	3.41	0	0	6th
***DARREN ELIOT** • *b. Hamilton, Ontario, November 26, 1961*									
1984	2	40	0–0–0	2	0	3.00	0	0	4th
FRED ETCHER • *b. Oshawa, Ontario, August 23, 1932*									
1960	7	9	12	21	0	S			
KEN FARMER • *b. Ste. Anne de Bellevue, Quebec, July 26, 1912*									
1936	8	10	4	14	0	S			
HUGH FARQUHARSON • *b. November 14, 1912*									
1936	8	11	8	19	2	S			
***CHRIS FELIX** • *b. Toronto, Ontario, May 27, 1964*									
1988	6	1	2	3	2	4th			
FRANK FISHER • *b. Barlieboro, Ontario, January 1, 1901*									
1928	1	1	—	1	—	G			

YEAR	GP	G	A	P	Pim	Pos			
YEAR	GP	W-L-T	Mins	GA	SO	Avg	A	Pim	Pos
***PAT FLATLEY** • *b. Toronto, Ontario, October 3, 1963*									
1984	7	3	3	6	70	4th			
BOB FORHAN • *b. Newmarket, Ontario, March 27, 1936*									
1960	6	1	5	6	0	S			
1964	7	7	0	7	0	4th			
Totals	13	8	5	13	0	S			
***FRANK FREDRICKSON** • *b. Winnipeg, Manitoba, June 11, 1895*									
1920	3	12	—	12	2	G			
CHRIS FRIDFINSSON • *b. Unknown*									
1920	3	1	—	1	—	G			
***DAVE GAGNER** • *b. Chatham, Ontario, December 11, 1964*									
1984	7	5	2	7	6	4th			
GEORGE GARBUTT • *b. Unknown*									
1932	1	1	0	1	0	G			
DONALD GAUF • *b. Fort Saskatchewan, Alberta, January 1, 1927*									
1952	7	3	0	3	4	G			
BILLY GIBSON • *b. Lethbridge, Alberta, April 22, 1927*									
1952	8	15	7	22	6	G			
***CURT GILES** • *b. The Pas, Manitoba, November 30, 1958*									
1992	8	1	0	1	6	S			
***BRIAN GLENNIE ("Blunt")** • *b. Toronto, Ontario, August 29, 1946*									
1968	7	0	1	1	10	B			
MAGNUS "Mike" GOODMAN • *b. March 18, 1898*									
1920	3	3	—	3	—	G			
***MARIO GOSSELIN ("Goose")** • *b. Thetford Mines, Quebec, June 15, 1963*									
1984	7	4–3–0	380	14	0	2.21	0	2	4th
GRANT GORDON • *b. Unknown*									
1928	1	0	—	0	—	G			
JOE GRANT • *b. Sudbury, Ontario, January 23, 1957*									
1980	6	0	1	1	2	6th			
JEAN-ORVAL GRAVELLE ("Carrot Top") • *b. Aylmer, Ontario, December 7, 1927*									
1948	7	3	0	3	4	G			
***RANDY GREGG** • *b. Edmonton, Alberta, February 19, 1956*									
1980	6	1	1	2	2	6th			
1988	8	1	2	3	8	4th			
Totals	14	2	3	5	10	—			
PATRICK "Patsy" GUZZO ("the Bird") • *b. Ottawa, Ontario, October 14, 1914*									
1948	8	5	7	12	8	G			
***MARC HABSCHEID** • *b. Swift Current, Saskatchewan, March 1, 1963*									
1988	8	5	3	8	6	4th			
***JIM HAGGARTY** • *b. April 14, 1914*									
1936	3	2	3	5	0	S			
WALLY HALDER • *b. Toronto, Ontario, September 15, 1925*									
1948	8	21	8	29	20	G			
***HALDOR "Slim" HALDERSON** • *b. Winnipeg, Manitoba, January 6, 1900*									
1920	3	9	—	9	—	G			

YEAR	GP	G	A	P	Pim	Pos			
YEAR	GP	W-L-T	Mins	GA	SO	Avg	A	Pim	Pos
***DAVE HANNAN** • *b. Sudbury, Ontario, November 26, 1961*									
1992	8	3	5	8	8	S			
RALPH HANSCH • *b. Edmonton, Alberta, May 20, 1924*									
1952	6	5–0–1	360	12	0	2.00	0	0	G
TED HARGREAVES • *b. Foam Lake, Saskatchewan, November 4, 1943*									
1968	7	1	1	2	0	B			
***DAVID HARLOCK** • *b. Toronto, Ontario, March 16, 1971*									
1994	8	0	0	0	8	S			
***DON HEAD** • *b. Windsor, Ontario, June 30, 1933*									
1960	7	5–1–0	385	12	2	1.87	0	0	S
TED HIBBERD • *b. Ottawa, Ontario, April 22, 1926*									
1948	8	3	4	7	4	G			
***DAVE HINDMARCH** • *b. Vancouver, British Columbia, October 15, 1958*									
1980	6	3	4	7	4	6th			
ROY HINKEL • *b. Unknown*									
1932	6	2	1	3	6	G			
***COREY HIRSCH** • *b. Medicine Hat, Alberta, July 1, 1972*									
1994	8	5–2–1	495	18	0	2.18	0	2	S
***TODD HLUSHKO** • *b. Toronto, Ontario, February 7, 1970*									
1994	8	5	0	5	6	S			
ALFRED "Buddy" HORNE • *b. Toronto, Ontario, October 4, 1933*									
1956	3	1	0	1	0	B			
***FRAN HUCK** • *b. Regina, Saskatchewan, December 4, 1945*									
1968	7	4	5	9	10	B			
Dr. LOU HUDSON • *b. Ontario, May 16, 1898*									
1928	3	4	—	4	—	G			
HAROLD "Boat" HURLEY • *b. Stratford, Ontario, November 16, 1930*									
1960	1	1–0–0	35	3	0	5.14	0	0	S
ART HURST • *b. Toronto, Ontario, May 2, 1923*									
1956	8	3	3	6	22	B			
***GORD HYNES** • *b. Montreal, Quebec, July 22, 1966*									
1992	8	3	3	6	6	S			
CONNIE JOHANNESSON • *b. August 10, 1896*									
1920	3	2	—	2	—	G			
***GREG JOHNSON** • *b. Thunder Bay, Ontario, March 16, 1971*									
1994	8	0	3	3	0	S			
***MARSHALL JOHNSTON ("Marsh"/"Hayseed")** • *b. Birch Falls, Saskatchewan, June 6, 1941*									
1964	7	0	3	3	6	4th			
1968	7	2	6	8	4	B			
Totals	14	2	9	11	10	B			
FABIAN JOSEPH • *b. Sydney, Nova Scotia, December 5, 1965*									
1992	8	2	1	3	2	S			
1994	8	0	2	2	2	S			
Totals	16	2	3	5	4	S/S			
***BOB JOYCE** • *b. St. John, New Brunswick, July 11, 1966*									
1988	4	1	0	1	0	4th			

YEAR	GP	G	A	P	Pim	Pos			
YEAR	GP	W-L-T	Mins	GA	SO	Avg	A	Pim	Pos
***JOE JUNEAU** • *b. Pont-Rouge, Quebec, January 5, 1968*									
1992	8	6	9	15	4	S			
***PAUL KARIYA** • *b. Vancouver, British Columbia, October 16, 1974*									
1994	8	3	4	7	2	S			
VAUGHN KARPAN • *b. The Pas, Manitoba, June 20, 1961*									
1984	7	0	0	0	0	4th			
1988	8	0	0	0	2	4th			
Totals	15	0	0	0	2	—			
***TREVOR KIDD** • *b. St. Boniface, Manitoba, March 29, 1972*									
1992	1	1-0-0	60	0	1	0.00	0	0	S
WALTER "Pud" KITCHEN • *b. December 18, 1912*									
1936	6	2	2	4	0	S			
BYRLE KLINCK • *b. Elmira, Ontario, June 20, 1934*									
1956	4	0	2	2	4	B			
***PAUL KNOX** • *b. Toronto, Ontario, November 23, 1933*									
1956	8	7	7	14	2	B			
***CHRIS KONTOS** • *b. Toronto, Ontario, December 10, 1963*									
1994	8	3	1	4	2	S			
ANDRÉ LAPERRIÈRE • *b. Montreal, Quebec, June 12, 1925*									
1948	8	1	1	2	14	G			
ANDRÉ LAPERRIÈRE (Goal)									
1948	1	1	0–0–0	0	0	0.00			
** played 8 seconds on January 30, 1948 when goalie Dowey penalized at 19:52 of 3rd*									
KEN LAUFMAN • *b. Hamilton, Ontario, January 30, 1932*									
1956	8	1	10	11	4	B			
1960	4	0	4	4	0	S			
Totals	12	1	14	15	4	S/B			
***PATRICK LEBEAU** • *b. St. Jerome, Quebec, March 17, 1970*									
1992	8	1	3	4	4	S			
LOUIS LECOMPTE • *b. Ottawa, Ontario, July 27, 1914*									
1948	8	2	3	5	12	G			
HOWIE LEE • *b. Toronto, Ontario, October 13, 1929*									
1956	8	2	3	5	12	B			
***DOUG LIDSTER** • *b. Kamloops, British Columbia, October 18, 1960*									
1984	7	0	2	2	2	4th			
***CHRIS LINDBERG** • *b. Fort Frances, Ontario, April 16, 1967*									
1992	8	1	4	5	4	S			
VICTOR LINDQUIST • *b. Wabigoon, Ontario, March 22, 1908*									
1932	5	3	6	9	2	G			
***ERIC LINDROS** • *b. Toronto, Ontario, February 28, 1973*									
1992	8	5	6	11	6	S			
JIM LOGAN • *b. September 17, 1933*									
1956	8	7	8	15	0	B			
***KEN LOVSIN** • *b. Peace River, Alberta, December 4, 1966*									
1994	8	0	0	0	8	S			

YEAR	GP	G	A	P	Pim	Pos			
YEAR	GP	W-L-T	Mins	GA	SO	Avg	A	Pim	Pos
***DARREN LOWE** • *b. Toronto, Ontario, October 13, 1960*									
1984	7	2	1	3	0	4th			
***BARRY MacKENZIE ("the Bear")** • *b. Toronto, Ontario, August 16, 1941*									
1964	7	0	2	2	4	4th			
1968	7	0	2	2	8	B			
Totals	14	0	4	4	12	B			
***JACK MacKENZIE** • *b. High River, Alberta, December 12, 1937*									
1956	8	7	5	12	9	B			
***PAUL MacLEAN** • *b. Grostenquin, France, March 9, 1958*									
1980	6	2	3	5	6	6th			
***BILLY MacMILLAN** • *b. Charlottetown, Prince Edward Island, March 7, 1943*									
1968	6	1	2	3	0	B			
***MERLIN MALINOWSKI ("the Magician")** • *b. North Battleford, Saskatchewan, September 27, 1958*									
1988	8	3	2	5	0	4th			
NORM MALLOY • *b. Unknown*									
1932	5	3	2	5	4	G			
***KENT MANDERVILLE** • *b. Edmonton, Alberta, April 12, 1971*									
1992	8	1	2	3	0	S			
GEORGE MARA • *b. Toronto, Ontario, December 12, 1921*									
1948	8	17	9	26	6	G			
FLOYD "Butch" MARTIN • *b. Floradale, Ontario, June 6, 1926*									
1956	8	2	5	7	12	B			
1960	7	6	6	12	14	S			
Totals	15	8	11	19	26	S/B			
***SETH MARTIN** • *b. Rossland, British Columbia, May 4, 1933*									
1964	6	4-1-0	247	5	0+	1.21	0	2	4th
+ shared a shutout with Ken Broderick on January 29, 1964 vs. Switzerland									
***KEVIN MAXWELL** • *b. Edmonton, Alberta, March 30, 1960*									
1980	6	0	5	5	4	6th			
***DEREK MAYER** • *b. Rossland, British Columbia, May 21, 1967*									
1994	8	1	2	3	18	S			
***BERT McCAFFERY** • *b. Listowel, Ontario, 1893*									
1924	5	20	—	20	—	G			
BOB McKNIGHT • *b. North Bay, Ontario, March 19, 1938*									
1960	3	2	2	4	0	S			
HAROLD McMUNN • *b. 1901*									
1924	5	5	—	5	—	G			
BOB MEYERS • *b. Edmonton, Alberta, August 11, 1924*									
1952	2	2	0	2	0	G			
DAVID MILLER • *b. North Battleford, Saskatchewan, December 15, 1925*									
1952	8	10	2	12	2	G			
RAY MILTON • *b. August 27, 1912*									
1936	2	0	0	0	0	S			
WALTER MONSON • *b. Winnipeg, Manitoba, November 29, 1908*									
1932	6	7	4	11	4	G			

YEAR	GP	G	A	P	Pim	Pos			
YEAR	GP	W-L-T	Mins	GA	SO	Avg	A	Pim	Pos
STEVE MONTEITH • *b. Stratford, Ontario, September 21, 1943*									
1968	7	1	0	1	0	B			
***ANDY MOOG** • *b. Penticton, British Columbia, February 18, 1960*									
1988	4	4–0–0	240	9	1	2.25	0	0	4th
FRANCIS "Dinty" MOORE • *b. Toronto, Ontario, October 29, 1900*									
1936	5	4–1–0	225	5	2	1.33	0	0	S
KENNETH MOORE • *b. Unknown*									
1932	1	1	0	1	0	G			
***MORRIS MOTT** • *b. Creelman, Saskatchewan, May 25, 1946*									
1968	7	5	1	6	2	B			
NORBERT "Stuffy" MUELLER • *b. Ontario, February 14, 1906*									
1928	1	1–0–0	45	0	1	0.00	0	0	G
***KIRK MULLER** • *b. Kingston, Ontario, February 8, 1966*									
1984	6	2	1	3	0	4th			
***DUNC MUNRO** • *b. Toronto, Ontario, January 19, 1900*									
1924	5	16	—	16	2	G			
HERMAN MURRAY • *b. December 5, 1909*									
1936	8	5	0	5	2	S			
ARTHUR "Jackie" NASH • *b. September 5, 1914*									
1936	3	3–0–0	135	2	2	0.89	0	0	S
***PETR NEDVED** • *b. Liberec, Czechoslovakia, December 9, 1971*									
1994	8	5	1	6	6	S			
DAVE NEVILLE • *b. May 9, 1908*									
1936	7	8	3	11	6	S			
***JIM NILL** • *b. Hanna, Alberta, April 11, 1958*									
1980	6	1	2	3	4	6th			
***DWAYNE NORRIS** • *b. St. John's, Newfoundland, January 8, 1970*									
1994	8	2	2	4	4	S			
TERRY O'MALLEY ("Mo") • *b. Toronto, Ontario, October 21, 1940*									
1964	7	0	0	0	4	4th			
1968	6	0	2	2	2	B			
1980	6	0	3	3	0	6th			
Totals	19	0	5	5	6	B			
***DANNY O'SHEA** • *b. Ajax, Ontario, June 15, 1945*									
1968	7	3	2	5	10	B			
***PAUL PAGEAU** • *b. Montreal, Quebec, October 1, 1959*									
1980	4	2–1–0	238	11	1	2.77	0	0	6th
***GREG PARKS** • *b. Edmonton, Alberta, March 25, 1967*									
1994	8	1	2	3	10	S			
***JAMES PATRICK** • *b. Winnipeg, Manitoba, June 14, 1963*									
1984	7	0	3	3	4	4th			
ERIC PATTERSON • *b. Edmonton, Alberta, September 11, 1929*									
1952	2	2–0–0	120	2	1	1.00	0	0	G
***CLIFF PENNINGTON** • *b. April 18, 1940*									
1960	4	0	2	2	6	S			

YEAR	GP	G	A	P	Pim	Pos			
YEAR	GP	W-L-T	Mins	GA	SO	Avg	A	Pim	Pos
***JIM PEPLINSKI** • *b. Renfrew, Ontario, October 24, 1960*									
1988	7	0	1	1	6	4th			
***GERRY PINDER** • *b. Saskatoon, Saskatchewan, September 15, 1948*									
1968	7	1	0	1	2	B			
HERB PINDER • *b. Boston, Massachusetts, December 24, 1946*									
1968	2	1	0	1	2	B			
BRAD PIRIE • *b. Guelph, Ontario, October 21, 1955*									
1980	6	1	2	3	2	6th			
***ADRIEN PLAVSIC** • *b. Montreal, Quebec, January 30, 1970*									
1992	8	0	2	2	0	S			
BERT PLAXTON • *b. April 22, 1901*									
1928	1	2	—	2	—	G			
***HUGH PLAXTON** • *b. Bruno, Saskatchewan, May 16, 1904*									
1928	3	12	—	12	—	G			
ROGER PLAXTON • *b. June 2, 1904*									
1928	1	0	—	0	—	G			
TOM POLLOCK • *b. August 1, 1925*									
1952	8	2	1	3	6	G			
JOHN "Red" PORTER • *b. Toronto, Ontario, January 21, 1904*									
1928	3	3	—	3	—	G			
***KEVIN PRIMEAU** • *b. Edmonton, Alberta, January 3, 1956*									
1980	6	4	1	5	6	6th			
AL PURVIS • *b. Trochu, Alberta, January 9, 1929*									
1952	8	2	0	2	2	G			
***BEATTIE RAMSAY** • *b. Lumsden, Saskatchewan, 1895*									
1924	5	10	—	10	—	G			
***DAN RATUSHNY** • *b. Windsor, Ontario, October 29, 1970*									
1992	8	0	0	0	4	S			
***CRAIG REDMOND** • *b. Dawson Creek, British Columbia, September 22, 1965*									
1984	7	2	0	2	4	4th			
ALBERTO "Ab" RENAUD • *b. Ottawa, Ontario, October 2, 1920*									
1948	8	4	10	14	6	G			
ROMEO RIVERS • *b. Unknown*									
1932	6	5	3	8	0	G			
GORDON ROBERTSON • *b. June 25, 1926*									
1952	8	4	6	10	9	G			
DON ROPE • *b. Winnipeg, Manitoba, February 2, 1929*									
1956	8	4	2	6	4	B			
1960	7	4	3	7	0	S			
Totals	15	8	5	13	4	S/B			
***BOBBY ROUSSEAU** • *b. Montreal, Quebec, July 26, 1940*									
1960	7	5	4	9	2	S			
***JEAN-YVES ROY** • *b. Rosemere, Quebec, February 17, 1969*									
1994	8	1	0	1	0	S			

YEAR	GP	G	A	P	Pim	Pos			
YEAR	GP	W-L-T	Mins	GA	SO	Avg	A	Pim	Pos
SERGE ROY • *B. Sept-Iles, Quebec, June 25, 1962*									
1988	5	0	7	7	4	4th			
RALPH ST. GERMAIN • *B. October 19, 1904*									
1936	4	6	5	11	0	S			
GEORGE SAMOLENKO • *B. Saskatchewan, December 20, 1930*									
1960	7	8	4	12	0	S			
***BRIAN SAVAGE** • *B. Sudbury, Ontario, February 24, 1971*									
1994	8	2	2	4	6	S			
***BRAD SCHLEGEL** • *B. Strathroy, Ontario, July 22, 1968*									
1992	8	1	2	3	4	S			
1994	8	0	0	0	6	S			
Totals	16	1	2	3	10	S/S			
GEORGE SCHOLES • *B. Toronto, Ontario, November 24, 1928*									
1956	8	5	5	10	2	B			
***WALLY SCHREIBER** • *B. Edmonton, Alberta, April 15, 1962*									
1988	8	1	2	3	2	4th			
1992	8	2	2	4	2	S			
1994	8	1	0	1	2	S			
Totals	24	4	4	8	6	S/S			
REG SCHROETER • *B. Ottawa, Ontario, September 11, 1921*									
1948	8	12	5	17	2	G			
LOUIS SECCO • *B. January 18, 1927*									
1952	8	2	3	5	2	G			
***ROD SEILING** • *B. Elmira, Ontario, November 14, 1944*									
1964	7	4	2	6	4	4th			
***GORD SHERVEN** • *B. Gravelbourg, Saskatchewan, August 21, 1963*									
1988	8	4	4	8	4	4th			
HAROLD "Hack" SIMPSON • *B. August 13, 1893*									
1932	5	6	1	7	6	G			
ALEX SINCLAIR • *B. June 28, 1911*									
1936	5	3	3	6	0	S			
HARRY SINDEN • *B. Toronto, Ontario, September 14, 1932*									
1960	7	4	5	9	6	S			
CYRIL "Sig" SLATER • *B. 1897*									
1924	5	4	—	4	—	G			
***DARRYL SLY** • *B. Collingwood, Ontario, April 3, 1939*									
1960	7	1	1	2	9	S			
***RANDY SMITH** • *B. Saskatoon, Saskatchewan, July 15, 1965*									
1992	8	1	7	8	4	S			
***REGINALD "Hooley" SMITH** • *B. Toronto, Ontario, January 7, 1905*									
1924	5	18	—	18	4	G			
***DON SPRING** • *B. Maracaibo, Venezuela, June 16, 1959*									
1980	6	0	1	1	0	6th			
***WAYNE STEPHENSON** • *B. Fort William, Ontario, January 29, 1945*									
1968	3	2–0–0	140	3	1	1.29	0	0	B

YEAR	GP	G	A	P	Pim	Pos			
YEAR	GP	W-L-T	Mins	GA	SO	Avg	A	Pim	Pos
***TONY STILES** • *b. Calgary, Alberta, August 12, 1959*									
1988	5	0	0	0	0	4th			
FRANK GERALD SULLIVAN • *b. Toronto, Ontario, June 26, 1898*									
1928	3	2	—	2	—	G			
***FRANK ("Sully") SULLIVAN** • *b. June 7, 1917*									
1952	8	5	5	10	2	G			
Dr. JOE SULLIVAN • *b. Toronto, Ontario, January 8, 1901*									
1928	2	2–0–0	90	0	2	0.00	0	0	G
HUGH SUTHERLAND • *b. Winnipeg, Manitoba, February 2, 1907*									
1932	6	1	5	6	4	G			
***GEORGE SWARBRICK ("Swiggy")** • *b. Moose Jaw, Saskatchewan, February 16, 1942*									
1964	7	3	3	6	2	4th			
***STEVE TAMBELLINI** • *b. Trail, British Columbia, May 14, 1958*									
1988	8	1	3	4	2	4th			
IRVING TAYLOR • *b. Ottawa, Ontario, August 13, 1919*									
1948	1	0	0	0	0	G			
ROSS TAYLOR • *b. Toronto, Ontario, October 2, 1905*									
1928	1	2	—	2	—	G			
GERRY THÉBERGE • *b. St. Hyacinthe, Quebec, December 18, 1930*									
1956	8	9	2	11	8	B			
***CHRIS THERIEN** • *b. Ottawa, Ontario, December 14, 1971*									
1994	4	0	0	0	4	S			
***BILL THOMSON** • *b. Ayshire, Scotland, March 23, 1914*									
1936	8	7	0	7	2	S			
***DAVE TIPPETT** • *b. Moosomin, Saskatchewan, August 25, 1961*									
1984	7	1	1	2	2	4th			
1992	7	1	2	3	10	S			
Totals	14	2	3	5	12	S			
***DAVE TROTTIER** • *b. Pembroke, Ontario, June 25, 1906*									
1928	3	12	—	12	—	G			
***BRIAN TUTT** • *b. Small Well, Alberta, June 9, 1962*									
1992	8	0	0	0	4	S			
***CLAUDE VILGRAIN** • *b. Port au Prince, Haiti, March 1, 1963*									
1988	6	0	0	0	0	4th			
STANLEY WAGNER • *b. Unknown*									
1932	1	1–0–0	45	0	1	0.00	0	0	G
***TODD WARRINER** • *b. Blenheim, Ontario, January 3, 1974*									
1994	4	1	1	2	0	S			
HARRY E. WATSON ("Moose") • *b. St. John's, Newfoundland, July 14, 1898*									
1924	5	36	—	36	2	G			
ROBERT WATT • *b. June 24, 1927*									
1952	8	3	3	6	2	G			
***TIM WATTERS** • *b. Kamloops, British Columbia, July 25, 1959*									
1980	6	1	1	2	0	6th			
1988	8	0	1	1	2	4th			
Totals	14	1	2	3	2	—			

YEAR	GP	G	A	P	Pim	Pos			
YEAR	GP	W-L-T	Mins	GA	SO	Avg	A	Pim	Pos
***BRAD WERENKA** • *b. Two Hills, Alberta, February 12, 1969*									
1994	8	2	2	4	8	S			
BOB WHITE • *b. Stratford, Ontario, July 22, 1935*									
1956	8	2	3	5	2	B			
***CAREY WILSON** • *b. Winnipeg, Manitoba, May 19, 1962*									
1984	7	3	3	6	6	4th			
ALISTON "Stoney" WISE • *b. Unknown*									
1932	5	2	0	2	0	G			
DAN WOOD • *b. Scarborough, Ontario, October 31, 1962*									
1984	7	0	1	1	2	4th			
KEITH WOODALL • *b. Elmira, Ontario, August 4, 1926*									
1956	4	3–1–0	240	4	2	1.00	0	0	B
ALLAN "Huck" WOODMAN • *b. Unknown*									
1920	3	1	—	1	—	G			
***JASON WOOLLEY** • *b. Toronto, Ontario, July 27, 1969*									
1992	8	0	5	5	4	S			
***KEN YAREMCHUK** • *b. Edmonton, Alberta, January 1, 1964*									
1988	8	3	3	6	2	4th			
***TRENT YAWNEY** • *b. Hudson Bay, Saskatchewan, September 29, 1965*									
1988	8	1	1	2	6	4th			
***ZARLEY ZALAPSKI** • *b. Edmonton, Alberta, April 22, 1968*									
1988	8	1	3	4	2	4th			
STELIO ZUPANCICH • *b. Toronto, Ontario, April 7, 1958*									
1980	6	1	3	4	2	6th			

CANADA'S TEAM CAPTAINS

1920	Frank Fredrickson
1924	Dunc Munro
1928	Red Porter
1932	William Cockburn*
1936	Herman Murray
1948	George Mara
1952	Billy Dawe
1956	Jack MacKenzie
1960	Harry Sinden
1964	Hank Akervall
1968	Marshall Johnston
1980	Randy Gregg
1984	Dave Tippett
1988	Trent Yawney
1992	Brad Schlegel
1994	Fabian Joseph

** only goalie to be team captain*

OLYMPIC MEDALISTS AND STANLEY CUP CHAMPIONS

Only nine Canadians have won both an Olympic medal and the Stanley Cup:

	Medal	Stanley Cup
1. Frank Fredrickson	G 1920	1925 (Victoria) /1929 (Boston)
2. Slim Halderson	G 1920	1925 (Victoria)
3. Bert McCaffery	G 1924	1930/1931 (Canadiens)
4. Dunc Munro	G 1924	1926 (Maroons)
5. Hooley Smith	G 1924	1927 (Ottawa)/1935 (Maroons)
6. Dave Trottier	G 1928	1935 (Maroons)
7. Dave Hannan	S 1992	1988 (Edmonton)/1996 (Colorado)
8. Bobby Rousseau	S 1960	1965/1966/1968/1969 (Canadiens)
9. Wayne Stephenson	B 1968	1975 (Philadelphia)

HOCKEY HALL OF FAME

Only four hockey players who have represented Canada at the Olympics have been inducted into the Hockey Hall of Fame:

Frank Fredrickson	1920
Harry Sinden*	1960
Hooley Smith	1924
Harry E. Watson	1924

** inducted as a Builder*

Canada's All-Time Coaching Register

* played in the NHL
ˣ coached in the NHL
GC = games coached
Pos = team finish
G = Gold
S = Silver
B = Bronze

YEAR	GC	W	L	T	Pos
***BOBBY BAUER** • *B. Waterloo, Ontario, February 16, 1915*					
1956	8	6	2	0	B
1960	7	6	1	0	S
Totals	15	12	3	0	S/B
FATHER DAVID BAUER • *B. Waterloo, Ontario, November 2, 1924*					
1964	7	5	2	0	4th
***FRANK BOUCHER** • *B. Ottawa, Ontario, October 7, 1901*					
1948	8	7	0	1	G
***LORNE DAVIS (co-coach)** • *B. Prince Albert, Saskatchewan, July 16, 1957*					
1980	6	3	3	0	6th
CLARE DRAKE (co-coach) • *B. Yorkton, Saskatchewan, October 9, 1928*					
1980	6	3	3	0	6th
***LOU HOLMES** • *B. England, January 29, 1911*					
1952	8	7	0	1	G
JACK HUGHES • *B. Unknown*					
1932	6	5	0	1	G
ˣDAVE KING • *B. North Battleford, Saskatchewan, December 22, 1947*					
1984	7	4	3	0	6th
1988	8	5	2	1	4th
1992	8	6	2	0	S
Totals	23	15	7	1	S
***JACKIE McLEOD** • *B. Unknown*					
1968	7	5	2	0	B
***AL PUDAS** • *B. Unknown*					
1936	8	6	1	1	S
FRANK RANKIN • *B. Stratford, Ontario, April 1, 1889*					
1924	5	5	0	0	G
ˣTOM RENNEY • *B. Cranbrook, British Columbia, March 1, 1955*					
1994	8	5	2	1	S
GORDON SIGURJONSON • *B. Unknown*					
1920	3	3	0	0	G
ˣCONN SMYTHE • *B. Toronto, Ontario, February 1, 1895*					
1928	3	3	0	0	G
ˣTOM WATT (co-coach) • *B. Toronto, Ontario, June 17, 1935*					
1980	6	3	3	0	6th

HOCKEY HALL OF FAME

Five men who have coached Canada at the Olympics have also been inducted into the Hockey Hall of Fame:

Bobby Bauer	1956/60
Father David Bauer	1964
Frank Boucher	1948
Frank Rankin	1924
Conn Smythe	1928

Canada's Hockey Records

RECORD BY OLYMPICS

YEAR	GP	W	L	T	GF	GA	POS
1920	3	3	0	0	29	1	1st
1924	5	5	0	0	110	3	1st
1928	3	3	0	0	38	0	1st
1932	6	5	0	1	32	4	1st
1936	8	7	1	0	54	7	2nd
1948	8	7	0	1	69	5	1st
1952	8	7	0	1	71	14	1st
1956	8	6	2	0	53	12	3rd
1960	7	6	1	0	55	15	2nd
1964	7	5	2	0	32	17	4th
1968	7	5	2	0	28	15	3rd
1980	6	3	3	0	29	18	6th
1984	7	4	3	0	24	16	4th
1988	8	5	2	1	31	21	4th
1992	8	6	2	0	37	17	2nd
1994	8	5	2	1	27	19	2nd
Totals	**107**	**82**	**20**	**5**	**719**	**184**	—

MEDALS SUMMARY FOR HOCKEY

16 OLYMPICS

GOLD	6
SILVER	4
BRONZE	2
4TH PLACE	3
6TH PLACE	1
Total	16

OVERALL RECORD • Canada vs. Other Countries

TEAM	GP	W	L	T	GF	GA
Austria	4	4	0	0	48	3
Czechoslovakia	14	10	3	1	86	25
Czech Republic	1	1	0	0	3	2
Finland	7	4	3	0	34	22
France	3	3	0	0	15	8
Germany	12	12	0	0	89	11
Great Britain	4	3	1	0	37	4
Holland	1	1	0	0	10	1
Hungary	1	1	0	0	15	0
Italy	3	3	0	0	31	4
Japan	2	2	0	0	25	1
Latvia	1	1	0	0	11	0
Norway	3	3	0	0	29	3
Poland	7	7	0	0	59	2
Slovakia	1	0	1	0	1	3
Sweden	14	11	2	1	81	23
Switzerland	7	7	0	0	78	5
Unified Team	2	0	2	0	5	8
United States	13	8	2	3	48	29
USSR	7	1	6	0	14	30
Totals	**107**	**82**	**20**	**5**	**719**	**184**

CHRONOLOGICAL RECORD • Canada vs. Other Countries

(from longest rivalry to most recent)

SWEDEN

year	score	result
1920	12-1	W
1924	22-0	W
1928	11-0	W
1948	3-1	W
1952	3-2	W
1956	6-2	W
1960	5-2	W
1960	6-5	W
1964	3-1	W
1968	3-0	W
1984	0-2	L
1988	2-2	T
1994	3-2	W
1994	2-3+	*L

** won in shootout*

+ overtime

Canada vs. Sweden

OVERALL RECORD

GP	W	L	T	GF	GA
14	11	2	1	81	23

CZECHOSLOVAKIA

year	score	result
1920	15-0	W
1924	30-0	W
1936	7-0	W
1948	0-0	T
1952	4-1	W
1956	6-3	W
1960	4-0	W
1964	1-3	L
1968	3-2	W
1980	1-6	L
1984	0-4	L
1988	6-3	W
1992	5-1	W
1992	4-2	W

Canada vs. Czechoslovakia

OVERALL RECORD

GP	W	L	T	GF	GA
14	10	3	1	86	25

UNITED STATES

year	score	result
1920	2-0	W
1924	6-1	W
1932	2-1+	W
1932	2-2+	T
1936	1-0	W
1948	12-3	W
1952	3-3	T
1956	1-4	L
1960	1-2	L
1964	8-6	W
1968	3-2	W
1984	4-2	W
1994	3-3	T

+ overtime

Canada vs. United States

OVERALL RECORD

GP	W	L	T	GF	GA
13	8	2	3	48	29

GERMANY

year	score	result
1932	4-1	W
1932	5-0	W
1936	6-2	W
1952	15-1	W
1956	4-0	W
1956	10-0	W
1960	12-0	W
1964	4-2	W
1968	6-1	***W
1968	11-0	**W
1988	8-1	***W
1992	4-3+	*W

** won in shootout*

*** East Germany*

**** West Germany*

+ overtime

Canada vs. Germany

OVERALL RECORD

GP	W	L	T	GF	GA
12	12	0	0	89	11

POLAND

year	score	result
1932	9-0	W
1932	10-0	W
1936	8-1	W
1948	15-0	W
1952	11-0	W
1980	5-1	W
1988	1-0	W

Canada vs. Poland

OVERALL RECORD

GP	W	L	T	GF	GA
7	7	0	0	59	2

SWITZERLAND

year	score	result
1924	33-0	W
1928	13-0	W
1948	3-0	W
1952	11-2	W
1964	8-0	W
1988	4-2	W
1992	6-1	W

Canada vs. Switzerland

OVERALL RECORD

GP	W	L	T	GF	GA
7	7	0	0	78	5

FINLAND

year	score	result
1952	13-3	W
1964	6-2	W
1968	2-5	L
1980	3-4	L
1984	4-2	W
1988	1-3	L
1994	5-3	W

Canada vs. Finland

OVERALL RECORD

GP	W	L	T	GF	GA
7	4	3	0	34	22

USSR

year	score	result
1956	0-2	L
1960	8-5	W
1964	2-3	L
1968	0-5	L
1980	4-6	L
1984	0-4	L
1988	0-5	L

Canada vs. USSR

OVERALL RECORD

GP	W	L	T	GF	GA
7	1	6	0	14	30

AUSTRIA

year	score	result
1936	5-2	W
1948	12-0	W
1956	23-0	W
1984	8-1	W

Canada vs. Austria

OVERALL RECORD

GP	W	L	T	GF	GA
4	4	0	0	48	3

GREAT BRITAIN

year	score	result
1924	19-2	W
1928	14-0	W
1936	1-2	L
1948	3-0	W

Canada vs. Great Britain

OVERALL RECORD

GP	W	L	T	GF	GA
4	3	1	0	37	4

FRANCE

year	score	result
1988	9-5	W
1992	3-2	W
1994	3-1	W

Canada vs. France

OVERALL RECORD

GP	W	L	T	GF	GA
3	3	0	0	15	8

ITALY

year	score	result
1948	21-1	W
1956	3-1	W
1994	7-2	W

Canada vs. Italy

OVERALL RECORD

GP	W	L	T	GF	GA
3	3	0	0	31	4

NORWAY

year	score	result
1952	11-2	W
1984	8-1	W
1992	10-0	W

Canada vs. Norway

OVERALL RECORD

GP	W	L	T	GF	GA
3	3	0	0	29	3

JAPAN

year	score	result
1960	19-1	W
1980	6-0	W

Canada vs. Japan

OVERALL RECORD

GP	W	L	T	GF	GA
2	2	0	0	25	1

UNIFIED TEAM

year	score	result
1992	4-5	L
1992	1-3	L

Canada vs. Unified Team

OVERALL RECORD

GP	W	L	T	GF	GA
2	0	2	0	5	8

CZECH REPUBLIC

year	score	result
1994	3-2+	W

Canada vs. Czech Republic

+ *overtime*

OVERALL RECORD

GP	W	L	T	GF	GA
1	1	0	0	3	2

HOLLAND

year	score	result
1980	10-1	W

Canada vs. Holland

OVERALL RECORD

GP	W	L	T	GF	GA
1	1	0	0	10	1

HUNGARY

year	score	result
1936	15-0	W

Canada vs. Hungary

OVERALL RECORD

GP	W	L	T	GF	GA
1	1	0	0	15	0

LATVIA

year	score	result
1936	11-0	W

Canada vs. Latvia

OVERALL RECORD

GP	W	L	T	GF	GA
1	1	0	0	11	0

SLOVAKIA

year	score	result
1994	1-3	L

Canada vs. Slovakia

OVERALL RECORD

GP	W	L	T	GF	GA
1	0	1	0	1	3

CHRONOLOGICAL ORDER OF ALL CANADIAN OLYMPIC HOCKEY GAME RESULTS

1920

April 24 • Canada 15 Czechoslovakia 0
April 25 • Canada 2 United States 0
April 26 • Canada 12 Sweden 1

1924

January 28 • Canada 30 Czechoslovakia 0
January 29 • Canada 22 Sweden 0
January 30 • Canada 33 Switzerland 0
February 1 • Canada 19 Great Britain 2
February 3 • Canada 6 United States 1

1928

February 16 • Canada 11 Sweden 0
February 18 • Canada 14 Great Britain 0
February 19 • Canada 13 Switzerland 0

1932

February 4 • Canada 2 United States 1 (OT)
February 6 • Canada 4 Germany 1
February 7 • Canada 9 Poland 0
February 8 • Canada 5 Germany 0
February 9 • Canada 10 Poland 0
February 13 • Canada 2 United States 2 (OT)

1936

February 6 • Canada 8 Poland 1
February 7 • Canada 11 Latvia 0
February 8 • Canada 5 Austria 2
February 10 • Great Britain 2 Canada 1
(counted twice in standings)
February 12 • Canada 15 Hungary 0
February 13 • Canada 6 Germany 2
February 15 • Canada 7 Czechoslovakia 0
February 16 • Canada 1 United States 0

1948

January 30 • Canada 3 Sweden 1
February 1 • Canada 3 Great Britain 0
February 2 • Canada 15 Poland 0
February 3 • Canada 21 Italy 1
February 5 • Canada 12 United States 3
February 6 • Canada 0 Czechoslovakia 0
February 7 • Canada 12 Austria 0
February 8 • Canada 3 Switzerland 0

1952

February 15 • Canada 15 Germany 1
February 17 • Canada 13 Finland 3
February 18 • Canada 11 Poland 0
February 19 • Canada 4 Czechoslovakia 1
February 21 • Canada 11 Switzerland 2
February 22 • Canada 3 Sweden 2
February 23 • Canada 11 Norway 2
February 24 • Canada 3 United States 3

1956

January 26 • Canada 4 Germany 0
January 27 • Canada 23 Austria 0
January 28 • Canada 3 Italy 1
January 30 • Canada 6 Czechoslovakia 3
January 31 • United States 4 Canada 1
February 1 • Canada 10 Germany 0
February 2 • Canada 6 Sweden 2
February 4 • USSR 2 Canada 0

1960

February 18 • Canada 5 Sweden 2
February 20 • Canada 19 Japan 1
February 22 • Canada 12 Germany 0
February 24 • Canada 4 Czechoslovakia 0
February 25 • United States 2 Canada 1
February 27 • Canada 6 Sweden 5
February 28 • Canada 8 USSR 5

1964

January 29 • Canada 8 Switzerland 0
January 30 • Canada 3 Sweden 1
February 2 • Canada 4 Germany 2
February 3 • Canada 8 United States 6
February 5 • Canada 6 Finland 2
February 7 • Czechoslovakia 3 Canada 1
February 8 • USSR 3 Canada 2

1968

February 6 • Canada 6 West Germany 1
February 8 • Finland 5 Canada 2
February 9 • Canada 11 East Germany 0
February 11 • Canada 3 United States 2
February 13 • Canada 3 Czechoslovakia 2
February 15 • Canada 3 Sweden 0
February 17 • USSR 5 Canada 0

1980

February 12 • Canada 10 Holland 1
February 14 • Canada 5 Poland 1
February 16 • Finland 4 Canada 3
February 18 • Canada 6 Japan 0
February 20 • USSR 6 Canada 4
February 22 • Czechoslovakia 6 Canada 1

1984

February 7 • Canada 4   United States 2
February 9 • Canada 8   Austria 1
February 11 • Canada 4   Finland 2
February 13 • Canada 8   Norway 1
February 15 • Czechoslovakia 4   Canada 0
(counted twice in the standings)
February 17 • USSR 4   Canada 0
February 19 • Sweden 2   Canada 0

1988

February 14 • Canada 1   Poland 0
February 16 • Canada 4   Switzerland 2
February 18 • Finland 3   Canada 1
(counted twice in standings)
February 20 • Canada 9   France 5
February 22 • Canada 2   Sweden 2
(counted twice in standings)
February 24 • USSR 5   Canada 0
February 26 • Canada 8   West Germany 1
February 27 • Canada 6   Czechoslovakia 3

1992

February 8 • Canada 3   France 2
February 10 • Canada 6   Switzerland 1
February 12 • Canada 10   Norway 0
February 14 • Canada 5   Czechoslovakia 1
February 16 • Unified Team 5   Canada 4
February 18 • Canada 4   Germany 3
(OT & shootout)
February 21 • Canada 4   Czechoslovakia 2
February 23 • Unified Team 3   Canada 1

1994

February 13 • Canada 7   Italy 2
February 15 • Canada 3   France 1
February 17 • Canada 3   United States 3
February 19 • Slovakia 3   Canada 1
February 21 • Canada 3   Sweden 2
February 23 • Canada 3   Czech Republic 2 (OT)
February 25 • Canada 5   Finland 3
February 27 • Sweden 3   Canada 2
(OT & shootout)

OLYMPIC PLAYERS WHO HAVE PLAYED IN THE NHL

Of the 234 players to have represented Canada at the Olympics, 115 have played in the NHL:

TORONTO MAPLE LEAFS • 22
G. Anderson, Boisvert, Bradley, T. Clancy, B. Conacher, Courtnall, Gagner, Glennie, Halderson, Hannan, Harlock, Knox, B. MacMillan, Manderville, McCaffery, Muller, Ramsay, Seiling, Sly, Sullivan, Warriner, K. Yaremchuk

CALGARY FLAMES • 17
Bartel, Bradley, Dahl, Gagner, Habscheid, Hindmarch, Hlushko, Kidd, Lindberg, Patrick, Peplinski, Schlegel, Stiles, Tambellini, C. Wilson, Yawney, Zalapski

VANCOUVER CANUCKS • 16
Aucoin, Bartel, Berry, Bradley, Courtnall, Daigneault, Gregg, Hirsch, Lidster, Nedved, Nill, Plavsic, K. Primeau, Sly, Tambellini, Vilgrain

MINNESOTA NORTH STARS • 15
Archibald, Broderick, Courtnall, G. Dineen, Gagner, Giles, Habscheid, Johnston, B. MacKenzie, K. Maxwell, O'Shea, Rousseau, Sherven, Sly, R. Smith

NEW YORK RANGERS • 15
G. Anderson, Archibald, Driver, Flatley, Gagner, Giles, Hirsch, Kontos, Lidster, Nedved, Patrick, Rousseau, Roy, Seiling, C. Wilson

EDMONTON OILERS • 13
G. Anderson, Berry, Cote, Donnelly, Dupuis, Gregg, Habscheid, Hannan, Manderville, Moog, C. Redmond, Sherven, Werenka

ST. LOUIS BLUES • 13
G. Anderson, Daigneault, Giles, Huck, Lidster, P. MacLean, Martin, Nedved, Nill, O'Shea, Plavsic, Seiling, Stephenson

BOSTON BRUINS • 12
Benson, Broderick, Donnelly, Fredrickson, Head, Hynes, Joyce, Juneau, Moog, Nill, Pennington, H. Smith

MONTREAL CANADIENS • 12
Boisvert, Courtnall, Daigneault, Haggarty, Huck, Lebeau, McCaffery, Muller, Munro, Pennington, Rousseau, Savage

DETROIT RED WINGS • 10
B. Conacher, Eliot, Fredrickson, Habscheid, Halderson, G. Johnston, P. MacLean, Nill, Thomson, Trottier

PHILADELPHIA FLYERS • 10
Daigneault, K. Dineen, Hlushko, Hynes, Lindros, Stephenson, Swarbrick, Therien, Tippett, Vilgrain

WASHINGTON CAPITALS • 10
Felix, Joyce, Juneau, Lovsin, Schlegel, Seiling, Stephenson, Tippett, Tutt, Woolley

HARTFORD WHALERS • 9
Burke, K. Dineen, Gosselin, Malinowski, Patrick, Sherven, Tippett, C. Wilson, Zalapski

CHICAGO BLACKHAWKS • 8
D. Donnelly, O'Shea, Pinder, Sullivan, Thomson, Werenka, K. Yaremchuk, Yawney

PITTSBURGH PENGUINS • 8
Daigneault, Hannan, Kontos, Lowe, Nedved, Swarbrick, Tippett, Zalapski

LOS ANGELES KINGS • 7
Glennie, Kontos, C. Redmond, Watters, Eliot, Gosselin, Pageau

NEW JERSEY DEVILS • 7
Burke, Driver, Malinowski, K. Maxwell, Muller, Tambellini, Vilgrain

NEW YORK ISLANDERS • 5
Flatley, B. MacMillan, Muller, Parks, Tambellini

OAKLAND (California Golden) SEALS • 5
T. Clancy, Johnston, Mott, Pinder, Swarbrick

WINNIPEG JETS • 5
Joyce, P. MacLean, Nill, Spring, Watters

QUEBEC NORDIQUES • 4
Gosselin, Lindberg, Norris, Werenka

BUFFALO SABRES • 3
Astley, Eliot, Hannan

DALLAS STARS • 3
Courtnall, Gagner, Moog

MIGHTY DUCKS OF ANAHEIM • 3
Kariya, Lebeau, Norris

MONTREAL MAROONS • 3
H. Plaxton, H. Smith, Trottier

OTTAWA SENATORS (II) • 3
Archibald, Mayer, Roy

TAMPA BAY LIGHTNING • 3
Bradley, Kontos, Plavsic

ATLANTA FLAMES • 2
B. MacMillan, Seiling

COLORADO AVALANCHE • 2
Hannan, Malinowski

COLORADO ROCKIES • 2
K. Maxwell, Tambellini

FLORIDA PANTHERS • 2
Muller, Wooley

PITTSBURGH PIRATES • 2
Fredrickson, McCaffery

NEW YORK AMERICANS • 1
H. Smith

OTTAWA SENATORS (I) • 1
H. Smith

Team Canada at the Winter Olympic Games

ALL-TIME TEAM AND INDIVIDUAL RECORDS

ALL-TIME TEAM RECORDS

LONGEST WINNING STREAK

16 games April 24, 1920-February 9, 1932

9 games February 12, 1936-February 5, 1948
February 7, 1948-February 23, 1952

LONGEST UNDEFEATED STREAK

24 games February 12, 1936-January 30, 1956

20 games April 24, 1920-February 8, 1936

LONGEST LOSING STREAK

3 games February 15, 1984-February 19, 1984

2 games February 7, 1964-February 8, 1964
February 20, 1980-February 22, 1980

LONGEST WINLESS STREAK

3 games February 15, 1984-February 19, 1984

2 games February 7, 1964-February 8, 1964
February 20, 1980-February 22, 1980
February 22, 1988-February 24, 1988
February 17, 1994-February 19, 1994

LONGEST SHUTOUT SEQUENCE FOR, TEAM (IN MINUTES) (for Individual, see goalie records)

225:25 January 30, 1948-February 3, 1948

206:50 February 5, 1948-February 15, 1952

203:15 February 3, 1924-February 4, 1932

164:19 February 20, 1960-February 25, 1960

160:00* April 26, 1920-February 1, 1924

138:19 February 6, 1932-February 13, 1932

* time rounded off to nearest five minutes

LONGEST SHUTOUT SEQUENCE AGAINST, TEAM (IN MINUTES)

186:04 February 13, 1984-February 14, 1988

GOAL SCORING RECORDS, TEAM

SCORELESS GAMES

February 6, 1948 vs. Czechoslovakia

MOST GOALS FOR, GAME

33 January 30, 1924 vs. Switzerland

30 January 28, 1924 vs. Czechoslovakia

23 January 27, 1956 vs. Austria

22 January 29, 1924 vs. Sweden

21 February 3, 1948 vs. Italy

19 February 1, 1924 vs. Great Britain
February 20, 1960 vs. Japan

15 April 24, 1920 vs. Czechoslovakia
February 12, 1936 vs. Hungary
February 2, 1948 vs. Poland
February 15, 1952 vs. Germany

MOST GOALS AGAINST, GAME

6 February 3, 1964 vs. United States
February 20, 1980 vs. USSR
February 22, 1980 vs. Czechoslovakia

5 February 27, 1960 vs. Sweden
February 28, 1960 vs. USSR
February 8, 1968 vs. Finland
February 17, 1968 vs. USSR
February 20, 1988 vs. France
February 24, 1988 vs. USSR
February 16, 1992 vs. Unified Team

MOST GOALS BOTH TEAMS, GAME

(both teams scoring)

22 February 3, 1948 • Canada 21 Italy 1

21 February 1, 1924 • Canada 19 Great Britain 2

20 February 20, 1960 • Canada 19 Japan 1

16 February 15, 1952 • Canada 15 Germany 1
February 17, 1952 • Canada 13 Finland 3

MOST GOALS FOR, PERIOD

14 January 28, 1924 vs. Czechoslovakia (2nd period)
January 30, 1924 vs. Switzerland (3rd period)

11 January 30, 1924 vs. Switzerland (2nd period)
February 3, 1948 vs. Italy (1st period)
January 27, 1956 vs. Austria (2nd period)

10 April 24, 1920 vs. Czechoslovakia (1st half)
January 29, 1924 vs. Sweden (3rd period)

MOST GOALS AGAINST, PERIOD

5 February 22, 1980 vs. Czechoslovakia (1st period)

4 February 27, 1960 vs. Sweden (1st period)
February 20, 1980 vs, USSR (3rd period)

MOST GOALS BOTH TEAMS, PERIOD

(both teams scoring)

10 February 20, 1988 vs. France (1st period)
Canada 7 goals, France 3 goals

8 February 1, 1924 vs. Great Britain (1st period)
Canada 6 goals, Great Britain 2 goals
February 17, 1952 vs. Finland (1st period)
Canada 6 goals, Finland 2 goals
February 20, 1960 vs. Japan (2nd period)
Canada 7 goals, Japan one goal

ALL TIE SCORES

3-3 Canada vs. United States, February 24, 1952
Canada vs. United States, February 17, 1994

2-2 Canada vs. United States, February 13, 1932
Canada vs. Sweden, February 22, 1988

0-0 Canada vs. Czechoslovakia, February 6, 1948

ALL OVERTIME GAMES

February 4, 1932 • Canada 2 United States 1 (10:00 OT)

February 13, 1932 • Canada 2 United States 2 (30:00 OT)

February 18, 1992 • Canada 4 Germany 3 (10:00 OT & shootout)

February 23, 1994 • Canada 3 Czech Republic 2 (Kariya 5:54 OT)

February 27, 1994 • Sweden 3 Canada 2 (10:00 OT & shootout)

ALL OVERTIME GOALS

Victor Lindquist, February 4, 1932 vs. United States

Eric Lindros, February 18, 1992 vs. Germany (shootout penalty shot)

Paul Kariya (pp), February 23, 1994 vs. Czech Republic

ALL POWER-PLAY AND SHORT-HANDED GOALS RECORDS, FOR AND AGAINST

(since 1952, when penalty times accurately kept)

	FOR		AGAINST	
	PP	SH	PP	SH
1952	3	0	1	0
1956	3	2	2	1
1960	6	0	3	0
1964	2	0	2	0
1968	4	0	3	1
1980	5	0	0	2
1984	4	0	2	1
1988	6	1	2	0
1992	9	0	2	0
1994	5	0	8	2

MOST POWER-PLAY GOALS, TEAM, ONE OLYMPICS

9 **1992** (Dave Archibald (3), Joe Juneau (3), Gord Hynes, Eric Lindros, Stephane Lebeau)

6 **1960** (Fred Etcher (3), Bob Attersley (2), Bobby Rousseau)
1988 (Ken Berry, Serge Boisvert, Marc Habscheid, Merlin Malinowski, Wally Schreiber, Trent Yawney)

MOST POWER-PLAY GOALS, TEAM, ONE GAME

3 February 18, 1960 vs. Sweden
February 12, 1980 vs. Holland
February 20, 1988 vs. France
February 10, 1992 vs. Switzerland
February 14, 1992 vs. Czechoslovakia

MOST POWER-PLAY GOALS, TEAM, ONE PERIOD

2 February 18, 1960, 3rd period, vs. Sweden
February 12, 1980, 3rd period, vs. Holland
February 20, 1988, 1st period, vs. France
February 26, 1988, 3rd period, vs. West Germany
February 13, 1994, 1st period, vs. Italy

MOST POWER-PLAY GOALS ALLOWED, ONE OLYMPICS

8 **1994** (Sweden (3), United States (2), Finland, France, Slovakia)

3 **1960** (Sweden, United States, USSR)
1968 (Finland, USSR, West Germany)

MOST POWER-PLAY GOALS AGAINST, GAME

2 February 17, 1994 vs. United States
February 27, 1994 vs. Sweden

MOST POWER-PLAY GOALS AGAINST, PERIOD

Canada has never given up more than one power-play goal in any one period of Olympic hockey.

MOST SHORT-HANDED GOALS FOR, GAME & PERIOD

Canada has never scored more than one short-handed goal in any Olympic period or game.

MOST SHORT-HANDED GOALS AGAINST, GAME & PERIOD

Canada has never given up more than one short-handed goal in any Olympic period or game.

ALL-TIME INDIVIDUAL RECORDS

MOST OLYMPICS PARTICIPATED IN

3 Terry O'Malley (1964, 1968, 1980)
Wally Schreiber (1988, 1992, 1994)

MOST MEDALS WON

2 Fabian Joseph (Silver '92/Silver '94)
Brad Schlegel (Silver '92/Silver '94)
Wally Schreiber (Silver '92/Silver '94)

Ken Laufman (Silver '60/Bronze '56)
Butch Martin (Silver '60/Bronze '56)
Don Rope (Silver '60/Bronze '56)

MOST OLYMPIC GAMES PLAYED

24 Wally Schreiber (1988/92/94)

19 Terry O'Malley (1964/68/80)

16 Fabian Joseph (1992/94)
Brad Schlegel (1992/94)

15 Vaughn Karpan (1984/88)
Butch Martin (1956/60)
Don Rope (1956/60)

MOST POINTS, CAREER

36 Harry Watson (1924)

29 Wally Halder (1948)

26 George Mara (1948)

22 Billy Gibson (1952)

21 Fred Etcher (1960)

20 Bert McCaffery (1924)

19 Hugh Farquharson (1936)
Butch Martin (1956/60)

18 Bob Attersley (1960)
Hooley Smith (1924)

17 Reg Schroeter (1948)

16 Dunc Munro (1924)

15 Joe Juneau (1992)
Ken Laufman (1956/60)
Jim Logan (1956)

MOST POINTS, ONE OLYMPICS

36 Harry Watson (1924)

29 Wally Halder (1948)

26 George Mara (1948)

22 Billy Gibson (1952)

21 Fred Etcher (1960)

20 Bert McCaffery (1924)

MOST GOALS, ONE OLYMPICS & CAREER

36 Harry Watson (1924)

21 Wally Halder (1948)

20 Bert McCaffery (1924)

18 Hooley Smith (1924)

17 George Mara (1948)

16 Dunc Munro (1924)

15 Billy Gibson (1952)

12 Frank Fredrickson (1920)
Hugh Plaxton (1928)
Reg Schroeter (1948)
Dave Trottier (1928)

11 Hugh Farquharson (1936)

10 Ken Farmer (1936)
David Miller (1952)
Beattie Ramsay (1924)

MOST ASSISTS, CAREER

14 Ken Laufman (1956/60)

12 Bob Attersley (1960)
Fred Etcher (1960)

11 Butch Martin (1956/60)

10 Ab Renaud (1948)

9 Marshall Johnston (1964/68)
Joe Juneau (1992)
George Mara (1948)

8 Gary Dineen (1964/68)
Hugh Farquharson (1936)
Wally Halder (1948)
Jim Logan (1956)

MOST ASSISTS, ONE OLYMPICS

12 Bob Attersley (1960)
Fred Etcher (1960)

10 Ab Renaud (1948)
Ken Laufman (1956)

9 George Mara (1948)
Joe Juneau (1992)

8 Hugh Farquharson (1936)
Wally Halder (1948)
Jim Logan (1956)

MOST PENALTY MINUTES, CAREER

70* Pat Flatley (1984)

26 Butch Martin (1956/60)

22 Art Hurst (1956)

20 Wally Halder (1948)

18 Dave Archibald (1992)
Moe Benoit (1960)
Derek Mayer (1994)

16 Gary Dineen (1964/68)
Sean Burke (1988/92)

14 Jim Connelly (1960)
André Laperrière (1948)

* includes match misconduct penalty of 60 minutes

MOST PENALTY MINUTES, ONE OLYMPICS

70* Pat Flatley (1984)

22 Art Hurst (1956)

20 Wally Halder (1948)

18 Dave Archibald (1992)
Moe Benoit (1960)
Derek Mayer (1994)

* includes match misconduct penalty of 60 minutes

MOST GOALS, ONE GAME (ALL HAT TRICKS)

13 goals Harry Watson
January 30, 1924 vs. Switzerland

11 goals Harry Watson
January 28, 1924 vs. Czechoslovakia

8 goals Bert McCaffery
January 30, 1924 vs. Switzerland

7 goals Slim Halderson
April 24, 1920 vs. Czechoslovakia

Frank Fredrickson
April 26, 1920 vs. Sweden

6 goals Harry Watson
January 29, 1924 vs. Sweden

Hugh Plaxton
February 18, 1928 vs. Great Britain

Wally Halder
February 5, 1948 vs. United States

5 goals Beattie Ramsay
January 29, 1924 vs. Sweden

Dunc Munro
January 30, 1924 vs. Switzerland

Hooley Smith
January 30, 1924 vs. Switzerland

Bert McCaffery
February 1, 1924 vs. Great Britain

Dave Trottier
February 16, 1928 vs. Sweden

Dave Trottier
February 19, 1928 vs. Switzerland

Ken Farmer
February 12, 1936 vs. Hungary

Wally Halder
February 3, 1948 vs. Italy

George Mara
February 3, 1948 vs. Italy

David Miller
February 15, 1952 vs. Germany

Paul Knox
January 27, 1956 vs. Austria

4 goals Frank Fredrickson
April 24, 1920 vs. Czechoslovakia

Hooley Smith
January 28, 1924 vs. Czechoslovakia

Hooley Smith
January 29, 1924 vs. Sweden

Dunc Munro
February 1, 1924 vs. Great Britain

Hooley Smith
February 1, 1924 vs. Great Britain

Hugh Plaxton
February 19, 1928 vs. Switzerland

Bill Thomson
February 6, 1936 vs. Poland

Hugh Farquharson
February 7, 1936 vs. Latvia

Hugh Farquharson
February 12, 1936 vs. Hungary

George Mara
February 5, 1948 vs. United States

Wally Halder
February 7, 1948 vs. Austria

George Mara
February 7, 1948 vs. Austria

Billy Gibson
February 15, 1952 vs. Germany

Bobby Rousseau
February 20, 1960 vs. Japan

Morris Mott
February 9, 1968 vs. East Germany

3 goals Bert McCaffery
January 28, 1924 vs. Czechoslovakia

Harold McMunn
January 28, 1924 vs. Czechoslovakia

Dunc Munro
January 28, 1924 vs. Czechoslovakia

Beattie Ramsay
January 28, 1924 vs. Czechoslovakia

Bert McCaffery
January 29, 1924 vs. Sweden

Dunc Munro
January 29, 1924 vs. Sweden

Harry Watson
February 1, 1924 vs. Great Britain

Harry Watson
February 3, 1924 vs. United States

Ralph St. Germain
February 7, 1936 vs. Latvia

Wally Halder
February 2, 1948 vs. Poland

Reg Schroeter
February 2, 1948 vs. Poland

Patsy Guzzo
February 3, 1948 vs. Italy

Ted Hibberd
February 3, 1948 vs. Italy

Reg Schroeter
February 7, 1948 vs. Austria

Billy Gibson
February 17, 1952 vs. Finland

George Abel
February 18, 1952 vs. Poland

Sully Sullivan
February 21, 1952 vs. Switzerland

Billy Gibson
February 23, 1952 vs. Norway

Gerry Théberge
January 26, 1956 vs. Germany

Jack MacKenzie
January 27, 1956 vs. Austria

Gerry Théberge
January 27, 1956 vs. Austria

Fred Etcher
February 20, 1960 vs. Japan

George Samolenko
February 20, 1960 vs. Japan

Jack Douglas
February 22, 1960 vs. Germany

Brian Conacher
February 3, 1964 vs. United States

Bob Forhan
February 5, 1964 vs. Finland

Ken Berry
February 12, 1980 vs. Holland

Dave Gagner
February 13, 1984 vs. Norway

Gord Sherven
February 27, 1988 vs.Czechoslovakia

MOST HAT TRICKS, ONE OLYMPICS & CAREER

5 Harry Watson (1924)

4 Wally Halder (1948)
Bert McCaffery (1924)
Dunc Munro (1924)
Hooley Smith (1924)

3 Billy Gibson (1952)
George Mara (1948)

MOST POINTS, ONE GAME

13 Harry Watson (13 goals, 0 assists)
January 30, 1924 vs. Switzerland

11 Harry Watson (11 goals, 0 assists)
January 28, 1924 vs. Czechoslovakia

10 George Mara (5 goals, 5 assists)
February 3, 1948 vs. Italy

8 Bert McCaffery (8 goals, 0 assists)
January 30, 1924 vs. Switzerland

7 Slim Halderson (7 goals, 0 assists)
April 24, 1920 vs. Czechoslovakia

Frank Fredrickson (7 goals, 0 assists)
April 26, 1920 vs. Sweden

Hugh Farquharson (4 goals, 3 assists)
February 7, 1936 vs. Latvia

Wally Halder (6 goals, 1 assist)
February 5, 1948 vs. United States

Wally Halder (4 goals, 3 assists)
February 7, 1948 vs. Austria

Paul Knox (5 goals, 2 assists)
January 27, 1956 vs. Austria

Ken Laufman (1 goal, 6 assists)
January 27, 1956 vs. Austria

Fred Etcher (3 goals, 4 assists)
February 20, 1960 vs. Japan

6 Harry Watson (6 goals, 0 assists)
January 29, 1924 vs. Sweden

Hugh Plaxton (6 goals, 0 assists)
February 18, 1928 vs. Great Britain

Wally Halder (3 goals, 3 assists)
February 2, 1948 vs. Poland

Wally Halder (5 goals, 1 assist)
February 3, 1948 vs. Italy

Wally Halder (6 goals, 0 assists)
February 5, 1948 vs. United States

Billy Gibson (4 goals, 2 assists)
February 15, 1952 vs. Germany

David Miller (5 goals, 1 assist)
February 15, 1952 vs. Germany

Jim Logan (2 goals, 4 assists)
January 27, 1956 vs. Austria

MOST ASSISTS, ONE GAME

6 Ken Laufman, January 27, 1956 vs. Austria

5 George Mara, February 3, 1948 vs. Italy

4 Ab Renaud, February 3, 1948 vs. Italy
Jim Logan, January 27, 1956 vs. Austria
Fred Etcher, February 20, 1960 vs. Japan
Bob Attersley, February 28, 1960 vs. USSR
Joe Juneau, Februry 12, 1992 vs. Norway

MOST POINTS, ONE PERIOD

6 Harry Watson (6 goals, 0 assists)
2nd period, January 28, 1924 vs. Czechoslovakia

5 Harry Watson (5 goals, 0 assists)
2nd period, January 30, 1924 vs. Switzerland

Hugh Farquharson (2 goals, 3 assists)
3rd period, February 7, 1936 vs. Latvia

George Mara (3 goals, 2 assists)
1st period, February 3, 1948 vs. Italy

4 Frank Fredrickson (4 goals, 0 assists)
2nd half, April 26, 1920 vs. Sweden

Bert McCaffery (4 goals, 0 assists)
3rd period, January 30, 1924 vs. Switzerland

Harry Watson (4 goals, 0 assists)
1st period, January 30, 1924 vs. Switzerland

Harry Watson (4 goals, 0 assists)
3rd period, January 30, 1924 vs. Switzerland

Wally Halder (3 goals, 1 assist)
1st period, February 3, 1948 vs. Italy

Billy Gibson (2 goals, 2 assists)
1st period, February 15, 1952 vs. Germany

David Miller (3 goals, 1 assist)
2nd period, February 15, 1952 vs. Germany

Charlie Brooker (2 goals, 2 assists)
2nd period, January 27, 1956 vs. Austria

Paul Knox (3 goals, 1 assist)
1st period, January 27, 1956 vs. Austria

Ken Laufman (1 goal, 3 assists)
2nd period, January 27, 1956 vs. Austria

MOST GOALS, ONE PERIOD

6 Harry Watson, 2nd period,
January 28, 1924 vs. Czechoslovakia

5 Harry Watson, 2nd period,
January 30, 1924 vs. Switzerland

4 Frank Fredrickson, 2nd half,
April 26, 1920 vs. Sweden

Bert McCaffery, 3rd period,
January 30, 1924 vs. Switzerland

Harry Watson, 1st period,
January 30, 1924 vs. Switzerland

Harry Watson, 3rd period,
January 30, 1924 vs. Switzerland

3 Frank Fredrickson, 1st half,
April 26, 1920 vs. Sweden

Hooley Smith, 1st period,
January 28, 1924 vs. Czechoslovakia

Harry Watson, 1st period,
January 28, 1924 vs. Czechoslovakia

Hooley Smith, 3rd period,
January 29, 1924 vs. Sweden

Harry Watson, 2nd period,
January 29, 1924 vs. Sweden

Harry Watson, 3rd period,
January 29, 1924 vs. Sweden

Hooley Smith, 3rd period,
January 30, 1924 vs. Switzerland

Bert McCaffery, 1st period,
February 1, 1924 vs. Great Britain

Dunc Munro, 2nd period,
February 1, 1924 vs. Great Britain

Hugh Plaxton, 2nd period,
February 18, 1928 vs. Great Britain

Dave Trottier, 3rd period,
February 19, 1928 vs. Switzerland

Bill Thomson, 1st period,
February 6, 1936 vs. Poland

Ken Farmer, 2nd period,
February 12, 1936 vs. Hungary

Hugh Farquharson, 2nd period,
February 12, 1936 vs. Hungary

Wally Halder, 1st period,
February 3, 1948 vs. Italy

George Mara, 1st period,
February 3, 1948 vs. Italy

David Miller, 2nd period,
February 15, 1952 vs. Germany

Paul Knox, 1st period,
January 27, 1956 vs. Austria

MOST ASSISTS, ONE PERIOD

3 Hugh Farquharson, 3rd period,
February 7, 1936 vs. Latvia

Wally Halder, 1st period,
February 2, 1948 vs. Poland

Ab Renaud, 1st period,
February 3, 1948 vs. Italy

Ken Laufman, 2nd period,
January 27, 1956 vs. Austria

Bob Attersley, 1st period,
February 28, 1960 vs. USSR

LONGEST POINT-SCORING STREAK

8 games Billy Gibson (1952)

5 games Gary Dineen (1964)
Billy Gibson (1952)
Wally Halder (1948)
George Mara (1948)
Butch Martin (1960)
Bert McCaffery (1924)
Dunc Munro (1924)
Reg Schroeter (1948)
Hooley Smith (1924)
Harry Watson (1924)

LONGEST GOAL-SCORING STREAK

5 games Billy Gibson (1952)
Wally Halder (1948)
George Mara (1948)
Bert McCaffery (1924)
Dunc Munro (1924)
Reg Schroeter (1948)
Hooley Smith (1948)
Harry Watson (1924)

LONGEST ASSIST-SCORING STREAK

5 games Ab Renaud (1948)

4 games Fred Etcher (1960)
Paul Knox (1956)

PENALTY SHOTS

Only once has Canada been involved in a penalty shot (for or against). On February 17, 1994 Petr Nedved (Canada) beat Garth Snow at 12:09 of the 2nd period vs. the United States.

SHOOTOUT RECORDS

Canada has been involved in two shootouts in Olympic competition, February 18, 1992 vs. Germany (4–3 win) and February 27, 1994 vs. Sweden (3–2 loss). Here is a total and breakdown of those shootout results:

SHOOTERS

player	*shots*	*goals*	*misses*
Paul Kariya	2	1	1
Eric Lindros	2	1	1
Petr Nedved	2	1	1
Wally Schreiber	1	1	0
Jason Woolley	1	1	0
Dave Archibald	1	0	1
Greg Johnson	1	0	1
Joe Juneau	1	0	1
Dwayne Norris	1	0	1
Greg Parks	1	0	1

GOALIES

goalie	*shots*	*saves*	*goals allowed*
Sean Burke	6	4	2
Corey Hirsch	7	4	3

EMPTY NET GOALS

Only once has a Canadian scored an empty net goal in Olympic competition:

Gord Sherven (sh-unassisted) • 19:51
February 27, 1988 • Canada 6 Czechoslovakia 3

ALL GOALTENDER RECORDS

SHUTOUTS FOR & AGAINST, ALL OLYMPICS, TEAM

Year	*For*	*Against*
1920	2	0
1924	3	0
1928	3	0
1932	3	0
1936	4	0
1948	5	1
1952	1	0
1956	3	1
1960	2	0
1964	1	0
1968	2	1
1980	1	0
1984	0	3
1988	1	1
1992	1	0
1994	0	0
Total	**32**	**7**

MOST SHUTOUTS, CAREER

5 Murray Dowey (1948)

2 Wally Byron (1920)
Jack Cameron (1924)
William Cockburn (1932)
Don Head (1960)
Dinty Moore (1936)
Jackie Nash (1936)
Joe Sullivan (1928)
Keith Woodall (1956)

1 Ken Broderick (1968)*
Denis Brodeur (1956)
Ernie Collett (1924)
Trevor Kidd (1992)
Andy Moog (1988)
Stuffy Mueller (1928)
Paul Pageau (1980)
Eric Patterson (1952)
Wayne Stephenson (1968)
Stanley Wagner (1932)

* also shared a shutout with Seth Martin, January 29, 1964

MOST OLYMPICS PARTICIPATED IN, GOALIE

2 Ken Broderick (1964/68)
Sean Burke (1988/92)

MOST GAMES PLAYED, GOALIE, CAREER

11 Ken Broderick (1964/68)
Sean Burke (1988/92)

MOST MINUTES PLAYED, CAREER

669	Sean Burke (1988/92)
495	Corey Hirsch (1994)
480	Murray Dowey (1948)
453	Ken Broderick (1964/68)
385	Don Head (1960)
380	Mario Gosselin (1984)
360	Ralph Hansch (1952)

MOST WINS, GOALIE, CAREER

7 Murray Dowey (1948)

6 Sean Burke (1988/92)

5 Ralph Hansch (1952)
Don Head (1960)
Corey Hirsch (1994)

MOST WINS, GOALIE, ONE OLYMPICS

7 Murray Dowey (1948)

5 Corey Hirsch (1994)
Sean Burke (1992)
Don Head (1960)
Ralph Hansch (1952)

MOST LOSSES, GOALIE, CAREER

4 Sean Burke (1988/92)

3 Ken Broderick (1964/68)
Mario Gosselin (1984)

2 Bob Dupuis (1980)
Corey Hirsch (1994)

MOST LOSSES, GOALIE, ONE OLYMPICS

3 Mario Gosselin (1984)

2 Sean Burke (1992)
Sean Burke (1988)
Bob Dupuis (1980)
Ken Broderick (1968)
Corey Hirsch (1994)

MOST SHUTOUTS, ONE OLYMPICS

5 Murray Dowey (1948)

MOST CONSECUTIVE SHUTOUTS

3 Murray Dowey (1948)

2 Wally Byron (1920)
William Cockburn (1932)
Murray Dowey (1948)
Don Head (1960)

BEST GOALS AGAINST AVERAGE, ONE OLYMPICS & CAREER

(minimum three games and 180 minutes played)

0.62	Murray Dowey (1948)
0.91	William Cockburn (1932)
1.00	Keith Woodall (1956)
1.21	Seth Martin (1964)
1.33	Dinty Moore (1936)

LONGEST SHUTOUT SEQUENCE (MINUTES)

225:25	Murray Dowey, January 30-February 3, 1948
195:30	Murray Dowey, February 5-February 8, 1948
164:19	Don Head, February 20-February 25, 1960

SHUTOUTS IN FIRST OLYMPIC GAME PLAYED

Wally Byron	April 24, 1920
Jack Cameron	January 28, 1924
Ernie Collett	January 29, 1924
Joe Sullivan	February 16, 1928
Stuffy Mueller	February 18, 1928
Stanley Wagner	February 9, 1932
Jackie Nash	February 7, 1936
Eric Patterson	February 18, 1952
Denis Brodeur	January 26, 1956
Keith Woodall	January 27, 1956
Seth Martin/ Ken Broderick	January 29, 1964*
Andy Moog	February 14, 1988
Trevor Kidd	February 12, 1992

* The only time two Canadian goalies have shared an Olympics shutout

LONGEST WINNING STREAK

5 games Murray Dowey (1948)

4 games William Cockburn (1932)
Mario Gosselin (1984)
Don Head (1960)

LONGEST UNBEATEN STREAK

8 games Murray Dowey (1948)

LONGEST LOSING STREAK

3 games Mario Gosselin (1984)

LONGEST WINLESS STREAK

3 games Mario Gosselin (1984)

2 games Sean Burke (1988)
Corey Hirsch (1994)

ALL GOALIE PENALTY MINUTES

16 Sean Burke

2 Murray Dowey
Mario Gosselin
Corey Hirsch
Seth Martin

GOALIE ASSISTS

No Canadian goalie has ever been credited with an assist in Olympic play.

ALL SHOTS ON GOAL RECORDS, TEAM

(since 1952, when this became an official Olympics statistic)

MOST SHOTS FOR, GAME

76 January 27, 1956 vs. Austria
February 20, 1960 vs. Japan

61 January 29, 1964 vs. Switzerland

58 February 24, 1952 vs. United States

51 February 9, 1968 vs. East Germany

MOST SHOTS AGAINST, GAME

52 February 16, 1992 by Unified Team

51 February 3, 1964 by United States

46 January 30, 1964 by Sweden

42 February 27, 1994 by Sweden

41 February 7, 1964 by Czechoslovakia

MOST SHOTS BOTH TEAMS, GAME

90 January 27, 1956
Canada 76 Austria 14
February 20, 1960
Canada 76 Japan 14

89 January 29, 1964
Canada 61 Switzerland 28

88 February 3, 1964
United States 51 Canada 37

77 February 7, 1984
United States 39, Canada 38

76 February 18, 1992
Canada 46, Germany 30

MOST SHOTS FOR, PERIOD

29 1st period, February 20, 1960 vs. Japan

24 2nd period, February 20, 1960 vs. Japan
1st period, January 29, 1964 vs. Switzerland
2nd period, January 29, 1964 vs. Switzerland

23 3rd period, February 20, 1960 vs. Japan
3rd period, February 18, 1980 vs. Japan

21 1st period, February 20, 1988 vs. France

20 3rd period, February 15, 1952 vs. Germany
1st period, February 22, 1960 vs. Germany
2nd period, February 25, 1960 vs. United States

MOST SHOTS AGAINST, PERIOD

19 1st period, January 30, 1964 by Sweden
3rd period, February 8, 1964 by USSR
2nd period, February 7, 1984 by United States
1st period, February 16, 1992 by Unified Team
3rd period, February 16, 1992 by Unified Team

18 3rd period, February 3, 1964 by United States
3rd period, Febraury 20, 1980 by USSR

MOST SHOTS BOTH TEAMS, PERIOD

37 1st period, January 29, 1964
Canada 24, Switzerland 13

33 1st period, February 20, 1960
Canada 29, Japan 4
1st period, February 20, 1988
Canada 21, France 12

32 3rd period, February 20, 1960
Canada 23, Japan 9
2nd period, January 29, 1964
Canada 24, Switzerland 8
1st period, January 30, 1964
Sweden 19, Canada 13

FEWEST SHOTS FOR, GAME

15 February 17, 1984 vs. USSR

17 February 8, 1964 vs. USSR
February 24, 1988 vs. USSR

19 February 16, 1992 vs. Unified Team

FEWEST SHOTS AGAINST, GAME

7 February 17, 1952 by Finland
February 18, 1952 by Poland

9 February 22, 1952 by Sweden
February 4, 1956 by USSR

10 February 15, 1994 by France

13 February 24, 1952 by United States
February 18, 1980 by Japan

FEWEST SHOTS BOTH TEAMS, GAME

32 February 4, 1956 • Canada 23 USSR 9

45 February 18, 1952 • Canada 38 Poland 7
February 22, 1952 • Canada 36 Sweden 9
February 15, 1994 • Canada 35 France 10

46 February 14, 1988 • Canada 29 Poland 17

47 January 26, 1956 • Canada 30 Germany 17

48 February 22, 1980 •
Czechoslovakia 27 Canada 21
February 8, 1992 • Canada 29 France 19

FEWEST SHOTS FOR, PERIOD

3 3rd period, February 24, 1988 vs. USSR

4 1st period, February 8, 1964 vs. USSR
1st period, February 16, 1992 vs. Unified Team
1st period, February 19, 1994 vs. Slovakia

5 3rd period, February 15, 1968 vs. Czechoslovakia
3rd period, February 15, 1968 vs. Sweden
3rd period, February 22, 1980 vs. Czechoslovakia
1st period, February 17, 1984 vs. USSR
2nd period, Fenruary 17, 1984 vs. USSR
3rd period, February 17, 1984 vs. USSR
3rd period, February 22, 1988 vs. Sweden
1st period, February 25, 1994 vs. Finland

FEWEST SHOTS AGAINST, PERIOD

0 3rd period, February 12, 1992 by Norway

1 3rd period, February 18, 1952 by Poland
2nd period, February 20, 1960 by Japan
2nd period, February 15, 1994 by France

2 1st period, February 18, 1952 by Poland
2nd period, February 22, 1952 by Sweden
3rd period, February 18, 1980 by Japan
3rd period, February 20, 1988 by France
1st period, February 15, 1994 by France

FEWEST SHOTS BOTH TEAMS, PERIOD

8 3rd period, February 12, 1992
Canada 8 Norway 0

10 3rd period, February 18, 1952
Canada 9 Poland 1

11 2nd period, February 22, 1980
Canada 7 Czechoslovakia 4

1st period, February 25, 1994
Finland 6 Canada 5

12 1st period, February 11, 1968
Canada 7 United States 5

1st period, February 19, 1984
Canada 8 Sweden 4

3rd period, February 14, 1988
Canada 7 Poland 5

ALL PENALTY RECORDS

PENALTY-FREE GAMES, BOTH TEAMS

February 7, 1948 vs. Austria
February 14, 1980 vs. Poland

PENALTY-FREE GAMES, CANADA

April 24, 1920 vs. Czechoslovakia
February 9, 1932 vs. Poland
February 6, 1936 vs. Poland
February 7, 1936 vs. Latvia
February 8, 1936 vs. Austria
February 15, 1936 vs. Czechoslovakia
February 22, 1988 vs. Sweden
February 18, 1992 vs. Germany

MOST PENALTY MINUTES, TEAM, GAME

70* February 19, 1984 vs. Sweden

29 February 18, 1960 vs. Sweden

26 February 14, 1992 vs. Czechoslovakia

24 February 1, 1948 vs. Great Britain
February 8, 1948 vs. Switzerland

22 January 28, 1956 vs. Italy
February 21, 1994 vs. Sweden

* including 60-minute match misconduct penalty

MOST PENALTY MINUTES, TEAM, PERIOD

62* 2nd period, February 19, 1984 vs. Sweden

20 2nd period, February 14, 1992 vs. Czechoslovakia

16 3rd period, February 27, 1960 vs. Sweden

14 2nd period, February 18, 1960 vs. Sweden

12 2nd period, January 28, 1956 vs. Italy
3rd period, February 3, 1964 vs. United States
2nd period, February 21, 1994 vs. Sweden

* including 60-minute match misconduct penalty

MOST PENALTY MINUTES, BOTH TEAMS, GAME

76* February 19, 1984
Canada 70 Sweden 6

51 February 10, 1992
Switzerland 31 Canada 20

47 February 18, 1960
Canada 29 Sweden 18

42 February 1, 1948
Canada 24 Great Britain 18

38 February 8, 1948
Canada 24 Switzerland 14

February 21, 1994
Canada 22 Sweden 16

37 February 19, 1952
Canada 21 Czechoslovakia 16

* including 60-minute match misconduct penalty

MOST PENALTY MINUTES, BOTH TEAMS, PERIOD

64* 2nd period, February 19, 1984
Canada 62 Sweden 2

27 3rd period, February 10, 1992
Switzerland 21 Canada 6

24 3rd period, January 30, 1948
Sweden 16 Canada 8

2nd period, February 14, 1992
Canada 20 Czechoslovakia 4

21 3rd period, February 18, 1960
Sweden 14 Canada 7

20 3rd period, February 27, 1960
Canada 16 Sweden 4

2nd period, February 18, 1980
Canada 10 Japan 10

2nd period, February 8, 1992
Canada 10 France 10

* including 60-minute match misconduct penalty

MOST PENALTIES, TEAM, GAME

12 (all minors) February 1, 1948 vs. Great Britain

11 (all minors) January 28, 1956 vs. Italy
(all minors) February 21, 1994 vs. Sweden

10 (all minors) February 3, 1964 vs. United States
(all minors) February 10, 1992 vs. Switzerland

MOST PENALTIES, TEAM, PERIOD

6 (all minors) 2nd period,
January 28, 1956 vs. Italy

(all minors) 3rd period,
February 3, 1964 vs. United States

(five minors, one misconduct) 2nd period,
February 14, 1992 vs. Czechoslovakia

(all minors) 2nd period,
February 21, 1994 vs. Sweden

MOST PENALTIES, BOTH TEAMS, GAME

21 February 1, 1948 vs. Great Britain
Canada 12 penalties, Great Britain 9 penalties

20 February 10, 1992 vs. Switzerland
Canada 10 penalties, Switzerland 10 penalties

19 February 21, 1994 vs. Sweden
Canada 11 penalties, Sweden 8 penalties

18 February 18, 1980 vs. Japan
Canada 7 penalties, Japan 11 penalties

MOST PENALTIES, BOTH TEAMS, PERIOD

10 2nd period, February 18, 1980 vs. Japan
Canada 5 penalties, Japan 5 penalties

2nd period, February 8, 1992 vs. France
Canada 5 penalties, France 5 penalties

9 2nd period, February 1, 1948 vs. Great Britain
Canada 4 penalties, Great Britain 5 penalties

3rd period, February 3, 1964 vs. United States
Canada 6 penalties, United States 3 penalties

MOST PENALTY MINUTES, INDIVIDUAL, GAME

60 Pat Flatley (match misconduct),
February 19, 1984 vs. Sweden

12 Wally Halder (two majors, one minor),
February 8, 1948 vs. Switzerland

Butch Martin (minor & misconduct),
February 18, 1960 vs. Sweden

10 Jim Connelly (one misconduct),
February 27, 1960 vs. Sweden

Sean Burke (misconduct),
February 14, 1992 vs. Czechoslovakia

8 Patsy Guzzo (all minors),
February 1, 1948 vs. Great Britain

Louis Lecompte (all minors),
February 5, 1948 vs. United States

Dave Archibald (all minors),
February 10, 1992 vs. Switzerland

Derek Mayer (all minors),
February 21, 1994 vs. Sweden

MOST PENALTY MINUTES, INDIVIDUAL, PERIOD

60 Pat Flatley (match misconduct)
2nd period, February 19, 1984 vs. Sweden

12 Butch Martin (minor & misconduct)
2nd period, February 18, 1960 vs. Sweden

10 Jim Connelly (misconduct)
3rd period, February 27, 1960 vs. Sweden

Sean Burke (misconduct)
2nd period, February 14, 1992 vs. Czechoslovakia

6 Howie Lee (all minors)
2nd period, January 28, 1956 vs. Italy

Dave Archibald (all minors)
2nd period, February 10, 1992 vs. Switzerland

MOST PENALTIES, INDIVIDUAL, GAME

4 Patsy Guzzo (all minors),
February 1, 1948 vs. Great Britain

Louis Lecompte (all minors),
February 5, 1948 vs. United States

Dave Archibald (all minors),
February 10, 1992 vs. Switzerland

Derek Mayer (all minors),
February 21, 1994 vs. Sweden

3 Wally Halder (all minors),
February 1, 1948 vs. Great Britain

Wally Halder (two majors, one minor),
February 8, 1948 vs. Switzerland

Howie Lee (all minors),
January 28, 1956 vs. Italy

Ray Cadieux (all minors),
February 3, 1964 vs. United States

Pat Flatley (all minors),
February 13, 1984 vs. Norway

Dave Tippett (all minors),
February 16, 1992 vs. Unified Team

MOST PENALTIES, INDIVIDUAL, PERIOD

3 Howie Lee (all minors)
2nd period, January 28, 1956 vs. Italy

Dave Archibald (all minors)
2nd period, February 10, 1992 vs. Switzerland

ALL SPEED RECORDS

FASTEST GOAL FROM START OF GAME

20 seconds Herman Murray
February 12, 1936 vs. Hungary

25 seconds Bruce Dickson
February 23, 1952 vs. Norway

27 seconds Pat Flatley
February 7, 1984 vs. United States

FASTEST GOAL FROM START OF PERIOD

9 seconds Ray Cadieux
2nd period, February 6, 1968 vs. West Germany

10 seconds Wally Halder
3rd period, February 3, 1948 vs. Italy

13 seconds Kirk Muller
2nd period, February 9, 1984 vs. Austria

18 seconds Hugh Farquharson
3rd period, February 7, 1936 vs. Latvia

FASTEST TWO GOALS FROM START OF GAME, TEAM

1:55 April 26, 1920 vs. Sweden
Halderson 1:15, Fridfinnson 1:55

1:59 February 23, 1952 vs. Norway
Dickson 0:25, Pollock 1:59

FASTEST TWO GOALS FROM START OF GAME, INDIVIDUAL

2:00 February 6, 1936 vs. Poland
Bill Thomson at 0:30 and again at 2:00

FASTEST TWO GOALS, TEAM

4 seconds February 2, 1948 vs. Poland
Halder scored at 7:50 of 2nd, Mara at 7:54

5 seconds February 18, 1952 vs. Poland
Gauf scored at 9:05 of 3rd, Davies at 9:10

8 seconds February 15, 1952 vs. Germany
Robertson scored at 16:05 of 1st, Gibson at 16:13

10 seconds February 3, 1948 vs. Italy
Schroeter scored at 6:50 of 1st, Halder at 7:00

10 seconds January 27, 1956 vs. Austria
Théberge scored at 14:00 of 2nd, Scholes at 14:10

FASTEST TWO GOALS, INDIVIDUAL

12 seconds Fred Etcher,
February 22, 1960 vs. Germany
Scored at 6:58 and 7:10 of 1st

13 seconds George Mara,
February 3, 1948 vs. Italy
Scored at 5:48 and 6:01 of 1st

15 seconds Frank Fredrickson,
April 26, 1920 vs. Sweden
Scored at 9:15 and 9:30 of 2nd

18 seconds Brian Conacher,
January 29, 1964 vs. Switzerland
Scored at 3:18 and 3:36 of 3rd

FASTEST THREE GOALS, TEAM

20 seconds February 15, 1952 vs. Germany
Robertson 16:05/Gibson 16:13/Miller 16:25 of 1st

40 seconds February 15, 1952 vs. Germany
Gibson 16:13/Miller 16:25/Watt 16:53 of 1st

48 seconds February 18, 1952 vs. Poland
Gauf 9:05/Davies 9:10/Dickson 9:53 of 3rd

57 seconds January 27, 1956 vs. Austria
Laufman 13:13/Théberge 14:00/Scholes 14:10 of 2nd

59 seconds February 3, 1948 vs. Italy
Mara 6:01/Schroeter 6:50/Halder 7:00 of 1st

FASTEST THREE GOALS, INDIVIDUAL

2:15 Dave Trottier,
February 19, 1928 vs. Switzerland
Scored at 3:10, 3:40, 5:25 of 3rd

3:12 George Mara,
February 3, 1948 vs. Italy
Scored at 5:48, 6:01, 9:00 of 1st

3:25 Ken Farmer,
February 12, 1936 vs. Hungary
Scored at 6:25, 7:00, 9:50 of 2nd

FASTEST FOUR GOALS, TEAM

48 seconds February 15, 1952 vs. Germany
Robertson 16:05/Gibson 16:13/Miller 16:25/
Watt 16:53 of 1st

1:12 February 3, 1948 vs. Italy
Mara 5:48/Mara 6:01/Schroeter 6:50/
Halder 7:00 of 1st

1:18 January 27, 1956 vs. Austria
MacKenzie 12:52/Laufman 13:13/
Théberge 14:00/Scholes 14:10 of 2nd

FASTEST FIVE GOALS, TEAM

2:30 January 27, 1956 vs. Austria
MacKenzie 12:52/Laufman 13:13/Théberge 14:00/Scholes 14:10/White 15:22 of 2nd

2:35 February 12, 1936 vs. Hungary
Farmer 6:25/Farmer 7:00/Murray 7:35/Farquharson 8:05/Farquharson 9:00 of 2nd

2:50 February 12, 1936 vs. Hungary
Farmer 7:00/Murray 7:35/Farquharson 8:05/Farquharson 9:00/Farmer 9:50 of 2nd

2:58 February 3, 1948 vs. Italy
Hibberd 4:02/Mara 5:48/Mara 6:01/Schroeter 6:50/Halder 7:00 of 1st

FASTEST FIVE GOALS, BOTH TEAMS

2:23 February 20, 1988 vs. France
Yaremchuk (Can) 16:57/Malinowski (Can) 17:24/Bozon (Fr) 17:57/Habscheid (Can) 18:58/Tambellini (Can) 19:20 of 1st

FASTEST SIX GOALS, TEAM

3:25 February 12, 1936 vs. Hungary
Farmer 6:25/Farmer 7:00/Murray 7:35/Farquharson 8:05/Farquharson 9:00/Farmer 9:50 of 2nd

3:48 February 3, 1948 vs. Italy
Dunster 3:12/Hibberd 4:02/Mara 5:48/Mara 6:01/Schroeter 6:50/Halder 7:00 of 1st

4:00 February 12, 1936 vs. Hungary
Farmer 7:00/Murray 7:35/Farquharson 8:05/Farquharson 9:00/Farmer 9:50/Sinclair 11:00 of 2nd

FASTEST SIX GOALS, BOTH TEAMS

3:04 February 20, 1988 vs. France
Richer (Fr) 16:16/Yaremchuk (Can) 16:57/Malinowski (Can) 17:24/Bozon (Fr) 17:57/Habscheid (Can) 18:58/Tambellini (Can) 19:20 of 1st

FASTEST SEVEN GOALS, TEAM

4:35 February 12, 1936 vs. Hungary
Farmer 6:25/Farmer 7:00/Murray 7:35/Farquharson 8:05/Farquharson 9:00/Farmer 9:50/Sinclair 11:00 of 2nd

FASTEST EIGHT GOALS, TEAM

5:25 February 12, 1936 vs. Hungary
Farmer 6:25/Farmer 7:00/Murray 7:35/Farquharson 8:05/Farquharson 9:00/Farmer 9:50/Sinclair 11:00/Thomson 11:50 of 2nd

FASTEST NINE GOALS, TEAM

8:15 February 12, 1936 vs. Hungary
Farmer 6:25/Farmer 7:00/Murray 7:35/Farquharson 8:05/Farquharson 9:00/Farmer 9:50/Sinclair 11:00/Thomson 11:50/Farquharson 14:40 of 2nd

FASTEST TWO POWER-PLAY GOALS, TEAM

36 seconds February 12, 1980 vs. Holland
Devaney 10:35 of 3rd, Berry 11:11

1:11 February 20, 1988 vs. France
Boisvert 9:36 of 1st, Yawney 10:47

FASTEST TWO POWER-PLAY GOALS, INDIVIDUAL

4:29 Fred Etcher,
February 18, 1960 vs. Sweden
Scored at 11:37 of 3rd, and again at 16:06

FASTEST POWER-PLAY GOAL FROM START OF OPPONENT'S MAN ADVANTAGE

4 seconds February 18, 1960 vs. Sweden
Swedberg (Swe) penalized at 16:59 of 1st,
Bob Attersley (Can) scored at 17:03

5 seconds February 23, 1994 vs. Czech Republic
Horak (CR) penalized at 5:49 of OT,
Paul Kariya (Can) scored at 5:54

6 seconds February 14, 1992 vs. Czechoslovakia
Zemlicka (Cz) penalized at 3:27 of 1st,
Joe Juneau (Can) scored at 3:33

FASTEST SHORT-HANDED GOAL FROM START OF OPPONENT'S MAN ADVANTAGE

35 seconds January 26, 1956 vs. Germany
Martin (Can) penalized at 5:10 of 3rd
Jim Logan (Can) scored at 5:45

YOUNGEST TO PLAY FOR TEAM CANADA

18 years, one day	Kirk Muller
18 years, 45 days	Jack MacKenzie
18 years, 118 days	J.J. Daigneault
18 years, 138 days	Craig Redmond
18 years, 345 days	Eric Lindros

OLDEST TO PLAY FOR TEAM CANADA

39 years, 124 days	Terry O'Malley
38 years, 184 days	Harold Simpson
36 years, one day	George Abel
35 years, 110 days	Dinty Moore
34 years, 262 days	Sully Sullivan

LONGEST TIME BETWEEN FIRST OLYMPIC GAME AND LAST

16 years, 14 days	Terry O'Malley

BROTHERS AND SONS AND FATHERS

(b)= brother (f)= father (s)= son

Bauer,	Bobby (b) • David (b)
Pinder,	Gerry (b) • Herb (b)
Plaxton,	Bert (b) • Hugh (b)
Sullivan,	Joe (b) • Frank (b)

TEAM CANADA REGISTER BY BIRTHPLACE

Total number of players • 234

ONTARIO • 92

Akervall, W. Anderson, Attersley, Aucoin, Bradley, Broderick, Brooker, Burke, Cadieux, Cameron, Clancy, Colvin, Conacher, Conlin, Connelly, D'Alvise, Delahey, Douglas, Dowey, Driver, Dunster, Dupuis, Eliot, Etcher, Felix, Fisher, Flatley, Forhan, Gagner, Glennie, Grant, Gravelle, Guzzo, Halder, Hannan, Harlock, Head, Hibberd, Hlushko, Horne, Hudson, Hurley, Hurst, Johnson, Klinck, Knox, Kontos, Laufman, Lecompte, Lee, Lindberg, Lindquist, Lindros, Lowe, B. MacKenzie, Mara, F. Martin, McCaffery, McKnight, Monteith, Moore, Mueller, Muller, Munro, O'Malley, O'Shea, Peplinski, Pirie, Porter, Ratushny, Renaud, Savage, Schlegel, Scholes, Schroeter, Seiling, Sinden, Sly, H. Smith, Stephenson, F. Sullivan, J. Sullivan, I. Taylor, R. Taylor, Therien, Trottier, Warriner, White, Wood, Woodall, Woolley, Zupancich

ALBERTA • 29

Astley, Bourbonnais, Brost, Davies, Dawe, Devaney, Donnelly, Gauf, Gibson, Gregg, Hansch, Hirsch, Lovsin, J. MacKenzie, Manderville, Maxwell, Meyers, Miller, Nill, Parks, Patterson, Primeau, Purvis, Schreiber, Stiles, Tutt, Werenka, Yaremchuk, Zalapski

SASKATCHEWAN • 19

Bartel, Begg, Dahl, Davidson, Habscheid, Hargreaves, Huck, Johnston, Malinowski, Mott, G. Pinder, H. Plaxton, Ramsay, Samolenko, Sherven, R. Smith, Swarbrick, Tippett, Yawney

QUEBEC • 18

Benoit, Boisvert, Brodeur, Daigneault, G. Dineen, K. Dineen, Farmer, Gosselin, Hynes, Juneau, Laperrière, Lebeau, Pageau, Plavsic, Rousseau, J.Y. Roy, S. Roy, Théberge

BRITISH COLUMBIA • 13

G. Anderson, Archibald, Berry, Courtnall, Hindmarch, Kariya, Lidster, S. Martin, Mayer, Moog, Redmond, Tambellini, Watters

MANITOBA • 12

Benson, Duncanson, Fredrickson, Giles, Halderson, Karpan, Kidd, Monson, Patrick, Rope, Sutherland, Wilson

NEWFOUNDLAND • 2

Norris, Watson

NEW BRUNSWICK • 1

Joyce

NOVA SCOTIA • 1

Joseph

PRINCE EDWARD ISLAND • 1

MacMillan

UNKNOWN • 40

Abel, Byron, Cockburn, Collett, Crowley, Deacon, Dickson, Farquharson, Fridfinsson, Garbutt, Goodman, Gordon, Haggarty, Hinkel, Johannesson, Kitchen, Logan, Malloy, McMunn, Milton, K. Moore, Murray, Nash, Neville, Pennington, B. Plaxton, R. Plaxton, Pollock, Rivers, Robertson, St. Germain, Secco, Simpson, Sinclair, Slater, S. Sullivan, Wagner, Watt, Wise, Woodman

PLAYERS WHO HAVE PLAYED HOCKEY FOR CANADA AT THE OLYMPICS BUT WERE BORN IN ANOTHER COUNTRY

Paul MacLean • Grostenquin, France

Petr Nedved • Liberec, Czechoslovakia

Herb Pinder • Boston, United States

Don Spring • Maracaibo, Venezuela

Bill Thomson • Ayshire, Scotland

Claude Vilgrain • Port au Prince, Haiti

JERSEY NUMBERS

0 • Ralph Hansch

1 • Murray Dowey, Eric Patterson, Keith Woodall, Denis Brodeur, Don Head, Harold Hurley, Seth Martin, Ken Broderick, Bob Dupuis, Darren Eliot, Sean Burke, Corey Hirsch

2 • John Davies, Harry Sinden, Byrle Klinck, Terry O'Malley, Warren Anderson, Robin Bartel, Tim Watters, Dan Ratushny

3 • Frank Dunster, Bob Meyers, Floyd Martin, Rod Seiling, Paul Conlin, Brad Pirie, Craig Redmond, Serge Roy, Brian Tutt, Adrian Aucoin

4 • Louis Lecompte, Al Purvis, Howie Lee, Darryl Sly, Barry MacKenzie, Randy Gregg, Doug Lidster, Tony Stiles, Gord Hynes, Derek Mayer

5 • André Laperrière, Billy Dawe, Art Hurst, Jack Douglas, Brian Glennie, Tim Watters, Warren Anderson, Trent Yawney, Jason Woolley, Brad Werenka

6 • Wally Halder, Don Gauf, Moe Benoit, Hank Akervall, Ron Davidson, Kevin Dahl, Kevin Lovsin

7 • Irving Taylor, Robert Watt, Bob Attersley, Gary Dineen, Joe Grant, Wally Schreiber, Adrien Plavsic, Todd Hlushko

8 • George Mara, George Abel, Gerry Théberge, Cliff Pennington, Roger Bourbonnais, Don Spring, Dave Tippett, Brian Bradley, Fabian Joseph

9 • Bruce Dickson, Paul Knox, Bob Forhan, Gary Dineen, Fran Huck, Glenn Anderson, James Patrick, Ken Berry, Joe Juneau, Paul Kariya

10 • Reg Schroeter, David Miller, Billy Colvin, George Samolenko, Marshall Johnston, Gord Sherven, Dave Hannan, Dwayne Norris

11 • Ted Hibberd, Sully Sullivan, Jim Logan, Paul Conlin, Ted Hargreaves, Kevin Maxwell, Steve Tambellini, Chris Lindberg

12 • Ab Renaud, Louis Secco, Jack MacKenzie, Bob McKnight, George Swarbrick, Billy MacMillan, Jim Nill, Serge Boisvert, Dave Archibald, Greg Johnson

13 • Billy Gibson, Brian Conacher, Ken Yaremchuk

14 • Gordon Robertson, Don Rope, Fred Etcher, Bob Forhan, Herb Pinder, Darren Lowe, Marc Habscheid, Brian Savage

15 • Tom Pollock, George Scholes, Floyd Martin, Gary Begg, Gerry Pinder, John Devaney, J.J. Daigneault, Bob Joyce, Dave Tippett

16 • Orval Gravelle, Don Rope, Buddy Horne, Terry Clancy, Ray Cadieux, Kevin Dineen, Merlin Malinowski, Wally Schreiber

17 • Patsy Guzzo, Ken Laufman, Steve Monteith, Paul MacLean

18 • Jim Connelly, Ray Cadieux, Charlie Brooker, Danny O'Shea, Dan D'Alvise, Russ Courtnall, Claude Vilgrain, Kent Manderville, Todd Warriner

19 • Bob White, Ken Berry, Dave Gagner, Vaughn Karpan, Todd Brost

20 • Bobby Rousseau, Morris Mott, Dave Hindmarch, Carey Wilson, Patrick Lebeau

21 • Wayne Stephenson, Kevin Primeau, Randy Gregg

22 • Stelio Zupancich, Dan Wood, Randy Smith, Greg Parks

23 • Dave Donnelly, Chris Felix

24 • Terry O'Malley, Jim Peplinski, Mark Astley

25 • Bruce Driver, Zarley Zalapski, Jean-Yves Roy

26 • Pat Flatley

27 • Kirk Muller, Chris Kontos

28 • Brad Schlegel, David Harlock

29 • Paul Pageau

31 • Vaughn Karpan

33 • Mario Gosselin, Chris Therien

35 • Andy Moog

37 • Trevor Kidd

44 • Kurt Giles, Brad Schlegel

88 • Eric Lindros

93 • Petr Nedved

Canada at the World Hockey Championships

* A strictly political decision to withdraw the team by Prime Minister Louis St. Laurent decrying the Russian Red Army's quelling of the Hungarian Revolution in November 1956.

** In 1972 and 1976, it was decided that in addition to the Olympics a World Championship would also be held. In previous Olympic years, the gold medal winner was also considered the world champion. In 1980, the old format was reinstated and the Worlds were not held in Olympic years again until 1994.

YEAR	HOST COUNTRY	CHAMPION	RUNNER-UP	CANADA
1930	France, Germany, Austria	CANADA	Germany	1st
1931	Poland	CANADA	United States	1st
1933	Czechoslovakia	United States	CANADA	2nd
1934	Italy	CANADA	United States	1st
1935	Switzerland	CANADA	Switzerland	1st
1937	Great Britain	CANADA	Great Britain	1st
1938	Czechoslovakia	CANADA	Great Britain	1st
1939	Switzerland	CANADA	United States	1st
1940–46	no competition			
1947	Czechoslovakia	Czechoslovakia	Sweden	DNP
1949	Sweden	Czechoslovakia	CANADA	2nd
1950	Great Britain	CANADA	United States	1st
1951	France	CANADA	Sweden	1st
1953	Switzerland	Sweden	West Germany	DNP
1954	Sweden	USSR	CANADA	2nd
1955	West Germany	CANADA	USSR	1st
1957	USSR	Sweden	USSR	DNP*
1958	Norway	CANADA	USSR	1st
1959	Czechoslovakia	CANADA	USSR	1st
1961	Switzerland	CANADA	Czechoslovakia	1st
1962	United States	Sweden	CANADA	2nd
1963	Sweden	USSR	Sweden	4th
1965	Finland	USSR	Czechoslovakia	4th
1966	Yugoslavia	USSR	Czechoslovakia	3rd
1967	Austria	USSR	Sweden	3rd
1969	Sweden	USSR	Sweden	3rd
1970	Sweden	USSR	Sweden	DNP
1971	Switzerland	USSR	Czechoslovakia	DNP
1972	Czechoslovakia	Czechoslovakia	USSR	DNP**
1973	USSR	USSR	Sweden	DNP
1974	Finland	USSR	Czechoslovakia	DNP
1975	West Germany	USSR	Czechoslovakia	DNP
1976	Czechoslovakia	Czecholsovakia	USSR	DNP**
1977	Austria	Czechoslovakia	Sweden	4th
1978	Czechoslovakia	USSR	Czechoslovakia	3rd
1979	USSR	USSR	Czechoslovakia	4th
1981	Sweden	USSR	Sweden	4th
1982	Finland	USSR	Sweden	3rd
1983	West Germany	USSR	Czechoslovakia	3rd
1985	Czechoslovakia	Czechoslovakia	CANADA	2nd
1986	USSR	USSR	Sweden	3rd
1987	Austria	Sweden	USSR	4th
1989	Sweden	USSR	CANADA	2nd
1990	Switzerland	USSR	Sweden	4th
1991	Finland	Sweden	CANADA	2nd
1993	Germany	Russia	Sweden	4th
1994	Italy	CANADA	Finland	1st
1995	Sweden	Finland	Sweden	3rd
1996	Austria	Czech Rep.	CANADA	2nd
1997	Finland	CANADA	Sweden	1st

ALLAN CUP CHAMPIONS • 1919–62

1919-20	Winnipeg Falcons*
1920-21	University of Toronto
1921-22	Toronto Granites
1922-23	Toronto Granites*
1923-24	Sault Ste. Marie Greyhounds
1924-25	Port Arthur
1925-26	Port Arthur
1926-27	University of Toronto Graduates*
1927-28	University of Manitoba
1928-29	Port Arthur
1929-30	Montreal AAA
1930-31	Winnipeg Hockey Club*
1931-32	Toronto Nationals
1932-33	Moncton Hawks
1933-34	Moncton Hawks
1934-35	Halifax Wolverines
1935-36	Kimberley Dynamiters
1936-37	Sudbury Tigers
1937-38	Trail Smoke Eaters
1938-39	Port Arthur
1939-40	Kirkland Lake Blue Devils
1940-41	Regina Rangers
1941-42	Ottawa RCAF
1942-43	Ottawa Commandos
1943-44	Quebec Aces
1944-45	no competition
1945-46	Calgary Stampeders
1946-47	Montreal Royals
1947-48	Edmonton Flyers
1948-49	Ottawa Senators
1949-50	Toronto Marlboros
1950-51	Owen Sound Mercurys
1951-52	Fort Francis Canadiens
1952-53	Kitchener-Waterloo Dutchmen
1953-54	Penticton V's
1954-55	Kitchener-Waterloo Dutchmen*
1955-56	Vernon Canadiens
1956-57	Whitby Dunlops
1957-58	Belleville McFarlands
1958-59	Whitby Dunlops
1959-60	Chatham Maroons
1960-61	Galt Terriers
1961-62	Trail Smoke Eaters

* represented Canada at the Olympics

ALL CANADIAN WINTER OLYMPIC MEDALS • 1920–94

YEAR	CITY	G	S	B	T
1920	Antwerp	1	0	0	1
1924	Chamonix	1	0	0	1
1928	St. Moritz	1	0	0	1
1932	Lake Placid	1	1	5	7
1936	Garmisch-Partenkirchen	0	1	0	1
1948	St. Moritz	2	0	1	3
1952	Oslo	1	0	1	2
1956	Cortina d'Ampezzo	0	1	2	3
1960	Squaw Valley	2	1	1	4
1964	Innsbruck	1	0	2	3
1968	Grenoble	1	1	1	3
1972	Sapporo	0	1	0	1
1976	Innsbruck	1	1	1	3
1980	Lake Placid	0	1	1	2
1984	Sarajevo	2	1	1	4
1988	Calgary	0	2	3	5
1992	Albertville	2	3	2	7
1994	Lillehammer	3	6	4	13
Total		**19**	**20**	**25**	**64**

CANADIAN MEDALS BY SPORT AT THE WINTER OLYMPIC GAMES • 1920-1994

SPORT	G	S	B	T
Speed Skating	3	8	7	18
Figure Skating	2	6	9	17
Hockey	6	4	2	12
Alpine Skiing	4	1	5	10
Biathlon	2	0	1	3
Freestyle skiing	1	1	1	3
Bobsleigh	1	0	0	1
Total	**19**	**20**	**25**	**64**

OLYMPIC WINTER GAMES BY NUMBERS

YEAR	CITY	N	A	M	W	C
1920	Antwerp	10	86	74	12	—
1924	Chamonix	16	258	245	13	12
1928	St. Moritz	25	464	438	26	25
1932	Lake Placid	17	252	231	21	53
1936	Garmisch-Partenkirchen	28	668	588	80	30
1948	St. Moritz	28	669	592	77	36
1952	Oslo	30	694	585	109	39
1956	Cortina d'Ampezzo	32	820	688	132	37
1960	Squaw Valley	30	665	522	143	44
1964	Innsbruck	36	1091	891	200	62
1968	Grenoble	37	1158	947	211	71
1972	Sapporo	35	1006	800	206	50
1976	Innsbruck	37	1123	892	231	60
1980	Lake Placid	37	1072	839	233	59
1984	Sarajevo	49	1274	1000	274	69
1988	Calgary	57	1423	1110	313	117
1992	Albertville	64	1801	1313	488	117
1994	Lillehammer	67	1737	1217	520	104

N=competing nations; A=total number of athletes; M=total number of men competing; W=total number of women competing; C=number of Canadians

CANADIAN MEMBERS OF THE IOC

Sir George McLaren Brown	1928-1939
Sidney Dawes	1947-1967
John Hanbury-Williams	1911-1921
Carol Anne Letheren	1990-present
James Merrick	1921-1946
John Coleridge Patterson	1946-1954
Richard Pound	1978-present
James Worrall	1967-1989

HOCKEY PLAYERS IN THE CANADIAN OLYMPIC HALL OF FAME

Incredibly, of the 341 members of the Canadian Olympic Hall of Fame, only two have represented Canada in hockey at the Winter Games:

Ken Farmer (1936)
George Mara (1948)

OTHER HOCKEY OFFICIALS IN THE CANADIAN OLYMPIC HALL OF FAME

Sydney Dawes
Sydney Halter
Jack Hamilton
Dave King
William Northey
Claude Robinson

Photo Credits

CANADIAN OLYMPIC ASSOCIATION • 6, 14, 16, 26, 43, 44, 46, 90, 91, 116, 137, 138, 139, 141, 147, 148, 151, 152, 159, 160, 163, 164, 173, 174, 175, 176, 177, 183, 184, 185, 186, 187, all colour inserts

IOC/OLYMPIC MUSEUM COLLECTIONS • 114

HOCKEY HALL OF FAME • 11, 17, 28, 41, 42, 89, 92, 94

DOUG MACLELLAN/HOCKEY HALL OF FAME • 196, 198, 199, 200

DENIS BRODEUR • 79, 82, 130, 131

MURRAY DOWEY • 53, 54, 56, 58, 59, 61

AL PURVIS • 67, 68, 69, 72, 73

NATIONAL ARCHIVES • 1, 3, 4

CANAPRESS • 117, 118

AP/WIDE WORLD PHOTOS • 101, 102, 103, 104, 105

METROPOLITAN TORONTO REFERENCE LIBRARY • 33, 34, 35, 36, 37

CANADIAN SPORTS HALL OF FAME • 113

UNIVERSITY OF TORONTO ARCHIVES • 23, 24

A RACE FOR REAL SAILORS

THE BLUENOSE AND THE INTERNATIONAL FISHERMEN'S CUP, 1920–1938

KEITH McLAREN

A RACE FOR REAL SAILORS

DOUGLAS & McINTYRE

To the memory of Richard John LeBlanc
January 21, 1945–April 2, 1993
A fine shipmate and friend.

First paperback printing, 2021
1 2 3 4 5 25 24 23 22 21

Douglas and McIntyre (2013) Ltd.
PO Box 219, Madeira Park, BC, V0N 2H0
www.douglas-mcintyre.com

Library and Archives Canada Cataloguing in Publication

Title: A race for real sailors : the Bluenose and the International Fishermen's Cup, 1920-1938 / Keith McLaren.

Names: McLaren, Keith, 1950- author.

Description: Originally published: Vancouver : Douglas & McIntyre, ©2006. | Includes bibliographical references and index.

Identifiers: Canadiana (print) 20200401270 | Canadiana (ebook) 20200401289 | ISBN 9781771622677 (softcover) | ISBN 9781771622684 (EPUB)

Subjects: LCSH: Bluenose (Schooner) | LCSH: International Fishermen's Race—History. | LCSH Sailboat racing—History. | LCSH: Sailboat racing—Nova Scotia—History.

Classification: LCC GV832 .M28 2021 | DDC 797.1/4—dc23

Editing by Jonathan Dore
Cover design by Jessica Sullivan
Text design by Peter Cocking and Jessica Sullivan
Front cover painting: *Racing Schooners, circa 1921,*
by Dusan Kadlec, portrays the *Bluenose* and the *Elsie* racing off Halifax. Reproduced by kind permission of the artist.
Back cover photographs (left to right): Leslie Jones, Boston Public Library (p.66); Edwin Levick, Mariners' Museum, Newport News, Virginia (p.182); Wallace MacAskill, Nova Scotia Archives and Records Management (p.54)
Printed and bound in China

Douglas and McIntyre acknowledges the support of the Canada Council for the Arts, the Government of Canada, and the Province of British Columbia through the BC Arts Council.

CONTENTS

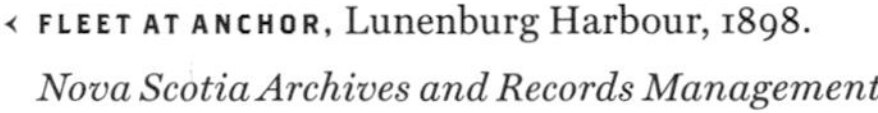

‹ **FLEET AT ANCHOR**, Lunenburg Harbour, 1898.
Nova Scotia Archives and Records Management

PREFACE

ON A CHILLY DAY in late October 1938, a crowd of thousands gathered on the shores of Nahant Bay, northeast of Boston, arriving from all over the eastern seaboard of the United States and Canada. They were about to witness the concluding chapter in a two-decade-old challenge between the fishing-schooner fleets of Canada and the United States.

The schooner fishery was one of the last all-sail commercial fleets left in the Western world. At its zenith, hundreds of large offshore boats filled the ports from Newfoundland south to Massachusetts. This was the culmination of a traditional way of life that had evolved over two and a quarter centuries. When the International Fishermen's Cup races were first proposed in

1920, the fishing schooner was already on its way out, being rapidly replaced by power-driven trawlers. This transformation occurred much more quickly in the United States than in Canada, which hung on and even actively resisted the introduction of the mechanized trawler to its fishing ports. Americans embraced the new technology, steadily forcing the older, traditional fishermen from the market. Although her time was nearly done, the fishing schooner remained a presence on the banks, an anachronism in the modern era, for far longer than anyone would have predicted. As the number of working sailing vessels decreased, their romantic appeal with the public rose. The fishermen's races became a fond last hurrah for a fast-disappearing way of life.

The timing of the races fitted neatly into that tumultuous period between the two world wars and became for a time the most popular sailing event in North America. Heralded as "a race for real sailors," the series began as a friendly match between the schooner fleets of Lunenburg, Nova Scotia, and Gloucester, Massachusetts, the two largest fishing communities on the east coast. They were originally proposed in response to the perceived timidity demonstrated in the America's Cup races, where the elite sailed beautiful but tender vessels barely capable of withstanding a decent breeze. In contrast, the fishermen's races were to be a working man's event, a tough, no-holds-barred affair, with few rules and fewer regulations; a showcase for a rugged, rigorous way of life that was on its way out.

The series, scheduled for the fall of each year, became instantly popular and initially ran like clockwork. The spectacle greatly appealed to the public and soon eclipsed even the venerable America's Cup as the race of choice to a generation. Unfortunately, the growing attention from the public and media provoked the well-meaning committee members to expand and elaborate the rules, ostensibly to ensure the competition remained true to its mandate. In so doing, a rather simple and straightforward affair became a complicated and confusing business, fraught with interpretations of legalities, much to the dismay and consternation of the competitors. Even though the series continued to draw a huge following, the tone often became rancorous and bitter, with competitors accusing the various committees of everything from favouritism to corruption. The fact that it carried on as long as it did is a testament to the single-mindedness of the competitors and to the passion for sail in the quest for the title "Queen of the North Atlantic Fishery."

While researching this book, I was immediately struck by the tremendous popularity of these races. Reading accounts published in contemporary magazines and newspapers, I was overwhelmed [illegible] ible amount of coverage given over to them. Although the series was [illegible] sporting event, the reportage was almost never in the sporting pag [illegible] e exposure and banner headlines heralded each new series, with top [illegible] photographers from major newspapers in Canada and the United S [illegible] d to cover every angle, no matter how insignificant. Even in 1938, wit [illegible] ed on the brink of war, the races dominated the front page alongside [illegible] ws from Nazi Germany.

My own interest began in my g [illegible] se, where a model of the *Bluenose,* given to him by Captain Ang [illegible] his retirement in 1934, held a place of honour on the mantel abo [illegible]. The stories of the schooner from Lunenburg highlighted my youth [illegible] ecured a berth on the replica schooner *Bluenose II* and spent two se [illegible] n her, expanding my knowledge of her predecessor's skipper, Ang [illegible] her illustrious past. There has been much written about the race [illegible], especially in Canada, but many writers have tended to oversimpl [illegible] ate, too often ignoring the controversies and rancour that frequen [illegible] event. I wanted to explore the story as fairly as I could, which mea [illegible] fro [illegible] sides of the border, so, to that end, I visited Massachusetts and Nova Sco [illegible] a to gain insight into their respective points of view. What I found, after much reading and talking, was that the debate and passion about one of the great maritime tales of North America, with a cast of characters whose egos and eccentricities were second to none, is still very much alive. Far from diminishing the power of the story by examining its flesh-and-blood details, I hope this book will help bring to life an amazing chapter in maritime history. Readers unfamiliar with nautical or fishing terms will find a glossary of these on page 236.

My sources in Gloucester and Boston provided me with mountains of material—rivalling anything I found in Canada—and it took months to organize and compile it into a usable form. During my visits to Massachusetts and Nova Scotia, I was given extraordinary help and assistance by many; everyone, it seemed, had a unique story to tell. The debate about which was the fastest schooner lives on in Gloucester and Lunenburg, as if the races had been held only yesterday. National pride and passion, when it comes to the working schooner, run deep.

2
1

‹ **THE *BLUENOSE*** and the *Columbia* run with the wind at the start of the first race in 1923. The grey-hulled American boat was probably the most closely matched schooner to compete against the *Bluenose.* Her ability to sail closer to the wind than her rival made her a serious contender. *Wallace MacAskill Collection, Nova Scotia Archives and Records Management*

INTRODUCTION

THE REAL QUESTION is, why would anyone still care?

A century ago, schooners were the workhorses of the east coast. A Cape Breton neighbour once told me that when he was a boy, a constant stream of schooners sailed past his boyhood home on the Great Bras d'Or, carrying gypsum and shingles, coal and potatoes.

"It must have been a beautiful sight to see," I said.

He shrugged.

"Never thought about it," he said. "Do you go ooh and aah over every eighteen-wheeler that goes down the road?"

If you think of the International Fishermen's Cup races as contests among eighteen-wheelers, why would we still care about them? What would prompt

› VIEW OF Gloucester Harbour, *c.* 1900. *Cape Ann Historical Association*

a successful twenty-first-century mariner like Keith McLaren to write yet another book about them? And if such a man did write such a book, would he find anything new to say about the ships and the races and the people involved?

Amazingly enough, he would. Captain McLaren is interested in the overall story of the races as seen from both sides. As a result, this is perhaps the most fair and even-handed account of them yet written—fair not only to the competitors and their boats, but to the story itself, in all its mythological splendour, intrigue, glory and outright venality.

Our culture cherishes a sentimental notion that sporting events encourage sportsmanship and fair play. Perhaps they do—but they equally encourage greed, pride, envy, anger and various other sins both deadly and venial. The international schooner races were no exception. They were loaded with meaning: working fishermen versus the plutocrats' fragile America's Cup racers; Lunenburg versus Gloucester; Canada versus the United States. Because they meant so much, people cared passionately about the races—and when people care that much, they compete right out to the uttermost limits of fair play. And even a bit beyond.

The races were also the defiant valedictory flourish of a fading culture of canvas, wood and handlining against a corporate culture of steel motor vessels that would ultimately destroy the fishery altogether.

In 1920, when the races began, fishing schooners were already obsolescent; in 1938, when they ended, the vessels were completely obsolete. As McLaren notes, even by 1930, when *Bluenose*'s last challenger was launched, the notion that the races were competitions between working fishermen was being tacitly ignored. *Gertrude L. Thebaud* went fishing to qualify, but she was never going to pay for herself as a fishing vessel. She was built to beat the *Bluenose.*

Bluenose herself, of course, had also been built to race. But that was ten years earlier, when a Grand Banks schooner could still pay her own way in the fishery. After 1930, even *Bluenose* had difficulty justifying herself economically. Still, the appeal of the schooners—though they had represented innovative fishing technology in an earlier day—was never entirely economic, and even as they died out, they recalled a more human way of relating to the world.

There is nothing beautiful about a trawler. It is hard to imagine anyone loving one. A trawler is an expensive corporate-owned fish-killing machine and nothing more. But a schooner could be built in any little notch of the coast by a gang of skilled men with access to wood, a building site and sharp hand tools. And the same men could sail their schooner, fish it, trade with it and prosper. The

schooners represented beauty versus force, honed skills versus raw power, human strength versus mechanical energy, art versus engineering.

The Lunenburg shipwright David Stevens, the great heir of that great tradition, liked to say that a ship was more like a living thing than anything else a man could build with his hands. The truth of the observation can be seen throughout Captain McLaren's book. There is something alive and individual, something like a personality, in each of the racing schooners—the quick and sturdy little *Esperanto,* the unlucky and out-of-sync *Haligonian,* the aristocratic and isolated *Mayflower,* the swift and ethereal *Columbia* and the fleet-winged *Puritan,* running through the fog so fast that she killed herself on Sable Island.

And, of course, the powerful, indomitable *Bluenose.*

Was there some extra quality, something akin to a greatness of heart, in the champion schooner from Lunenburg? Angus Walters, her captain, certainly acted as though there were. In moments of stress he would coax her, cajole her, shout at her. And she would always respond.

But maybe the unconquerable greatness of heart was in Angus himself, who knew and loved his vessel as few vessels have ever been known and loved. He was not an amiable or easygoing character, nor was he a particularly gracious winner. As Captain McLaren reminds us, he needled his opponents mercilessly, and, like them, he was not above a little discreet chicanery. But even the marine historian Howard Chapelle, who detested him, admitted that Angus Walters was "a prime sailor."

The races took place at a unique moment in history, a period that produced a great many legends in sports, exploration, the arts and entertainment—Joe Louis and Babe Ruth, Greta Garbo and Clark Gable, Amelia Earhart and Seabiscuit and Duke Ellington. The reasons are complex—the interwar period was a transitional time in many respects—but the 1920s were a period of dizzying change, and the 1930s were a decade of economic catastrophe.

So the public was in need of distraction, and at that very moment, the new technology of mass communication meant spectacular events could be reported to millions of people simultaneously, as they occurred. As McLaren notes, the schooner races were given astonishing play in the newspapers, and they were among the first sporting contests to be broadcast live. In today's multi-channel world, the mass audience has fragmented; only colossal events are reported to everyone. In the 1930s, however, the same newscast reached the whole audience and "fame" meant something it never meant before or since.

The echoes still linger. During his research, McLaren reports, he learned that the debate and passion about the races is still very much alive. Indeed it is; people still do care. When Canadians compete with their larger, more powerful neighbour, they normally lose—but this time they didn't, and since the races can never be held again, that victory is permanent. It has become one of the legends of our national life, and Canadians remember it every time they look at a Canadian dime. No wonder we care about it.

Americans naturally care much less about the story, but those who remember it care for the exact opposite reason. The Marines are supposed to land, the cavalry is supposed to arrive, the Revolution is supposed to succeed, everything is supposed to come out right in the final reel, and this story is a galling exception. It jest ain't fittin'. Americans feel, with some justification, that they *could* have won, perhaps *should* have won, but the prize is now forever out of reach.

Nova Scotians care particularly strongly because the races symbolize both our capacity and our decline. At one point in the nineteenth century, Nova Scotia was the fourth-largest trading nation in the world—or would have been, had it actually been a nation—and it entered Canada as the most prosperous of the founding provinces. That prosperity was based on wooden shipbuilding and resolute seafaring, and by the 1930s it was only a mirage in the communal memory. But *Bluenose* emerged from that history, and her triumphs forever remind Nova Scotians of what they once were, and what they could be again.

And sailors everywhere care because the races were a supreme moment of glory in an art they cherish, hard-fought contests using a style of sailing vessel that was at its peak of development just at the moment it was poised to disappear.

The enduring appeal of the schooners is their beauty and their ordinariness. Fundamentally, these were working boats sailed by working men, not high-tech wonders sailed by scientifically enhanced athletes. There was harmony and balance not only in the way they sailed, but also in the way they lived. They raced for fun and for fame, and then they went fishing.

These sailors were amateurs in the root sense of the word, men who competed for the sheer love of the thing itself, testing their mastery against that of their peers. That's what echoes down through the years—the beauty and danger of a working life under sail, and the pride of the men who did it.

SILVER DONALD CAMERON
2006, D'Escousse, Nova Scotia · www.silverdonaldcameron.ca

< **A COMMON METHOD** of distributing a crew across a fishing ground was called a flying set. The dories would be lowered over the side and allowed to drift astern, then tied to the after rail. Once all the dories were out, the skipper would head towards the area he wanted to fish and drop his dories off, one at a time at intervals. He would then jog back and forth along his line of men, tending them like a mother hen. *F.W. Wallace Collection, Maritime Museum of the Atlantic*

1

THE GRAND BANKS

FOR CENTURIES the Grand Banks, situated off the east coast of Canada, were considered one of Earth's most important fishing grounds, feeding much of the Western world. The banks are undersea plateaus that rise from the continental shelf, a relatively shallow part of the North Atlantic that extends just under two hundred miles from the shore before the ocean bottom drops 6,000 feet (1,800 metres). There are over twenty individual banks, ranging from the largest, the Grand Bank of Newfoundland, in the northeast, to Georges Bank off Cape Cod in the south, and they are known collectively as the Grand Banks. The water depth on these plateaus descends from 100 to 600 feet (30 to 180 metres). The icy Labrador Current, flowing south over most of the banks, mixes with

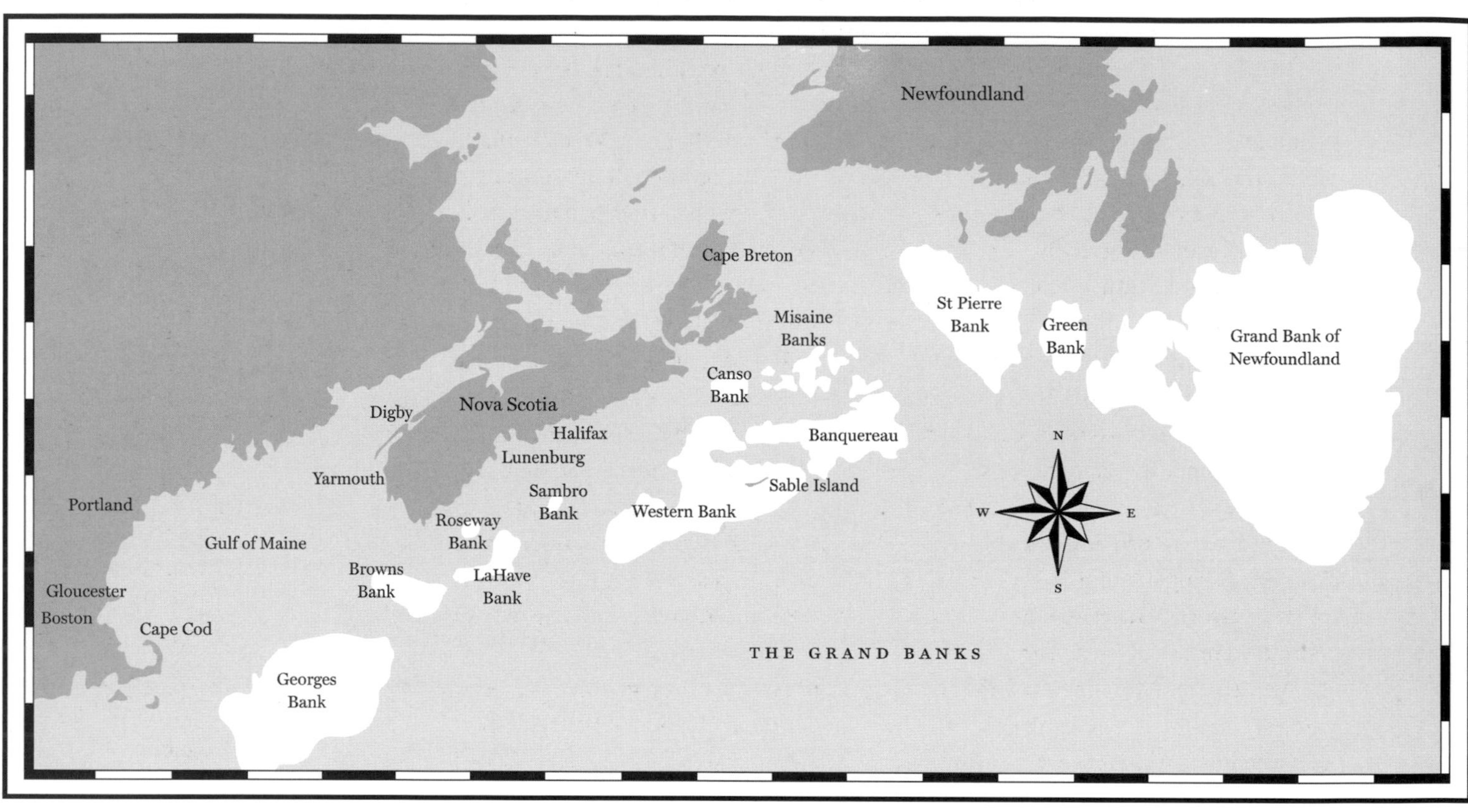
Newfoundland
Cape Breton
Misaine Banks
St Pierre Bank
Green Bank
Grand Bank of Newfoundland
Canso Bank
Nova Scotia
Digby
Halifax
Lunenburg
Banquereau
Yarmouth
Sambro Bank
Sable Island
Portland
Roseway Bank
Western Bank
Gulf of Maine
Browns Bank
LaHave Bank
Gloucester
Boston
Cape Cod
THE GRAND BANKS
Georges Bank
N
W
E
S

the warm waters of the Gulf Stream sweeping north along the eastern coast, as well as the freshwater currents flowing down from the Gulf of St. Lawrence. The swirling and mixing of the currents over the banks, along with the shallow water depth, creates a nutrient-rich environment that produces a dense growth of phytoplankton, the first link in the marine food chain.

Until recently, this habitat sustained a tremendous population of groundfish (those living near the bottom). The most important species to grow there was the Atlantic cod. This fish alone was primarily responsible for the early settlement and colonization of North America. Cod was easy to catch and, when dried and salted, could be preserved for long periods, allowing for transportation to markets in Europe. Basque fishermen were the first to discover the potential of the fishery, in the fifteenth century, and they kept its location a secret until John Cabot stumbled across it in 1497 on his first voyage of discovery to North America. Cabot reported to his English masters that the waters off Newfoundland were so thick with fish that the progress of his vessel was impeded. Inspired by this vivid description, the powers of Europe rushed to stake their claims on the fertile fishing ground. By the mid-1500s, more than half of the fish eaten in Europe was from that source, and by the time the Pilgrims arrived at Plymouth Rock in 1620, the banks were providing an income to over a thousand vessels from England, France, Portugal and Spain. The fishery had quickly become an important part of the western European economy, supplying markets with thousands of tons of salted Atlantic cod each year.

< **MAP** of the Grand Banks

As settlement became established along the northeast coast of North America, communities such as Gloucester and Lunenburg became homes to large fleets of offshore boats. Until the turn of the twentieth century, fishing methods remained virtually unchanged from the days of the early Basque fishermen. Wind-powered vessels and hook-and-line fishing were the standard methods of the time. Although the banks had been heavily fished for four centuries, the techniques used were relatively sustainable until modern methods were introduced. Overfishing, combined with the use of the indiscriminate wire mesh trawl, which dragged the bottom and destroyed everything in its path, brought about the demise of the fishery. The seas that had fed the mouths of hungry North Americans and Europeans for hundreds of years are now considered by some to be a marine desert. Unable to support human demands, the Grand Banks fishery is likely to remain in a state of collapse for many years to come.

‹ **WITH HIS BACK** to the weather, a fisherman on board the schooner *Corinthian* hunches over his trawl bucket as he finishes baiting his line. A mere snow squall would not slow work on a banker. Life was often cold, wet and miserable, but work would cease only if the sea became too rough to launch the dories—and even that was at the discretion of the master. *Edwin Cooper, Thomas Collection, Cape Ann Historical Association*

2

FISHING UNDER SAIL

ON THE WATERFRONT in Gloucester, there is a hauntingly beautiful sculpture of a fisherman grasping the wheel of a banks schooner. Wearing traditional oilskins and sou'wester, he appears to be straining every muscle to hold his schooner on course. His face is etched with tension as he gazes intently at the unseen sails aloft. The rough grey-green patina of the bronze casting has been permanently streaked by rain and sea spray. Below, the inscription reads: THEY THAT GO DOWN TO THE SEA IN SHIPS, 1623–1923. The memorial commemorates the many lives lost at sea in Gloucester's first three centuries and is now surrounded by ten tablets listing the names of more than five thousand fishermen. In Lunenburg, near the Fisheries Museum, is another monument—not, like its Gloucester cousin, a figurative representation, but equally powerful and poignant. Eight polished black granite slabs rise up from the earth in a Stonehenge-like cairn, each positioned on the directional points of a compass, with a ninth pillar in the centre. Names of the dead, a seemingly endless list of them, are etched into the surfaces. The two communities share a common bond of loss, a bond further strengthened by the fact that twelve hundred of the names on the Gloucester memorial belong to Nova Scotians who crewed Gloucester vessels.

Back in Gloucester and just up the street from the famous Man at the Wheel is perhaps the most moving monument of all. It was commissioned in August 2001 by the Gloucester Fishermen's Wives' Association to commemorate the families, the women and children, left to mourn those lost at sea. It is a simple statue of a mother and two children facing seaward, searching for a glimpse of the tall masts of the husband's and father's schooner. The sculpture strikes an even deeper chord than do the other two, speaking to the awful grief of the survivors who must somehow find a way to cope with the desolation of loss and carry on. The lives of those who depended on fishing for a living were always hard and too often ended in tragedy.

There was no romance in a working life at sea. The dirty and often brutally exhausting labour took place in uncertain and perilous conditions, where survival depended on constant vigilance and good fortune. Simply slipping from a footrope or being struck by a swinging boom could end a life in an instant. Many were swept overboard, lost in heavy fog or swamped in dories holding too many fish. Sometimes entire vessels and crews would go missing, smashed to pieces on a lee shore, run down by an Atlantic steamer in thick fog or torn apart in a hurricane, leaving no clues as to their passing. However, the promise of better pay than for work ashore, the camaraderie and the pride in doing the job well were viewed as compensation for the constant risk. Fishing was always a gamble, dependent on nature and the market for a reasonable return. Companionable shipmates, a competent skipper, a good cook and reasonable fo'c'sle crew made any hardship tolerable.

Life aboard a fishing schooner was more of a co-operative venture than the rigid hierarchy of the merchant marine. Fishermen worked as shareholders, and so their livelihood depended on the fortunes of their vessel and how hard they worked. They were engaged on a share system, their compensation paid out in proportion to the catch, after the vessel's costs had been deducted: the food, bait, salt, ice and wages for the paid members of the crew (the cook and perhaps one or two deckhands). In addition there could be one or two children on board who were paid a small wage to work as "throaters" or "headers," until they were considered old enough to work the dories. These children were often as young as ten or eleven, sent to sea to help out their families and learn the trade. The largest share went to the boat's owners—for the hire of the vessel—followed by the skipper, who normally took twice that of his crew. The rest was divided among the fishermen in one of two ways. If the crew were known to the skipper as hard-working men, he would generally give them "even shares," regardless of how many fish were caught in each dory. If, on the other hand, he had a crew of strangers whose fishing abilities were unknown to him, the skipper would have the catch divided "by the count." With two men to a boat, dory-mates were credited with the number of marketable fish they caught as a pair, and those catching the most took the highest share. Although there were reasonable arguments to be made for both systems, some skippers insisted on "by the count" on all occasions because they thought it encouraged competition and therefore greater catches. Those that counted highest were ranked "high dory," whereas those who consistently came out "low dory" often lost their jobs. "Even shares" was considered more democratic and fair by some, as the loss of gear and fish was often the result of bad luck rather than incompetence. But a good skipper had to be sure of his crew before he offered "even shares."

The crew of a typical banks schooner consisted of sixteen to twenty-four men. If a schooner was running eight dories, it would require a crew of sixteen. In addition to the crew, there was the skipper, a cook and one or two paid hands, who did not fish but tended to the ship and the needs of the men. These hands were also available to launch and recover dories and work the ship until the crew returned. When not fishing or on passage, the fishermen were required to help stand watches, provide lookouts, steer the vessel and handle sail. Once on the banks, they were either fishing or sleeping—and usually very little of the latter. When handling sail, even for the smallest job the entire crew would be called out, so there would be no accusations of favouritism.

Depending on the distance between port and the fishing ground, it could be hours or days until the men began to fish. Once on the banks, the day usually started at about three or four in the morning when they began putting bait on their trawls and readying their boats. The reason for starting so early was explained to

› **ATLANTIC COD**, the mainstay of the northern fishery, is forked from the dory, over the rail and onto the deck. The fish would be headed, gutted and split, then taken below to be either packed in ice (if being sold fresh) or salted down (to preserve it for the longer term). Livers would be stored separately in barrels, to be sold for cod liver oil. *Cape Ann Historical Association*

writer Fred Wallace by Captain Harry Ross of the schooner *Dorothy M. Smart.* It was "better," he said, "to begin your fishing early than to fish late. When you swing 'em over at two, or three or four—'specially during broken weather—the men have daylight ahead of them should it breeze or shut down thick. I'd sooner be caught with my dories astray in a fog or a snowstorm at four in the morning than at four in the afternoon. More chances of pickin' 'em up."[1] Once the crew was "baited up," the skipper would sing out to cast off, with his schooner slowly jogging along or hove to under foresail and jumbo sails. The top dory in each nest would be readied with all her thwarts or seats, plugs and gear securely in place, and was then lifted over the side by means of dory tackle descending from the main and fore mastheads. The two-man crew would carefully time their jump into the boat once it was over the rail, illuminated only by lantern and guttering kerosene torches, often with quite a sea running. The dory was then allowed to drift astern and was tied up to the quarter rail. After each was let go, it would be led aft and made fast to the others until there was a long string of boats behind the schooner. With all the boats in the water, the skipper would head off to a favourite fishing spot and let the dories go, one at a time, along a line several miles long. This was known as a flying set. The schooner would then act as a mother hen tending her chicks, jogging up and down the line or heaving to, ready at any time to service the boats. Once a dory crew had set their trawl, they would row back to the schooner and go aboard for a coffee break or mug-up before heading out again to haul in the trawl. The dorymen would signal the schooner when their boat was full of fish, by raising an oar or waving one of the torches, and the schooner would come alongside to pick up the load.

Some skippers preferred another method whereby they anchored their boats and had their dories fan out in all directions, like the spokes of a wheel. The dory crew would row to a likely spot, sometimes a mile from the schooner, to set their trawls. This was a method favoured by salt fishermen, but it had its drawbacks. If the wind and sea picked up, the men left aboard the schooner would be unable to raise the anchor on their own except by cutting the cable, and those dories on the leeward side would have a hard pull upwind to safety. On the other hand, if thick fog were to settle in, the dory crew would have a good idea of the direction and distance in which to find their schooner.

The dory was the workhorse of the Grand Banks fishery. It was a small, flat-bottomed craft with flared sides, a pointed bow and a tombstone stern, cheap to

build and stout enough to withstand the rigours of offshore fishing. It could easily be handled on and off the schooner and, after the thwarts were removed, nested onto another, so taking up little space on deck. An 18-foot (5.5-metre) dory seemed a mere sliver on a distant sea but had the capacity to carry more than two tons of fish without swamping. The banks dory was legendary for its stability when laden, and a crew of skilled fishermen could keep it afloat in very rough seas. The dory was not only a workhorse but also the lifeline of the fishermen, who depended on its famous durability and stability to keep them safe in almost any weather. A pair of oars, a small mast and sail, pen boards to contain the fish, a bailer, a water jar, a bait knife, a compass, a small wooden winch called a hurdy gurdy, a fish gaff, and the tubs, trawls, floats and anchors used to set gear was all that was required to equip it.

In the early days of fishing on the banks, fishermen worked from the deck of a schooner, standing along the rails and handlining for groundfish from the relative safety of a stable platform. Each man would tend several weighted lines to jig fish from the bottom, not much different from the method employed by the sports fisherman of today. It was a slow and labour-intensive method that did not produce a large catch. The introduction and adaptation of dory trawling in the late 1800s made the industry far more efficient, but at the cost of considerably increasing the risk to the fishermen. Hundreds of hooks could be laid out at a time, but the men handling them were no longer comfortably ensconced aboard a mother vessel. They were alone in a small boat, often miles away.

After a dory was dropped from the schooner, one man would ship the oars and row his boat as directed by the skipper, while his dory-mate attached the end of the first tub of line to a small anchor and tossed it over the side; standing in the stern, he would flick the baited hooks and line into the sea with a short wooden stick. Three, sometimes four tubs of line were attached together and laid out across the ocean floor. At the other end another anchor would be set to keep the trawl in place. Often a mile of line with thousands of baited hooks was laid out, marked at the ends with only a small flag or black ball. After setting the trawl and enjoying a mug-up aboard the schooner, the men would return to tend the gear. The man at the bow would now haul the line out of the water over a small wooden roller. The fish caught on the line were twisted off the hooks with a deft flick of the wrist and chucked into the bottom of the boat, and the line would either be coiled back into the tubs or "under-run"—rebaited and returned to the water for another set. The man at the oars would also be keeping a wary eye on the sea, ready to twist the boat into any oncoming waves to prevent a swamping. Once a ton or two of fish had been caught, they would either row or sail back to the schooner or signal it to come and off-load the catch. After a day of fishing, the night would be spent gutting, splitting and cleaning. Only when all the fish had been salted or iced in the hold could heads be put down for an hour or two of sleep.

A typical day on the banks was described in an article in a Lunenburg newspaper in 1911 as follows:

> All get up at three o'clock, cut bait, and row to their trawls before getting any breakfast; if the trawls have not been parted during the night, either by sharks or chafing against rocks, they haul them up, take off the fish, rebait, and return to the vessel at half after five, and have breakfast. They stay on board until nine thirty when they revisit their trawls, and repeat the same work mentioned above. Those who have been unfortunate enough to have had their trawls parted are not able to return until eleven thirty. In the meantime the other dories have landed two loads. The usual dinner hour is about twelve thirty, and after which meals they return to the trawls, and get back in time for tea served at half after three. Four o'clock sees them on their fourth trip, which is usually the last except when the fish are plentiful and the weather is fine they make five or six. In the night after the fourth meal all help to dress the fish, that is, cut off the heads, split them open, clean them and sprinkle them thoroughly with salt. They are then piled away in the hold of the vessel.[2]

It was cold, wet, back-breaking work, with the constant threat of being swamped in a squall or "going astray" in heavy fog. Fog was the worst enemy of a doryman. A day that started out fine and clear could quickly change and disappear under a thick blanket of heavy mist. The warm, moist air of the Gulf Stream drifting over the cold Labrador Current could produce some of the heaviest and most persistent fogs in the world, especially in summertime. Jimmy Connolly, writing in the 1920s, witnessed the conditions first-hand:

> Clear weather or thick, those men put out from the vessel. They put out one night at two o'clock in what fishermen call black vapour—heavy black fog. Each dory left with a lighted flambeaux, a great torch with a two-inch wick. The flambeaux

> were for the dories to show, to keep track of each other in the black night. The vapour so thick that even the flare of the big torches could not be seen from one dory to another. The men then had to halloo from dory to dory so as not to go astray. *Hi-oh! Hi-oh-h! Hi-oh-h-h!* To be standing on the vessel's deck and hearing them call to each other and not be able to see them—it was as if a lot of dead men had come to life and were calling to each other in some graveyard.[3]

Masters were always wary of changing conditions, but they often walked a fine line when it came to stopping fishing and calling back the men. Keeping track of boats spread out over the ocean was a demanding and tricky business in thick weather. Some skippers had an uncanny ability to locate their men in any conditions, but for many it was more luck than skill, and fishermen disappeared. Fortunate were those who were picked up by other schooners or passing steamers; most had to fend for themselves, waiting out the weather or rowing to safety, sometimes a hundred miles away.[4] Too many perished, drowned in a swamped dory, froze to death or simply died of dehydration, but there were also many incredible stories of survival. As Connolly wrote, "Men that go in for this life are not worrying overmuch about being lost. They may not enjoy the prospect of it, but the thought never overburdens them. If they feared death overmuch they would hardly be trying to make a living at banks fishing."[5]

One of the greatest survival stories was that of Howard Blackburn, a young Nova Scotian who joined the crew of the Gloucester boat *Grace L. Fears* in January 1883. He and Tom Welch, his dory-mate, lost their schooner in a blinding snowstorm on Burgeo Bank, off Newfoundland's south shore. In desperation, they headed for shore, more than sixty miles away, fighting mountainous seas and freezing rain. After Blackburn lost his mittens overboard on the first day, he froze his hands around the oars so that he could continue rowing. He and Welch had to constantly pound the ice forming on the dory and bail to stave off capsizing. Blackburn's hands became battered wrecks and Welch froze to death, succumbing to the bitter cold on the second night of their ordeal. With his dead partner in the stern, Blackburn continued to pull for shore, bail the water that sometimes rose to his knees and pound off the ice, all the while trying to stay on course for land. After five days with no rest, food or water, and in constant fear of capsizing, he finally made it to a desolate south shore settlement. The astonished inhabitants nursed him back to health and, although he lost all of his fingers and half of each thumb as well as a number of toes, he survived, eventually making his way back to Gloucester. His fellow citizens were so taken with his heroic journey that they raised enough money to buy him a saloon on the Gloucester waterfront. He was also paid his share from the halibut trip of the *Grace L. Fears,* $86. This legendary figure in the Cape Ann community further enhanced his reputation by twice crossing the Atlantic single-handed in later years.

The relationship of a banks skipper with his men was not defined by the shipping acts and articles of agreement, which gave masters in the merchant marine a great deal of authority. On a fishing schooner, life was much more informal. The skipper was in charge only by common consent, and the men were not bound to the schooner in any manner. There was no rank, and there were few rules regarding behaviour and none regarding dress. Men shared the same food and slept wherever a bunk was available, often in the master's aft cabin. The skipper's authority was based largely on his personal reputation and the confidence he inspired in his crew. Ultimately, the success of any trip depended on his abilities as a navigator, sailor and fisherman, and as a manager of men. Reporting to the United States Fish Commission, Captain Joseph Collins wrote in 1887 that a fishing skipper

> must be a natural leader, and generally gifted with superior intellect and tact, in order to get along with the crew, there being no special laws like those of the merchant service, which give him authority over his men. In cases of insubordination he must have recourse to his physical strength. If he cannot sustain himself in this manner, his influence over his crew is gone.[6]

Once ashore, skippers could easily get rid of troublemakers or unproductive crews, a threat that kept most crew members on their toes.

Fishing skippers began their careers young, learning the trade from the bottom up as ordinary fishermen, gutting and cleaning fish. By the time they were grown, they knew everything that was to be known about men and boats, fish, weather and markets. It was not an overly crowded profession, as most fishermen preferred to follow rather than lead. There were no formal qualifications, and training depended on finding a skipper willing to teach. Because authority had to be earned, a skipper had to prove himself before he could become successful. It is little wonder that many became larger-than-life personalities with reputations that took on almost mythic proportions. A skipper who was known to be a "sail

dragger and fish killer" would have no trouble attracting a top-notch crew, no matter how hard he worked them at sea. When a schooner came upon a productive area, the men were expected to fish until they literally dropped, sometimes working for days on end without sleep. Some skippers were ruthless when it came to crew safety, launching dories under terrible conditions. Any reluctant crew member would be landed ashore at the first opportunity and branded a coward. All too often a returning schooner came home with a flag at half-mast, marking the loss of life that resulted from the actions of an overzealous skipper. One disillusioned fisherman explained the indifference to the men's safety as follows:

> The skipper'd send you out as long as you could get out—long as you could get the dories off an' get out. Some of 'em was pretty rusty characters... hardly ever stop you from goin' off. He'd care only about the fish... and he's sleepin' while you was out haulin'. The one Cap'n I was with—he kept a dog aboard, see. There was many a night... blowin' a gale an' stormin'... why he'd call that dog in an' leave the men out. The men were out an' they'd stay out... on deck or in the dories. Made no difference to him. He must o' lost seven or eight men when I was with him... more or less.[7]

The promise of income made men endure the hardships inflicted on them by these ambitious and merciless souls. On the other hand, if a skipper could not find fish and fared poorly on the banks, he would have a hard time finding a boat, let alone a crew.

The master of a fishing schooner had to have the confidence and skill to be able to sail miles from shore in variable sea conditions, tidal currents and poor visibility. A crew's livelihood and safety depended on his being able to pinpoint a prime fishing spot, sometimes hundreds of miles from the home port, and make landfall safely after the trip was finished. There were no radars, radios or electronic navigation aids of any kind. A few skippers could use a sextant to perform celestial sights, but most were content with the basic navigational tools: a compass, a chart, a lead line and the confidence that comes from years of experience and local knowledge. As Fred Wallace explained in his excellent book, *The Roving Fisherman:*

> [The skipper's] sense of location, of tidal and current sets, of wind, is guided by compass indications. Coupled with this continual mental plotting of courses and fixing of positions, is his intimate knowledge of what is underneath the ocean

‹ **TWO FISHERMEN** of the Gloucester schooner *Killarney* haul on the forward dory tackle, as a third steadies it for launching. Another dory can be seen in the distance, already pulling away from the schooner. After being hauled out of her nest, the dory would be loaded with thwarts, oars, sail, trawl tubs and a variety of other items needed for a day's fishing before being sent on its way. *Al Barnes Collection, Mariners' Museum, Newport News, Virginia*

> surface in depth of water and character of bottom. Give him but one or two casts of the sounding lead, and the whole layout of the fishing ground he is working upon spreads out before his mind's eye... The average fishing skipper of the old days was superior to most deepwater merchantship masters in keeping "a grip on the bottom" and knowing where they were at any time.[8]

Wallace supplied proof of the skipper's knowledge after a trip with Captain John Apt of Yarmouth in 1912. While Wallace found the ship's position by using a sextant and making calculations from the appropriate tables—a skill he had learned from his father—Apt, after scribbling a few notations on a stovepipe with a nail, came up with the same location in half the time. There were even stories of masters whose knowledge of the coast was so detailed they could navigate by identifying the bark of a dog ashore. At the very least this would tell a skipper he was close to land!

A bad cook could doom a trip to the banks before it started. A good one played a major role in the maintenance of crew morale, especially on long trips. The cook was expected to have good grub available at all times of the day and night, three square meals as well as numerous "mug-ups." A "quick lunch locker" was to be kept well stocked and a pot of coffee always available on the stove. Some cooks were legendary for the extraordinary meals they could produce and their seemingly unlimited capacity to keep a crew satisfied.

Along with cooking duties, cooks kept an inventory of provisions, especially water, to ensure there was enough for the trip home. They usually tried to have water available for the men to clean up when heading in, but this was not always possible. Keeping track of stores was a prodigious job, especially on a salt banker, which could be at sea for months at a time. Provisions were a considerable investment for the owners, who hoped to more than recoup the expense at the end of the trip. The following list was from the Atlantic Supply Company for their schooner *Columbia* in April 1923:

> 16 barrels of flour, 1,100 pounds of sugar, 60 pounds of tea, 40 pounds of coffee, 7 bushels of beans, 75 pounds raisins, 100 cans of evaporated apples, 120 gallons of kerosene, 16 cases of milk, 15 gallons of molasses, 1 bushel of dry beans, 50 pounds of rice, 60 bushels of potatoes, 150 pounds of onions, 5 bushels of turnips, 11 barrels of beef, 1 barrel of corned shoulders, 300 pounds of salt spare ribs,

1 barrel of salt pork, 200 pounds of smoked ham, four cases of eggs, 300 cans of beets, squash, blueberries, string beans, clams, corn, peas, peaches, and tomatoes, 40 pounds of crackers, 40 pounds of baking powder, 15 cans of cream of tartar, 15 pounds of saleratus, from two to four pounds each of nutmeg, pepper, allspice, clove, ginger, cassia, mustard, etc., 20 packages of corn starch, 30 boxes of salt, 60 pounds of jam, 30 pounds of lemon pie filling, 20 pounds of mince meat, 24 boxes of lemon extract, 24 bottles of vanilla extract, 25 pounds of prunes, 48 packages of pudding, 24 bottles of ketchup, 12 mugs of prepared mustard, 25 packages of currants, 15 pounds of barley, 25 pounds of evaporated peaches, 100 pounds of fresh meat, 24 pounds of cheese and 100 pounds of slack salted polluck, also 40 bars of soap, 25 packages of washing powder, 24 packages of soap powder, 24 gross matches. In addition to the supplies for the men are included six tons of coal, four feet of wood, 450 hogsheads of salt, three gross of wax candles, 20 yards of towelling, 25 yards of torch wicking, one dozen torches, four coils buoy line, 30 dozen seven-pound lines, 10 dozen twenty-two-pound lines, 700 pounds of lead to be melted and used for jigger hooks, 24 dory gaffs, 18 fish forks, 20 pairs of oars, 32 two-pound anchors, 20 gallons of gasoline, 36 pairs of rubber boots, 20 dozen pairs of cotton gloves, five dozen pairs cotton mitts, 150 yards cotton cloth for dory sails, four dozen suits of oil skins, one dozen oiled petticoats, 24 bail buckets, 28 mattresses, 24 water jugs, besides the dishes, silverware, crockery, cooking utensils, tools, dory tackle and painters, etc.[9]

Cooks were also required to be on deck to tend to the vessel when the men were away fishing, and they would often supplement their wages by jigging for fish from the deck of the schooner while the dories were gone.

The forecastle, or fo'c'sle, was the heart of a schooner. This was where the crew ate, slept and relaxed. It was also the liveliest part of the boat, up in the bow, under the foremast. Men could feel the hull slicing and crashing through rough seas and hear the timbers creak and groan. Rows of bunks were set into the sloping bulkheads of the hull, and a large, wedge-shaped table on which food was served and cards were played thrust out between the rows. A large cast-iron cook's stove, sitting at the after end, would be kept well stoked throughout a trip to warm the men and dry their constantly sodden clothes. The galley and larder, also located near the stove, were home to the cook in his endless preparation of meals. The fo'c'sle was a tight but comfortable space. Wet clothing was hung everywhere; only the outer layers—woollen socks, sweaters and oilskins—were laid out to dry. The inner layers stayed on for the night, in case the men were called out to fish or tend sail. The smells of the stove, sodden wool clothing and as many as twenty working men—blending with the aromas of tobacco, fish, cooked food and the pungent bouquet of fishy brine from an unpumped bilge—made life in the forecastle an experience for the senses.

Schooners were seldom still, except on those rare days of perfect calm. All too often they pitched and rolled, making life on board, especially when hove to in a gale, far from easy. Every movement on board would become an effort, a simple walk across the deck a frantic dash from one post to another. Muscles were strained and sore from attempts to stay upright. Fishing would usually cease once it became impossible to launch the dories, and everyone would lie low, only standing watches, until the gale was over. The constant rolling and plunging, not to mention the danger of being thrown out of your bunk, made a good night's sleep impossible. However, a seasoned crew would weather it out and relax as best they could, knowing the seas would eventually settle and they would soon be back fishing.

For the men that went down to the sea in ships it was a hard, tough life for little return. Unless they were with a particularly good highline skipper, they would always be just dollars away from the poorhouse. There was always the promise of the large haul but, averaged over the year, they were not going to get rich. It was little wonder that men from the Maritimes migrated south in large numbers, since the work back home was usually seasonal and paid less. The New England fishery, by contrast, was year-round, to satisfy the large American market. Winter fishing paid more, but the perils were greater. It is hardly surprising that few landlubbers were attracted to the life, but, with all its drawbacks, for the men who worked the seas there was little alternative. The job of their grandfathers, fathers, brothers, neighbours and sons was all they knew, or wanted to do.

NOTES

In the notes following each chapter, citation by surname indicates an entry in the Selected Bibliography.

1 Wallace, *The Roving Fisherman,* p. 43
2 *Lunenburg Progress Enterprise,* n.d., 1911
3 Connolly, *The Book of the Gloucester Fishermen,* p. 37
4 All references to miles in this book are as used by mariners—*nautical* miles. A nautical mile is defined as one minute of arc of a great circle (such as the equator), or one-sixtieth of one degree. In practice this equals 1,854 metres, or 1.15 statute miles. Speed over water is expressed in knots, which is a measure of nautical miles per hour.
5 Connolly, *The Book of the Gloucester Fishermen,* p. 21
6 Goode, *The Fisheries and Fishery Industries of the United States*
7 Barss, *Images of Lunenburg County,* p. 41
8 Wallace, *The Roving Fisherman,* p. 54.
9 *Gloucester Daily Times,* April 25, 1923

‹ **SEVERAL CREW** members struggle to furl the stiff, sodden headsails of a banker during a fast passage from Maine to Nova Scotia in 1912. Commonly known as "widow-makers," the bowsprits on banks schooners were perilous places to work. Fishermen who slipped from the footropes could be dragged under by their heavy, bulky oilskins and seaboots, and they would often disappear without a trace. *F.W. Wallace Collection, Maritime Museum of the Atlantic*

3

A SKIPPING STONE

THE SCHOONERS of the east coast fishing fleet at the beginning of the twentieth century were the product of more than two hundred years of evolution. By the second decade of the century, the schooner had reached its peak in design but ironically was teetering on the verge of extinction. The introduction of reliable marine engines into the fishing industry had made sail obsolete. The use of sail—one of the oldest forms of propulsion, dating back to the beginnings of human history—could not compete with the superior power and reliability of the marine engine, and the schooner found itself quickly replaced by the dull but dependable trawler. Even so, it would take several decades before the working schooner made its final departure from the banks.

For the last half century of its existence, the schooner was greatly admired and often described as the finest fishing vessel in the world. Its powerful hull, seaworthiness and versatile sail plan made it perfectly suited to the harsh, demanding job of offshore fishing. The hull was staunchly built and rugged enough to withstand the most relentless of seas, and the configuration of sails was so flexible that the amount of canvas carried could be adapted to any weather, from light airs to hurricane-force winds. Schooners were fast, stable and could work their way to windward, a huge advantage in the variable wind conditions of the east coast. They also required fewer men to work them than other fishing vessels, something that appealed to both owners and fishermen. It is no wonder that the schooner could be found fishing and trading from Labrador to South America and Europe. The last all-sail schooners built in the 1920s were breathtakingly beautiful, with long, graceful hulls, upswept spoon bows and overhanging transoms. Their masts, over one hundred feet (thirty metres) tall, soared skyward, often carrying more than 10,000 square feet (930 square metres) of canvas. A design that combined aesthetic beauty and practical perfection would become a source of pride to owners, skippers and fishermen alike.

The schooner first appeared in North America on the shores of Cape Ann in Massachusetts in the early years of the eighteenth century. The precise origins are hard to place, as there are no plans, documents or models that have survived from the period. There is evidence in early Dutch engravings that the schooner rig was used in Europe in the mid-1700s, but the unique American version seems to have evolved independently earlier in the century. The local lore in Gloucester has it that a Captain Andrew Robinson invented the schooner in 1713 while building a new fishboat on the eastern shore of the harbour. According to legend, a spectator watching the passage of the unusual vessel was heard to remark, "Oh, how she scoons!" (A possible derivation of "scoon" is a Scots verb meaning to skip over the water like a flat stone.) The delighted builder is reputed to have replied, "A scooner let her be!"[1] The term "schooner" applied more to the rig than the hull, and with a relatively simple repositioning of the masts it became easily adaptable to existing colonial craft. The schooner rig was so practical that even fishermen, who were notoriously resistant to change, could immediately see the benefits of the innovation. The schooner was faster, easier to handle, and could carry more canvas than any existing craft.

Prior to the development of the schooner, the colonial ports in both Canada and the United States were populated by sailing craft that had been either brought over from Great Britain or built locally to a familiar design. The shallop was a small, open boat, propelled by an oar or sail, carrying a large for-and-aft main sprit-sail or rigged two-masted with square sails. These were suitable only for the inshore fishery that was then accessible to the developing colonies, as there were plenty of fish to be caught in the nearby fishing grounds.

The more likely forerunner to the schooner, however, was the ketch, which carried two masts, one larger mainmast forward and a smaller mizzen mast aft. It was generally larger and more seaworthy than the shallop, having a covered, flush deck. Both types were popular throughout the colonies, on each side of the border, but both were generally unsuitable for the harsh, variable wind and sea conditions, especially in winter. It does not take much to imagine Captain Andrew Robinson, or a kindred spirit, experimenting with the ketch and coming up with the more efficient schooner rig. All that was needed was to move the smaller mizzen mast from its aft position to forward of the mainmast, rig it with both fore and aft sails, and the schooner was born.

These colonial vessels were replaced by a specialized fishing vessel called the Marblehead schooner, which was a far cry from the elegant fishing schooners of the early twentieth century but met the needs of the coastal fishery. The design originated in the town of Marblehead, Massachusetts, the state's largest fishing port until the rise of Gloucester in the mid-nineteenth century, and spread rapidly around the New England coast and into Canada. There were many variations, but most had finer lines and were faster sailers than the earlier forms. They had a bluff bow, high stern and were bulky enough to carry a substantial cargo of fish. There were no bulwarks forward of the quarterdeck, since it was then regarded as unsafe to prevent the unobstructed sweep of water across the main deck. As a result, except on very calm days, fishing was done from the relative safety of the higher, drier quarterdeck. Schooners gradually grew in length, some up to sixty feet (eighteen metres), making them better suited to offshore fishing, and some were used to trade cargo as far south as the West Indies. There is little record of the earlier models, but later depictions show a high, proud stern, which made them look like an upturned shoe—hence the nickname "heeltapper." Their reputation for speed was noted during the American Revolution, Napoleonic Wars

and the War of 1812, when schooners were appropriated by the fledgling U.S. Navy and by the British and French for use as privateers. Sailing to windward, schooners were easily able to outdistance the heavier, more cumbersome square-rigged vessels in pursuit.[2]

Immediately after the American Revolution, the depletion of fishing boats virtually crippled the industry in New England. Two distinctly new schooner designs appeared as cheap alternatives to the Marblehead: the Chebacco boat and the Pinky. The Chebacco was very popular and was built in huge numbers on the Cape Ann peninsula. It was a smallish craft and carried two masts, schooner-fashion, with the foremast up in the bow. As there was no bowsprit, the sail arrangement had no jibs, foresails nor, for that matter, topsails. Some such schooners were double-enders and others, called "dogsbodies," were built with square ends. Because of their size, they were usually restricted to the inshore fishery.

The evolution of the other schooner design, the Pinky, paralleled that of the Chebacco boat and became equally accepted off the New England coast. The Pinky was a fast sailer with a double-ended hull but, unlike the Chebacco, had a bowsprit, allowing for fore- and topsails. These schooners were seldom longer than fifty feet (fifteen metres) and had a distinctive stern that swept gracefully upwards into a narrow tombstone transom. The hulls were so symmetrical from front to back that they would constantly pitch like a rocking horse in any seaway. However, the Pinky's superior ability to sail to windward was a quality much sought-after in the prevailing wind conditions off the east coast ports. After the War of 1812, a more refined version was developed that was suitable for working farther from home. Squabbles over fishing treaties between the United States and Great Britain ended with the imposition of a three-mile limit around the shoreline of Britain's North American territories and the barring of Americans from fishing in those waters. Bays and harbours that were previously open to Yankee fishermen were now closed; as fishermen always followed the fish rather than the law, the ban led to wide-scale poaching. Their illegal activities made "clipper Pinkies," a larger, faster version of the boat, well known in the Maritime provinces, where they were adopted in turn by the Canadian fishery. They remained in common use up to the 1830s, when they were gradually replaced by the broad-hulled, low-quarterdecked schooner that began to dominate the industry. The Pinky's popularity may have waned, but the design continued to be favoured by many well into the twentieth century.

‹ **THE WRITER** Fred Wallace was able to take this dramatic photograph of the *Effie M. Morrissey* by climbing out on the bowsprit with her captain, Harry Ross. Shortly after this was taken, the helmsman let her "come-to" a little, burying the whole lee side and thoroughly soaking the pair forward. *F.W. Wallace Collection, Maritime Museum of the Atlantic*

The development of larger, more substantial schooners called "market fishermen" or "bankers," which could range farther out to sea and carry far greater loads of fish, was a response to the pressures of the rapidly growing American domestic market. Most of these larger vessels could sail great distances from port, going to anchor on a likely spot and fishing until full before returning with a cargo of gutted, split and salted fish. The new boats were met with suspicion by many fishermen, their natural aversion to change reinforced by news of the loss of many of these boats and their crews in winter gales. Critics called them unsafe. Writing in the *Gloucester Advertiser,* Captain Joseph Collins made "invidious comments" on the new boats, stating that "these schooners were very slow sailers—more suited to drifting than sailing—and not weatherly. In addition, their lack of depth and, in fact, their general form, made them liable to being knocked down and swamped in a gale."[3] As Howard Chapelle has observed, supplying the market and making a profit came first:

> While all these were practical objections to the type, none of them were really valid reason for disregarding the old model, for the safety of fishermen and vessel property were not always prime considerations in the improvement of vessels, the brutal facts being that the men lost cost the shipowner nothing, and insurance could take care of the loss of vessel property.[4]

Unfortunately, this sentiment prevailed among shipowners, not only in the fishing industry but also in the commercial shipping trade.

The next changes in schooner design were a radical departure from the older, fuller-hulled vessels of the past and were a response to the need for speed to meet the demand for fresh fish in the American market. In the 1840s, the introduction of crushed ice as a means of preserving fish changed the industry almost overnight. Fishing took on a far more competitive tone. It was now a race to the grounds and a race to be the first back to port with a fresh cargo. Shipowners had a compelling financial incentive to underwrite changes to schooner design, and designers competed with each other to come up with the best new vessel. Faster boats meant higher profits, since the first boat to the pier with a load of prime, iced cod or halibut earned the best price from dealers ashore. These early "sharpshooters," as they were called, had long, straight keels with almost flat bottoms, shallow-drafted to suit the shoal water in Gloucester Harbour. The biggest departure was the long, pointed, "sharp" bow, a feature that added to the racy character of the boat. Again, the local fishermen had grave doubts about the seaworthiness of the new designs. They were felt to be too dangerous without a full, bluff bow, as many thought that if the vessels dived into a head sea they would never recover.

This period of intense rivalry among both shipowners and designers became a frenetic pursuit of speed. As the demand for fresh seafood grew, the tendency was to build longer, shallower, extremely sharp vessels with a minimum of ballast. Huge piles of sail were crowded on, to the extent that the vessels became dangerous; their flat bottoms meant stability depended almost entirely upon the width of their beam. In fair weather, these boats could carry as much sail as possible, but in a blow they often met with disaster. If a vessel heeled over too far, the centre of gravity was not sufficiently low to right her, often resulting in capsizing and the loss of the crew. The madness continued throughout the seventies and eighties: in the ten years from 1874 to 1883, the town of Gloucester lost eighty-two schooners and 895 men. It was obvious to anyone with a rudimentary knowledge of ship design that the answer lay in increasing the vessel's draft and lowering the centre of gravity.

One man with a desire to put things right was Captain Joseph W. Collins, a highly respected, self-educated fishing master who had spent most of his life at sea. He began a personal crusade to reform the industry and make it a safer business. He was horrified by the tremendous losses he saw around him and began writing articles critical of current fishing practices and vessel design. As a member of the United States Fish Commission, he was able to persuade the government to build an experimental schooner that would incorporate all the practical innovations he and designer Dennison J. Lawlor had been advocating. The schooner, *Grampus*, represented a huge leap ahead of common practice. She was narrower of beam, had a deeper draft, a plumb stem, and an altered sail plan resulting from changes to the masts and rigging. Special attention was given to the vessel's stability; the ballast and cargo were properly secured to prevent shifting, and limits were put on the weight aloft. At the same time, it was essential to preserve qualities that would ensure the vessel could be competitive. Although keenly aware of the objections to the adoption of a deep hull because of the shallowness of Gloucester Harbour, Collins and Lawlor insisted that safety should be paramount. "Safety of life and property should supersede all other considerations and will."[5]

The *Grampus* and other similarly designed schooners were great improvements on the older, "sharp" vessels. They proved to be fast as well as safe. With deeper holds and a lower centre of gravity, they could not only stow more fish but also could carry sail without fear of capsizing. The "sharp," hollow lines of the earlier boats were replaced with the long, easy curves that typify the modern schooner. The graceful stern was narrowed considerably, ending in a long, overhanging transom, and the elegant clipper bow was fuller on the waterline. The model proved fast and seaworthy and quickly became a favourite of fishermen and owners alike. This style of schooner went through further evolutions in the coming years, but the basic template became the norm for the industry until the end of the all-sail era. Hulls became larger, especially in Canada where the salt-fish trade continued, and that meant longer, deeper keels that could carry great amounts of sail aloft. The round, spoon bow that marked the next generation would make these beauties even more impressive. The final incarnations of the type, which were built to race in the international competitions of the 1920s, were the ultimate in the refinement of commercial schooner design, their almost yacht-like appearance belying their blue-collar purpose.

If this narrative seems heavily American in its description of the evolution of schooner design, it is because New England, with its far greater population base than the Maritimes' and consequently huge market demands, provided the most fertile ground for schooner development in North America. Their geographical proximity meant that the Maritimes naturally benefited from innovations from the south, and they were quick to adapt new designs for their own use. Canada had many fine designers and master builders, but, with a few exceptions, adaptation, not innovation, was the rule. The Tancook whaler, for instance, was a distinctly Nova Scotian variant. It was a double-ended schooner, similar to the Pinky but with a finer entry, more rake in the ends and a clipper bow. Generally, however, when Nova Scotians saw a new vessel from the United States they took what they could from its design and applied it to their own. David Stevens, a master builder from Second Peninsula in Nova Scotia, related a story of his grandfather building the first spoon-bowed schooner in the province.

> He was fishing on the Grand Banks... and saw what he thought was a very strange vessel coming down close by. He couldn't take his eyes off her... About two weeks later he was in port and here was that vessel laying alongside at the wharf, so he took a piece of paper and a pencil and got off on the side and he drew a profile of

> the shape. It was a spoon bow schooner out of Gloucester with a transom stern... He brought the drawing home to his father and his father immediately made a half model and began to build what is known as the Tancook Schooner.[6]

It was always a matter of pride for schooner masters to carry a lot of sail and carry it well. Reputations were built on how hard a vessel could be pushed and how much speed could be squeezed out of her hull. A "highliner" was a master who could not only catch fish but also could drive his vessel to market in record time. It is no wonder that when vessels met at sea there were often spontaneous hookups and unspoken challenges, when all thoughts of fish and markets were put aside for the joy of a race. Egged on by their crews, masters threw caution to the wind, sometimes losing dories and gear over the side. Howard Chapelle felt compelled to comment on this practice in his superb book *The American Fishing Schooners:*

> In the late 1800s and early 1900s carrying a heavy press of sail on all occasions was common practice among fishing skippers. One of these hard-driving skippers lost five sets of spars during his career, with even greater damage to rigging and sails. This characteristic of many fishing skippers was the result of the work of a great short-story writer, James B. Connolly, whose tales of the Gloucester fishermen attracted widespread attention during this period. Connolly glorified and publicized hard-driving skippers, so a reputation for being a sail carrier became much sought after, though the result was sometimes an exhibition of recklessness.[7]

Americans generally hold that the first fishermen's race occurred in Boston in the mid-1880s. However, an earlier contest was held in Halifax, Nova Scotia, at the Great Aquatic Festival in 1871. Although the four-day festival was primarily a rowing regatta, bringing together the best rowers in the world, it was also a showcase for Nova Scotia fishermen, and one of the event's features was a fishing-schooner race. There were several races, each designed for a different class of boat, including two categories of schooners, wherries, gigs and whalers. The star of the series was a small forty-ton schooner called *Flash,* which was entered in the second class of schooners (fifty tons and under). Although her race started half an hour after that of the first class (fifty tons or over), the *Flash* not only won but crossed the finish a mere two minutes behind the leader of the larger group, a sixty-six-ton vessel called the *Ida E.* The *Flash*'s spectacular performance astonished the race watchers.[8] Twenty schooners had entered the competition, and although this was a fairly modest affair, it was likely the first time fishermen had had the opportunity to show off their racing skills to a hometown crowd.

Fishing-schooner racing on a formal basis proved to be a popular though rather sporadic sport over the next half century or so. Fishermen were understandably more interested in earning a living than in playing games and could ill afford to take time off to race. Thomas McManus, a naval architect and the self-professed "Father of the Fishermen's Races," organized a competition in Boston in May 1886 when a strike by fish handlers ashore was forcing the schooners to lie idle. The young designer could not bear to see the fleet inactive, so he arranged for a no-handicaps "boat for boat" contest. Vessels were allowed to be hauled out and cleaned, but nothing else. It was a fairly dull and listless event with little wind, but it pleased the spectators just the same and McManus's own boat, the *John H. McManus,* designed by himself and named for his father, won the race.

There were no more than eight official fishermen's races from 1871 until the start of the International Fishermen's Cup series in 1920. Several, sponsored by the international sportsman Sir Thomas Lipton, were held off Boston and Gloucester. The Brittain Cup series, named for the owner of a fish plant, was held in Digby, Nova Scotia, at the end of the first decade of the new century and inspired the young writer Frederick Wallace to chronicle the fishing industry in North America. But it was the race off Gloucester in 1892 that attained a legendary stature that made it the yardstick by which future races were measured. James Connolly did not witness the race, but he coined the phrase "the race it blew" when he wrote about it years later and modelled many fictional characters in his later books after the real-life participants in this race.

In the summer of 1892, the town of Gloucester was marking the 250th anniversary of its incorporation with a six-day celebration, capped off with a fishing-schooner race on August 26. Ten vessels entered to race the long, forty-one-mile triangular course that would take them around Massachusetts Bay. A southwest leg to Nahant Bay followed the start at Gloucester. From there, the route went south to Minot's Ledge and then returned to Gloucester along a seventeen-mile leg. There were two categories of vessels; the class of eighty-five feet (twenty-six metres) and over drew seven entries, and three competed in the eighty-five-foot-and-under. Most of the boats had arrived early to prepare, but one schooner, the *Harry L. Belden,* did not arrive in town until the evening before the race. Maurice Whalen, her skipper, had been out fishing for mackerel but was hit by light airs that delayed his arrival back home. Whalen had no time to off-load his cargo, let alone paint or trim his vessel.

On the morning of the race the weather appeared ominous, with a grey, scudding sky, slashing rain and, in answer to the prayers of many, plenty of wind. Governor William Russell of Massachusetts was to have been a guest on board one of the competing vessels, the *James S. Steele,* but after observing the conditions prudently declined the invitation. Off Eastern Point, the racing committee was tossed about in the heavy sea and could barely see the contestants for the wind and spray. As they waited for the start, none of the competitors saw fit to shorten sail in the growing breeze.

Then the race was on. It is said that the wind picked up to fifty knots halfway to Nahant Bay and the sea was getting wilder by the minute, with mountainous, white-capped waves washing over each vessel as she staggered along. The lead boat, the *Ethel B. Jacobs,* broke her main gaff while jibing around the first mark and was forced to take in her mainsail and retire from the course. Two others, the *Grayling* and the *James S. Steele,* also found conditions too trying and stood off with the spectators. The rest of the fleet managed to hang on as they headed towards Minot's Ledge with a howling gale just forward of the beam. Arthur Millet of the *Gloucester Daily Times* wrote:

> With every sheet hauled flat and every sail drawing, they pounded and staggered into the heavy seas, burying their bowsprits and washing decks at every jump. Lee rails were buried and the water was up to the hatches as the schooners laid over before the strength of the fierce northeaster. Sea after sea they shipped and sometimes dove into them to the foremasts.[9]

The madness continued as the remaining boats in the fleet pressed for home on a windward beat. Captain Tommie Bohlin, the skipper of the *Nannie C. Bohlin,* must have regretted shedding a few tons of ballast, since his vessel had difficulty staying upright in the storm-force winds. Nonetheless, he was hot on the tail of the *Belden,* which had taken over the lead from the *Ethel B. Jacobs.* Dr. William Hale, a guest on the *James S. Steele,* described the drama.

> During the long thrash to windward, every vessel sailed on her lee rail, with deck buried to the hatches. Huge seas broke continually over the staunch flyers and swept the decks. The brave, laboring craft would roll under surging seas to the second and third ratlines; then would follow awful moments of suspense, as the unflinching crew, with teeth set and hands clenched, watched to see if their craft would stagger up again, or go down under her grievous load. Desperate as the chances were, not a vessel luffed or reefed, as to be the first to reef would make her the laughing stock of the town, and there was not a skipper in the fleet who would not carry away both sticks rather than be branded as a coward.[10]

The *Belden,* with her eighty thousand pounds of mackerel on board, "stood up like a church" in the heavy weather as she made for the finish, but even as Whalen tacked one final time, his jib tore away and flogged to pieces as he passed the finish in the lead. Although it bordered on insanity to be racing in such conditions, it did prove one major point: In their ability to withstand such adverse conditions, the schooners had shown they were far superior to and much safer than the earlier designs, and schooner skippers would not miss a chance to prove it.

Sadly, by the second decade of the twentieth century the schooner fleet and the days of sail were coming to an end. There were good, rational and practical reasons to move into the power-driven era, and few would regret the old ways. The uncertainty and danger that went along with sailing was soon replaced by the predictability, safety and almost monotonous regularity of engine power. The industry could now be run with far less loss of life and property than in the past, but the dull, graceless hull of a dragger, powering along under a pall of smoke, could never replace the splendour of a schooner under full sail with a gut-load of fish, racing to market. Those who had sailed them loved them and mourned their passing.

NOTES

1 Garland, *Down to the Sea,* p. 5; Dear and Kemp, *Pocket Oxford Guide to Sailing Terms,* p. 159
2 Greenhill, *Schooners*
3 Chapelle, *American Fishing Schooners,* p. 64
4 Ibid., p. 64
5 Ibid., p. 136
6 Gordon McGowan, "Two Tall Ships," CBC interview, n.d.
7 Chapelle, *American Fishing Schooners,* p. 210
8 *Morning Chronicle,* August 18, 1871
9 *Gloucester Daily Times,* August 27, 1892
10 Hale, *Memorial of the Celebration*

‹ **A BOISTEROUS SEA** and a stiff wind were common fare to east coast schooner fishermen who spent their lives battling the elements to earn a living. The sturdy banks schooner was the workhorse of the North Atlantic. *Nova Scotia Archives and Records Management*

4

"A RACE FOR REAL SAILORS": 1920

ON JULY 24, 1920, two slender-hulled sailboats jockeyed about in the turbulent waters off Sandy Hook, New York, awaiting a decision from the committee boat nearby. Both the British *Shamrock IV* and the American *Resolute* were rigged for weather, their mains reefed and storm sails forward. The masters of these two thoroughbreds watched for the sign that the race was on.

Begun in 1851 by the Royal Yacht Squadron in Cowes, England, the America's Cup series was the world's premier yachting event. The Yankee schooner *America*, sponsored by the New York Yacht Club, had sailed to Britain for the first race and won it, and American boats had held onto the cup ever since. The silver trophy, donated to the New York club in 1857 by the *America* syndicate, had been given the name "America's Cup" for the first winning boat. The 1920 series was the thirteenth since the inception of the race, and the Irish tea baron Sir Thomas Lipton was making his fourth attempt to return the coveted trophy to Britain. Sir Thomas had entered a succession of boats in the 1899, 1901 and 1903 series. In 1914 he had sailed the *Shamrock IV* across the Atlantic to compete, but the outbreak of World War I forced the cancellation of the race. The series had remained in limbo until the summer of 1920. Both the British and the American vessels matched to race before the war now had another chance. Spectator enthusiasm was ripe for such a contest in the post-war years, and the series proved to be an exciting match.

The first race was beset by thunderstorms, rain squalls and shifting winds. The *Resolute* led throughout, but as she came up to the last mark, the peak halyard on her main gaff parted and dropped, cutting off a good portion of the mainsail. The crew's effort to lower the rest of the sail and carry on with only a jib proved inadequate, forcing them to give up and retire from the course. Charles Adams, the *Resolute*'s skipper, was heavily criticized for not using more seamanship to at least finish the race.

The second contest brought light and fluky winds. The *Shamrock*'s start was spoiled when her large balloon jib became tangled and would not fill. William Burton, her master, ordered the crew to clear the sail, but it tore in the process and had to be removed. Meanwhile, the *Resolute* flew along with a fully filled ballooner, steadily inching away from her competitor. Burton jury-rigged a flying jib, which set well, and the *Shamrock* slowly gained on the sleek white hull of her competitor. She not only had to beat the *Resolute* but also to make up a seven-minute handicap assigned to compensate for the difference in hull length. When she crossed the finish line first, she did so to a roar from twenty-five thousand cheering spectators, winning the second race by two and a half minutes on corrected time in the best-of-five race series. With two wins to her credit, all the *Shamrock* needed was one more to take the cup home.

The next day, the public anticipated a spectacular contest and was not disappointed. The beat to windward was a long haul for the *Shamrock*, unable to point nearly as high as could the *Resolute*. She tacked almost twenty times to keep pace with the American boat. Downwind, it was another story. She flew along, steadily gaining on her rival, to cross the finish line in the lead, but not by enough to make up the handicap.

During the fourth race, the boats appeared evenly matched and both were superbly handled. Nathaneal Herreshoff, the aged designer of the *Resolute,* had appeared on the scene to oversee adjustments to her rigging and sail plan. The buoyed crew of the American boat worked her like clockwork and the *Resolute* took her second win by a full ten minutes.

The stage was now set for a nail-biter of a fifth race. With the series tied at two apiece, the public was in a frenzy of anticipation. The morning of Saturday, July 24, brought the first real wind of the series. The *Resolute* and the *Shamrock,* both with shortened sail, ventured out from the shelter of Sandy Hook into a boisterous seaway. The *Boston Globe* reporter wrote that "short work was made by both vessels on the run out to the light vessel, the 20-knot southwester carrying them along at express train speed... It was the kind of day that one reads that real sailormen like to weigh anchor in and head seaward with their craft carrying every sail."[1] Sails snapped loudly and nerves were pulled as tight as the halyards as the winds whipped through, while both crews watched for the start signal from the committee boat.

A *Toronto Telegram* sportswriter commented: "The race committee was in a quandary... it was rough, very rough. The committee possibly had some 'inside' information to that effect. And in this rough weather either vessel might break down. *Resolute* might break down. And that meant the loss of the cup... the committee made a seasick signal: 'Do you consent to the race being called off for the day?' "[2] Both skippers agreed. The regatta committee justified its ruling by stating that, with heavy seas sweeping the decks, great damage to the boats, and possibly loss of life among the crew, was a strong possibility.

The decision to call off the race was received by many with disappointment and disbelief. What should have been an exciting finish to a close series was, in the opinion of the spectators, ruined by the timidity of the racers. The *Toronto Telegram* reporter noted that "it was blowing only a wholesale breeze Saturday. Highest estimates of the wind velocity were 28 miles per hour. That is only 'half a gale' and the registering instruments were at a great level. On the lower level it is questionable if the wind was blowing harder than 20 knots."[3] The weather had not prevented local fishermen from being out in their small skiffs; nor had the fleet of spectators stayed away. It was reported that even a forty-foot (thirteen-metre) Long Island Sound schooner had carried full sail, and carried it well.[4] The cancellation and the ensuing hue and cry made the last race, when it was finally held on the following Monday, and won by the *Resolute*, into a mere footnote. The cup returned to its home at the New York Yacht Club, but the debate raged on.

The yachting pages in the North American papers were awash with discussion of what had become of the America's Cup series. The fact that these boats were too delicate to sail in anything but light winds troubled most devotees of the sport. The *Boston Globe* said that "neither *Resolute* nor *Shamrock* are like the cup boats of 25 years ago. They are of lighter construction and rigging and in addition have extremely tall rigs for boats of their length. Therefore they are not at all suitable for racing in strong breezes."[5] The correspondent for the *Toronto Telegram* was more critical when he wrote that Burton, as master of the *Shamrock*, could have done more to emphasize the absurd rules and conditions by insisting on a race. "It would have been worthwhile if he had split *Shamrock* from stem to stern doing so."[6] But it was the *New York Globe* that was most scathing when it referred to the contenders as "paper napkin" boats and suggested the race would have been far more exciting had it been held in a bathtub.[7] The public clearly wanted more from their heroes than mere competitiveness. They wanted a spectacle, a show of courage, steadfastness, resolve and mastery of the elements.

All this was not lost on the commercial fishing community, which was still dominated by the banks schooner. The fishermen's interest in the races was more professional. As men who worked under sail, they felt they had the credentials to assess the contest with a true sailor's eye. The cancellation became a popular topic of conversation in sail lofts, taverns and smoke-filled fo'c'sles in ports up and down the eastern seaboard. The series was discussed, chewed over and spat out in disgust by fishermen from Massachusetts to Newfoundland. To men who made their living at sea, it seemed ridiculous that sportsmen in their highly refined racing machines were cowed by a little bit of breeze. Twenty knots of wind would barely press the wrinkles out of the sails of a banks schooner. The timidity of the America's Cup yachtsmen was too much for the fishermen of the North Atlantic, and they began to talk about a real test, a contest between the men who worked the schooners that sailed the great offshore banks. Now that *would* be a race.

It was Colin McKay, the great-grandson of the famous clipper-ship designer Donald McKay, who brought the subject forward to the public when he wrote an editorial for both the *Halifax Herald* and the *Montreal Daily Star* on August 11, 1920, asking simply: "Why not a fishermen's race between Canada and United States?"[8] He suggested that such a race would be a fitting way of inaugurating a fishing treaty the two nations were expected to sign shortly, and he said the only conditions needed for such a race would be that the vessels have the same waterline length and sail plan as when they entered the fishery. This aroused a great deal of interest, and the idea was taken up immediately by magazines and newspapers all across the Maritime provinces. In the opinion of many, such a regatta would enhance the image of the fishery, stimulate improved vessel design and raise the profile of the North Atlantic fishing industry, inspiring more people to eat fish! Whatever the side benefits, the primary goal was expressed by the Sydney correspondent of the *Halifax Herald:* "Old salts and fishermen, he says, want to see a real race—not a lady-like saunter of fair weather freaks."[9]

William Dennis, the owner of both the *Halifax Herald* and Halifax's *Evening Mail,* had also reacted with derision when he read about the America's Cup fiasco. He agreed that the series had become far too refined and, focussing on the local fishery, proposed a true sailors' contest for the fishermen of Nova Scotia, a real ocean race, not of the "pink tea" variety that had recently been witnessed off New York.[10] The race could be a "sort of a preliminary canter to an International Sailing Race," to be held the following year between American and Canadian schooners, to be run off Halifax in the first week of October.[11] Only working, bona fide fishermen and true banks boats that had completed at least one full season offshore could participate. Dennis put up a cup with the cumbersome name "The Halifax Herald and Evening Mail Nova Scotia Fishing Vessel Championship Trophy" and promised to raise a suitable purse by public subscription. The course would be a large triangle, beginning in Halifax Harbour and running well out to the open ocean, beyond Chebucto Head, a true test of a vessel's sailing capabilities. Nine schooners, "the pride of the Lunenburg fleet," immediately signed up for the event.[12]

Public interest grew daily, and subscriptions for prize money came pouring in. It was believed by many that the event would put Halifax on the international stage. The excitement was tangible in every editorial and article on the subject. "Never in this generation has Nova Scotia attempted the like—It must be made a success." "They are making elaborate preparations to make the race the greatest event ever held in North American waters."[13] The organizers planned everything to the last detail: waterfront merchants and ship owners were requested to decorate their premises and boats; factories and ships were asked to blast their whistles; fire bells were to ring and cannons to fire from the Halifax Citadel when the boats neared the finish. Four forty-mile courses were mapped out, giving the race organizers alternative choices depending on the wind directions on the day of the race.[14]

> **THE AMERICA'S CUP** contenders the *Shamrock IV* and the *Resolute* face off in the light winds of the 1920 series near Sandy Hook, New York. What schooner fishermen disparagingly referred to as the timidity of these racers when faced with a good breeze provided the impetus to develop another series, hailed as a test for "real sailors." *Edwin Levick, Mariners' Museum, Newport News, Virginia*

Halifax was in the mood for celebration, as it was only just recovering from a devastating event in 1917. The city had been the North American staging point for convoys carrying troops, munitions and relief supplies to the battlefields in Europe. On the morning of December 6, 1917, the Belgian-relief ship *Imo* was departing Halifax Harbour when she collided with the incoming French munitions vessel *Mont Blanc*, carrying 2,500 tons of TNT, benzol, picric acid and gun cotton. Twenty minutes after the collision, when large crowds of citizens had gathered on the foreshore to watch the burning ships, the *Mont Blanc* erupted, causing the biggest man-made explosion of the pre-nuclear age. In a single moment, Halifax was transformed from a bustling wartime port into a shattered relic. The blast, which broke windows fifty miles away, immediately killed more than 1,600 people and injured 9,000 others. The whole north end of the city was levelled, and its people were crippled beyond belief. Relief poured in from the Canadian and British governments and from as far away as New Zealand and China. Haligonians were most grateful for the quick response of a volunteer relief committee from the state of Massachusetts, which was among the first to deliver funds and goods to the stricken citizens. The rebuilding of the city was nearing completion by 1920, and its citizens were ready, willing and able to put the past behind them and to take on the joyful task of hosting such an important event.

In the United States, there was only passing interest in the proposed schooner race in Halifax, as most of the Massachusetts boats were then at sea. The fishermen of both nations used the same fishing grounds and caught the same catch, cod and halibut, but they processed the fish differently. The Nova Scotian crews worked a "salt fishery" that was seasonal, from early May until mid-September. Their boats would stay out for extended periods and, since their catch was split and salted down, there was no need for refrigeration. Fishermen came into port only when their holds were full or when they were in need of supplies such as salt or bait.

The Americans, on the other hand, had developed a fresh-fish industry. Boats went out for shorter periods and the catch was gutted, iced and delivered to port while it was still fresh. As theirs was a year-round occupation, when Nova Scotians started talking about schooner racing Americans were paying little attention. While the entire fleet was in port in Lunenburg, there were few boats alongside or at anchor in Boston and Gloucester. The first indication of any American interest

in the race up north was a small article in the *Gloucester Daily Times* on October 1, 1920, but aside from the writer, nobody seems to have taken much notice.

On October 11, nine boats—the *Delawana,* the *Gilbert B. Walters,* the *Alcala,* the *Mona Marie,* the *Bernice Zink,* the *Freda L. Himmelman,* the *Democracy,* the *Ruby Pentz* and the *Independence*—headed out into Halifax Harbour under a clear blue October sky. The local correspondent for the *Evening Mail* wrote:

> To the landlubber who awakened early this morning, the swishing curtains at the bedroom window bespoke a wind, and a wind meant a race... No tugs were needed to get the vessels from their berths today. Under part sail, they majestically rode from the docks. Out they came, one at a time, and each as trim and pretty as the other.[15]

With the wind blowing at about fifteen knots, whitecaps spread across the harbour and the sails of the great schooners flapped loudly as they waited for the start. Thousands of the citizenry crowded vantage points along the docks and out along the shore at Point Pleasant Park. The *Mail* reporter continued:

> It was a glorious day for such a grand event. The sky was never bluer, the sun was never brighter, the breeze was never more favourable and the weather man in general, never was in better humor than he was this morning, when the great sea classic for which thousands have awaited news for days, was started.[16]

It was nervous work as the nine schooners jockeyed about at the start in the fresh nor'westerly breeze. A signal indicating course number 1 was hoisted on the flag halyard at the breakwater and, at the gun, they were off.[17] The *Gilbert B. Walters,* with Captain Angus Walters at the helm, was first across the starting line. Forty-five seconds later, Captain Tommy Himmelman of the *Delawana* was hot on his heels. The breeze blew straight down the harbour and all the boats carried every stitch of canvas aloft. The schooners made a glorious sight as they headed out on the course, most of them running down to the Inner Automatic Buoy with their sails wing and wing. The romance of the occasion was not lost on reporters. "It was a sight for angels and men the way those boats made the buoy, their great sails bellying in the wind and giving a spread of white over the blue waters wonderfully fine."[18]

The fleet was now making a steady nine and a half knots out of the harbour. Even the venerable old committee boat, *Tyrian*, failed to keep up and steadily lost ground to the schooners. The *Walters* passed the first mark leading, with the *Delawana* close on her tail, followed by a progression of boats tight on her stern. Himmelman was pushing Walters hard, but lost ground passing the second mark, the Outer Automatic Buoy. On a beam reach to the Sambro Lightship Buoy, the boats increased speed to more than ten knots. Six of the fleet passed the third mark within seven minutes of each other. "The craft had all sail set and looked like great white and black birds in an elongated flock of life and action," stated the evening paper.[19]

But it was the *Delawana* and the *Walters*, "with spray flying in splendid sheen from the bows of each of the swiftly moving craft," that provided the real race.[20] Himmelman steadily gained on his rival, cutting the lead to one minute, forty seconds by the third mark. They now faced a windward beat down the harbour and headed towards the fourth mark with a wind blowing at twenty knots. It was hard to tell from the committee boat which was in the lead, but the *Walters* had the windward advantage. She was barely holding her own, however, as both vessels matched tack for tack up the harbour on the six-mile run to the finish. Eight minutes after passing the final buoy, the fore-topmast on the *Walters* snapped and came crashing down. Confusion on deck, as the crew sorted out the mess, meant even more time was lost. After over four hours of hard sailing, Tommy Himmelman passed his rival at Marr's Rock and proceeded to gain on every tack, crossing the finish line four minutes, twenty-seven seconds ahead. Whether the *Walters* would have beaten the *Delawana* with her fore-topmast undamaged is open to speculation, but Captain Walters showed nothing but high regard for the winning skipper and offered his hearty congratulations.

When the fleet returned to the harbour, the noise of the crowd, whistles, horns and sirens was deafening. The city went wild with delight and jubilation. The event had lived up to its promise, and Haligonians had every reason to be proud. A large banquet held at the Carleton Hotel in honour of the participants was attended by the lieutenant-governor, the city's mayor and many other local dignitaries. The idea of an international race was raised again and received with much enthusiasm, but with a winning schooner and crew ready to compete, a race committee already in place and the courses laid out, the obvious question was: why wait a year? William Dennis proposed holding the international series immediately and sent off a

challenge to the fishing fleet of Gloucester, offering as prize the "Halifax Herald North Atlantic Fishermen's International Trophy."

A sad end to the festivities occurred when the youngest skipper in the racing fleet drowned as his boat, the *Ruby Pentz,* left harbour the next day. Captain Calvin Lohnes was knocked overboard by the main boom and died before he could be rescued.

The good citizens of Gloucester, Massachusetts, opened their newspapers on October 13, 1920, to find a challenge from the Nova Scotia Ocean Racing Committee awaiting them:

> Committee in charge of ocean race met tonight and carefully considered all details of proposed race between a Nova Scotia fishing vessel and an American vessel. It was decided to hold the race over 40 mile course off Halifax not later than three weeks hence for a suitable silver trophy and a prize of $5,000, $4,000 to the winner and $1,000 to the loser, under the following conditions:
>
> 1. Vessel must be bonafide fisherman with at least one year's experience on the banks.
> 2. Vessels to carry inside ballast only.
> 3. Sails used in race to be made of commercial duck and be of no greater area than those in ordinary use on banks and to be limited to mainsail, foresail, jumbo, jib, jib topsail, and fore and main working gaff topsails and fisherman staysails.
> 4. Crew to be limited to 25 men.
> 5. Skipper to be bonafide fisherman captain with at least one year's experience on the banks.
> 6. Vessels to be not more than 150 feet overall.
> 7. Notification of acceptance of this challenge must be received within one week from receipt of these conditions.
> 8. Race to be sailed boat for boat without time allowances.
> 9. The decisions of the sailing committee on which you will have representation to be regarded as final in the interpretation of the above conditions.
>
> Please let us have definite answer by wire if you mean business and representatives of our committee will leave for Gloucester at once to arrange final details.[21]

‹ **THE AMERICANS** were caught unprepared by the challenge to participate in the proposed International Fishermen's Cup race, to be held in Halifax in the fall of 1920. They had few boats in port from which to choose and no time for an elimination race as most of their fishing fleet was still at sea. The schooner *Esperanto* was hurriedly made ready for the race and the legendary Gloucester skipper Marty Welsh was chosen to command her. *Wallace MacAskill, Nova Scotia Archives and Records Management*

This news was met with delight by the fishermen of the port of Gloucester, followed by lively debate as skippers and crews argued over which boats were the most likely candidates to represent their town. Even before the proposal was brought officially to the Board of Trade for discussion, a consensus among fishermen had it that schooners such as the *Stiletto,* the *Joffre,* the *Catherine Burke,* the *Esperanto* or the *Marechal Foche* could easily win against anything that Lunenburg could produce.[22] The Gloucester skippers wanted all the particulars so that the details could be worked out quickly. National pride was at stake! No red-blooded Yankee could turn down such a challenge. Nova Scotia and Massachusetts had long shared fishing grounds, mingling and jostling on the banks like jealous brothers at sea. Ironically, countless captains and crews of the American boats were former Maritimers or their relations who had headed south across the border in search of better pay or the exciting city life found in Boston and New York.

However, the challenge also represented for Gloucester a problem that lay in the nature of the year-round fishery. Most of the boats the town had in mind were either at sea or otherwise unavailable, and captains and crews were too occupied in making a living to take time out for racing. As they had not kept abreast of events in Canada, they were unprepared for the challenge. Although there were a few possible contenders available, there was too little time to organize an elimination race. With only days to spare, the fishing firm Gorton-Pew offered as challenger its schooner *Esperanto,* which had just arrived back in port. For captain they recruited the highly respected veteran Marty Welsh. The *Gloucester Daily Times* wired the *Halifax Herald* that the challenge had been accepted, and the *Herald* immediately answered that representatives were on their way to work out the details.

"A RACE FOR REAL SAILORS," declared the Halifax press. "Nova Scotia's Great Epic of the Sea."[23] This series promised the excitement and drama that the America's Cup race lacked; it would be a true ocean classic. No careful measurement of hulls or exhaustive comparisons with tape and rule. This would be a real race with no frills, no handicaps and no nonsense, a straight boat-for-boat affair with no favours given. It would be a true working man's race, sailed in the rough waters off Chebucto Head. The International Fishermen's Cup race, it was hoped, would easily eclipse the America's Cup in popularity. Gloucester's only addition to the rules was that instead of a single race, there should be a best-of-three series in order that the American crew, who were not as familiar with the waters off Halifax, should not be at a disadvantage.

Some Gloucestermen figured the odds were against them already, since the Nova Scotian boat was chosen, tested and in racing trim. Most, however, were decidedly optimistic about the odds and figured that, with any significant wind at all, their boat would be a runaway winner. When the *Esperanto* was hauled out of the water to have her propeller and shaft removed, she was soon beleaguered by a mob of curious Gloucester townsfolk, eager to inspect the challenger. A large gang of riggers, painters, caulkers, carpenters and sailmakers descended upon her to work late into the night, bringing her up to fighting trim in the short time left. It is doubtful whether any vessel in the port, before or since, has been given as exhaustive and thorough an overhaul in such a short time as was the *Esperanto*.

Although he had never before stepped aboard this schooner, the choice of Marty Welsh as skipper was met with universal approval along the waterfront. He was highly regarded as a fisherman and sail carrier who had worked in the industry since boyhood. There was no lack of talent from which to pick his crew. Eager captains and experienced fishermen all lined up to sign on in anticipation of a chance for glory. Comparing the experience and knowledge of the crews from both sides, the *Gloucester Daily Times* concluded that, though the Gloucestermen had a reputation along the coast for taking greater chances, "if the skipper of the Nova Scotian is the same Himmelman about whom they used to tell the story of knocking off the revenue cutter's figurehead with his main boom, the race is likely to be a lively one."[24]

The *Esperanto* came off the ways after her refit looking like a new boat. "Her spars and rigging and new paint glistened like a pot of gold in the early morning sun... One could hardly realize that she was the same *Esperanto* which came in less than two weeks ago after a long summer's hand lining trip to the Grand Banks."[25] On October 25, she slipped her moorings and headed out of the harbour to the roar of the thousands who had lined the docks. She was off to Halifax to win—or blow her sticks out in the attempt!

In Halifax, one would have been hard pressed to find anyone who did not have some opinion on the upcoming race. The newspapers were full of the progress of the Gloucester challenger, with articles covering everything from the refitting of the vessel to vignettes of the captain and crew. Journalists from all the over the east coast arrived to cover the race, and tourists packed the hotels. The *Boston*

Post alone sent one photographer and three reporters in an attempt to get as much coverage as possible. The young George Holland would write from the deck of the *Delawana;* James Brendan Connolly, the famous American writer of sea stories, was to be aboard the *Esperanto,* and James T. Kinsella, who was one of the best "waterfront" men in Boston, would follow the race from the committee boat. Frank Palmer Sibley, star reporter from the *Boston Globe,* arrived during the week to add his perspective, also from the deck of the American boat.

The *Delawana* departed from Lunenburg on Thursday with great fanfare, escorted by the *Gilbert B. Walters.* Like the *Esperanto,* the *Delawana* had had no end of willing hands to sand, paint and tidy her up. Even a prominent local clergyman was noticed wielding a paintbrush.[26] The small army of outfitters that boarded the vessel left nothing to chance. Everything that could be overhauled was stripped down and reassembled. A new topmast was stepped into place, the sails carefully mended, the topsides painted with a fresh coat of black and the underbody with a rich green, a broad three-inch white stripe indicating the waterline. Thus transformed from a traditional black-and-red fisherman to a snappy-looking racer, she sailed off to Halifax on Thursday morning anxious to meet her rival.[27]

When a grey dawn broke on the following Saturday, October 30, 1920, heavy cloud was hanging over the harbour. The wind that had raged all night had exhausted itself into a mere breath, and the *Delawana* and *Esperanto* lay quietly side by side at the Mitchell and Campbell wharves. The Union Jack and Old Glory hanging from their masts fluttered lazily in the zephyrs that floated down from the citadel. By seven, the boats were alive with activity as their crews readied them for the day. By the time the *Esperanto* was towed out into the stream, the first puffs of wind were ruffling the surface. The large crowd of Lunenburgers took this as a cue to begin chanting *"Delawana! Delawana!"* The two contenders, now out in the harbour, quickly hoisted sail in the growing wind and gracefully dipped their hulls into the swells.[28] The dozens of spectators who were dockside in the early hours had steadily grown in number, and the crowd now covered the breakwater and Point Pleasant Park so thickly that its presence actually changed the dark silhouette of the shoreline.

As the nine o'clock start approached, the light southwesterly breeze began to freshen, and the race committee raised the signal for course number 4.[29] The *Delawana* was leading slightly and leaning well over in the breeze, her captain working for the favourable windward berth. Marty Welsh calmly sucked on his pipe, watching the Lunenburger tacking and filling across the harbour, carefully observing local conditions before making his move. At the gun, the sun broke through the clouds and the sails of the two schooners glowed a brilliant white against the blue wavelets sparkling across the water. Forty seconds later, the *Delawana* surged across the line with *Esperanto* twenty-five seconds behind. As the boats shrank into the distance towards the first mark, the American was gaining.

Marty Welsh wrapped himself around the wheel of the *Esperanto* and did not relinquish it for a moment during the entire race. With his crew lying low along the windward rail and the lee scuppers awash, he caught the *Delawana* off the first mark. The men on the Canadian boat saw a fleeting glimpse of the gilt lettering on the stern of their rival when they rounded the Inner Automatic Buoy. Heading for the second mark, the Yankee was well away and sailing faster. " 'Don't let her beat us, Captain Tommy,' pleaded one of his men, appeal in heart and eyes."[30] The Nova Scotian crew was still hopeful they would catch her on the windward leg but began to fear the worst as the distance between the two vessels increased. If the lads on the *Esperanto*, tucked under the rail and hugging the deck, were feeling pleased with themselves, they did not show it—they still had a long way to go.

By the time the boats reached the open sea and the Outer Automatic Buoy, the wind had picked up to twenty knots. It was a long way short of the gale everyone hoped for, but at least it had some snap to it. On board the *Esperanto*, steadily gaining on the run down to the third mark off Shut In Island, "the white stuff was whish-shing past our quarter and more white stuff coming in fine waterfalls over our lee bow."[31] Although the crew of the *Delawana* admitted they might have met their match in the *Esperanto* in the off-wind work, they still had hopes that their boat would prove her worth during the windward leg.

Optimism returned to the crew of the Lunenburger as they watched the American boat falter around the third buoy. The wind shifted briefly while they were settling into the windward work. The *Delawana*'s gains on her run for the buoy were short-lived, for the *Esperanto* shook off her sluggishness and began to work to windward again. During that long, close-hauled leg, the Yankee did the most damage to the Nova Scotian boat, masterfully riding through the white-topped swells on her way to the last mark while the *Delawana* appeared to slam heavily and hesitate. "When Captain Himmelman went below for chow at noon he predicted the race's finish. She's way to windward. We'll not be coming on her no more today."[32]

Just after three o'clock, the *Esperanto* crossed the finish line to a huge roar from the crowd along the shoreline. It seemed all work in the city had ceased that day and the whole population had turned out to witness the spectacle. Throughout the race, the crew had been holding its collective breath until the last inshore buoy was cleared. At last the men were able to rise up and give the boat and skipper a fine cheer. She had beaten her rival on every point of sail.[33] The *Delawana* crossed the finish eighteen minutes later. As they came into the harbour there were filled eyes among the disappointed crew when they, too, received the cheers of thousands. "Passing the first dock Mate Roger Conrad leapt atop of a dory yelling, all together boys, three cheers for the *Esperanto* and remember Monday's another day!"[34]

› **THE LUNENBURG** schooner *Delawana,* under the command of Captain Tommy Himmelman, won the right to sail against the Americans in 1920 after winning a hard-fought contest in the first Nova Scotia Fishermen's Regatta. She only barely bested another Lunenburger, the *Gilbert B. Walters,* skippered by Angus Walters, after the *Walters* lost her foretopmast during the last leg of the race. *Wallace MacAskill, Nova Scotia Archives and Records Management*

After being beaten so decisively in Saturday's race, Himmelman decided to lighten the *Delawana* and replace the stone ballast with iron. As Sunday was a legal day of rest in Nova Scotia and no work was allowed, this had to be done surreptitiously. The captain had the boat towed out beyond Georges Island, where he and the crew discreetly set about the arduous task of removing the weight from inside her hull. One hundred and thirty tons of good Lunenburg stone was heaved, a bucket at a time, over the side. At four in the morning, the *Delawana* was hauled up to the dockyard, where sixty tons of chain was manhandled into her. On her return to Mitchell's wharf, her trim was further refined by adding more iron and bags of salt, bringing her slightly down at the head. The work finished just in time to hoist sail and make ready for the race. A decidedly lighter, better-trimmed *Delawana*—with an exhausted crew—was now ready to take on her rival.

The morning was foggy and grey, with a light westerly breeze. Despite the poor visibility, spectators were filling the vantage points along the shore. However, the lack of wind quickly raised doubt as to whether there would be a race at all. As the schooners slowly made their way to the start, the crew of the *Esperanto* commented on the increase in the green-painted underbody showing on the *Delawana*'s hull. "Sixty tons they say they have taken out her? Seems more like a hundred," Marty Welsh was heard to say. "Let this wind stay light and she'll worry us," reported writer Jimmy Connolly.[35] The wind was just tickling the surface of the harbour, barely creating a ripple, but blowing enough to give the craft headway as they closed in on the start. When the gun fired, Welsh got the jump on the Lunenburger, but only by a little over a minute.

Neither boat was making much headway, but the *Delawana* was footing faster. Eager to avenge her loss, the Canadian boat slowly and relentlessly closed on the

DELAWAN

Yankee's quarter as they headed off on the same course as in the previous race. In a mere three minutes, the *Delawana* had overlapped her opponent, and in five she was well past and making better headway. There was no doubt that removing the ballast had improved her performance. When they came out from under the land and into a fresher breeze, both boats picked up the pace. As Himmelman rounded the first mark, his lead had improved by almost five minutes and, at the second mark, on a flat sea and in steady rain, she was one mile ahead. Desperate for wind and in true fisherman fashion, the men on the *Esperanto* appealed to the wind god by whistling loudly and tossing out coins.[36] Nerves were on edge as they watched their opponent increasing her lead.

On the third leg, the *Delawana* lost ground. Heavy mist had obscured the turning buoy off Shut In Island and, even with a lookout posted aloft in the spreaders, she overshot her mark by a good two miles, astonishing both the crew of the *Esperanto* and those on the committee boat. The *Esperanto*'s sailors could not believe their luck. By the time the Canadian finally found her bearings and made for the buoy, the American had gained and was closing on the leader. After rounding the mark, both skippers held well away to leeward of the next mark, fearing that the wind would come up from the west again and head them up. Well off the course, the vessels sailed towards the north shore. Three times the *Esperanto* attempted to come up the *Delawana*'s windward side, but Himmelman luffed and held her off. Since he did not have the speed to cross her bow, Welsh tried a different tactic and attempted to sail through her lee.

Coming up fast was a rocky shoal sticking out from Devil's Island. The *Esperanto,* on the *Delawana*'s lee, was pinched between her opponent—who was still playing the luffing game—and the breaking surf. Welsh could call for the right-of-way, as vessels cannot be forced ashore, but he chose to say nothing and hold his course. Presently his vessel was only two boat lengths off the beach, close enough to make the lightkeepers on the island light their lens to warn him off.[37] The *Delawana*'s continuing effort to crowd the *Esperanto* made the Halifax pilot aboard her nervous enough to warn Captain Welsh of the danger. Welsh nodded to signify he had heard the warning but continued on his course. He was now in so close that falling off would mean fetching up on the beach. Drawing a foot less than her opponent, the *Delawana* kept pushing her towards the shoaling water. "Captain, you have now less than a foot of water under your keel," said the pilot, and from aloft, Mikey Hall, the masthead man, yelled down that he could see the kelp on the bottom. Welsh looked at Russell Smith, whose father was part owner of Gorton-Pew, and said, "You represent the owners, Russell." To which Smith's response was blunt: "To hell with the owners." Welsh stuck to his course.[38]

Himmelman was also in a bind. If he held on too long, both ships were in danger of running aground, but if he came about, he would lose the coveted weather berth and possibly the race to his rival. Ultimately, he had no choice but to swing his vessel to port, allowing his opponent sea room. Both ships turned so tightly that the main boom on the *Esperanto* hung over the stern quarter of her rival.

With wind freshening, both vessels sheeted hard, running side by side for the next three miles to the last mark. When they rounded the Inner Automatic Buoy, they were so close that while the peak of the leader's gaff was flying the American flag, the bowsprit of the Canadian was over the stern of *Esperanto*. Both crews seemed to work in tandem, trimming sheets and beating it, tack for tack, in the driving rain up the harbour, but the *Esperanto* held the advantage in the windward work, and in six short miles she had gained so much on her rival that she finished seven minutes ahead. Whereas the first race had been a rather easy victory, this race had had it all: drama, brinkmanship, a crucial error and excellent seamanship. It was as fine a race as anyone could ask for and a fitting end to the series.

The following day a luncheon held at the Halifax Hotel to present the cup and to honour the contestants was attended by dignitaries such as the mayor of Halifax, the lieutenant-governor, the premier of Nova Scotia and a representative of the governor of Massachusetts. Grand speeches were made extolling the fine nature of the contest and the sportsmanship shown by both sides. Lavish praise was heaped on the winning skipper, Captain Marty Welsh, who sat through the occasion with his face flushed, embarrassed by all the attention. The general manager of Gorton-Pew Fisheries, Mr. Carroll, who accepted the cup on behalf of the owners of the *Esperanto,* spoke enthusiastically of her captain: "No better man ever sailed out of any harbour in the world. No better man ever walked the deck of a vessel or the streets of a city." Welsh was then called upon to respond. The highly skilled mariner, able to face any manner of danger at sea, was clearly out of his element. "He gurgled in his throat in the effort to speak, but couldn't make it. So he just bobbed his head a couple of times, grinned amiably and sat down again and the guests nearly took the roof off at his eloquence."[39]

A giant siren that had been set up outside the *Times* office in Gloucester was cranked up at the news of the triumph. Soon every bell and whistle in the town was pealing out in "the greatest conglomeration of noise since the armistice was signed."[40] Schoolchildren just dismissed from classes were dancing in the street, and staid old fishermen were shouting and laughing with delight.[41] When the *Esperanto* arrived back several days later, a victory broom tied to her masthead, she was greeted like a conquering hero. A huge banquet was held in the drill hall of the State Armoury where, once again, the reluctant man of the hour, Marty Welsh, blushed brilliantly with every compliment bestowed upon him. The American vice-president-elect, Calvin Coolidge, saw the bravery and courage of the crew as a "Triumph of Americanism... Your wonderful victory shows to all the world what Massachusetts stands for and what America is bound to accomplish."[42] The victory was hailed by every newspaper across the United States. The *New York Tribune,* at the end of a long editorial, nominated the win as "the supreme sporting event of 1920."[43] In Nova Scotia, however, the mood was quite the opposite. Devastated by the unexpected defeat, plans were already underway to make certain America would not keep the cup for long.

NOTES

1 *Boston Sunday Globe,* July 25, 1920
2 *Toronto Telegram,* July 25, 1920
3 Ibid.
4 Ibid.
5 *Boston Globe,* July 25, 1920
6 *Toronto Telegram,* July 25, 1920
7 *New York Globe,* July 25, 1920
8 *Montreal Daily Star,* August 11, 1920; *Halifax Herald,* August 11, 1920
9 *Canadian Fisherman,* September 1920, p. 195
10 *Toronto Telegram,* October 2, 1920
11 *Canadian Fisherman,* September 1920, p. 190
12 *Evening Mail,* October 5, 1920
13 Ibid.
14 See course maps, pp. 230–31
15 *Evening Mail,* October 11, 1920
16 Ibid.
17 See course maps, pp. 230–31
18 *Evening Mail,* October 12, 1920
19 Ibid.
20 Ibid.
21 *Gloucester Daily Times,* October 13, 1920
22 *Gloucester Daily Times,* October 14, 1920
23 *Evening Mail,* October 19, 1920
24 *Gloucester Daily Times,* October 19, 1920
25 *Gloucester Daily Times,* October 23, 1920
26 *Halifax Herald,* October 26, 1920
27 *Evening Mail,* October 26, 1920
28 *Evening Mail,* October 30, 1920
29 See course maps, pp. 230–31
30 George Holland, *Boston Post,* November 1, 1920
31 James B. Connolly, *Boston Post, Evening Mail,* November 1, 1920
32 Holland, *Boston Post, Evening Mail,* November 1, 1920
33 Connolly, *Boston Post, Evening Mail,* November 1, 1920
34 Holland, *Boston Post, Evening Mail,* November 1, 1920
35 Connolly, *Boston Post, Evening Mail,* November 2, 1920
36 Frank P. Sibley, *Boston Globe,* November 2, 1920
37 Ibid.
38 Connolly, *Boston Post,* November 2, 1920
39 Sibley, *Boston Globe,* November 3, 1920
40 *Gloucester Daily Times,* November 1, 1920
41 *Gloucester Daily Times,* November 2, 1920
42 *Gloucester Daily Times,* November 9, 1920
43 *Canadian Fisherman,* November 1920

‹ **CAPTAIN ANGUS WALTERS** takes time out between races in the 1923 series to instruct his sons on the finer points of steering the *Bluenose*. *Leslie Jones, Boston Public Library*

5

THE LUNENBURG FLYER: 1921

NOVA SCOTIANS were left shocked and humbled by the defeat of their beloved *Delawana*. To have their boat so soundly beaten, and the new trophy whisked out of their arms with such apparent ease, had been unthinkable. Race enthusiasts did not take long to figure out that the boats in the large Lunenburg fleet were too heavily modelled to be real competition for the Americans. Nova Scotian craft were designed for packing large quantities of cargo rather than for fast sailing. In summer these boats were out for months at a time salt fishing, and in the winter they carried dried fish or lumber south to the West Indies and South America, bringing salt back to Canada on the return trip. A schooner that could pay its way with large cargoes usually had only moderate sailing

UENOSE

qualities. The type of craft preferred in Gloucester, by contrast, was generally smaller and quicker than the Nova Scotians', with less cargo capacity and an ability to engage in the quick turnaround of the fresh-fish industry, so vital to the economy of the eastern U.S. fishery. Speed was essential to the Americans, and the Nova Scotians realized they needed a finer hull design to compete.

It is said that within ten minutes of the *Esperanto* crossing the finishing line, funds were committed to the building of a worthy contender for the next series.[1] A group of like-minded Nova Scotians, drawing on the affectionate nickname for the people of their province, formed the Bluenose Schooner Company to fund the building of the new boat and invited Captain Angus Walters, the feisty Lunenburg skipper of the *Gilbert B. Walters*, to sign on as her master. A young naval architect named William Roué was approached and asked to design a schooner that would outsail any fisherman afloat. Roué was familiar with the races, as he had sat on the sailing committee of the first series, but he was more of a hobbyist than a full-fledged designer, his primary income coming from his family's soft-drink business. Despite his lack of experience as a naval architect, he had successfully designed a small number of yachts and working boats; he realized that taking on something as large as a banks schooner would be an opportunity to make his name, so he threw himself into it heart and soul. By December 1920 he had presented his plans to Walters and the company and won their approval—scarcely dreaming of the impact his schooner design would have on the outcome of the races of the coming years, nor of the resulting fame that would come his way.

‹ **THOUSANDS** crowded the Lunenburg shore around the Smith and Rhuland shipyard in March 1921 to witness the launching of the schooner *Bluenose*. Built to beat the Americans in the Fishermen's Cup races, she proved to be not only fast under her wily skipper, Angus Walters, but also one of the highline fishermen on the coast. *Wallace MacAskill, Nova Scotia Archives and Records Management*

The conclusion of the 1920 races had brought about several changes to the organization of the event. The first series had been thrown together quickly with little thought to the future interpretation of the dozen or so rules that dictated how the races would be run.[2] With the huge success of the event, and its continuation apparently assured, William Dennis and his committee set about drafting a proper deed of gift for the disposition of the trophy.[3] A testament to the importance of the International Fishermen's Cup is the list of trustees set down in the deed; they include the premier of Nova Scotia, the mayor of Halifax and the governor of Massachusetts.[4] The rules regarding the qualification of vessels were tightened, with the intention of keeping the competition fair, limiting the races to "bona fide" fishermen and keeping out "freak" vessel designs that could threaten the character of the series. Several of the changes had a significant impact on future races: the overall length of vessels was reduced from 150 to 145 feet (45.73

to 44.20 metres), the all-important maximum waterline length was set at 112 feet (34.15 metres) and the vessel draft limited to 16 feet (4.88 metres). The most technical change came with the measurement of the total sail area, which was to be no bigger than 80 per cent of the square of the waterline length as expressed in feet. Although this rule did not apply to vessels built prior to 1920, it affected all vessels built after that date and later led to a major disruption in the series.

In December the keel of the new Nova Scotian vessel was laid at the Smith and Rhuland shipyard in Lunenburg, and on the nineteenth of the month the governor general of Canada, the Duke of Devonshire, arrived from Ottawa to drive in the ceremonial spike. The solemnity of the occasion was somewhat diminished by the actions of some His Excellency's friends, who had absconded with him prior to the event and plied him with drink. When he was called upon to perform the deed, he found that his spirit was willing but his eyesight was not—he missed the spike with the first swing of the maul, much to the dismay and disapproving looks of the staid spectators in the crowd. After several more equally errant and dismal attempts, a kind soul rescued the heavy maul from his grasp and drove the spike home.[5]

Angus Walters fussed over his new boat through all stages of construction, like a worried mother over a newborn child. When the ribs of the 143-foot (43.6-metre) schooner began to take shape, Walters insisted on one controversial change: he required the freeboard in the bow to be raised by eighteen inches (forty-five centimetres) to provide more headroom in the fo'c'sle for the crew. This fuelled speculation later that the change greatly enhanced the boat's windward capabilities. However, it is unlikely that this modification significantly improved her sailing performance, though it did make the boat drier forward and the fo'c'sle more comfortable. On March 26, 1921, Audrey Smith, Walters's niece and the daughter of the shipbuilder, Richard Smith, christened the glistening black hull of the *Bluenose*. The people of Nova Scotia were known on the east coast as "Bluenosers," perhaps referring to the blue mittens worn at sea—often used to wipe runny noses—or perhaps to noses made blue by the frigid temperatures. In front of hundreds of onlookers, the vessel slid down the ways and into the placid waters of Lunenburg Harbour.

Angus Walters was not the only Nova Scotian captain caught up in racing fever. Captain Joe Conrad, a popular skipper from LaHave, postponed his retirement and engaged the seventy-one-year-old designer and builder Amos Pentz to draw up plans for another contender. On April 6, the powerful-looking, 138-foot (42-metre) hull of the *Canadia* slid down the ways of the old McGill shipyard in Shelburne. Admirers found her hull a little finer and a trifle racier than anything previously turned out by Pentz, and on her shakedown cruise she made a very fast run from LaHave to Halifax, proving she was a more than capable sailer. Word also came in from Newfoundland that at least one vessel would be ready from that colony for the elimination races in October. No matter where one went in fishing circles, the chief topic of conversation was fast fishing schooners.

In the United States, excitement was brewing over a new vessel under construction in the J.F. James and Son yard in Essex, Massachusetts. Work on this schooner, the *Mayflower,* had not begun until February 4, allowing little time for completion considering the necessity of putting in a full season of fishing to qualify for the races. She was backed by a group of disgruntled Boston businessmen who had felt more than a little put out that the 1920 series had been offered exclusively to the Gloucester fleet. "It seems that the Gloucester people have felt right all along that the international races were intended solely for Gloucester and Nova Scotia fishing vessels," said an editorial in the *Atlantic Fisherman.*[6] Fred Pigeon, who headed Schooner Mayflower Associates, hired the distinguished yacht designer Starling Burgess to draw up plans for a fast fishing schooner that was to be built with Boston money and crewed and captained by Boston men. Only modern methods were to be employed in her construction; she was to be engineered with mathematical precision instead of the rule-of-thumb shipyard techniques that were then the norm. Due to the tight time frame, a gang of Boston shipwrights was brought up to Essex to rush construction along, something that did not sit well with the local shipyard workers.

Grumbling about the Boston boat began from the outset, the main bone of contention being that the *Mayflower* was too "yacht-like." In fact, all the new vessels—the *Bluenose* and the *Canadia* included—were coming under fire for being "racers" and not true "banks" schooners, but it was the *Mayflower* that looked the most radical and bore the brunt of the criticism. The Cape Ann fishermen were the most vocal in their condemnation, due perhaps in part to what they perceived as the superior attitude of the Bostonians. The Gloucester fishermen had yet to decide which boat was to represent them in the upcoming races. A Boston magazine patronizingly admonished the old fishing community for not coming up with an entry. "Too bad Gloucester is not represented by a vessel of her own. Somehow the prospect of a fishermen's race without a Gloucester entry loses much of its charm."[7] That must have ratcheted up regional resentment by a few notches!

In lengthy editorials, the Boston papers attempted to deflect any criticism of what they considered their boat, but this proved to be an uphill battle. Much was made of the *Mayflower*'s "radical design," referring to her shorter, stubby transom, intended to reduce pounding in a seaway. A dolphin striker and upswept laminated spreaders added to her yacht-like appearance. In an attempt to silence opposition, the owners invited delegations of race trustees to visit Essex to view the launching. The Canadian delegation, arriving on a boat from Yarmouth on April 11, was met at the dock by Wilmot Reed, the secretary of the Gloucester committee. The *Mayflower* representatives arrived shortly afterwards, and the heated discussion between them and Reed ended with Reed left alone on the steamship wharf and the embarrassed Canadians, in the company of the Boston men, departing for their hotel.[8] Among the Canadian group was William Roué, the designer of the *Bluenose*, and he, along with the others, had ample time to examine the hull on the slipway before the launch. Eight thousand spectators were on hand the following day to watch the *Mayflower* be christened by the designer's daughter, Starling Burgess, and slide gracefully into the Essex River.[9] Unfortunately, the long-winded speeches had thrown off the schedule, and the falling tide had lowered the water level in the river enough for the vessel to become stuck on a mudbank half a mile away from the shipyard. As Dana Story, whose father owned the shipyard next door, suggested years later, "perhaps it was an omen of things to come."[10]

› **THE SCHOONER** *Mayflower* was built to take on the Canadians in 1921 but was barred from racing for being too yacht-like. Gloucester fishermen refused to sail against the Boston-owned boat in an elimination series to choose a defender and the Canadian trustees denied her bid to participate in the series. She carried a dolphin striker forward, laminated spreaders and a truncated stern that was not in keeping with the traditional design of the fishing schooner. *Edwin Levick, Mariners' Museum, Newport News, Virginia*

After inspecting the *Mayflower*, the Canadian delegation declared themselves satisfied that there was no material difference in the construction of this boat and that of any other American fishing schooner. They kept well clear of the conflict between Boston and Gloucester by saying her eligibility for the coming international race was up to the Americans, and thus in the hands of the race committee in Gloucester. The *Mayflower* was towed to the famous T-wharf in Boston, where a swarm of riggers worked furiously to step new masts and rig her for sea. The vessel had less than a month to be on her way to the banks to put in a full season fishing. A constant crowd of admirers looked on as work progressed, and the general opinion was that the fine, smooth hull looked every inch a match for anything on the sea. At 143 feet (43.6 metres), she equalled the new Canadian schooners, *Bluenose* and *Canadia*, in almost every respect, including sail area.

On April 28, two days before the deadline, her master, Henry Larkin, took his vessel out to sea, heading first to Shelburne, Nova Scotia, to pick up two crew members. Shortly after leaving Gloucester Harbour, he came across Felix Hogan, an old friend, in command of another recently built Essex schooner, the *L.A. Dunton*. Hogan suggested a race to Shelburne, and Larkin was more than eager to oblige. The two vessels set off in thick weather and lumpy seas but did not stay together for long. The *Mayflower* soon showed her heels to the *Dunton*, making her way alone in the heavy headwinds and lying snug in Shelburne Harbour a full seven hours before the *Dunton* arrived. The following day both vessels headed out together again, this time to Canso to take on ice. The Boston boat once more proved herself handy in a breeze and beat the *Dunton* by nine hours. Canso in Nova Scotia was the end of the race; the boats parted ways and the *Mayflower* went on to the Magdalen Islands for bait before sailing to the Grand Banks.[11]

Despite her time as a working boat, the controversy around the *Mayflower* would not go away. She was still thought to be a "schooner-yacht" and her efforts at the fishery were met with suspicion; she was accused of heading to the Grand Banks only to lounge around and catch a token amount of fish in order to comply with the rules. However, as the Canadian delegation had given her the thumbs-up, the American committee had little choice but to allow the schooner to participate in the upcoming elimination race to choose the official defender. Local resentment persisted, and the Gloucester masters and crews demonstrated their anger by vowing not to race the *Mayflower*. In their opinion, she was little more than a camouflaged yacht, and the competition between her and a bona fide schooner would not be fair. With no competitors, the race was cancelled and the *Mayflower* was declared the defender by default.

The trustees of the international trophy in Halifax had been happy to let Boston and Gloucester fight it out over the eligibility of the *Mayflower*, no doubt expecting that the Boston boat would eventually be disqualified. Now that she had been declared the defender, they were forced to face their own concerns about the vessel. Even though their delegation had given the *Mayflower* a clean bill of health, members of the fishing fraternity of Nova Scotia became more and more sceptical about her right to call herself a genuine schooner. As early as May, editorials in the *Halifax Herald* began to voice an opinion on the matter and questioned whether, by permitting the *Mayflower* to race, the series would deviate from its mandate as a venue for honest-to-goodness fishermen. In an attempt to shake off the growing criticism that his schooner was unable to withstand the rigours of winter fishing, Captain Larkin of the *Mayflower* threw out an open challenge to all other fishermen for an open-sea contest to be held at any time of the year. He specifically targeted Angus Walters, as his vessel was the biggest of the new Canadian schooners. Walters apparently agreed, but suggested a race "with a cargo of salt fish from Newfoundland to Brazil, thence to Turk's Island for a lading of salt to be carried to a port in Nova Scotia."[12] Neither skipper followed up on the other's offer. By mid-September, the decision had been made by the trustees to refuse the American entry on the grounds that her design was too yacht-like and extreme for a fisherman and her inclusion would violate the spirit of the deed of gift. Besides, they decided, she had taken too long to get to the banks to start fishing. Representatives of the *Mayflower* were dispatched to Halifax to plead her case, but to no avail. The American race committee, heavily weighted in Gloucester's favour, had plenty of chances to protest the Canadian decision but was only too happy to accept the judgement. It moved quickly to strip the *Mayflower* of her title of cup defender.

The Americans reorganized an elimination contest off Gloucester for mid-October. Five local schooners entered: the *Arthur James,* the *Elsie,* the *Philip P. Manta,* the *Elsie G. Silva* and the *Ralph Brown.* There was certainly no question that all of these schooners were "bona fide" fishermen; not one was less than five years old, and the oldest, the *Philip P. Manta* from Provincetown, had been built in 1902. Her good-natured captain, Ben Pine, had never skippered a fishing schooner before and had borrowed her for the races. He knew the elderly little schooner would not be a match for the others, but he was eager to participate. The clear favourite now was the little *Elsie,* whose masterful skipper, Marty Welsh, had commanded the *Esperanto* to victory the year before. Sadly, the *Esperanto* herself was missing from the contest. On May 30 she had hit a submerged wreck off Sable Island in heavy fog and sunk shortly after; the crew escaped in dories just before she went down. Ironically, the vessel that rescued them was none other than the *Elsie.* On October 12 and 14, she handily won both races in the elimination contest, fairly romping around the course and leaving her adversaries in her wake. The eleven-year-old veteran of the banks was formally declared the cup defender.

Enthusiasm for the international race may have dimmed somewhat in Boston with the exclusion of its vessel, but the people of Gloucester were over the moon about their entry. Boston papers initially groused about the unfairness of it all but

were soon caught up in the spirit and gave over the front page for coverage. Racing fever was definitely in the air. The only question remaining was which Canadian boat the *Elsie* would be facing. Eight schooners had entered to race in the elimination Nova Scotia Fishing Schooner Regatta: the *Uda R. Corkum*, the *Bluenose*, the *J. Duffy*, the *Donald J. Cook*, the *Independence*, the *Canadia*, the *Alcala* and the old favourite, the *Delawana*. All the boats were handy and fast, but the two new ones, *Bluenose* and *Canadia*, were considered the ones to watch. The *Canadia*, with her bottle-green hull, looked smart and capable, her clean, true lines inspiring as much confidence as did her master, Captain Conrad, the venerable old salt who had nearly six decades of schooner fishing behind him. The *Bluenose*, the other favourite, was sparred and rigged to a queen's taste. Everything about her was perfect, from the truck to the keel—"fit to be put on a mantle [sic]," as one wag declared.[13] She was not yet ready for Captain Walters, who, determined not to be defeated for a second time, took the vessel through a trimming spin and adjusted her ballast. Another vessel worth watching was Captain Albert Himmelman's *Independence*, sporting a new bowsprit that would definitely improve her windward work from the previous year's. Her informal sorties with the *Bluenose* outside the harbour had caused much excitement. And, of course, the *Delawana* was not to be discounted. Since 1920's races, she had acquired a much larger mainsail and a new thirty-foot (nine-metre) keel shoe that would help her keep a greater grip on the wind. As news broke from Gloucester of the *Elsie*'s win, anticipation intensified at the thought of another contest against Marty Welsh.

In the first race of the Canadian eliminations the *Bluenose* demonstrated her superiority, winning by four minutes ahead of her nearest rival, the *Canadia*. The second race was decidedly different. The *Delawana* put up a game fight and took an early lead, holding onto it during the runs and reaches. It must have given the backers of the new boats pause to see their vessels upstaged by the old-timer. Not until the windward thrash did the *Bluenose* wake up and take off like a scared dog to the finish, crossing the line fifteen minutes ahead of the fleet after four and a half hours of sailing. Her nose for weather showed her to be a true sea hound. Unfortunately, the *Canadia* made a poor showing. Her ballast had been badly distributed and she proved exceedingly tender in the choppy seas, disappointing both captain and crew. She followed her rival across the finish line forty-five minutes later. It was obvious that the design of the *Bluenose* gave her a distinct advantage over the others in the Lunenburg fleet. She seemed to come alive in the

‹ **IF CARRYING SAIL** alone could win a race, the *Elsie* would have prevailed in the 1921 series, but she needed more hull in the water, not more sail aloft. In a fruitless attempt to overhaul the *Bluenose*, her skipper had crowded on more sail than was prudent and, over-canvassed, she lost her fore-topmast in the heavy wind. Her bow plunging deeply, Welsh continues with the race as his crew fights to drag in the headsails. *Wallace MacAskill Collection, Nova Scotia Archives and Records Management*

windward work, especially in rough water and choppy seas. Gloucestermen had long held the view that, compared with their own sleeker, faster craft, the Nova Scotian boats were comfortable and stable sea-going arks: "Great vessels to pack a cargo of fish, ye know, but not much for travelling."[14] News of the *Bluenose* win made them sit up and take notice.

As the *Elsie* and her crew made their way up the coast to Halifax, grumbling began to surface from the New York papers about the differences between the two vessels. The complaints that had been made about the *Mayflower* now found their way to another target; the familiar charge was that the *Bluenose* had been specifically designed to win the race and the *Elsie* was built solely as a deep-sea fisherman. The *Bluenose* was much larger than the Gloucester boat, with a longer waterline and much more sail, and then there was the issue of the eleven-year age difference between the two. "It is a simple matter to argue from this that the *Bluenose* should be faster than the *Elsie*," said the *New York Herald*.[15]

Critics agreed that the real test would occur when the skills of Marty Welsh were pitted against those of Angus Walters. Welsh had a reputation as a remarkable sail handler in rough weather. In Halifax, speculation about the two vessels grew every day and, by the time the *Elsie* arrived on October 20, superlatives used to describe the features of the ship and the character of her captain were causing a good deal of nervousness in the Canadian camp. Rumour had it that the *Elsie* had topped the unlikely speed of seventeen knots during her voyage north. Reports of Welsh's crew's extraordinary ability to handle sail must have given the jitters to Walters. He recruited Commander Beard, the captain of the Canadian naval destroyer *Patriot*, to drill his crew in sail handling and tacking. Hours were spent in Bedford Basin in the early mornings before the race with Beard running the *Bluenose* crew through its paces.[16]

Walters had a formidable reputation himself. He had been only thirteen in 1895 when he had first gone fishing and was still in his early twenties when he became master of his first ship. He was known as a "driver," a no-nonsense, hard-nosed skipper with a flinty character and a caustic edge to his tongue. He was blessed with a remarkable ability to carry sail and a sixth sense when it came to fishing; his vessel was always amongst the top boats when the biggest catches of the season were reckoned.

The *Elsie*, designed by Thomas McManus, was built in Essex, Massachusetts, in 1910. She was a smart-looking vessel, lean and low in the sides, with black topsides, a red underbody and a broad green strip along her waterline. Her white hawse pipes made a distinctive feature at the forward end. In contrast, the *Bluenose* had longer overhangs, higher sides and a lengthier hull. Her black body carried a yellow moulding stripe with a white boot-top and a copper-brown underbelly. Once Welsh caught sight of the *Bluenose,* the size of the schooner, nearly twenty feet (six metres) longer than his own, must have given him pause for thought. However, the dimensions of the *Bluenose* were not unusual. Nova Scotian boats were generally larger than the Americans', and nearly a fifth of the Lunenburg fleet was of similar size. The two boats may not have been evenly matched as far as size went, but the Gloucester vessel had exceedingly sweet lines, and her sails fit like a glove. Neither captain nor crew of the *Elsie* voiced any objection to the *Bluenose.*

Saturday, October 22, 1921, was crisp and frosty, with a fresh breeze. It was the perfect day for a race, the northwest wind rising from twenty to thirty knots as the race progressed over the forty-mile course off Halifax. Everything that could float was on the water: Government steamers, cable ships, fishing boats, yachts, tugs and ferries—all loaded heavily with spectators—wallowed near the start. At the five-minute gun, both schooners swung into position, the *Elsie* easing her sheets and running the line towards McNab's Island, while all on board hoped for the seconds to pass quickly. The signal cannon from the breakwater sounded the start and Welsh cranked over the helm, shooting over the line ten seconds later. With the Stars and Stripes snapping at the main peak and a twenty-knot nor'westerly snorting over her starboard quarter, the *Elsie* flew down the course as if she had an engine in her. She was several boat lengths ahead of the *Bluenose* at the outset. Observers aboard the steamer *Lady Laurier* felt the Nova Scotian had been caught napping and began to experience that unpleasant "all gone" sensation.[17]

However, it was not long before the *Bluenose* perked up and fairly smoked after the *Elsie.* A luffing match on the broad reach for the first mark ended when the *Elsie* crossed over her opponent's bow and took the weather berth. Walters attempted to pass on her weather side, but Welsh sheeted in and stood up towards the unyielding granite rocks of the western shore, two miles to windward of the course. Walters put his wheel hard up and swung across the *Elsie*'s wake, making for the Inner Automatic Buoy. The *Elsie* followed suit and covered her rival. The two fairly flew across the water, all sails filled in the stiff quartering breeze and hulls rolling heavily in the deep chop. "The end of *Bluenose*'s 80-ft. boom was now in the water, now half way up to the masthead as she gained on her rival. The

› **LIKE A PROUD** parent, Angus Walters poses at the helm of his brand-new schooner in October 1921. The *Bluenose*'s main boom can be seen resting in its crutch, with the quarter tackles in place. No one could have predicted the impact of Walters and his boat on the Fishermen's Cup series over the next two decades. *Leslie Jones, Boston Public Library*

Elsie rolled still harder and three times brought her main boom across the *Bluenose*'s deck, between the fore and main rigging."[18] It was a constant battle for the weather berth, with members of both crews either handling lines or working aloft or hugging the windward rails. Anyone daring to raise his head above the weather rail on the *Bluenose* caught the edge of Walters's caustic tongue. The skippers strained at the wheels of their vessels, see-sawing back and forth in increasingly heavy seas. Walters finally gave up the fight for the windward berth and managed to shoot past the *Elsie* by coming up under her lee. By this time, both vessels were logging twelve to thirteen knots, the *Elsie* a mere minute and a half astern of the *Bluenose* as she rounded the Inner Automatic Buoy.

As they turned the mark, the wind piped up to twenty-five knots. It was a good fisherman's sea, with plenty of "lop" to it. The competitors eased off on their sheets for the run to the Outer Buoy, just over six miles away. Every kite was flying, booms were off to port and lee rails buried in the boisterous sea. The spray smoked off the crests at each plunge. It must have been a wild ride for the masthead men, whipped around the sky in that cool October wind. The *Elsie* stuck to the stern of her rival and hung on during the run to the second mark. At times, the *Bluenose* would haul ahead and then the *Elsie* would come up on her weather side, her main boom dipping over the stern of her rival. Back and forth they went. As they neared the mark, both doused their staysails and clewed up the fore-topsails, preparing to jibe around the buoy. The big Lunenburger rounded first, followed a mere thirty seconds later by the tough little Gloucesterman. "The great booms swung across the decks and fetched up on the patent gybers with staggering shocks as the crews roused the sheets in for the reach to Shut In Island bell buoy."[19] It was during this leg that the *Bluenose* began to run away from the defender, and she made the nine-mile reach in just forty-two minutes, taking the buoy two minutes ahead of her opponent.

Now began the real test: the thrash to windward. The ability to drag herself off a lee shore in a gale and claw her way to safety proves the real worth of any vessel. When the *Bluenose* rounded the mark and sheeted in hard on a starboard tack for the upwind trial, the wind was cresting at thirty knots. Her staysail and fore-topsail doused, and a roaring "bone in her teeth," the *Bluenose* began plunging into the heavy sea, burying her lee rail. The *Lady Laurier* observers could see her entire deck as she heeled to an angle of forty degrees. The boat appeared to revel in it, her long body punching through the heavy sea and her crew stuffed up under

the windward rail "like bats to a barn rafter," with Walters and his mate at the lee and weather sides of the wheel.[20]

As he passed the mark, Welsh threw his helm over and quickly hoisted his ballooner. The old *Elsie* rolled over onto the starboard tack with every sail aloft. Welsh could not have enjoyed seeing the big Lunenburger flying away from him and desperately raced after her. If carrying more sail alone could win a race, it would have been the *Elsie*'s.

In his article for *Yachting* magazine, F.W. Wallace wrote:

> Now there is this difference between a fisherman and a skilled yachtsman. The latter knows something about the science of spreading canvas and will forebear to drive his craft under a press of sail when she will make better sailing without too much muslin hung. Not so with the average fishing skipper. He is out to carry the whole patch and nothing gladdens his heart so much as to see his hooker lugging the whole load with her lee rail under and everything bar-taut and trembling under the strain. A roaring bow wave, a boiling wake, and an acre of white water to loo'ard looks good to him, and he often imagines this to be a sign that his vessel is smoking through it at a rate of knots.[21]

Perhaps these skippers lacked the refinement of the yachtsman, but they had far more experience and skill in handling their boats under these rugged conditions. The America's Cup contenders would most certainly have been hunkered down under the lee of Sandy Hook waiting for the weather to settle. This was not the environment for those fined-tuned yachts, but a real fishermen's race that James Connolly later called "the greatest race ever sailed over a measured course."[22]

The combination of wind and too much sail proved to be more than the *Elsie* could bear. First to go was her jib topsail halyard. As a crewman scampered out onto her bowsprit to re-reeve the halyard, the bow plunged deeply into the sea, burying the bowsprit to the third hank of her jib. Moments later, the foremast snapped off at the cap and both jib topsail and staysail came down in a mess of wire stays and rigging. Without missing a beat, the crew set about clearing up the wreckage. The mate and a couple of fishermen headed out on the bowsprit to cut away the jib topsail that was now dragging under the forefoot. "Down into the jumping sea went the bowsprit and the three sailors were plunged under five feet of water. They cut away the sail and brought it in with the crew behind them hauling it inboard thru the green-white smother."[23] Those aloft worked frantically to secure the topmast, assorted wires, blocks and halyards.

Within six minutes the *Elsie,* under forcefully shortened sail, appeared to be making better time than she had before. Angus Walters reacted in the spirit of sportsmanship by immediately dousing his own jib topsail and clewing up his main topsail. Marty Welsh stood inshore on a port tack and raised his main gaff topsail and, by so doing, could have risked losing his main topmast. Once again he was carrying more sail than his rival in the thirty-knot breeze. However, what he needed was more hull in the water, not more sail aloft. *Bluenose* streaked for home "like a kerosened cat through Hades," with her lee rail buried so deep that, according to the press on board the *Lady Laurier,* "we reckoned you could drown a man in her lee scuppers."[24]

After four and a half hours of hard sailing over a distance of about fifty miles, the *Bluenose* ploughed a furrow of white water across the finish. Walters and his crew became instant heroes, arriving home to a chorus of steam whistles and sirens. The valiant *Elsie* followed twelve and a half minutes later. The Gloucester crew was beaten but not defeated, and their captain remained steadfastly optimistic about their chances, saying, "The best boat won in the weather of the day, but there's another race and maybe two, acoming."[25] Russell Smith, the Gloucester observer on board the *Bluenose,* stated that "Captain Angus Walters sailed one of the finest races it has ever been my privilege to witness," but he added, "There are two handles on that old trophy—and you fellows have hold of one of them. It is not a case of perhaps there will be three races; there WILL be three races."[26] Captain Walters, when asked about the race, commented that "the man and boat that are out to beat Marty Welsh and the *Elsie* have no small job on their hands; they have a fine boat and a real racing skipper to go up against."[27] The city of Halifax was delirious with excitement.

The second race, on October 24, appeared to be more to the Americans' liking, with lighter winds over a smoother sea. The little *Elsie,* sporting new topmasts, streaked across the start at nine knots, a full minute and a half ahead of her challenger. *Bluenose* had loafed too far back and, as she moved lethargically to the start, one wag was heard to comment that "Angie must have stayed up late last night."[28] Observers became even less charitable when the Yankee banker began to widen the gap. Walters later rebuffed his critics: "It ain't who crosses the starting line first that counts. If we can cross the finish line first—that's the main thing."[29]

It was a grand, crisp, clear day for sailing, the ruffled blue water flecked with snappy white crests. The experts predicted the *Elsie* would show her stern to the Lunenburger in such weather and, at the start, it looked as if they were right. Both vessels' sails filled beautifully with eased sheets and booms over their port quarters, an absolute delight to the eye in the brilliance of the morning sun. The *Bluenose* finally found her stride and began, slowly, to foot on her rival, passing the Inner Automatic Buoy only forty seconds behind as they hauled up west-southwest and headed seaward to the Sambro Lightship Buoy, more than eleven miles away. Both vessels moved closer inshore under Chebucto Head, where the wind picked up under the land. The *Bluenose* appeared to surge ahead in the puffs until she was slapping the *Elsie*'s wake.

At this point, a familiar boat appeared from seaward. The *Mayflower*, under four lowers and in winter rig with no topmasts, was paralleling the course of the two racers. Bound for the banks with twenty dories nested on her deck and loaded down with ice and fishing gear, the Bostonian was in no trim to race but had come over to have a look at the contest. Her appearance caused a commotion among the journalists, who immediately began pumping out wild commentaries over the wireless. The Boston schooner kept to leeward of the racers and was really too far out to do any true pacing, but she did run with the committee boat for a time. She appeared to move quickly under her short rig, but was very wet forward. Most observers agreed she would have been a marvel in light winds and that the *Elsie* and the *Bluenose* were likely far better in rough seas.

Both racers jibed around the Sambro Buoy, where the wind was now blowing twenty knots, the *Bluenose* twenty-six seconds behind the *Elsie*. Walters kept tight onto Welsh's weather quarter, looking for a break on the nine-and-a-half-mile leg to the Outer Buoy. For twenty-seven miles the little Gloucester schooner had led the way and it was beginning to look as if she might come home the winner. The undaunted supporters of the Lunenburger, however, were waiting for the windward work to begin. When the vessels closed in on the Outer Automatic Buoy, Walters performed a masterful bit of helmsmanship and capitalized on the small opening between the *Elsie* and the buoy. He came up on her inside, leaving only a foot between his boat and the buoy, a feat that inspired a *Toronto Telegram* reporter to write that "the buoy (was shaved) so closely that, while it was properly cleared, it must have felt like shrieking for witch-hazel and talcum powder."[30]

‹ **HER CREW** clinging to the windward rail "like bats to a barn rafter," the *Bluenose* streaks to the finish and victory in the 1921 series. Her big, powerful hull, enormous sail area and tenacious skipper, Captain Angus Walters, proved too much for the little American schooner *Elsie* and her determined master, the defending cup-holder Captain Marty Welsh. *Wallace MacAskill, Nova Scotia Archives and Records Management*

The *Elsie*'s slim lead at the buoy gave her no chance to tack and cover her rival. Both vessels sheeted hard and boiled along, but it was the *Bluenose* that could point higher. "They were showing twelve knots and the big white bone which the *Bluenose* carried in her teeth suggested the old comparison of a big growling mastiff and a little fighting terrier."[31] Despite a valiant effort, it was all over for the *Elsie*. She could not sail as close to the wind, and there was no overcoming her rival's powerful hull. The *Bluenose* had the windward legs and walked away from her opponent. Bunting and flags flying from scupper to truck, the great Lunenburger entered the harbour a champion. "When they tied up to the dock, Angus Walters was, as someone graphically remarked, like a piece of chewed string after almost five and a half hours of constant strain and anxiety."[32] The International Fishermen's Cup race was over and the trophy was back in Canadian hands.

The 1921 series brought all the excitement and thrills expected of a working fishermen's race. In spite of the ensuing argument over the difference in size of the vessels, the public on both sides of the border thought they had received their money's worth. Although the series had been taken in only two races, there had been no shortage of anxiety and high drama, largely due to Welsh's superb seamanship. He had proved to be a tenacious sailor and a splendid tactician, who had pushed his boat to her limits. Had his vessel been on more even terms, the outcome might have been different. Walters was every bit his equal, and had more than demonstrated his ability to drive his boat hard, and his willingness to take chances when necessary. Perhaps the result was simply proof of the old adage: a good big boat will always beat a good small boat. The one certainty was that *Bluenose* would not remain unchallenged for long, and next year's contest was going to be in American waters.

NOTES

1 *Atlantic Fisherman,* May 1921, p. 15
2 See Appendix, (1), (2)
3 See Appendix, (1), (3)
4 The Halifax Herald North Atlantic Fishermen's International Trophy was also known as the Fisherman's Cup, Herald Cup, Denis Cup and the International Fishermen's Cup. I have chosen to limit the names to the International Fishermen's Cup and Herald cup or trophy to avoid confusion.
5 Backman, *Bluenose,* p. 36
6 *Atlantic Fisherman,* February 1921, p. 7
7 *Atlantic Fisherman,* April 1921, p. 3
8 Story, *Hail Columbia!,* p. 35
9 Miss Burgess was named Starling after her father, but would later assume the name Tasha Tudor and become famous as a writer and illustrator.
10 Ibid.
11 *Atlantic Fisherman,* May 1921, p. 2
12 *Canadian Fisherman,* June 1921, p. 130
13 *Evening Mail,* October 14, 1921
14 *Canadian Fisherman,* November 1921, p. 252
15 *New York Herald,* October 20, 1921
16 *Canadian Fisherman,* November 1921, p. 257
17 Ibid., p. 253
18 Snider, *Rudder,* December 1921, p. 4
19 *Canadian Fisherman,* November 1921, p. 253
20 Wallace, *Yachting,* November 1921, p. 215
21 Ibid.
22 James Connolly, *Evening Mail,* October 24, 1921
23 Ibid.
24 *Canadian Fisherman,* November 1921, p. 254
25 Wallace, *Yachting,* November 1921, p. 215
26 *Evening Mail,* October 24, 1921
27 Ibid.
28 *Canadian Fisherman,* November 1921, p. 254
29 Wallace, *Yachting,* November 1921, p. 255
30 Snider, *Rudder,* December 1921, p. 44
31 Connolly, *Evening Mail,* October 25, 1921
32 *Canadian Fisherman,* November 1921, p. 256

1
7

‹ **RUNNING NECK** and neck on a starboard tack, the *Henry Ford* and the *Bluenose* compete in the first official race of the 1922 series. The previous day, a race won by the *Henry Ford* had been declared unofficial by the race committee as both boats had crossed the starting line early. The skippers had decided to race anyway. *Wallace MacAskill Collection, Nova Scotia Archives and Records Management*

6

TURMOIL IN GLOUCESTER: 1922

THE 1921 SERIES and the triumph of the *Bluenose* left the Americans with the realization that this was no longer an event for "off the shelf" boats. The *Bluenose* had been built well within the specifications of the deed of gift, but her design was not that of the "comfortable sea-going ark" that Gloucester fishermen associated with the Nova Scotian fleet. Her size was a problem for the Americans, not because she was a "freak," since the Lunenburg boats were generally larger than those of the Americans, but she was faster than the general run of Lunenburg vessels and so a much more challenging competitor. There was no question that she could fish and carry "highliner" loads of over 225 tons of salt cod, but her hull was finer than the average boat and everyone knew she had been built to beat the Yankee challenge.

As the defeat of the *Delawana* had spurred the Nova Scotians to develop the *Bluenose,* so the *Elsie*'s loss gave the Americans reason to do the same. If they were going to be able to compete effectively, they were going to have to build a fast schooner of comparable size. Shortly after the end of the 1921 series, a group of Gloucestermen met over dinner at the Halifax Hotel to discuss the situation. There was much more than just civic pride at stake; winning the race had become an issue of international honour. Captain Jeff Thomas, his brother Bill, Ben Pine and several others from the Gloucester business community agreed they would build their own boat to be ready for competition the following year. Pine, who was still soaking in the exhilaration of crewing on the *Elsie* under Marty Welsh, was especially eager to take part. A critical look at the fleet in Gloucester had left the group convinced they had nothing that could come close to challenging the black-hulled beauty from Lunenburg. The organization called itself the Manta Club after the little schooner Pine had skippered the previous year. No one could question the pedigree of the backers of the new boat, all of whom were closely associated with the fishing industry and with Gloucester.

Only three days after the *Elsie*'s defeat, the club announced that a new challenger, to be named the *Puritan,* would be built in Essex.[1] Curiously, the club hired Starling Burgess, who had designed the *Mayflower,* to draw up a hull. His new design proved to be quite similar to that of the Boston boat but smaller, with a longer, traditional, overhanging transom and none of the *Mayflower*'s "yachty" features.

Great efforts were made from the outset to assure all parties that the vessel was to be a fisherman first, putting to rest any fears that she might be too refined. Apart from the need to abide by the deed of gift, the vessel had to be a money-maker, as none of the investors had cash to throw away. As further proof of their intentions, the Manta Club announced that her size would be smaller than that of the *Bluenose,* 137 feet (41.8 metres) in length and 105 feet (32 metres) on the waterline, since a larger boat would not be profitable in the fresh-fish trade. "If she shows us anything," said Captain Thomas, in his characteristically blunt style, "you will hear from us in the races next Fall; If she doesn't, well, you won't."[2]

Another Cape Ann skipper caught up in racing fever was Clayton Morrissey, known locally as Captain Clayte. He was a tall, lean, quiet-spoken family man with a solid reputation as a sail dragger and fisherman, and his schooner, the *Arethusa,* was one of the largest, fastest knockabouts in the fleet. George Hudson

‹ **SHORTLY AFTER** launching in 1922, the *Henry Ford* fell victim to a series of unfortunate incidents. First she became stuck in marsh weed after she slid down the way and then, as she was being towed from Essex to Gloucester for fitting out, she came up hard on a bar at the mouth of the Essex River. Unbelievably, she was left unattended until morning by the tug crew and, during the night, floated off on a tide, fetching up on Coffin's Beach, perilously close to some rocky outcroppings. Fortunately, she suffered only minor damage and was floated off four days later. *Peabody Essex Museum*

of the *Boston Herald* remarked on Morrissey's skillful handling of sail: "He hangs the duds aloft until it pipes and pipes, but lowers away and furls in the nick of time and fools the gale. Morrissey is quite clever that way."[3] However, the *Arethusa* was getting on in years, and Morrissey found himself itching for a newer, faster boat that might be able to meet the *Bluenose* challenge. His quiet ways and habitual stammer disguised a forceful, determined and short-tempered personality. He sold the *Arethusa* to Captain Bill McCoy, who changed her name to the *Tomaka* and put her to use "bottle fishing," the term given to rum-running in the early days of Prohibition. Morrissey and his wife, Bessie, joined forces with three of Gloucester's exclusive Eastern Point residents, Jonathan Raymond, F. Wilder Pollard and Frank C. Pearce, along with the boat builder Arthur D. Story, who often took a financial interest in the vessels he was constructing when he found a skipper to his liking. Morrissey then hired the venerable old boat designer Thomas McManus to draw up plans. McManus had been the obvious choice for Morrissey because, apart from being the grand old man of fishing-schooner design, he had also been the designer of the *Arethusa*. At sixty-six, he had produced more than four hundred often-copied designs, and he was already working on a plan when Morrissey called. The defeat of the *Elsie*, which had been one of his personal favourites, plus a detailed description of the *Bluenose* from Marty Welsh, had driven him to the drafting table. He quickly turned out plan number 419 for Morrissey's approval.[4]

By April, two new challengers sat on the ways in Essex—the *Henry Ford* at the A.D. Story yard and the *Puritan* at the J.F. James and Son yard. There was so much interest and speculation about both vessels that the town of Essex became a favourite destination for touring "automobilists" and sightseers. Both hulls had very similar dimensions, though Morrissey's boat was a little fuller and longer on the waterline.

The *Puritan* was launched first, on March 15, before a crowd of two thousand, and christened with champagne by Ray Adams, a young female friend of Ben Pine's. A month later, after being rigged and fitted for sea, the *Puritan* was turned over to her captain, Jeff Thomas. She left Gloucester under the tow of a converted submarine chaser—accompanied by cheers, whistles and cannon fire—on her maiden trip "halibutting" to the banks. Her sails began to feel the press of wind as she left the outer harbour and she quickly overhauled her tow, which was going a steady eleven knots. It was an auspicious beginning to a sea-going career and left the residents of Gloucester with little doubt that she could be counted on to recover the honour they believed to be theirs.

On her return in early May, loaded with halibut, Captain Thomas fairly bubbled over with enthusiasm for his new vessel, calling her "fast on every point without playing any tricks."[5] By all accounts she was the fastest vessel yet to come off the ways at Essex, a reputation enhanced by an impromptu matchup with the *Mayflower*, which she met off Cape Cod on her maiden voyage. She left the Boston boat trailing in her wake. By June 17, Thomas had made two successful fishing trips, and he headed out on a third, to Sable Bank. After stopping at Booth Bay to pick up ice and bait, he took the *Puritan* east on a fateful trip to Sable Island, the notorious mistress of sunken ships, with her treacherous coastline of shifting sands. Thick fog and strong southerly winds accompanied them as they worked their way through the heavy swells for the banks at the north end of the island. The boat was going at twelve knots and carrying a full kit of sail when she hit a bar. She had been making such good speed that she had overrun her dead-reckoning position by a good twenty miles. The impact was so hard that it broke her back and ripped free a lengthy section of keel. Sea water quickly poured in and breakers crashed over the bulwarks as the crew worked frantically to launch the dories. The first dory off capsized, and the three men aboard were tossed into the sea. Two were dragged back, but the third, Christopher Johnson, was lost. Seven men pulled for shore in the pounding surf, while the other fifteen rowed offshore, where they were eventually picked up by a passing schooner.[6] Nine days after the trip had begun, and barely three months after her launching, a short telegram arrived in Gloucester announcing the loss of the *Puritan*: "Struck Northwest Bar, Sable Island, about 7:30 p.m., 23rd."[7] Although all but one member of the crew were still alive, the hopes of the *Puritan*'s backers were not.

Hit hard by the disaster, Ben Pine and his associates nonetheless hardly skipped a beat. So keen was their interest in participating in the international races, they immediately looked for an alternative vessel. Pine went into partnership with Marion Cooney, a sail maker, and chartered the 138-foot (43-metre) knockabout schooner the *Elizabeth Howard,* another fast McManus boat belonging to William Howard of New York. She was quickly fitted out and sailed to the banks in order to qualify for the fall elimination races. The Howard had reputedly made sixteen knots under sail and had even been offered up to the *Mayflower* owners as a trial horse to race against their boat the previous year.[8]

› **THE TALL** and lanky figure of Captain Clayton Morrissey confers with the designer Thomas McManus on board the schooner *Henry Ford.* The pair's fiery protestations concerning the treatment of their vessel by the race committee led to heated discussions that almost ended the 1922 series. McManus was considered to be the grandfather of fishing-schooner design and produced more than 450 often-copied designs during his long and prolific career. *Rosenfeld Collection, Mystic Seaport Museum Inc.*

The public was still keenly interested in the new designs and, after the loss of the *Puritan,* pinned its hopes on the *Henry Ford,* launched a month later on April 11. As they had for her rival, people turned out in droves to see the launching of the *Ford.* With a gold stripe along her black hull, carvings on her stem and transom and new bunting fluttering in the northeast breeze, she was christened by Clayton Morrissey's fourteen-year-old daughter, Winnie. The schooner had been named by Morrissey's wife, who held the automobile maker Henry Ford in such high regard that she insisted on naming the vessel in his honour. Once off her blocks, the *Ford* slid into the Essex River so quickly that she had to be hauled off the marsh weeds on the opposite side. This was not the only setback that day. After two tugs had taken her in tow for the trip downriver, she went aground for a second time on the bar at the river mouth. Unbelievably, the tugs failed to stand by their charge and abandoned her until the following morning. At midnight, the *Ford* came off the bar with the tide and floated onto the sandy shore, coming precariously close to the rocky ledges at Coffin's Beach, where she was in imminent danger of breaking up. It took four days of continuous work, with pontoons and tugs, to get her off the beach. Fortunately, fears that the damage would leave her severely warped or hogged proved unfounded. Apart from a strained rudder stock, several broken planks and chunks missing from her shoe, she seemed to have suffered little from the grounding. The repairs and fitting-out caused unavoidable delays and, as the race rules stipulated the vessel must be on her way to the banks by April 30, a dispensation was requested by Morrissey from the trustees. Luckily, they agreed. It took until June 2 to ready her for sea.

With the *Puritan* gone, the *Ford* might have been considered the only contender now in the running. However, the backers of the *Mayflower* renewed their efforts for recognition, certain their schooner could not be barred from competition a second time. She had put in another full season on the banks, carrying respectable loads to market and as well proving herself capable of surviving extreme weather conditions, riding out gales on the banks when others were dismasted or damaged. As far as the *Mayflower* group was concerned, she had paid her dues and demonstrated beyond a shadow of a doubt that she was, in fact, a bona fide fisherman. They applied to the American race committee for qualification and, in August, the *Mayflower* and the *Henry Ford,* the *Elizabeth Howard* and two Boston boats, the *L.A. Dunton* and the *Yankee,* were accepted

for the elimination races that were due to begin on October 12. The inclusion of the *Mayflower* set off another storm of protest concerning her eligibility, but she now had many supporters, as well as detractors, both in the United States and in Canada. Ultimately, it was up to the trustees in Halifax to determine her fate, and although they initially appeared unimpressed by arguments in her favour, they chose to forestall making a decision until September.

Newspapers editorials on each side of the border argued for and against. In contrast to the previous year, in Gloucester a "no *Mayflower*—no race" sentiment was beginning to take hold. The *Mayflower* group, supported by the American race committee, sent representatives, including the boat's designer, Starling Burgess, to plead their case with the trustees in Halifax, but they could see no reason to alter their decision, as there had been no structural changes made to the boat. The decision made the previous year had been based on the argument that the *Mayflower* was too radical and yacht-like in design and the capacity of her hold far too small for her size. As far as they were concerned, therefore, the fact that she had put in a full season on the banks was irrelevant, and there was no basis upon which to alter her status. Angus Walters was disappointed with the decision and put it down to a lack of courage on the part of the trustees, later commenting that "the Committee was scared of us racing the *Mayflower,* though I would have been happy to do so. I had a good look at her on the marine railway once, and I knew then she'd be no trouble. I told them so, but they stuck to their guns."[9]

The American race committee was split on whether to abide by the decision or stand as one to continue the pressure to have it reversed. In a special meeting held at the Gloucester Chamber of Commerce, impassioned debate raged on for five hours. The argument was so intense that at times it could clearly be heard through the closed doors of the committee room by those awaiting the outcome in the hallway outside. After all argument had been exhausted, a compromise that would have allowed the *Mayflower* to race was reached, and a telegram was sent off to Halifax voicing opposition to the trustees' decision and suggesting instead "that the race for the Halifax Herald Cup be suspended for this year, pending a revision and amplication [sic] of the deed of gift, and that in its place, a free-for-all race be held, for a suitable cup and purse between the fastest vessels in the Canadian and American fishing fleets."[10] Knowing that feelings for a fishermen's race ran deep in Gloucester, the American committee was unwilling to give up the series entirely. When the trustees turned down this request, the committee felt it had no choice but to relent. The *Mayflower* group withdrew its entry, but issued a challenge to the winner of the Herald trophy for a separate and entirely independent event.

In Nova Scotia, four vessels entered elimination races, which began on October 7. The odds-on favourite, the *Bluenose,* had put in another successful season on the banks and, by all reports, was sailing better than ever now that Walters had become even more familiar with his charge. The *Canadia,* skippered by Captain Conrad, was also entered and expected to do much better this year as well. She had greatly improved her trim and had had her mainsail recut. Conrad welcomed a second chance at taking on Walters and the *Bluenose.* Two "dark horses" were also in the mix, the *Mahaska* and the *Margaret K. Smith.* There had been considerable interest in the *Mahaska.* Under her skipper, Captain Mack, she had proved herself to be a fast boat during the season, and some expected her to give the others a run for their money. Little was known about the *Smith*; as she had been launched only in August, she would in any case be ineligible for the international series should she win the trials.

The first race on Saturday was a near disaster for the champion. As it was later said, the *Bluenose* won in spite of those on board. Walters was left flat-footed at the start as the *Smith* grabbed the windward berth, shooting across the line ten seconds after the gun, followed closely by the *Canadia* and *Mahaska* less than a minute behind. Sitting off to leeward, Walters found himself caught in irons and could not bring his boat around. When her sails finally filled, she crossed the starting line a full five minutes late. The anxious crew of the defender were busy whistling for wind and making offerings over the side. "Save your wind for the sails," cut in Walters. "Out pipes and overboard with cigars and cigarettes, boys, till the race is over. Keep your heads down and hands ready."[11] The *Bluenose* finally came alive when the breeze freshened on the first leg, and she began to move up on her rivals. Twenty minutes after crossing the start, she was in second place, chasing the *Smith*'s tail. With winds picking up to eighteen knots, the *Bluenose* flew past the *Smith* and made for the Inner Automatic Buoy. She thundered by the mark, leaving it on her starboard side, with the *Smith* close in on her wake.

Jerry Snider, the reporter for the *Toronto Telegram,* was on board to cover the event; he had been reading the race program when they passed the buoy, and "what struck [his] eye like a blast of cinders" was that they had taken the buoy on the wrong side.[12] He broke the news to Walters, who, as he had seen Captain Whynacht on the *Smith* do the same, took some convincing. But the print was plain. Although

the sailing committee had clearly indicated course number 2, nobody on the two leading boats had taken the time at the start to read the program properly and both were headed off in the wrong direction. When Walters realized his mistake, he wasted no time in roaring out orders to come about, lubricating the commands with seasoned curses and sending "thirty oil-skinned figures jump[ing] like scalded cats to various stations."[13] The *Smith* countered quickly and came about for the right side of the buoy before the *Bluenose*. The *Canadia* was now in the lead with *Mahaska* in her wake and, once again, it was a stern chase for the *Bluenose*. "Spit on your hands and never say die, boys," called out an undeterred Walters. "It was my mistake; I got us into this hole, but maybe the *Bluenose* will get us out."[14] Although the *Canadia* was a mile ahead, the *Bluenose*'s persistent forging up to weather paid off. "By speed superiority alone she ate and ate and ate down the long gap that separated her from the LaHave vessel," as Snider described it. Those on board the committee boat could see that when the two leaders reached the Sambro Buoy, the *Bluenose* was going to take it.

‹ **TAKEN FROM** the main cabin roof, this photograph shows the *Bluenose* punching through a heavy sea as she shoulders a comber on her port rail. The *Bluenose* stood up better to the weather than the *Henry Ford* in the 1922 series and barely wet her decks. *Author's collection*

Conrad's *Canadia* fought a good race but in the end was no match for the Lunenburg flyer. The fact that the *Bluenose* could recover from not one but two blunders—at the start and at the buoy—and still make up so much time was a testament to the Roué hull and the skills of the skipper. *Bluenose* was declared the defender after the two follow-up events were abandoned due to insufficient winds. She headed for Gloucester on October 12.

"Damn a light sail! Give me four lowers and wind enough to bury her rail—and that's what I call a racing combination," was all Captain Morrissey could say of the light winds in Gloucester's first elimination race on Thursday, October 12. Even so, the light sail was too much for Ben Pine on the *Elizabeth Howard*. He surprised the fleet and crossed first at the gun, but ten minutes later lost his topmast when the crosstree cracked at his main top. Always game, he continued for an hour, but the unfortunate *Howard* was clearly out of the contest. In spite of a listless race and a bad start, the day belonged to Morrissey and the *Henry Ford*. With the neck of his blue sweater rolled up under his chin and a cigar stub clamped firmly in the corner of his mouth, Morrissey drove his vessel around the course, taking the race by nearly eighteen minutes. Before the race he had expressed some apprehension about the *Yankee* from Boston, but she and the *Dunton* finished well behind. Ed Millet, the *Halifax Herald* correspondent aboard the *Ford*, enthusiastically described the vessel to his readers: "The wake is barely perceptible. She leaves no dead water behind her, and throws but little on her decks. She is very quick in stays and her best point is heading into it."[15] Her captain was far less impressed by the *Ford*'s performance, finding her sluggish and unresponsive during the contest. He spent the next day with Tom McManus correcting her ballast, while Pine repaired his masthead trestle. On Saturday, the *Ford* seemed to sail much better and proved her superiority on just about every point of sail. Pine on the *Howard* gave Morrissey a race but came in second by over five minutes, with the *Yankee* following ten minutes later and the *Dunton* a further half hour behind. The *Henry Ford* had clearly won the honour of challenging the *Bluenose*.

While the citizens of Gloucester slept, the *Bluenose* stole into the harbour unannounced in the early hours of Saturday morning, October 14, 1922. She had left Halifax under the tow of the HMCS *Patriot*, travelling through rough and foggy weather. Their tether soon parted in the boisterous seas and both vessels went their separate ways. News of the *Bluenose*'s arrival in Gloucester spread quickly, when dawn revealed her anchored near Ten Pound Island. As she made her way from her anchorage to the Gloucester Gas Company wharf, she was soon surrounded by a small flotilla of sailing craft. Alerted by the shrieking of sirens and whistles from the boats and factories, crowds began to stream towards the waterfront for a glimpse of the now-famous schooner and, by Sunday, Gloucester had taken on a decidedly holiday spirit. "All that was lacking was the street peddler with his balloons and popcorn to make the carnival scene complete," said the reporter for the *Herald*.[16] American dignitaries such as Governor Channing Cox of Massachusetts, Secretary of State Frederic W. Cook, Senator Henry Cabot Lodge and Secretary of the Navy Edwin Denby were scheduled to arrive, along with an official delegation from Canada, including Lieutenant-Governor MacCallum Grant of Nova Scotia and the province's premier, G.H. Murray. Hotel accommodation became a scarce commodity in the old fishing port. A grand Fishermen's Ball, set for Friday night, drew over fifteen hundred people.

On the day of his arrival, Walters and some Gloucester friends took the opportunity to view the final elimination race from a high knoll on the Magnolia shore. As he was standing there, taking in every detail, a surprise delegation from the *Mayflower* group, headed by Fred Pigeon and Captain Henry Larkin, descended on Walters and attempted to negotiate a race with the *Bluenose*, in the event of her winning the Herald cup. Unwilling to make any commitment, the always cagey Walters suggested they take up the matter with the American race committee. As a result of this discussion, a meeting held later that night between members of the committee and representatives of both vessels resulted in an agreement with Walters that he would race the *Mayflower*, provided the same offer be made to the *Henry Ford*. The date set for the race was two days after the international race was completed.

The following days were filled with last-minute fittings-out and trial spins around the course. One of the first orders of business was the official measuring of both vessels. George Owens, professor of marine technology at the Massachusetts Institute of Technology, had been invited to be the official measurer, but, as he was unable to attend, Evers Burtner, his young assistant, took his place. Burtner was the official measurer for the Yacht Racing Union of Massachusetts and had plenty of experience with yachts, though none with fishing schooners. He was instructed to measure each vessel's waterline and calculate the allowable sail area stipulated by the Eighty Per Cent Rule in the 1921 deed of gift. On Thursday the *Bluenose* went under the tape and was found to be in compliance, as she carried 228 square feet (21.2 square metres) of sail under her allowable limit. The following day the thunderbolt struck when Burtner, in the company of the race officials, measured the *Ford* and found that her sail area exceeded the limit by 490 square feet (45.5 square metres). Burtner proceeded to mark the boom where the excess sail needed to be cut.[17] Morrissey was astounded. His suit of sails had served him well on the banks and he could see no reason to change them now. Tom McManus, the designer, was livid. He had not been allowed to view the measuring and insisted she was in compliance. However, the officials were not to be argued with and at 7 PM that evening, less than twenty-four hours before the first race, Morrissey was forced to cut his sail. "They may cut us all to pieces," he defiantly declared, "but we'll race her anyhow, under bare poles if necessary."[18] Throughout the night, a gang worked on the sails in the United Sail Loft under Morrissey's supervision, liberally assisted by bootlegged refreshment. Two twenty-inch (fifty-centimetre) cloths were removed from the leech of the mainsail and a similar amount from the fore gaff topsail. They finished the job at 8 AM, leaving the crew with barely enough time to bend on the mainsail for the ten o'clock start. Tempers aboard the American boat had begun to smoulder.

In light airs, on October 21, the two competitors were ready to face off near the start of the race at the entrance to Gloucester Harbour. The sailing committee aboard the USS *Paulding* decided the winds were inadequate and postponed the race, hauling up the appropriate signals. The two skippers, however, felt differently. Angus hailed his rival, "What say Clayte, Let's have a race. I'm going to race if I have to sail alone."[19] That was all the challenge it took and, as with any impromptu hookup at sea, the two skippers were off. The sailing committee's attempts to recall the vessels met with failure. After more signalling, a motor launch was sent to stop them, but by the time it caught up, the racers had covered a mile and a half. As no race officials were on board the launch, and both skippers were more interested in racing than in following yachting rules, the recall was ignored. The committee finally gave up trying to stop them, hauled anchor and gave chase in order to mark the times at the turns, giving every indication that the race was now sanctioned. The committee was privately hoping the winds would peter out completely, leaving the competitors unable to finish. To the thousands ashore and in the spectator fleet, it certainly looked as if the race was on. The *Ford* favoured light winds and gained an early and commanding lead, holding onto it for the duration. She crossed the finish a mile and half ahead of the *Bluenose*. All the anger over the sail slashing vanished with the victory, and the town of Gloucester went wild with jubilation.

› **THE DIMINUTIVE** Angus Walters is almost dwarfed by the Halifax Herald North Atlantic Fishermen's International Trophy. His victory over the Americans in 1921 quickly made him a household name in Canada, and his antagonistic manner fuelled the fierce and sometimes bitter rivalry between the Lunenburg and Gloucester fishermen. *Wallace MacAskill Collection, Nova Scotia Archives and Records Management*

That night, the sailing committee dropped a bombshell just after the schooners had tied up, declaring "no official race on account of both of the contestants having made false starts," as it was reported by Leonard Fowle.[20] To make matters worse, the official measurer, Evers Burtner, unaware of the uproar his actions would cause and the criticism that would follow him for the rest of his days, dropped another bomb by stating the cutting of the *Ford*'s mainsail had not been done correctly, and she was still not in compliance: another 53 square feet (4.9 square metres) would have to come off. It was obvious to the incensed fishermen that yachting attitudes were beginning to dominate what had been a working man's affair. There was little reaction from the skippers, and what they did say was short and to the point: from Morrissey, "I'm going fishing Monday," and from Walters, "It was a race and the best boat won."[21] He told the race committee to "tally one up for Clayte, he won it—give it to him."[22] Morrissey appealed and the committee went into closed session to review the ruling. His was a difficult position; he was loath to recut his mainsail, his crew was on the point of revolt, but he also wanted to be ready to race again. Feeling there was no recourse open to him, he sent off the sail to be recut.

Speculation ran rampant through the town, and a crowd gathered round the chamber offices all through Sunday while the committee members discussed the issue of the validity of the race. At 1:30 AM on Monday the decision was announced: the ruling would stand. The race on Saturday was unofficial and would therefore not count.

Morrissey's crew's response was out-and-out mutiny. They marched through the streets, shouting that they were through with racing and race committees. They were "good and mad" at having their sails slashed, and they were not going to have any more of it. They were not going to race—and Captain Morrissey was not forcing them. As far as they and many Gloucestermen were concerned, the series had been taken over by yachtsmen, who were instituting yachting rules and regulations. But at eight in the morning, when they headed to the *Ford* to clear out their gear, they were met by Mrs. Jack Raymond (the wife of one of the owners) and Edwin Denby, the secretary of the navy. The feisty lady sailor begged, cajoled and pleaded with the crew to stay the course, "for the glory of Gloucester and in the spirit of sportsmanship." Her pleas fell on deaf ears. The boys would have none of it, so Denby stepped in and appealed to their patriotism, giving them a rousing speech about how the *Ford* represented the United States and it was their duty to man her for the race. Knowing most of the crew originally hailed from Nova Scotia, he pleaded, "Never let it be said the men of Clark's Harbour, the Pubnico's [sic] and Barrington, helped trail Old Glory in the dust."[23] The crew remained unmoved until finally swayed by Morrissey's deep, gruff voice: "Come on boys, let's pick up the sail and bend her on."[24] If Captain Clayte was willing, then they were, too. All but four jumped to it and went aboard. The dissenters were quickly replaced by eager fishermen from the crowd of bystanders that had been watching events unfold. Half an hour later, the *Ford* slipped into the stream and headed out to race.

The first "official" race began in light winds, once again to the *Ford*'s liking. It was an electrifying start as the *Ford* shot across the *Bluenose*'s wake and the two boats crossed the line as one. The *Ford* nosed up alongside her rival, squeaking between her and the committee boat, the USS *Paulding,* and almost scraping the destroyer's stern. Cheers broke out on the deck of the *Paulding* as the *Ford* took the *Bluenose*'s wind and shot into the lead. At the first mark, the *Ford* led by forty seconds, and she continued to gain steadily, proving once more her superiority in lighter winds. By the fourth mark, she had a lead of over four minutes. Then the wind picked up to almost fifteen knots and both close-hauled boats began to smash through the seas, boiling down to the line with their lee rails buried for the first time that day. The Lunenburger finally began to stretch her legs on her best point of sail and moved up on the *Ford,* but it proved to be too late. After forty miles and five hours of sailing, the best Walters could do was close the gap and cross the finish two and a half minutes after his rival.

The *Bluenose* had sailed the race under protest, as she had a splintered keel. During the night, she had settled on a rock at low tide while alongside the gas company's wharf, and when the crew had swept the hull with a rope in the morning they had come up with a four-foot (1.3-metre) splinter of wood. Whether or not this affected the schooner's performance is open to speculation, but in Walters's mind, it had. He complained that his boat had felt sluggish. "When the wind was light today," he told the *Telegram* reporter, "she went so dead that she disgusted me... she sailed worse on the starboard tack than on the port one."[25] The protest flag had flown from her port rigging from the start, but, by that time, the committee was so fed up with complaints it had told Walters to go on with the race and disallowed the protest.

The American boat again headed into Gloucester victorious, but Morrissey had had enough. As far as he was concerned, he had won two races, the first of which even his adversary had conceded was his, and he was not prepared to compete again the following day. He began to ready the *Ford* to go fishing, loading ten tons of ballast rock on board. At this point, it seemed the whole event was beginning to unravel. Tempers began to boil over on the streets of Gloucester, and the banquet held that night at the armoury to honour the crews was boycotted by many. Dignitaries tried their best to reignite the patriotic fervour of the *Ford*'s crew, but Morrissey's men stood firm. They would not race again. Ben Pine was approached to see if he would skipper the *Elizabeth Howard* in the event the *Ford*'s crew remained intransigent. Angus Walters was nonplussed by the attitude of his opponent and expressed his intention to be there, waiting at the start and ready to sail the course—alone if need be.

In a secret session held in the basement of the armoury, the race committee debated whether or not the Herald cup could be awarded to the *Ford* on the strength of her two wins. One member on the American side forcefully declared that "we would be yellow curs if we, as a majority, voted to take the cup. We want to win it fairly and squarely. Let's race for it as we should."[26] In the end it was decided that rules must be obeyed and the first race disallowed. All the debate and acrimony drove the correspondent for the Halifax papers to write:

Since arrival here we have been given few thrills on the water, but ashore all has been impossibility and chaos. The flock of rumours has been bewildering. Somehow or other, this has not struck me as sport. During the past couple of days I have begun to feel more like a war correspondent than a peaceful newspaperman of a peaceful country.[27]

Alarmed by the turn of events and the possibility of the situation developing into an international incident, Jack Raymond, one of the owners of the *Ford*, took matters into his own hands. He invited Captain Morrissey and his crew for a quiet dinner at the Ramparts, his summer home on Eastern Point. As requested, two dozen fishermen arrived at his doorstep to partake of a rather hastily prepared meal cooked by Raymond's mother and sister (the staff had all been dismissed in preparation for shutting the house up for the winter). After the dinner—and a liberal libation of Prohibition whiskey—Raymond took the crew into his drawing room for a fireside chat. What was said there was never fully revealed, but in essence, the crew was told that far more was at stake than they could realize. There had been a great deal of money bet on the races, upwards of $100,000—and, unpatriotically, not all of it wagered on the hometown boat. Whatever the case, Raymond won them over, and the crew voted to continue with the series. All they would afterwards admit about the evening was that "everything had been explained to us at dinner. Now we're going out to fight and win!"[28]

On Tuesday, the ships sat idle while a thirty-five-knot gale howled outside the harbour. Captain Morrissey fell ill and the committee granted the *Ford* a postponement, leaving the *Bluenose* crew grumbling and chafing for a race. This was the kind of weather they had been looking for, and the idea of sitting it out was frustrating and disappointing. Walters's attempt to take advantage of the postponement by having the hull checked was also thwarted, as another schooner was occupying the marine railway all day. Now it was the Canadian's turn to lose patience and he lashed out at the opposition, saying, "I knew it would blow hard today. I told you so last night. How did I know? My barometer told me. Clayte has a barometer too," implying that the Gloucester fisherman was afraid to race in such weather.[29] Nothing could have been farther from the truth. Not only was Morrissey laid up with a painful hernia, but his son was dying. He had been implored by his grief-stricken wife not to continue with the series. Morrissey had lost his appetite to race and desperately wanted to have done with it.

‹ **"ATA BOY,** Henry, go it old socks, she's a hound, I tell you, she's a hound," the ecstatic crewmen of the *Henry Ford* reportedly cried as they casually leaned against the windward rail during the 1922 series. With her lee rail buried so deep that half her main deck was submerged, the schooner laboured heavily under a tremendous press of wind. The strain and drag proved too much, and shortly after this photograph was taken, the fore-topmast let go. *Rosenfeld Collection, Mystic Seaport Museum Inc.*

Early Wednesday morning, with a wind piping up outside the harbour, the *Ford*'s men were back on board removing the stone ballast to bring her back to racing trim. When they raised the foresail, they found the bolt rope on the leech of the sail slashed in three places, in what appeared to be a deliberate attempt at sabotage. Morrissey made light of it and had the damage quickly repaired. His wife, Bessie, and her sister boarded the vessel and, in the most dramatic scene yet, pleaded with him to give up the whole affair and come home. "Come ashore, Clayton; let some one [else] sail her. You're sick, I'm sick and my boy is sick to the point of death; let's get rid of this miserable business."[30] She cried out to the crew:

> "Boys, I appeal to you as sons and husbands, don't go out. Think of my boy dying at death's door... Think of your own mothers and your own wives. Why should you go out at the point of your lives for the pleasure and profit of a lot of miserable millionaires who have money up on this race? You've won two races already. Why should you risk your lives to win a third? Angus Walters says he is willing to call both races you won yours and let the contest go at that."[31]

As she was a principal shareholder in the vessel, Morrissey told his crew, it was only fair to listen to her, and he offered to go over and talk to Walters himself. He arrived at the *Bluenose* to find the Nova Scotians all smiles at the prospect of a heavy-weather sail. The crew poured down into the cabin to hear what was being said, but Walters ordered them back on deck. Initially, Angus seemed to be willing to oblige Clayton: "We're good friends, Clayte," said Captain Walters, "but there's a lot around here trying to make us bad friends. If you lay to the wharf I'm willing to lay to the wharf and if you go out I'll go out," reported Jerry Snider, who witnessed the meeting.[32] After five more minutes of talking, they decided to "cut the knot by racing." Morrissey arrived back at his boat and, speaking to his anxious wife, told her, "Be a good girl and go home now. I must go, they've got me." With tears in his eyes, he ordered his crew to cast off.[33]

The HMCS *Patriot,* having taken over the role of committee boat, stood by with its four-inch gun at the ready to start the race. The twenty-five-knot wind that had been raging all morning had diminished to half that by the time the two competitors moved into position. In a start very similar to that of Monday's race, both vessels hit the line almost simultaneously, but this time with the *Bluenose* in a slight lead. She had outmanoeuvred the *Ford* by coming up to windward at the last moment and blanketing the American. So close did they come together that a crew member could have leapt from one vessel to the other, but no foul was declared. Tension on board the competing boats rose sharply as caustic slurs began to erupt from both sides. "There was a tremendous broadside of language from both ships and it must be confessed that while the Nova Scotians vocabulary is extensive, Gloucester plumbs the depths and scales the heights of expression which Canada cannot attempt," wrote Jerry Snider on board the *Henry Ford*.[34] The *Bluenose* sailed easily to a boat length ahead, while Morrissey held off for a time to escape the blanket. After the great main boom of his rival cleared, he swung down hard on his wheel, crossing the Lunenburger's wake and coming up to windward like an express train. The first leg was a back-and-forth affair, with each boat taking a turn at the lead. When the first serious dips into the ocean swell began, it looked as though both vessels were in danger of losing their main tops. Neither crew had remembered to set backstays, and the slender spruce topmasts curled forward like whips against the sky. "So close were the schooners that the shouts of the men working on the backstay wires of the two seemed to come from one quarterdeck,"[35] wrote Snider.

Bluenose rounded the first mark in the lead by half a minute, and the race continued with both vessels in tandem, tack for tack. The second leg was a real luffing match, with Morrissey fighting for the weather berth and Walters trying to hold onto it. The vessels worked themselves far up to windward as they bore down on the second mark, when the *Ford* finally had a chance to move ahead, gaining her only advantage in the race. The *Bluenose* soon outfooted her and resumed the lead after passing the mark. On the fourth leg it was a close reach, with the wind blowing at over twenty-five knots. Both boats flew along at thirteen knots, the *Bluenose* appearing to stand up stiffer to the weather, and aside from the occasional spurt of water coming up through her scuppers, remaining dry. Captain Albert Himmelman, who was working as a crewman on the *Bluenose*, reputedly walked the deck all day without bothering with seaboots. Snider described how the *Ford*, on the other hand, staggered under the press of wind

> until the blue brine poured in solid torrents over her waist and quarter bulwarks and were heaved up in great deep swibs to the lee comings of her hatches nine feet inboard. The sheer poles of the *Ford* were nearly ten feet above the level of the deck and at times the lee ones were almost buried.

The crew of the *Ford* was ecstatic, crying out, "Ata boy, Henry, go it old socks, she's a hound, I tell you, she's a hound."[36]

The last five-mile leg was dead to wind, a "real muzzler," as the boats hauled almost due west. Both vessels sheeted hard and made for weather. Approaching the last turn, Albert Himmelman rushed to the stern and shouted back to the *Ford*, "If you gentlemen got anything further to say, say it now. From now on it'll cost you... postage."[37] Even Morrissey was struck by the *Bluenose*'s windward work. "She spins like a top and her crew do know how to handle her canvas. I don't mind saying that in a breeze of wind she is too much for us going to windward."[38]

› **PERCHED HIGH** above the deck, the "top men" of the schooner *Henry Ford* await the next tack before springing into action. These men often provided much entertainment to their adoring public. Observers watched with awe the daring acrobatics of the likes of Jack Sparrow and his rival aboard the *Bluenose*, Fred Rhodenhiser, who worked the upper sails as the schooners tore along, with the wind sometimes shrieking through the rigging and the slender topmasts bending like whips against the sky. *Cape Ann Historical Association*

It was an exciting thrash home against the darkening evening sky, with one last bit of high drama to cap it off. When the crew lowered the *Bluenose*'s fisherman's staysail for the next tack, one of the halyards caught crewman Ernie Hiltz around the ankle, snatching him from the deck and shooting him aloft. "While the sail thundered and flailed and threatened to beat him to bits, his shipmates swarmed up the rigging to cut him adrift. Others rushed to the waist ready to catch him should he be hurled clear."[39] After a five-minute battle to cut him free of the halyard, they got him into the crosstrees but in the process loosened the quadrilateral sail, which flogged and flailed itself into a dozen pieces before flying off to leeward. Hiltz survived the ordeal with a badly fractured leg.

Even this mishap failed to slow the *Bluenose* significantly, and she gained three minutes over her rival on the final leg. She crossed the finish seven minutes, twenty-three seconds ahead of the *Ford*, once again proving her mastery of heavy weather. With the series officially tied at a race apiece, the Lunenburg boat was still in the game.

The following morning, both captains had divers down to inspect their hulls before the next race. The atmosphere around the two boats had been poisoned with antipathy, rumour and paranoia. A member of the *Ford* crew had noticed an unfamiliar diver hanging around the wharf the day before, and someone else had reported that on the *Henry Ford* a plank had been fastened across the keel, the rudder damaged and the sails slashed. These stories proved to be groundless; all Morrissey discovered were some small pieces adrift on his keel, and he had a diver remove them. The problems with the steering gear needed only minor mechanical adjustment. The diver on the *Bluenose* found much more; the keel had been gouged and splintered severely, but not through sabotage. The damage had been done when the boat had sat on the rock at low tide. Walters called for an hour's

postponement while the diver pared down a 12-foot (3.6-metre) section of the shoe. By the time the two boats met off the breakwater for the eleven o'clock start, the wind was puffing up a fresh nor'westerly breeze. Morrissey was still feeling poorly and had brought Captain Al Malloch, one of Gloucester's great "drivers," aboard to help him out. Both the boats, under four lowers, killed time dodging around the HMCS *Patriot* before the start.

When the cannon fired, the wind had flopped to a mere twelve knots, catching the boats well behind the line. The start was a poor one; the boats crossed the line more than a minute behind the gun. The *Bluenose* took an early lead by several boat lengths, moving faster than her rival in the long ocean swells. The day seemed to be right for the Nova Scotians when the wind picked up to real fishermen's weather, at times topping thirty knots. "Captain Morrissey's *Ford* appeared in the puffs much the tenderer, heeling down until her lee rail was in the water. The *Bluenose,* standing up straight in the gusts, slowly drew away, all the way down the shore," wrote Leonard Fowle of the *Boston Globe.*[40] On the second leg the *Ford* fared better when the wind eased off to about ten knots and she chased down the *Bluenose.* From his position on the cabin roof, hunched over to ease the pain of his hernia, Morrissey kept an eye on his sails while Al Malloch handled the wheel. Just as the *Ford* was about to overhaul her rival, the wind picked up slightly and gave the Lunenburger a chance to escape. When Walters characteristically spat on his hands and gave his wheel a hard spin at the second mark, the *Ford* almost overhauled the *Bluenose* again. The Americans were not quite as efficient at shifting the staysail as were the Canadians, and "as the boats were only seconds apart, quick sail handling counted heavily and the *Bluenose* gained 20 yards."[41]

On the third leg, the *Ford* gripped onto the stern of the *Bluenose* as if attached by a tow line, never more than one hundred yards behind. When the wind rose again, however, the *Bluenose* took off. There was only a minute between them when they passed the next mark, but the Nova Scotian was back in her element. The *Ford* hung on, only a few hundred yards behind. "Both vessels were carrying too much sail, as the wind hardened again and they were smothered in the puffs; but neither skipper would start a halyard and both hung on to their kites and drove them while the steel rigging hummed."[42] At this point in the race, the crew of the *Ford* noticed a small split in the staysail and had to cast off the halyard to bring it in. They had barely smothered the billowing sail on the deck when, with a blistering crack, away went the top ten feet (three metres) of the fore topmast. The rigging held, but the broken mast carried off the fore gaff topsail and the ballooner. The crew worked like demons to clear away the mess and haul in the loosened sail. She seemed to sail better with her top-hamper gone, but was still well behind her opponent. Seeing the problems on board the *Ford,* Angus, in a show of sportsmanship, quickly hauled in matching sails, so both were now smoking along under the same set of canvas. Jerry Snider, on board the *Ford,* described the scene on deck as she bravely fought towards the finish.

> Driving her to the limit she was awash from for'ard of the fore rigging to the taffrail. When she dipped to the heaviest puffs she had a roaring millstream of water on her decks extending inboard ten feet from the scuppers. The upper deadeyes of her shrouds are away above a man's head as he stands on the deck. She was heeled until these were buried in the broken water of her track. The gangway between her cabin house and the lee rails is three or four feet wide and house and rail are each two feet or more above the quarterdeck. This gangway was filled to the brim with roaring water and it swirled up three feet or more past the lee side of the house, nothing could be seen on the lee rail except one little piece of the bow.[43]

The *Bluenose,* on the other hand, barely had her decks wet as she crossed the finish more than seven minutes ahead of the *Ford.* The *Boston Globe* reporter lamented: "Today's meeting proved conclusively that the *Henry Ford* is no match for the *Bluenose* in a breeze from 15 to 30 knots in strength. While the Nova Scotian stood up and seemed to enjoy the puffs, the harder the better, the *Henry Ford* was close to being overpowered along toward the close."[44] When asked later about the weather on the course, Angus replied in his characteristically cocky manner, "Well I tell you, I never wore no coat or oilskins and if there was any spray flyin' I never felt it. Certainly not the kind of weather you look for a topmast to go in. Leastaways, ours didn't."[45]

Although the controversies over sail cutting and the disallowing of races raged on, the series was officially over and Nova Scotia the winner of the cup. Four races had been run, the *Ford* proving herself better in lighter airs and the *Bluenose* standing up to a "fisherman's wind." The relative merits of each vessel would be talked about long and hard over the coming winter.

The dissent, misgivings and generally ugly mood that accompanied the races did not go away. The *Ford* lodged four official protests against the *Bluenose.* First,

BLUENOSE.
UNENBURG,N.S.

there had been no American observer on board the *Bluenose* during the last two races. The original observer, Russell Smith, had resigned, and the new man had failed to appear. As this was found to be the committee's responsibility and not Captain Walters's, this protest was not allowed to stand. Second, a replacement staysail used in the final race had not been measured. The first one had been blown to pieces when Ernie Hiltz had his mishap. It had been replaced by a smaller, older sail, which was found acceptable by the committee. The third protest concerned the material used in the sail canvas of the *Bluenose*, reputedly of finer quality than that used by an ordinary fisherman. Since her arrival, remarks had been made about the fine Egyptian-cotton yacht sails given to Walters by an English admirer. Speculation had been further fuelled by the set of sail covers on her booms, a highly unusual and suspicious feature in the eyes of fishermen, as no other banks schooner carried them. This charge was quashed when the sail was inspected and found to be of a common grade. The last protest accused the *Bluenose* crew of shifting ballast between races, but as no evidence of this manoeuvre could be found, this charge was also dismissed. The fact that all four protests came to naught did nothing to dispel the bitterness felt by both sides and only served to convince their opponents that the Americans were sore losers.

‹ **ANGUS WALTERS** poses for cameramen at the wheel of the *Bluenose* the day after winning the highly contentious 1922 series against Clayton Morrissey and the *Henry Ford*. A news reporter compared the atmosphere in Gloucester to that of a war zone, with citizens boiling over with anger at the outcome of the series. Walters vowed never to race in American waters again. *Leslie Jones, Boston Public Library*

Astonishingly, Captain Morrissey expressed a desire for one more race. "I raced after winning the first two times. We have now won two each. I hope Angus will meet me again."[46] Jonathan Raymond raised $2,000 for the matchup, but Walters, satisfied that the best boat had won two races in a "fisherman's breeze," flatly refused to entertain the idea. The race committee felt it had performed its functions and would not act further on the matter. Suspicion around the series continued to fester. Members of the race committee were accused of having rigged the series in favour of the *Bluenose*. When Captain George Peeples, the committee chairman, got wind of a rumour that he had bet on the *Bluenose*, he posted a $100 reward for anyone who could prove it. Most believed too many yachting interests had become involved in the event, and the only hope of continuing the series lay in yachtsmen and their fancy rules being excluded in the future.

Walters had no desire to remain in these unfriendly waters and wanted to pick up his winnings and head home as quickly as possible. He had lost all interest in competing against the *Mayflower* and announced unequivocally that he would not race again in the United States that year. Then rancour turned to grief when an announcement was made during a noon-hour banquet to present the prize money and trophy to Walters and his crew that Bert Demone, Walters's nephew and *Bluenose* shipmate, had been found dead, face down in the mud at the foot of a wharf behind the Olympic Theater. The night before, Demone had requested money to go ashore, but Walters had turned him down, feeling that, as tempers were high in town, his crew would be safer aboard. Despite Walters's warning to stay close to the boat, Demone headed ashore. What transpired remains a mystery. Walters always maintained his nephew must have got hold of some liquor and probably fell in with a bad crowd, one of whom shoved him off the wharf, drowning him. A police inquiry later found no evidence of foul play. For Walters, added to the trouble about the races and the two men he had in hospital—Ernie Hiltz with his broken leg and Randolph Stevens with appendicitis—this news was more than enough reason to end the celebration. He recalled his crew and sent the *Bluenose* home under the command of his mate, Ammon Zinck, while he remained behind to escort the body of his nephew. It was a sad departure, perhaps appropriate for a bitter and disappointing series. Not a whistle blew nor bell rang out as onlookers silently watched the black-hulled schooner slip out of the harbour, her ensign flying halfway down her peak.

At that moment, the future of the series looked remarkably bleak. Fred Wallace, the eminent editor of *Canadian Fisherman* magazine, wrote years later in his book, *The Roving Fisherman*, "After the acrimony and ill-feeling engendered by the races of October 1922, I lost all interest in the event. Skippers and crews were all right. It was the newspapers and sports writers and yachting enthusiasts, by injecting their ideas into the business, that ruined it."[47]

NOTES

1 *Evening Mail,* October 27, 1921; Story, *Hail Columbia!,* p. 43; *Atlantic Fisherman,* June 1922, p. 17
2 *Evening Mail,* October 27, 1921
3 George Hudson, *Boston Sunday Herald,* February 5, 1922
4 Dunne, *Thomas F. McManus,* p. 323
5 *Atlantic Fisherman,* June 1922, p. 18
6 Garland, *Adventure,* p. 23
7 *Atlantic Fisherman,* July 1922, p. 5
8 Ibid., p. 6
9 Backman, *Bluenose,* p. 42
10 *Evening Mail,* September 30, 1922
11 Jerry Snider, *Evening Mail,* October 9, 1922
12 Ibid.
13 Ibid.
14 Ibid.
15 Ed Millet, *Halifax Herald,* October 13, 1922
16 *Halifax Herald,* October 16, 1922
17 See Appendix, (4)
18 *Boston Globe,* October 21, 1922
19 Ibid.
20 Leonard Fowle, *Boston Globe,* October 22, 1922
21 Ibid.
22 Edgar Kelly, *Halifax Herald,* October 23, 1922
23 Merkel, *Schooner Bluenose,* p. 37
24 Fowle, *Boston Globe,* October 24, 1922
25 Snider, *Toronto Telegram,* October 24, 1922
26 *Boston Post,* October 25, 1922
27 Kelly, *Halifax Herald,* October 25, 1922
28 Garland, *Eastern Point*
29 Snider, *Toronto Telegram,* October 25, 1922
30 *Boston Globe,* October 25, 1922
31 Snider, *Toronto Telegram,* October 26, 1922
32 Ibid.
33 *Boston Globe,* October 25, 1922
34 Snider, *Toronto Telegram,* October 26, 1922
35 Ibid.
36 Ibid.
37 *Maclean's,* June 15, 1950, p. 48
38 Snider, *Toronto Telegram,* October 26, 1922
39 Ibid.
40 Fowle, *Boston Globe,* October 27, 1922
41 *Gloucester Daily Times,* October 26, 1922
42 *Yachting,* November 1922, p. 258
43 Snider, *Toronto Telegram,* October 27, 1922
44 Fowle, *Boston Globe,* October 27, 1922
45 Backman, *Bluenose,* p. 43
46 *Boston Globe,* October 27, 1922
47 Wallace, *Roving Fisherman,* p. 422

COLUMBIA

‹ **THE *COLUMBIA*** was the last all-sail schooner to be built for the American fishery. Even though most American schooners had been motorized and turned to the fresh-fish trade, *Columbia*'s backers felt there was still a dollar to be made in salt fish. It was obvious that her primary function was to beat the Canadians, but, as she was built as a salt banker, there could be no argument about her being a true fisherman under the race regulations. *Author's collection*

7

"I AM NOT A SPORTSMAN": 1923

IF THERE WAS ANY lingering ill will in 1923 after the turmoil of the previous series in Gloucester, it did not appear in the popular press. There was too much public interest to allow the International Fishermen's Cup series to be overshadowed by bad feeling, and the Americans also wanted another opportunity to win back the cup. The papers were full of stories anticipating the upcoming series and celebrating the last. Ironically, one New York newspaper went so far as to suggest that the 1922 series should be nominated as the sporting event of the century. The Fishermen's Cup had often been favourably compared to the illustrious America's Cup, which was now held infrequently, depending on the whim of Sir Thomas Lipton. Enthusiasts were eager for an ocean race that could be counted on to run like clockwork every fall, and so far the Fishermen's Cup had done exactly that for three years running. The perception that it was a working man's race gave it greater credibility with the general populace, and the uproar of the previous year was generally dismissed as growing pains. The Fishermen's series had all but eclipsed the "millionaire's races," and most believed they could go on indefinitely.

One man still with an axe to grind was Captain Larkin of the schooner *Mayflower*. His long battle for acceptance into this select group of fishermen had been denied time and again. After he had finally fixed a match with the *Bluenose* for the end of the 1922 series, he arrived in Gloucester only to find that Walters had sent his ship home. Fit to be tied, Larkin fired off a telegram accusing Walters of reneging on the deal and challenging him again, this time for a purse of $5,000. "I have tried for two solid years to get this man to race," Larkin declared in an open letter to the papers.[1] Larkin attempted to embarrass Walters into a match, but Angus, playing to the hometown crowd, countered that it was he who had been slighted. "For two years the master and owners of the *Mayflower* have studiously ignored our offer to race the *Bluenose* against the *Mayflower* for a side bet of ten thousand dollars, vessels to sail from Newfoundland to West Indies with equal cargo of fish, proceeding to Turk's Island, load equal cargo of salt and return to Newfoundland."[2] A frustrated Larkin finally gave up his attempts to race the *Bluenose* over a measured course and never followed up on Walters's offer. In a move that seemed to substantiate the international race committee's original claim that she was no fisherman, the owners of the *Mayflower* decided she was not commercially viable, and in March 1923 had her hauled up on the marine railway in Gloucester, an engine installed and her lofty spars cut down to a workmanlike size.

Another schooner was under construction in Essex over the winter. Ben Pine had wanted to compete with his own boat ever since his first taste of racing with Marty Welsh on the *Elsie*. Thus far, his two attempts had yielded disappointing results. His first had been with the beautiful but short-lived schooner *Puritan* and his second with the *Elizabeth Howard*, which had proved incapable of beating the *Henry Ford*. Former members of the Manta Club agreed to finance the building of a new schooner and again engaged Starling Burgess, the designer of both the *Puritan* and the *Mayflower*, to draw up plans. Contrary to the American practice of the time, which favoured building boats for the fresh-fish industry, Pine decided his vessel would be a true salt banker. He believed there was still money to be made in that market, and that this would no doubt discourage any argument about whether his boat was a true fisherman. Her owners declared emphatically that she was built for banking, pure and simple, but it was also clear she was a prime candidate for Fishermen's Cup honours. The new schooner, *Columbia,* was built at the A.D. Story yard in Essex. As with the *Henry Ford* before her, Arthur Story invested in her.

Pine was an interesting character in Gloucester. Although he never really spent much time on schooners, he was an invaluable member of the fishing community. Born in Belleoram, Newfoundland, in 1883 (then a British colony separate from Canada), he had moved to Gloucester when he was only ten years old.[3] Like many of his compatriots from the Maritimes, he no doubt believed the future in New England looked brighter than that offered by his Newfoundland outport settlement. As a "rag and bone" man servicing the maritime industry, he scoured Gloucester Harbour, buying dories and selling and salvaging anything that could make him a dollar. He would occasionally go fishing to supplement his income but spent most of his youth developing a keen business sense as a junk dealer. In 1905 he went into a trading partnership with Joe Langsford, selling ship supplies and buying shares in fishing vessels. By 1922, he had started the Atlantic Supply Company, a ship's chandlery that also managed a fleet of schooners. Pine often went into partnership with a fisherman by jointly purchasing a schooner and equipping it from his chandlery. If his partner needed dories, sails, trawls, line or any other equipment required in the running of an offshore boat, Pine supplied it, marking it up against his co-owner's side of the ledger. After a few years, the partner might want to sell his share—only to find that he had little value left from his original purchase. Pine could thus cheaply buy out his partner and add a new boat to his private fleet.

Although Pine was a steely businessman who drove a hard bargain and knew the value of a dollar, when it came to schooners he was soft to the core. He loved them, and he loved the industry. He must have been able to foresee the end of the all-sail fleet, because there was an urgency in his desire to make his mark as a racing fisherman in those twilight days of sail. His utter lack of experience as master of a fishing schooner did not deter him in the least. He appeared to have a natural talent for ship handling by virtue, some said, of just being born a Newfoundlander. Whatever it was, he felt completely comfortable at the helm of a big banks schooner, and he had the tenacity and ambition needed to compete. The fact that "Piney" was not a true fisherman did not seem an issue in the fishing community of Gloucester, nor would it affect his participation in the International Fishermen's Cup series.

› **CAPTAIN BEN PINE** is pictured at the helm of the *Columbia*. He was a prominent figure on the Gloucester waterfront who ran a marine salvage and supply business. Although he never sailed as a working skipper on a fishing schooner, his close ties to the industry and his unmatched desire to beat the Canadians left his credentials unchallenged. *Wallace MacAskill Collection, Nova Scotia Archives and Records Management*

Crews began work on the *Columbia* in December 1922 and continued through one of the most vicious winters in living memory. Sea ice choked the harbours, and the Cape Ann peninsula was swept with snowstorms. In spite of the slow progress caused by the weather, the sweet, graceful lines of the hull of the 141-foot (43-metre) schooner soon emerged. In March, when normally milder temperatures should have allowed work to speed up, another snowstorm put the builders further behind schedule. When the grey-and-white hull was launched on April 17, there was little time left before the deadline of April 30 in which to complete the rigging and fitting. The vessel was quickly towed to Gloucester and, in record time, masts were stepped, rigging was hung and the ship fitted out and readied for sea by April 26. She left under the command of Captain Alden Geele, to pick up a crew and a load of dories in Shelburne, Nova Scotia. Carrying only a minimum of sail, she was a disappointing sight to the spectators in the harbour, but because of the time constraints and the necessity of putting in a season of fishing before the races, there had been no choice. She had no mainsail or topsails and carried only a small triangular storm sail, a foresail, jumbo and jib. After arriving in Shelburne, where he picked up twenty-four dories (for a much lower price than in the United States), Geele was forced to wait for crew until another storm abated. Crews for fishing schooners were becoming increasingly hard to find in Gloucester, and the skippers and owners relied on Nova Scotia men to fill the depleted ranks. The *Columbia* finally put out to sea on her first fishing trip on May 8. Pine applied to the international committee in Halifax for dispensation caused by the delays, and received assurances that his entry would be accepted.

In Nova Scotia, another contender for the international series was launched in late April from Mahone Bay. Captain Albert Himmelman, on the *Independence*, had lost the Canadian elimination races to the *Bluenose* in 1921. Rather than watch from the sidelines, he had signed on as part of the *Bluenose* racing crew and sailed with Walters against both the *Elsie* and, in 1922, the *Henry Ford*. Himmelman, brother of Tommy Himmelman, was a successful and popular fishing skipper who loved to race and was determined to captain his own craft to victory. In the fall of 1922 he sold the *Independence* and ordered a new craft, the *Keno*, to be built at the John McLean and Sons yard in Mahone Bay. Having studied the *Bluenose*, Himmelman was determined to build an even faster boat. Walking her decks he had been heard to say, "She'll be a foot or so narrower than this one and she won't have the shoulders on her."[4] At 140 feet (42.7 metres), the *Keno* was very similar in size to

the champion, but delays in her construction meant she did not get onto the banks until late spring—too late to qualify. So Nova Scotians would have to wait another year to see what stuff she was made of. According to Jerry Snider, writing in the *Toronto Telegram,* her passage from Lunenburg to Louisbourg in Cape Breton "was the fastest ever made by such a vessel in the memory of living man."[5]

Gloucester was gearing up for a big birthday bash in 1923. It was the three hundredth anniversary of the founding of the community, and the city fathers were planning a week-long celebration to begin on August 25. The centrepiece of the tercentenary festivities was to be a locally run fishermen's race that would, with any luck, successfully erase the memory of last year's debacle. Attempting to demonstrate to the trustees of the international event how to run a fishermen's race properly, Gloucester's was declared open to all fishing schooners, regardless of size, with no limitations on ballast or sail area. Notice of the event went out to all comers from Maine to Newfoundland. The great America's Cup contender Sir Thomas Lipton was asked to donate a cup for the race.

Although half a dozen owners initially expressed interest, only three boats participated. Ben Pine's *Columbia* was unfortunately out of the running as she had suffered damage in a collision with the French beam trawler *La Champlain,* while sitting at anchor off Sable Island. The *Columbia* had been struck on the port side and her forward rigging, bowsprit and bulwarks were damaged, and some of her seams had opened up. She was towed to St. Pierre and temporarily patched up but was clearly not going to be repaired in time for the contest. Unable to resist a race, Pine borrowed the *Elizabeth Howard* once again and entered her. Two Boston boats, the *Yankee* and the *Mayflower,* considered it, but bailed out at the last moment. Captain Clayton Morrissey would be there with the *Henry Ford* if he could get back in time from fishing, and a brand new schooner, the *Shamrock*—fresh from the Story yard in Essex—would also race. She had been built for the O'Hara brothers of Boston, who had hired Captain Marty Welsh to skipper her. No Canadian or Newfoundland boats attended.

Weather conditions on the day of the race, a Wednesday, were so miserable—thick fog and little wind—that officials were forced to postpone until the next day. The contenders did their best on Thursday in a light, eight-knot wind, but it became a drifting match, ending two miles off the finish line when the time limit expired. On Friday, weather at the beginning of the race was not much better. The three vessels started well, within thirty-five seconds of each other, but coasted over a glassy sea towards the first mark. The *Ford* took an early lead and kept it throughout the race, with the *Howard* challenging when the wind freshened through the latter part of the race. The *Shamrock* fell behind right from the start—to no one's surprise, since the schooner was only a week old and Welsh had not had time to try her out or adjust her trim. On the windward beat of the second leg, Pine capitalized on Morrissey's mistake of standing too far inshore, cutting down the *Ford*'s two-minute lead. For the first time in the event, both vessels were scuppering as their lee rails dipped. The race continued to be close, with Pine pressing his vessel for every second of gain, finally crossing the finish line only fifty seconds behind Morrissey. The Lipton Cup and the $1,000 purse were Morrissey's, and Pine and Welsh both came away with the $800 apiece for second and third prize. More entertaining than the actual race was watching Sir Thomas Lipton being dragged from pillar to post in Gloucester for photo opportunities and receptions. The race may have been a fairly lacklustre affair, especially when compared with "the race it blew" of 1892, but it did revive interest in the upcoming international series in Halifax. Talk about the town was focussed now on the absent *Columbia* and how she might perform against the *Henry Ford* and the *Bluenose*.

The *Columbia* returned in mid-September from her misadventure with the French trawler. It appeared after the collision that the crew had thought their schooner was about to sink and had abandoned ship. According to Dana Story,

> Captain Geele ordered the crew to return and save her. Believing their ship was doomed, the crew refused the order. For one of the two times in his long career as a master, Captain Geele was forced to threaten the men with his pistol. He assured them he would use it unless they returned and manned the pumps. In the face of this threat the men re-boarded the vessel and were able to lower the water and keep ahead of it while the trawler which had struck them towed *Columbia* to St. Pierre.[6]

Once back in Gloucester, the *Columbia*'s cargo of salt cod was off-loaded and her repairs completed. The American Fishermen's Cup race committee dearly wanted an elimination race between the *Henry Ford* and the *Columbia*, but as the *Ford* had returned to sea, time was slipping away. On October 14 the Americans appealed to the trustees in Halifax for a postponement, and the Canadians agreed to delay the event until October 27. The Americans were in a quandary. Still awaiting the return of the *Ford,* they held a meeting on October 17 in the Master Mariners Association rooms in Gloucester and decided they would give the *Ford* twenty-four hours to return, after which the *Columbia* would be chosen to contest the 1923 Fishermen's Cup by acclamation. The following day at noon, and only a few hours before the *Columbia* was due to become the certified challenger, the *Henry Ford* sailed into the harbour with 90 tons of fish on board. As soon as Captain Morrissey stepped ashore, he was accosted by members of the committee and grilled about his willingness to race.[7] Unaware of the negotiations and debate that had preceded his arrival, Morrissey announced he was rather cool to the idea. The previous year's series had soured him. He had an enormous amount of work to do in unloading his ship and felt that the *Columbia,* skippered by the enthusiastic Ben Pine, should be Gloucester's challenger.

That night, after another meeting of the race committee, Pine finally persuaded the reluctant Morrissey to compete. With little time and even less inclination, Morrissey set about readying his ship to race on Sunday, October 21, only a week before the international series was to begin. All through Friday and into the night the shore crew worked to remove the fish from the *Ford*'s hold, and on Saturday riggers installed a borrowed topmast and replaced a boom. Although there was no time to haul the *Ford* out and clean her bottom, she was as ready as she was going to be by Sunday morning. The frantic preparations built up the excitement in the town, and any ill will held over from 1922 evaporated with the frenzied pace of events. There was a genuine feeling of optimism, very similar to that of the 1920 race, when the *Esperanto* had been similarly rushed into service.

Regrettably, after all the anxiety, preparation, pleading and cajoling, the elimination race was a bust. Morrissey's *Ford* did not live up to the expectations placed on her, and Pine's *Columbia* effortlessly led the way through a listless race that ended unfinished. After five and half hours of sailing over the thirty-one-mile course, the committee decided to cancel the race before the boats were near the end. The *Columbia* was leading the *Ford* by almost twenty minutes, and it was obvious to all that she should be the challenger. On the following Tuesday morning, amid tremendous cheering, the *Columbia* left Gloucester, accompanied by the USS *Bushnell.* The noise of the crowd had barely died away when the schooner came up hard on Great Round Rock off the Dog Bar breakwater. She was hurriedly escorted back to the harbour and put up on the ways, where a twelve-foot (three-and-a-half-metre) section of her shoe was found to be badly splintered. It took the rest of the day, in heavy rain and high wind, for workers to repair the keel. Wednesday's departure was postponed because of storm-force winds, so Pine and the *Columbia* could not begin their trip until October 25. Faced with the further delay, the trustees agreed to move the opening race date to Monday, October 29.

In Nova Scotia, planning for the series was in its final stages. Requests had been made to competitors for a fleet elimination race, but none had entered, leaving the *Bluenose* to defend the cup unchallenged. Walters had finished off another successful season on the banks with a record catch of 213 tons of fish, making him the season highliner of the Lunenburg fleet. The *Bluenose* had been well prepared. She was hauled out of the water, scrubbed, painted, ballasted and trimmed by many willing hands under the careful supervision of Captain Walters and William Roué. Walters had decided the vessel was too deep during the 1922 series, particularly in the stern, so he lightened the weight of ballast by about ten tons. The *Bluenose* and Walters had by now become household names across Canada, and William Roué, although still working at his family's carbonated-water plant in Halifax, was steadily gaining a reputation as a naval architect. The prominent firm of Ford and Paine in New York asked him to join it as an associate member. He agreed to supply designs to the New York firm but remained based in Halifax, and did not become a full-time boat designer until 1929.

The *Columbia* and the USS *Bushnell* made the 360-mile trip to Halifax in just thirty-eight hours, in good time for the first race. The bickering started almost immediately. Questions were raised over the eligibility of the American boat and the credentials of her skipper. The trustees responded quickly by stating that, in their opinion, "no question regarding the eligibility of Capt. Pine has arisen, and he was designated to handle the *Columbia* in the match if he so desires."[8] Angus Walters then insisted the American boat be hauled out and measured, just as his boat had been for the two previous years.

> We are going to finish this series without a hitch and without ill-feeling if we can. We are not worrying about technicalities. All we ask is a fair field and no favors. We do not want any of the trouble and hard feeling we had at Gloucester last Fall. The request that the *Columbia*, a new vessel, be hauled out and measured is quite an ordinary one.[9]

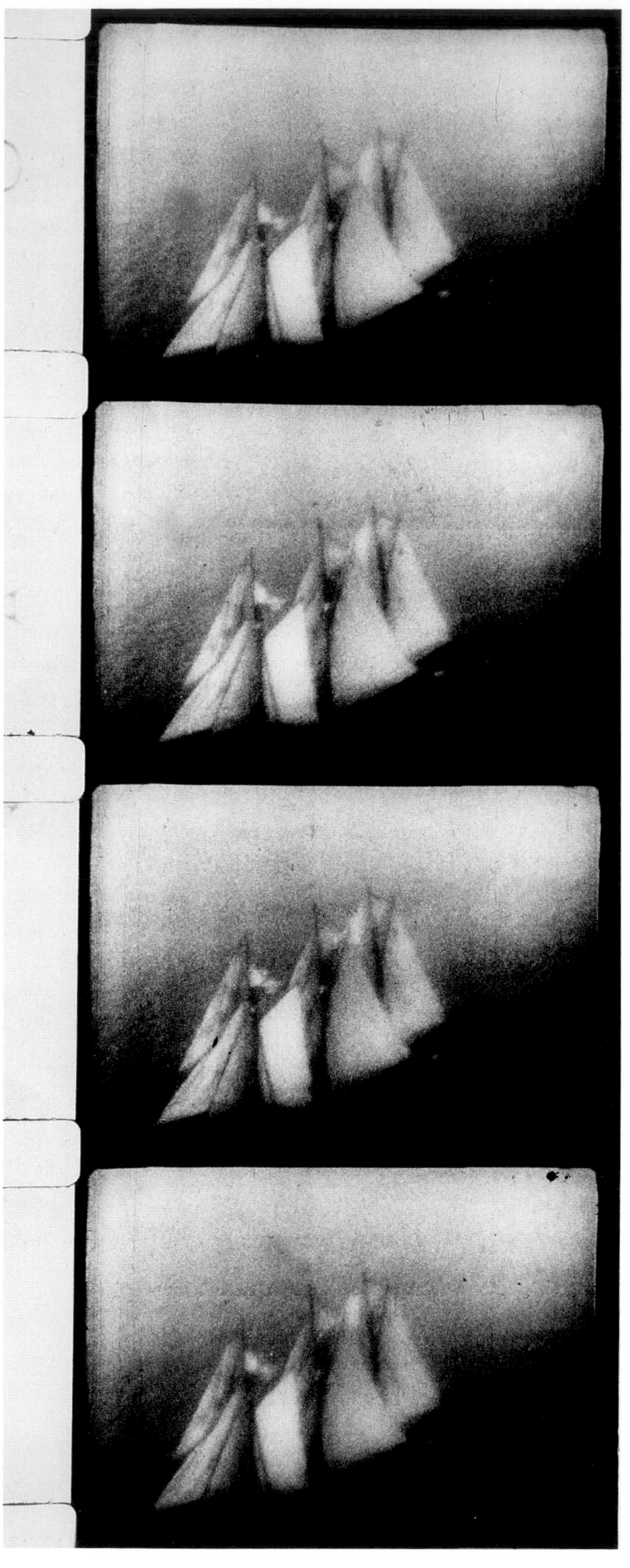

Trouble about the *Columbia*'s eligibility had been brewing throughout August and September. After the 1922 series the trustees had seen fit to further amend the regulations, adding new rules concerning the tonnage and the freeboard measurements.[10] The American race committee accused the Canadians of stacking the deck in favour of their own boat, and the Canadians responded by insisting that the owners of the *Columbia* send the ship's drawings to be inspected by the race officials. After much correspondence, the Americans yielded and sent off the plans. The trustees found the *Columbia* to be a few inches short of the freeboard dictated by the new regulations, but at length they agreed to waive the new rule. They assured the *Columbia* associates that they would accept the measurements of the vessel at face value and nothing further would be required before the race. So it was an already highly annoyed Ben Pine who reluctantly agreed to a compromise that, should he win, his vessel would be put under the tape.

On Monday morning, the competitors were greeted by a brooding October sky. It was dark and rainy, with a fresh breeze from the west. The harbour was full of pleasure craft huddled about the start line, and hordes of citizens under umbrellas gathered on the headlands. The *Columbia* was first to make sail, leaving her berth at the Pickford and Black wharf shortly before eight o'clock, followed by the *Bluenose,* which left from the Plant wharf. Both vessels jogged under four lowers and awaited the fifteen-minute gun. Signals from the flagstaff on the breakwater indicated course number 2. According to the *Gloucester Daily Times,* both skippers seemed tentative and "unduly gun shy, particularly so with the Yankee as she gingerly approached the line. Seldom in an International trophy race have skippers gone about their work in such a leisurely fashion."[11] With a Canadian Air Force service plane roaring overhead, the *Bluenose* crossed the line first, five boat lengths ahead of her rival and one minute, twenty seconds after the gun.

It was a close reach down to the Inner Automatic Buoy, with a squally wind and wicked puffs coming down off the land. The *Columbia* buried her lee rail in one puff and the sea washed over her deck as high as her cabin top, reminiscent of the *Henry Ford* the previous year. Her crew quickly eased sheets and stood her up again. The *Bluenose* gained on the first leg and passed the mark one minute, sixteen seconds in the lead. American observers on board the warship *Bushnell* looked on in dismay as the Canadian boat seemed to be walking away with the race. After both vessels left the confines of the harbour, they faced a stiffer breeze and a choppier sea. Easing the sheets on the broad reach to the Outer Buoy,

‹ **DURING THE FIRST** race off Halifax in 1923, Angus Walters in the *Bluenose* was crowded towards the rocky shore when he attempted to overtake the *Columbia* to windward. Ben Pine continued to pinch his rival towards the shoal marker off Duncan's Cove, but an undeterred Walters ran inside the marker and overtook the *Columbia.* Forced to either run ashore or turn into the *Columbia,* he chose the latter and struck the American boat with his main boom. The collision set off a storm of protest and indignation from both parties. *Author's collection*

Walters made further gains, passing the next mark more than two minutes ahead of the *Columbia*. Thus far, the *Bluenose* had proved to be the better vessel on runs and reaches. When the boats rounded the second mark and headed towards the Sambro Lightship Buoy, the wind picked up and moved around to the southeast and a heavier sea tumbled in from offshore. The Yankee was finally in her element and both boats revelled in the weather, pounding along a starboard tack with sheets flattened. With water streaming over her bridge, the committee boat *Lady Laurier* had a rough ride, frequently disappearing in the hollows of waves.[12]

Things began to get exciting when the *Columbia*'s superior windward ability allowed her to point higher than her rival and sail as fast. After two long tacks towards the Sambro Buoy, Ben Pine attempted to seize the windward berth between the *Bluenose* and the next mark. Pine drove his vessel as far offshore as he dared before coming about, forcing Walters to over-stand the mark. The Americans' superior handling of sail allowed the *Columbia* to come about in half the time of her rival. Past the buoy, the *Columbia* gained the lead for the first time in the race but by only a few seconds.

On the long eleven-mile reach back to the Inner Automatic, the *Bluenose* attempted to regain the weather berth, sailing slightly behind her opponent, her bowsprit never more than a few yards from the *Columbia*'s stern. To the spectators ashore it began to look like a repeat of the 1920 race, when Marty Welsh and Tommy Himmelman had fought a duel alongside the shoals of Devil Island. Pine pinched his vessel higher towards the shoals off Chebucto Head with Walters tenaciously hanging on and gradually inching his vessel ahead, until her bow began to overlap the American on her port side. Pine pinched higher, forcing the race closer to the shore and farther from the course line. The Canadian observer on the *Columbia* described the scene: "Both vessels were tearing towards the Inner Automatic buoy, with the iron fangs of Chebucto Head gnashing at them close aboard. *Bluenose* was regaining ground she had lost by over standing, and the *Columbia* kept luffing her… until both vessels were almost on the rocks."[13] With the *Bluenose* threatening to overtake the *Columbia,* Pine fought hard to hold on to his position, pushing the *Bluenose* closer towards the shore. "The schooners tore along, the *Bluenose* not more than a biscuit toss from the Three Sisters, one of the most dreaded shoals on the coast." When they barrelled down on Bell Rock Buoy, marking another inshore shoal, members of his crew reported that Pine all but "scraped the whiskers off the buoy" in an attempt to force Walters to fall off under his stern. Undeterred, the Lunenburger shot through the "green waters inside the buoy" and committed the *Bluenose* to the dangerous path of passing between it and the shoal.[14] Continuing her gains, the *Bluenose* overlapped her rival and steadily began to overtake her. Unwilling to give his opponent an inch, Pine kept his course and deliberately kept on luffing his rival towards the shore.

On board the *Bluenose,* the Halifax harbour pilot shouted to Albert Himmelman, spelling off Angus Walters at the helm, that he must bear away from shore. "Bear away and we strike him," Himmelman replied. "Strike him, or we strike the rocks," was the pilot's terse response. It was becoming obvious to all that the *Bluenose* had no choice, so she bore off with eased sheets, allowing the booms to run free in the now-following breeze. Walters doused his staysail and flung his foresail to port, wing and wing. Pine could have fallen off but continued on his course until the vessels converged, the eighty-one-foot (twenty-four-metre) boom of the *Bluenose* looming towards the *Columbia*'s afterdeck. The great wings of the Nova Scotian swallowed *Columbia*'s wind, stalling her as she crossed her bow. When the *Bluenose* surged ahead, the main boom, standing out forty feet (twelve metres) to leeward, struck the main shrouds of the *Columbia,* scraping clear and hitting the fore shrouds, buckling the one-inch-thick (twenty-five-millimetre) sheer pole in half like an iron hoop. The boom then skidded forward, catching on the jib stay and holding there, actually towing the challenger for a minute or two before being wrenched free. On board the *Bluenose,* the drag on the boom end unshipped the jaws from the mast, sending the boom forward several feet past the mainmast and leaving the mainsail hanging like a broken wing. With Herculean effort, seven brawny Lunenburgers manhandled the massive boom back into place.[15]

The *Columbia* recovered her speed and resumed the chase, but the *Bluenose* turned the last mark just over one minute ahead. Along the last six-mile broad reach up the harbour, the *Bluenose* once again showed her superior ability on the reaches and gained a few more seconds, crossing the finish one minute, twenty seconds ahead. The two ships received a tumultuous welcome from the crowd. The race had been one of the most stubbornly contested in the history of the International Fishermen's Cup series. The *Columbia* was, without a doubt, a good match for the Nova Scotian, and her determined skipper, Captain Ben Pine, every bit the equal of the tenacious and obstinate Angus Walters.

› **LIGHT AIRS** often plagued the races and lengthened the series. Although insufficient wind caused the cancellation of the second race in the 1923 series, it provided a scenic opportunity for the lens of Nova Scotian photographer Wallace MacAskill. *Wallace MacAskill Collection, Nova Scotia Archives and Records Management*

The *Columbia*'s crew and supporters cried for blood after being fouled by the *Bluenose,* believing it had cost them the race. But, although it was clear that the Lunenburg boat had struck them, Ben Pine refused to lodge a protest. Both boats had been on a beam reach, with the *Bluenose* gaining steadily, when the incident occurred. It stood to reason that the *Bluenose* had to have been even with or slightly forward of the beam for her to start taking the American's wind when she bore off and crossed. Pine had forced Walters's hand by crowding him farther into the shore off Duncan's Cove, but according to rule 6 of the race regulations he was obliged to give sea room only after being hailed by the other vessel. This, he insisted, had not happened. However, as both boats had Halifax pilots aboard, neither could argue that they were unaware of their proximity to shore and of the dangers close by. Pine would have been blind not to have realized his opponent would either have to alter course immediately or risk piling up on the shore. His own course was a good forty degrees away from the course line to the next buoy. He had chosen to continue crowding his rival in order to keep the weather berth, instead of easing his sheets for the run to the buoy.

Walters and Himmelman, on the other hand, felt they had cause for protest. Whether or not they had actually hailed for sea room remains unclear, but it appeared obvious from the film footage taken from an aircraft above the race that, minutes before the incident, the *Bluenose* had already overtaken the *Columbia* and was quickly running out of sea room. It was indisputable that Pine remained on course while the *Bluenose* bore off towards him, indicating that he was willing to incur a collision rather than give way. In the Canadians' minds, Pine's refusal to give way had caused the collision. Both sides decided in the end that there would be no advantage in pursuing the matter. The sailing committee made it clear that there would be no similar occurrences in the future, however, by drafting a set of "special rules" to cover the rest of the series. It listed all the buoys and specifically ordered that all of them be passed to seaward.[16]

On Tuesday, dense fog and lack of wind caused the postponement of the second race. Pine used the day off to trim his vessel. He was unhappy with her steering and thought she was sluggish in her turns. Captain Geele had brought this to Pine's attention during the fishing season, but Pine had not considered it a serious problem until now. He also thought the surface area of the rudder was inadequate and hired a diver to spike planks to it. H.R. Silver, the chairman of the trustees, advised him that such an action, while the series was underway, was

unwise. Pine relented, but he and his crew had another problem to deal with: They were upset with their Canadian observer, Jerry Snider, and wanted him removed. Snider, who had been the observer on the *Henry Ford* the previous year, was a well-known reporter for the *Toronto Telegram* and often wrote in the Halifax papers. His partisan and inflammatory account of the race had incensed the American crew and, charging that he "had a camera aboard and took copious notes concerning the tactics of the Yankee crew," they complained that his presence on board affected morale. His "observations both during and after Monday's race, proved very obnoxious to the men."[17] The race committee thought it prudent to have him replaced, and was roundly applauded by the Gloucester crew.

More favourable conditions seemed likely for Wednesday's race, as the remnants of a gale that had whipped up through the night left heavy rain and a light northwest breeze. Pine's alterations to the *Columbia*'s trim appeared to improve her performance in the light airs, and she outpaced the *Bluenose* throughout the race. After the boats had taken three and half hours to cover less than half the course, however, the sailing committee acknowledged there was no possibility of finishing the contest and called it off. Ironically, the wind picked up to fifteen knots soon after the committee boat hailed the vessels and sent the racers scurrying back into harbour. Had timing been better, it would have made for a splendid race. The *Bluenose* came to life and easily overhauled her rival as they headed up into the harbour.

On Thursday morning, the men had their mug-up early so that they could dry out the sails left sodden after a heavy overnight downpour. The clouds were scudding across the sky and the air was raw, with a fine breeze of about twenty knots blowing from the northeast. Conditions seemed made to order and the course chosen for the day was number 2, the same as for the first race. Both schooners crossed the start within forty seconds of each other, and the *Bluenose* had a thirteen-second lead on the run for the Inner Automatic. Pine's attempt to work his boat to windward of the *Bluenose* failed due to lack of speed. The wind grew stronger, and the sea began to build as they passed the Inner Automatic, leaving the fleet of spectator boats pitching and rolling in the waves behind them. As they neared the second mark, the Outer Automatic Buoy, the schooners had every stitch of canvas aloft and were now outpacing the steamer *Lady Laurier,* which was moving along at twelve knots. Only the Canadian destroyer *Patriot,* which carried the race officials, could keep pace with the flying fishermen. The *Columbia* was splitting the oncoming waves, throwing off sheets of green water to either side, and the *Bluenose*'s fuller bow was smashing into the seas and sending off a blinding smother of foam.[18]

Both boats jibed and heeled over hard around the second mark, "a feat calling for heroic courage considering the half gale and the nearly 10,000 feet of canvas, hard as iron, under tons of pressure, that spired 150 feet above the sea."[19] Blocks squealed as the crews manned the sheets and the massive eighty-foot (twenty-four-metre) booms were hurled from port to starboard, coming up hard on the shock-absorbing preventers. It was the roughest day of the series, with a wind blowing thirty knots. The *Bluenose* quickly righted herself as she made the mark one minute, twenty seconds ahead of the *Columbia*. On the run for the Sambro Buoy, both boats were wing and wing, wallowing and rolling in the growing seas. The American had a harder time of it as her main boom dipped and dragged in the combers, which affected the quality of her steering. Since her mainsail was cut much higher on the foot, the *Bluenose* did not drag her boom. The effort required to maintain the course took its toll. On board the *Columbia*, Ben Pine and another crew member struggled with the wheel, "as no one man has the physical strength to steer a wildly rearing vessel of some 260 tons displacement hour after hour."[20] Although the *Columbia* had been slowly gaining on her rival, she lost ground when her fore topsail was taken in too soon at the Sambro Buoy.

The sea around the buoy was rough and choppy, with stiff squalls picking off the crests into sheets of spray. The eighteen-mile stretch for home would be a real test for both as they made the close-hauled thrash to windward. The vessels stood out for a long starboard tack towards the Sambro Ledges, and there the *Bluenose* showed her best performance of the day. The *Columbia* seemed to have trouble with the wind and fell off course badly as her crew struggled to clew up the fore-topsail, which had sagged to leeward. Walters kept pinching his vessel on the wind, pointing higher, footing faster and finally leaving his rival half a mile behind. Neither boat could make the mark, and both were forced to tack as they approached the Inner Automatic Buoy, but when the *Columbia* came about, a wave swept over the lee rail, carrying crew member Steve Post into the sea-foamed scuppers and washing him over the side. Five men grabbed him by his oilskins as he swept past the quarter, dragged him back on board and threw him on the cabin roof. He suffered only scratches and bruises, commonplace on a banks schooner.

The *Bluenose* had problems of her own. The wind—shrieking through the rigging and exerting tremendous pressure on the masts—had parted a backstay to

the main topmast. The thick wire whipped and flailed about the deck, coming within inches of the American observer and several others. It then snaked about the stern of the vessel, where the captain was stationed. The *Gloucester Daily Times* reported that "it caught a turn about Capt. Angus Walters's arm as he crouched at the steering wheel and held his ground in the face of death. This wire, almost as thick as one's wrist, could sever his body yet the plucky Lunenburger hardly flinched, fists gripping throbbing spokes and the mad sea a maelstrom."[21] The crew quickly took in the staysail until the wire could be secured, but in the process the main topmast became badly sprung. The *Bluenose* remained firmly in the lead past the final mark, but the *Columbia* fought back during the continuous series of tacks up the harbour to the finish. After nearly five and half hours of hard sailing, and well over fifty miles of ocean covered, the big Lunenburger crossed the line only two minutes, forty-five seconds ahead of her rival. It was by far the strongest challenge for the championship yet. Ben Pine had given the *Bluenose* the toughest competition of her career and pushed her to the limit, but she had prevailed. The reception at the finish was extraordinary, as the city and harbour erupted into a cacophony of whistles, horns and sirens.

A celebration banquet was scheduled that night at the Halifax Hotel to present the trophy and prize money, but early in the evening it became clear that something had gone wrong. Shortly before the banquet was to have begun, an announcement had been made that representatives of the *Columbia* had lodged a formal protest with the sailing committee concerning the day's race. All the events of the evening were put on hold while the committee convened. H.R. Silver made a brief announcement that there was now some doubt as to the outcome of the race because of the protest, and he asked for co-operation and patience from the crowd as the committee worked through the process. Pine had accused Walters of passing one of the buoys—the Lighthouse Bank—on the wrong side, and both men were asked for an account. Walters admitted he had passed on the landward side of the buoy in question, simply because he had missed it. He said "that he did not see it in time to pass it on that side, and that if he had so seen it he would have passed the buoy on the seaward side."[22] Since the action contravened the new special rules, which had included the Lighthouse Bank Buoy as one that had to be passed to seaward, the committee had little choice but to rule in favour of the *Columbia* and disqualify the *Bluenose*. The committee, which that year consisted of three Canadians and two Americans, decided that since the

‹ **LAID OVER** and flying across the finish "like the hounds of hell were after her," the *Bluenose* wins her final race against *Columbia* by two minutes, forty-five seconds. The *Bluenose* proved to be the faster vessel in two races, but this victory was overturned by a technical protest. The 1923 series came to a premature end when Walters and his crew sailed off in disgust, leaving the series unfinished. *Wallace MacAskill Collection, Nova Scotia Archives and Records Management*

race series was now 1–1, there would have to be a third race, to be held on Saturday, November 3, which would give Walters and his crew enough time to repair the sprung topmast.

A furious Walters reported the decision to his crew who, to a man, vowed not to sail another race. In their minds, they had won the race fair and square and were not about to give any weight to ridiculous yachting rules. They had sailed the same "bee line" on a reach from the eastern side of the start line to the Inner Automatic Buoy as the *Columbia* had from closer to the western side of the line. Both vessels had covered the same amount of water to reach the first mark, and it had given them absolutely no advantage to pass on the wrong side. Walters said he would participate in another race only if the last one was declared "no contest" and Pine were denied the victory. The sailing committee could not support this demand. It insisted that a contest without rules was an invitation to chaos and the sacrifice of safety. If rules were not followed, the resulting "go as you please" affair would be better abandoned altogether.[23] Walters found himself in much the same position as had Clayton Morrissey the previous year. He, too, was implored by men of power and persuasion to race again for the good of the series. Premier E.H. Armstrong vainly tried to appeal to Walters, at one point trying to make light of it by saying, "After all, it was only sport," to which the peppery Lunenburger replied that it was "working sport."[24] It *was* hard work, and he suggested that if the premier did not think so, he should come aboard and see for himself. Men like Walters and Morrissey were unused to being told what to do; as sea captains, they made the decisions and did not stand for any argument. Morrissey had succumbed to pressure and agreed to race against his better judgement and the protestations of his family and crew; Walters showed his flinty resolve by belligerently digging in his heels. He would not race, and that was final.

A.H. Zwicker, the managing owner of the Bluenose Schooner Company, decided that if the present crew were unwilling to race, he would replace them with a scratch crew from Lunenburg. But Angus proved to be resourceful as well as stubborn, and he quickly ordered his vessel to sail for home. As the major shareholder and master of the boat, he had every right to do so, and at 1:30 PM on Friday he took a tow and slipped out into the stream. Captain Ben Pine was given the option of sailing the course alone on Saturday, but he declined. He was there to beat the *Bluenose*, and he took no joy in the idea of winning the cup by default. The international committee therefore had no other choice but to declare the 1923 series incomplete. It awarded the *Columbia* $2,500, which was half the prize money, and put the cup in the hands of the trustees until the next series. Pine left the next morning for Gloucester.

The series ended on a note of surprising civility when the American officials lavishly praised the Canadians for their efforts during the races. W.W. Lufkin, representing the president of the United States, said: "It has been a wonderful contest between two of the finest fishing vessels in the entire world, the most wonderful in the history of this great International sport." He congratulated the race committee for doing its best to leave "no stone unturned" in its efforts to avoid this unfortunate ending.[25] In the interest of continuing the series, the committee invited both parties to Gloucester the following year.

The press, on the other hand, had a field day. Not surprisingly, the *Halifax Herald* played down the affair as best it could, clearly siding with the *Bluenose* and characterizing the protest as a "trivial matter." The writers questioned the *Columbia*'s right to protest in what, in their opinion, should have been a matter between the *Bluenose* and the committee, adding that "any decision arrived at could never rob *Bluenose* of the honour of coming home in front yesterday."[26] Others were not so charitable. James Connolly, writing for the *Boston Post*, said Walters "may have been so overpowered by righteous indignation as to forget every obligation of a racing fishing captain in a contest of this kind, but the belief of the Gloucester men here is that he was overcome with cold feet."[27] The *Evening Transcript* in Moncton, New Brunswick, wrote that Walters "failed miserably to live up to the fine traditions of British seamen. He has proved that he is not worthy of the name of good sport."[28] Another *Boston Post* writer was more philosophical in his approach:

> There has been too much insistence on technicalities and too much disposition to win at all hazards. Somehow we cannot help thinking that the time honored idea of sport for sports sake, which has been a great virtue of the English speaking people, has suffered somewhat a decline... Most of us expected that the fishermen's races would develop the highest type of sportsmanship. That they did not is a sad reflection on both Americans and Canadians.[29]

The *Boston Herald* went even further by saying that, although it could not justify what Walters had done, it could understand:

> Before we talk about bad sportsmanship, Let us remember that the *Bluenose* is a fishing vessel, made primarily to catch fish and not to win an International race.

> Even on the near perfect state, we should not look for the ethics and practices of the Tennis court and the Polo field on the decks of a deep sea fishing schooner.[30]

Walters tried to weather the storm of criticism directed at him and his crew, but the adverse commentary and editorials on the subject took their toll. On Monday, November 5, he made a public statement: "On reflection I regret the effects of my action. I was under great strain. I am a fisherman, not a sportsman. I acted hurriedly, and did not realize that other people were so largely interested." He offered to race the *Columbia* again. "I am prepared to correct the situation if humanly possible and am willing to meet the challenger *Columbia* under conditions to be agreed."[31] His statement was condemned in an editorial in the *Weekly Bulletin* of the Halifax Commercial Club. Walters's excuse for his behaviour as being that of a fisherman and not a sportsman was hardly justifiable, they wrote, and "should be resented by the fishermen in the spirit of fair play." In their opinion,

> adherence to rules should mark all phases of life whether in sport or in work. We can only say that Captain Walters and his crew have cast a reflection upon our fair Province from the effects of which we shall suffer for years to come. If it lay within our power we would disqualify them from ever taking part in any international races.[32]

After his return to Gloucester, Ben Pine was asked if there would be another race against the *Bluenose* that year. He replied, "We went 700 miles to race him and he ran away from us. No, Sir, there'll be no match for the *Columbia* this year. That's final. Tomorrow we get ready for fishing."[33] Whether or not another race could have been organized is doubtful. The international committee had washed its hands of the matter, declaring the series unfinished and repossessing the Herald trophy. What was certain was that the year's match, however sullied by controversy and accusation, was in sailing terms the finest, most exciting and most evenly matched contest in the history of the International Fishermen's Cup series. The second race had been lost on a technicality, but the *Bluenose* had outsailed the *Columbia* and Pine knew it. He also knew, however, that his vessel was quite capable of beating the champion, and he would not be satisfied until given another chance to prove it. The *Bluenose* and Walters had become a thorn in the side of the Gloucesterman.

NOTES

1 *Halifax Herald,* November 5, 1922
2 Ibid.
3 Newfoundland was a colony until 1949, when it voted to join Canada and did so.
4 Jerry Snider, *Lunenburg Progress Enterprise,* January 30, 1924
5 Ibid.
6 Story, *Hail Columbia!,* p. 93
7 *Atlantic Fisherman,* October 1923, p. 10
8 *Gloucester Daily Times,* October 27, 1923
9 *Halifax Herald,* October 29, 1923
10 See Appendix, (5)
11 *Gloucester Daily Times,* October 30, 1923
12 *Halifax Herald,* October 30, 1923
13 *Toronto Telegram, Halifax Herald,* October 30, 1923
14 *Boston Globe,* October 30, 1923
15 *Halifax Herald, Boston Globe, Gloucester Daily Times,* October 30, 1923; *Atlantic Fisherman,* November 1923
16 See Appendix, (5) (A)
17 *Gloucester Daily Times,* October 31, 1923
18 *Atlantic Fisherman,* November 1923, p. 15
19 *Gloucester Daily Times,* November 2, 1923
20 Ibid.
21 Ibid.
22 *Halifax Herald,* November 1, 1923
23 *Halifax Herald,* November 3, 1923
24 Gillespie, *Bluenose Skipper*
25 *Gloucester Daily Times,* November 3, 1923
26 *Halifax Herald,* November 2, 1923
27 *Boston Post,* November 3, 1923
28 *Evening Transcript,* November 4, 1923
29 *Boston Post,* November 3, 1923
30 *Boston Herald,* November 3, 1923
31 *Halifax Herald,* November 6, 1923
32 *Boston Globe,* November 9, 1923
33 *Gloucester Daily Times,* November 5, 1923

‹ **THE FISHERMEN'S CUP** races were extremely popular, as can be seen in the crowds lining the shore by the thousands and in spectator boats in 1923. The *Bluenose* crosses the finish well ahead of the *Columbia* and is photographed dropping her fisherman's staysail. *Author's collection*

8

THE STORM YEARS: 1924–29

THE DISAPPOINTING OUTCOME of the 1923 series gave rise to a decision by the race trustees to forgo the 1924 series and give schooner racing a break. In a telegram sent to the American race committee, they explained "that the interests of the event would be best served by not having a race this year."[1] They also stated that when races resumed in 1925, Canada would be represented by "a boat and crew... prepared to abide by the decision of the International committee."[2] The reference was an obvious dig at Walters and his crew, whose actions had caused them great embarrassment. The trustees knew that the *Bluenose*'s position as cup defender was firmly established, and her supporters were legion—not only in Nova Scotia, but across Canada. They also knew Walters was unlikely to compete if the races were held in Gloucester. He had left no doubt after the 1922 series that he would never race in the American port again, and his anger over that series was still smouldering. Relations between the trustees and Walters were therefore understandably less than cordial. In fact, shortly after the 1923 series ended, the Bluenose Schooner Company sent a letter to the trustees stating that as it was entitled to the trophy and its share of the prize money, legal action would be taken unless both were handed over. Opinion in Lunenburg was that if any vessel were to race the Americans it should be the *Bluenose,* and no other skipper was likely to enter his boat if Angus Walters refused.[3] Tragically, Captain Albert Himmelman, who had built his schooner *Keno* specifically to compete against the *Bluenose,* had been lost at sea without a trace—along with the *Keno*—on a trip to Newfoundland in early January 1924. All in all, it looked highly unlikely that 1924 would see another fishermen's race.

The sad fact was that the once-large fleet of schooners in Nova Scotia was slowly disappearing, and there were fewer boats available for fishing, let alone racing. In 1920 the fleet had numbered 130 schooners, but by 1924 only 80 or so remained in service. Prohibition in the United States and in Canada opened up an illicit trade in alcohol smuggling, and in those economically hard times many boats were eagerly pressed into service. Rum-running was immensely popular with Nova Scotians, so much so that the once-proud fishing industry began to take a back seat. Trade magazines lamented that if the trend towards "bottle fishing" continued, there would soon be fewer fish to market.

After the fiasco of 1923, Captain Ben Pine was more determined than ever to win the international championship. He knew the days of the fishing schooner were coming to an end, and he wanted one more crack at the Fishermen's Cup before it all finished. His schooner, the *Columbia,* was the last to come out of Essex without auxiliary power and there was no question that although she had been expected to make money at the salt fishery, her main purpose was to beat the *Bluenose.* Most of the schooners in Gloucester, including the *Henry Ford* skippered by Pine's old friend Clayton Morrissey, had taken on engines, and large, reliable, steam-driven trawlers, with smaller crews, were steadily taking over the industry. But racing fever had taken hold of Pine and he determined to field a competitor, no matter what the cost. He did face obstacles. Although the *Columbia* had made a couple of trips freighting salt herring from Newfoundland, it was hard to convince investors there was much money to be made any more from the salt fishery. At the same time, it was getting progressively more difficult to find a crew that wanted to go dory fishing. The *Columbia* was not paying her way.

Pine was forced to dig deep into his own pockets to keep *Columbia* in racing trim while he tried to organize a race. There was some cause for optimism, as a new schooner named the *Haligonian,* designed by *Bluenose*'s William Roué, was under construction in Nova Scotia. On March 25, 1925, the *Haligonian* slid off the ways in Shelburne. She had been built for a group of Halifax businessmen as a viable challenger to the *Bluenose,* with hull and sail area nearly identical to the older boat. Most race aficionados had assumed the series would begin again in the fall of 1925, but the trustees were divided on its date and location. The Canadians felt a combined elimination and cup race should be held in Halifax in late November, an idea that had little appeal to the Americans, who wanted the usual series to be held in Gloucester earlier in the month. Talks remained deadlocked while the opportunity to hold the races passed. With no Fishermen's Cup for two years in a row, editorials predicted the demise of the series.

In 1926, it seemed Ben Pine's dream of beating the *Bluenose* would never be realized; the *Columbia* was sold at public auction in February. She had become a financial drain on her shareholders, and Arthur Story, who had built her for $35,000 three years earlier, foreclosed on the mortgage and bought her for the bargain price of $10,000. Undeterred, Pine found new partners and quickly bought her back in March. In April, he sent her off to sea again on a handlining trip to ensure compliance with the race rules. The outing was disappointing. Near the end of the month, she ran aground off Canso when seeking shelter from bad weather and was almost lost. Leaking badly, she was towed to Halifax for repairs. It was mid-May before the vessel was ready to fish, but after heading back to the banks, she found the fishing so poor that she was forced to return to Gloucester in July—a miserable showing for four months at sea.

In Nova Scotia, the Lunenburg fleet was hit by some of the worst weather fishermen had seen in twenty-five years. Storm followed storm, forcing many boats to return to harbour to replace lost and damaged gear. About ten schooners came home in early March with unused bait, causing further financial drain. The *Alachua* was lost, though her crew was saved, and the *Bluenose* was battered twice. The first time, she lost both her anchors, three hundred fathoms of cable,

her foresail and most of her fishing gear. The second occasion was even more dramatic. She was caught by a storm on April 24 when anchored off the Northwest Bar off Sable Island. A huge sea mounted her deck and parted her cable, carrying away fourteen stanchions and part of the rail and bulwarks. Under storm trysail, a reefed foresail and one headsail, Walters lashed himself to the wheel and struggled all night to hold her off the bar. The wind finally changed direction and he was able to drag her away from the deadly grip of Sable Island.

› SOMETIMES friendly but more often at odds with each other, the rival skippers of the *Gertrude L. Thebaud* and the *Bluenose* knew the value of publicity. Angus Walters's aggressive and fiery character contrasted greatly with that of the amenable and good-natured Ben Pine, something that played well with the media and kept interest in the races high. *Leslie Jones, Boston Public Library*

August has always been a time for bad weather on the banks. Hurricanes that develop in the south sometimes reach as far as the northern United States and Canada, whipping the banks with their vicious tails. What are referred to by the locals—with classic understatement—as the "August breezes" start as a whisper of wind off the African coast, move across the Atlantic Ocean with the trade winds and build in intensity until they become a tropical depression. Most fizzle out, but some, through the alchemy of atmospheric conditions, turn into the full-blown hurricanes that regularly harass the Gulf of Mexico and the eastern seaboard of North America. Occasionally one of these huge depressions makes its way farther north, cutting swaths through fishing fleets and battering northern coastlines. With no offshore weather broadcasting system in the 1920s, fishermen were always at the mercy of the elements. They depended upon a good eye and a barometer to give fair warning, but tropical depressions and hurricanes often move too swiftly to be detected early. By the time the glass drops, there is often nothing to be done but to hunker down and hope or pray for the best.

On August 7, 1926, hurricane-force winds of over one hundred miles per hour hit Sable Bank and battered the fleet. Known as "the Graveyard of the Atlantic," Sable Island is a sliver of shifting sands, twenty miles long and less than a mile wide. Its treacherous shoaling waters extend miles out from the exposed shore and have claimed more than 350 ships since 1583. So many have died that "wearing sand in your shirt" became a euphemism for drowning off Sable Island. Fishermen and merchant sailors alike dreaded and feared the island, which sits alone, 180 miles southeast of Halifax, but fishermen could not stay away; the rich and fertile fishing ground that surrounds the island provided them with a livelihood.

Boats at anchor in the shoal water off the lee shore of Sable faced a desperate situation on August 7, relying on the thin thread of an anchor hawser to keep them from destruction. Schooners offshore in deeper water stood a better chance, but as the storms came up so quickly there was little time to secure the decks. Captain W. Conrad, aboard the schooner *Mary Ruth,* gave a detailed description of the devastation.

> At eight o'clock in the evening it started to blow. I had all hands on deck doing our best to secure everything… At 10:30 we parted cable. We hoisted a single reef foresail. In five minutes it went to pieces… shortly after that the wind came west—and we crossed the nor'-west Bar on Sable Island on an angle in eleven and twelve fathoms of water. And there is where the sea did its damage. The sea would break from the bottom and strike us. The deck was swept clean by the gigantic seas. It took our boats and all our moveable gear. It smashed the skylight; the cabin door and the cabin side. The stove and everything else was smashed. The cabin was half full of water and the men washed around in the cabin and beat to pieces. Two men were washed overboard. We just saved them—that was all. Nine men were injured with broken ribs and injured limbs and one man at the pump was half beaten to pieces with the terrific seas. George Locke, one of our best fishermen, was so badly injured that he has since died… It was the hardest thing I have ever endured in my life.[4]

Most of the vessels in the path of the 1926 storm were badly battered, but they survived. However, two schooners from the Lunenburg fleet were not so lucky. The *Sylvia Mosher* broke up in the surf on Sable Island, tumbling end over end until she lay smashed on the beach. Her remains stood there for years before the sand claimed them. Another, the *Sadie Knickle,* disappeared without a trace. Both crews, a total of forty-eight men, died in the wild weather of August 7. Ironically, though the storm of 1926 was the worst in living memory, the catch was the biggest on record, over 17,200 tons of fish. This, unfortunately, did not translate into profit, because of low fish prices and the expense of repairing the heavily damaged schooners.

A memorial service was held in October for the fifty-four men of the Lunenburg fleet who had perished that season. The families of fishermen were often hit harder by tragedy than those in other occupations, as family members frequently sailed together. It was not unusual to lose a father and a son or brother on one vessel. The service was attended by over seven thousand people, more than would have attended the annual Fishermen's Picnic, normally held at that time of year but cancelled in 1926 out of respect for the dead.

There had been efforts made earlier in the season to get the International Fishermen's Cup race going. Ben Pine attempted to draw out the Canadians by writing an editorial suggesting Gloucester was ready and willing to resume the series at any time. Angus Walters replied in his trademark manner, intended to get under the skin of the Americans: "Well, I'd like you to let Captain Pine and everybody else that doubts it to know that Nova Scotia doesn't have to get ready for Gloucester—Nova Scotia is always ready."[5] The Americans were becoming weary of trying to corner the stubborn Lunenburger, and their frustration began to show. "The thing that rankles is his arbitrary attitude. Why can't he take a win or a loss and display a semblance of sporting blood? Nobody would hold it against him if he got licked like a man. Neither would he be made the king of Kickapoo if he was to win" were a few lines from a lengthy article in the July issue of *Atlantic Fisherman.*[6] Soon after, a promising telegram arrived from the Canadians, saying there would be an elimination race in October and the winner would sail to Gloucester. The American race committee took this as a response to the challenge and sent word to Halifax that October 12 would be a suitable date.

In early September, Clayton Morrissey confronted Ben Pine at his Atlantic Supply Company office in Gloucester and proclaimed good-naturedly that he thought his *Henry Ford* was far superior to the *Columbia,* and he was willing to prove it. Pine responded to the challenge from his friend by enthusiastically agreeing to a race. Gloucester now had a contest—maybe not the one it was hoping for, but a race just the same. The race committee originally agreed upon October 2, 4 and 5, but then wisely changed the date to the following week, so as not to conflict with the upcoming baseball World Series. The Americans had not given up on an international event, but could not get any commitment from Nova Scotia. Captain Walters had cagily suggested he would be interested in a race if the "rules, committee and purse were satisfactory, but not otherwise," and he went on to say he believed any race should be held off Halifax.[7] On September 30, the following message was received by the Nova Scotians:

> American Fishermen's Race Committee invite the entry of the *Mayotte* [another recently built schooner that had shown good speed], the *Haligonian,* and the *Bluenose* in an open fishing schooner race to be sailed off Gloucester

> October 11th, 12th and 13th. Races open to all vessels of the North Atlantic, to be sailed fishermen's orders, no restriction, sails, rig or crews. Valuable silver trophies and generous cash prizes. Gloucester schooners *Columbia* and *Henry Ford* have entered. Kindly answer. Signed W.A. Reed.[8]

This began a series of correspondence between Gloucester and Lunenburg that could only be characterized as voluminous, with the Americans leaving no stone unturned in their attempts to entice the schooners from Nova Scotia.

The owners of the *Bluenose* and the *Mayotte* replied immediately and briefly that it would be utterly impossible for them to attend, but gave no explanation. The owners of the *Haligonian* responded by saying: "Thanks for the telegram. Damage to sails and rigging occasioned by stranding at Canso makes it impossible for the *Haligonian* to compete in your contest as cost of suitable equipment too expensive." Undeterred, the Americans offered up aid. "We are allowing Gloucester schooners $1000 each expense money for conditioning vessels. Committee will allow owners *Haligonian* $1000 for same purpose in order to have city of Halifax represented."[9] H.L. Montague, representing the owners, wired back that although they "cordially appreciate your very generous offer," they needed a day's postponement of the race in order to be able to participate. The race committee met and reluctantly decided it could allow no further delays. Montague then replied that "every effort being made dispatch *Haligonian* Friday morning. Hope succeed... will telegraph when vessel sails." The citizens of Gloucester, who had been following the discourse in the local paper, found reason to be optimistic that there would be a Nova Scotian boat in their upcoming series. Both Morrissey and Pine agreed to race the *Haligonian* even if she arrived too late for the main event. "They would race for money or peanuts and settle their supremacy and let the fastest boat take on the *Haligonian*," reported the *Gloucester Daily Times*.[10] The bubble burst when a telegram arrived the following day: "Regret advise that although everything possible had been done cannot arrange berth on slip and complete sails for time to race *Haligonian* next week." In a last futile attempt, the Americans offered up an available slip in Gloucester for the Nova Scotian boat, but this, too, was declined. William Roué, the designer of the *Bluenose* and the *Haligonian*, was so disgusted with the pettiness and the unenthusiastic response from Nova Scotia that he commented it would be "very poor advertising for this Province... They are calling our bluff... and we are allowing them to do it. The

humiliating thing about the whole business is that it will appear Halifax cannot afford to send a schooner, even when Gloucester is putting up the money."[11]

The following day, an announcement was made in Halifax that there would be a provincial championship race on October 16 between the *Bluenose* and the *Haligonian*. Many embittered Gloucestermen believed that, after all the back-and-forth and dangling of carrots, the holding of their own series was the real reason for the reluctance of the Nova Scotians to sail south. Mr. Corbett, the chairman of the Halifax race committee, suggested that the winner of the Nova Scotia series might challenge the champion of the Gloucester races. Pine and Morrissey were willing to await the outcome and take on the challenger. When asked if he would compete against the Canadians, Morrissey replied that "he would race the Nova Scotian for a brass can and that Captain Pine undoubtedly feels the same."[12]

Over the Columbus Day holiday the two Gloucester boats, the *Columbia* and the *Henry Ford*, faced off against each other before huge crowds drawn to the peninsula by the fine weather. The *Columbia* prevailed, beating the *Ford* in two closely matched races and taking the open championship. Pine immediately sent a telegram to the Halifax newspapers:

> Will you please announce through the columns of your paper that I hereby challenge the winner of the Provincial Fishing Vessel Contest to be sailed in the near future off Halifax, to a race the week of October 25th off Gloucester, best two out of three, for prizes $2500 and $1500 under conditions which governed the race series just concluded here.[13]

Curiously, at a well attended reception that followed the Gloucester races, Pine appeared to bow out of future competition when he announced his "racing days were over and that never again would he hold the wheel of a racing vessel in a formal contest."[14] He went on to name Clayton Morrissey as his successor should the *Columbia* enter the International Fishermen's Cup race. Both he and Morrissey booked passage to Halifax to watch the Nova Scotians race in the provincial championship.

Captain Moyle Crouse, the master of the *Haligonian*, welcomed a match with the Yankees with open arms. "Race Ben Pine off Gloucester?" he said. "Sure why not?" Angus Walters, on the other hand, gave the challenge a more predictable reception: "Off Boston, perhaps. Off Halifax, maybe. But off Gloucester, never!"[15]

› **DESIGNED BY** William Roué, the *Haligonian* was built to the same specifications as the *Bluenose* but never lived up to expectations. She failed to prove herself and could not even come close to her sister ship in the 1926 Nova Scotia Fishermen's Regatta for the provincial championship, leaving her backers mystified. *R. Walker Collection*

Captain Joe Conrad, the master of the *Canadia*, was unimpressed with the attitudes coming from his side of the border, and in a letter to a friend wrote: "I saw in one of the papers last week where both the *Haligonian* and *Bluenose* could beat the *Columbia* with the foresail and jib down. All I hope is that *Columbia* beats her [*Bluenose*]. They are no sports there, only bags of wind."[16]

The first provincial race, held on Saturday, October 16, had an ideal start with a fine fifteen-knot breeze behind the boats. A crowd of thousands held its collective breath as it watched the *Haligonian* cross the start line two seconds before the gun went off. Both vessels were immediately informed of the false start, but as Walters declined to protest, the race went on. A confident Walters had earlier predicted the victor. "I don't like to make any prophecies. But I'll tell you... bring a couple of boxes of good cigars down to meet us when we get in after tomorrow's race. I and my boys will have them half smoked before *Haligonian*'s got a line ashore."[17]

The *Haligonian* held her lead until the first buoy, after which the *Bluenose* took over and surged ahead. She continued to be ahead throughout the forty-mile course and crossed the finish in four hours and sixteen minutes, beating her previous record for the course by a quarter of an hour. The *Haligonian* crossed the finish a full half an hour later. No one had expected such a thrashing, and the same question appeared to be on everyone's mind. "The city seemed to be one huge interrogation mark... The poor *Haligonian* never seemed to get going at any stage in the race... She appeared listless, 'sick'—labouring under some kind of burden all the way."[18] Her size and shape were comparable to the *Bluenose* but had not translated into similar speed and, as her sails seemed a good fit, her trim would have to be improved in order for her to make a better showing. After William Roué, the designer of both boats, had observed every move, a shift was made in her ballast.

On Monday, the *Haligonian* looked to be in better shape and got off to a good start by leading the *Bluenose* across the line. Her advantage was short-lived, however, and the *Bluenose* once again pushed ahead in the twenty-knot breeze. After the wind hauled due north on the last leg, the schooners took so long to make way, tacking repeatedly, that the time limit had expired by eleven minutes when *Bluenose* finally crossed the finish. "No race" was declared. Although the *Haligonian*'s performance had been better this time, she had still lost by the considerable margin of twenty-two minutes, leaving her followers wondering where the difference lay between these almost identical boats. After the race, Angus Walters

decided he had had enough and announced that his vessel had proved her superiority and he should be allowed to take the trophy and go home. The officials disagreed and insisted the races be completed. Perhaps tempered by lingering guilt over his behaviour after the 1923 international series, Angus relented. The third race was a repetition of the second, with neither vessel completing the course before the allotted time. Once again, the *Haligonian*'s skipper, Crouse, got the better start and maintained the lead for a short period during a luffing match that took them far off the course line. After the first mark, Walters began to draw ahead. When both vessels jibed around the second mark, Crouse foresaw danger and called for sea room. The *Bluenose* refused to alter course and was struck by the *Haligonian* on the starboard side, breaking two stanchions. Both boats told different stories about the accident, but neither skipper filed a protest. In the end, Walters led his rival across the finish by thirty minutes, leaving the *Haligonian*'s supporters again scratching their heads. Some blamed her dismal showing on the fact that she had run aground off Cape Breton earlier in the year; perhaps the damage to her hull had been more severe than believed, possibly leaving it twisted. In any event, a frustrated Walters was becoming weary of the contest and declared that, as he had beaten his rival three times and his crew was tiring of the races, he would head for home. Once again the race committee stood its ground and, in the end, sportsmanship prevailed.

The fourth and final race of the series was the closest. The wind was lighter, and from the northwest at the start. It hauled around to the southwest later on, allowing the racers to sail "downhill" all the way on runs and reaches. The lack of windward work, which was always *Bluenose*'s best point of sail, probably accounts for the closeness of the race. She won by just over six minutes and held onto the championship of the Nova Scotia fishing fleet, decisively beating her rival in all four races, two of which were declared official. When Walters finally sailed for home with the silver cup and the prize money, he left the backers of the *Haligonian* wondering what they should have done differently.

While they were in Nova Scotia, captains Pine and Morrissey had used every opportunity they could to promote the international series. After the first provincial race on Saturday, Pine had restated the challenge: "We want an International Race. We are prepared to race the winner of this series off Gloucester for The Halifax Herald International Trophy and the prize money called for by the International Race regulations."[19] After the *Bluenose* victory, he continued to press but insisted the race be held off Gloucester. Walters repeated his refusal to race there: "I made a solemn vow that I would not race off Gloucester again and I cannot be expected to break it. I am ready and willing to race off Halifax."[20] He insisted that this was not just a matter of personal preference but was more to do with the inferiority of the Gloucester course and the fact that it was time to have the series off his home port of Lunenburg. In the end, neither moved from his respective position, and Walters began the dismantling of his boat for winter lay-up.

Apart from Ben Pine and some of his friends on the American race committee, few cared to pursue the competition further. The dull and predictable series off Halifax, added to the losses suffered by the fleet during the "August breezes," had had a decidedly dampening effect on public interest. Pine put the disappointment of 1926 behind him and set his sights on 1927, swearing that, if all else failed, he would send his schooner to Halifax in the fall and stand by in the harbour until he had a race.

On August 24, 1927, hurricane-force winds again tore across Nova Scotia and the offshore banks. Apple orchards in the Annapolis Valley were torn up and barns flattened, and on the coast, fishing stages were ruined and an unknown number of boats smashed. In a repeat of the "August breezes" of 1926, the fleet on Sable Bank was hit hard, and those ashore prayed and braced themselves for bad news. *Canadian Fisherman* magazine reported:

> In a few days vessels that had been fishing around Sable Island, where the storm was at its worst, began limping into port, with their sails gone and their decks swept of everything and their captains and crews telling of marvellous escapes from the treacherous sand bars... Some vessels were so near destruction that the sand from the bars washed over their decks.[21]

The second day after the storm, the battered schooner *Edith Newhall* arrived back in port after a narrow escape. Her captain, Gordon Mosher, related that his vessel had been caught in the storm while fishing near the treacherous Northeast Bar and that when the gale struck he was forced to sail right over it. Huge seas, tossed up from the seabed, crossed his decks and tore away hatches and skylights before flooding the engine room. Waves broke the main boom and stanchions and carried away the light boxes in the rigging. When they arrived in port, the crew reported they had passed a lot of debris from another vessel also hit by the storm.

Angus Walters had to head back for repairs to the *Bluenose.* She had been able to ride out the storm in open water, losing only an anchor cable and trawls and having her sails badly ripped. Walters commented on the ferocity and sudden appearance of the storm: "There was no canvas ever made to stand such a gale. In all my seagoing experience I've never seen the barometer go down and come up as quick as it did on that occasion."[22]

The difficult part for those ashore was the waiting. With no radio communication, there was no way to find out if something was wrong with a boat at sea. If a schooner was undamaged, its crew would simply continue fishing and not come in until the holds were full or the bait gone, so it could be weeks, even months, before anyone knew the fate of these vessels. Schooners heading home often carried letters from other boats to be posted ashore, and the masters and crews would pass on the latest news from the banks, but all a desperate family could do was to wait and hope for the return of their men or for news of their safety.

The first sign of tragedy arising from the August 24 storm appeared on September 3 when the steamer *Albertolite* sighted debris in the water. It found a sea chest belonging to a crew member of the *Joyce M. Smith,* a schooner that had carried eighteen men. By mid-September, it became clear that three more schooners from the Lunenburg fleet were missing: the *Clayton Walters,* the *Mahala* and the *Uda R. Corkum.* All were overdue and, by the month's end, presumed lost. A total of eighty fishermen perished. In those two years, 1926 and 1927, 130 fishermen from Lunenburg had lost their lives to the sea. The 1927 storm had travelled to Newfoundland's shores, striking without warning on a clear, cloudless day. Winds of more than ninety miles per hour had taken five schooners, the *Vienna,* the *John C. Lochlan,* the *Hilda Gertrude,* the *Annie Healey* and the *Effie May,* all of them lost with all hands.

In Gloucester, the storm did no more than dump heavy rains on the Cape Ann peninsula, so it did little to arouse concern for the fleet at sea. Then news began to trickle in about the destruction caused by the path of the storm across Nova Scotia, and soon Gloucester boats returned home with tales of their own narrow escapes from disaster. One of Ben Pine's schooners, the *Marion McLoon,* was lost on the Nova Scotia shore. She had dropped anchor in Yankee Harbour, near Whitehead, where she had seemed snug and secure until the wind suddenly began to howl. The crew rushed up on deck just in time to see the anchor windlass pulled clean out. They desperately tried to secure the hawser around the foremast, but were driven ashore before they could finish. As one of the crew recounted:

‹ THE *COLUMBIA* and *Henry Ford* fight it out off Gloucester in 1926 in an "open" championship the Canadians declined to contest. The *Columbia* won hands down, but both skippers, Ben Pine and Clayton Morrissey, headed to Halifax in a fruitless attempt to entice the Nova Scotians to race the *Columbia* and resume the International Fishermen's Cup series. *Cape Ann Historical Association*

> The waves were dashing all over her, and it was not possible to stay on deck, nor was it possible to launch a boat and get ashore. There was about 150 feet of boiling water between us and the rocks and the old craft was pounding her life out. We took to the rigging and there we hung praying, and praying, that the wind would stop.[23]

After three hours, the wind died down and the crew made it safely ashore, though the boat could not be salvaged.

Another schooner arrived at the Boston Fish Pier with her flag at half-mast. The popular skipper Alvaro Quadros had been swept from the deck of his schooner during the height of the storm. Members of the crew had been fighting for their lives, with the decks awash and water pouring in the fo'c'sle and aft cabin, and it was hours before anyone noticed their captain was gone.

Pine also had his beloved schooner *Columbia* at sea. She had been out since July 2, on her second handlining trip of the season. When reports of the storm arrived in Gloucester, they did not concern Pine, who was confident that his boat and her master, Lewis Wharton, could ride it out. Even when he heard early news that debris, battered dories and oars bearing the *Columbia*'s name had been recovered on Sable Island on September 13, Pine could not believe they came from his boat; he had recently sold a load of old *Columbia* dories and suspected those found had come off another schooner. Reports from another master that placed *Columbia* on Western Bank later in the summer indicated to Pine that she was too far away from Sable Island to have arrived there before the storm. The *Columbia* was not expected back in port until the first week of October.

As hope for the return of the missing Canadian schooners began to fade, anxiety about the *Columbia* grew. The American coast guard cutter *Tampa* was dispatched to Sable Island to search for clues to her fate. Bits and pieces of dories and oars were found on the island but nothing conclusive. An undaunted Pine refused to give up hope. Finally, on October 27, a local haddock boat, the *Mary Sears,* arrived at the Boston Fish Pier with a dory that had the name "Columbia" painted on her side and, inside, a bait knife with the letter "M" carved on the handle and known to have belonged to a crew member of the *Columbia*. This was irrefutable evidence that something awful had happened to the schooner, and the amount of sea growth on the bottom of the dory was an indication that it had occurred some time before. Pine was finally forced to acknowledge the loss of his treasured schooner and her crew of twenty-two. The *Columbia*'s crew was mostly Nova Scotian, adding more names to the province's list of victims of the August breezes, and bringing further misery and grief to the families.

The two years of tragic losses hit the industry hard, especially in Nova Scotia. Gloucester had steadily surrendered to the pressures and demands of modernization, and its fleet had been taken over by steam-driven trawlers that required smaller crews and could work year-round in almost any weather. There were few fishing schooners left in American ports, and their numbers were quickly dwindling. Most of the remaining schooners had had engines installed and their masts cut down to convert them into trawlers. In Canada, however, the banks schooner still dominated the industry, and fishermen accustomed to traditional methods were resisting the introduction of mechanization to their fleet. However, two disastrous seasons brought about a change in attitude and direction in the fishery. Now that an alternative technology was available, most men, particularly those new to the industry, were no longer willing to risk their lives in a dory when they could work from the relative comfort and safety of a trawler. As fewer schooner men remained wedded to the old ways, even the best fishing skippers, like Angus Walters—men whose reputations could guarantee a crew—came to the realization that the glory days of the fishing schooner were numbered. Modernization was expensive; it cost thousands of dollars to install an engine in a vessel, which took years to pay off, but no crew meant no fish.

The following year, a postscript was added to the story of the *Columbia*. In the early morning hours of January 1, 1928, the steam trawler *Venosta* was dragging the bottom about forty miles southwest of Sable Island when her trawl became entangled in wreckage. When the men hauled it up, they saw it was the hull of a schooner. Her top masts, boom and bowsprit were gone, but apart from that, she was in remarkable condition. There was little sea growth, and most of her rigging appeared intact. Even the paint on her hull was in good shape. The stunned crew watched in disbelief for a few minutes before the heavy steel cables parted and the ghostly apparition slid back into the sea. Although she was never positively identified, those who had known the *Columbia* were certain that this was indeed the famous Gloucester schooner.

Ben Pine's obsession with fishing-schooner racing seemed to wane after the sinking of his pride and joy. His favourite racing mate, the *Henry Ford,* was also gone; she had run aground and broken up on Whaleback Reef off Newfoundland on June 16, 1928. Perhaps it was time to admit that his dream of beating his rival would remain a dream. To add insult to injury, the Canadian government immortalized the *Bluenose* on a postage stamp in 1928, a reminder to Pine of his failure every time he received a piece of Canadian mail.

Modern trawlers may have been the future of fishing, but the sight of them could not hope to match the silent majesty and beauty of a fleet of schooners under full sail. Promoters could still count on a race's appeal to the viewing public, and in 1929 the beating of the drum for another series began. Gloucestermen still loved a schooner race and the American committee reconvened to organize a local event. There were a few older schooners available, but none was of the class of the *Henry Ford* or the *Columbia*. Four entered, the most famous being the *Elsie,* which had raced against and lost to the *Bluenose* in 1921. Pine entered his schooner the *Arthur D. Story,* built in Essex in 1912, and announced that, contrary to his assertion in 1926 that he was retiring from racing, he would be taking the helm. The other two were the *Thomas S. Gorton,* the oldest (1905), and the *Progress* (1913), which at ninety-six feet (twenty-nine metres) was the smallest. The *Progress* was originally to be skippered by Captain Marty Welsh, who, after his doctor advised him to stay ashore, gave up his position to Captain Manuel Domingoes. The fact that the schooners were four old workhorses did not diminish the race in the eyes of the public; after three dry years (and six years since the last international race), the public was hungry for a return to racing. Subscription money poured in, and the required amount of $20,000 was quickly met, then exceeded.

The competition was held during the last days of August, but light winds plagued the racers. The first and second races ended without completion after passing the seven-hour time limit. The third race, held on Labor Day, was won by the little schooner *Progress,* an unlikely victor considering her size. Captain Domingoes trailed Ben Pine on the *Arthur D. Story* for thirty miles before he overhauled him, taking the lead and winning the race by ten minutes. With no assurance of better conditions for the following days and unwilling to see the American open series become a prolonged and dull affair, the committee put an end to it and gave the cup to the *Progress,* allowing victory celebrations to begin. Officially, the series was reduced from a best of three to a one-off in the interests of restoring normality to the fishing industry, but it is more likely that the contestants and organizers were anxious to get on with the party.[24] The races may have been disappointing, but they reawoke "race fever" in Gloucester, and plans were soon in the offing to build another contender to challenge the Nova Scotians once again.

NOTES

1 *Canadian Fisherman,* October 1924, p. 281
2 Ibid.
3 Ibid.
4 *Canadian Fisherman,* September 1926, p. 274
5 *Atlantic Fisherman,* July 1926, p. 7
6 Ibid.
7 *Gloucester Daily Times,* September 29, 1926
8 *Gloucester Daily Times,* September 30, 1926
9 *Halifax Herald,* October 1, 1926
10 *Gloucester Daily Times,* October 6, 1926
11 *Gloucester Daily Times,* October 5, 1926
12 *Gloucester Daily Times,* October 7, 1926
13 *Gloucester Daily Times,* October 13, 1926
14 *Halifax Herald,* October 13, 1926
15 *Gloucester Daily Times,* October 14, 1926
16 Letter from Joe Conrad, October 21, 1926, Maritime Museum of the Atlantic
17 *Maclean's,* June 15, 1950, p. 48
18 *Halifax Herald,* October 18, 1926
19 Ibid.
20 *Halifax Herald,* October 22, 1926
21 *Canadian Fisherman,* October 1927, p. 303
22 Story, *Hail Columbia!*, p. 151
23 *Gloucester Daily Times,* August 29, 1927
24 *Atlantic Fisherman,* September 1929, p. 17

GERTRUDE L. THEBAUD

‹ **BRIGHT AND SHINY** as a new penny, the recently launched *Gertrude L. Thebaud* is put through her paces off Gloucester in 1930. Her owner, Ben Pine, often arranged exclusive excursions, such as this, for the wealthy members of the yacht clubs of Marblehead and Newport. *Leslie Jones, Boston Public Library*

9

THE LIPTON CUP: 1930

AFTER THE INTERMINABLE difficulties of the latter half of the 1920s, it seemed to many that the cup races were beyond revival. There were no schooners in Gloucester or Boston able to compete against the Canadians, and there was little incentive to build new boats. In Gloucester, an elderly insurance man from New York named Louis A. Thebaud came to the rescue. After spending a few weeks each year with his family in a cottage near Rockport just up the coast, Thebaud had bought a summer home close to Gloucester. Bored with the tedium of summer life, he engaged a local garage owner, Joseph Mellow, to act as his driver and companion. Through Joe, Thebaud was introduced in 1929 to the Master Mariners Association, where he learned about the fishing industry and was captivated by the stories of schooner racing and the long-standing rivalry between Gloucester and Lunenburg. The thrill and passion of these tales must have struck a chord, because he immediately wrote a cheque for $2,000 to go towards financing the local schooner races to be held that summer. Before he left the hall he was not only granted membership in the elite club of fishing skippers but was also put on the race committee and given the honorary title of captain.

Mellow took Thebaud down to the wharves, where he became friendly with the local skippers and crews, turning up regularly to chat and listen to tales of the sea. Ben Pine frequently took the old man out fishing and further broadened his knowledge of the fishermen's races and the role played by the *Columbia* before her tragic loss. Thebaud spent hours on the docks observing preparations for the upcoming races, and when Mellow casually remarked that it would be nice to have a schooner that could race the Canadians, Thebaud jumped at the idea. On September 12, he turned up at Mellow's garage with a cheque for $10,000 in his hand. Mellow's confused reaction got a quick response from Thebaud: "Don't you remember after the races on Labor Day, when we agreed there wasn't a good racer here in Gloucester; well here's $10,000 toward a vessel that CAN race. Speak up now; who shall I make the check out to?" Mellow stammered, "Make it out to Ben Pine and myself."[1]

This windfall resurrected Pine's hopes of beating the Nova Scotians, but, after looking around at prospective purchases, he and Mellow decided there was only one schooner capable of racing, and that was the *Mayflower,* the only American "racing fisherman" still afloat. She had been sold to the British government, which had coppered her bottom and was using her as a freighter in the West Indies. Inquiries were made, but the asking price of $28,000 was considered too much for the eight-year-old schooner. When they told the news to Thebaud, he instantly wrote them a cheque for an additional $20,000 and told them to build a new one. The dumbfounded duo were further astonished when Thebaud's wife entered and handed them another cheque for $10,000. The pair headed back to Pine's Atlantic Supply Company offices to talk things through. One thing was clear: this schooner was going to be built to race, and any consideration of her being a fisherman was almost an afterthought.

In spite of the generosity of the Thebauds, $40,000 was not enough to cover the expense of building a schooner. Fortunately, their friends were persuaded to join in: Wetmore Hodges, a wealthy Gloucester businessman, Bassett Jones, an electrical inventor from New York, and Thebaud's brother-in-law, Robert H. McCurdy, each invested $5,000. Ben Pine and his pal Joe Mellow enthusiastically paid the difference up to $73,000, making the boat the most expensive fishing schooner ever built. Normally, fishing vessels were financed by selling $100 shares, which were usually bought by those close to the industry, but this project was quickly becoming a rich man's hobby.

Frank Paine, the Boston designer of the *Yankee,* an America's Cup contender (not the Boston schooner of the same name), was engaged to draw up the plans. The new vessel was to be called the *Gertrude L. Thebaud* after the principal owner's wife, and any pretensions that this was to be anything but a racer were put to rest with Paine's design. *Rudder* magazine reported there were substantial differences between this schooner and the average Gloucester boat. "The *Thebaud* is more cut away forward and her after sections are quite yacht-like."[2] The *Gloucester Daily Times* wrote that she "has an underbody like a yacht, in fact closely [resembling] that of the *Yankee.*"[3] And *Yachting* magazine added that the design followed "more or less, the lines of some of [Paine's] recent yachts, though of course a more burdensome vessel."[4] She was equipped with all the amenities, such as electric lights, and her cabin was of solid mahogany, a luxury unheard of on a banks schooner. Her holds were small—she carried far less than the *Mayflower,* which had been barred from racing in part for just that reason. Had the *Thebaud* been built five years earlier, her eligibility for the Fishermen's Cup would have been out of the question. Identifying her as a bona fide banks fisherman was little more than a charade, but by 1930 it seemed no one cared to notice. In the early years of the Depression, and with schooner fishing representing a dying way of life, the spectacle and tourism potential of another International Fishermen's Cup race was clear on both sides of the border; there seemed little to be gained by quibbling about the qualifications of the contestants. However, it looked as though the race of working men in working schooners was about to be reduced to the "pink tea" variety, in total opposition to the original intent.

On St. Patrick's Day, March 17, 1930, three months after the keel was laid in the A.D. Story yard, the slender hull of the *Gertrude L. Thebaud* slid down the ways into the Essex River. Huge crowds were on hand, and every available parking space in town was taken. It was a grand occasion, flavoured with nostalgia, as the *Thebaud* was one of the last schooner hulls to be built in this historic yard. The Thebauds themselves were unable to attend because of preparations for a trip to Europe. The vessel was 124 feet (37.8 metres) long, 99 feet (30.2 metres) on the waterline with a 14-foot, 8-inch (4.5-metre) draft, smaller than the *Bluenose* by 19 feet (5.8 metres) and carrying 3,000 fewer square feet (278 square metres) of sail. Those who knew boats predicted she would be fast in light to moderate weather, but likely would be beaten by the *Bluenose* in a heavy blow; still, they hoped she would prove more nimble than her older rival. Although the *Thebaud* was rigged with topmasts and carried more than 7,000 square feet (650 square metres) of canvas, her main source of propulsion was a 180-horsepower Fairbanks Morris diesel engine. In the months after her launch, little effort was made to prove she was a sailing fisherman. Unless she was racing, she seldom unfurled her sails.

› **UNDER FOUR** lowers, the *Bluenose* is laid over so far that her keel is exposed during the second race of the 1930 series. With winds blowing over forty knots, the schoonermen finally had the "fishermen's wind" they had all been hoping for. Unfortunately, as the high winds had flattened the highliner poles marking the course, making them difficult to see, the sailing committee decided to call off the race, much to the fury of Walters, who was by that time well in the lead. *Leslie Jones, Peabody Essex Museum*

Enticing the competition from Nova Scotia to race once again proved difficult. The American race committee wanted a match with the *Bluenose,* if only to be able to take the contentious Angus Walters down a peg or two. Walters still had a habit of goading the Americans whenever possible. The previous March, after making a voyage from Lunenburg to Halifax in record time, he had boasted: "From now on I will refuse to race the *Bluenose* against any other vessel unless we take the mainsail off of her. Otherwise there would be no interest in it for me. If we race a United States craft we will probably tow an anchor over the side as well."[5] Just when it seemed possible that the Lunenburg schooner might race in the fall, she ran aground off Argentia, Newfoundland. Walters's brother, John, had taken her there on a caplin-bait trip in June, prior to heading out to the banks. She went ashore at Point Riche at the entrance to the harbour and sat there, grinding her bottom on the gravel beach, for five days until the Canadian government hospital ship *Arras* pulled her off. Although there appeared to be no serious damage, this did nothing but strengthen Walters's resolve not to race.

With well-heeled investors eager for a contest, the American race committee continued to pressure the trustees in Halifax for a race in October. Ben Pine had been actively wooing the wealthy yachting fraternities of Gloucester, Marblehead and Newport by organizing exclusive sailing excursions on the *Gertrude L. Thebaud.* An exhibition race between the *Thebaud* and the America's Cup contender *Yankee* was under consideration. Sir Thomas Lipton, back in the United States to challenge for the America's Cup for the fifth and final time, was persuaded to donate another huge silver cup for the proposed fishermen's race. Any idea of sending the *Thebaud* off fishing was almost an afterthought to drumming up support for the coming event. Finally, a delegation was sent off to Halifax to see what could be done.

After lengthy discussions, agreement was reached in August that not one but two races would be held in the fall. Walters was persuaded to race Pine off Gloucester in early October on condition that the championship of the International Fishermen's Cup was not at stake. It would be an exhibition race only, and the "true" Fishermen's Cup race would be held later off Halifax in October or early November. Walters insisted the agreement be drawn up and all conditions of the exhibition race spelled out. If they were "not strictly adhered to by the Gloucester signatories, then all races [would] be called off."[6] Even the proposed name, the International Fishermen's Challenge Trophy, was considered too contentious and was changed to the Lipton Cup. (This would be the third Lipton Cup; the first was donated in 1907 and the second in 1923.) Gloucester had succeeded in getting a race, but only on Walters's terms.

After the grounding in Newfoundland in June, the *Bluenose* continued to fish on the Grand Banks, returning to Lunenburg in early September. Walters was anxious to inspect her hull and found that half her keel and some planking had been damaged and needed to be replaced. Over the next two weeks the schooner was repaired and groomed, had a new set of sails cut and part of her rigging replaced. A fishermen's regatta held in Lunenburg on October 1, 1930, was the finale of a three-day Fisheries Exhibition, and four vessels were entered to race: the *Haligonian,* the *Margaret K. Smith,* the *Alsatian* and the *Bluenose.* For Angus Walters, it was an opportunity to fine-tune his vessel before heading out to Gloucester. In his typically arrogant fashion, he requested that his competitors be given a ten-minute handicap because of the *Bluenose*'s superior speed. This show of hubris proved unfortunate, as the *Haligonian,* under the command of Captain Moyle Crouse, put on a fine show for the first time in her existence, beating the *Bluenose* by eight minutes. "It was easily seen here that the *Haligonian* had advanced to a new place in the contest and was calling upon all observers to sit up and take notice... When he came about he put the *Bluenose* and *Smith* well to leeward, making it impossible for either schooner to get anywhere near him for the finish," reported the *Halifax Herald.*[7] Keen disappointment was felt by the legions of loyal *Bluenose* supporters, who were left to wonder whether the old champion was still fit to be representing Canada in the upcoming Gloucester race. All hoped the *Bluenose* would show better form in more favourable winds. Meanwhile, her international rival was on the marine railway in Gloucester having her engine removed in preparation for the contest.

The *Bluenose* set off for Gloucester in convoy with the *Arras* and the Canadian naval destroyer *Champlain,* but quickly lost sight of both in the heavy seas. When the wind picked up, she broke her foresail gaff during an attempt to jibe, and the crew took an hour to repair it. She continued with reduced sail but still beat the government ships to harbour. Upon her arrival in Gloucester on the night of Sunday, October 5, after a thirty-five-hour run from Lunenburg, she received a boisterous and rousing welcome, in stark contrast to the solemnity and melancholy that had accompanied her last departure from the port, in 1922. The following night, the crews from the rival schooners and the *Champlain,* along with local military, coast guard and several marching bands, paraded together through the town in a torchlit procession. Putting their differences behind them, skippers Angus Walters and Ben Pine looked forward to a promising and uncomplicated contest in their exhibition race for the Lipton Cup.

On Wednesday, October 8, 1930, the competition almost ended before it started when the *Gertrude L. Thebaud* ran into trouble the day before the first race. She had been out on the course for a trial run when her hull sprang a serious leak. One of several problems that had plagued her construction had been a shortage of full-length timbers. The shorter timber used meant more butt ends, which tended to work open at sea, causing serious leakage.[8] The crew had been puzzled by the lifeless and unresponsive handling of their vessel and found, when they went below, that there was three feet (a metre) of water in the hold. Five miles off Thatcher's Island, she was taking on water at such an alarming rate that three pumps were unable to keep up with the flow. She immediately headed for home and was lucky that the marine railway was free when she arrived—had she been farther offshore, it is doubtful she would have made it back. The worst leak came from a weak seam in the deadwood in the stern, but at least a dozen other seams had also opened. A six-foot (two-metre) plank and another, smaller insert were replaced near her bow. Pine took the incident in stride and appeared confident his boat would be on the water the following day, "dry as a bone."[9]

With the Columbus Day holiday on Monday and an American Legion convention in nearby Boston, Gloucester was in a festive mood and expecting up to thirty thousand visitors over the weekend. A small fifteen-mile triangular course, which would be followed twice by the schooners, promised to give shore-bound spectators an optimal view. The local press went to great lengths to inspire enthusiasm for the contest, describing the vessels as the "two fastest fishermen on the North

Atlantic, manned by crews of hard-bitten, frost-touched men of the sea," adding that "for anyone that wants a two-fisted, he-man, crest-crushing and wave-breaking contest, 100 per cent satisfaction is guaranteed all comers."[10] It was ironic that the race being touted as a true test of fishing schooners and fishing captains included a vessel owned by a junk dealer, a taxi man and a wealthy insurance broker. Nevertheless, the races were billed as the highlight of a well-planned weekend, and wireless reports from a U.S. Coast Guard boat following the race were to be broadcast live from a Boston radio station. Overwhelmed with the fanfare and flattered to be on radio for the first time, a jocular Walters threatened to stay: "It's wonderful the way they received us, and if things keep on, the women folk down in Lunenburg shouldn't expect us home until Christmas."[11]

The first race began on Thursday morning and both boats got off to a sluggish start. Once on the course, however, the *Thebaud* took off like a whippet and quickly established herself in the lead position. The *Bluenose* staggered behind, her new set of sails so hopelessly stretched out of shape that a *Yachting* magazine reporter commented they "looked like insufficiently re-cut circus tents."[12] Local fishermen watching from the shore agreed she carried a "clumsy suit of sails." Even when the gaffs were raised as high as they could go, they remained baggy. The stretching of her sails was later blamed on the high winds she had encountered on the trip to Gloucester. Nonetheless, Walters gamely chased the *Thebaud* along the roundabout course and, at times, the *Bluenose* showed some of her old class, when she was able pick up speed to twelve knots. But the die was cast, and the *Thebaud* seemed only to be toying with her before delivering the knockout punch. "It was a walkaway and disappointing to racing experts. But to those who sought only spectacle, there was nothing to moan about... Leaning on the shoulders of a 15-mile breeze, both boats gave an unforgettable picture as they dug into the water and sent the spray flying," wrote John Griffin of the *Boston Post*.[13] The *Gertrude L. Thebaud* romped home fifteen minutes, thirty-seven seconds ahead of the *Bluenose,* to an enthusiastic reception from the hundreds of boats that lay along the finish line.

As soon as he was alongside, Walters had the huge 4,000-square-foot (370-square-metre) mainsail unbent and sent ashore with his two topsails and foresail. He personally supervised the cutting of the sails and removed as much as five feet (one and a half metres) from the foot of the mainsail and a similar amount from the others. He also ordered ten tons of ballast removed.

‹ **DURING THE SAME** race as in the photo on page 167, the *Gertrude L. Thebaud* was less successful at coping with the high seas and wind and was unable to keep up with her opponent. On several occasions, she could not properly answer her helm and became caught in irons, forced to watch her rival soaring ahead. *Leslie Jones, Peabody Essex Museum*

The next two races were abandoned for lack of wind. In the first of these, on Saturday, the *Thebaud* got the jump on the *Bluenose,* leading across the starting line by about a minute. She opened up the lead in a disappointing wind that never picked up above eight knots and occasionally fell away to nothing. Every time there was a light puff, the *Thebaud* would respond like a yacht and spring ahead. But by the end of the first half of the course it had become obvious that, barring a full gale, the vessels could not possibly finish in time. The *Bluenose* seemed to sail better with her recut sails but still could not gain sufficiently on her rival. Walters's reaction to an announcement that the races would resume the next day, a Sunday, was emphatic: "We never fish on Sunday and we won't race on Sunday."[14] The race was rescheduled for Monday, when once again the boats were beset by light airs. The *Thebaud* once more beat the *Bluenose* to the gun and led at the start by one minute, but on the close reach to the first mark the Lunenburger began, astonishingly, to overhaul her rival. Foot by foot, she worked her way up, turning the mark thirty-seven seconds in the lead. On the next leg and in the lightest breeze the *Thebaud* worked up alongside the *Bluenose,* "so close that the rival crew could nearly shake hands with each other." In response to a ribald hail from the Americans, the high-spirited Nova Scotian crew pelted their rivals with a barrage of Annapolis Valley apples.[15] Camaraderie was high between the crews, but the wind was not as friendly. An hour and a half later, the race was called for the second time.

This series was developing into one of the longest to date, and Tuesday morning promised more of the same weather, so the race was cancelled well before the start. The Lipton Cup was turning into a listless, drawn-out affair that satisfied no one, sailors and onlookers alike. However, later that day thickening clouds heralded a possible change in the weather.

What the previous races lacked, Wednesday's contest had in abundance—wind, and plenty of it. In contrast to the pleasant but dull days that had characterized the series thus far, this day was dark and stormy, with driving rain and winds raging from twenty-five to forty knots. For the first time, the weather was worthy of fishermen; it "had enough weight and teeth and punch in it to suit the toughest sail-dragger who ever raced a schooner."[16] It was a race that Ben Pine was sadly obliged to miss; he had been ordered to stay ashore by his doctor because of a sinus infection, and he had turned over the helm to Captain Charles Johnson. The strong northeasterly and torrents of rain had reduced visibility to a few hundred yards when the *Thebaud,* sheeted hard to windward, flew across the start, forty-six seconds ahead of the *Bluenose. Thebaud* took off like a runaway freight train, heeled over so far that her keel was visible from the press boat, and a grey-green sea washed over her deck. The *Bluenose* was hard on her heels and "charging after her like a mad thing."[17] John Griffin of the *Boston Post* described the dramatic scene: "The crews were clinging to whatever was handy, and probably the most unenviable position in the world at that moment was occupied by the men who went aloft in the swaying rigging. Great tumbling seas smashed against the side of the schooners and climbing aboard, rushed down the decks and slid swishing off the stern."[18] This was, perhaps, the race both sides had been waiting for: one that would finally settle the question of which schooner was the fastest in wind that could honestly be called fishermen's weather.

The *Bluenose* had been built for conditions like this, and she was revelling in it. The six-mile beat straight to windward going towards the first mark was obscured by fog and rain, and the battle between the two went largely unseen by the observers ashore. Johnson was having difficulty tacking his vessel in the heavy weather, and three times she was caught in irons, allowing her rival to forge ahead. The *Bluenose* made for the slim, flagged highliner pole that marked the first turn six minutes and one mile ahead. On board the *Thebaud*, one huge wave after another was washing over the deck and the crew was desperately trying to hang on. One crew member, Carlin Powers, was washed over the side by one wave and tossed back by the next. Another, Kellogg Birdseye, was saved from being thrown overboard only because his foot had tangled in a line, holding him long enough to be rescued. The *Thebaud* lost a further six minutes on the run down to the second mark and fell two miles behind.

Trouble began for the *Bluenose* when she failed to find the third mark, a slim pole with a red flag on top. The committee boat, which was supposed to keep station close to it, had also been unable to locate it. The Nova Scotian continued searching for the mark and fell well off to leeward on a broad reach, in the area the eighteen-mile mark should have been, and all the time the *Thebaud* was closing in. The marker might have been blown flat on the grey heaving seas or simply have broken loose. Whatever the case, the sailing committee called off the race, blaming the heavy rain that continued to obscure vision. Whether this was a disastrous mistake is a moot point, but it brought to a premature end the only race so far that had offered the kind of excitement and drama expected of a true fishermen's race, and which many have compared to the legendary "race it blew" of 1892.

› THE *GERTRUDE L. THEBAUD* leads the *Bluenose* across the finish in the 1930 Lipton Cup exhibition series off Gloucester. After a seven-year hiatus from international competition, Angus Walters and the *Bluenose* suffered their first defeat at the hands of the Americans. This was a sad moment for Walters, but he accepted it graciously and blamed himself, not his beloved schooner, for the loss. The stage was now set for a resumption of the International Fishermen's Cup series the following year off Halifax. *Mariners' Museum, Newport News, Virginia*

The two skippers were furious, and both were scathing in their criticism of the committee's decision. Walters quite rightly noted that the visibility at the beginning of the race had been equally poor and added that fishermen were quite used to finding buoys in poor weather. "Let us stay out there until something blows away. That's our hard luck. We were perfectly satisfied to carry on," he said during a long harangue that scorched the air in the committee room.[19] Captain Knickle of Lunenburg, a Canadian member of the committee, attempted to pour some oil on the troubled waters by acknowledging that, though the sailing committee had had no right to call off the race, it was probably the correct thing to have done, pointing out that "the men of both boats were wet and cold and if the race had continued we might have lost a man or two from one of the vessels."[20] In an attempt to mollify the two skippers, the committee decided that for future races, a boat would be stationed at each mark.

The next day the boats lay idle, in order to give Walters a chance to repair damage to the crosstrees of the foremast. One of the "hams" that supported the rigging had splintered and the *Bluenose* had come close to losing her foremast. Walters emphatically denied there was anything seriously wrong with his vessel and claimed the *Bluenose* would have finished the previous race with no problem. A gang of carpenters worked until early the following morning to replace the splintered piece.

The final race was held on a beautiful sunny Friday morning, October 17, with a fifteen-knot nor'westerly blow and no sea running. The *Thebaud* again led at the start, but by only a boat length, with the Lunenburger slightly to weather and gaining. The Gloucester boat seemed slow to respond to her helm and had trouble making headway. Walters quickly overtook his rival and, after twenty minutes, was three boat lengths ahead, running with the wind and with sheets well off. The *Bluenose* was a minute ahead in a freshening breeze at the first mark and held her own on the next six-mile leg to the southwest mark, adding a further fifteen seconds to her lead. After rounding the second mark, disaster struck the *Bluenose*. Walters mistakenly elected to head inshore on a port tack on the first windward leg of the race. Almost immediately, adverse currents that ran the shore caught the *Bluenose* and pushed her farther leeward of the buoy. Johnson wisely stayed on the starboard tack and ran farther offshore, steering clear of the inshore tidal movement. This action won him the race. With one more tack, he was able to make the third mark, while Walters continued to struggle against inshore currents. After

2

four lengthy tacks, the *Bluenose* finally made the buoy fifteen minutes behind the *Thebaud* and gallantly tried to make up the difference, gaining on every leg of the second turn around the course. But the damage done to her chances was irreparable, and the *Gertrude L. Thebaud* sailed home the winner, the *Bluenose* crossing the finish eight minutes behind. A humbled Angus Walters would later admit that because of his mistake the *Thebaud* had beaten him rather than his boat.[21] He deeply regretted straying from the old racing wisdom of staying between the other fellow and the mark and not splitting tacks. No one, however, could argue that the result was not fair and square, and the victory gave Gloucestermen every reason to celebrate.

Bill Taylor of *Yachting* magazine argued that the series was not so much a celebration of speed and strategy as a homage to a quickly disappearing way of life:

> The interest in the races off Gloucester lies not in the extreme speed of the vessels nor in the exhibition of consummate racing tactics, but in the spectacle itself and its traditions—in that the few remaining commercial sailing vessels can still scare up the will and the way to put on a race at all.[22]

All things considered, the 1930 Lipton Cup series was a good-natured affair, unmarred by the wrangling and bitterness that had marked the previous decade. The proposed resumption of the International Fishermen's Cup series that was planned for Halifax in November was postponed to the following year. The trustees felt that in view of the economic hard times and the necessity of raising funds through public subscription, holding another race so soon after the Lipton Cup could not be justified.[23]

NOTES

1 Frank Jason, "Avast Ye Lubbers," *Boston Post,* March 16, 1930
2 *Rudder,* December 1930, p. 60
3 *Gloucester Daily Times,* October 5, 1930
4 *Yachting,* December 1930, p. 108
5 *Bridgewater Bulletin,* March 19, 1929
6 *Halifax Herald,* September 1, 1930
7 *Halifax Herald,* October 2, 1930
8 Dana Story in conversation with the author, October 2003
9 *Boston Post,* October 9, 1930
10 Ibid.
11 *Gloucester Daily Times,* October 7, 1930
12 *Yachting,* December 1930, p. 81
13 *Boston Post,* October 10, 1930
14 *Halifax Herald,* October 13, 1930
15 *Gloucester Daily Times,* October 14, 1930
16 *Halifax Herald,* October 16, 1930
17 *Atlantic Fisherman,* October 1930, p. 15
18 *Boston Post,* October 16, 1930
19 Ibid.
20 Tom Horgan, Associated Press, October 16, 1930
21 *Halifax Herald,* October 20, 1930
22 *Yachting,* December 1930, p. 108
23 *Canadian Fisherman,* November 1930, p. 24

‹ **THE *GERTRUDE L. THEBAUD*** is heeled over on her starboard side and trimmed to perfection as a comber of brine bursts over her rail. *Cape Ann Historical Association*

10

THE REVIVAL: 1931

THE GREAT DEPRESSION that began in 1929 hit the fishing industry hard, especially in Lunenburg, where the demand for salt cod had been on the decline for the second half of the 1920s. This was due in part to the expansion of the fresh-fish market in the United States, but also to fierce competition in salt cod from Iceland and Norway, which had effectively closed out Nova Scotia from its traditional markets in the West Indies, South America and Europe. Although Lunenburg's cod was still considered the finest available, other countries had improved the salting process and were now able to undercut Lunenburg's prices. The fresh seafood market in Canada was not yet a viable option, and duties on Canadian fish made the American market prohibitive. The lean years took a heavy toll on the Lunenburg fleet, forcing many owners to sell or lay up their boats. Three years after 1929, when there had been over seventy boats in the fleet, there remained only twenty-six.[1]

Angus Walters laid up the *Bluenose* for the first time in her career in 1931. She had always been a highliner, consistently catching impressive amounts of fish, but with the dramatic drop in price, it was cheaper to stay ashore no matter how much was caught. South of the border, things were not much better. The market was steadier but the prices still miserably low. Trawlers had squeezed all but the few remaining schooners out of business, and even the venerable old *Elsie* had turned to greener pastures, serving as a summer training vessel for Sea Scouts. Despite an adequate halibut-fishing season, the *Gertrude L. Thebaud* could not pay her way, and she too was laid up before summer's end.

When talk of a 1931 Fishermen's Cup series surfaced, interest in Gloucester was lukewarm until Louis Thebaud once again stepped up to the plate. Though his friend Ben Pine thought better of it, reminding him that "times are hard" and "people are not interested enough to subscribe money," Thebaud pulled out his cheque book and offered $5,000 to get things moving.[2] Pine turned the money over to the American race committee, urging it to immediately challenge the Nova Scotian fleet. When this was received by Halifax in mid-September, it was immediately accepted. With his beloved *Bluenose* laid up, Walters was more than willing to take on the Americans, seeing this as an opportunity to redeem his poor showing of the previous year and to win a substantial purse that could help pay his expenses. He knew inadequate preparation and his own poor racing strategy had let the *Bluenose* down in 1930. There would be no excuses this time: his vessel would be properly groomed and ballasted, with her sails well cut and in perfect condition. The course off Halifax would, in his opinion, be a far better one; it would be deep-sea course, not the tiny roundabout circuit offered by Gloucester with its "baby buoys" that went missing in a breeze. A civic appeal went out in the press in Nova Scotia for a subscription fund—a further $6,000 was needed to help cover the expenses and prize money.

Contrary to Pine's pessimistic view of the public's likely response, the promise of a new series was welcomed with enthusiasm, offering as it did an escape from the dreary economic realities of day-to-day life during the Depression, with its collapsing businesses, soup kitchens, idleness and despair. Races and other forms of entertainment were hugely popular during those hard times and the citizens of the fishing communities, so badly affected by the Depression, saw in the Fishermen's Cup race an occasion for optimism and hope.

After the *Esperanto* had beaten the *Delawana* in the first series of 1920, Americans had thought of themselves as rightful owners of the cup, never truly reconciling themselves to its loss to the *Bluenose* by the *Elsie* in 1921. There was still the lingering feeling that they had been "robbed." It had been nine long years since the *Bluenose* had last won the series in 1922, and this time she would be facing a competitor that had already proved her worth in the Lipton Cup. The dominance demonstrated by the *Thebaud* in the previous fall's races gave Gloucestermen cause to anticipate that the Fishermen's Cup would finally be returning. And, for the first time, the date of the races did not have to be determined by the fishing season, as both boats were available and in port. October 17 was agreed upon—earlier than usual, but, with the benefit of better weather and a bit of luck, it would attract larger crowds.

Both skippers began to prepare seriously for the contest. Angus Walters took the *Bluenose* out on a trial run against the schooner that had just won that year's Lunenburg fishermen's regatta, the *Alsatian*. In fairly light winds, she showed fine form, handily beating the *Alsatian* on all points of sail. When asked about his chances against the Americans, Walters replied with customary bravado that "the wood is not yet growing of the vessel that will beat the *Bluenose*."[3] Ben Pine took his own boat out of the water and gave her a thorough overhaul. The *Boston Post* reported of the *Gertrude L. Thebaud:*

> A corps of workmen swarmed over her, smoothing her seams and painting her sleek hull. Below the waterline she was painted a ruddy copper, red as a fish's gills. Along the waterline a boot top of bright green contrasted pleasingly with her more subdued under body. A coat of glistening black hid the scars the fishing banks had left on her topsides.[4]

Pine expected more wind on the Halifax course and consequently wanted more ballast on board. Her designer, Frank Paine, reluctantly agreed to deepen her with more pig iron, as long as her waterline length, then 99 feet (30.2 metres), grew no longer than 101 feet (30.8 metres). When she was measured in Halifax before the first race, she taped in at 103 feet (31.4 metres), well within the rules of

the deed of gift but an obvious indication that she was a much heavier vessel than she had been the previous year.[5]

Pine arranged a trial match with the *Elsie*, probably the only other schooner left in the port of Gloucester that could put up a challenge. With borrowed topmasts and a crew of Sea Scouts, the *Elsie* seemed not to have lost her old form and gave the *Thebaud*'s backers a fright. In the first race, the *Elsie* started late but within fifteen minutes forged ahead and took the lead. The *Thebaud*, looking sluggish in the brisk southerly wind, finally bounced back, narrowly taking the win by only two and a half minutes. This was a cause of much concern in Gloucester to those who had expected far more from the *Thebaud*. "It was a severe blow to Gloucester hopes of recovering the blue ribbon of the North Atlantic fishing banks," reported Tom Horgan in the *Boston Post*.[6] The *Thebaud* looked in better form during the second race and beat the *Elsie* by more than eight minutes, but the margin of victory had been augmented by a mishap; a broken backstay had forced the crew of the *Elsie* to douse her topsails. Confidence in the *Thebaud* was not restored until her trip north to Halifax on October 13. Skippered by Captain John Matheson, the *Thebaud* clocked an impressive 365 miles in just over thirty hours, mostly under four lowers, making astonishing speeds of between twelve and fifteen knots. The crew was ecstatic about her performance and felt they could have pushed her even harder had they not wanted to avoid taxing the rigging and sails before the race. They were so sure of the trouncing they were about to give the *Bluenose*, they felt sorry for her.[7] Ben Pine could only hear about the trip; he had been forced to go by rail because of his recurrent sinus troubles, though he would skipper the *Thebaud* on race day.

On October 17, thirty thousand spectators arrived on the shores of Halifax to watch the great sea challenge. An easterly gale had blown hard all night but blew out by morning, leaving a nasty, steep swell rolling across the course. The race was a stern-chase from the start for the *Thebaud*. The *Bluenose* crossed first and within ten minutes had opened up a lead of several boat lengths. She appeared to rise easily with each swell and work her way well to windward on the beat down to the first mark. Her rival, on the other hand, could not overcome the boisterous seaway and plunged and butted into each swell. She looked as if she was "wallowing around like a punch-drunk prize fighter," according to reporter John Griffin of the *Boston Post*.[8] Those aboard the official spectator boat, the *Lady Laurier*, watched as the Lunenburger sailed away from her rival, and they predicted the

‹ **WITH THE SHEETS** hauled bar-taut and sailing close to weather, the crew of the *Bluenose* struggles to stay upright on a heaving, wave-swept deck while working lines at the mainmast. *Edwin Levick, Mariners' Museum, Newport News, Virginia*

result long before the first buoy was reached. They quickly lost interest in the race and "devoted all their time to being seasick" as the wildly tossing government steamer tried to keep pace with the lead boat. The *Bluenose* tore around the course, leading the *Thebaud* by more than four miles, but with about six miles left to the finish, Walters hit an ebb tide and the wind died, leaving him barely half an hour to beat the clock. This he failed to do, leaving the committee to call an end to it and saving the *Thebaud* from an ignominious defeat.

The second day of the series, Monday, October 19, seemed far more suited to the American sailer. The sea was flat and smooth, with a fresh offshore breeze. After the first race, Ben Pine had realized belatedly that his increased ballast was hindering his boat and he wished to have it removed, something the rules did not allow after the series was underway. His appeal to the race committee to grant a dispensation depended on his getting the consent of his rival. Walters refused and pointed out that the American skipper had had plenty of opportunity before the series to properly adjust his ballast; he had raced the *Elsie* off Gloucester, sailed up the coast and made several trial runs around the Halifax course. All Pine could do was attempt to improve the *Thebaud*'s performance by shifting the ballast on board, and initially this appeared to work. He outmanoeuvred Walters and took off from the start, twelve seconds ahead. For the next half hour, the *Thebaud* stood her ground and both vessels were neck and neck until the big Lunenburger came through on the weather side of the *Thebaud* and got down to business. By the first mark, in a wind of twelve to fourteen knots, she was four lengths ahead and steadily gaining. In contrast to the *Bluenose* ploughing forward under a great press of sail, the *Thebaud* appeared to be standing still, her dismal performance causing one wag on board the press boat to shout for her to pull up her anchor.[9] The only thrill left in the contest was packed into the last few miles when Walters again had to fight the clock. At 3 PM the *Bluenose* was off Thrumcap Shoal, only four and a half miles from the finish, and she had forty-five minutes to go before the time limit expired. Walters threw his vessel from one tack to another, fighting his way up the harbour and finally making the breakwater a mere six minutes and thirty-one seconds before time ran out. When the cannon roared, "Captain Angus smiled and his men tumbled about the deck in handsprings," wrote the correspondent for the *Boston Post*.[10] Steam whistles, horns and sirens screeched approval. A dejected *Gertrude L. Thebaud* arrived thirty-two minutes later and was given, upon arrival at her dock, three rousing cheers from the *Bluenose* crew.

A disappointed Ben Pine took the defeat graciously, but he knew his vessel, in its over-ballasted state, was no match for the Lunenburg flyer. He explained that he had sailed against the wishes of his doctor as he did not want his alternate, Captain John Matheson, to bear sole responsibility for the *Thebaud*'s defeat, which he felt certain was coming.[11] Pine's health was deteriorating and he would not sail again in that series. Angus Walters revelled in the *Bluenose*'s obvious superiority, but complained about his competition. "You know, it was kinda lonely out there today, *Thebaud* wasn't any company—in either race, for that matter—and a feller don't get much fun out o' racing the clock all the time."[12]

Conditions for the next race on October 20 were a repetition of the first's, with the sea as smooth as a ballroom floor and a good sailing breeze from the northwest. The *Bluenose* crossed the line first, fifteen seconds after the gun, with the *Thebaud,* this time under John Matheson, only seconds behind. Both vessels settled into the seventeen-mile run to the Sambro Lightship Buoy with their sails wing and wing. There appeared to be little or nothing to choose between them. Though the conditions were virtually identical to those that had brought her defeat the day before, the *Thebaud* surprisingly held her own. Hope sprang up in the Gloucester camp when, for the first time in the series, she seriously challenged the ten-year-old Lunenburger. After jockeying back and forth to the buoy, never more than a couple of boat lengths apart, the *Bluenose* finally came alive in the windward thrash for home. Slowly and steadily, the *Thebaud* fell astern while the *Bluenose* ate up the wind on her tacks down the harbour and, an hour after turning the Sambro Buoy, she left the *Thebaud* several miles behind. The *Bluenose* surged home in five hours, six minutes, well under the time limit, with the *Thebaud* crossing twelve minutes later. The American boat had proved handier in the second race but was still no match for the Nova Scotian.

The crowds went wild in Halifax and Lunenburg in celebration of their heroes, the victorious team of Walters and the *Bluenose.* The usually staid *Yachting* magazine summed it up:

> The *Thebaud* is a good vessel, but the *Bluenose* is a better one... Gloucester had sent a boy to do a man's job, and a boy with his pockets full of pig iron at that. In perfect trim, the *Thebaud* could probably beat the *Bluenose* she met last year at Gloucester. But it was a different *Bluenose* she met this time... and a *Bluenose* better sailed. Angus was taking no more chances on splitting tacks. He had the

> *Thebaud* covered all the time, no matter how far back she was, and he sailed his vessel with the loving touch of a master playing an old violin.[13]

Captain Ben Pine did not go away empty-handed. Not only did he receive his portion of the prize money, but he was also praised for his enthusiasm and competitive spirit. The premier of Nova Scotia, G.S. Harrington, in presenting him with a silver cup marking his ten years of participation in fishing-schooner racing, remarked:

> Captain Pine, may I tell you with genuine sincerity how much we all appreciate your fine sportsmanship, as displayed in these great contests almost from their inception... We all realize the sacrifices you have made and the greatest of these is your devotion to your duties and the handicap of ill health.[14]

The *Bluenose*'s success was, to her fervent supporters, as much a vindication as a triumph. All the bitterness and ill will that had permeated the previous decade seemed to dissolve into the past. However, the victory was bittersweet. There was an underlying feeling of sadness about the series. People sensed the inevitability that the races—and the life they represented—were coming to an end.

NOTES

1 Balcom, *Lunenburg Fishing Industry,* p. 51
2 *Boston Post,* September 17, 1931
3 *Halifax Herald,* October 15, 1931
4 *Boston Post,* October 12, 1931
5 *Yachting,* Decembcr 1931, p. 39
6 Tom Horgan, Associated Press, October 9, 1931
7 *Evening Mail,* October 14, 1931
8 John Griffin, *Boston Post,* October 18, 1931
9 Ibid.
10 Griffin, *Boston Post,* October 19, 1931
11 *Boston Post,* October 20, 1931
12 Backman, *Bluenose,* p. 49
13 *Yachting,* December 1931, p. 40
14 *Halifax Herald,* October 21, 1931

‹ **PICTURE-PERFECT** and escorted by two police launches, the *Bluenose* departs Toronto Harbour in September 1934 on her way out of the Great Lakes and back home to Nova Scotia. She had been invited to represent Canada at the World's Fair in Chicago the previous year. *Library and Archives Canada*

11

THE LAST FISHERMEN'S RACE: 1938

THE GREAT DEPRESSION settled heavily over North America in the early 1930s. The fishing industry on both sides of the border was faltering and many boat owners were forced into bankruptcy. At best, most considered themselves lucky to be able to cover operating costs and provide a subsistence wage for their crews. Even those former fishermen involved in the illegal liquor trade were forced to look elsewhere for income when Prohibition in the United States ended with the repeal of the Volstead Act in 1933.

Trading on their celebrity status, the *Gertrude L. Thebaud* and the *Bluenose* both took on new roles. The *Thebaud* began to function as an emissary for the

› **ALONGSIDE HER** berth at the Century of Progress Exposition in Chicago in 1933, the *Gertrude L. Thebaud* is ready for another day of public cruises. Both the *Thebaud* and her rival the *Bluenose* attended the World's Fair at the behest of their respective governments. The popularity of these two ships was so great that they often had 2,500 people crossing their decks daily. Both vessels worked a tight schedule of cruises and charters that helped finance the boats during the exposition. *D. Ward Pease, Chicago Historical Society*

ailing fishing industry. She sailed to Washington in April 1933 carrying a large delegation of prominent fishing skippers and industry chiefs from most of the coastal ports in the New England states to meet the newly elected U.S. president, Franklin D. Roosevelt. They provided his administration with a detailed report on the industry and requested they be included in the government's labour programs, which were then being instituted to reinvigorate the American economy. The *Thebaud* and her complement of hardy, nearly legendary fishing captains were welcomed to the United States capital with much excitement. "The *Thebaud* party while in Washington received honors usually reserved for the highest potentates. Crowds stormed the navy yard where the *Thebaud* was tied up to inspect the vessel."[1] The visitors were wined and dined in Congress and even had tea with Eleanor Roosevelt in the White House, leaving with hope and promises that the administration would do all it could to provide assistance by developing a national market for fish products. The *Thebaud* also made appearances in New York at the famous Fulton Market to help stimulate sales.

In Canada, there was much talk of preserving the *Bluenose* as a training ship for merchant and naval services, but neither the federal nor the provincial government was willing to contribute any funding. As the *Bluenose* began to fall on hard times, Angus Walters soon realized he could capitalize on the celebrity status of his vessel. He found a public eager to pay to sail on his schooner, and so began a new career touring his vessel for profit. The *Bluenose* spent the next few years on intermittent charters as well as fishing. In 1933 Walters was invited by the Canadian government to take the *Bluenose* to Chicago for the Century of Progress Exposition. This was the first time the schooner had travelled to the Great Lakes, and Walters found she had enormous appeal to the citizens of communities that bordered the waterway. He had her fish holds gutted and replaced with cabins on the starboard side and a showcase of the Lunenburg fishery—complete with scale models and exhibits—installed on the port side. She was funded by a newly formed company of businessmen, Lunenburg Exhibitors Limited, who saw this as an opportunity to promote Lunenburg sea products.

In Chicago, she tied up near her old rival, the *Gertrude L. Thebaud,* representing the state of Massachusetts at the exposition. Like the *Bluenose,* the *Thebaud* had had her fish pens removed and extensive alterations made to accommodate guests, crew, and exhibits on loan from the Cape Ann Historical Association. The mass appeal of both schooners was obvious as hordes of visitors, more than 2,500

HOLLYWOOD
Gertrude L. Thebaud
STEAMBOATS
GERTRUDE L. THEBAUD

a day, descended on them. There were many calls for a race between the two old combatants, but neither skipper was interested.

Walters had his hands full, committing his vessel to a busy schedule of charters, until he ran afoul of a dissatisfied customer who sued him for not adequately catering to his needs. Although the case was eventually thrown out of court, it brought the vessel to the attention of the U.S. customs and excise service, which began to investigate the schooner for customs infractions. Chicago's sinister side came uncomfortably close to the *Bluenose* when a gangster shootout resulted in a bullet-riddled body being dumped astern of her in the early morning. It could be that Angus felt safer in a hurricane at sea than spending a winter in Al Capone's Chicago; he decided in late fall that it was time to head home.

Back in Canadian waters, the *Bluenose* was met by Walters's old newspaper chum, Jerry Snider, who persuaded him to stay for a while in Toronto. Snider had arranged a berth for the boat and a hero's welcome for Walters in Canada's largest city. Over the spring and summer, the *Bluenose* continued in her new career as a showboat for hire. Although she was very popular, she did not meet with the same success as in Chicago, and by the fall of 1934 Walters and his partners decided there was little profit to be made in staying any longer. They headed back home to fish.

In 1935 the *Bluenose* was once again in demand, this time as Canada's ambassador to Great Britain, to attend the silver jubilee of King George V's coronation. Angus made the passage to Plymouth in seventeen days. There, the *Bluenose* found herself anchored among the long lines of British battleships to be reviewed by the king, where her presence was noted and appreciated. Walters was later summoned to the royal yacht to be received by His Majesty and his three sons. The diminutive fishing skipper from Lunenburg found himself sought after by the British elite. He was wined and dined and had the time of his life swapping tales with the rich and famous. When his boat was challenged to a friendly match against a schooner from the Royal Yacht Squadron on a course around the Isle of Wight—where the America's Cup races had begun—he could hardly refuse. The *Bluenose* was clearly outclassed by the refined racing schooner *Westward,* but even so the feisty Walters figured she had given her a run for her money. After this successful foray into British society, he left for home on September 11. The bad weather that accompanied his departure turned steadily worse, until he and the crew were forced to heave to in hurricane-strength winds. Walters later proclaimed the weather was the worst he had ever encountered at sea. For four days they were pounded by fierce headwinds that caused considerable damage to the vessel, and a week after departing England, the Nova Scotian schooner limped back to Plymouth for repairs.

Both the *Bluenose* and the *Thebaud* survived the lean years of the 1930s by making ends meet in any way they could. They continued to fish, bringing in reasonable catches but for paltry returns. In 1936, in an attempt to remain competitive, Walters finally succumbed to the indignity of having diesel engines installed in his beloved schooner, at a cost of $12,000. His efforts to have his vessel officially recognized as a national treasure, with a permanent berth as a museum ship, failed to arouse interest with either local or provincial governments. South of the border, Ben Pine had little more financial luck with the *Thebaud*, as fish prices remained miserably low. In 1937, he chartered his vessel to the renowned Arctic explorer Donald MacMillan for use on a lengthy scientific expedition to the Arctic. After having given so much entertainment and excitement to a generation, each boat seemed to be fading into oblivion.

Two things occurred in 1937 that brightened prospects for both. The likeness of the *Bluenose* was minted onto the Canadian ten-cent piece (where it remains to this day), breathing new life into Walters's campaign to preserve his legendary boat. The other event was the resurrection of Gloucester's glory days of schooner fishing by Hollywood, when MGM Pictures made the Rudyard Kipling classic, *Captains Courageous*, into a movie starring Spencer Tracy as Manuel, a Portuguese fisherman. The story revolved around the character of a spoiled rich brat, played by Freddie Bartholomew, who falls off an Atlantic liner en route to Europe. He is rescued by Manuel, who is out fishing from his dory, and taken back to Manuel's schooner, the *We're Here*. The hard-working, fair-minded skipper has no intention of making a special trip into port to return his errant cargo and puts the little stranger to work gutting fish. The moral lesson taught to the rich child by the industrious, no-nonsense fishermen on board a Cape Ann schooner resonated with the American public, still suffering from economic hard times. The high drama of the last scenes of the movie rang especially true, when two genuine Gloucester schooners, the *Oretha F. Spinney* and the *Imperator*, were used to portray the boats in the film, racing neck and neck under full sail with the sea guttering over the leeward rails. Even today, the excitement of watching the two old schooners race is a powerful testament to the magnetic attraction of the power of sail.

The enormous success of the movie rekindled Gloucester's love affair with schooner racing. The members of the Master Mariners Association met in December to discuss the possibility of reviving the International Fishermen's Cup series. The American race committee was resurrected after seven years of dormancy, and the indefatigable Ben Pine happily threw in his hat. The Halifax trustees were contacted but were not seriously interested in taking part, instead officially handing over the race trophy to Angus Walters and leaving the decision in his hands. Angus was happy to have the chance to race, not only to see his beloved schooner once again in the spotlight, but also to benefit from the occasion by having her fitted out and, with any luck, using the prize money to help pay off the cost of her engines. The Bluenose Schooner Company was in financial difficulty and had not been able to come up with adequate funds.

‹ IN 1935, Angus Walters and the *Bluenose* were invited by the Canadian government to attend the silver jubilee celebrations of King George V's reign. The sight of such a small fishing craft among the fleet of battleships on review at Plymouth in England delighted the king, who insisted on an audience with the Nova Scotian fishing master. Walters can be seen with cap in hand behind the large gentleman on the far right. *Times* (London)

The American race organizers felt they could better capitalize on the event by having a best-of-five series run off two locations, Gloucester and Nahant Bay, near Boston. A longer series in both locations would maximize the tourism potential. They promoted the series to be held in 1938 as an idyllic romp into a bygone age with two legendary skippers squaring off for battle one more time. Steadfastness and courage under the banner of true competition would be the order of the day. Hoping for a friendly contest that would be in keeping with the romantic spirit of the movie, they neglected to take into account the reality of the personalities involved, more specifically that of Captain Angus Walters, who was there not to entertain the public but to win.

Pine himself still had an axe to grind, and seven years had done little to soften his fierce desire to beat the combative Lunenburger. Walters made his intentions clear the moment he arrived in Boston in October 1938. When the mayor greeted the *Bluenose* from the deck of a U.S. Coast Guard cutter and invited Walters to a luncheon in his honour, Angus declined, saying to his crew, "Let them spout. I'm getting ready to race."[2] Nor was he about to keep silent about his views on the organization of the race. When the race committee let it be known it had decided on a short course to enable the race to be better viewed from the shore, Walters went ballistic and fired off the first of a series of broadsides at the race committee, and in particular its chairman, Captain Lyons. Calling it a "merry-go-round," Walters said "he would positively not allow his vessel to be sailed over any course that required going over it twice to complete a race."[3] He was no doubt remembering his defeat at the hands of the *Thebaud* on a twice-around course at the exhibition race in 1930. He went on to protest the lack of Canadians on the committee and found fault with the regulations being used. He let his full fury fly when he accused Captain Lyons of being unfit for the post of chairman, telling him to go back to the farm where he belonged.[4] As the "shrapnel burst and the storm of words raged," Captain Ed Proctor of the committee dug in his heels, remarking that he "saw no reason why [the panel] should buckle under to suit Angus." However, a compromise was needed, and in the end the seven-member committee agreed to a variety of long and short courses and reduced its American membership to three, adding two Canadians. Proctor resigned in disgust but later changed his mind. Ben Pine said that although he would go along with any arrangement, he found the fact that there were no Gloucester fishermen on the committee insulting. All this did not bode well for the future tone of the event, and the cantankerous Angus Walters had just begun. Denying he was making life difficult, he said "he would race in a puddle of brimstone for a counterfeit Chinese centime to settle the championship once and for all."[5] Initially, at least, the combative attitude of the Canadian skipper played well with the press, and reports of the controversy drove up enthusiasm and interest in the series.

The first race was held on October 9 off Nahant Bay. The *Bluenose* was the odds-on favourite going into the race, as most felt the smaller *Thebaud* had little chance against the big Nova Scotian defender in spite of her showing in the 1930 Lipton Cup. The race began in light winds, which picked up quickly into a brisk northwest breeze. The *Bluenose* shot off at the start and secured the weather berth, leaving the *Thebaud* trailing badly eight boat lengths behind. The schooners carried every inch of canvas and flew around the short, eighteen-mile "merry-go-round" course that Walters so despised. Neither would shorten sail, even though both were labouring under the heavy press of wind and shipping huge deck-loads of water. The *Bluenose* blew out one of her foresails on the first leg, but this did not slow her down. It was a wonderful race for the thousands of spectators who were able to view it in its entirety from the shore and hear the crisp, booming sound of rippling canvas on every tack. The Gloucester mistress soon found her legs and began seriously battling the Lunenburger, advancing on each turn, taking only thirty seconds to come about while the *Bluenose* took more than a minute. On the last leg, about three miles from the finish, a sharp crack was heard from aloft on the *Bluenose*. Walters was forced to douse both his fore and jib topsails to ease the pressure on a fractured fore-topmast. The accident slowed the *Bluenose*, but she had already been overtaken by her rival when the mishap occurred. The *Thebaud* soared across the finish nearly three minutes in the lead. With surprising good humour, Angus congratulated Ben Pine, saying: "It was a great race, the finest I have ever sailed and there are no complaints. You know, two boats can't win and Ben sure knows how to sail."[6]

The *Thebaud*'s win was totally unexpected, and it galvanized the American public and the crew. Few had seriously expected her to beat "the big brute from Lunenburg," though the *Thebaud* had never looked so good. She was in great trim, properly ballasted, and her new suit of sails, hand-stitched by Marion Cooney, fitted like a glove. Americans suddenly felt confident of her chances of victory over the Canadians. Despite the glorious sight she made at sea, the *Bluenose* was showing little of her previous form. She seemed far too tender in the gusty wind, rolling heavily and exposing too much weather bilge. When she had arrived from Lunenburg, Walters had had her engines as well as tons of iron ballast removed in preparation for the races. Her seventeen years of life as a fisherman had taken their toll: her sea-ravaged hull had run aground, battled innumerable storms and soaked up so much water over the years that it was now hard to determine her proper ballasting needs. As it was, she was longer on the waterline than she should have been for the competition. She was also hogged—her bow and stern sagged distinctly from the middle—and the strain of the overhang at either end was giving way to gravity. Most boats of her age were retired from fishing and had been sold off to freight cargo in the south.

The next race moved to Gloucester, and then came the first of a barrage of protests from the Americans that the *Bluenose* was breaking the rules by being too deep on the waterline. A survey revealed she was a full fourteen inches longer than permitted. When they had measured her in Boston, Walters had cunningly kept his crew out of sight below decks, moving the men to the stern when the measurer was at the bow and to the bow when the measurer was at the stern, thus making her appear farther out of the water, and therefore lighter than she actually was.[7] In answering the charge, Angus shot back that the *Thebaud* was also in violation by having 50 square feet (4.6 square metres) over the allowable limit of sail, whereas he was nearly 800 square feet (74 square metres) under. Captain Lyons, tired of the protests, insisted the races continue with both vessels in "as-is" condition, and they would discuss the differences at a later date.

The race of October 11 was called off due to lack of wind, but only after it had been allowed to continue for nearly the entire six hours. (The race duration varied between six and seven hours, depending on the course for this series.) Both

Walters and Pine were furious that it had been allowed to continue when it had taken the schooners more than four hours to cover one twelve-mile leg. At one point, a bored Ben Pine called over to Walters, "Hey Angus, you haven't a canoe aboard, have you?"[8]

The schooners did not sail on the twelfth, as both were invited to the dedication of the brand new Gloucester Community Fish Pier. At the time, it was a state-of-the-art facility with a freezer capacity of nearly 1,600 tons of fish and capable of producing 50 tons of ice daily, paid for by federal, state and local money under the Public Works Administration. Thousands toured the new building as well as the *Bluenose* and the *Thebaud*, which were tied up alongside. While the officials and politicians made their speeches on the dock, the fishermen were having their own private party on board the *Bluenose*. *Thebaud* crewman Sterling Hayden gave a delightful description of the party in his book, *Wanderer*:

› **SMASHING INTO** a head sea, the *Gertrude L. Thebaud* momentarily stalls, spilling wind from her jib. Such conditions made for dramatic moments during the series. *Peabody Essex Museum*

> From the fish hold of the *Bluenose* come the sound of a trumpet muted by the three inch pine... Fishermen guard each hatch, for the party below is by invitation only—given by the crews of the schooners in their honor, and maybe that of the press. No one else is welcome... Here ninety men are assembled out of the sun, away from the politicians and tourists, the kids and the wives. They're assembled this day to bury some hatchets and kill a few kegs of rum. Up and down this cave long bundles of sails are spread, with flags nailed to the inner hull. Hymie Rodenhauser [sic], one of the *Bluenose*'s mastheadmen, straddling a keg in a cradle, is blasting loose with his trumpet. A bedlam of laughter and singing and wild gesticulations seen through a pall of smoke... A figure bursts into the hold, blowing the cook's tin whistle. "All right, you bassards, up, up, everybo'y up on the goddam deck! Hear me? The governor's gonna make us his honorin' speech, an' the mayor wants every friggin' one o' you on th' deck... An leave the booze down here... An' no more friggin' noise! Hear?" No one moves. "Drink up!" roars O'Toole. You can hear the Legion band playing the National Anthem. All rise. When the Anthem expires, they sit.[9]

Clearly these hard-bitten fishermen had their own agenda, which was to drink and have fun, with no interest in the ceremonies going on outside.

The second official race occurred on October 13 off Eastern Point, in light winds that only occasionally reached eighteen knots. It was a decent sailing breeze, much

2

suited to the *Bluenose,* and she quickly overhauled her rival and finished twelve minutes in the lead, despite blowing out her staysail. Among the spectators was a very seasick Greta Garbo, a guest aboard a pleasure yacht. Both race skippers were infuriated at the use of trawl buoys to mark the course; these marks disappeared in the swells and were easily confused with the other fishing markers strewn over the water. Pine had so much difficulty locating the buoys that, at one point, the *Thebaud* wasted two tacks in overshooting one mark by more than two miles. Walters wired friends in Halifax: "We won despite the baby buoys."[10] The captains also objected to a new rule that all crew members had to stay on deck during the entire race so that there could be no one below shifting ballast. The series now sat at 1–1, with the next race scheduled for the following day. Because of unfavourable conditions, this race was postponed six times before it was finally sailed.

If the captains were the ringmasters of the show, the men who worked the topsails were the acrobats entertaining the masses. Working eighty feet (twenty-four metres) aloft, men like Fred Rhodenhiser, the main topman of the *Bluenose,* constantly wowed the crowd. Rhodenhiser would casually do a tightrope act across the spring stay between the two masts and inform the public that it was no more difficult to do than walking across the deck. The masthead man of the *Thebaud,* Sterling Hayden, attracted many admirers, primarily women, to the docks to watch his displays of fine seamanship aloft and enjoy his handsome good looks. The local paper, the *Gloucester Daily Times,* plastered his photo across the front page with a headline proclaiming "*Thebaud* Sailor Like Movie Idol," calling him a "Fine Masculine Specimen." Hayden was a superb sailor and navigator, but he was eventually drawn to Hollywood, partly due to the Associated Press reporter Tom Horgan, who arranged a screen test for him.

The next two attempts to race off Gloucester were called off due to light airs. Argument then erupted between the rival skippers and the committee about the location of the next race. The committee wanted it moved to Nahant Bay to satisfy Bostonians' desire to see the race closer to home, but Pine vehemently refused to move from Gloucester. He had hauled out the *Thebaud* to repair a splintered shoe after bumping a ledge in the harbour, and he was determined to have the next race off his home port. Walters was expecting to race off Nahant Bay and had already moved the *Bluenose* to an East Boston boatyard to have a new bowsprit installed. The wrangling continued for three days while the boats were being repaired. The committee was at first deadlocked over what to do, but it finally capitulated to Pine's demand and ordered the *Bluenose* to return to Gloucester. A furious Walters responded: "What do they think I have here, a Halifax ferry boat? I'll have to get a passenger license to navigate between Boston and Gloucester."[11] A disgusted Canadian member of the race committee, Wallace MacAskill, resigned and headed back to Halifax, announcing that his membership on the committee was superfluous. An unexpected visit to the *Bluenose* by John Roosevelt, a son of the American president, managed to calm the waters somewhat and caused Walters to tone down his robust attacks.[12] Leonard Fowle, writing for the *Boston Globe,* could not resist parodying the latest developments:

> The reason for the latest postponements was the inability of Capts. Ben Pine and Angus Walters, who are rivals for the hero's role, to promise to produce their feminine leads, *Gertrude L. Thebaud* and *Bluenose,* on the same stage tomorrow. Captain Ben Pine stated he could not bring his fair lady to Boston in time for a start off Nahant and Capt. Walters was equally certain that his Nova Scotian beauty could not possibly rise early enough to reach Gloucester.[13]

Finally, on Wednesday, October 19, both boats were on the line and ready to race off Gloucester. Captain Cecil Moulton had replaced Ben Pine as master of the *Thebaud,* as Pine was again suffering from a recurrence of his sinus infection. Walters was impatient to race, saying he had spent far too long lying alongside. "I've spent enough time tied up here to the dock for the average Nova Scotia boy to become a full-fledged master in sail."[14] The day held great promise; a spanking twenty-knot breeze was blowing in from the southwest and both crews were more than ready. Suddenly, it was all over before it had started. Five minutes before the starting gun sounded, a bronze composition nut that held the steering wheel in place broke on the *Bluenose,* and the heavy, cast-iron Lunenburg Foundry wheel clattered to the deck. Walters hoisted his ensign to half-mast indicating his boat was disabled, and the race was once again postponed. The vessels returned to port to allow him to repair the damage.

Walters also had a ballast problem. He knew he would need more weight deep in the *Bluenose*'s belly if he were going to race successfully in any substantial wind, but his waterline was already too long. He and his crew had begun surreptitiously loading forty-pound iron ingots in the pre-dawn hours, in clear violation of the rules. Captain Ed Proctor heard a rumour concerning ballast-shifting and had

been closely watching the *Bluenose* over a period of five nights in an attempt to catch the crew in the act. On the night of October 19, he sprinkled sand over a big pile of ingots sitting in a shed on the Pew wharf and asked the night watchman, Manuel Silva, to keep an eye on them. At 4:30 AM on October 20, Proctor received a phone call from the watchman telling him the door to the shed had been opened during the night; when Silva had gone to investigate, he had scared off about fourteen men. In the morning, Proctor found footprints of rubber boots in the sand and several tons of ballast missing. He took his findings to Captain Moulton, who delivered a protest to Captain Lyons on board the committee boat *Thetis,* demanding an investigation. Lyons brushed the complaint aside, saying he had had enough of protests and talk "about a little ballast," and he ordered the race to continue regardless.[15]

The news of the nocturnal ballasting episode spread quickly, and Gloucestermen prayed for the light wind that would work against the *Bluenose.* Their prayers may have been answered too well, for once again the race was cancelled after four and a half hours due to insufficient winds. The *Bluenose* had appeared sluggish during the race to that point and the *Thebaud* was in the lead by more than ten minutes when it was finally called off. When the boats returned to harbour, suspicions were aroused when a zealous "Angus watcher" saw Walters dock at the newly dedicated Community Fish Pier instead of at the Pew wharf. This turn of events was reported to Ray Adams, a friend and associate of Ben Pine's at the Atlantic Supply Company who later became his wife. She sped down to the fish pier and apparently caught Walters and his crew in the act of unloading ballast. When Miss Adams asked Angus outright what he was doing, he admitted he was removing ballast he had loaded that morning.[16] He said it was his ballast and he could do with it as he pleased. The open admission left Captain Lyons with little option but to order the boats be measured again and to postpone the race set for the following day. Miss Adams arranged for the police to guard the *Bluenose* through the night until the measuring was completed.

Walters telegraphed the boat's designer, William Roué, asking him to hurry down from Halifax to help with the problem of bringing his vessel back up to a 112-foot (34-metre) waterline. Instead of removing any more iron ballast, which was located deep in the hull, Roué told the crew to rip up the deck and take out five oil tanks, three air tanks, a generating plant and about five tons of other equipment, explaining that "she was carrying too much weight above the waterline. With that

‹ **THE OPENING** of the new Gloucester Fish Pier provided a brief pause in the 1938 series, and the two famous fishing schooners were a main attraction. As thousands poured across the decks of the *Bluenose* and the *Gertrude L. Thebaud,* the rival crews danced, sang and drank in a private party in the hold of the Nova Scotian boat. Over several kegs of rum, the crew members buried the hatchet for a brief while, before resuming the battle for the Fishermen's Cup. *Cape Ann Historical Association*

weight carried high she was tender and sluggish."[17] He later acknowledged that, in the condition she was then in, it was impossible to give the *Bluenose* adequate ballast for a stiff breeze while still holding her up to the required waterline. She was old and hogged, and her waterline was simply not straight any more.[18] The Americans took great delight in seeing the much lighter *Bluenose,* judging that she would now be far too tender in a breeze to carry much sail and prayed for wind. Any vestige of friendliness between the competing crews had been severely tested by this time, and when Angus was asked to comment, he responded: "They've pushed me too far. I will now give them a beating they won't forget."[19] Frustrated by all the delays, one of the *Bluenose* crew, Sam Shaw, facetiously remarked: "We can only stay in this country six months under the immigration laws and our time will soon be up."[20]

The protests from the Americans seemed to have backfired when, on October 23, a rejuvenated *Bluenose* sailing the "merry-go-round" course off Gloucester outraced her rival by nearly seven minutes. Judging from her performance, it might have been better for the *Thebaud* if the *Bluenose* had been allowed to go on loading ballast, as the Canadian boat now appeared to be in her best trim since the start of the series. As Lester Allen of the *Boston Post* wrote, the *Bluenose* swooped by the *Thebaud* "like a hawk over a chicken yard."[21] A grim, determined Walters had worked his crew like automatons, squinting hard at the sails and roaring out orders that sent the men madly scurrying about the vessel. The defeated crew of Gloucestermen returned to Boston licking its wounds, the series now heading towards the finish with the Canadians up 2–1.

The following day, the Americans evened the score by beating the *Bluenose* over an irregular thirty-five-mile triangular course off Boston. Although the *Thebaud* trailed the *Bluenose* for the first leg of the race, her victory was all but assured on the second twelve-mile leg to windward in a piping southerly breeze. The *Bluenose* had problems with her gear. On the first tack to windward, the block on the fisherman's staysail fouled and would go neither up nor down. As sails lashed and flogged about, Fred Rhodenhiser clung precariously to the spring stay high above the deck and struggled to clear the block. When the *Bluenose* rounded the second mark, a backstay parted and Walters was forced to come up into the wind to lower the jib topsail, which cost him valuable time. The breeze fluctuated in velocity from eight to twenty-five knots, and whenever the wind strengthened, the *Thebaud* drew away from the big defender.[22] At times both vessels were logging twelve to fourteen knots, and the crews were working waist-deep in the green water along the lee rail. It was no picnic on board the *Thebaud* as she hurtled through the smother of sea and spray. Aloft, Sterling Hayden and Jack Hackett fought their way out to the end of the mainsail gaff in the howling wind to secure a block that was threatening to tear away. Lester Allen described the scene: "From afar the yellow oilskinnned figures of the *Thebaud*'s crew seemed to swim around, while working at the leeward gear, like little yellow dabs of butter on a smoking oyster stew."[23] When the *Thebaud* finally crossed the finish, there was some confusion about on which side of the mark she should pass, so having gone past on one side, Moulton came about and repassed it on the other, just to be sure. The lead she had on her rival varied from three to five minutes, according to different sources. The committee boat had great difficulty keeping up with the racers and became lost in the rain and fog, so the finish was not officially timed. When asked how he won, a gloating Moulton said, "The *Bluenose* simply couldn't take it."[24] Walters blurted out: "*Thebaud* beat us—enough said."[25] Echoing the simmering tension between the two competitors, the vessels turned their sterns to each other and went off in opposite directions. The *Thebaud* headed back to Gloucester and the *Bluenose* to East Boston, where it was reported the police had their eyes on her to make sure no more ballast was shifted.[26] Through blinding rain squalls and a boisterous sea, the crew of the *Thebaud* had put the *Bluenose* crew on notice that they were still in the game.

With the series now even and the Americans on a roll, Moulton was furious when the committee cancelled the race the following day. Storm warnings posted all along the coast forced Lyons to call it off to protect the men and vessels. Ben Pine, now out of hospital, charged that Lyons should have consulted the rival skippers beforehand. "Captain Lyons has sent us out day after day when there was no wind and we knew we could not finish, but when everyone knew there would be a breeze he called it off and he wouldn't if he had to pay the expenses of one of these vessels."[27] Both Moulton and Pine went on to accuse Lyons of everything from being seasick to being in collusion with Walters. Their protests concerning the weather appeared to be well founded, since the day passed with clear skies and a twenty-eight-knot northwest breeze, possibly the best conditions since the series had opened.

The fifth and deciding race was held off Boston on October 26. The two old competitors again squared off for the final act in a two-decade-old drama, the likes of which would never be seen again. The previous day, both skippers had

› **NOT ABOUT** to give his opponent an inch, Angus Walters handles the helm of the *Bluenose* like a fine instrument. He was often criticized by his rivals for his flinty and abrasive personality, but not even they could fault his superior seamanship. *Leslie Jones, Boston Public Library*

been involved in the repair of their vessels. Walters had the broken stay and frayed gear to mend, and Moulton, leaving nothing to chance, had had the *Thebaud* hauled out for the fourth time in the series to have her hull scraped and painted. The *Bluenose* crossed the start fifteen seconds ahead of the *Thebaud* when the gun boomed at noon precisely. On the first leg of the thirty-six-mile triangle, Walters sent his charge plunging out past Graves Light with every inch of canvas flying. As the *Thebaud* trailed slightly behind, Walters's small figure, in its trademark faded blue sweater, could be seen behind the heavy Lunenburg Foundry wheel, carefully adjusting direction one spoke at a time. Under a moderate southwest breeze, the *Bluenose* ripped along at eleven knots and gradually pulled farther away, yard by yard, from her rival. On board, the crew huddled under the windward rail, no one stirring but all ready to move at a moment's notice.

On the second leg, the *Thebaud* began to chase down her rival and for the first time started to gain on her. Cecil Moulton, who would have much preferred a good blow, nursed every ounce of the 15-knot wind that flowed across her sails. As Lester Allen described it, Moulton "had an odd trick of rocking back and forth like a lad on a sled, trying to urge his vessel on—and throughout yesterday's race, with eyes cocked up at the fluttering leech of the mainsail, he rocked and rocked and rocked."[28] Conditions on the first two legs did not allow for a luffing match or a strategic tacking duel. Both crews sat idle during the long reaches, except to trim a sail now and then. This part of the race belonged to the skippers, who used all their knowledge and skill to coax every bit of speed they could out of the wind.

The real fight began on the last leg to the finish, when the two big schooners had to work the nine-mile beat to windward. The *Thebaud* crew, which had been far quicker at sail handling than their rivals, found themselves matched on this point for the first time. There was simply too much at stake, and both crews worked with clockwork precision. When they tacked around the last buoy, Walters kept his boat well to windward and was able to point higher than his rival. He sailed so close to the wind that his sails were constantly on the verge of luffing and losing air. The crews went to work in earnest for the first time during this part of the race as both vessels tacked again and again. When the wind freshened to twenty knots, the *Thebaud* was able to gain a little ground on each tack, but she ran out of time. The *Bluenose* was out of reach and flew across the finish two minutes, fifty seconds in the lead. In the closing minutes, the topsail halyard of the *Bluenose* had parted. Had this happened earlier, the result might

have been different, but breaking so close to the finish it did not matter. Lester Allen was magnanimous in his praise of the Lunenburg skipper, writing that Walters and the *Bluenose* were an unbeatable combination. "Walters sailed a magnificent race... He didn't miss a strategic bet anywhere along the 36-mile course. At all times he was the master of both the *Bluenose* and the *Gertrude L. Thebaud*."[29]

The Gloucestermen were disconsolate. There were no smiling faces or caps tossed in the air, only silent groups of men braced against the heel of the deck, with thumbs in the suspenders of their oilskins, silently examining their boots. Each knew this had been the last chance to take on the Nova Scotians.

On the *Bluenose,* the crew were already into the rum and prepared to party. When they made their way into the dock in East Boston, Fred Rhodenhiser, the indomitable foretop man, tooted a merry parody of "The Music Goes Round and Round" on his trumpet, while the crew sang lustily and loudly some uncomplimentary verses about the "merry-go-round" course their skipper so detested.[30] The *Bluenose* had retained her title of Queen of the North Atlantic and her triumphant skipper, Angus Walters, could not have been happier. "Today's race was beautiful, but if the *Thebaud* couldn't beat the *Bluenose* today, she never could and never will."[31]

Although the racing had finally ended, the accusations and recriminations continued. From the start Captain Lyons, the chairman of the race committee, had come under intense criticism from both sides for his handling of the series. A highly disgruntled Cecil Moulton wasted no time in accusing him of favouritism and blamed him for the result. "*Thebaud* was not beaten by *Bluenose,* but by Capt. Lyons. He sent us out day after day when there wasn't enough wind for a real race and kept us in port when there was a good breeze."[32] In Moulton's opinion, the final race was nothing but a drifting match, with no windward work, which favoured the *Bluenose*. "Angus says they haven't got a vessel here that can beat the *Bluenose,* does he? Well, all I can say is that there is no boat can beat him in a drifting match. The *Thebaud* is a racer, not drifter."[33] Captain Proctor, the Gloucester member of the race committee, supported Moulton and agreed that the *Thebaud* was robbed of victory by being forced to stay in port every day there was fishermen's weather. An equally irate Ben Pine said he would never again challenge for the International Fishermen's Cup. "We took two races sailed in a good breeze. *Bluenose* got three sailed in weather I don't consider fit for a fisherman's race. I don't want any more of it."[34]

Walters had also had enough of the series and was glad to see it over. In a brief statement to the press, he said, "I will never sail *Bluenose* again in American waters in a race with an American vessel. I have been treated unfairly. All the tricks they tried on me in Gloucester didn't do them any good, and I'm through with them for good and all."[35] Unfortunately, his problems with the race committee were only just beginning. The promised prize money plus expenses, totalling $9,000, were unavailable as meagre donations and poor sales of subscriptions to the race fund had left the organizers struggling to come up with funds. But Walters had entered into the series with a contract stipulating that he would be paid in full, and he was not about to leave without it; nor was Ben Pine about to let Walters depart with any money until he had received his own share. As John Griffin said in the *Boston Post,* "It would take the talents of the proverbial Philadelphia lawyer to set things in order, and even then it is doubtful that all hands would be satisfied."[36] To make matters worse, the International Fishermen's Cup, which had been on prominent display in a Boston department store window, went missing.

News of the trophy's disappearance brought great amusement along the waterfront in Gloucester. Although no one admitted to stealing it, most thought it had been "borrowed" as a prank. Pine said he had no interest in the trophy and had only raced to "beat Angus," but, he added, "it was a great joke that the trophy was gone, and wondered how Angus could ever convince the Nova Scotians that he had beat the *Thebaud* if he couldn't produce the trophy."[37] The insurance company that held a policy on the cup put up a $500 reward for its return, with no result. Walters was not amused and told the race directors, "You better get it back or else." He ordered the *Bluenose* to depart for Lunenburg, "before she too disappeared."[38] He was not about to wait around to have the engines installed, either, as he did not "want to have anything more to do with Gloucester." In fact, at the time Angus probably felt the same way about Boston; to add insult to injury, a confidence man there robbed him of $10 he had put down on a new suit.

Cecil Moulton could not shake off his bitterness over the outcome and refused to let things rest. He desperately wanted another chance to take on the *Bluenose* in "real fishermen's weather" and sent a telegram to Walters, stating, "I hereby challenge you to one race over your own course in Massachusetts waters in any breeze of 25 miles an hour or more velocity. You and I put up $500 each and race under deed of gift. Put up or shut up. Winnings go to winning crew."[39] Walters was unmoved and replied through the press that he had "more important things on his mind now," referring to his upcoming marriage to Mildred Butler of

Halifax. Nonetheless, he could not resist a jab at Moulton and upped the ante: "Five hundred dollars, Bah! That's only poker money those Gloucester folks are talking about. Let's get this thing settled for once and for all. Let's race for $5,000, from Boston to Bermuda, around the island and back to Halifax, winner-take-all. Let them think that over instead of spouting about chicken feed."[40] Neither challenge was accepted, and both skippers adamantly refused to negotiate.

‹ CARRYING LESS sail and almost twice the age of her rival, the *Bluenose* manages to creep up on the *Gertrude L. Thebaud* during a race off Gloucester in 1938. That Fishermen's Cup series became the longest and most contentious in the history of these races; it also turned out to be the last. *Leslie Jones, Boston Public Library*

At the same time, Walters—still in Boston—was basking in the attention given to him as victor, secure in the knowledge that the International Fishermen's Cup was now his forever. He was wined and dined and, at a victory dinner put on by the Canadian Club at the Chamber of Commerce in his honour, his rivals, Ben Pine and Cecil Moulton, as well as Captain Lyons, were all on hand to congratulate him and his crew. If there was any ill feeling between the rival skippers at that point, it was well hidden, as each congratulated the other for fine sportsmanship. Walters was invited to speak to the Massachusetts House of Representatives, and told the assembled politicians he was confident the prize money would be forthcoming and the trophy soon found. The opportunity to speak before the house, he said, had given him the greatest pleasure he'd had since arriving in Boston. The representatives gave him a rousing round of cheers and enthusiastic applause. Walters was by now enjoying his reception so much that he made hints he might return with his new bride to settle in the city.

The errant trophy finally resurfaced, mysteriously appearing unharmed on the Boston doorstep of the New England Home for Little Wanderers. The culprits were never identified, but there was a rumour the Boston press had been responsible. No one was more puzzled than Elizabeth Beyer, the matron of the home, when she found the parcel on her steps on Halloween morning. Like a foundling child, the cup lay carefully wrapped, with a bottle of cod liver oil beside it and a poem reading:

> Here's to Angus, good old sport,
> Whose challenge sort of takes us short.
> Send us a gale that blows at thirty,
> And we'll bet our shirts on little Gerty.[41]

The irony of the 1938 series was that, in a reversal of roles from their previous encounters, the *Gertrude L. Thebaud* was probably the better boat in a strong breeze and the *Bluenose* better in light airs. From the beginning of her career, the *Bluenose* had made her name in heavy-weather sailing and was always considered at her best going to windward in a strong blow. She had beaten the *Elsie,* the *Henry Ford* and the *Thebaud* over long courses in heavy weather. Only the *Columbia* had come close to matching her, boat for boat, in a gale of wind. The *Thebaud,* on the other hand, always seemed out of trim and improperly ballasted until the 1938 series. In 1930, during the second race of the Lipton Cup series, she floundered so badly in the forty-knot breeze that she was caught in irons and barely able to manoeuvre before the race was abandoned, while the *Bluenose* had soared ahead. But in 1938 it appeared the *Thebaud* was in her prime, giving the best performance of her career, far superior in a strong breeze than her opponent. The *Bluenose* was by then too old and sea-worn to be racing at all, but she had honours and a skipper's pride to defend—and engines to pay off. She was now a very different boat than she had been the last time she raced, in 1931. If the final race of 1938 had been run on October 25, when the wind was blowing hard, the series might have had a different outcome. The *Bluenose* needed the lighter air to race effectively because her lack of proper ballasting made her too tender for a strong breeze. Even Ed Kelly, the *Halifax Herald* writer who had followed the *Bluenose*'s career from the time she was built, admitted she was too old and too tender for racing:

> Imagine it! *Bluenose*—the "heavy weather vessel"—wanting a "light breeze." We would have called it ridiculous, if we had not realized by then it was true... Heavily handicapped by years, woefully out of condition, in no shape to do what she used to do, this splendid old Champion came through yesterday with the greatest triumph of her long career.[42]

With the trophy now handed back to him, Walters returned home to a hero's reception, though still without the promised prize money. It would take months, and the help of lawyers, to sort out the financial wrangling. In the end, Walters received only a portion of his winnings and expenses.

NOTES

1 *Atlantic Fisherman,* May 1933, p. 5
2 *Boston Post,* October 8, 1938; Hayden, *Wanderer,* p. 218
3 *Gloucester Daily Times,* October 6, 1938
4 Ibid.
5 *Boston Sunday Post,* October 9, 1938
6 *Boston Post,* October 10, 1938
7 Cameron, *Schooner,* p. 60
8 *Halifax Herald,* October 12, 1938
9 Hayden, *Wanderer,* p. 221
10 *Halifax Herald,* October 14, 1938
11 *Boston Globe,* October 17, 1938
12 Ibid.
13 *Boston Globe,* October 18, 1938
14 *Boston Post,* October 19, 1938
15 *Gloucester Daily Times,* October 21, 1938
16 *Gloucester Daily Times,* October 21, 1938; *Halifax Herald,* October 22, 1938
17 *Boston Post,* October 24, 1938
18 *Halifax Herald,* October 27, 1938
19 *Boston Sunday Post,* October 23, 1938
20 *Boston Post,* October 21, 1938
21 *Boston Post,* October 24, 1938
22 *Halifax Herald,* October 25, 1938
23 *Boston Post,* October 25, 1938
24 Ibid.
25 *Halifax Herald,* October 25, 1938
26 *Gloucester Daily Times,* October 25, 1938
27 *Halifax Herald,* October 26, 1938
28 *Boston Post,* October 27, 1938
29 Ibid.
30 Ibid.
31 *Boston Herald,* October 27, 1938
32 *Gloucester Daily Times,* October 27, 1938
33 *Boston Herald,* October 27, 1938
34 Ibid.
35 Ibid.
36 *Boston Post,* October 28, 1938
37 *Gloucester Daily Times,* October 28, 1938
38 *Boston Post,* October 28, 1938
39 *Boston Post,* October 28, 1938
40 *Halifax Herald,* October 29, 1938
41 *Gloucester Daily Times,* November 1, 1938
42 *Halifax Herald,* October 27, 1938

‹ **A MERE** "biscuit toss" away, the *Bluenose* steadily gains on the *Gertrude L. Thebaud* and attempts to take her wind during the 1938 series. As ribald comments are tossed back and forth between the schooners, the *Bluenose* crew hauls on her mainsheet, trying to coax every ounce of speed out of the seventeen-year-old hull. *Cape Ann Historical Association*

12

IN THE WAKE

AS BITTER AND ACRIMONIOUS as the 1938 series was, the competition did serve as a swan song for the schooner fishery. The sight of tall spars marking a harbour beyond a headland was by then already becoming a distant memory, and the end of an era could not have come with more finality than with the beginning of the Second World War. Even as the *Gertrude L. Thebaud* and the *Bluenose* were facing off for their first race of the 1938 series, the prime minister of Great Britain, Neville Chamberlain, was attempting to negotiate a peaceful resolution to Nazi aggression with Adolf Hitler in Germany. Despite the fuss and fanfare, to most of the world riveted to news of events in Europe, the last Fishermen's Cup races were really only a bit of nostalgic entertainment for some.

In 1939, Angus Walters had a tough time trying to keep his vessel afloat financially. The marauding German U-boats had effectively closed the sea lanes off North America and the banks fishery had entirely collapsed, leaving the *Bluenose* and the rest of the Lunenburg fleet no option but to remain tied up at the dock. The Bluenose Schooner Company could not make payments on her engines, so the mortgage was foreclosed and the *Bluenose* went up for auction on November 14, 1939. Walters had retired from life at sea in 1939 and and opened a dairy in Lunenburg, but he could not bear to part with his treasured schooner. One hour before she was due to go under the auctioneer's hammer, he rescued her with $7,000 of his own savings. "I think it a disgrace the schooner be threatened with the auction block. I still will protect the *Bluenose* with all that I have as she has served me so faithfully to be let down," the impassioned skipper later declared.[1] He continued to lobby hard to have her taken over by the government and preserved as a national monument, but without a groundswell of support, there could be little hope of success. He appealed to his own community and beyond to help save her, and he tried to organize a nationwide campaign to sell non-dividend-bearing shares at a dollar apiece. The timing could not have been worse. An old fishing schooner in Lunenburg could not compete with a world war. By 1942, Angus could no longer afford to keep his schooner and was forced to sell her to the West Indies Trading Company Ltd. for $20,000; she was put to work as an itinerant freighter carrying cargoes of rum, bananas, sugar, dynamite and fuel oil throughout the Caribbean. It is not hard to imagine his grief when he cast off her lines in May 1942 and, knowing he would likely never see her again, watched her go. "We've seen a lot together in fair weather and foul, and the *Bluenose* was like a part of me," he said after she departed. He remained bitter that the province and his own community had failed to preserve the schooner that had served so faithfully for eighteen years and brought fame and glory to Lunenburg, Nova Scotia and Canada.

As Walters predicted, the *Bluenose* did not return to Nova Scotian waters. Her new career in the West Indies was a short one, coming to an abrupt end in January 1946 when she struck a reef off Haiti and sank. Too late, her loss finally struck a nerve in Canada, and as the *Halifax Herald* lamented, "her passing is a national sorrow; the ignominy of her death, a national shame."[2] As a Lunenburg resident put it more poignantly years later, "*Bluenose!* You know how Loun'burg feels? Like somebody just buried their mother. Home now after the funeral, they sit in the kitchen and remember they didn't treat her very good when she was alive."[3] In a letter to the *Chronicle Herald* in 1953, Walters wrote, "I feel it is to the shame of the Province and the town of Lunenburg, and the citizens who were in a position to have set up the *Bluenose* as a permanent memorial of a fast dying way of fishing that she was allowed to go South to founder and to rest on a bed of rocks."[4]

Sadly, the sinking of the *Bluenose* seemed to be part of a pattern affecting the schooners that took part in the International Fishermen's Cup series; many of them came to similar tragic ends. Her rival, the *Gertrude L. Thebaud,* passed the war years on loan to the United States Navy, acting as a flagship for the Corsair fleet of volunteer pleasure boats that patrolled the Atlantic and Gulf coasts looking for German submarines. In the spring of 1944, with a wheelhouse added and bowsprit removed, she was returned to her owner. As Ben Pine had little use for his antiquated schooner, he sold her to a New Yorker who sent her south, like the *Bluenose,* to cart cargo around the Caribbean and South America. She left Gloucester for the last time in May 1945 and met her end not far from her famous rival, smashed against a breakwater in Laguaira Harbour, Venezuela, in February 1948.

Both schooners from the first series of 1920 were lost, the *Esperanto* off Sable Island in the summer of 1921 and the *Delawana* in a storm off Guysburo County in April 1924. The little *Elsie* foundered in the Gulf of St. Lawrence in January 1936, and the *Henry Ford* broke up on Whaleback Ledge on the west coast of Newfoundland in June 1928. The *Columbia* never did race the *Bluenose* again after the 1923 series, and she sank with all hands, off Sable Island, in August 1927. Many of the vessels that competed in the elimination races, or were built to compete, also met with disaster. Both the *Puritan* and the *Keno* had their racing careers cut short before they had a chance to prove their worth, the *Puritan* sinking off Sable Island in June 1922 and the *Keno* on her way to Newfoundland in January 1924. Others, such as the *Uda R. Corkum,* the *Mayotte,* the *Mahaska,* the *Arthur James,* the *Elizabeth Howard* and the *Elsie G. Silva,* fell victim to the sea in one way or another. The tragic endings were blamed on the jinx of the Fishermen's Cup races, but in reality they were no different from the fates of many fishing schooners at the time. One need only remember the monuments to drowned fishermen in Lunenburg and Gloucester to realize how many schooners and men were lost at sea.

Despite the sometimes heated bluster of their public comments, Ben Pine remained friendly with Angus Walters and had a cordial relationship with his rival until his death at the age of seventy in February 1953. He was buried in Gloucester under a headstone that bears an image of his favourite schooner, the

Columbia. Although he never sailed as a working skipper on any of the fishing boats he owned, his title of "captain" was well earned through his untiring efforts to promote an industry he loved and his almost single-handed efforts to keep schooner racing alive through the late 1920s and the 1930s. He was plagued with illness and could not always be at the wheel when he wished, but he always showed great sportsmanship and, given the opportunity, a masterful handling of his schooners. His one remaining regret was that he never had a second chance to take on his nemesis, the *Bluenose,* with the *Columbia,* which he considered the finest and fastest fishing schooner ever built.

On July 24, 1963, Angus Walters watched history repeat itself at the Smith and Rhuland yard in Lunenburg. Three years earlier, the shipyard had built a replica of HMS *Bounty* to be used in the film *Mutiny on the Bounty.* The sight of a large wooden sailing ship in the waterfront shipyard generated much excitement and fuelled speculation that a replica of the *Bluenose* could be next. The boom days of the salt fishery and shipbuilding were long gone, but there was enough expertise left in the town to do the job. A local Halifax business, Oland and Son Brewery, understood the enormous potential in advertising and underwrote the building of the replica of the famous Nova Scotian schooner to promote its new label, "Schooner Beer." Both Walters and William Roué were consulted on the construction details. The hull, sail plan and rigging were identical to the original, but the interior was altered to suit her new role as floating ambassador for the province. Walters was thrilled to see his old charge brought back to life in replica, and when he took the wheel on her sea trials in 1963, after studying her lines and the set of her sail, he announced, "She'll do fine."[5] Walters passed away in 1968, secure in the knowledge that his legacy would be passed on for some time to come.

Walters has been seen as hero or villain, depending on the side of the Canada–United States border. Although he was known for his caustic tongue and for playing hard and fast with the rules, even his worst critics could not fault his superior seamanship. The American maritime historian Howard Chapelle later called him "an aggressive, unsportsmanlike, and abusive man," but acknowledged him as "a prime sailor."[6] North of the border, Walters was a champion who contributed greatly to a spirit of nationhood in a young country so often overshadowed by her neighbour to the south. This was especially true during the depths of the Great Depression, when Canada desperately needed larger-than-life heroes who were tough and resourceful. The *Bluenose* became a national icon, her image

‹ **THE *BLUENOSE*** sails off in the distance with her sails "wing and wing," or, as old sailors like to say, "reading both pages." A following breeze and a fair wind was a joy to sailor and fisherman alike. *Wallace MacAskill Collection, Nova Scotia Archives and Records Management*

appearing on everything from soft drinks to underwear. Today, her likeness remains engraved on the Canadian ten-cent coin.

Although the advance of technology forever changed the fishing industry, until the 1950s the few stalwart souls who clung to tradition continued to work from dories with hook and line. The schooners still at sea seemed to be almost ghosts from the past, come to haunt the trawlers and draggers operating offshore. They were objects of awe and wonder to modern fishermen who, though shaking their heads in disbelief, would make way for their revered elders on the banks. Though their time was long past, the harsh and dangerous life they represented still commanded respect. Today, aside from the expensively restored historic vessels lying alongside museum wharves, there is little left of the traditional fishing schooner.

The irony of the passing of the banks schooners is that they are now seen as symbols of romance. The passage of time has all but eliminated the memory of a working life under sail and, to some extent, the last schooner races served to reinforce the ideal that was also popularized by contemporary writers. Walters, Morrissey, Welsh, Himmelman and Pine have become picturesque folk heroes to a public that admires their skill, resourcefulness and courage and neglects their all-too-human qualities that, at the time, added to the excitement and drama of the races.

The series may have elevated the status of the humble fisherman, but it failed in other respects. Its goal of expanding the fish market proved to be beyond its powers and the anticipated improvements in schooner design did not materialize, as that would have been a pointless exercise for an almost obsolete vessel. Although the International Fishermen's Cup often became mired in controversy and contention and fell victim to pettiness and patriotism, the "race for real sailors" succeeded in giving working boats—and their designers, builders, skippers and crews—an opportunity to prove their worth on a grand scale and the public a last look at those beautiful vessels crewed by a dying breed of fishermen, before both sailed off into the horizon.

NOTES

1 Backman, *Bluenose,* p. 21
2 *Halifax Herald,* n.d.
3 *Maclean's,* June 15, 1950, p. 45
4 *Chronicle Herald,* 1953
5 Backman, *Bluenose,* p. 84
6 Chapelle, *American Fishing Schooners,* p. 296

APPENDIX: RACE RULES, 1920–38

(1) **PROPOSED RACE RULES**, as published in the *Gloucester Daily Times*, October 13, 1920

1. Vessel must be a *bona-fide* fisherman with at least one year's experience on the banks.
2. Vessels must carry inside ballast only.
3. Sails used in the race to be made of ordinary commercial duck and to be of no greater area than those in ordinary use on the banks and to be limited to mainsail, foresail, jumbo, jib, jib topsail, fore and main working gaff topsails and fisherman's staysail.
4. Crew to be limited to twenty-five men.
5. Skipper to be *bona-fide* fishing captain with at least one year's experience on the banks.
6. Vessels to be not more than 150 feet [45.7 metres] overall length.
7. Race to be sailed boat for boat without any time allowance.
8. Decisions of the sailing committee, on which both sides are to be represented, to be regarded as final in the interpretation of the above conditions.
9. Trophy to be awarded to the winner of the best two out of three races.

(2) **THE RACE RULES 1920**, as published in the *Evening Mail*, October 29, 1920

1. One vessel only to represent Nova Scotia and one only to represent Gloucester.
2. Crew to consist of Twenty-five (25) men including Master; also one representative of the opposing boat. Owners to have the privilege of taking Two (2) invited guests on each boat, one whom may be a Pilot if desired, making the maximum total of Twenty-eight (28) on each boat.
3. The Trophy Cup to be a Perpetual Challenge Trophy. The Cup to remain in possession of the Municipality or some responsible organization. A formal Document to be prepared stating that the Cup is open to yearly challenge. The present series to be the best two out of three Races. Trophy to be raced for this year, 1920, and next year, 1921, off Halifax, and afterwards in accordance with the Deed of Gift.
4. Start to be at 9 a.m. Time Limit nine hours. In case of a later start and the Race not concluded it is to be called off at 6 p.m.
5. Racing Rules: the regular rules of the road.
6. Length of Course: Forty (40) Miles. Weather conditions permitting, one of the first two races shall be a windward or a leeward if possible, the others to be triangle, over course laid down. Sailing Committee to have full jurisdiction over the Race and to notify competitors One Hour before the start what course is selected. Race every day unless postponement for sufficient reasons.
7. Dates, 1920 Race: Saturday, Oct. 30, Monday, Nov. 1, Tues. Nov. 2.
8. Sails: Those only to be used which are a regular part of a fishing vessel outfit, viz: 4 lowers, 2 topsails, 1 jib topsail, 1 staysail.
9. Ballast Rocks or Iron: Owner's option. No shifting of ballast allowed after the firing of the Fifteen Minute preparatory Gun.

10. Guns: One at fifteen minutes before the start, one at five minutes before the start, and the Starting Gun. Competing schooners to be notified of any postponement of the time of starting.
11. All time to be from the foremast of the vessels.
12. Gloucester to appoint a representative to act on the Race Committee.

(3) 1921 DEED OF GIFT

To all Men Greetings

Be it known that William H. Dennis, representing the proprietors of The *Halifax Herald* and The *Evening Mail* newspapers, published in the City of Halifax, in the Province of Nova Scotia, Canada, recognizing the great importance and value of the deep sea fishing industry to the inhabitants of this Province of Nova Scotia, and realizing the necessity of the best possible type of craft being employed in the pursuit of the industry and believing that this can best be obtained by engendering a spirit of friendly competition among the fishermen of this Province and also with the fishermen engaged in similar methods of fishing in the other Maritime Provinces of Canada, the dominion of Newfoundland and the United States of America, has donated and placed under the control of Trustees to be named herein, a TROPHY, of which a photograph and description thereof shall be attached hereto, to be known as:

The Halifax Herald North Atlantic Fishermen's International Trophy

to be sailed for annually under the Rules and Conditions which follow, which may be added to, taken from or modified from time to time to meet changing conditions of the Industry by the Trustees herein appointed or their successors. The said Rules or any modification thereof being always drawn in such manner as to safeguard and continue the intention of the Donors of the Trophy, which is the development of the most practical and serviceable type of fishing schooner combined with the best sailing qualities, without sacrificing utility. For the purpose of maintaining this principle the Trustees are empowered to disqualify from all or any competition any vessel which in their opinion is of such a type or dimensions as would contravert the intention of the Donors and such decisions of the Trustees shall be final; the Trustees shall, however, do nothing which will change the spirit of the intention of the Donors, that the competitors shall be confined to vessels and crews engaged in practical commercial fishing.

The Trustees in whom the control of the Trophy is vested are The Honourable The Premier of Nova Scotia, His Worship The Mayor of Halifax, Messrs. H.R. Silver, H.G. DeWolf, R.A. Corbett, H.G. Lawrence, W.J. Roué, F.W. Baldwin, Capt. V.C. Johnson, being Members of the Original Committee; any vacancies arising to be filled by a majority vote of the remaining Trustees, who, in conference with the representatives of the Gloucester Committee in charge of the races held in the year Nineteen Hundred and Twenty, have drawn the following Rules and Regulations, which shall govern all future races until and unless good and sufficient reason arises for their modifications in such manner as the Trustees may consider advisable.

1. This Trophy is being presented by the proprietors of the The *Halifax Herald* and The *Evening Mail*, as a perpetual International Championship Trophy, to be raced for annually.

2. All Races for this Trophy shall be under the control and management of an International Committee of Five, which shall be elected for each series of races; the Trustees will nominate the two members of the Committee to represent Nova Scotia, and the Governor of the Commonwealth of Massachusetts, in conjunction with the local United States Committee handling the Race, shall name the two members of the Committee to represent the United States. The Chairman of this Committee shall be named by the two members of the Committee representing the country in which the Race is to be held.

3. The Race shall be sailed in the year 1921 off the Harbour of Halifax, Nova Scotia, and alternately thereafter off Gloucester (or a course in Massachusetts Bay to be mutually agreed upon by the International Committee in charge of the Race) and off Halifax, Nova Scotia. The dates on which the Races are to be sailed shall be decided by the International Committee, but shall be fixed so as not to unduly interfere with the business in which the craft are engaged.

4. The only vessels which can compete for the trophy shall be *bona-fide* fishing vessels, which have been engaged in commercial deep sea fishing for at least one season previous to the Race. A fishing season for the purpose of these Rules is considered as extending from the month of April to September, and any vessel competing must have actually sailed from her last port of departure for the Fishing Banks not later than April thirtieth in any year and have remained on the fishing grounds in all weather as customary, until the month of September, excepting necessary returns to port for landing cargo and refitting. Fishing Banks shall mean all off-shore Banks, such as George's, Western, Grand, etc., and vessels engaged in shore fishing and making port in bad weather shall not be eligible.

5. The Captain and Crew of each competing vessel shall be *bona-fide* fishermen, actively engaged in deep sea fishing, and the number of the crew shall be fixed by the International Committee. A list of the crew of each vessel and substitutes therefore shall be forwarded to the International Committee one week before the Series takes place, and each vessel competing shall be furnished with a copy of the Crew List of the opposing vessel or vessels.

6. All competing vessels shall be propelled by sails only and must comply with the following measurements and conditions:
   (a) OVERALL LENGTH, Not to exceed one hundred and forty-five (145) feet [44.2 metres], from outside of stem to outside of taffrail.
   (b) WATER LINE LENGTH, in racing trim, not to exceed one hundred and twelve (112) feet [34.1 metres] from the outside of the stem at point of submersion to the point of submersion at the stern.
   (c) DRAUGHT OF VESSEL, in racing trim shall not exceed sixteen (16) feet [4.9 metres] from the lowest point of the keel to the racing water line, measured vertically.
   (d) NO OUTSIDE BALLAST shall be used.
   (e) INSIDE BALLAST shall consist of any material of a not greater specific gravity than iron.
   (f) COMPETING VESSELS shall race with the same spars, including booms and gaffs (which must all be solid), as are used in fishing.

(g) COMPETING VESSELS must be of the usual type, both in form and construction, sail plan and rigging, as customary in the fishing industry, and any radical departure therefrom may be regarded as a freak and eliminated.

7. (a) The Sails used in racing shall be made of the ordinary commercial duck of the same weight and texture as generally used in the class of vessel and shall have been used at least one season in fishing.

(b) SAILS TO BE USED are Mainsail, Foresail, two Jibs (including Jumbo), Jib Topsail, Fore and Main Gaff Topsails and fisherman's Staysail.

(c) THE TOTAL SAIL AREA, not including fisherman's staysail, to be no greater than Eighty Percent (80%) of the square of the water line length, in racing trim, as expressed in square feet. This stipulation not to apply to vessels built previous to the 1920 Races, but such existing vessels shall not increase their sail area to exceed 80% of the square of the water line if it does not already do so.

(d) THE COMBINED AREA of the Mainsail and the Main Gaff Topsail shall not be more than Fifty percent (50%) of the maximum total sail area, as provided in the preceding subsection "c".

8. The area of the sails shall be calculated as follows:

- MAINSAIL By the universal rule for mainsails, with the exception that the "B" of the formulae shall be measured from the after-side of the mainmast to the outer clew iron hole.
- MAIN GAFF TOPSAIL Universal rule
- FORESAIL AND FORE GAFF TOPSAIL By the universal rule for actual measurement of the sails used and not a percentage of space between the masts.
- HEAD SAILS Universal rule for Head Sails.

If more than one Staysail or Jibtopsail are on the vessel they must be of the same area and only one be set at a time.

9. NO BALLAST shall be taken on or put off the competing vessels during the Series and no ballast shall be shifted after the Fifteen Minute Preparatory Gun is fired before each Race.

10. THE INTERNATIONAL COMMITTEE shall have power to arrange all details of the Races in accordance with the Deed of Gift and shall appoint such Sub-Committees as may be necessary to properly carry them out.

11. THE SAILING COMMITTEE shall be a sub-committee, appointed by the International Committee, and shall be an independent body having no financial interest in the competing vessels. They will lay out the courses for each Series, decide the Course to be sailed for each Race, make the necessary sailing regulations and have them carried out.

12. THE COURSES laid down by the sailing committee shall not be less than thirty-five or more than forty nautical miles in length and be so arranged as to provide windward and leeward work. The time limit of each Race shall be nine hours. There shall be no handicap or time allowance, each vessel shall sail on its merits.

13. THE TROPHY shall be awarded to and remain in the possession for one year of the Vessel winning Two of Three Races over Courses as laid down by the sailing committee each year, and a responsible person or corporation representing the Owners of the winning vessel shall give to the Trustees of the Trophy an official receipt therefore, together with a Bond for $500.00 obligating them to return the Trophy to the Trustees previous to the next Race, or to replace the Trophy if it becomes lost or destroyed through accident or otherwise; and to return same to the Trustees if it has not been raced for during a period of five years.

14. THE TOTAL CASH PRIZES awarded in connection with this Race in any one year shall not exceed the sum of five Thousand Dollars ($5,000) for each Series and the distribution of the money shall be decided by the International Committee. The money for these prizes to be provided by the Committee representing the country in which the Race is held.

If for any reason there should be no International Competition for this Trophy for any period of five consecutive years it shall be within the power of the Trustees to make such use of the Trophy as they may consider advisable in connection with the development of the Fishing Industry in the Province of Nova Scotia.

IN WITNESS WHEREOF we have hereunto set our hands and affixed our seals this 23rd day of March in the year of our Lord One Thousand Nine Hundred and Twenty-One A D.

In the presence of

(SND.) W.H. DENNIS

For the Proprietors of The *Halifax Herald* and The *Evening Mail.*

(SND.) H.R. SILVER

For the Trustees.

(4) **EXPLANATION** of Eighty Per cent Rule for the 1922 Series

The Eighty Per Cent Rule was added to the deed of gift after the 1920 series. The idea was to keep the sail area within an acceptable range of a typical banks schooner and deter "freak" rig and sail development. The measurement was 80 per cent of the square of the waterline as measured before a race. Information concerning the Eighty Per Cent Rule was widely circulated after it was incorporated into the 1921 rules. It certainly would have been a popular topic of discussion among those interested in the series; Thomas McManus would most certainly have known about the rule prior to designing the *Henry Ford.*

The measurements below were those given by the measurer, Evers Burtner, to the *Gloucester Daily Times,* October 21, 1922:

› *Bluenose*

Draft: 15.66 feet [4.77 metres]

Waterline: 111.8 Feet [34.08 metres]

111.8 squared = 12,499 square feet x 0.8 = 9999.39 square feet [928.97 square metres]

Allowed sail area: 9999.39 square feet [928.97 square metres]
Actual sail area: 9771.0 square feet [907.76 square metres]
Difference: 228.39 square feet [21.21 square metres] under the allowed limit

› *Henry Ford*
Draft: 15.12 feet [4.6 metres]
Waterline: 109.47 feet [33.37 metres]
109.47 squared = 11,983.68 square feet x 0.8 = 9586.94 square feet [890.66 square metres]
Allowed sail area: 9586.94 square feet [890.66 square metres]
Actual sail area: 10,077.0 square feet [936.18 square metres]
Difference: 490.06 square feet [45.52 square metres] over the allowed limit

The first cut of the sail of the *Henry Ford* took off 437 square feet [40.6 square metres] and the second cut took away an additional 53 square feet [4.92 square metres]. It should be pointed out in defence of Evers Burtner that he did not make a mistake in his initial measuring, as was implied in the popular press at the time. Rather, the crew had ignored his marks the first time and cut off too little.

(5) ADDITIONAL RULES, 1923

Freeboard and tonnage measurements were added to the 1921 rules before the 1923 series, but so far they are only known from references in other documents; a copy of the actual rules has not been found.

(A) Special Rules, 1923 (also used for the 1931 series)

1. PASSING TO WINDWARD. An overtaken vessel may luff as she pleases to prevent an overtaking vessel passing her to windward, until she is in such a position that the bowsprit end, or stem if she has no bowsprit, would strike the overtaking vessel abaft the main shrouds, when her right to prevent the other having a free passage to windward shall cease.
2. PASSING TO LEEWARD. An overtaken vessel must never bear away to prevent another vessel passing her to leeward—the lee side to be considered that on which the leading vessel of the two carries her main boom. The overtaking vessel must not luff until she has drawn clear ahead of the vessel which she has overtaken.
3. RIGHTS OF NEW COURSE. A vessel shall not become entitled to her rights on a new course until she has filled away.
4. PASSING AND ROUNDING MARKS. If an overlap exists between two vessels when both of them, without tacking, are about to pass a mark on a required side, then the outside vessel must give the inside vessel room to pass clear of the mark. A vessel shall not, however, be justified in attempting to force an overlap and thus force a passage between another vessel and the mark after the latter has altered her helm for the purpose of rounding.
5. OVERLAP. An overlap is established when an overtaking vessel has no longer a free choice on which side she will pass, and continues to exist as long as the leeward vessel by luffing, or the weather vessel by bearing away, is in danger of fouling.

6. OBSTRUCTION TO SEA ROOM. When a vessel is approaching a shore, shoal, rock, vessel or other dangerous obstruction, and cannot go clear by altering her course without fouling another vessel, then the latter shall, on being hailed by the former, at once give sea room; and in case one vessel is forced to tack or to bear away in order to give sea room, the other shall also tack or bear away as the case may be, at as near the same time as is possible without danger of fouling. But if such obstruction is a designated mark of the course, a vessel forcing another to tack under the provisions of this section shall be disqualified.
7. If any competing vessels foul a buoy marking the course or foul another competing vessel during the race, she may be disqualified by the Sailing Committee and in the event of disqualification shall score no points in such race.
8. If a vessel crosses the line before the starting gun is fired, her number will be displayed at the end of the "Breakwater" and she will have to return and recross the starting line, otherwise she shall be disqualified from the race.
9. All protests regarding any race shall be made in writing and delivered to the Chairman of the Sailing Committee on the day of the race. Such protests shall be heard and considered by the Sailing Committee and its decision thereon shall be final.
10. Starting and finishing line to be a line from the end of breakwater at Point Pleasant Park, extending easterly across the harbour, and marked by two poles in line with the breakwater.

Vessels starting and finishing must pass between Ives Knoll and Reid Rock Buoys.

(B) Additional Amended Rules after the First Race, October 31, 1923

By the unanimous vote of the Sailing Committee, at a meeting held this morning, it was decided that the special rules governing the 1923 series of the International Fishing Vessel Championship Race should be amended by adding the following rules thereto, which rules shall be effective this date.

11. Competing vessels shall pass on the seaward side of any buoy indicating shoal water or the approach to shoal water; provided, however that this rule shall not apply to mark buoys of the course being sailed, nor to the following buoys, namely: Middle Ground, Mars Rock, Lichfield, Neverfail, Portuguese Shoal, and Rock Head Shoal buoys.
12. A buoy which must be passed on its seaward side shall be deemed to be an obstruction to sea room under Rule 6.

You will please, therefore, understand that all future races of the present series will be governed by the rules already communicated to you amended above.

(6) **SPECIAL RULES, 1930** (also used for the 1938 series)

1. No restriction as to Sails, Crews or Ballast.
2. Passing to Windward. An overtaken vessel may luff as she pleases to prevent an overtaking vessel passing her to windward, until she is in such a position that the bowsprit end, or stem if she has no

bowsprit, would strike the overtaking vessel abaft the main shrouds, when her right to prevent the other having a free passage to windward shall cease.

3. Passing to Leeward. An overtaken vessel must never bear away to prevent another vessel passing her to Leeward—the lee side to be considered that on which the leading vessel of the two carries her main boom. The overtaking vessel must not luff until she has drawn clear ahead of the vessel which she has overtaken.
4. Rights of New Course. A vessel shall not become entitled to her rights on a new course until she has filled away.
5. Passing and Rounding Marks. If an overlap exists between two vessels when both of them, without tacking, are about to pass a mark on the required side, then the outside vessel must give the inside vessel room to pass clear of the mark. A vessel shall not, however, be justified in attempting to force an overlap and thus force a passage between another vessel and the mark after the latter has altered her helm for the purpose of rounding.
6. Overlap. An overlap is established when an overtaking vessel has no longer a free choice on which side she will pass, and continues to exist as long as the leeward vessel by luffing, or the weather vessel by bearing away, is in danger of fouling.
7. Obstruction of Sea Room. When a vessel is approaching a shore, shoal, rock, vessel or other dangerous obstruction, and cannot go clear by altering her course without fouling another vessel, then the latter shall, on being hailed by the former, at once give room; and in case one vessel is forced to tack or to bear away in order to give room, the other shall also tack or bear away as the case may be, at as near the same time as is possible without danger of fouling. But if such obstruction is a designated mark of the course, a vessel forcing another to tack under the provisions of this section shall be disqualified.
8. If Any Competing Vessel Fouls a buoy marking the course or fouls another competing vessel during the race, she may be disqualified by the Sailing Committee.
9. If a Vessel crosses the line before the starting gun is fired, her number will be displayed from the Judges' Boat and attention will be called to it by two blasts of the whistle and she will have to return and recross the starting line, otherwise she shall be disqualified from the race.
10. All Protests regarding any race shall be made in writing and delivered to the Chairman of the Sailing Committee on the same day of the race. In case any damage should occur to any contending sailing vessel during the intervening time between races notice shall be made in writing and delivered to the Chairman of the Sailing Committee prior to 8 a.m. on the day of the race. The decision of the Committee shall be final.

(7) ADDITIONAL SAILING RULES, October 13, 1931

- LEAVING HARBOUR: Point Pleasant Buoy and Bell Rock Buoy must be left to starboard; Horse Shoe shoal buoy, Lighthouse Bank buoy and Thrumcap Shoal buoy must be left to port.
- ENTERING HARBOUR: Thrumcap Shoal buoy, Lighthouse Bank buoy and Horse Shoe shoal buoy must be left to starboard; Bell Rock buoy and Point Pleasant buoy must be left to port.

COURSES OFF HALIFAX

AS PUBLISHED—ALL COURSES MAGNETIC

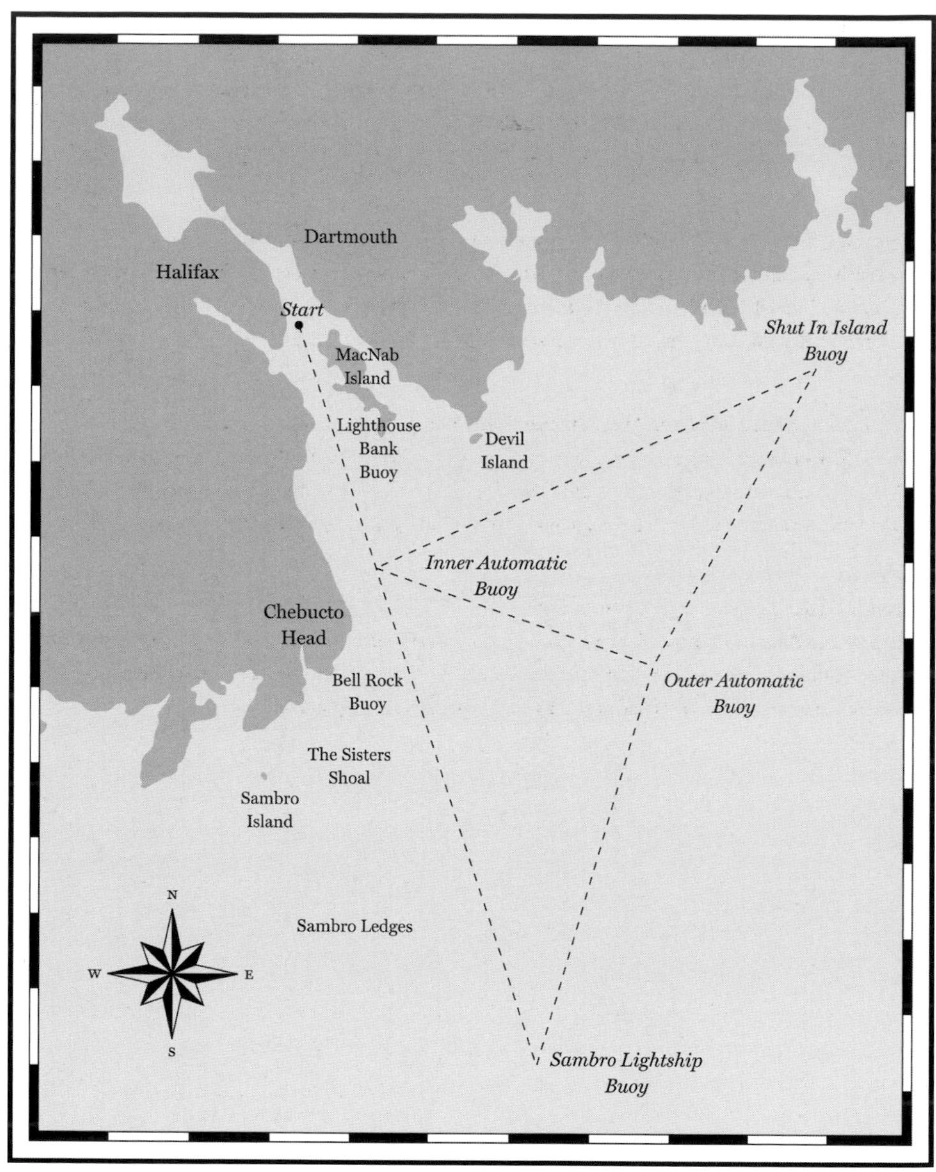

COURSE 1

From starting line south 6.3 miles to the Inner Automatic, leaving buoy to starboard; thence south by west 3/4 west. 11.25 miles to Sambro Lightship, leaving ship to port; thence north east 7/8 east 9.6 miles to Outer Automatic, leaving buoy to port; thence northwest 1/2 north 6.4 miles to Inner Automatic, leaving buoy to starboard; thence north 6.3 miles to finish line. 39.85 miles.

COURSE 2

From starting line south 6.3 miles to the Inner Automatic, leaving buoy to port; thence southeast 1/2 south 6.4 miles to Outer Automatic, leaving buoy to starboard; thence southwest 7/8 west 9.6 miles to Sambro Lightship, leaving ship to starboard; thence north by east 3/4 east 11.25 miles to Inner Automatic, leaving buoy to port; thence north 6.3 miles to finish line. 39.85 miles.

COURSE 3

From starting line south 6.3 miles to the Inner Automatic, leaving buoy to port; thence southeast 1/2 south 6.4 miles to Outer Automatic, leaving buoy to port; thence northeast 3/4 east 9 miles to Shut In Island Bell buoy, leaving the buoy to port; thence west 1/4 south 11.3 miles to Inner Automatic, leaving buoy to starboard; thence north 6.3 miles to finish line. 39.3 miles.

COURSE 4

From starting line south 6.3 miles to Inner Automatic, leaving buoy to port; thence east 1/4 north 11.3 miles to Shut In Island Bell buoy, leaving buoy to starboard; thence southwest 3/4 west 9 miles to Outer Automatic, leaving buoy to starboard; thence northwest 1/2 north 6.4 miles to Inner Automatic, leaving buoy to starboard; thence north 6.3 miles to finish line. 39.3 miles.

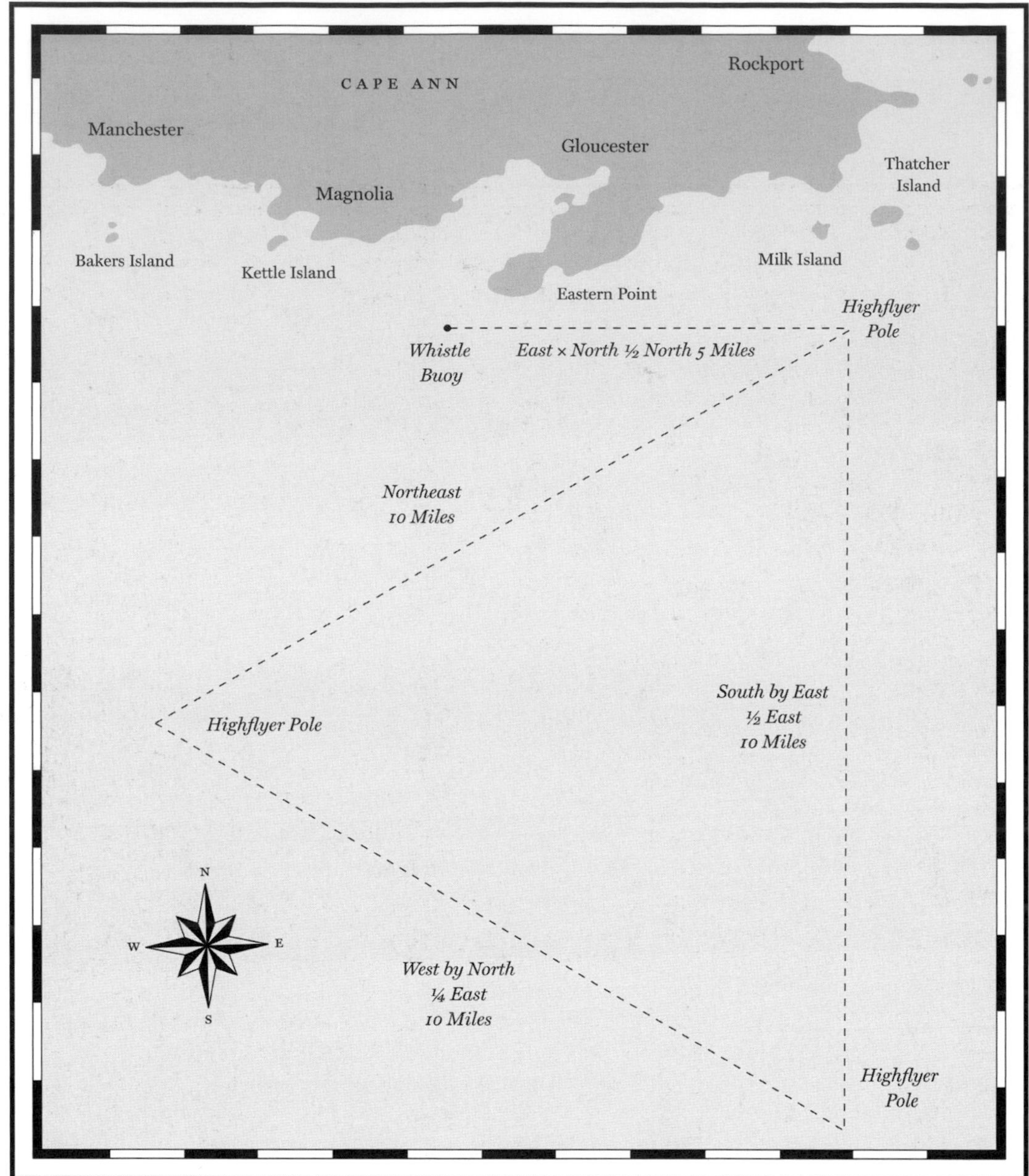

GLOUCESTER LONG COURSE

To and across the starting line between the Mark Buoy and the Judges' Boat; thence east by north ½ north 5 miles to a mark, leaving it to starboard; thence south by east ½ east 10 miles to a mark, leaving it to starboard; thence west by north ¼ north 10 miles to a mark buoy, leaving it to starboard; thence northeast 10 miles to a mark, leaving it to port; thence west by south ½ south 5 miles to the finish line. 40 miles.

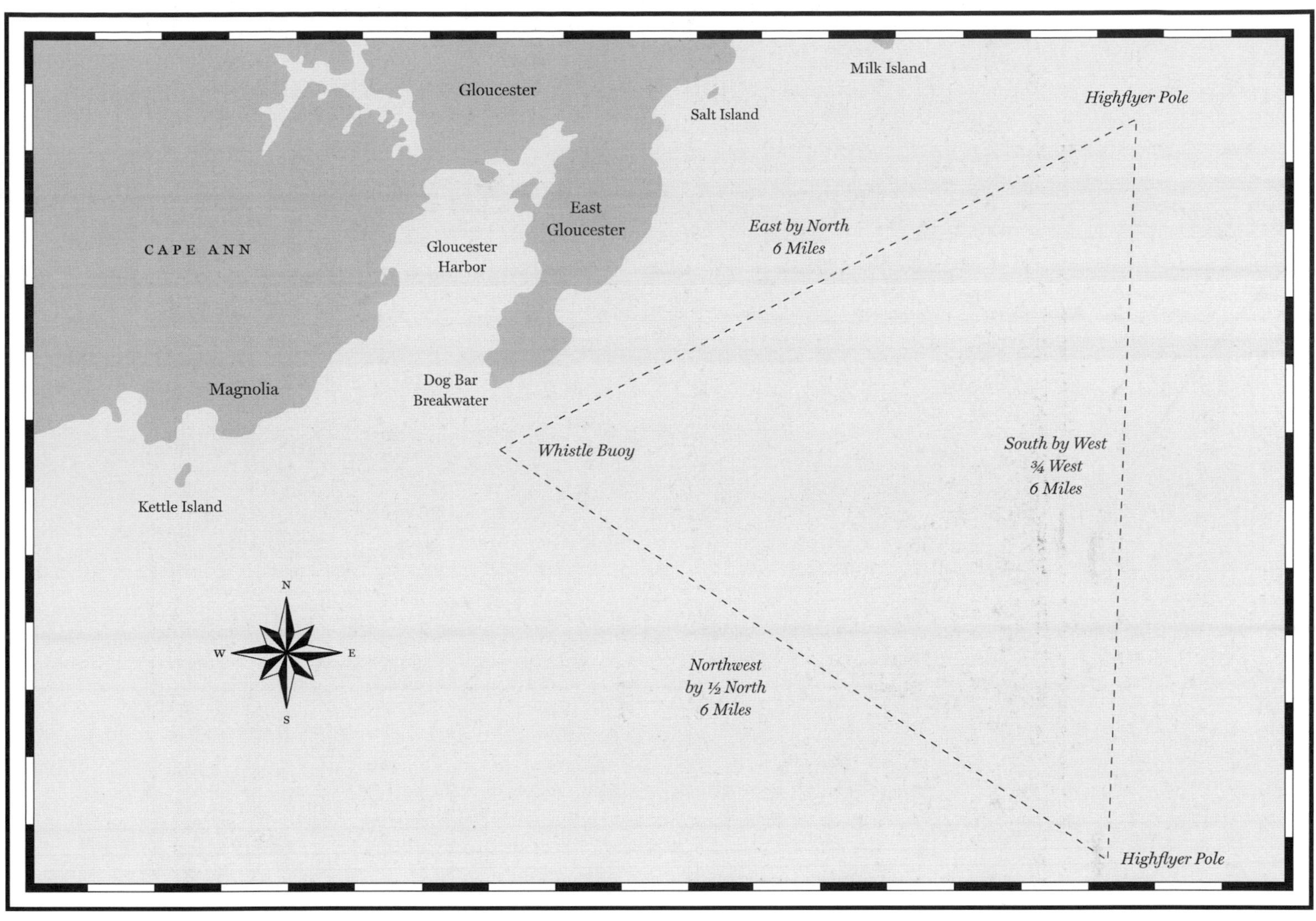

GLOUCESTER SHORT COURSE

To and across the starting line between the Mark Buoy and the Judges' Boat; thence east by north 6 miles to a mark buoy, leaving it to starboard; thence south by west ¾ west 6 miles to a mark buoy, leaving it to starboard; thence northwest ½ north 6 miles to a mark buoy; thence repeating entire triangle to finish line. 36 miles.

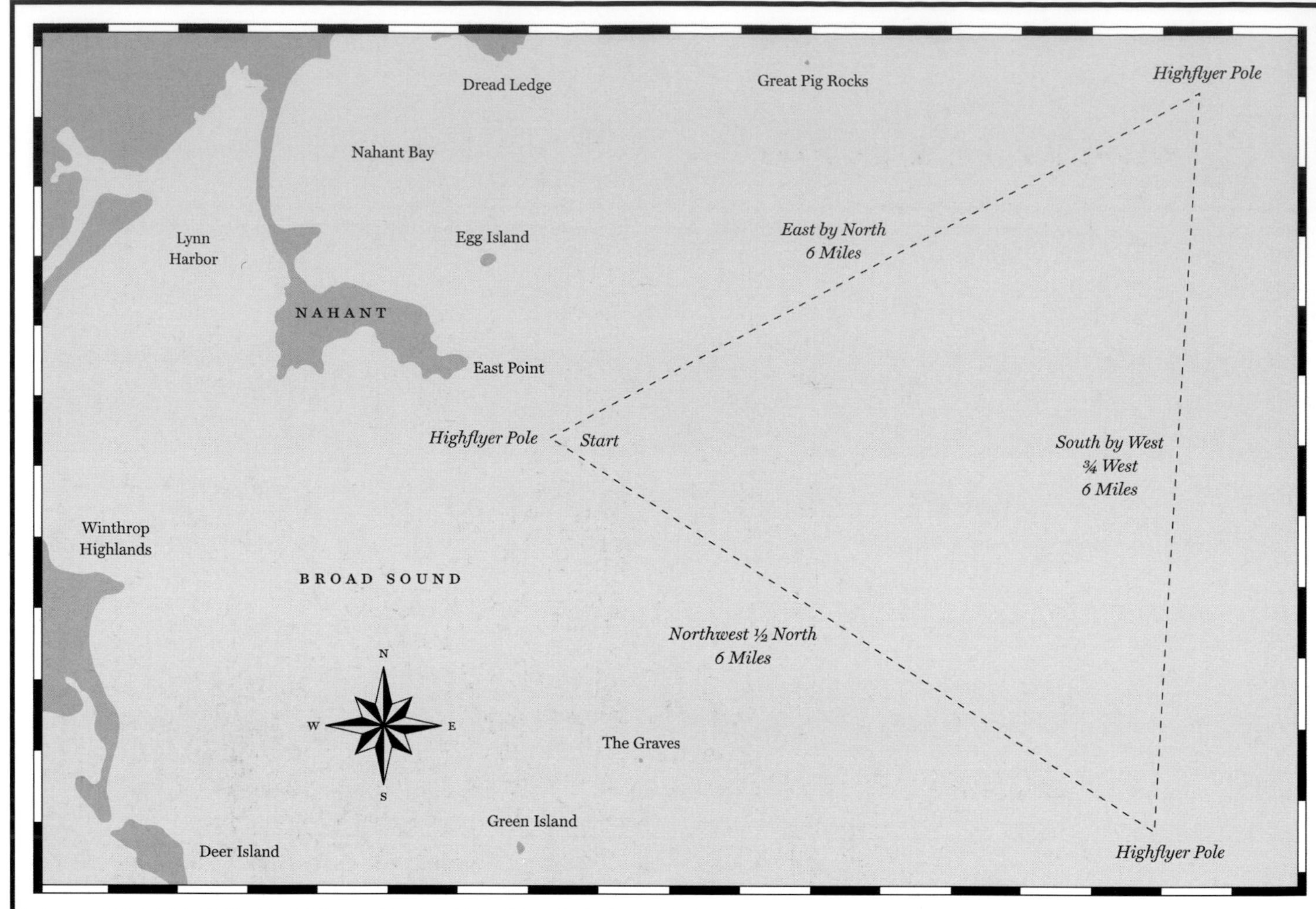

BOSTON SHORT COURSE

To and across the starting line between the Mark Buoy and the Judges' Boat; thence east by north 6 miles to a mark buoy, leaving it to starboard; thence south by west ¾ west 6 miles to a mark buoy, leaving it to starboard; thence northwest ½ north 6 miles to a mark buoy; thence repeating entire triangle to finish line. 36 miles.

BOSTON LONG COURSE

The 1938 series was originally set up with only short courses off Boston and Gloucester. After Captain Walters complained about these "merry-go-round" courses, a compromise of short and long in both locations was agreed upon. The long courses were not published in the race program, as it had been already printed. The long course off Gloucester was mapped out in the local paper, but the only references found to the long course off Boston were in newspapers, which described it as being an irregular 36-mile triangle. The first leg began off the tip of the Nahant Peninsula and led southeast by east, 14 ½ miles to an offshore highliner buoy; the course then ran north-northwest, 12 miles to the Newcomb Ledge Whistle Buoy, and the last leg headed west-southwest, 9 ½ miles back to the finish line.

SCHOONER SAIL PLAN AND SPARS

GLOSSARY

AFT: The stern (or "after") part of the vessel, i.e., towards the rear.

BACKSTAYS: Movable or running rigging that supports the upper masts and counteracts the forward pressure of the sails.

BALLOONER: Uppermost of the three headsails on a schooner; also known as jib topsail, balloon jib or flying jib—see illustration on p. 235.

BALLOON JIB: *See ballooner*

BEAM: A direction or bearing at right angles to the fore and aft line of a ship.

BEAR OFF/BORE OFF: To change course farther away from the wind direction.

BEATING IT: Sailing a vessel to windward, i.e., into the wind.

BEND: To attach a sail to a boom or gaff.

BLANKETING: To take the wind from an opponent's sails by blocking the wind with your own sails.

BLOCK: A pulley used to increase the mechanical advantage of ropes when handling sails.

BOLT ROPE: A rope that is sewn around the edge of a sail to keep it from fraying.

BONE IN HER TEETH: The foam or bow wave caused by a ship's motion through the water.

BOOT-TOP: A painted line just above the waterline.

BOWSPRIT: A large spar projecting forward from the bow that carries headsails and provides support to the fore-topmast.

BULWARKS: The wooden planking running along a vessel's sides above the deck, which stops the sea from washing over the deck and prevents crew and equipment from being washed overboard.

CAP RAIL: A flat rail attached to the top of the bulwark.

CAUGHT IN IRONS: A condition that occurs when a vessel's bow is facing into the wind and she is unable to tack in either direction.

CLEW UP: A term used when hauling in the topsails.

CLOSE-HAULED: The vessel is sailing as close to the wind direction as possible.

COMBER: A large wave that rolls and crests.

CROSSTREES: Also known as spreaders or trestles, these are timbers laid across the upper end of a mast to support the topmast and increase the span of the upper shrouds.

DOLPHIN STRIKER: A short, perpendicular spar under the bowsprit to spread the angle of the stay leading to the end of the bowsprit.

DOUBLE-ENDER: A vessel that is pointed at both ends.

DRAWING/DRAFT: The depth of a vessel under the water.

DUDS: A colloquial term for sails.

ENTRY: The shape of the bow under the waterline, which determines how the vessel moves through the water.

FO'C'SLE: *See forecastle*

FOOT: The lower edge of a sail.

FOOTING: A colloquial term for moving quickly through the water.

FORECASTLE: The term used for the crew's living space in the forward end of a ship.

FORESAIL: Gaff-rigged sail between the fore and main mast—see illustration on p. 235.

FORGING UP TO WEATHER: Sailing a vessel towards the wind direction.

FORWARD OF THE BEAM: The wind crossing the hull just ahead of the beam.

GAFF: The spar to which the top or head of a four-sided sail is secured.

GIG: A small open craft often used as a ship's boat for transporting crew ashore.

GLASS DROPS: A drop in atmospheric pressure (the "glass" was a mercury-filled glass barometer).

HAM: Wooden block that supports the crosstrees. Also known as a cheek or hound.

HANK: A small ring or hoop that attaches a sail to a wire stay.

HATCH: A rectangular opening in the deck that provides access from one deck to another.

HAWSE PIPE: A pipe or opening in the upper bow through which the anchor cable is led to the anchor windlass.

HAWSER: A heavy line or rope usually used for mooring or anchoring a vessel.

HEADER: A person employed on board a fishing vessel to remove the head from the caught fish.

HEADSAIL: The collective name for all the sails forward of the foremast, jumbo, jib and jib topsail.

HEAD SEA: A heavy sea coming from the direction of the bow of a ship.

HIGHLINE SKIPPER: A fishing skipper who catches the most fish.

HOGGED: As the result of strain on an aging vessel, the hull droops both fore and aft, leaving the middle arched.

HOVE TO: To move the windward bow of the vessel just off the wind and hold that position while making little or no headway, usually to ride out a storm.

JIB: The middle of the three headsails—see illustration on p. 235.

JIBING: Shifting a sail from one side to another while sailing with the wind aft of the beam.

JIB TOPSAIL: *See ballooner*—see illustration on p. 235.

JUMBO SAIL: The aftermost of the three headsails on a schooner, normally fitted with a boom at the foot—see illustration on p. 235.

KEEL SHOE: A strip of wood fitted along the bottom of a keel to protect it, easily replaced if damaged.

KNOCKABOUT: A schooner that does not carry a bowsprit.

KNOT: A nautical measure of speed. One knot equals one-tenth of a nautical mile (6,080 feet) or 608 feet per hour.

LEECH: The after or outside edge of a sail.

LEE RAIL: The rail on the side of the vessel opposite to the direction of the wind.

LEE SHORE: Shoreline that lies off the lee side of a boat. A lee shore from a sailor's point of view is a windward shore to a person on land.

LIGHT AIRS: A common nautical term for a very light wind of one to three knots.

LIGHT BOXES: Shallow shelves that hold the navigational lights and are located on the port and starboard fore shrouds.

LOO'ARD: A colloquial term for leeward, or the side opposite to the direction of the wind.

LOWERS: The four lower sails on a schooner: mainsail, foresail, jumbo and jib—see illustration on p. 235.

LUFF: The leading edge of a for-and-aft sail; to sail as close to the wind as possible.

MADE FOR WEATHER: Sailing close to the wind.

MIZZEN MAST: A shorter after mast on a small craft.

ON PASSAGE: Sailing to a destination.

PATENT GYBER: A shock absorber on the sheets of the main and foresails, used to ease the strain on the deck when tacking or jibing.

PEAK HALYARD: The block and tackle that hoists the peak or outer end of the gaff on the fore or main sails.

PINCH HIGHER: To sail closer to the wind than another vessel.

PIPES: A colloquial term for an increase in wind.

PLUMB STEM: A bow that is straight up and down.

POINT HIGH: To sail close to the wind.

POINTS OF SAIL: Various headings in relation to the wind. e.g., close-hauled, reaching or running.

PORT: The left-hand side of a vessel, looking forward.

PORT TACK: Sailing with the wind coming from the port side.

QUARTERDECK: A raised portion of deck on the aft part of a ship.

QUARTER RAIL: The railing that surrounds the aft part of the quarterdeck.

QUICK IN STAYS: A description of a vessel that can move quickly from one tack to another.

RATLINES: The footropes on the main and fore shrouds, used for climbing aloft.

REACH: To sail with the wind on or just forward or just aft of the beam.

Beam reach: a point of sailing where the vessel is at right angles to the wind.

Broad reach: a point of sailing where the vessel is sailing away from the wind, but not directly downwind.

Close reach: a point of sailing where the wind is forward of the beam, at a point between a beam reach and close-hauled.

REEF: To reduce the sail area by gathering up the lower portion of the sail and securing it to the boom.

REEVE: A term used when running rope through blocks to form a tackle and more generally used when passing a rope-end through anything.

RUNNING THE LINE: Moving parallel to the start line.

SAIL THROUGH HER LEE: To sail up the leeward side of another vessel.

SALT BANKER: A fishing schooner that works the Grand Banks and salts its catch.

SALT FISHERMAN: A fisherman who works on a salt banker.

SALT FISHERY: The fishing industry that deals with salted fish.

SCUPPERING: Leaning the boat over so far that the sea pours in through the scuppers in the bulwarks.

SCUPPERS: The openings at deck level that allow water to flow off the deck.

SHEER POLE: A metal pole lashed across the shrouds to prevent twisting.

SHEET: A line or purchase used to trim or control the position of a sail.

SHOAL WATER: Shallow water.

SHOE: *See keel shoe*

SHROUDS: The permanent rigging that supports the masts and is rigged from the masthead to the side of the ship.

SPOON BOW: A bow that has a shallow curve similar to the underside of a spoon.

SPREADERS: *See crosstrees*

SPRING: To split or break loose.

SPRIT-SAIL: A four-sided, for-and-aft sail with a long spar stretching diagonally across it and supporting the peak.

STANCHIONS: Wooden pillars that support the bulwarks and rail.

STAND ON: To maintain a course in a particular direction.

STARBOARD: The right-hand side of a vessel, looking forward.

STARBOARD TACK: Sailing with the wind coming from the starboard side.

STICKS: A colloquial term for masts.

STORM TRYSAIL: A small, heavy triangular sail that replaces the mainsail in stormy weather.

SWIBS: A type of wave or comber.

TACK: To work a vessel to windward (sail into the wind) by a zigzag manoeuvre on either side of the windward direction, alternately changing courses from a port tack to a starboard tack.

THROATER: A person employed on board a fishing vessel to remove the stomach from the caught fish.

THWART: Transverse removable wooden seat in a dory.

TOP-HAMPER: A colloquial term for upper, light-air sails.

TRANSOM: The planking that forms the flat stern of a vessel.

TRAWL: A tarred cotton ground line, often over a mile in length, to which are tied, at intervals, shorter and lighter lines with baited hooks at the ends. These are laid over the ocean floor and buoyed at each end.

TRESTLE: *See crosstrees*

TRUCK: A circular wooden cap affixed to the top of a vessel's topmast.

UNDER FOUR LOWERS: Sailing with the mainsail, foresail, jumbo and jib.

UNSHIP THE JAWS: The wooden saddle at the forward end of the boom is pulled back, away from the mast, and comes adrift.

UPPERS: The four upper sails on a schooner: the main gaff topsail, fore gaff topsail, fisherman's staysail and jib topsail—see illustration on p. 235.

WEATHER BILGE: The portion of a vessel's hull adjacent to the keel when exposed due to extreme heeling.

WHALER: A small open boat with fine lines, easy to row. Used originally in the whaling industry to chase whales.

WHERRIE: A small open craft often used to fish inshore or carry small amounts of cargo.

WINDLASS: A mechanical device used for hauling in the anchor.

WINDWARD BERTH: A vessel's position when sailing on the windward side of another vessel.

WING AND WING: Running before the wind (i.e., sailing downwind) with the sails set on both sides, also known as "goose-winged" or "reading both pages."

WORK ONE'S WAY TO WINDWARD: Sail in the direction the wind is coming from, by means of an indirect, zigzagging course (tacking).

ACKNOWLEDGEMENTS

TO BEGIN, I would like to thank my wife, Judy, for her guidance and wisdom in moving this book towards completion. Her tireless efforts researching and carefully editing, and her endless patience, helped tremendously with the writing of this book. To all my friends in Nova Scotia who assisted me with my quest and made me welcome whenever I visited, especially Ben and Marilyn Verburgh, please accept my gratitude. I am also indebted to many others who have helped along the way, particularly Joe Garland, the master storyteller of Gloucester, who not only gave so much help and insight answering my questions but did so with great humour and warmth. His home at Eastern Point allowed me to daydream of fleets of schooners from a bygone age gracing Gloucester Harbour, which it overlooks. Also, the late Dana Story, of Essex, added so much depth and local insight to the history of schooners and shipbuilding that his loss will be greatly felt by those wishing to keep the history alive. Thanks to Bill Garden for use of his landing grid and his advice on all things nautical. Others, such as Ben Verburgh, Captain Doug Himmelman, Captain Phil Watson, Captain Martyn Clark and Bill Wolferstan, gave freely of their time to read the manuscript and add comments and corrections. I am also grateful to those wonderful people who fill the ranks of museums, libraries and archives, those guardians of our past who give so much time and assistance to the researcher: Andy Price, Gordon Miller, Peggy Tate Smith, Ellen Nelson, Ralph Getson, Gary Shutlak, Aaron Schmidt, Ellen Lampson, Erik Ronnberg, Suzanne Boudet, Debbie Vaughan, Claudia Jew, Michael Lapides, James Craig, Christine Michelini and Stephanie Buck. Without their dedication to the preservation of the past, projects such as this would never be launched. I would also like to acknowledge those great writers and reporters such as George Hudson, Leonard Fowle, Tom Horgan, Jerry Snider, Fred Wallace, Colin McKay, Jimmy Connolly, Frank Sibley, Charlton Smith, William Taylor and Ed Kelly, to name just a few, whose enthusiasm for the subject fills the thousands of pages of print from the 1920s and 1930s. A special thanks to Dusan Kadlec, who allowed me to use his wonderful painting for the cover. Jonathan Dore, Wendy Fitzgibbons and Susan Rana worked so diligently throughout the editing process. Special thanks also to Silver Donald Cameron for writing the introduction. Of course, this book would not be a reality without a publisher, Scott McIntyre, whose faith and support I have enjoyed over the years.

The following museums, libraries and archives provided material for this book:

Boston Public Library, Boston, Massachusetts
The Bostonian Society, Boston, Massachusetts
Canadian Nautical Research Society
Cape Ann Historical Society, Gloucester, Massachusetts
Chicago Historical Society, Chicago, Illinois
Essex Shipbuilding Museum, Essex, Massachusetts
Fisheries Museum of the Atlantic, Lunenburg, Nova Scotia

Fisheries Research Centre, Nanaimo, British Columbia
G.W. Blunt White Library, Mystic Seaport Museum, Mystic, Connecticut
Library and Archives Canada, Ottawa, Ontario
Maritime Museum of the Atlantic, Halifax, Nova Scotia
Maritime Museum of British Columbia, Victoria, British Columbia
Mariners' Museum, Newport News, Virginia
Mystic Seaport Museum Archives, Mystic, Connecticut
National Maritime Museum, Greenwich, United Kingdom
New Bedford Whaling Museum, New Bedford, Massachusetts
Nova Scotia Archives and Record Management, Halifax, Nova Scotia
Peabody Essex Museum, Salem, Massachusetts
Sawyer Free Library, Gloucester, Massachusetts

SELECTED BIBLIOGRAPHY

BOOKS

Backman, Brian, and Phil Backman, *Bluenose*, Toronto: McClelland and Stewart, 1965

Balcom, B.A., *History of the Lunenburg Fishing Industry*, Lunenburg, NS: Lunenburg Marine Museum Society, 1977

Barss, Peter, *Images of Lunenburg County*, Toronto: McClelland and Stewart, 1978

Cameron, Silver Donald, *Schooner: Bluenose and Bluenose II*, Toronto: McClelland and Stewart, 1984

Campbell, Lyall, *Sable Island Shipwrecks*, Halifax: Nimbus, 1994

Chapelle, Howard I., *The History of American Sailing Ships*, New York: Norton, 1935

——, *American Small Sailing Craft: Their Design, Development, and Construction*, New York: Norton, 1951

——, *The American Fishing Schooners, 1825–1935*, New York: Norton, 1973

Church, Albert C., and James B. Connolly, *American Fishermen*, New York: Norton, 1940

Connolly, James B. *The Book of the Gloucester Fishermen*, New York: John Day, 1927

Darrach, Claude K., *Race to Fame: The Inside Story of the Bluenose*, Hantsport, NS: Lancelot Press, 1985

Dear, Ian, *The America's Cup: An Informal History*, New York: Dodd, Mead, and London: S. Paul, 1980

Dear, Ian, and Peter Kemp, *The Pocket Oxford Guide to Sailing Terms*, Oxford and New York: Oxford University Press, 1987

Dunne, W.M.P., *Thomas F. McManus and the American Fishing Schooners: An Irish-American Success Story*, Mystic, CT: Mystic Seaport Museum, 1994

Garland, Joseph E., *Lone Voyager*, Boston: Little, Brown, 1963; reprinted as *Lone Voyager: The Extraordinary Adventures of Howard Blackburn, Hero Fisherman of Gloucester*, New York: Simon and Shuster, 2000

——, *Eastern Point: A Nautical, Rustical, and Social Chronicle of Gloucester's Outer Shield and Inner Sanctum, 1606–1950*, Peterborough, NH: Noone House, 1971

——, *Down to the Sea: The Fishing Schooners of Gloucester*, Boston: David R. Godine, 1983

——, *Adventure: Queen of the Windjammers*, Camden, ME: Down East Books, 1985; reprinted as *Adventure: Last of the Great Gloucester Dory-Fishing Schooners*, Gloucester: Curious Traveller Press, 2000

——, *Gloucester on the Wind: America's Greatest Fishing Port in the Days of Sail*, Dover, NH: Arcadia, 1995; reprinted, Charleston, SC: Arcadia, 2005

Gillespie, G.J., *Bluenose Skipper*, Fredericton: Brunswick Press, 1955

Goode, G. Brown, *The Fisheries and Fishery Industries of the United States*, 8 vols, Washington: U.S. Commission of Fish and Fisheries, 1884–87

Greenhill, Basil, *Schooners*, Annapolis, MD: Naval Institute Press, 1980

Hale, William, *Memorial of the Celebration of the 250th Anniversary of the Incorporation of the Town of Gloucester, Massachusetts, August 1892*, Boston, 1901

Hayden, Sterling, *Wanderer*, New York: Knopf, 1963

Herreshoff, L. Francis, *The Common Sense of Yacht Design*, 2 vols, New York: Rudder, 1946–48; reprinted, Jamaica, NY: Caravan Maritime, 1973

Innis, Harold A., *The Cod Fisheries: The History of an International Economy*, Toronto: Ryerson, and New Haven: Yale University Press, 1940; revised edition, Toronto: University of Toronto Press, 1954, reprinted 1978

Jenson, L.B., *Bluenose II: Saga of the Great Fishing Schooners*, Halifax: Nimbus, 1994

Kipling, Rudyard, *Captains Courageous: A Story of the Grand Banks*, London: Macmillan, and New York: Century, 1897

Kurlansky, Mark, *Cod: A Biography of the Fish that Changed the World*, Toronto: Knopf, and New York: Walker, 1997

Lipscomb, F.W., *A Hundred Years of the America's Cup*, Greenwich, CT: New York Graphic Society, 1971

McLaren, R. Keith, *Bluenose and Bluenose II,* Willowdale, ON: Hounslow Press, 1981

Merkel, Andrew, *Schooner Bluenose,* Toronto: Ryerson, 1948

Roué, Joan E., *A Spirit Deep Within: Naval Architect W.J. Roué and the Bluenose Story,* Hantsport, NS: Lancelot Press, 1995

Santos, Michael Wayne, *Caught in Irons: North Atlantic Fishermen in the Last Days of Sail,* Selinsgrove, PA: Susquehanna University Press, 2002

Story, Dana A., *Frame Up!: A Story of Essex, Its Shipyards and Its People,* Barre, MA: Barre Press, 1964; reprinted, Charleston, SC: History Press, 2004

——, *Hail Columbia!,* Barre, MA: Barre Press, 1970

Thomas, Gordon W., *Fast and Able: Life Stories of Great Gloucester Fishing Vessels,* Gloucester, MA: Gloucester 350th Anniversary Celebration, 1973

Wallace, Frederick M., *The Roving Fisherman: An Autobiography Recounting Personal Experiences in the Commercial Fishing Fleets and Fish Industry of Canada and the United States, 1911–1924,* Gardenvale, QC: Canadian Fisherman, 1955

Ziner, Feenie, *Bluenose, Queen of the Grand Banks,* Philadelphia: Chilton, 1970; third edition, Halifax: Nimbus, 1986

ARTICLES

Newspaper articles are detailed in the chapter notes and thus omitted here; magazine articles without a byline are listed alphabetically by publication title, chronologically for each publication. If not specified, page numbers are unknown.

Aerenburg, H.R., "The Famous Fishing Fleet of Lunenburg," *Canadian Fisherman,* May 1925, 115–16

Ahlers, H.E., "The Glorious, *Gertrude L. Thebaud,*" *Ships & Sailing,* April 1952, 26–30

The American Neptune, "American and Canadian Fishing Schooners," 1966

Atlantic Fisherman, "Preparations for Fisherman's Races," February 1921, 7–8

——, "Contenders Nearing Completion," March 1921, 2

——, "Fishermen's Cup Contenders," April 1921, 3–4, 18–19

——, "The Story of the *Canadia,*" August 1921, 6–8

——, "Races Given a Severe Blow," September 1921, 11

——, "How the Big *Bluenose* Beat the Little *Elsie,*" November 1921, 5–7

——, "The Story of the *Mayflower,*" May 1921, 14–27

——, "Schooner *Henry Ford* Out of Difficulties," May 1922, 6

——, "The Story of the *Puritan,*" June 1922, 17–19

——, "*Puritan* and *Henry Ford* Quality Fishermen," June 1922, 20, 28

——, "Schooner *Henry Ford*—A McManus Design," June 1922, 27

——, "The Unhappy Fate of the *Puritan,*" June 1922, 5–6

——, "The Case of the Schooner *Mayflower,*" September 1922, 7–8

——, "*Bluenose* a True Champion," October 1922, 9, 13, 29

——, "Programs and Regulations Governing 1922 International Fishermen's Races," October 1922, 19–30

——, "Schooner *Columbia,* Salt Banker," April 1923, 7–9

——, "Special Rules Governing the Open Fishermen's Race in Connection with Gloucester Tercentenary," August 1923, 19–21

——, "Talk of the Fishermen's Races," April 1925, 7–8

——, "Nova Scotia Is Always Ready," July 1926, 7

——, "The Fishermen's Races," October 1926, 19, 33–35

——, "Program Open Fishermen's Race," October 1926, 24–32

——, "New Fishing Schooner Built for International Racing," April 1930

——, "Nova Scotia Accepts Gloucester Race Challenge," October 1931, 6–9

Canadian Fisherman, "The Racing Fishermen," April 1920

——, "The Toll of the Sea," August 1920

——, "Schooner Races First Class Publicity," September 1921, 200

——, "Rules and Conditions Covering International Schooner Race," September 1921, 206

——, "The International Fisherman's Race," November 1921, 251–57

——, "Nova Scotia Fishermen's Regatta," November 1921, 247–50

——, "Gossip About Fishermen's Race," March 1922, 50

——, "Rules for Fishermen's Race Amended," September 1922, 191

——, "*Bluenose* Once More the Champion," November 1922, 243–45

——, "Former Bankers Are Now Rum-Running," April 1923, 101
——, "About Those Racing Rules," August 1923, 206
——, "Races Thrill Till Beans Spill," November 1923, 283–85
——, " 'Bank' Fleet Hit Hard," February 1924
——, "Prospect Brightens Lunenburg Fleet," May 1924, 103
——, "In the Wake of the Storm," September 1924, 250
——, "Third Trip for Lunenburgers," July 1925, 311–12
——, "To Race or Not to Race," November 1925, 331–32
——, "The End of International Schooner Races," February 1926, 33–34
——, "*Bluenose* Shows her Quality," June 1926, 197
——, "Capt. Walters Willing to Race," July 1926, 197
——, "Storm Warnings Urgently Needed," September 1926, 263
——, "Tragic Loss Hits Lunenburg," September 1926, 273–74
——, "Next Year's Races," November 1926, 323
——, "*Bluenose* Again Champion Schooner," November 1926, 327–29
——, "Hope Abandoned for Eighty Fishermen and Four Schooners," October 1927, 303–34
——, "Why Should Fishermen Fight the Steam Trawlers?" November 1927, 325
——, "Lunenburg Honours Her Fishermen Lost at Sea," December 1929
——, " '*Bluenose*' Skipper will Not Race in U.S. Waters," June 1930, 27
——, "*Bluenose* will Meet *Gertrude L. Thebaud* in Exhibition Races off Gloucester," October 1930
——, " '*Bluenose*' Tastes Defeat's Dregs in Gloucester Series," November 1930, 24
——, "Lunenburg Fleet had Worst Season in Many Years," November 1930, 21
——, " '*Bluenose*' to Defend Cup at Halifax," October 1931, 23
——, "Make the *Bluenose* a Training Ship," December 1931, 14
——, "*Bluenose* to get New Mainboom for Races," July 1938, 16
——, "*Bluenose* in Peak Condition," September 1938, 13
——, "Fishermen Win Sailing Honours for British Empire," November 1938, 59–67
Church, Albert C., "The Evolution and Development of the American Fishing Schooner," *Yachting,* May–June 1910
——, "The Evolution of the American Fishing Schooner," *The Atlantic Fishermen's Almanac,* n.d., 53–57
——, "The Three New Yankee Flyers," *Atlantic Fisherman,* June 1922, 5–6, 10
——, "The Gloucester Open Fishermen's Race," *Atlantic Fisherman,* September 1923, 5–6, 9, 14
——, "Selecting the Challenger to Meet *Bluenose,*" *Atlantic Fisherman,* October 1923, 9–10
——, "The Race at Halifax," *Atlantic Fisherman,* November 1923, 7–10, 15, 18, 30
Conlon, James H., "The Flying Gloucestermen," *Collier's Weekly,* December 25, 1920
——, "Walters' Faux Pas," *Canadian Fisherman,* November 1923
Day, Thomas F., "The Schooner," *Rudder,* March 1906
Dennis, W. Alexander, "The Canadian Races," *Atlantic Fisherman,* November 1926, 16–17, 23
Edson, Merritt A., "The Schooner Rig: A Hypothesis," *The American Neptune,* April 1965
Goodick, E.A., "Schooner Progress Wins North Atlantic Title," *Atlantic Fisherman,* September 1929, 15–18
——, "The '*Thebaud*' Wins the First Race of the Fishermen's Series," *Atlantic Fisherman,* October 1930, 13–16
——, " '*Bluenose*' Retains Title as Queen of the North Atlantic," *Atlantic Fisherman,* November 1931, 6–7
Haliburton, M.A., "The American Fishermen and the Modus Vivendi," *Canadian Fisherman,* June 1925, 187–88
Hudson, George Story, "How the *Esperanto* Won the Fisherman's Races," *Yachting,* December 1920, 296–98
Johnson, Captain V.C., "How the Fishermen's Race Was Sailed," *Yachting,* December 1921, 277–79, 307
Jubien, E.E., "Nova Scotia: Growth and Outlook," *Canadian Fisherman,* June 1925, 167–68, 196
Kelsey, Arthur E., " '*Bluenose*' Still Queen of Atlantic Fishing Fleets," *Canadian Fisherman,* November 1931, 9–11
Kenyon, Paul, "*Bluenose* vs. *Gertrude L. Thebaud,*" *Gloucester Magazine,* n.d., 5–8, 16–20
Knowles, A.H., "Ringing the Bell," *Canadian Fisherman,* September 1938, 11

McKay, Colin, "Fishermen's Vessels Race," *Canadian Fisherman,* September 1920, 195–96
——, "The Knockabout Schooner," *Canadian Fisherman,* October 1920, 221–22
——, "Speculation on Fishermen's Races," *Canadian Fisherman,* July 1922, 145
——, "A Substitute for Schooner Races," *Canadian Fisherman,* February 1926, 68
——, "The Machine Age with Its Trawler and Its Relation to Our Off Shore Fishermen," *Canadian Fisherman,* December 1927, 365–66
McManus, Thomas F., "Tom McManus, Designer of the *Henry Ford* Writes His Opinion of Races," *Atlantic Fisherman,* December 1922, 10
McQuire, Agnes G., "The Racing Fishermen," *Canadian Fisherman,* May 1921, 112
Newsweek, "Fishing Schooners' Race," November 7, 1938
Nickerson, Arthur E., "The Sacred Cod," *Canadian Fisherman,* November 1937, 12–13
The Rudder, "*Esperanto* Wins Fishermen's Race," December 1920, 18, 36
——, "Discord Ends Fishermen's Race," December 1923, 1
——, "The Racing Fisherman, *Gertrude L. Thebaud,*" December 1930, 60
Sidney, F.H., "Fishermen Race Again," *The Rudder,* November 1923, 35
Smith, Charlton L., "American Fishermen's Elimination Race," *Atlantic Fisherman,* October 1921, 7–8
——, "The First of the New Contenders Launched," *Atlantic Fisherman,* March 1922, 5–6
——, "The Launching of the *Henry Ford,*" *Atlantic Fisherman,* April 1922, 5–6
——, "Schooner *Henry Ford* Wins Right to Challenge *Bluenose,*" *Atlantic Fisherman,* October 1922, 7–8
——, "The International Fiasco," *Atlantic Fisherman,* November 1922, 5–6, 12
——, "The Open Fishermen's Races," *Atlantic Fisherman,* November 1926, 13–15
——, "The First Fishermen's Race," *Yachting,* January 1939, 64–65, 213–14
Snider, C.H.J., "The Fishermen's Race," *The Rudder,* December 1921, 3–6, 44–45
——, "The International Fishermen's Race," *The Rudder,* December 1922, 3–5
Stone, Herbert L., "How the *Bluenose* Won the Fishermen's Races," *Yachting,* November 1922, 229–33, 258
Time, "Fishermen's Finale," November 7, 1938, 18
Taylor, William H., "Gloucester Once More Holds Fishermen's Championship," *Yachting,* December 1930, 81, 108
Wallace, Frederick M., "A Sailing Race Between American and Canadian Fishermen," *Canadian Fisherman,* August 1920, 169–73
——, "Fishing Schooner Race," *Canadian Fisherman,* November 1920, 240–42
——, "The Yankee *Bluenose* Victory," *Canadian Fisherman,* November 1920, 237
——, "Racing Fishermen Excite Nationwide Interest," *Canadian Fisherman,* June 1921, 130
——, "Life on the Grand Banks," *National Geographic Magazine,* July 1921, 1–28
——, "The International Fishermen's Race," *Yachting,* November 1921, 213–15, 255–56
Walters, Angus J., "The Truth About the *Bluenose,*" *Ships and the Sea,* October 1952, 22–26

INDEX

Page numbers in *italics* indicate figures and captions. Subentries that refer to specific dates are in chronological order, after general subentries.